Essentials of Business Communication

Eighth Edition

Mary Ellen Guffey

Professor Emerita of Business

Los Angeles Pierce College

Dana Loewy

Contributing Editor

Business Communication Program

California State University, Fullerton

SOUTH-WESTERN
CENGAGE Learning™

Australia • Brazil • Japan • Korea • Mexico • Singapore • Spain • United Kingdom • United States

SOUTH-WESTERN
CENGAGE Learning™

Essentials of Business Communication, Eighth Edition

Mary Ellen Guffey

Vice President of Editorial, Business:
Jack W. Calhoun

Editor-in-Chief: Melissa S. Acuña

Senior Acquisitions Editor: Erin Joyner

Senior Developmental Editor: Mary Draper

Executive Marketing Manager:
Kimberly Kanakes

Marketing Manager: Mike Aliscad

Marketing Communications Manager:
Sarah Greber

Senior Content Project Manager:
Tamborah Moore

Managing Media Editor: Pam Wallace

Media Editor: John Rich

Manufacturing Coordinator: Diane Gibbons/
Beverly Breslin

Production Service: LEAP Publishing
Services, Inc.

Compositor: ICC Macmillan, Inc.

Permissions Account Manager, Text:
Roberta Broyer

Permissions Account Manager, Images:
Amanda Groszko

Photo Researcher: Terri Miller

Senior Art Director: Stacy Jenkins Shirley

Cover and Internal Designer:
Craig Ramsdell

Cover Image: © Veer/PhotoAlto

ExamView® is a registered trademark of eInstruction Corp. Windows is a registered trademark of the Microsoft Corporation used herein under license. Macintosh and Power Macintosh are registered trademarks of Apple Computer, Inc. used herein under license.

© 2010 Cengage Learning. All Rights Reserved.

Library of Congress Control Number: 2008940428

Pkg ISBN-13: 978-0-324-58800-2

Pkg ISBN-10: 0-324-58800-3

ISBN-13: 978-0-324-58799-9

ISBN-10: 0-324-58799-6

South-Western Cengage Learning
5191 Natorp Boulevard
Mason, OH 45040
USA

Cengage Learning products are represented in Canada by Nelson Education, Ltd.

For your course and learning solutions, visit **academic.cengage.com**

Purchase any of our products at your local college store or at our preferred online store **www.ichapters.com**

Printed in the United States of America
4 5 6 7 12 11

Dear Business Communication Students:

Essentials of Business Communication, 8e, brings you a four-in-one learning package including (a) an authoritative textbook, (b) a convenient workbook, (c) a self-teaching grammar/mechanics handbook, and (d) a fully supported student Web site at **www.meguffey.com.**

Although much copied, **Essentials** maintains its leadership in post-secondary markets because of its effective grammar review, practical writing instruction, and exceptional support materials. In revising this Eighth Edition, we examined every topic and added new coverage with two themes in mind: professionalism and the relevance of this course to your future career success. Let me describe a few of the major improvements and features in the Eighth Edition:

- **Workplace relevance.** At the request of reviewers, this edition stresses the practical and immediate importance of this course to success in your career.
- **Office Insider feature.** To help you understand employers' expectations and to better connect what you are learning to your future job performance, Office Insider presents workplace facts and advice.
- **Updated communication technologies.** The Eighth Edition updates and expands coverage of blogs, instant messaging, wikis, and other current technologies.
- **New grammar and writing improvement exercises.** Many new grammar review and writing improvement exercises help you review the basics and hone your skills.
- **New chapter on professionalism.** To reinforce the focus on marketable skills and career success, this edition teaches business etiquette, team behavior, and other professional soft skills.
- **Job-search and interviewing coverage.** The Eighth Edition presents the latest trends in résumés and employment interviews.
- **Premier Web site at www.meguffey.com.** All students with new books have access to chapter review quizzes, PowerPoint slides, and a wide assortment of learning resources.

The many examples and model documents in ***Essentials of Business Communication,*** including résumés and cover letters, have made this book a favorite to keep as an on-the-job reference.

I wish you well in your studies!

Cordially,

Mary Ellen Guffey

UNDERSTANDING THE IMPORTANCE OF GOOD COMMUNICATION...
IT'S JUST THAT EASY!

Strong business communication skills will serve you well throughout college, your careers, and entire lives. Guffey helps you learn to communicate effectively and professionally in today's workplace, no matter what career path you choose to follow. The exciting, new *Essentials of Business Communication, 8e,* is packed with resources to make learning business communication easier and more enjoyable. With the book's grammar focus, coverage of current workplace technologies, and an unmatched ancillary package, you will find that learning business communication can be ... *just that easy.*

Essentials offers a four-in-one learning package that gets results:

- Authoritative textbook
- Practical workbook
- Self-teaching grammar/mechanics handbook
- Fully supported student support Web site – www.meguffey.com

Mary Ellen Guffey continues to be your partner in learning.

Award-winning author Mary Ellen Guffey provides unparalleled resources to help you learn and retain business writing techniques. When you use a Guffey text, you get dynamic learning resources that help you succeed in the course.

In this edition Dr. Dana Loewy joins Mary Ellen as a major contributor and coauthor. Learn more about both authors on the "About the Authors" page.

Emphasis on Grammar

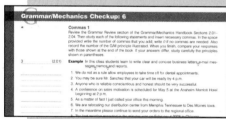

Throughout the text, you are encouraged to build on your basic grammar skills. Grammar/ Mechanics Check-ups, Grammar/ Mechanics Challenges, and Web-based grammar activities help you practice and sharpen your skills.

Emphasis on Writing Plans

Ample, step-by-step writing plans help you get started quickly on organizing and formatting messages.

From the emphasis on professionalism to new *Workplace in Focus* photo essays, Guffey has updated tools and created new ways to keep you interested and engaged. The following six pages describe features that will help make learning with Guffey... *just that easy.*

g Associates, to help find an appropriate service s. Without realizing it, Catherine had mentioned ces, Inc.) that her client was considering hiring an . An overeager salesperson from Payroll Services us angering the client. The client had hired the f intrusion. Alliance did not want to be hounded vices.

oblem, the first thing consultant Catherine to explain and apologize. She was careful to king. A low-pitched, deliberate pace gives the clearly, logically, and reasonably—not emo- ally. However, she also followed up with the tter not only confirms the telephone conversa- of formality. It sends the nonverbal message seriously and that it is important enough to

OFFICE INSIDER

"As soon as you realize there is a problem, let your client know by phone or, if possible, in person. It's better to let them hear bad news from you than to discover it on their own because it establishes your candor."

ething they are not entitled to or something you nd warranties or make unreasonable demands. nhappy with a product or service, they are emo- *no* to emotionally involved receivers will prob- mmunication task. As publisher Malcolm Forbes lisagreeing—that's an art." [11] -refusal plan helps you be empathic and artful in denial letters you will need to adopt the proper if they are at fault. Avoid *you* statements that *known that cash refunds are impossible if you* al, objective language to explain why the claim g resale information to rebuild the customer's ganization. In Figure 7.6 on page 176 the writer fference between the price the customer paid for

Office Insider
To accentuate how excellent communica- tion skills translate into career success, the *Office Insider* demonstrates the importance of communication skills in real-world practice.

Emphasis on Professionalism

The Eighth Edition increases its emphasis on professional workplace behaviors and illustrates the importance of professionalism. Businesses have a keen interest in a professional workforce that effectively works together to deliver positive results that ultimately boost profits and bolster a company's image. In this edition, you'll discover the professional characteristics most valued in today's competitive workplace.

Career Relevance

Because employers often rank communication skills among the most requested competencies, the Eighth Edition emphasizes the link between excellent communication skills and career success—helping you see for yourself the critical role business communication will play in your life.

Abundant Activities and Cases

Chapter concepts are translated into action as you try out your skills in activities designed to mirror "real-world" experiences.

I really like the updates in Essentials, and the focus on using technology as a communication medium in the 21st century workplace and classroom.

— DEBORAH J. BUELL, CY-FAIR COLLEGE, NORTH HARRIS MONTGOMERY COMMUNITY COLLEGE DISTRICT, TEXAS

More Before-and-After Model Documents

Before-and-after sample documents and descriptive callouts create a road map to the writing process, demonstrating the effective use of the skills being taught, as well as the significance of the revision process.

FIGURE 7.4 Refusing an Internal Request

DATE: June 22, 200x

TO: Zachary Stapleton
            Chief Information Officer

FROM: Victoria M. Blaylock
            VP, Management Information Systems

SUBJECT: Request

This is to let you know that attending that conference in October, Zach, is out of the question. Perhaps you didn't remember that budget-planning meetings are scheduled for that month.

We really need your expertise to help keep the updating of our telecommunications network on schedule. Without you, the entire system—which is shaky at best— might fall apart. I'm really sorry to have to refuse your request to attend the conference. I know this is small thanks for the fine work you have done for us. Please accept our humble apologies.

In the spring I'm sure your work schedule will be lighter, and we can release you to attend a conference at that time.

MAGELLAN ENTERPRISES

MEMORANDUM

DATE: June 22, 200x

TO: Zachary Stapleton
            Chief Information Officer

FROM: Victoria M. Blaylock *VMB*
            VP, Management Information System

SUBJECT: Your Request to Attend October Conference

Buffer: Includes sincere praise

The entire Management Council and I are pleased with the excep you have provided in setting up video transmission to our regiona of your genuine professional commitment, Zach, I can understand attend the conference of the Telecommunication Specialists of A October 23-27 in Phoenix.

Reason: Tells why refusal is necessary

The last two weeks in October have been set aside for budget p and I know, we have only scratched the surface of our teleconfe for the next five years. Because you are the specialist and we rely expertise, we need you here for these planning sessions.

Bad news: Implies refusal

Closing: Contains realistic alternative

If you are able to attend a similar conference in the spring and permit, we will try to send you then. You are our most valuable Zach, and we are grateful for the quality leadership you provide Information Systems team.

That Easy!

Communication Workshops

Communication Workshops develop critical thinking skills and provide insight into special business communication topics such as ethics, technology, career skills, and collaboration.

Communication Workshop: Intercultural Issues

Presenting Bad News in Other Cultures

To minimize disappointment, Americans generally prefer to present negative messages indirectly. Other cultures may treat bad news differently, as illustrated in the following:

- In Germany business communicators occasionally use buffers but tend to present bad news directly.
- British writers tend to be straightforward with bad news, seeing no reason to soften its announcement.
- In Latin countries the question is not how to organize negative messages but whether to present them at all. It is considered disrespectful and impolite to report bad news to superiors. Therefore, reluctant employees may fail to report accurately any negative situations to their bosses.
- In Thailand the negativism represented by a refusal is completely alien; the word *no* does not exist. In many cultures negative news is offered with such subtleness or in such a positive light that it may be overlooked or misunderstood by literal-minded Americans.
- In many Asian and some Latin cultures, one must look beyond an individual's actual words to understand what is really being communicated. One must consider the communication style, the culture, and especially the context. Consider the following phrases and their possible meanings:

Phrase	Possible Meaning
I agree.	I agree with 15 percent of what you say.
We might be able to . . .	Not a chance!
We will consider . . .	*We* will consider, but the real decision maker will not.
That is a little too much . . .	That is outrageous!
Yes.	Yes, I'm listening. *OR:* Yes, you have a good point. *OR:* Yes, I understand, but I don't necessarily agree.

Career Application. Interview fellow students or work colleagues who are from other cultures. Collect information regarding the following questions:

- How is negative news handled in their cultures?
- How would typical business communicators refuse a request for a business favor (such as a contribution to a charity)?
- How would typical business communicators refuse a customer's claim?
- How would an individual be turned down for a job?

Your Task

Report the findings of your interviews in class discussion or in a memo report. In addition, collect samples of foreign business letters. You might ask foreign students, your campus admissions office, or local export/import companies whether they would be willing to share business letters from other countries. Compare letter styles, formats, tone, and writing strategies. How do these elements differ from those in typical North American business letters?

---

*I'm really enjoying using **Essentials.** The detail and pedagogical design of the book are truly inspiring. I really get a kick out of reading all of the positive and grateful student comments about the book at the end of the semester when I distribute an instructor/course evaluation.*

— BRIAN WILSON, COLLEGE OF MARIN, CALIFORNIA

heard and that they have been treated fairly. In canceling funding for a program, board members provided this explanation: *As you know, the publication of* Urban Artist *was funded by a renewable annual grant from the National Endowment for the Arts. Recent cutbacks in federally sponsored city arts programs have left us with few funds. Because our grant has been discontinued, we have no alternative but to cease publication of* Urban Artist. *You have my assurance that the board has searched long and hard for some other viable funding, but every avenue of recourse has been closed before us. Accordingly, June's issue will be our last.*

WORKPLACE IN FOCUS

The ChicoBag Company knows that it is not what you say but how you say it that matters. While some environmental activists make strident calls to ban plastic bags that "hurt the earth," the California-based bag business takes a humorous approach to the issue. To illustrate the drawbacks of single-use plastic bags, ChicoBag dispatches Bag Monsters to roam the streets in high-visibility locations, such as on the streets at Mardi Gras or in front of the White House. The gimmicky-but-good-natured promotional effort helps the company sell its reusable nylon bags while muting the sometimes-negative tone taken by other eco-minded organizations. *Why is it important to accentuate the positive side of things?*

New Workplace in Focus Photo Essays

Vivid photos with intriguing stories demonstrate real-world applicability of business communication concepts. Each photo essay concludes with a critical thinking question.

hat Easy!

Writing Improvement Exercises

These exercises will develop your writing skills and allow you to practice the concepts explained in the chapter.

---

15. What are some channels that large organizations may use when delivering bad news to employees?

Writing Improvement Exercises

Passive-Voice Verbs

Passive-voice verbs may be preferable in breaking bad news because they enable you to emphasize actions rather than personalities. Compare these two refusals:

Example Active voice: I cannot authorize you to take three weeks of vacation in July.
Example Passive voice: Three weeks of vacation in July cannot be authorized.

Revise the following refusals so that they use passive-voice instead of active-voice verbs.

16. We will no longer be accepting credit cards for purchases under $5.

17. Our hospital policy forbids us from examining patients until we have verified their insurance coverage.

18. We cannot offer health and dental benefits until employees have been on the job for 12 months.

19. The manager and I have made arrangements for the investors to have lunch after the tour.

20. Your car rental insurance does not cover large SUVs.

21. Because management now requires more stringent security, we are postponing indefinitely requests for company tours.

Tips for Preparing Business Messages

Tips boxes summarize practical suggestions for creating effective business messages. Study them before completing your writing assignments.

Director, Administrative Operations
Alliance Resources International
538 Maricopa Plaza, Suite 1210
Phoenix, AZ 85008

Dear Mr. Nasserizad:

You have every right to expect complete confidentiality in your transactions with an independent consultant. As I explained in yesterday's telephone call, I am very distressed that you were called by a salesperson from Payroll Services, Inc. This should not have happened, and I apologize to you again for inadvertently mentioning your company's name in a conversation with a potential vendor, Payroll Services, Inc.
— Opens with agreement and apology

All clients of Paragon Consulting are assured that their dealings with our firm are held in the strictest confidence. Because your company's payroll needs are so individual and because you have so many contract workers, I was forced to explain how your employees differed from those of other companies. Revealing your company name was my error, and I take full responsibility for the lapse. I can assure you that it will not happen again. I have informed Payroll Services that it had no authorization to call you directly and its actions have forced me to reconsider using its services for my future clients.
— Explains what caused the problem and how it was resolved
— Takes responsibility and promises to prevent recurrence

A number of other payroll services offer outstanding programs. I'm sure we can find the perfect partner to enable you to outsource your payroll responsibilities, thus allowing your company to focus its financial and human resources on its core business. I look forward to our next appointment when you may choose from a number of excellent payroll outsourcing firms.
— Closes with forward look

Sincerely,

PARAGON CONSULTING ASSOCIATES

Catherine Martinez

Catherine Martinez
Partner

Tips for Resolving Problems and Following Up
- Whenever possible, call or see the individual involved.
- Describe the problem and apologize.
- Explain why the problem occurred.
- Take responsibility, if appropriate.
- Explain what you are doing to resolve the problem.
- Explain how it will not happen again.
- Follow up with a letter that documents the personal contact.
- Look forward to positive future relations.

Guffey helps you learn to communicate effectively and professionally in today's workplace, no matter what career path you choose to follow. The exciting, new *Essentials of Business Communication, 8e,* is packed with resources to make learning business communication easier and more enjoyable. The all-new student Web site houses powerful resources to help make learning with Guffey ... *just that easy.*

NEW! Student Support Web Site

www.meguffey.com gives you one convenient place to find the support you need. You can study with self-teaching grammar/mechanics activities, PowerPoint® slides, chapter review quizzes, Beat the Clock quizzes, and other valuable study tools.

Just That Easy!

Beat-the-Clock Interactive Quizzes

These fun **but challenging** interactive quizzes, available at **www.meguffey.com,** give you an opportunity **to review chapter concepts and make quick decisions** in a game-like environment.

Chapter Review Quizzes

Chapter review quizzes help you prepare for tests and check your understanding of the most important concepts in each chapter. Plus, each question includes feedback to help you understand why your answers are right or wrong.

Grammar/Mechanics Checkups

Improve your grammar skills by completing these Grammar/Mechanics Checkups. Available in the textbook and at the student Web site, these Checkups review all sections of the Grammar/Mechanics Handbook.

Grammar/Mechanics Challenge Documents

Build your language skills by finding and correcting errors in the Grammar/Mechanics Challenge Documents. Save time re-keying these documents by downloading them from the Web site.

Personal Language Trainer

Our Personal Language Trainer program helps you improve your language skills through a three-part plan that reviews, strengthens, and measures your knowledge. With immediate feedback, it's like having your own private language trainer coaching you as you work at a comfortable pace.

Online Writing Labs

This rich collection of Web sites provides relevant and publicly accessible online "handouts," style guides, and writing tips to help you in this course. You will find a variety of topics including citation formats, test-taking tips, grammar, and the writing process.

Dr. Guffey's Business Etiquette Guide

Do your table manners need to be polished before your next business dinner? Dr. Guffey explores 17 different business etiquette topics, including business dining, of interest to both workplace newcomers and veterans.

PowerPoint® Slides

You can review the most important topics of each chapter in these professionally designed PowerPoint slides. Study them before tests to check your understanding of key concepts.

> " *I have used the Guffey textbooks for years, and I think they offer the best exercises and supplemental materials in the market.* "

— DEBRA BOHLMAN, RASMUSSEN COLLEGE, ST. CLOUD, MINNESOTA

Accessing the Guffey Student Web site is *just that easy.* Follow the steps below to reach all of the study resources available.

Accessing the Guffey Student Web Site

1. Go to **www.meguffey.com.**

2. Click on the book cover for *Essentials of Business Communication, 8e.* Then click **Student: Companion Site.**

3. Click **Register.**

4. Follow the online prompts to create an account and enter your Access Code *exactly* as it appears on the access card that came with your new textbook.

5. Record your e-mail address and password and store it in a secure location for future visits.

SIGN IN

Already registered? Click here to sign in as a returning user.

REGISTER

Register your access code that came packaged with your new textbook. **NOTE:** If you have already created an account for a Cengage textbook, you can use that account information to register for www.meguffey.com after entering your access code.

ust That Easy!

Now that you've bought the textbook . . .

Get the best grade in the shortest time possible!

Visit **www.iChapters.com** to receive 25 percent off over 10,000 print, digital, and audio study tools that allow you to practice, review, and master course concepts using printed guides and manuals that work hand in hand with each chapter of your textbook.

Join the thousands of students who have benefited from **www.iChapters.com.** Just search by author, title, or ISBN, and then filter the results by "Study Tools" and select the format best suited for you.

www.iChapters.com

Brief Contents

Contents

Unit 3: Communicating at Work 97

Unit 4: Reporting Workplace Data 221

Unit 5: Professionalism, Teamwork, Meetings, and Speaking Skills 303

Unit 6: Employment Communication 371

Contents

Appendixes A-1

Grammar/Mechanics Handbook GM-1

About the Authors

Dr. Mary Ellen Guffey

A dedicated professional, Mary Ellen Guffey has taught business communication and business English topics for over thirty years. She received a bachelor's degree, *summa cum laude,* from Bowling Green State University; a master's degree from the University of Illinois, and a doctorate in business and economic education from the University of California, Los Angeles (UCLA). She has taught at the University of Illinois, Santa Monica College, and Los Angeles Pierce College.

Now recognized as the world's leading business communication author, Dr. Guffey corresponds with instructors around the globe who are using her books. She is the author of the award-winning *Business Communication: Process and Product,* the leading business communication textbook in this country and abroad. She has also written *Business English,* which serves more students than any other book in its field; *Essentials of College English* (with Carolyn M. Seefer), and *Essentials of Business Communication,* the leading text/workbook in its market. Dr. Guffey is active professionally, serving on the review boards of the *Business Communication Quarterly* and *The Journal of Business Communication,* participating in all national Association for Business Communication meetings, and sponsoring business communication awards.

A teacher's teacher and leader in the field, Dr. Guffey acts as a partner and mentor to hundreds of business communication instructors nationally and internationally. Her workshops, seminars, teleconferences, newsletters, articles, teaching materials, and Web sites help novice and veteran business communication instructors achieve effective results in their courses.

Dr. Dana Loewy

New to this edition, Dana Loewy brings extensive international expertise, broad business communication teaching experience, and exceptional writing skills. Born in former Czechoslovakia and raised in Germany, Dana Loewy earned a *magister artium* (M.A.) degree in English, linguistics, and communication from Rheinische Friedrich-Wilhelms-Universität Bonn, where she also studied Slavic languages and literatures and took business administration courses. Before receiving a master's degree and PhD from the University of Southern California, Dr. Loewy gained considerable teaching experience in freshman writing at USC. She also taught English—composition, reading, and grammar—at local two-year colleges.

A longtime professional translator, writer, and consultant, Dr. Loewy has published several books, articles, and translations, both poetry and prose. For the last 13 years, she has been teaching business communication at the largest business college on the West Coast, California State University, Fullerton. Dr. Loewy is excited to join Dr. Guffey, whom she considers a mentor and leader in the discipline.

Acknowledgments

I gratefully acknowledge the following reviewers whose excellent advice and constructive suggestions helped shape the Eighth Edition of *Essentials of Business Communication*:

Mary Y. Bowers
Northern Arizona University

Maryann Egan Longhi
Dutchess Community College

JoAnn Foth
Milwaukee Area Technical College

Gail Garton
Ozarks Technical Community College

Bonnie Jeffers
Mt. San Antonio College

Pamela R. Johnson
California State University, Chico

Rose Marie Kuceyeski
Owens Community College

Ruth E. Levy
Westchester Community College

Paula Marchese
State University of New York College at Brockport

For their contributions to previous editions, I warmly thank the following professionals:

Faridah Awang
Eastern Kentucky University

Joyce M. Barnes
Texas A & M University—Corpus Christi

Patricia Beagle
Bryant & Stratton Business Institute

Nancy C. Bell
Wayne Community College

Ray D. Bernardi
Morehead State University

Karen Bounds
Boise State University

Jean Bush-Bacelis
Eastern Michigan University

Cheryl S. Byrne
Washtenaw Community College

Steven V. Cates
Averett University

Lise H. Diez-Arguelles
Florida State University

Dee Anne Dill
Dekalb Technical Institute

Jeanette Dostourian
Cypress College

Nancy J. Dubino
Greenfield Community College

Cecile Earle
Heald College

Valerie Evans
Cuesta College

Bartlett J. Finney
Park University

Christine Foster
Grand Rapids Community College

Pat Fountain
Coastal Carolina Community College

Marlene Friederich
New Mexico State University—Carlsbad

Nanette Clinch Gilson
San Jose State University

Robert Goldberg
Prince George's Community College

Margaret E. Gorman
Cayuga Community College

Judith Graham
Holyoke Community College

Bruce E. Guttman
Katharine Gibbs School, Melville, New York

Tracey M. Harrison
Mississippi College

Debra Hawhee
University of Illinois

L. P. Helstrom
Rochester Community College

Jack Hensen
Morehead State University

Rovena L. Hillsman
California State University, Sacramento

Karen A. Holtkamp
Xavier University

Michael Hricik
Westmoreland County Community College

Sandie Idziak
University of Texas, Arlington

Karin Jacobson
University of Montana

Edna Jellesed
Lane Community College

Edwina Jordan
Illinois Central College

Sheryl E. C. Joshua
University of North Carolina, Greensboro

Diana K. Kanoy
Central Florida Community College

Ron Kapper
College of DuPage

Lydia Keuser
San Jose City College

Linda Kissler
Westmoreland County Community College

Deborah Kitchin
City College of San Francisco

Frances Kranz
Oakland University

Keith Kroll
Kalamazoo Valley Community College

Richard B. Larsen
Francis Marion University

Mary E. Leslie
Grossmont College

Nedra Lowe
Marshall University

Elaine Lux
Nyack College

Margarita Maestas-Flores
Evergreen Valley College

Jane Mangrum
Miami-Dade Community College

Maria Manninen
Delta College

Tim March
Kaskaskia College

Paula Marchese
SUNY College at Brockport

Kenneth R. Mayer
Cleveland State University

Karen McFarland
Salt Lake Community College

Bonnie Miller
Los Medanos College

Mary C. Miller
Ashland University

Willie Minor
Phoenix College

Nancy Moody
Sinclair Community College

Nancy Mulder
Grand Rapids Junior College

Paul W. Murphey
Southwest Wisconsin Technical College

Jackie Ohlson
University of Alaska—Anchorage

Richard D. Parker
Western Kentucky University

Martha Payne
Grayson County College

Catherine Peck
Chippewa Valley Technical College

Carol Pemberton
Normandale Community College

Carl Perrin
Casco Bay College

Jan Peterson
Anoka-Hennepin Technical College

Kay D. Powell
Abraham Baldwin College

Jeanette Purdy
Mercer County College

Carolyn A. Quantrille
Spokane Falls Community College

Susan Randles
Vatterott College

Diana Reep
University of Akron

Ruth D. Richardson
University of North Alabama

Carlita Robertson
Northern Oklahoma College

Vilera Rood
Concordia College

Judy Sunayama
Los Medanos College

Rich Rudolph
Drexel University

Dana H. Swensen
Utah State University

Joanne Salas
Olympic College

James A. Swindling
Eastfield College

Rose Ann Scala
Data Institute School of Business

David A. Tajerstein
SYRIT College

Joseph Schaffner
SUNY College of Technology, Alfred

Marilyn Theissman
Rochester Community College

Susan C. Schanne
Eastern Michigan University

Lois A. Wagner
Southwest Wisconsin Technical College

James Calvert Scott
Utah State University

Linda Weavil
Elan College

Laurie Shapero
Miami-Dade Community College

William Wells
Lima Technical College

Lance Shaw
Blake Business School

Gerard Weykamp
Grand Rapids Community College

Cinda Skelton
Central Texas College

Beverly Wickersham
Central Texas College

Estelle Slootmaker
Aquinas College

Leopold Wilkins
Anson Community College

Clara Smith
North Seattle Community College

Charlotte Williams
Jones County Junior College

Nicholas Spina
Central Connecticut State University

Almeda Wilmarth
State University of New York—Delhi

Marilyn St. Clair
Weatherford College

Barbara Young
Skyline College

In addition to honoring these friends and colleagues, I extend my warmest thanks to the many skillful professionals at Cengage Learning/South-Western including president Jonathan Hulbert; vice president of editorial business, Jack Calhoun; editor in chief, Melissa Acuña; acquisitions editor, Erin Joyner; marketing manager, Mike Aliscad; senior content project manager, Tamborah Moore; senior art director, Stacy Shirley, and media editor, John Rich. Special gratitude goes to my unsurpassed developmental editor and friend, Mary Draper for her remarkable insights, unflappable manner, professional support, steady guidance, and always sunny disposition.

For their outstanding work in developing testing and quiz materials, I thank Carolyn Seefer, Diablo Valley College; Catherine Peck and Jane Flesher, Chippewa Valley Technical College; and John Donnellan, University of Texas. For the exciting PowerPoint program, I am indebted to Corinne Livesay, Bryan College, and Dana Loewy, California State University, Fullerton. In recognition of excellent editing, I commend Malvine Litten and her staff at LEAP Publishing Services Inc. I am especially grateful to Dr. Dana Loewy, my coauthor, who brings to this edition a remarkable combination of teaching, international, and writing expertise.

Finally, I express deep gratitude to my husband, Dr. George R. Guffey, professor emeritus of English, University of California, Los Angeles, for his continuing technical and editorial advice, and, most of all, for his love, strength, and wisdom.

Mary Ellen Guffey

Communicating in Today's Workplace

Chapter 1
Career Success Begins With Communication Skills

Career Success Begins With Communication Skills

OBJECTIVES
After studying this chapter, you should be able to

- Understand the importance of education and especially the value of communication skills in relation to your income and success in today's changing workplace.

- Clarify the process of communication.

- Discuss techniques for becoming an effective listener.

- Analyze nonverbal communication and explain techniques for improving nonverbal communication skills.

- Explain how culture affects communication and describe methods to improve intercultural communication.

- Identify specific techniques that improve effective communication among diverse workplace audiences.

Communication Skills: Your Ticket to Work or Your Ticket Out the Door

Whether you are already working or are about to enter today's workplace, one of the fastest ways to ensure your career success is to develop excellent communication skills. Today's workplace revolves around communication. How good are your skills? If your communication skills are top notch, they can be your ticket to work. If not, they can be your ticket out the door. This textbook and this course can immediately help you improve your communication skills. Because the skills you are learning will make a huge difference in your ability to find a job and to be promoted, this will be one of the most important courses in your entire college career.

The Importance of Communication Skills to Your Career

Communication skills are critical to your job placement, performance, career advancement, and organizational success.

Surveys of employers consistently show that communication skills are critical to effective job placement, performance, career advancement, and organizational success.[1] In making hiring decisions, employers often rank communication skills among the most requested competencies. Many job advertisements specifically ask for excellent oral and written communication skills. In a poll of recruiters, oral and

WORKPLACE IN FOCUS

Today's graduates are light-years ahead when it comes to computer know-how. However, the long hours they spend instant messaging and "twittering" could be hampering important career skills. Nearly two thirds of employers say that college students are not prepared to work in the global economy, and communication is the skill that professionals find most lacking among new recruits. Tech-savvy youth are certainly expert at sending cryptic text messages at rapid-fire speed; however, analysts spot a correlation between prolonged use of electronic communication and the erosion of solid writing and speaking abilities. *What specific communication skills are essential for career success?*

written communication skills were by a large margin the top skill set sought.[2] In another poll, executives were asked what they looked for in a job candidate. The top choices were teamwork skills, critical thinking, analytical reasoning skills, and oral and written communication skills.[3]

When we discuss communication skills, we generally mean reading, listening, nonverbal, speaking, and writing skills. In this book we focus on listening, non-verbal, speaking, and writing skills. We devote special attention to writing skills because they are difficult to develop and increasingly significant.

Why Are Writing Skills Increasingly Important?

Writing skills are particularly important on the job today because people are writing more than ever before. Technology enables us to transmit messages faster, farther, and more easily than in the past. You will probably be writing many e-mail messages, such as that shown in Figure 1.1. In fact, e-mail is "today's version of the business letter or interoffice memo."[4] Because electronic mail has become the primary channel of communication in today's workplace, business e-mail messages must be clear, concise, and professional. Notice that the message in Figure 1.1 is more businesslike and more professional than the quick e-mail messages you might send to friends. Learning to write professional e-mail messages will be an important part of this course.

Writing skills are also increasingly significant today because many people work together but are not physically together. They stay connected through spoken and written messages. Writing skills, which were always a career advantage, are now a necessity.[5] A survey of American corporations revealed that two thirds of salaried employees have some writing responsibility. About one third of them, however, do not meet the writing requirements for their positions.[6]

"Businesses are crying out—they need to have people who write better," said Gaston Caperton, business executive and College Board president.[7] The ability to write opens doors to professional employment. People who cannot write and communicate clearly will not be hired. If already working, they are unlikely to last long enough to be considered for promotion. Writing is a marker of high-skill, high-wage, professional work, according to Bob Kerrey, president of New School University in New York and chair of the National Commission on Writing. If you can't express yourself clearly, he says, you limit your opportunities for many positions.[8]

Note: Small superscript numbers in the text announce information sources. Full citations begin on page N-1 near the end of the book. This edition uses a modified American Psychological Association (APA) format.

Advancements in technology mean that writing skills are increasingly important because more messages are being transmitted.

FIGURE 1.1 Businesslike, Professional E-Mail Message

Because e-mail messages are rapidly replacing business letters and interoffice memos, they must be written carefully, provide complete information, and sound businesslike and professional. Notice that this message is more formal in tone than e-mail messages you might send to friends.

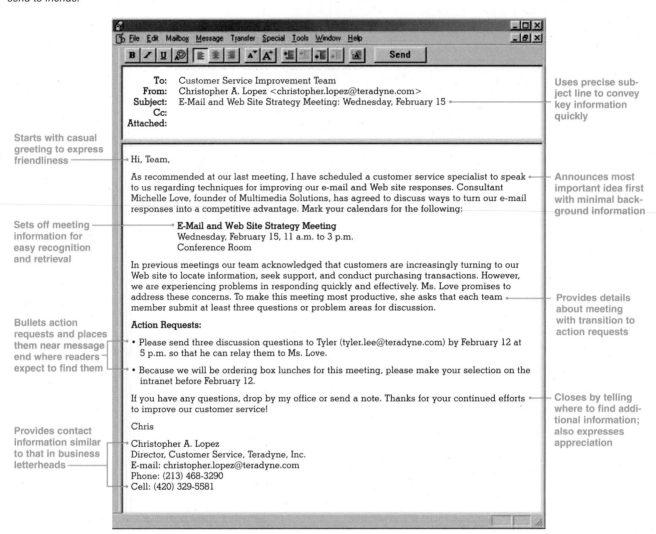

Uses precise subject line to convey key information quickly

Starts with casual greeting to express friendliness

Announces most important idea first with minimal background information

Sets off meeting information for easy recognition and retrieval

Bullets action requests and places them near message end where readers expect to find them

Provides details about meeting with transition to action requests

Closes by telling where to find additional information; also expresses appreciation

Provides contact information similar to that in business letterheads

You may be thinking that jobs in technical fields do not require communication skills. For example, communication has traditionally NOT been a necessary skill for finance and accounting professionals. However, times are changing. A recent poll of 1,400 chief financial officers sponsored by Accountemps revealed that 75 percent said that verbal, written, and interpersonal skills are more important today than they were in the past.[9] Even technical specialists must be able to communicate with others and explain their work clearly. A survey of Web professionals showed that those with writing and copyediting skills were far less likely to have their jobs sent offshore.[10] Another survey conducted by the Society for Information Management revealed that network professionals ranked written and oral communication skills among the top five most desired skills for new-hires.[11]

Professionalism Counts With Employers

In addition to expecting employees to write clearly, businesses expect employees to act in a businesslike and professional manner on the job. One employer was surprised that many of her new-hires had no idea that excessive absenteeism or tardiness was grounds for termination. The new employees also didn't seem to know that they were expected to devote their full energy to duties when on the job. One young man wanted to read Harry Potter novels when things got slow.[12]

Projecting and maintaining a professional image can make a real difference in helping you obtain the job of your dreams. Once you get that job, you are more likely to be taken seriously and promoted if you look and sound professional. New-hires can sabotage their careers when they carry poor college habits into the business world. Banish the flip-flops, sloppy clothes, and IM abbreviations. Think twice about sprinkling your conversation with *like, you know*, and uptalk (making declarative sentences sound like questions). You don't want to send the wrong message with unwitting and unprofessional behavior. Figure 1.2 reviews areas you will want to check to be sure you are projecting professionalism.

Looking and sounding professional gains you credibility on the job.

How Does Your Education Affect Your Income?

Because the U.S. economy is increasingly knowledge based, education is extremely important. Two thirds of all new jobs require some kind of postsecondary education. The more education you have, the more you can expect to earn and the less likely you will be unemployed, as shown in Figure 1.3. Notice that graduates with bachelor's degrees can expect to earn nearly three times as much as high school dropouts.

Writing is one aspect of education that is particularly well rewarded. A *Fortune* magazine article reported this finding: "Among people with a two- or four-year

Those with four-year degrees will earn nearly three times as much as high school dropouts.

FIGURE 1.2 Projecting Professionalism When You Communicate

	Unprofessional	Professional
Speech habits	Speaking in *uptalk*, a singsong speech pattern that has a rising inflection making sentences sound like questions, using *like* to fill in mindless chatter, substituting *go* for *said*, relying on slang, or letting profanity slip into your conversation.	Recognizing that your credibility can be seriously damaged by sounding uneducated, crude, or adolescent.
E-mail	Writing messages with incomplete sentences, misspelled words, exclamation points, IM slang, and senseless chatting. Sloppy, careless messages send a nonverbal message that you don't care, don't know, or aren't smart enough to know what is correct.	Including subjects, verbs, and punctuation marks. Employers don't recognize IM abbreviations. Call it crazy, but they value conciseness and correct spelling, even in brief e-mail messages.
Internet	Using an e-mail address such as *hotbabe@ hotmail.com, supasnugglykitty.@yahoo.com*, or *buffedguy@aol.com*.	An e-mail address should include your name or a relevant, positive, businesslike expression. It should not sound cute or like a chat room nickname.
Voice mail	An outgoing message with strident background music, weird sounds, or a joke message.	An outgoing message that states your name or phone number and provides instructions for leaving a message.
Telephone	Soap operas, thunderous music, or a TV football game playing noisily in the background when you answer the phone.	A quiet background when you answer the telephone, especially if you are expecting a prospective employer's call.
Cell and smart phones	Taking or placing calls during business meetings or during conversations with fellow employees; raising your voice (cell yell) or engaging in cell calls when others must reluctantly overhear; using a PDA during meetings.	Turning off phone and message notification, both audible and vibrate, during meetings; using your cell only when conversations can be private.

FIGURE 1.3 Income and Unemployment in Relation to Education

Education	Weekly Salary	Unemployment Rate
High school dropout	$ 522	7.1%
High school diploma	704	4.4%
Associate's degree	846	3.5%
Bachelor's degree or higher	1,393	2.1%

Source: E. L. Chao (2007, September 3). Knowledge fuels U.S. work force. Santa Barbara News-Press, p. A9.

college degree, those in the highest 20 percent in writing ability earn, on average, more than three times what those with the worst writing skills make."[13] One corporate president explained that many people climbing the corporate ladder are good. When he faced a hard choice between candidates, he used writing ability as the deciding factor. He said that sometimes writing is the only skill that separates a candidate from the competition.

Using This Book to Build Your Career Communication Skills

This book focuses on developing basic writing skills. You will also learn to improve your listening, nonverbal, and speaking skills. The abilities to read, listen, speak, and write effectively, of course, are not inborn. When it comes to communication, it is more *nurture* than *nature*. Good communicators are not born; they are made. Thriving in the dynamic and demanding new world of work will depend on many factors, some of which you cannot control. One factor that you *DO* control, however, is how well you communicate.

The goal of this book is to teach you basic business communication skills. These include learning how to write an e-mail, letter, or report and how to make a presentation. Anyone can learn these skills with the help of instructional materials and good model documents, all of which you will find in this book. You also need practice—with meaningful feedback. You need someone such as your instructor to tell you how to modify your responses so that you can improve.

We have designed this book, its supplements, and a new companion Web site at **www.meguffey.com** to provide you and your instructor with everything necessary to make you a successful business communicator in today's dynamic but demanding workplace. Given the increasing emphasis on communication, many businesses are paying large amounts to communication coaches and trainers to teach employees the very skills that you are learning in this course. Your instructor is your coach. So, get your money's worth! Pick your instructor's brains.

To get started, this first chapter presents an overview. You will take a quick look at the changing workplace, the communication process, listening, nonverbal communication, culture and communication, and workplace diversity. The remainder of the book is devoted to developing specific writing and speaking skills.

Succeeding in the Changing World of Work

The world of work is changing dramatically. The kind of work you will do, the tools you will use, the form of management you will work under, the environment in which you will be employed, the people with whom you will interact—all are undergoing a pronounced transformation. Many of the changes in this dynamic workplace revolve around processing and communicating information. As a result, the most successful players in this new world of work will be those with highly developed communication skills. The following business trends illustrate the importance of excellent communication skills:

Because communication skills are learned, you control how well you communicate.

Developing career-boosting communication skills requires instruction, practice, and feedback from a specialist.

Trends in the new world of work emphasize the importance of communication skills.

- **Flattened management hierarchies.** To better compete and to reduce expenses, businesses have for years been trimming layers of management. This means that as a frontline employee, you will have fewer managers. You will be making decisions and communicating them to customers, to fellow employees, and to executives.
- **More participatory management.** Gone are the days of command-and-control management. Now, even new employees like you will be expected to understand and contribute to the big picture. Improving productivity and profitability will be everyone's job, not just management's.
- **Increased emphasis on self-directed work groups and virtual teams.** Businesses today are often run by cross-functional teams of peers. You can expect to work with a team in gathering information, finding and sharing solutions, implementing decisions, and managing conflict. You may even become part of a virtual team whose members are in remote locations and who communicate almost exclusively electronically. Good communication skills are extremely important in working together successfully in all team environments, especially if members do not meet face-to-face.
- **Heightened global competition.** Because American companies are moving beyond local markets, you may be interacting with people from many cultures. As a successful business communicator, you will want to learn about other cultures. You will also need to develop intercultural skills including sensitivity, flexibility, patience, and tolerance.
- **Innovative communication technologies.** E-mail, fax, instant messaging, text messaging, the Web, company intranets, audio- and videoconferencing, wikis, voice recognition—all these innovative technologies are reshaping the way we communicate at work, as illustrated in Figure 1.4. You can expect to be communicating more often and more rapidly than ever before. Your writing and speaking skills will be showcased as never before.
- **New work environments.** Mobile technologies and the desire for a better balance between work and family have resulted in flexible working arrangements. You may become part of an increasing number of workers who are telecommuters or virtual team members. Working as a telecommuter or virtual team member requires even more communication, because staying connected with the office or with one another means exchanging many messages. Another work environment trend is the movement toward open offices divided into small work cubicles. Working in cubicles requires new rules of office etiquette and civility.
- **Focus on information and knowledge as corporate assets.** Corporate America is increasingly aware that information is the key to better products and increased profitability. You will be expected to gather, sort, store, and disseminate data in a timely and accurate fashion. This is the new way of business life.

> Today's employees must contribute to improving productivity and profitability.

> Increasing global competition and revolutionary technologies demand intercultural communication skills.

Understanding the Communication Process

As you can see, you can expect to be communicating more rapidly, more often, and with greater numbers of people than ever before. The most successful players in this new world of work will be those with highly developed communication skills. Because good communication skills are essential to your success, we need to take a closer look at the communication process.

Just what is communication? For our purposes *communication* is "the transmission of information and meaning from one individual or group to another." The crucial element in this definition is *meaning*. Communication has as its central objective the transmission of meaning. The process of communication is successful only when the receiver understands an idea as the sender intended it. This process generally involves five steps, discussed here and shown in Figure 1.5 on page 10.

> Communication is the transmission of information and meaning from one individual or group to another.

FIGURE 1.4 Communication and Collaborative Technologies

Communication Technologies: Reshaping the World of Work

Today's workplace is changing dramatically as a result of innovative software, superfast wireless networks, and numerous technologies that allow workers to share information, work from remote locations, and be more productive in or away from the office. We are seeing a gradual progression from basic capabilities, such as e-mail, instant messaging, and calendaring, to deeper functionality, such as remote database access, multifunctional devices, and Web-based collaborative applications. Becoming familiar with modern office and collaboration technologies can help you be successful in today's digital workplace.

Telephony: VoIP

Savvy businesses are switching from traditional phone service to voice over internet protocol (VoIP). This technology allows callers to communicate using a broadband Internet connection, thus eliminating long-distance and local telephone charges. Higher-end VoIP systems now support unified voice mail, e-mail, click-to-call capabilities, and softphones (phones using computer networking). Free or low-cost Internet telephony sites, such as the popular Skype, are also increasingly used by businesses.

Multifunctional Printers

Stand-alone copiers, fax machines, scanners, and printers have been replaced with multifunctional devices. Offices are transitioning from a "print and distribute" environment to a "distribute and print" environment. Security measures include pass codes and even biometric thumbprint scanning to make sure data streams are not captured, interrupted, or edited.

Open Offices

Widespread use of laptop computers, wireless technology, and VoIP have led to more fluid, flexible, and open workspaces. Smaller computers and flat-screen monitors enable designers to save space with boomerang-shaped workstations and cockpit-style work surfaces rather than space-hogging corner work areas. Smaller breakout areas for impromptu meetings are taking over some cubicle space, and digital databases are replacing file cabinets.

Handheld Wireless Devices

A new generation of lightweight, handheld smartphones provide phone, e-mail, Web browsing, and calendar options anywhere there is a wireless network. Devices such as the BlackBerry, the iPhone, and the Palm Treo now allow you to tap into corporate databases and intranets from remote locations. You can check customers' files, complete orders, and send out receipts without returning to the office.

Company Intranets

To share insider information, many companies provide their own protected Web sites called intranets. An intranet may handle company e-mail, announcements, an employee directory, a policy handbook, frequently asked questions, personnel forms and data, employee discussion forums, shared documents, and other employee information.

Voice Recognition

Computers equipped with voice recognition software enable users to dictate up to 160 words a minute with accurate transcription. Voice recognition is particularly helpful to disabled workers and to professionals with heavy dictation loads, such as physicians and attorneys. Users can create documents, enter data, compose and send e-mails, browse the Web, and control the desktop—all by voice.

Electronic Presentations

Business presentations in PowerPoint can be projected from a laptop or PDA or posted online. Sophisticated presentations may include animations, sound effects, digital photos, video clips, or hyperlinks to Internet sites. In some industries, PowerPoint slides ("decks") are replacing or supplementing traditional hard-copy reports.

Collaboration Technologies: Rethinking the Way We Work Together

Global competition, expanding markets, and the ever-increasing pace of business accelerate the development of exciting collaboration tools. New tools make it possible to work together without being together. Your colleagues may be down the hall, across the country, or around the world. With today's tools, you can exchange ideas, solve problems, develop products, forecast future performance, and complete team projects any time of the day or night and anywhere in the world. Blogs and wikis, part of the so-called Web 2.0 era, are social tools that create multidirectional conversations among customers and employees. Web 2.0 moves Web applications from "read only" to "read-write," thus enabling greater participation and collaboration.

Blogs, Podcasts, and Wikis

A *blog* is a Web site with journal entries usually written by one person and comments by others. Businesses use blogs to keep customers and employees informed and to receive feedback. Company developments can be posted, updated, and categorized for easy cross-referencing. *Podcasts* are usually short audio or video clips that users can either watch on a company Web site or download and view or listen to on their computers or MP3 players on the go. A *wiki* is a Web site that allows multiple users to collaboratively create and edit pages. Information gets lost in e-mails, but blogs and wikis provide an easy way to communicate and keep track of what is said. *RSS* (really simple syndication) *feeds* allow businesspeople and customers to receive updates automatically whenever podcasts, news stories, or blog entries become available on their favorite Web sites.

Voice Conferencing

Telephone "bridges" allow two or more callers from any location to share the same call. *Voice conferencing* (also called *audioconferencing*, *teleconferencing*, or just plain *conference calling*) enables people to collaborate by telephone. Communicators at both ends use enhanced speakerphones to talk and be heard simultaneously.

Videoconferencing

Videoconferencing allows participants to meet in special conference rooms equipped with cameras and television screens. Groups see each other and interact in real time although they may be continents apart. Faster computers, rapid Internet connections, and better cameras now enable 2 to 200 participants to sit at their own PCs and share applications, spreadsheets, presentations, and photos.

Web Conferencing

With services such as GoToMeeting, WebEx, Microsoft LiveMeeting, or the free Skype, all you need are a PC and an Internet connection to hold a meeting (*webinar*) with customers

or colleagues in real time. Although the functions are constantly evolving, Web conferencing currently incorporates screen sharing, chats, slide presentations, text messaging, and application sharing.

Presence Technology

Presence technology makes it possible to locate and identify a computing device as soon as users connect to the network. This technology is an integral part of communication devices including cell phones, laptop computers, PDAs, pagers, and GPS devices. Collaboration is possible wherever and whenever users are online.

Video Phones

Using advanced video compression technology, video phones transmit real-time audio and video so that communicators can see each other as they collaborate. With a video phone, people can videoconference anywhere in the world over a broadband IP (Internet Protocol) connection without a computer or a television screen.

FIGURE 1.5 The Communication Process

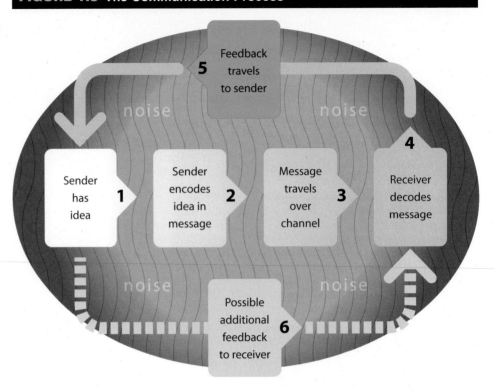

The communication process has five steps: idea formation, message encoding, message transmission, message decoding, and feedback.

1. **Sender has an idea.** The form of the idea may be influenced by the sender's mood, frame of reference, background, culture, and physical makeup, as well as the context of the situation.

2. **Sender encodes the idea in a message.** *Encoding* means converting the idea into words or gestures that will convey meaning. A major problem in communicating any message verbally is that words have different meanings for different people. That's why skilled communicators try to choose familiar words with concrete meanings on which both senders and receivers agree.

3. **Message travels over a channel.** The medium over which the message is transmitted is the *channel*. Messages may be sent by computer, telephone, letter, or memorandum. They may also be sent by means of a report, announcement, picture, spoken word, fax, or other channel. Because both verbal and nonverbal messages are carried, senders must choose channels carefully. Anything that disrupts the transmission of a message in the communication process is called *noise*. Channel noise ranges from static that disrupts a telephone conversation to spelling errors in an e-mail message. Such errors damage the credibility of the sender.

4. **Receiver decodes message.** The person for whom a message is intended is the *receiver*. Translating the message from its symbol form into meaning involves *decoding*. Successful communication takes place only when a receiver understands the meaning intended by the sender. Such success is often hard to achieve because no two people share the same background. Success is further limited because barriers and noise may disrupt the process.

5. **Feedback travels to sender.** The verbal and nonverbal responses of the receiver create *feedback*, a vital part of the entire communication process. Feedback helps the sender know that the message was received and understood. Senders can encourage feedback by asking questions such as, "Am I making myself clear?" and, "Is there anything you don't understand?" Senders can further

improve feedback by delivering the message at a time when receivers can respond. Senders should provide only as much information as a receiver can handle. Receivers can improve the process by paraphrasing the sender's message. They might say, "Let me try to explain that in my own words," or, "My understanding of your comment is . . ."

Improving Listening Skills

An important part of the communication process is listening. By all accounts, however, most of us are not very good listeners. Do you ever pretend to be listening when you are not? Do you know how to look attentive in class when your mind wanders far away? How about "tuning out" people when their ideas are boring or complex? Do you find it hard to focus on ideas when a speaker's clothing or mannerisms are unusual?

You probably answered *yes* to one or more of these questions because many of us have developed poor listening habits. In fact, some researchers suggest that we listen at only 25 percent efficiency. Such poor listening habits are costly in business. Messages must be rewritten, shipments reshipped, appointments rescheduled, contracts renegotiated, and directions restated.

To improve listening skills, we must first recognize barriers that prevent effective listening. Then we need to focus on specific techniques that are effective in improving listening skills.

Most individuals listen at only 25 percent efficiency.

Barriers to Effective Listening

As you learned earlier, barriers and noise can interfere with the communication process. Have any of the following barriers and distractions prevented you from hearing what has been said?

- **Physical barriers.** You cannot listen if you cannot hear what is being said. Physical impediments include hearing disabilities, poor acoustics, and noisy surroundings. It is also difficult to listen if you are ill, tired, uncomfortable, or worried.
- **Psychological barriers.** Everyone brings to the communication process a unique set of cultural, ethical, and personal values. Each of us has an idea of what is right and what is important. If other ideas run counter to our preconceived thoughts, we tend to "tune out" the speaker and thus fail to receive them.
- **Language problems.** Unfamiliar words can destroy the communication process because they lack meaning for the receiver. In addition, emotion-laden or "charged" words can adversely affect listening. If the mention of words such as *abortion* or *overdose* has an intense emotional impact, a listener may be unable to think about the words that follow.
- **Nonverbal distractions.** Many of us find it hard to listen if a speaker is different from what we view as normal. Unusual clothing, speech mannerisms, body twitches, or a radical hairstyle can cause enough distraction to prevent us from hearing what the speaker has to say.
- **Thought speed.** Because we can process thoughts at least three times faster than speakers can say them, we can become bored and allow our minds to wander.
- **Faking attention.** Most of us have learned to look as if we are listening even when we are not. Such behavior was perhaps necessary as part of our socialization. Faked attention, however, seriously threatens effective listening because it encourages the mind to engage in flights of unchecked fancy. Those who practice faked attention often find it hard to concentrate even when they want to.
- **Grandstanding.** Would you rather talk or listen? Naturally, most of us would rather talk. Because our own experiences and thoughts are most important to us, we grab the limelight in conversations. We sometimes fail to listen carefully because we are just waiting politely for the next pause so that we can have our turn to speak.

Barriers to listening may be physical, psychological, verbal, or nonverbal.

Most North Americans speak at about 125 words per minute. The human brain can process information at least three times as fast.

Keys to Building Powerful Listening Skills

You can reverse the harmful effects of poor habits by making a conscious effort to become an active listener. This means becoming involved. You can't sit back and hear whatever a lazy mind happens to receive. The following keys will help you become an active and effective listener:

- **Stop talking.** The first step to becoming a good listener is to stop talking. Let others explain their views. Learn to concentrate on what the speaker is saying, not on what your next comment will be.
- **Control your surroundings.** Whenever possible, remove competing sounds. Close windows or doors, turn off TVs and iPods, and move away from loud people, noisy appliances, or engines. Choose a quiet time and place for listening.
- **Establish a receptive mind-set.** Expect to learn something by listening. Strive for a positive and receptive frame of mind. If the message is complex, think of it as mental gymnastics. It is hard work but good exercise to stretch and expand the limits of your mind.
- **Keep an open mind.** We all sift and filter information through our own biases and values. For improved listening, discipline yourself to listen objectively. Be fair to the speaker. Hear what is really being said, not what you want to hear.
- **Listen for main points.** Heighten your concentration and satisfaction by looking for the speaker's central themes. Congratulate yourself when you find them!
  - **Capitalize on lag time.** Make use of the quickness of your mind by reviewing the speaker's points. Anticipate what is coming next. Evaluate evidence the speaker has presented. Don't allow yourself to daydream. Try to guess what the speaker's next point will be.
  - **Listen between the lines.** Focus both on what is spoken and what is unspoken. Listen for feelings as well as for facts.
  - **Judge ideas, not appearances.** Concentrate on the content of the message, not on its delivery. Avoid being distracted by the speaker's looks, voice, or mannerisms.
  - **Hold your fire.** Force yourself to listen to the speaker's entire argument or message before reacting. Such restraint may enable you to understand the speaker's reasons and logic before you jump to false conclusions.
- **Take selective notes.** In some situations thoughtful notetaking may be necessary to record important facts that must be recalled later. Select only the most important points so that the notetaking process does not interfere with your concentration on the speaker's total message.
- **Provide feedback.** Let the speaker know that you are listening. Nod your head and maintain eye contact. Ask relevant questions at appropriate times. Getting involved improves the communication process for both the speaker and the listener.

"How can I listen to you if you don't say the things I want to hear?"

© TED GOFF WWW.TEDGOFF.COM

Enhancing Your Nonverbal Communication Skills

Understanding messages often involves more than merely listening to spoken words. Nonverbal cues, in fact, can speak louder than words. These cues include eye contact, facial expression, body movements, space, time, territory, and appearance. All these nonverbal cues affect how a message is interpreted, or decoded, by the receiver.

Just what is nonverbal communication? It includes all unwritten and unspoken messages, whether intended or not. These silent signals have a strong effect on receivers. But understanding them is not simple. Does a downward glance indicate modesty? Fatigue? Does a constant stare reflect coldness? Dullness? Aggression? Do crossed arms mean defensiveness? Withdrawal? Or do crossed arms just mean that a person is shivering?

Messages are even harder to decipher when the verbal codes and nonverbal cues do not agree. What will you think if Scott says he is not angry, but he slams the door when he leaves? What if Alicia assures the hostess that the meal is excellent, but she eats very little? The nonverbal messages in these situations speak more loudly than the words.

When verbal and nonverbal messages conflict, receivers put more faith in nonverbal cues. In one study speakers sent a positive message but averted their eyes as they spoke. Listeners perceived the total message to be negative. Moreover, they thought that averted eyes suggested lack of affection, superficiality, lack of trust, and nonreceptivity.[14]

Successful communicators recognize the power of nonverbal messages. Although it is unwise to attach specific meanings to gestures or actions, some cues broadcast by body language are helpful in understanding the feelings and attitudes of senders.

How the Eyes, Face, and Body Send Silent Messages

Words seldom tell the whole story. Indeed, some messages are sent with no words at all. The eyes, face, and body can convey a world of meaning without a single syllable being spoken.

Eye Contact. The eyes have been called the windows to the soul. Even if they don't reveal the soul, the eyes are often the best predictor of a speaker's true feelings. Most of us cannot look another person straight in the eyes and lie. As a result, in American culture we tend to believe people who look directly at us. Sustained eye contact suggests trust and admiration; brief eye contact signals fear or stress. Good eye contact enables the message sender to see whether a receiver is paying attention, showing respect, responding favorably, or feeling distress. From the receiver's viewpoint, good eye contact, in North American culture, reveals the speaker's sincerity, confidence, and truthfulness.

Facial Expression. The expression on a person's face can be almost as revealing of emotion as the eyes. Experts estimate that the human face can display over 250,000 expressions.[15] To hide their feelings, some people can control these expressions and maintain "poker faces." Most of us, however, display our emotions openly. Raising or lowering the eyebrows, squinting the eyes, swallowing nervously, clenching the jaw, smiling broadly—these voluntary and involuntary facial expressions can add to or entirely replace verbal messages.

Posture and Gestures. A person's posture can convey anything from high status and self-confidence to shyness and submissiveness. Leaning toward a speaker suggests attraction and interest; pulling away or shrinking back denotes fear, distrust, anxiety, or disgust. Similarly, gestures can communicate entire thoughts via simple movements. However, the meanings of some of these movements differ in other cultures. Unless you know local customs, they can get you into trouble. In the United States and Canada, for example, forming the thumb and forefinger in a circle means everything is OK. But in Germany and parts of South America, the OK sign is obscene.

When verbal and nonverbal messages clash, listeners tend to believe the nonverbal message.

The eyes are thought to be the best predictor of a speaker's true feelings.

Nonverbal messages often have different meanings in different cultures.

DILBERT   By Scott Adams

"Sorry, Ridgely, but this area is my personal space."

What does your own body language say about you? To take stock of the kinds of messages being sent by your body, ask a classmate to critique your use of eye contact, facial expression, and body movements. Another way to analyze your nonverbal style is to videotape yourself making a presentation. Then study your performance. This way you can make sure your nonverbal cues send the same message as your words.

How Time, Space, and Territory Send Silent Messages

In addition to nonverbal messages transmitted by your body, three external elements convey information in the communication process: time, space, and territory.

Time. How we structure and use time tells observers about our personalities and attitudes. For example, when Donald Trump, multimillionaire real estate developer, gives a visitor a prolonged interview, he signals his respect for, interest in, and approval of the visitor or the topic to be discussed.

Space. How we order the space around us tells something about ourselves and our objectives. Whether the space is a bedroom, a dorm room, an office, or a department, people reveal themselves in the design and grouping of their furniture. Generally, the more formal the arrangement, the more formal and closed the communication style. The way office furniture is arranged sends cues about how communication is to take place. Former FBI director J. Edgar Hoover used to make his visitors sit at a small table below his large, elevated desk. Clearly, he did not want office visitors to feel equal to him.[16]

> The distance required for comfortable social interaction is controlled by culture.

Territory. Each of us has a certain area that we feel is our own territory, whether it is a specific spot or just the space around us. Your father may have a favorite chair in which he is most comfortable, a cook might not tolerate intruders in the kitchen, and veteran employees may feel that certain work areas and tools belong to them. We all maintain zones of privacy in which we feel comfortable. Figure 1.6 illustrates the four zones of social interaction among Americans, as formulated by anthropologist Edward T. Hall.[17] Notice that Americans are a bit standoffish; only intimate friends and family may stand closer than about 1½ feet. If someone violates that territory, Americans feel uncomfortable and defensive and may step back to reestablish their space.

FIGURE 1.6 Four Space Zones for Social Interaction

Intimate Zone
(1 to 1½ feet)

Personal Zone
(1½ to 4 feet)

Social Zone
(4 to 12 feet)

Public Zone
(12 or more feet)

Chapter 1: Career Success Begins With Communication Skills

How Appearance Sends Silent Messages

The physical appearance of a business document, as well as the personal appearance of an individual, transmits immediate and important nonverbal messages.

The appearance of a message and of an individual can convey positive or negative nonverbal messages.

Appearance of Business Documents. The way a letter, memo, or report looks can have either a positive or a negative effect on the receiver. Sloppy e-mail messages send a nonverbal message that you are in a terrific hurry or that you do not care about the receiver. Envelopes—through their postage, stationery, and printing—can suggest routine, important, or junk mail. Letters and reports can look neat, professional, well organized, and attractive—or just the opposite. In succeeding chapters you will learn how to create business documents that send positive nonverbal messages through their appearance, format, organization, readability, and correctness.

Personal Appearance. The way you look—your clothing, grooming, and posture—telegraphs an instant nonverbal message about you. Based on what they see, viewers make quick judgments about your status, credibility, personality, and potential. If you want to be considered professional, think about how you present yourself. One marketing manager said, "I'm young and pretty. It's hard enough to be taken seriously, and if I show up in jeans and a teeshirt, I don't stand a chance."[18] As a businessperson, you will want to think about what your appearance says about you. Although the rules of business attire have loosened up, some workers show poor judgment. You will learn more about professional attire and behavior in later chapters.

Keys to Building Strong Nonverbal Skills

Nonverbal communication can outweigh words in the way it influences how others perceive us. You can harness the power of silent messages by reviewing the following tips for improving nonverbal communication skills:

Because nonverbal cues can mean more than spoken words, learn to use nonverbal communication positively.

- **Establish and maintain eye contact.** Remember that in the United States and Canada, appropriate eye contact signals interest, attentiveness, strength, and credibility.
- **Use posture to show interest.** Encourage communication interaction by leaning forward, sitting or standing erect, and looking alert.
- **Improve your decoding skills.** Watch facial expressions and body language to understand the complete verbal and nonverbal messages being communicated.
- **Probe for more information.** When you perceive nonverbal cues that contradict verbal meanings, politely seek additional cues ("I'm not sure I understand," "Please tell me more about . . . ," or "Do you mean that . . .").
- **Avoid assigning nonverbal meanings out of context.** Don't interpret nonverbal behavior unless you understand a situation or a culture.
- **Associate with people from diverse cultures.** Learn about other cultures to widen your knowledge and tolerance of intercultural nonverbal messages.
- **Appreciate the power of appearance.** Keep in mind that the appearance of your business documents, your business space, and yourself sends immediate positive or negative messages to receivers.
- **Observe yourself on video.** Ensure that your verbal and nonverbal messages are in sync by recording and evaluating yourself making a presentation.
- **Enlist friends and family.** Ask friends and family to monitor your conscious and unconscious body movements and gestures to help you become an effective communicator.

How Culture Affects Communication

Comprehending the verbal and nonverbal meanings of a message is difficult even when communicators are from the same culture. When they come from different cultures, special sensitivity and skills are necessary.

Verbal and nonverbal messages are even more difficult to interpret when people come from different cultures.

With more than 1 billion people and a growing reputation as the second-largest English-speaking country, India has become a hot market for outsourced call center jobs. To accommodate the high demand for international customer support professionals in India, the city of Delhi offers more than 300,000 English and communication skills classes—and that is in addition to call center training offered locally through multinational corporations such as IBM and Wipro. *What challenges do India's call center professionals face when communicating with customers from across the globe?*

Negotiators for a North American company learned this lesson when they were in Japan looking for a trading partner. The North Americans were pleased after their first meeting with representatives of a major Japanese firm. The Japanese had nodded assent throughout the meeting and had not objected to a single proposal. The next day, however, the North Americans were stunned to learn that the Japanese had rejected the entire plan. In interpreting the nonverbal behavioral messages, the North Americans made a typical mistake. They assumed the Japanese were nodding in agreement as fellow North Americans would. In this case, however, the nods of assent indicated comprehension—not approval.

Every country has a unique culture or common heritage, joint experience, and shared learning that produce its culture. Their common experience gives members of that culture a complex system of shared values and customs. It teaches them how to behave; it conditions their reactions. Global business, new communication technologies, the Internet, and even Hollywood are spreading Western values throughout the world. However, cultural differences can still cause significant misunderstandings.

The more you know about culture in general and your own culture in particular, the better able you will be to adopt an intercultural perspective. In this book it is impossible to cover fully the infinite facets of culture. However, we can outline some key dimensions of culture and look at them from various points of view.

So that you will better understand your culture and how it contrasts with other cultures, we will describe five key dimensions of culture: context, individualism, formality, communication style, and time orientation.

Context

Low-context cultures (such as those in North America and Western Europe) depend less on the environment of a situation to convey meaning than do high-context cultures (such as those in China, Japan, and Arab countries).

Context is one of the most important cultural dimensions, yet it is among the most difficult to define. In a model developed by cultural anthropologist Edward T. Hall, context refers to the stimuli, environment, or ambience surrounding an event. Hall arranged cultures on a continuum, shown in Figure 1.7, from low to high in relation to context. Our figure also summarizes key comparisons for today's business communicators.

Communicators in low-context cultures (such as those in North America, Scandinavia, and Germany) depend little on the context of a situation to convey their meaning. They assume that listeners know very little and must be told practically everything. Low-context cultures tend to be logical, analytical, and action oriented. Business communicators stress clearly articulated messages that they consider to be objective, professional, and efficient. Words are taken literally.

FIGURE 1.7 Comparing High- and Low-Context Business Communicators

Culture has a powerful effect on business communicators. The following observations point out selected differences. Remember, however, that these are simplifications and that practices within a given culture vary considerably. Moreover, as globalization expands, low- and high-context cultures are experiencing change, and differences may be less pronounced.

Business Communicators in Low-Context Cultures	Business Communicators in High-Context Cultures
Assume listeners know little and must be told everything directly.	Assume listeners are highly "contexted" and require little background.
Value independence, initiative, self-assertion.	Value consensus, group decisions.
Rely on facts, data, and logic.	Rely on relationships rather than objective data.
Value getting down to business and achieving results.	Value relationships, harmony, status, and saving face.
Keep business and social relationships separate.	Intermix business and social relationships.
Expect negotiated decisions to be final and ironclad.	Expect to reopen discussions of decisions previously made.
Hold relaxed view toward wealth and power.	Defer to others based on wealth, position, seniority, and age.
Value competence regardless of position or status.	May value position and status over competence.
Have little problem confronting, showing anger, or making demands.	Avoid confrontation, anger, and emotion in business transactions.
Analyze meanings and attach face value to words.	May not take words literally; may infer meanings.

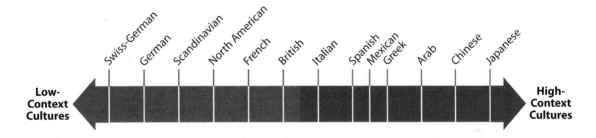

Communicators in high-context cultures (such as those in China, Japan, and Arab countries) assume that the listener is already "contexted" and does not need much background information.[19] Communicators in high-context cultures are more likely to be intuitive and contemplative. They may not take words literally. Instead, the meaning of a message may be implied from the social or physical setting, the relationship of the communicators, or nonverbal cues. For example, a Japanese communicator might say *yes* when he really means *no*. From the context of the situation, the Japanese speaker would indicate whether *yes* really meant *yes* or whether it meant *no*. The context, tone, time taken to answer, facial expression, and body cues would convey the meaning of *yes*.[20] Communication cues are transmitted by posture, voice inflection, gestures, and facial expression.

Individualism

An attitude of independence and freedom from control characterizes individualism. Members of low-context cultures, particularly Americans, tend to value individualism. They believe that initiative, self-assertion, and competence result in personal achievement. They believe in individual action and personal responsibility, and they desire a large degree of freedom in their personal lives.

Members of high-context cultures are more collectivist. They emphasize membership in organizations, groups, and teams; they encourage acceptance of group values, duties, and decisions. They typically resist independence because it fosters

Members of many low-context cultures value independence and freedom from control.

competition and confrontation instead of consensus. In group-oriented cultures such as those in many Asian societies, for example, self-assertion and individual decision making are discouraged. "The nail that sticks up gets pounded down" is a common Japanese saying.[21] Business decisions are often made by all who have competence in the matter under discussion. Similarly, in China managers also focus on the group rather than on the individual, preferring a "consultative" management style over an autocratic style.[22]

Many cultures, of course, are quite complex and cannot be characterized as totally individualistic or group oriented. For example, European Americans are generally quite individualistic, whereas African Americans are less so, and Latin Americans are closer to the group-centered dimension.[23]

Formality

Tradition, ceremony, and social rules are more important in some cultures than in others.

People in some cultures place less emphasis on tradition, ceremony, and social rules than do members of other cultures. Americans, for example, dress casually and are soon on a first-name basis with others. Their lack of formality is often characterized by directness. In business dealings Americans come to the point immediately; indirectness, they feel, wastes time, a valuable commodity in American culture.

This informality and directness may be confusing abroad. In Mexico, for instance, a typical business meeting begins with handshakes, coffee, and an expansive conversation about the weather, sports, and other light topics. An invitation to "get down to business" might offend a Mexican executive.[24] In Japan signing documents and exchanging business cards are important rituals. In Europe first names are used only after long acquaintance and by invitation. In Arab, South American, and Asian cultures, a feeling of friendship and kinship must be established before business can be transacted.

In Western cultures people are more relaxed about social status and the appearance of power.[25] Deference is not generally paid to individuals merely because of their wealth, position, seniority, or age. In many Asian cultures, however, these characteristics are important and must be respected. Deference and respect are paid to authority and power. Recognizing this cultural pattern, Marriott Hotel managers learned to avoid placing a lower-level Japanese employee on a floor above a higher-level executive from the same company.

Communication Style

Words are used differently by people in low- and high-context cultures.

People in low- and high-context cultures tend to communicate differently with words. To Americans and Germans, words are very important, especially in contracts and negotiations. People in high-context cultures, on the other hand, place more emphasis on the surrounding context than on the words describing a negotiation. A Greek may see a contract as a formal statement announcing the intention to build a business for the future. The Japanese may treat contracts as statements of intention, and they assume changes will be made as a project develops. Mexicans may treat contracts as artistic exercises of what might be accomplished in an ideal world. They do not necessarily expect contracts to apply consistently in the real world. An Arab may be insulted by merely mentioning a contract; a person's word is more binding.[26]

North Americans value a direct, straightforward communication style.

In communication style North Americans value straightforwardness, are suspicious of evasiveness, and distrust people who might have a "hidden agenda" or who "play their cards too close to the chest."[27] North Americans also tend to be uncomfortable with silence and impatient with delays. Some Asian businesspeople have learned that the longer they drag out negotiations, the more concessions impatient North Americans are likely to make.

Time Orientation

North Americans consider time a precious commodity. They correlate time with productivity, efficiency, and money. Keeping people waiting for business appointments wastes time and is also rude.

In other cultures time may be perceived as an unlimited and never-ending resource to be enjoyed. A North American businessperson, for example, was kept waiting two hours past a scheduled appointment time in South America. She wasn't offended, though, because she was familiar with Hispanics' more relaxed concept of time.

The perception of time and how it is used are culturally learned. In some cultures time is perceived analytically. People account for every minute of the day. In other cultures, time is holistic and viewed in larger chunks. Western cultures tend to be more analytical, scheduling appointments at 15- to 30-minute intervals. Eastern cultures tend to be more holistic, planning fewer but longer meetings. People in one culture may look at time as formal and task oriented. In another culture, time is seen as an opportunity to develop an interpersonal relationship. In the announcements of some international meetings, a qualifier may be inserted after the meeting time. For example, "The meeting starts at 10 A.M. Malaysian time." This tells participants whether to expect fixed or fluid scheduling.

Controlling Ethnocentrism and Stereotyping

The process of understanding and interacting successfully with people from other cultures is often hampered by two barriers: ethnocentrism and stereotyping. These two barriers, however, can be overcome by developing tolerance, a powerful and effective aid to communication.

Ethnocentrism. The belief in the superiority of one's own culture is known as *ethnocentrism*. This natural attitude is found in all cultures. Ethnocentrism causes us to judge others by our own values. If you were raised in North America, the values described in the preceding sections probably seem "right" to you, and you may wonder why the rest of the world doesn't function in the same sensible fashion. A North American businessperson in an Arab or Asian country might be upset at time spent over coffee or other social rituals before any "real" business is transacted. In these cultures, however, personal relationships must be established and nurtured before earnest talks may proceed.

Ethnocentrism is the belief in the superiority of one's own culture and group.

Stereotypes. Our perceptions of other cultures sometimes cause us to form stereotypes about groups of people. A *stereotype* is an oversimplified perception of a behavioral pattern or characteristic applied to entire groups. For example, the Swiss are hard-working, efficient, and neat; Germans are formal, reserved, and blunt; Americans are loud, friendly, and impatient; Canadians are polite, trusting, and tolerant; Asians are gracious, humble, and inscrutable. These attitudes may or may not accurately describe cultural norms. But when applied to individual business communicators, such stereotypes may create misconceptions and misunderstandings. Look beneath surface stereotypes and labels to discover individual personal qualities.

A *stereotype* is an oversimplified behavioral pattern applied to entire groups.

Tolerance. Working with people from other cultures demands tolerance and flexible attitudes. As global markets expand and as our society becomes increasingly multiethnic, tolerance becomes critical. *Tolerance*, here, does not mean "putting up with" or "enduring," which is one part of its definition. Instead, we use *tolerance* in a broader sense. It means learning about beliefs and practices different from our own and appreciating them. One of the best ways to develop tolerance is to practice *empathy*. This means trying to see the world through another's eyes. It means being nonjudgmental, recognizing things as they are rather than as they "should be."

Developing intercultural tolerance means practicing empathy, being nonjudgmental, and being patient.

For example, in China, the American snack foods manufacturer Frito-Lay had to accommodate yin and yang, the Chinese philosophy that nature and life must balance opposing elements. Chinese consider fried foods to be hot and avoid them in summer because two "hots" don't balance. They prefer "cool" snacks in summer; therefore, Frito-Lay created "cool lemon" potato chips dotted with lime specks and mint. The yellow, lemon-scented chips are delivered in a package showing breezy-blue skies and rolling green grass.[28] Instead of imposing the American view that potato chips are fine as a summer snack, Frito-Lay looked at its product through the eyes of its Chinese consumers and adjusted accordingly.

The following suggestions can help you prevent miscommunication in oral and written transactions across cultures.

How to Minimize Oral Miscommunication Among Intercultural Audiences

When you have a conversation with someone from another culture, you can reduce misunderstandings by following these tips:

- **Use simple English.** Speak in short sentences (under 20 words) with familiar, short words. Eliminate puns, sports and military references, slang, and jargon (special business terms). Be especially alert to idiomatic expressions that can't be translated, such as *burn the midnight oil* and *under the weather*.
- **Speak slowly and enunciate clearly.** Avoid fast speech, but don't raise your voice. Overpunctuate with pauses and full stops. Always write numbers for all to see.
- **Encourage accurate feedback.** Ask probing questions, and encourage the listener to paraphrase what you say. Don't assume that a *yes*, a nod, or a smile indicates comprehension or assent.
- **Check frequently for comprehension.** Avoid waiting until you finish a long explanation to request feedback. Instead, make one point at a time, pausing to check for comprehension. Don't proceed to B until A has been grasped.
  - **Observe eye messages.** Be alert to a glazed expression or wandering eyes. These tell you the listener is lost.
  - **Accept blame.** If a misunderstanding results, graciously accept the blame for not making your meaning clear.
  - **Listen without interrupting.** Curb your desire to finish sentences or to fill out ideas for the speaker. Keep in mind that North Americans abroad are often accused of listening too little and talking too much.
  - **Smile when appropriate.** Roger Axtell, international behavior expert, calls the smile the single most understood and most useful form of communication in either personal or business transactions. In some cultures, however, excessive smiling may seem insincere.[29]
  - **Follow up in writing.** After conversations or oral negotiations, confirm the results and agreements with follow-up letters. For proposals and contracts, engage a qualified translator to prepare copies in the local language.

© 1989 by NEA, Inc

BERRY'S WORLD © BY NEA, INC.

"He doesn't understand you. Try shouting a little louder."

How to Minimize Written Miscommunication Among Intercultural Audiences

When you write to someone from a different culture, you can improve your chances of being understood by following these suggestions:

- **Consider local styles.** Learn how documents are formatted and how letters are addressed and developed in the intended reader's country. Decide whether to use your organization's preferred format or adjust to local styles.
- **Consider hiring a translator.** Engage a professional translator if (a) your document is important, (b) your document will be distributed to many readers, or (c) you must be persuasive.
- **Use short sentences and short paragraphs.** Sentences with fewer than 20 words and paragraphs with fewer than 8 lines are most readable.
- **Avoid ambiguous wording.** Include relative pronouns (*that, which, who*) for clarity in introducing clauses. Stay away from contractions (especially ones such as *Here's the problem*). Avoid idioms (*once in a blue moon*), slang (*my presentation really bombed*), acronyms (*ASAP* for *as soon as possible*), abbreviations (*DBA* for *doing business as*), and jargon (*input, output, clickstream*). Use action-specific verbs (*purchase a printer* rather than *get a printer*).

- **Cite numbers carefully.** For international trade it is a good idea to learn and use the metric system. In citing numbers, use figures (*15*) instead of spelling them out (*fifteen*). Always convert dollar figures into local currency. Avoid using figures to express the month of the year. In North America, for example, *March 5, 2009*, might be written as *3/5/09*, while in Europe the same date might appear as *5.3.09*. For clarity, always spell out the month.

Capitalizing on Workforce Diversity

As global competition opens world markets, North American businesspeople will increasingly interact with customers and colleagues from around the world. At the same time, the North American workforce is also becoming more diverse—in race, ethnicity, age, gender, national origin, physical ability, and countless other characteristics. No longer, say the experts, will the workplace be predominantly male or Anglo-oriented. By 2020 many groups now considered minorities (African Americans, Hispanics, Asians, Native Americans) are projected to become 36 percent of the U.S. population. By 2050 these same groups are expected to surge to 47 percent of the U.S. population.[30] Women will become nearly 50 percent of the workforce. Moreover, it is estimated that the share of the population over 65 will jump dramatically from 13 percent now to 20 percent in 2050. Trends suggest that many of these older people will remain in the workforce.

While the workforce is becoming more diverse, the structure of businesses in North America is also changing. As you learned earlier, many workers are now organized by teams. Organizations are flatter, and rank-and-file workers are increasingly making decisions among themselves. What does all this mean for you as a future business communicator? Simply put, your job may require you to interact with colleagues and customers from around the world. Your work environment will probably demand that you cooperate effectively with small groups of coworkers. What's more, these coworkers may differ from you in race, ethnicity, gender, age, and other ways.

> You can expect to be interacting with customers and colleagues who may differ from you in race, ethnicity, age, gender, national origin, physical ability, and many other characteristics.

Benefits of a Diverse Workforce

A diverse work environment offers many benefits. Consumers want to deal with companies that respect their values and create products and services tailored to their needs. Organizations that hire employees with various experiences and backgrounds are better able to create the products these consumers desire.

At Procter & Gamble a senior marketing executive hit the nail on the head when he said, "I don't know how you can effectively market to the melting pot that this country represents without a workforce and vendors who have a gut-level understanding of the needs and wants of all of these market segments. . . . When we started getting a more diverse workforce, we started getting richer [marketing] plans, because they came up with things that white males were simply not going to come up with on their own."[31] At PepsiCo, work teams created new products inspired by diversity efforts. Those products included guacamole-flavored Doritos chips and Gatorade Xtremo aimed at Hispanics, as well as Mountain Dew Code Red, which appeals to African Americans. One Pepsi executive said that companies that "figure out the diversity challenge first will clearly have a competitive advantage."[32]

In addition, organizations that set aside time and resources to cultivate and capitalize on diversity will suffer fewer discrimination lawsuits, fewer union clashes, and less government regulatory action. Most important, though, is the growing realization among organizations that diversity is a critical bottom-line business strategy to improve employee relationships and to increase productivity. Developing a diverse staff that can work together cooperatively is one of the biggest challenges facing business organizations today.

"We need to focus on diversity. Your goal is to hire people who all look different, but think just like me."

Improving Communication Among Diverse Workplace Audiences

Integrating all this diversity into one seamless workforce is a formidable but vital task. Harnessed effectively, diversity can enhance productivity and propel a company to success well into the twenty-first century. Mismanaged, it can become a tremendous drain on a company's time and resources. How companies deal with diversity will make all the difference in how they compete in an increasingly global environment. This means that organizations must do more than just pay lip service to these issues. Harmony and acceptance do not happen automatically when people who are dissimilar work together. The following suggestions can help you and your organization find ways to improve communication and interaction:

- **Understand the value of differences.** Diversity makes an organization innovative and creative. Sameness fosters an absence of critical thinking called "groupthink." Case studies, for example, of the *Challenger* shuttle disaster suggest that groupthink prevented alternatives from being considered. Even smart people working collectively can make dumb decisions if they do not see different perspectives.[33] Diversity in problem-solving groups encourages independent and creative thinking.

- **Seek training.** Especially if an organization is experiencing diversity problems, awareness-raising sessions may be helpful. Spend time reading and learning about workforce diversity and how it can benefit organizations. Look upon diversity as an opportunity, not a threat. Intercultural communication, team building, and conflict resolution are skills that can be learned in diversity training programs.

- **Learn about your cultural self.** Begin to think of yourself as a product of your culture, and understand that your culture is just one among many. Try to stand outside and look at yourself. Do you see any reflex reactions and automatic thought patterns that are a result of your upbringing? These may be invisible to you until challenged by people who are different from you. Remember, your culture was designed to help you succeed and survive in a certain environment. Be sure to keep what works and yet be ready to adapt as your environment changes.

- **Make fewer assumptions.** Be careful of seemingly insignificant, innocent workplace assumptions. For example, don't assume that everyone wants to observe the holidays with a Christmas party and a decorated tree. Celebrating only Christian holidays in December and January excludes those who honor Hanukkah, Kwanzaa, and the Lunar New Year. Moreover, in workplace discussions don't assume that everyone is married or wants to be or is even heterosexual, for that matter. For invitations, avoid phrases such as *managers and their wives. Spouses* or *partners* is more inclusive. Valuing diversity means making fewer assumptions that everyone is like you or wants to be like you.

- **Build on similarities.** Look for areas in which you and others not like you can agree or at least share opinions. Be prepared to consider issues from many perspectives, all of which may be valid. Accept that there is room for various points of view to coexist peacefully. Although you can always find differences, it is much harder to find similarities. Look for common ground in shared experiences, mutual goals, and similar values. Concentrate on your objective even when you may disagree on how to reach it.[34]

> Successful communicators understand the value of differences, seek training, learn about their own cultures, make fewer assumptions, and build on similarities.

> In times of conflict, look for areas of agreement and build on similarities.

Visit www.meguffey.com
- **Chapter Review Quiz**
- **Flash Cards**
- **Grammar Practice**
- **PowerPoint Slides**
- **Personal Language Trainer**
- **Beat the Clock Quiz**

Summing Up and Looking Forward

This chapter described the importance of communication skills in today's information economy. Writing skills are particularly important because businesspeople are doing more writing than ever before. In addition, many of the changes in today's dynamic workplace revolve around processing and communicating information. Flattened management hierarchies, participatory management, increased emphasis on work teams, heightened global competition, and innovative communication technologies are all trends that increase the need for good communication skills. To improve your skills, you should understand the communication process. Communication doesn't take place unless senders encode meaningful messages that can be decoded and understood by receivers.

One important part of the communication process is listening. You can become a more active listener by keeping an open mind, listening for main points, capitalizing on lag time, judging ideas and not appearances, taking selective notes, and providing feedback. The chapter also described ways to help you improve your nonverbal communication skills.

You learned about the powerful effect that culture has on communication, and you became more aware of the cultural dimensions of context, individualism, formality, communication style, and time orientation. Finally, the chapter discussed ways that businesses and individuals can capitalize on workforce diversity.

The following chapters present the writing process. You will learn specific techniques to help you improve your written and oral expression. Remember, communication skills are not inherited. They are learned, and anyone can learn to be a good communicator. Writing skills are critical because they function as a gatekeeper. Poor skills keep you in low-wage, dead-end work. Good skills open the door to high wages and career advancement.[35]

Critical Thinking

1. Why is it important for business and professional students to develop good communication skills, and why are writing skills especially essential?

2. Recall a time when you experienced a problem as a result of poor communication. What were the causes of and possible remedies for the problem?

3. How are listening skills important to employees, supervisors, and executives? Who should have the best listening skills?

4. What arguments could you give for or against the idea that body language is a science with principles that can be interpreted accurately by specialists?

5. Because English is becoming the international language of business and because the United States is a dominant military and trading force, why should Americans bother to learn about other cultures?

Chapter Review

6. What percentage of new jobs require postsecondary education?

7. Are communication skills acquired by *nature* or by *nurture*? Explain.

8. List seven trends in the workplace that affect business communicators. Be prepared to discuss how they might affect you in your future career.

9. Give a brief definition of the following words:
   a. Encode
   b. Channel
   c. Decode

10. List 11 techniques for improving your listening skills. Be prepared to discuss each.

11. When verbal and nonverbal messages conflict, which are receivers more likely to believe? Give an original example.

12. Would your culture be classified as high- or low-context? Why?

13. What is ethnocentrism, and how can it be reduced?

14. List seven or more suggestions for enhancing comprehension when you are talking with nonnative speakers of English. Be prepared to discuss each.

15. List five suggestions for improving communication among diverse workplace audiences. Be prepared to discuss each.

Activities and Cases

1.1 Pumping Up Your Basic Language Muscles

You can enlist the aid of your author to help you pump up your basic language skills. As your personal trainer, Dr. Guffey provides a three-step workout plan and hundreds of interactive questions to help you brush up on your grammar and mechanics skills. You receive immediate feedback in the warm-up sessions, and when you finish a complete workout, you can take a short test to assess what you learned. These workouts are completely self-taught, which means you can review at your own pace and repeat as often as you need. *Your Personal Language Trainer* is available at your premium Web site, **www.meguffey.com**. In addition to pumping up your basic language muscles, you can also use *Spell Right!* and *Speak Right!* to improve your spelling and pronunciation skills.

Your Task. Begin using *Your Personal Language Trainer* to brush up on your basic grammar and mechanics skills by completing one to three workouts per week or as many as your instructor advises. Be prepared to submit a printout of your "fitness" (completion) certificate when you finish a workout module. If your instructor directs, complete the spelling exercises in *Spell Right!* and submit a certificate of completion for the spelling final exam.

E-MAIL

1.2 Getting to Know You

Your instructor wants to know more about you, your motivation for taking this course, your career goals, and your writing skills.

Your Task. Send an e-mail or write a memo of introduction to your instructor. See Chapter 5 for formats and tips on preparing e-mail messages. In your message include the following:

a. Your reasons for taking this class

b. Your career goals (both temporary and long-term)

c. A brief description of your employment, if any, and your favorite activities

d. An assessment and discussion of your current communication skills, including your strengths and weaknesses

For online classes, write a letter of introduction about yourself with the preceding information. Post your letter to your discussion board. Read and comment on the letters of other students. Think about how people in virtual teams must learn about each other through online messages.

TEAM

1.3 Small-Group Presentation: Getting to Know Each Other

Many business organizations today use teams to accomplish their goals. To help you develop speaking, listening, and teamwork skills, your instructor may assign team projects. One of the first jobs in any team is selecting members and becoming acquainted.

Your Task. Your instructor will divide your class into small groups or teams. At your instructor's direction, either (a) interview another group member and introduce that person to the group or (b) introduce yourself to the group. Think of this as an informal interview for a team assignment or for a job. You will want to make notes from which to speak. Your introduction should include information such as the following:

a. Where did you grow up?

b. What work and extracurricular activities have you engaged in?

c. What are your interests and talents? What are you good at doing?

d. What have you achieved?

e. How familiar are you with various computer technologies?

f. What are your professional and personal goals? Where do you expect to be five years from now?

To develop listening skills, team members should practice the good listening techniques discussed in this chapter and take notes. They should be prepared to discuss three important facts as well as remember details about each speaker.

1.4 Class Listening

Have you ever consciously observed the listening habits of others?

Your Task. In one of your classes, study student listening habits for a week. What barriers to effective listening did you observe? How many of the suggestions described in this chapter are being implemented by listeners in the class? Write a memo or an e-mail message to your instructor briefly describing your observations. (See Chapter 5 to learn more about e-mail messages and memos.)

1.5 How Good Are Your Listening Skills? Self-Checked Rating Quiz
You can learn whether your listening skills are excellent or deficient by completing a brief quiz.

Your Task. Take Dr. Guffey's Listening Quiz at **www.meguffey.com**. What two listening behaviors do you think you need to work on the most?

1.6 Silent Messages
Becoming more aware of the silent messages you send helps you make them more accurate.

Your Task. Analyze the kinds of silent messages you send your instructor, your classmates, and your employer. How do you send these messages? Group them into categories, as suggested by what you learned in this chapter. What do these messages mean? Be prepared to discuss them in small groups or in a memo to your instructor.

1.7 Body Language
Can body language be accurately interpreted?

Your Task. What attitudes do the following body movements suggest to you? Do these movements always mean the same thing? What part does context play in your interpretations?

a. Wringing hands, tugging ears

b. Bowed posture, twiddling thumbs

c. Steepled hands, sprawling sitting position

d. Rubbing hand through hair

e. Open hands, unbuttoned coat

1.8 Universal Sign for "I Goofed"
In an effort to promote peace and tranquillity on the highways, motorists submitted the following suggestions to a newspaper columnist.[36]

Your Task. In small groups consider the pros and cons of each of the following gestures intended as an apology when a driver makes a mistake. Why would some fail?

a. Lower your head slightly and bonk yourself on the forehead with the side of your closed fist. The message is clear: "I'm stupid. I shouldn't have done that."

b. Make a temple with your hands, as if you were praying.

c. Move the index finger of your right hand back and forth across your neck—as if you were cutting your throat.

d. Flash the well-known peace sign. Hold up the index and middle fingers of one hand, making a V, as in Victory.

e. Place the flat of your hands against your cheeks, as children do when they have made a mistake.

f. Clasp your hand over your mouth, raise your brows, and shrug your shoulders.

g. Use your knuckles to knock on the side of your head. Translation: "Oops! Engage brain."

h. Place your right hand high on your chest and pat a few times, like a basketball player who drops a pass or a football player who makes a bad throw. This says, "I'll take the blame."

i. Place your right fist over the middle of your chest and move it in a circular motion. This is universal sign language for "I'm sorry."

j. Open your window and tap the top of your car roof with your hand.

k. Smile and raise both arms, palms outward, which is a universal gesture for surrender or forgiveness.

l. Use the military salute, which is simple and shows respect.

m. Flash your biggest smile, point at yourself with your right thumb and move your head from left to right, as if to say, "I can't believe I did that."

1.9 Workplace Writing: Separating Myths From Facts
Today's knowledge workers are doing more writing on the job than ever before. Flattened management hierarchies, heightened global competition, expanded team-based management, and heavy reliance on e-mail have all contributed to more written messages.

Your Task. In teams or in class, discuss the following statements. Are they myths or facts?

a. Because I'm in a technical field, I will work with numbers, not words.

b. Secretaries will clean up my writing problems.

c. Technical writers do most of the real writing on the job.

d. Computers can fix any of my writing mistakes.

e. I can use form letters for most messages.

1.10 Translating Idioms

Many languages have idiomatic expressions that do not always make sense to outsiders.

Your Task. Explain in simple English what the following idiomatic expressions mean. Assume that you are explaining them to nonnative speakers of English.

a. can't hold a candle

b. class act

c. grey area

d. cold shoulder

e. early bird

f. get your act together

g. go ape

h. soldier on

i. the bottom of the barrel

E-MAIL

1.11 Analyzing Diversity at Reebok

Reebok grew from a $12 million a year sport shoe company into a $3 billion footwear and apparel powerhouse without giving much thought to the hiring of employees. "When we were growing very, very fast, all we did was bring another friend into work the next day," recalled Sharon Cohen, Reebok vice president. "Everybody hired nine of their friends. Well, it happened that nine white people hired nine of their friends, so guess what? They were white, all about the same age. And then we looked up and said, 'Wait a minute. We don't like the way it looks here.' That's the kind of thing that can happen when you are growing very fast and thoughtlessly."[37]

Your Task. In what ways would Reebok benefit by diversifying its staff? What competitive advantages might it gain? Outline your reasoning in an e-mail message to your instructor.

Video Resources

Two video libraries accompany Guffey's *Essentials of Business Communication*, 8e. These videos take you beyond the classroom to build the communication skills you will need to succeed in today's rapidly changing workplace.

Video Library 1, Building Workplace Skills, includes seven videos that introduce and reinforce concepts in selected chapters. These excellent tools ease the learning load by demonstrating chapter-specific material to strengthen your comprehension and retention of key ideas.

The recommended video for this chapter is **Communication Foundations**, which illustrates how strong communication skills can help you advance your career in today's challenging world of work. Be prepared to discuss critical-thinking questions your instructor may provide.

Video Library 2, Bridging the Gap, presents six videos transporting you inside high-profile companies such as Cold Stone Creamery, Ben & Jerry's, and Hard Rock Cafe. You will be able to apply your new skills in structured applications aimed at bridging the gap between the classroom and the real world of work.

We recommend three videos for this chapter:

Video Library 1: *Career Success Starts With Communication Foundations.* Made especially for Guffey books, this film illustrates the changing business world, flattened management hierarchies, the communication process, communication flow, ethics, listening, nonverbal communication, and other topics to prepare you for today's workplace. The film is unique in that many concepts are demonstrated through role-playing. Be prepared to discuss critical-thinking questions at the film's conclusion.

Video Library 1: *Intercultural Communication at Work.* This film illustrates intercultural misunderstandings when a Japanese businessman visits an American advertising agency that seeks his business. The agency owners, Rob and Ella, as well as the receptionist, Stephanie, make numerous cultural blunders because they are unaware of the differences between high- and low-context cultures. At the film's conclusion you will have an opportunity to make suggestions for improving Rob and Ella's cultural competence.

Video Library 2: *Understanding Teamwork: Cold Stone Creamery.* This video highlights teamwork at Cold Stone Creamery, a fast-growing ice cream specialty chain. It shows team members behind the counter but also provides the inside scoop through the insights of Kevin Myers, vice president, marketing. Viewers see how teamwork permeates every facet of Cold Stone's corporate culture. Look for a definition of *team*, as well as six kinds of teams and the characteristics of successful teams.

These checkups are designed to improve your control of grammar and mechanics. They systematically review all sections of the Grammar/Mechanics Handbook. Answers are provided near the end of the book. You will find Advanced Grammar/Mechanics Checkups with immediate feedback at your premium Web site, **www.meguffey.com**.

Nouns

Review Sections 1.02–1.06 in the Grammar/Mechanics Handbook. Then study each of the following statements. Underscore any inappropriate form, and write a correction in the space provided. Also record the appropriate G/M section and letter to illustrate the principle involved. If a sentence is correct, write C. When you finish, compare your responses with those provided. If your answers differ, study carefully the principles shown in parentheses.

Attorneys   (1.05d)

Example Attornies seem to be the only ones who benefit from class action suits.

inquiries

1. A huge number of inquirys overwhelmed their two Web sites.

C

2. Banks are installing multilingual ATMs to serve customers.

Companies

3. Some companys are giving up land lines for cell phones.

saturdays

4. Business is better on Saturday's than on Sundays.

turkey

5. Frozen turkies fill the grocery's lockers at Thanksgiving.

Bushes

6. Only the Bushs and the Sanchezes brought their entire families.

2000.

7. During the 2000's stock prices fluctuated extremely.

editors, chief

8. Both editor in chiefs instituted strict proofreading policies.

complexes

9. Luxury residential complexs are part of the architect's plan.

counties

10. Voters in three countys are likely to approve new school taxes.

cassidys

11. The instructor was surprised to find two Cassidy's in one class.

C

12. André sent digital photos of two valleys in France before we planned our trip.

liabilities

13. Most companies have copies of statements showing their assets and liabilitys.

C

14. My flat-screen monitor makes it difficult to distinguish between o's and a's.

women

15. Both of her sisters-in-law were woman with high principles.

The following letter has intentional errors in spelling, proofreading, noun plurals, and sentence structure. You may either (a) use standard proofreading marks (see Appendix B) to correct the errors here or (b) download the document from your companion Web site and revise at your computer. Study the guidelines in the Grammar/Mechanics Handbook to sharpen your skills.

FOREST COMMUNICATION SERVICES
259 Elm Street, Suite 400
Cambridge, MA 02124
(617) 830-2871
conferencing@forest.com

April 12, 200x

Ms. Rachel M. Fisher
Workplace Monthly Magazine
302 Northland Boulevard
Cincinnati, OH 45246

Dear Ms. Fletcher:

Thank you for giving Forrest Communication Services opportunity to contribute to the magazine article. That you are writing about Web conferencing for *Workplace Monthly Magazine*. My specialty here at Forest Communication is conferencing service's for North America.

Online meetings are definitely becomming more frequent. Web conferencing began in the 1990's, but it has grown rapidly in the 2000's. Many companys find that such meeting save time and money. Participants can hold live, interactive meetings and share documents and presentations. Without ever leaving their offices or homes. Web conferencing is simply more convenient then having to attend meeting in person. Let me summarize a few Web conferencing feature:

- **Participant ID.** This feature displays on your screen the name of all attendee's and indicates who is talking over the phone line.
- **PowerPoints/Document Sharring.** Presenters can show batchs of Web-based visuals and describe them by talking on the telephone.
- **Polling/Surveys.** A virtual "show of hands" can speed consensus and shorten a meeting. Many users consider this feature one of the real luxurys of Web conferencing.

Businessmen and businesswoman from countrys around the world are turning to Web conferances because of the many plus's and few minus's. Do you plan to discuss the pro's and con's of conferencing in your article? Our Web site has a list of FAQ's that you might find interesting. I would be happy to provide more information if you call me at (617) 830-8701.

Cordially,

Tamara Lippman
Director, Conferencing Services

Using Job Boards to Learn About Employment Possibilities in Your Field

Nearly everyone looking for a job today starts with the Web. This communication workshop will help you use the Web to study job openings in your field. Looking for jobs or internships on the Web has distinct advantages. For a few job seekers, the Web leads to bigger salaries, wider opportunities, and faster hiring. The Web, however, can devour huge chunks of time and produce slim results.

In terms of actually finding a job, the Web does not always result in success. Web searching seems to work best for professionals looking for similar work in their current fields and for those who are totally flexible about location. However, the Web is an excellent place for any job seeker to learn what is available, what qualifications are necessary, and what salaries are being offered. Thousands of job boards with many job listings from employers across the United States and abroad are available on the Web.

Career Application. Assume that you are about to finish your degree or certification program and you are now looking for a job. At the direction of your instructor, conduct a survey of electronic job advertisements in your field. What's available? How much is the salary? What are the requirements?

Your Task

- **Visit Monster.com (http://www.monster.com),** one of the most popular job boards.
- **Study the opening page.** Ignore the clutter and banner ads or pop-ups. Close any pop-up boxes.
- **Select keyword, category, city, and state.** Decide whether you want to search by a job title (such as *nurse, accountant, project manager*) or a category (such as *Accounting/ Finance, Administrative/Clerical, Advertising/Marketing*). Enter your keyword job title or select a category—or do both. Enter a city, state, or region. Click **Search.**
- **Study the job listings.** Click **Expand** to read more about a job opening. Click **More** to see a full description of the job.
- **Read job search tips.** For many helpful hints on precise searching, click **Job search tips.** Browsing this information may take a few minutes, but it is well worth the effort to learn how to refine your search. Close the box by clicking the X in the upper right corner.
- **Select best ads.** In your career and geographical area, select the three best ads and print them. If you cannot print, make notes on what you find.
- **Visit another site.** Try **http://www.collegerecruiter.com,** which claims to be the highest-traffic entry-level job site for students and graduates, or **http://www.careerbuilder.com,** which says it is the nation's largest employment network. Become familiar with the site's searching tools, and look for jobs in your field. Select and print three ads.
- **Analyze the skills required.** How often do the ads you printed mention communication, teamwork, computer skills, or professionalism? What tasks do the ads mention? What is the salary range identified in these ads for this position? Your instructor may ask you to submit your findings and/or report to the class.

Communication Workshops (such as the one on this page) provide insight into special business communication topics and skills not discussed in the chapters. These topics cover ethics, technology, career skills, and collaboration. Each workshop includes a career application to extend your learning and help you develop skills relevant to the workshop topic.

The Writing Process

CHAPTER 2

Planning Business Messages

OBJECTIVES

After studying this chapter, you should be able to

- Understand that business messages should be purposeful, persuasive, economical, and audience oriented.
- Identify and implement the three phases of the writing process.
- Appreciate the importance of analyzing the task and profiling the audience for business messages.
- Create messages that spotlight audience benefits and cultivate a "you" view.
- Develop a conversational tone and use positive, courteous language.
- Create messages that include inclusive language, plain expression, and familiar words.

The Basics of Business Writing

Business writing differs from other writing you may have done. In preparing high school or college compositions and term papers, you probably focused on discussing your feelings or displaying your knowledge. Your instructors wanted to see your thought processes, and they wanted assurance that you had internalized the subject matter. You may have had to meet a minimum word count. Business writers, however, have different goals. For business messages and oral presentations, your writing should be:

- **Purposeful.** You will be writing to solve problems and convey information. You will have a definite purpose to fulfill in each message.
- **Persuasive.** You want your audience to believe and accept your message.
- **Economical.** You will try to present ideas clearly but concisely. Length is not rewarded.
- **Audience oriented.** You will concentrate on looking at a problem from the perspective of the audience instead of seeing it from your own.

These distinctions actually ease the writer's task. You will not be searching your imagination for creative topic ideas. You won't be stretching your ideas to make them appear longer. Writing consultants and businesspeople complain that many college graduates entering industry have at least an unconscious perception that quantity enhances quality. Wrong! Get over the notion that longer is better. Conciseness and clarity are what counts in business.

The ability to prepare concise, audience-centered, persuasive, and purposeful messages does not come naturally. Very few people, especially beginners, can sit down and compose a terrific letter or report without training. However, following a systematic process, studying model messages, and practicing the craft can make nearly anyone a successful business writer or speaker.

The Writing Process for Business Messages and Oral Presentations

Whether you are preparing an e-mail message, memo, letter, or oral presentation, the process will be easier if you follow a systematic plan. Our plan breaks the entire task into three phases: prewriting, writing, and revising. As you can see in Figure 2.1, however, the process is not always linear. It does not always proceed from Step 1 to Step 2; often the writer must circle back and repeat an earlier step.

To illustrate the writing process, let's say that you own a popular local McDonald's franchise. At rush times, you face a problem. Customers complain about the chaotic multiple waiting lines to approach the service counter. You once saw two customers nearly get into a fistfight over cutting into a line. What's more, customers often are so intent on looking for ways to improve their positions in line that they fail to examine the menu. Then they are undecided when their turn arrives. You want to convince other franchise owners that a single-line (serpentine) system would work better. You could telephone the other owners. But you want to present a serious argument with good points that they will remember and be willing to act on when they gather for their next district meeting. You decide to write a letter that you hope will win their support.

> The writing process has three parts: prewriting, writing, and revising.

Prewriting

The first phase of the writing process prepares you to write. It involves *analyzing* the audience and your purpose for writing. The audience for your letter will be other franchise owners, some highly educated and others not. Your purpose in writing is to convince them that a change in policy would improve customer service. You are convinced that a single-line system, such as that used in banks, would reduce chaos and make customers happier because they would not have to worry about where they are in line.

Prewriting also involves *anticipating* how your audience will react to your message. You are sure that some of the other owners will agree with you, but others might fear that customers seeing a long single line might go elsewhere. In *adapting* your message to the audience, you try to think of the right words and the right tone that will win approval.

> The first phase of the writing process involves analyzing and anticipating the audience and then adapting to that audience.

FIGURE 2.1 The Writing Process

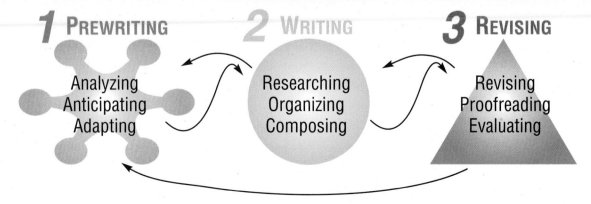

1 PREWRITING

Analyzing
Anticipating
Adapting

2 WRITING

Researching
Organizing
Composing

3 REVISING

Revising
Proofreading
Evaluating

Writing

The second phase involves researching, organizing, and then composing the message. In *researching* information for this letter, you would probably investigate other kinds of businesses that use single lines for customers. You might check out your competitors. What are Wendy's and Burger King doing? You might do some calling to see whether other franchise owners are concerned about chaotic lines. Before writing to the entire group, you might brainstorm with a few owners to see what ideas they have for solving the problem.

Once you have collected enough information, you would focus on *organizing* your letter. Should you start out by offering your solution? Or should you work up to it slowly, describing the problem, presenting your evidence, and then ending with the solution? The final step in the second phase of the writing process is actually *composing* the letter. Naturally, you will do it at your computer so that you can make revisions easily.

Revising

The third phase of the process involves revising, proofreading, and evaluating your message. After writing the first draft, you will spend a lot of time *revising* the message for clarity, conciseness, tone, and readability. Could parts of it be rearranged to make your point more effectively? This is the time when you look for ways to improve the organization and sound of your message. Next, you will spend time *proofreading* carefully to ensure correct spelling, grammar, punctuation, and format. The final phase involves *evaluating* your message to decide whether it accomplishes your goal.

Scheduling the Writing Process

Although Figure 2.1 shows the three phases of the writing process equally, the time you spend on each varies depending on the complexity of the problem, the purpose, the audience, and your schedule. One expert gives these rough estimates for scheduling a project:

- Prewriting—25 percent (planning and worrying)
- Writing—25 percent (organizing and composing)
- Revising—50 percent (45 percent revising and 5 percent proofreading)

These are rough guides, yet you can see that good writers spend most of their time on the final phase of revising and proofreading. Much depends, of course, on your project, its importance, and your familiarity with it. What's critical to remember, though, is that revising is a major component of the writing process.

It may appear that you perform one step and progress to the next, always following the same order. Most business writing, however, is not that rigid. Although writers perform the tasks described, the steps may be rearranged, abbreviated, or repeated. Some writers revise every sentence and paragraph as they go. Many find that new ideas occur after they have begun to write, causing them to back up, alter the organization, and rethink their plan.

Analyzing the Purpose and the Audience

We have just taken a look at the total writing process. As you begin to develop your business writing skills, you should expect to follow this process closely. With experience, though, you will become like other good writers and presenters who alter, compress, and rearrange the steps as needed. At first, however, following a plan is very helpful. The remainder of this chapter covers the first phase of the writing process. You will learn to analyze the purpose for writing, anticipate how your audience will react, and adapt your message to the audience.

Identifying Your Purpose

As you begin to compose a message, ask yourself two important questions: (a) Why am I sending this message? and (b) What do I hope to achieve? Your responses will determine how you organize and present your information.

Your message may have primary and secondary purposes. For college work your primary purpose may be merely to complete the assignment; secondary purposes might be to make yourself look good and to get a good grade. The primary purposes for sending business messages are typically to inform and to persuade. A secondary purpose is to promote goodwill: you and your organization want to look good in the eyes of your audience.

> The primary purpose of most business messages is to inform or to persuade; the secondary purpose is to promote goodwill.

Selecting the Best Channel

After identifying the purpose of your message, you need to select the most appropriate communication channel. Some information is most efficiently and effectively delivered orally. Other messages should be written, and still others are best delivered electronically. Whether to set up a meeting, send a message by e-mail, or write a report depends on some of the following factors:

- Importance of the message
- Amount and speed of feedback and interactivity required
- Necessity of a permanent record
- Cost of the channel
- Degree of formality desired
- Confidentiality and sensitivity of the message

> Choosing an appropriate channel depends on the importance of the message, the feedback required, the need for a permanent record, the cost, and the degree of formality, confidentiality, and sensitivity needed.

An interesting theory, called media richness, describes the extent to which a channel or medium recreates or represents all the information available in the original message. A richer medium, such as face-to-face conversation, permits more interactivity and feedback. A leaner medium, such as a report or proposal, presents a flat, one-dimensional message. Richer media enable the sender to provide more verbal and visual cues, as well as allow the sender to tailor the message to the audience.

Many factors help you decide which of the channels shown in Figure 2.2 is most appropriate for delivering a workplace message.

FIGURE 2.2 Choosing Communication Channels

Channel	Best Use
Blog	When one person needs to present digital information easily so that it is available to others.
E-mail	When you need feedback but not immediately. Lack of security makes it problematic for personal, emotional, or private messages.
Face-to-face conversation	When you need a rich, interactive medium. Useful for persuasive, bad-news, and personal messages.
Face-to-face group meeting	When group decisions and consensus are important. Inefficient for merely distributing information.
Fax	When your message must cross time zones or international boundaries, when a written record is significant, or when speed is important.
Instant message	When you are online and need a quick response. Useful for learning whether someone is available for a phone conversation.
Letter	When a written record or formality is required, especially with customers, the government, suppliers, or others outside an organization.
Memo	When you want a written record to clearly explain policies, discuss procedures, or collect information within an organization.
Phone call	When you need to deliver or gather information quickly, when nonverbal cues are unimportant, and when you cannot meet in person.
Report or proposal	When you are delivering considerable data internally or externally.
Voice mail message	When you wish to leave important or routine information that the receiver can respond to when convenient.
Video- or teleconference	When group consensus and interaction are important but members are geographically dispersed.
Wiki	When digital information must be made available to others. Useful for collaboration because participants can easily add, remove, and edit content.

"I sent you an e-mail and forwarded a copy to your PDA, cell phone, and home computer. I also faxed a copy to your office, your assistant, and laptop. Then I snail-mailed hard copies to you on paper, floppy, and CD. But in case you don't receive it, I'll just tell you what it said..."

© RANDY GLASBERGEN WWW.GLASBERGEN.COM

Switching to Faster Channels

Technology and competition continue to accelerate the pace of business today. As a result, communicators are switching to ever-faster means of exchanging information. In the past business messages within organizations were delivered largely by hard-copy memos. Responses would typically take a couple of days. However, that's too slow for today's communicators. They want answers and action now! Cell phones, instant messaging, faxes, Web sites, and especially e-mail can deliver that information much faster than can traditional channels of communication.

Within many organizations, hard-copy memos are still written, especially for messages that require persuasion, permanence, or formality. They are also prepared as attachments to e-mail messages. Clearly, the channel of choice for corporate communicators today is e-mail. It's fast, inexpensive, and easy. Thus, fewer hard-copy memos are being written. Fewer letters to customers are also being written. That's because many customer service functions can now be served through Web sites or by e-mail.

Whether your channel choice is e-mail, a hard-copy memo, or a report, you will be a more effective writer if you spend sufficient time in the prewriting phase.

Anticipating the Audience

A good writer anticipates the audience for a message: What is the reader or listener like? How will that person react to the message? Although you can't always know exactly who the receiver is, you can imagine some of that person's characteristics. Even writers of direct-mail sales letters have a general idea of the audience they wish to target. Picturing a typical reader is important in guiding what you write. One copywriter at Lands' End, the catalog company, pictures his sister-in-law whenever he writes product descriptions for the catalog. By profiling your audience and shaping a message to respond to that profile, you are more likely to achieve your communication goals.

Profiling the Audience

Visualizing your audience is a pivotal step in the writing process. The questions in Figure 2.3 will help you profile your audience. How much time you devote to answering these questions depends greatly on your message and its context. An analytical report that you compose for management or an oral presentation before a big group would, of course, demand considerable audience anticipation. On the other hand, an e-mail message to a coworker or a letter to a familiar supplier might require only a few moments of planning. No matter how short your message, though, spend some time thinking about the audience so that you can tailor your words to your readers or listeners. Remember that most readers or listeners will be thinking, "What's in it for me?" or, "What am I supposed to do with this information?"

By profiling your audience before you write, you can identify the appropriate tone, language, and channel for your message.

Responding to the Profile

Profiling your audience helps you make decisions about shaping the message. You will discover what kind of language is appropriate, whether you are free to use specialized technical terms, whether you should explain everything, and so on. You will decide whether your tone should be formal or informal, and you will select the most desirable channel. Imagining whether the receiver is likely to be neutral, positive, or negative will help you determine how to organize your message.

After profiling the audience, you can decide whether the receiver will be neutral, positive, or hostile toward your message.

Another advantage of profiling your audience is considering the possibility of a secondary audience. For example, let's say you start to write an e-mail message to your supervisor, Sheila, describing a problem you are having. Halfway through the message you realize that Sheila will probably forward this message to her boss, the vice president. Sheila will not want to summarize what you said; instead she will take the easy route and merely forward your e-mail. When you realize that the vice president will probably see this message, you decide to back up and use a more formal tone. You remove your inquiry about Sheila's family, you reduce your complaints, and you tone down your language about why things went wrong. Instead, you provide more background information, and you are more specific in identifying items the vice president might not recognize. Analyzing the task and anticipating the audience help you adapt your message so that you can create an efficient and effective message.

FIGURE 2.3 Asking the Right Questions to Profile Your Audience

Primary Audience	Secondary Audience
Who is my primary reader or listener?	Who might see or hear this message in addition to the primary audience?
What are my personal and professional relationships with that person?	How do these people differ from the primary audience?
What position does the person hold in the organization?	Do I need to include more background information?
How much does that person know about the subject?	How must I reshape my message to make it understandable and acceptable to others to whom it might be forwarded?
What do I know about that person's education, beliefs, culture, and attitudes?	
Should I expect a neutral, positive, or negative response to my message?	

Adapting to the Task and Audience

After analyzing your purpose and anticipating your audience, you must convey your purpose to that audience. Adaptation is the process of creating a message that suits your audience.

One important aspect of adaptation is *tone*. Conveyed largely by the words in a message, tone affects how a receiver feels upon reading or hearing a message. Skilled communicators create a positive tone in their messages by using a number of adaptive techniques, some of which are unconscious. These include spotlighting audience benefits, cultivating a "you" attitude, sounding conversational, and using positive, courteous expression. Additional adaptive techniques include using inclusive language and preferring plain language with familiar words.

"You haven't been listening. I keep telling you that I don't want a product fit for a king."

Empathy involves shaping a message that appeals to the receiver.

Audience Benefits

Focusing on the audience sounds like a modern idea, but actually one of America's early statesmen and authors recognized this fundamental writing principle over 200 years ago. In describing effective writing, Ben Franklin observed, "To be good, it ought to have a tendency to benefit the reader."[1] These wise words have become a fundamental guideline for today's business communicators. Expanding on Franklin's counsel, a contemporary communication consultant gives this solid advice to his business clients: "Always stress the benefit to the audience of whatever it is you are trying to get them to do. If you can show them how you are going to save them frustration or help them meet their goals, you have the makings of a powerful message."[2]

Adapting your message to the receiver's needs means putting yourself in that person's shoes. It's called *empathy*. Empathic senders think about how a receiver will decode a message. They try to give something to the receiver, solve the receiver's problems, save the receiver's money, or just understand the feelings and position of that person. Which version of the following messages is more appealing to the audience?

Sender Focus	Audience Focus
The Human Resources Department requires that the enclosed questionnaire be completed immediately so that we can allocate our training resource funds to employees.	By filling out the enclosed questionnaires, you can be one of the first employees to sign up for our training resource funds.
Our warranty becomes effective only when we receive an owner's registration.	Your warranty begins working for you as soon as you return your owner's registration.
We are proud to announce our new software virus checker that we think is the best on the market!	Now you can be sure that all your computers will be protected with our real-time virus scanning.

"You" View

Notice that many of the previous audience-focused messages included the word *you*. In concentrating on receiver benefits, skilled communicators naturally develop the "you" view. They emphasize second-person pronouns (*you, your*) instead of first-person pronouns (*I/we, us, our*). Whether your goal is to inform, persuade, or promote goodwill, the catchiest words you can use are *you* and *your*. Compare the following examples.

Because receivers are most interested in themselves, emphasize the word *you* to promote audience benefits.

WORKPLACE IN FOCUS

Employers are working hard to attract and retain Generation Y graduates for their organizations. Now reaching their mid-twenties, Gen Y-ers are generally optimistic, entrepreneurial, team oriented, and tech savvy. But they also have high workplace expectations and short attention spans—traits linked to the gotta-have-it-now digital culture. Accounting firms have begun using rap videos, online chat, and alternative work arrangements to recruit these young graduates before they lose interest and go elsewhere. *When creating a message for a Generation Y audience, what benefits would you stress?*

"I/We" View

I'm asking all employees to respond to the attached survey about working conditions.

I have granted you permission to attend the communication seminar.

We have shipped your order by UPS, and we are sure it will arrive in time for your sales promotion December 1.

"You" View

Because your ideas count, please complete the attached survey about working conditions.

You may attend the seminar to improve your communication skills.

Your order will be delivered by UPS in time for your sales promotion December 1.

Although you want to focus on the reader or listener, don't overuse or misuse the second-person pronoun *you*. Readers and listeners appreciate genuine interest; on the other hand, they resent obvious attempts at manipulation. Some sales messages, for example, are guilty of overkill when they include *you* dozens of times in a direct-mail promotion. What's more, the word can sometimes create the wrong impression. Consider this statement: *You cannot return merchandise until you receive written approval.* The word *you* appears twice, but the reader feels singled out for criticism. In the following version the message is less personal and more positive: *Customers may return merchandise with written approval.*

Another difficulty in emphasizing the "you" view and de-emphasizing *we/I* is that it may result in overuse of the passive voice. For example, to avoid *We will give you* (active voice), you might write *You will be given* (passive voice). The active voice in writing is generally preferred because it identifies who is doing the acting. You will learn more about active and passive voice in Chapter 3.

In recognizing the value of the "you" attitude, writers do not have to sterilize their writing and totally avoid any first-person pronouns or words that show their feelings. Skilled communicators are able to convey sincerity, warmth, and enthusiasm by the words they choose. Don't be afraid to use phrases such as *I'm happy* or *We're delighted*, if you truly are. When speaking face-to-face, communicators show sincerity and warmth with nonverbal cues such as a smile and a pleasant voice tone. In letters, memos, and e-mail messages, however, only expressive words and phrases can show these feelings. These phrases suggest hidden messages that say *You are important, I hear you,* and *I'm honestly trying to please you.*

Emphasize *you* but don't eliminate all *I* and *we* statements.

Strive for conversational
expression, but also
remember to be professional.

Conversational but Professional

Most instant messages, e-mail messages, business letters, memos, and reports replace conversation. Thus, they are most effective when they convey an informal, conversational tone instead of a formal, pretentious tone. Workplace messages should not, however, become so casual that they sound low-level and unprofessional.

Instant messaging (IM) enables coworkers to have informal, spontaneous conversations. Some companies have accepted IM as a serious workplace tool. With the increasing use of instant messaging and e-mail, however, a major problem has developed. Sloppy, unprofessional expression appears in many workplace messages. You will learn more about the dangers of e-mail in Chapter 5. At this point, though, we focus on the tone of the language.

To project a professional image, you must sound educated and mature. Overuse of expressions such as *totally awesome, you know,* and *like,* as well as reliance on needless abbreviations (*BTW* for *by the way*), make a businessperson sound like a teenager. Professional messages do not include IM abbreviations, slang, sentence fragments, and chitchat. We urge you to strive for a warm, conversational tone that avoids low-level diction. Levels of diction, as shown in Figure 2.4, range from unprofessional to formal.

Your goal is a warm, friendly tone that sounds professional. Although some writers are too casual, others are overly formal. To impress readers and listeners, they use big words, long sentences, legal terminology, and third-person constructions. Stay away from expressions such as *the undersigned, the writer,* and *the affected party.* You will sound friendlier with familiar pronouns such as *I, we,* and *you.* Study the following examples to see how to achieve a professional, yet conversational tone:

Unprofessional	Professional
Hey, boss, Gr8 news! Firewall now installed!! BTW, check with me b4 announcing it.	Mr. Smith, our new firewall software is now installed. Please check with me before announcing it.
Look, dude, this report is totally bogus. And the figures don't look kosher. Show me some real stats. Got sources?	Because the figures in this report seem inaccurate, please submit the source statistics.

FIGURE 2.4 Levels of Diction

Unprofessional (low-level diction)	Conversational (midlevel diction)	Formal (high-level diction)
badmouth	criticize	denigrate
guts	nerve	courage
pecking order	line of command	dominance hierarchy
ticked off	upset	provoked
rat on	inform	betray
rip off	steal	expropriate
Sentence example: If we just hang in there, we can snag the contract.	**Sentence example:** If we don't get discouraged, we can win the contract.	**Sentence example:** If the principals persevere, they can secure the contract.

Overly Formal	**Conversational**
All employees are herewith instructed to return the appropriately designated contracts to the undersigned.	Please return your contracts to me.
Pertaining to your order, we must verify the sizes that your organization requires prior to consignment of your order to our shipper.	We will send your order as soon as we confirm the sizes you need.

Positive Language

The clarity and tone of a message are considerably improved if you use positive rather than negative language. Positive language generally conveys more information than negative language does. Moreover, positive messages are uplifting and pleasant to read. Positive wording tells what *is* and what *can be done* rather than what *isn't* and what *can't be done*. For example, *Your order cannot be shipped by January 10* is not nearly as informative as *Your order will be shipped January 20*. Notice in the following examples how you can revise the negative tone to reflect a more positive impression.

Positive language creates goodwill and gives more options to receivers.

Negative	**Positive**
You failed to include your credit card number, so we can't mail your order.	We look forward to completing your order as soon as we receive your credit card number.
Your letter of May 2 claims that you returned a defective headset.	Your May 2 letter describes a headset you returned.
You cannot park in Lot H until April 1.	You may park in Lot H starting April 1.
You won't be sorry that . . .	You will be happy that . . .

Courteous Language

Maintaining a courteous tone involves not just guarding against rudeness but also avoiding words that sound demanding or preachy. Expressions such as *you should, you must,* and *you have to* cause people to instinctively react with *Oh, yeah?* One remedy is to turn these demands into rhetorical questions that begin with *Will you please . . . .* Giving reasons for a request also softens the tone.

Even when you feel justified in displaying anger, remember that losing your temper or being sarcastic will seldom accomplish your goals as a business communicator: to inform, to persuade, and to create goodwill. When you are irritated, frustrated, or infuriated, keep cool and try to defuse the situation. In dealing with customers in telephone conversations, use polite phrases such as *It was a pleasure speaking with you, I would be happy to assist you with that,* and *Thank you for being so patient.*

OFFICE INSIDER

"Negative tone can hurt your company in many ways. It can lose customers, it can generate lawsuits and, if inflammatory rhetoric is found in a discoverable e-mail or log notes, a few words might cost your company a whopping settlement and punitive damages in a bad-faith lawsuit."

Less Courteous	**More Courteous and Helpful**
You must complete the report before Friday.	Will you please complete the report by Friday.
You should organize a car pool in this department	Organizing a car pool will reduce your transportation costs and help preserve the environment.
This is the second time I've written. Can't you get anything right?	Please credit my account for $450. My latest statement shows that the error noted in my letter of April 2 has not been corrected.
Am I the only one who can read the operating manual?	Let's review the operating manual together so that you can get your documents to print correctly next time.

Sensitive communicators avoid language that excludes people.

Inclusive Language

A business writer who is alert and empathic will strive to use words that include rather than exclude people. Some words have been called *sexist* because they seem to exclude females. Notice the use of the masculine pronouns *he* and *his* in the following sentences:

> If a physician is needed, *he* will be called.

> Every renter must read *his* rental agreement carefully.

These sentences illustrate an age-old grammatical rule called "common gender." When a speaker or writer did not know the gender (sex) of an individual, masculine pronouns (such as *he* or *his*) were used. Masculine pronouns were understood to indicate both men and women. Today, however, sensitive writers and speakers replace common-gender pronouns with alternate inclusive constructions. You can use any of four alternatives.

Sexist/Noninclusive	Every attorney has ten minutes for *his* summation.
Alternative 1	All attorneys have ten minutes for their summations. (Use a plural noun and plural pronoun.)
Alternative 2	Attorneys have ten minutes for summations. (Omit the pronoun entirely.)
Alternative 3	Every attorney has ten minutes for *a* summation. (Use an article instead of a pronoun.)
Alternative 4	Every attorney has ten minutes for *his* or *her* summation. (Use both a masculine and a feminine pronoun.)

Note that the last alternative, which includes a masculine and a feminine pronoun, is wordy and awkward. Try not to use it frequently.

Other words are considered sexist because they suggest stereotypes. For example, the nouns *fireman* and *mailman* suggest that only men hold these positions. You can avoid offending your listener or reader by using neutral job titles, such as those shown here:

Noninclusive Job Titles		**Inclusive, Neutral Job Titles**	
chairman	stewardess	department head	flight attendant
fireman	waiter, waitress	firefighter	server
mailman	workman	letter carrier	worker
policeman		police officer	

Plain English

Business communicators who are conscious of their audience try to use plain language that expresses clear meaning. They avoid showy words, long sentences, and confusing expressions. Some business, legal, and government documents, however, are written in an inflated and confusing style that obscures meaning. This style of writing has been given various terms such as *legalese, federalese, bureaucratic gobbledygook, doublespeak,* and the *official style.*

Over the past 30 years, consumer groups and the government have joined forces in the Plain English movement. It encourages businesses, professional organizations, and government bodies to write any official document—such as a contract, warranty, insurance policy, or lease—in clear, concise language.[3] As a result of the Plain English movement, numerous states have passed laws requiring that business contracts and public documents be written in plain language. The nonprofit Center for Plain Language in Washington, D.C., urges government and business officials to use clear, understandable language in laws and business documents so that people can "find what they need, understand what they find, and act on that understanding."[4] That's exactly what business writers should do.

One branch of the government, the Securities and Exchange Commission, has even written "A Plain English Handbook." This booklet illustrates many of the principles of good writing, some of which are shown in Figure 2.5. Throughout this textbook we will be practicing these principles to help you improve your writing skills.

Don't be impressed by high-sounding language and legalese such as *aforementioned*, *herein*, *thereafter*, *hereinafter*, and similar expressions. Your writing will be better understood if you use plain English.

Familiar Words

Clear messages contain words that are familiar and meaningful to the receiver. How can we know what is meaningful to a given receiver? Although we can't know with certainty, we can avoid long or unfamiliar words that have simpler synonyms. Whenever possible in business communication, substitute short, common, simple words. Don't, however, give up a precise word if it says exactly what you mean.

Although you yourself may not use some of the words in the following list of unfamiliar words, you may see them in business documents. Remember that the simple alternatives shown here will make messages more readable for most people.

Familiar words are more meaningful to readers and listeners.

Less Familiar Words	Simple Alternatives	Less Familiar Words	Simple Alternatives
ascertain	learn	perpetuate	continue
compensate	pay	perplexing	troubling
conceptualize	see	reciprocate	return
encompass	include	remuneration	salary
hypothesize	guess	stipulate	require
monitor	check	terminate	end
operational	working	vis-à-vis	in relation to, about

FIGURE 2.5 Plain English Pointers

- Use the active voice with strong verbs (instead of *the stock was acquired by the investor*, write *the investor bought the stock*).
- Don't be afraid of personal pronouns (e.g., *I*, *we*, and *you*).
- Bring abstractions down to earth (instead of *asset*, write *one share of IBM common stock*).
- Omit superfluous words (instead of *in the event that*, write *if*).
- Use positive expression (instead of *it is not unlike*, write *it is similar*).
- Prefer short sentences.
- Remove jargon and legalese.
- Keep the subject, verb, and object close together.
- Keep sentence structure parallel.

As you revise a message, you will have a chance to correct any writing problems. Notice in Figure 2.6 what a difference revision makes. Before revision, the message failed to use familiar language. Many negative ideas could have been expressed positively. After revision, the message is shorter, is more conversational, and emphasizes audience benefits.

FIGURE 2.6 Improving the Tone in an E-Mail Message

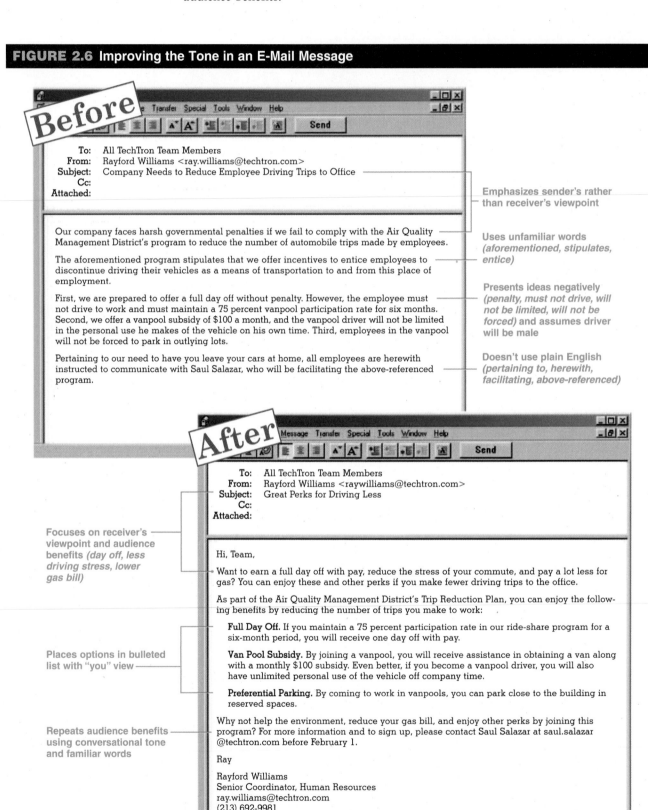

Chapter 2: Planning Business Messages

Summing Up and Looking Forward

In this chapter you learned that good business writing is audience centered, purposeful, persuasive, and economical. To achieve these results, business communicators typically follow a systematic writing process. This process includes three phases: prewriting, writing, and revising. In the prewriting phase, communicators analyze the task and the audience. They select an appropriate channel to deliver the message, and they consider ways to adapt their message to the task and the audience. Effective techniques include spotlighting audience benefits, cultivating the "you" view, striving to use conversational language, and expressing ideas positively. Good communicators also use courteous and inclusive language, plain English, and familiar words.

The next chapter continues to examine the writing process. It presents additional techniques to help you become a better writer. You will learn how to eliminate repetitious and redundant wording, as well as how to avoid wordy prepositional phrases, long lead-ins, needless adverbs, and misplaced modifiers.

Critical Thinking

1. Why do you think employers prefer messages that are not written like high school and college essays?

2. How can the three-phase writing process help the writer of a business report as well as the writer of an oral presentation?

3. Discuss the following statement: "The English language is a land mine—it is filled with terms that are easily misinterpreted as derogatory and others that are blatantly insulting. . . . Being fair and objective is not enough; employers must also appear to be so."[5]

4. Why is writing in a natural, conversational tone difficult for many people?

5. If computer software is increasingly able to detect writing errors, can business communicators stop studying writing techniques? Why or why not?

Chapter Review

6. How can a writer make a message audience oriented and develop audience benefits? Provide an original example.

7. List the three phases of the writing process and summarize what happens in each phase. Which phase requires the most time?

8. What six factors are important in selecting an appropriate channel to deliver a message? What makes one channel richer than another?

9. How does profiling the audience help a business communicator prepare a message?

10. List three specific techniques for developing a warm, friendly, and conversational tone in business messages.

11. Why is it OK to use instant messaging abbreviations (such as *BTW*) and happy faces in messages to friends but not OK in business messages?

12. Why does positive language usually tell more than negative language? Give an original example.

13. List five examples of sexist pronouns and nouns.

14. List at least five principles of the Plain English movement.

15. Why should business writers strive to use short, common, simple words? Does this "dumb down" business messages?

Activities

Selecting Communication Channels

Your Task. Using Figure 2.2, suggest the best communication channels for the following messages. Assume that all channels are available. Be prepared to explain your choices.

16. You want to know what team members are available immediately for a quick teleconference meeting. They are all workaholics and stuck to their computers.

17. As a manager during a company reorganization, you must tell nine workers that their employment is being terminated.

18. You need to know whether Thomas in Reprographics can produce a rush job for you in two days.

19. A prospective client in Italy wants price quotes for a number of your products—pronto!

20. As assistant to the vice president, you are to investigate the possibility of developing internship programs with several nearby colleges and universities.

21. You must respond to a notice from the Internal Revenue Service insisting that you did not pay the correct amount for last quarter's employer's taxes.

Writing Improvement Exercises

Audience Benefits and the "You" View

Your Task. Revise the following sentences to emphasize the perspective of the audience and the "you" view.

22. We regret to announce that the bookstore will distribute free iPods only to students in classes in which the instructor has requested these devices as learning tools.

23. Our safety policy forbids us from renting power equipment to anyone who cannot demonstrate proficiency in its use.

24. To prevent us from possibly losing large sums of money in stolen identity schemes, our bank now requires verification of any large check presented for immediate payment.

25. So that we may bring our customer records up-to-date and eliminate the expense of duplicate mailings, we are asking you to complete and return the enclosed card.

26. For just $219 per person, we have arranged a four-day, three-night getaway package to Orlando that includes hotel accommodations, theme park tickets, and complimentary breakfasts.

27. We find it necessary to request that all employees complete the enclosed questionnaire so that we may develop a master schedule for summer vacations.

28. To enable us to continue our policy of selling name brands at discount prices, we can give store credit but we cannot give cash refunds on returned merchandise

Conversational, Professional Tone

Your Task. Revise the following sentences to make the tone conversational yet professional.

29. Per your recent e-mail, the undersigned takes pride in informing you that we are pleased to be able to participate in the Toys for Tots drive.

30. Pursuant to your message of the 15th, please be advised that your shipment was sent August 14.

31. Yo, Jeff! Look, dude, I need you to pound on Ramona so we can drop this budget thingy in her lap.

32. BTW, Danika was totally ticked off when the manager accused her of ripping off office supplies. She may split.

33. He didn't have the guts to badmouth her 2 her face.

34. The undersigned respectfully reminds affected individuals that employees desirous of changing their health plans must do so before November 1.

Positive and Courteous Language

Your Task. Revise the following statements to make them more positive and courteous.

35. Employees are not allowed to use instant messaging until a company policy is established.

36. We must withhold authorizing payment of your consultant's fees because our CPA claims that your work is incomplete.

37. Plans for the new health center cannot move forward without full community support.

38. This is the last time I'm writing to try to get you to record my October 3 payment of $359.50 to my account! Anyone who can read can see from the attached documents that I've tried to explain this to you before.

39. Although you apparently failed to read the operator's manual, we are sending you a replacement blade for your food processor. Next time read page 18 carefully so that you will know how to attach this blade.

40. Everyone in this department must begin using new passwords as of midnight June 15. Because of flagrant password misuse, we find it necessary to impose this new rule so that we can protect your personal information and company records.

Inclusive Language

Your Task. Revise the following sentences to eliminate terms that are considered sexist or that suggest stereotypes.

41. Every employee must wear his photo ID on the job.

42. Media Moguls hired Sheena Love, an African American, for the position of project manager.

43. A skilled assistant proofreads her boss's documents and catches any errors he makes.

44. The conference will include special excursions for the wives of executives.

45. Serving on the panel are a lady veterinarian, a female doctor, two businessmen, and an Indian CPA.

Plain English and Familiar Words

Your Task. Revise the following sentences to use plain expression and more familiar words.

46. The salary we are offering is commensurate with remuneration for other managers.

47. To expedite ratification of this agreement, we urge you to vote in the affirmative.

48. In a dialogue with the manager, I learned that you plan to terminate our contract.

49. Did the braking problem materialize subsequent to our recall effort?

50. Pursuant to your invitation, we will interrogate our agent.

Video Resource

Video Library 1, Building Workplace Communication Skills. Your instructor may show you a video titled **Guffey's 3-x-3 Writing Process Develops Fluent Workplace Skills**. It shows three phases of the writing process including pre-writing, writing, and revising. You will see how the writing process guides the development of a complete message. This video illustrates concepts in Chapters 2, 3, and 4.

Grammar/Mechanics Checkup 2

Pronouns

Review Sections 1.07–1.09 in the Grammar Review section of the Grammar/Mechanics Handbook. Then study each of the following statements. In the space provided, write the word that completes the statement correctly and the number of the G/M principle illustrated. When you finish, compare your responses with those provided near the end of the book. If your responses differ, study carefully the principles in parentheses.

its _____ (1.09d)   **Example** The Employee Development Committee will make (its, their) recommendation soon.

1. I hoped Rhonda would call. Was it (she, her) who left the message?
2. Everyone on the men's soccer team must be fitted for (his, their) uniform.
3. Even instant messages sent between the manager and (he, him) will be revealed in the court case.
4. Does anyone in the office know for (who, whom) these DVDs were ordered?
5. It looks as if (her's, hers) is the only report that cites electronic sources correctly.
6. Thomas asked Matt and (I, me, myself) to help him complete his report.
7. My friend and (I, me, myself) were also asked to work on Saturdays.
8. Both printers were sent for repairs, but (yours, your's) will be returned shortly.
9. Give the budget figures to (whoever, whomever) asked for them.
10. Everyone except the broker and (I, me, myself) claimed a share of the commission.
11. No one knows that problem better than (he, him, himself).
12. Investment brochures and information were sent to (we, us) shareholders.
13. If any one of the female tourists has lost (their, her) scarf, she should see the driver.
14. Neither the glamour nor the excitement of the position had lost (its, it's, their) appeal.
15. Any new subscriber may cancel (their, his or her) subscription within the first month.

The following e-mail message has errors in spelling, proofreading, noun plurals, conversational tone, unfamiliar words, and other writing techniques studied in this chapter. You may either (a) use standard proofreading marks (see Appendix B) to correct the errors here or (b) download the document from your companion Web site and revise at your computer. Study the guidelines in the Grammar/Mechanics Handbook to sharpen your skills.

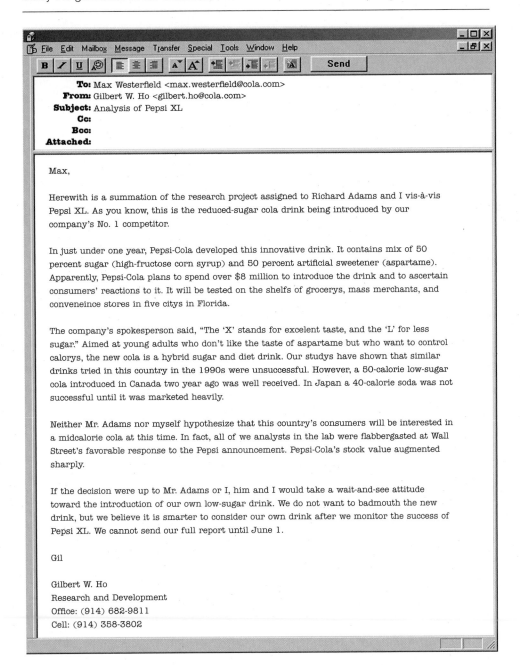

To: Max Westerfield <max.westerfield@cola.com>
From: Gilbert W. Ho <gilbert.ho@cola.com>
Subject: Analysis of Pepsi XL
Cc:
Bcc:
Attached:

Max,

Herewith is a summation of the research project assigned to Richard Adams and I vis-à-vis Pepsi XL. As you know, this is the reduced-sugar cola drink being introduced by our company's No. 1 competitor.

In just under one year, Pepsi-Cola developed this innovative drink. It contains mix of 50 percent sugar (high-fructose corn syrup) and 50 percent artificial sweetener (aspartame). Apparently, Pepsi-Cola plans to spend over $8 million to introduce the drink and to ascertain consumers' reactions to it. It will be tested on the shelfs of grocerys, mass merchants, and conveneince stores in five citys in Florida.

The company's spokesperson said, "The 'X' stands for excelent taste, and the 'L' for less sugar." Aimed at young adults who don't like the taste of aspartame but who want to control calorys, the new cola is a hybrid sugar and diet drink. Our studys have shown that similar drinks tried in this country in the 1990s were unsuccessful. However, a 50-calorie low-sugar cola introduced in Canada two year ago was well received. In Japan a 40-calorie soda was not successful until it was marketed heavily.

Neither Mr. Adams nor myself hypothesize that this country's consumers will be interested in a midcalorie cola at this time. In fact, all of we analysts in the lab were flabbergasted at Wall Street's favorable response to the Pepsi announcement. Pepsi-Cola's stock value augmented sharply.

If the decision were up to Mr. Adams or I, him and I would take a wait-and-see attitude toward the introduction of our own low-sugar drink. We do not want to badmouth the new drink, but we believe it is smarter to consider our own drink after we monitor the success of Pepsi XL. We cannot send our full report until June 1.

Gil

Gilbert W. Ho
Research and Development
Office: (914) 682-9811
Cell: (914) 358-3802

Communication Workshop: Career Skills

Sharpening Your Skills for Critical Thinking, Problem Solving, and Decision Making

Gone are the days when management expected workers to check their brains at the door and do only as told. Today, you will be expected to use your brains when thinking critically. You will be solving problems and making decisions. Much of this book is devoted to helping you solve problems and communicate those decisions to management, fellow workers, clients, the government, and the public. Faced with a problem or an issue, most of us do a lot of worrying before separating the issues or making a decision. You can change all that worrying to directed thinking by channeling it into the following procedure:

- **Identify and clarify the problem.** Your first task is to recognize that a problem exists. Some problems are big and unmistakable, such as failure of an air-freight delivery service to get packages to customers on time. Other problems may be continuing annoyances, such as regularly running out of toner for an office copy machine. The first step in reaching a solution is pinpointing the problem area.
- **Gather information.** Learn more about the problem situation. Look for possible causes and solutions. This step may mean checking files, calling suppliers, or brainstorming with fellow workers. For example, the air-freight delivery service would investigate the tracking systems of the commercial airlines carrying its packages to determine what is going wrong.
- **Evaluate the evidence.** Where did the information come from? Does it represent various points of view? What biases could be expected from each source? How accurate is the information gathered? Is it fact or opinion? For example, it is a fact that packages are missing; it is an opinion that they are merely lost and will turn up eventually.
- **Consider alternatives and implications.** Draw conclusions from the gathered evidence and pose solutions. Then weigh the advantages and disadvantages of each alternative. What are the costs, benefits, and consequences? What are the obstacles, and how can they be handled? Most important, what solution best serves your goals and those of your organization? Here is where your creativity is especially important.
- **Choose the best alternative and test it.** Select an alternative, and try it out to see if it meets your expectations. If it does, implement your decision and put it into action. If it doesn't, rethink your alternatives. The freight company decided to give its unhappy customers free delivery service to make up for the lost packages and downtime. Be sure to continue monitoring and adjusting the solution to ensure its effectiveness over time.

Career Application. Let's return to the McDonald's problem (discussed on page 33) in which some franchise owners are unhappy with the multiple lines for service. Customers don't seem to know where to stand to be the next served. Tempers flare when aggressive customers cut in line, and other customers spend so much time protecting their places in line that they are not ready to order. As a franchise owner, you want to solve this problem. Any new procedures, however, must be approved by a majority of McDonald's owners in a district. You know that McDonald's management feels that the multiline system accommodates higher volumes of customers more quickly than a single-line system. In addition, customers are turned off when they see a long line.

Your Task

- Individually or with a team, use the critical-thinking steps outlined here. Begin by clarifying the problem.
- Where could you gather information? Would it be wise to see what your competitors are doing? How do banks handle customer lines? Airlines?
- Evaluate your findings and consider alternatives. What are the pros and cons of each alternative?
- Within your team choose the best alternative. Present your recommendation to your class and give your reasons for choosing it.

CHAPTER 3

Composing Business Messages

OBJECTIVES

After studying this chapter, you should be able to

- Contrast formal and informal methods of researching data and generating ideas for messages.

- Organize information into outlines.

- Compare direct and indirect patterns for organizing ideas.

- Write effective sentences using four sentence types while avoiding three common sentence faults.

- Understand how to emphasize ideas, use active and passive voice effectively, achieve parallelism, and avoid dangling and misplaced modifiers.

- Draft powerful paragraphs that incorporate topic sentences, support sentences, and transitional expressions to build coherence.

© ISTOCKPHOTO.COM / WEBPHOTOGRAPHEER

Collecting Information to Compose Messages

Because all business and professional people—even those in technical positions—are exchanging more messages than ever before, you can expect to be doing your share of writing on the job. The more quickly you can put your ideas down and the more clearly you can explain what needs to be said, the more successful and happy you will be in your career. Being able to write is also critical to promotions. That's why we devote three chapters to teaching you a writing process, summarized in Figure 3.1. This process guides you through the steps necessary to write rapidly but, more important, clearly. Instead of struggling with a writing assignment and not knowing where to begin or what to say, you are learning an effective process that you can use in school and on the job.

The previous chapter focused on the prewriting stage of the writing process. You studied the importance of using a conversational tone, positive language, plain and courteous expression, and familiar words. This chapter addresses the second stage of the process: gathering information, organizing it into outlines, and composing messages.

No smart businessperson would begin writing a message before collecting the needed information. We call this collection process *research*, a rather formal-sounding term. For simple documents, though, the process can be quite informal. Research is

OFFICE INSIDER

"You can't move up without writing skills."

FIGURE 3.1 The Writing Process

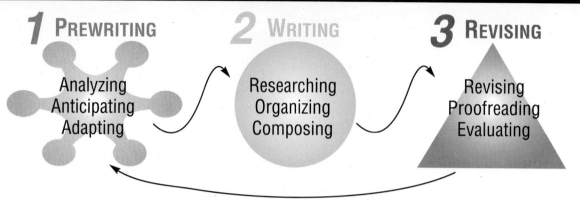

1 PREWRITING

Analyzing
Anticipating
Adapting

2 WRITING

Researching
Organizing
Composing

3 REVISING

Revising
Proofreading
Evaluating

necessary before beginning to write because the information you collect helps shape the message. Discovering significant data after a message is completed often means starting over and reorganizing. To avoid frustration and inaccurate messages, collect information that answers these questions:

- What does the receiver need to know about this topic?
- What is the receiver to do?
- How is the receiver to do it and when?
- What will happen if the receiver doesn't do it?

Whenever your communication problem requires more information than you have in your head or at your fingertips, you must conduct research. This research may be formal or informal.

Formal Research Methods

Formal research may include searching libraries and electronic databases or investigating primary sources (interviews, surveys, and experiments).

Long reports and complex business problems generally require some use of formal research methods. Let's say you are a market specialist for Coca-Cola, and your boss asks you to evaluate the impact on Coke sales of private-label or generic soft drinks (the bargain-basement-brand knockoffs sold at Kmart and other outlets). Or, assume you must write a term paper for a college class. Both tasks require more data than you have in your head or at your fingertips. To conduct formal research, you could:

WORKPLACE IN FOCUS

International product teams at PepsiCo recently introduced a new cola with a unique name: Pepsi Ice Cucumber. This is definitely not your garden-variety soda. With its emerald green color, vegetable flavor, and ice crystal packaging, Ice Cucumber is formulated to keep consumers feeling cool and refreshed in the summer heat. If cucumber-flavored cola doesn't sound very refreshing, you are probably not living in Japan. Pepsi's limited edition veggie drink was developed specifically for Japanese tastes. *What role does research play in creating new products and their brand-promotion messages?*

- **Search manually.** You will find helpful background and supplementary information through manual searching of resources in public and college libraries. These traditional sources include books and newspaper, magazine, and journal articles. Other sources are encyclopedias, reference books, handbooks, dictionaries, directories, and almanacs.
- **Access electronically.** Much of the printed material just described is now available from the Internet, databases, CDs, or DVDs that can be accessed by computer. College and public libraries subscribe to retrieval services that permit you to access most periodic literature. You can also find extraordinary amounts of information by searching the Web. You will learn more about using electronic sources in Chapters 9 and 10.
- **Go to the source.** For firsthand information, go directly to the source. For the Coca-Cola report, for example, you could find out what consumers really think by conducting interviews or surveys, by putting together questionnaires, or by organizing focus groups. Formal research includes structured sampling and controls that enable investigators to make accurate judgments and valid predictions.
- **Conduct scientific experiments.** Instead of merely asking for the target audience's opinion, scientific researchers present choices with controlled variables. Let's say, for example, that Coca-Cola wants to determine at what price and under what circumstances consumers would switch from Coca-Cola to a generic brand. The results of experimentation would provide valuable data for managerial decision making.

> Good sources of primary information are interviews, surveys, questionnaires, and focus groups.

Because formal research techniques are particularly necessary for reports, you will study resources and techniques more extensively in Chapters 9 and 10.

Informal Research and Idea Generation

Most routine tasks—such as composing e-mail messages, memos, letters, informational reports, and oral presentations—require data that you can collect informally. Here are some techniques for collecting informal data and for generating ideas:

- **Look in the files.** If you are responding to an inquiry, you often can find the answer to the inquiry by investigating the company files or by consulting colleagues.
- **Talk with your boss.** Get information from the individual making the assignment. What does that person know about the topic? What slant should be taken? What other sources would he or she suggest?
- **Interview the target audience.** Consider talking with individuals at whom the message is aimed. They can provide clarifying information that tells you what they want to know and how you should shape your remarks.
- **Conduct an informal survey.** Gather unscientific but helpful information by using questionnaires or telephone surveys. In preparing a memo report predicting the success of a proposed fitness center, for example, circulate a questionnaire asking for employee reactions.
- **Brainstorm for ideas.** Alone or with others, discuss ideas for the writing task at hand, and record at least a dozen ideas without judging them. Small groups are especially fruitful in brainstorming because people spin ideas off one another.

> Informal research may include looking in the files, talking with your boss, interviewing the target audience, conducting an informal survey, and brainstorming.

Organizing to Show Relationships

Once you have collected data, you must find some way to organize it. Organizing includes two processes: grouping and patterning. Well-organized messages group similar items together; ideas follow a sequence that helps the reader understand relationships and accept the writer's views. Unorganized messages proceed free-form, jumping from one thought to another. Such messages fail to emphasize important points. Puzzled readers can't see how the pieces fit together, and they become frustrated and irritated. Many communication experts regard poor organization as the greatest failing of business writers. Two simple techniques can help you organize data: the scratch list and the outline.

> Writers of well-organized messages group similar ideas together so that readers can see relationships and follow arguments.

FIGURE 3.2 Format for an Outline

Title: Major Idea or Purpose

I. First major component
   A. First subpoint
      1. Detail, illustration, evidence
      2. Detail, illustration, evidence
      3. Detail, illustration, evidence
   B. Second subpoint
      1.
      2.
II. Second major component
   A. First subpoint
      1.
      2.
   B. Second subpoint
      1.
      2.
      3.

Tips for Making Outlines

- Define the main topic in the title.
- Divide the topic into main points, preferably three to five.
- Break the components into subpoints.
- Don't put a single item under a major component if you have only one subpoint; integrate it with the main item above it or reorganize.
- Strive to make each component exclusive (no overlapping).
- Use details, illustrations, and evidence to support subpoints.

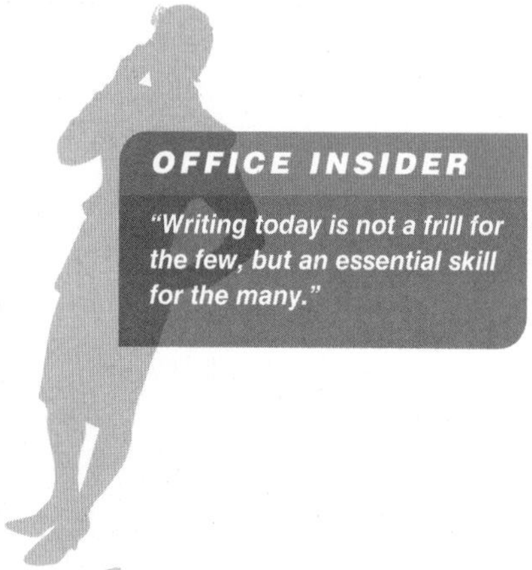

OFFICE INSIDER

"Writing today is not a frill for the few, but an essential skill for the many."

Business messages typically follow either (a) the direct pattern, with the main idea first, or (b) the indirect pattern, with the main idea following an explanation and evidence.

In developing simple messages, some writers make a quick scratch list of the topics they wish to cover. They then compose a message at their computers directly from the scratch list. Most writers, though, need to organize their ideas—especially if the project is complex—into a hierarchy, such as an outline. The beauty of preparing an outline is that it gives you a chance to organize your thinking before you get bogged down in word choice and sentence structure. Figure 3.2 above shows a format for an outline.

The Direct Pattern

After developing an outline, you will need to decide where in the message to place the main idea. Placing the main idea at the beginning of the message is called the *direct pattern*. In the direct pattern the main idea comes first, followed by details, an explanation, or evidence. Placing the main idea later in the message (after the details, explanation, or evidence) is called the *indirect pattern*. The pattern you select is determined by how you expect the audience to react to the message, as shown in Figure 3.3.

In preparing to write any message, you need to anticipate the audience's reaction to your ideas and frame your message accordingly. When you expect the reader to be pleased, mildly interested, or, at worst, neutral—use the direct pattern. That is, put your main point—the purpose of your message—in the first or second sentence. Compare the direct and indirect patterns in the following memo openings. Notice how long it takes to get to the main idea in the indirect opening.

Indirect Opening

For the past several years, we have had a continuing problem scheduling vacations, personal days, and sick time. Our Human Resources people struggle with unscheduled absences. After considerable investigation, the Management Council has decided to try a centralized paid time-off program starting January 1. This memo will describe its benefits and procedures.

Direct Opening

To improve the scheduling of absences, a new paid time-off program will begin January 1. The procedures and benefits are as follows.

FIGURE 3.3 Audience Response Determines Pattern of Organization

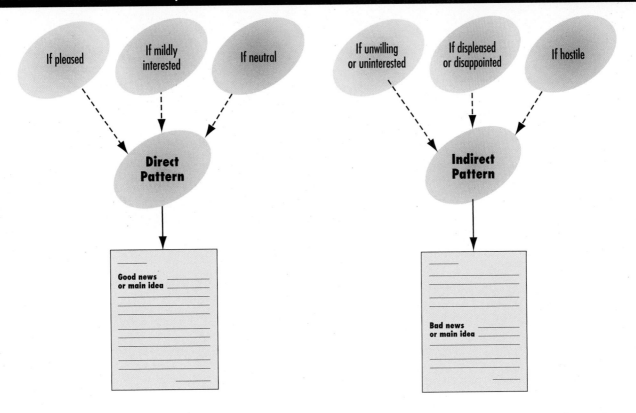

Explanations, background, and details should follow the direct opening. What's important is getting to the main idea quickly. This direct method, also called *front-loading,* has at least three advantages:

- **Saves the reader's time.** Many of today's businesspeople can devote only a few moments to each message. Messages that take too long to get to the point may lose their readers along the way.
- **Sets a proper frame of mind.** Learning the purpose up front helps the reader put the subsequent details and explanations in perspective. Without a clear opening, the reader may be thinking, *Why am I being told this?*
- **Prevents frustration.** Readers forced to struggle through excessive verbiage before reaching the main idea become frustrated. They resent the writer. Poorly organized messages create a negative impression of the writer.

This frontloading technique works best with audiences who are likely to be receptive to or at least not likely to disagree with what you have to say. Typical business messages that follow the direct pattern include routine requests and responses, orders and acknowledgments, nonsensitive memos, e-mail messages, informational reports, and informational oral presentations. All these tasks have one element in common: none has a sensitive subject that will upset the reader.

The Indirect Pattern

When you expect the audience to be uninterested, unwilling, displeased, or perhaps even hostile, the indirect pattern is more appropriate. In this pattern you don't reveal the main idea until after you have offered an explanation and evidence. This approach works well with three kinds of messages: (a) bad news, (b) ideas that require persuasion, and (c) sensitive news, especially when being transmitted to superiors. The indirect pattern has these benefits:

> Frontloading saves the reader's time, establishes the proper frame of mind, and prevents frustration.

> The indirect pattern works best when the audience may be uninterested, unwilling, displeased, or even hostile.

- **Respects the feelings of the audience.** Bad news is always painful, but the trauma can be lessened when the receiver is prepared for it.
- **Encourages a fair hearing.** Messages that may upset the reader are more likely to be read when the main idea is delayed. Beginning immediately with a piece of bad news or a persuasive request, for example, may cause the receiver to stop reading or listening.
- **Minimizes a negative reaction.** A reader's overall reaction to a negative message is generally improved if the news is delivered gently.

Typical business messages that could be developed indirectly include letters and memos that refuse requests, reject claims, and deny credit. Persuasive requests, sales letters, sensitive messages, and some reports and oral presentations also benefit from the indirect strategy. You will learn more about how to use the indirect pattern in Chapters 7 and 8.

In summary, business messages may be organized directly, with the main idea first, or indirectly, with the main idea delayed. Although these two patterns cover many communication problems, they should be considered neither universal nor unquestionable. Every business transaction is distinct. Some messages are mixed: part good news, part bad; part goodwill, part persuasion. In upcoming chapters you will practice applying the direct and indirect patterns in typical situations. Eventually, you will have the skills and confidence to evaluate communication problems and choose a pattern based on your goals.

Composing Effective Sentences

Vary your sentences to make your messages interesting and readable.

The most compelling and effective messages contain a variety of sentences rather than just one repeated pattern. Effective messages also avoid common sentence faults, and they achieve emphasis and parallelism with special sentence-writing techniques.

Achieving Variety With Four Sentence Types

Messages that repeat the same sentence pattern soon become boring. The way you construct your sentences can make your messages interesting and readable. To avoid monotony and to add spark to your writing, use a variety of sentence types. You have four sentence types from which to choose: simple, compound, complex, and compound-complex.

A **simple sentence,** shown in the following example, contains one complete thought (an independent clause) with a subject (underlined once) and predicate verb (underlined twice):

Our <u>team</u> <u>completed</u> the project.

A **compound sentence** contains two complete but related thoughts. The two thoughts (independent clauses) may be joined (a) by a conjunction such as *and, but,* or *or;* (b) by a semicolon; or (c) by a conjunctive adverb such as *however, consequently,* and *therefore.* Notice the punctuation in these examples:

The team <u>project</u> <u>was</u> challenging, and <u>we</u> <u>were</u> happy with the results.

The team <u>project</u> <u>was</u> challenging; <u>we</u> <u>were</u> happy with the results.

The team <u>project</u> <u>was</u> challenging; however, <u>we</u> <u>were</u> happy with the results.

A **complex sentence** contains an independent clause (a complete thought) and a dependent clause (a thought that cannot stand by itself). Dependent clauses are often introduced by words such as *although, since, because, when,* and *if.* When dependent clauses precede independent clauses, they always are followed by a comma.

When <u>we</u> <u>finished</u> the team project, <u>we</u> <u>held</u> a team party.

A **compound-complex sentence** contains at least two independent clauses and one dependent clause. Because these sentences are usually long, use them sparingly.

Although this team <u>project</u> <u>is</u> completed, soon <u>we</u> <u>will begin</u> work on another; however, <u>it</u> <u>will be</u> less challenging.

Controlling Sentence Length

Regardless of the type of sentence, remember that sentence length can influence readability. Because your goal is to communicate clearly, try to limit your sentences to about 20 or fewer words. The American Press Institute reports that reader comprehension drops off markedly as sentences become longer:

Sentence Length	Comprehension Rate
8 words	100%
15 words	90%
19 words	80%
28 words	50%

Sentences of 20 or fewer words have the most impact.

Avoiding Three Common Sentence Faults

As you craft your sentences, beware of three common traps: fragments, run-on (fused) sentences, and comma-splice sentences. If any of these faults appears in a business message, the writer immediately loses credibility.

Fragments. One of the most serious errors a writer can make is punctuating a fragment as if it were a complete sentence. A fragment is usually a broken-off part of a complex sentence.

Fragments are broken-off parts of sentences and should not be punctuated as sentences.

Fragment	**Revision**
Because most transactions require a permanent record. Good writing skills are critical.	Because most transactions require a permanent record, good writing skills are critical.
The recruiter requested a writing sample. Even though the candidate seemed to communicate well.	The recruiter requested a writing sample even though the candidate seemed to communicate well.

Fragments often can be identified by the words that introduce them—words such as *although, as, because, even, except, for example, if, instead of, since, such as, that, which,* and *when.* These words introduce dependent clauses. Make sure such clauses always connect to independent clauses.

When two independent clauses are run together without punctuation or a conjunction, a run-on (fused) sentence results.

Run-On (Fused) Sentences.
A sentence with two independent clauses must be joined by a coordinating conjunction (*and, or, nor, but*) or by a semicolon (;). Without a conjunction or a semicolon, a run-on sentence results.

Run-On	Revision
Most job seekers present a printed résumé some are also using Web sites as electronic portfolios	Most job seekers present a printed résumé. Some are also using Web sites as electronic portfolios.
One candidate sent an e-mail résumé another sent a traditional résumé.	One candidate sent an e-mail résumé; another sent a traditional résumé.

When two independent clauses are joined by a comma without a conjunction, a comma splice results.

Comma-Splice Sentences.
A comma splice results when a writer joins (splices together) two independent clauses with a comma. Independent clauses may be joined with a coordinating conjunction (*and, or, nor, but*) or a conjunctive adverb (*however, consequently, therefore,* and others). Notice that clauses joined by coordinating conjunctions require only a comma. Clauses joined by a coordinating adverb require a semicolon. Here are three ways to rectify a comma splice:

Comma Splice	Possible Revisions
Some employees responded by e-mail, others picked up the telephone.	Some employees responded by e-mail, and others picked up the telephone.
	Some employees responded by e-mail; however, others picked up the telephone.
	Some employees responded by e-mail; others picked up the telephone.

"Sentence fragments, comma splices, run-ons — who cares? I know what I meant!"

Improving Writing Techniques

Writers can significantly improve their messages by working on a few writing techniques. In this section we focus on emphasizing and de-emphasizing ideas, using active and passive voice strategically, developing parallelism, and avoiding dangling and misplaced modifiers.

Developing Emphasis

When you are talking with someone, you can emphasize your main ideas by saying them loudly or by repeating them slowly. You could even pound the table if you want to show real emphasis! Another way you could signal the relative importance of an idea is by raising your eyebrows or by shaking your head or whispering in a low voice. But when you write, you must rely on other means to tell your readers which ideas are more important than others. Emphasis in writing can be achieved primarily in two ways: mechanically or stylistically.

Achieving Emphasis Through Mechanics.
To emphasize an idea in print, a writer may use any of the following devices:

Underlining	<u>Underlining</u> draws the eye to a word.
Italics and boldface	Using *italics* or **boldface** conveys special meaning.
Font changes	Selecting a large, small, or *different* font draws interest.
All caps	Printing words in ALL CAPS is like shouting them.
Dashes	Dashes—used sparingly—can be effective.
Tabulation	Listing items vertically makes them stand out: 1. First item 2. Second item 3. Third item

You can emphasize an idea mechanically by using underlining, italics, boldface, font changes, all caps, dashes, and tabulation.

Other means of achieving mechanical emphasis include the arrangement of space, color, lines, boxes, columns, titles, headings, and subheadings. Today's software and color printers provide a wonderful array of capabilities for setting off ideas. More tips on achieving emphasis are coming in Chapter 4, where we cover document design.

Achieving Emphasis Through Style. Although mechanical means are occasionally appropriate, more often a writer achieves emphasis stylistically. That is, the writer chooses words carefully and constructs sentences skillfully to emphasize main ideas and de-emphasize minor or negative ideas. Here are four suggestions for emphasizing ideas stylistically:

- **Use vivid words.** Vivid words are emphatic because the reader can picture ideas clearly.

You can emphasize ideas stylistically by using vivid words, labeling the main idea, and positioning the main idea strategically.

General	Vivid
One business uses *personal* selling techniques	*Avon* uses *face-to-face* selling techniques.
Someone will *contact* you as soon as possible.	*Ms. Stevens* will *telephone* you *before 5 P.M. tomorrow, May 3.*

- **Label the main idea.** If an idea is significant, tell the reader.

Unlabeled	Labeled
Consider looking for a job online, but also focus on networking.	Consider looking for a job online; but, *most important*, focus on networking.
We shop here because of the customer service and low prices.	We like the customer service, but the *primary reason* for shopping here is low prices.

- **Place the important idea first or last in the sentence.** Ideas have less competition from surrounding words when they appear first or last in a sentence. Observe how the concept of *productivity* can be emphasized by its position in the sentence:

Unemphatic	Emphatic
Profit-sharing plans are more effective in increasing *productivity* when they are linked to individual performance rather than to group performance.	*Productivity* is more likely to be increased when profit-sharing plans are linked to individual performance rather than to group performance. Profit-sharing plans linked to individual performance rather than to group performance are more effective in increasing *productivity*.

- **Place the important idea in a simple sentence or in an independent clause.** Don't dilute the effect of the idea by making it share the spotlight with other words and clauses.

Unemphatic	Emphatic
Although you are the first trainee we have hired for this program, we had many candidates and expect to expand the program in the future. (Main idea is lost in a dependent clause.)	You are the first trainee we have hired for this program. (Simple sentence)
	Although we considered many candidates, you are the first trainee we have hired for this program. (Independent clause contains main idea.)

You can de-emphasize ideas by using general words and placing the ideas in dependent clauses.

De-emphasizing When Necessary. To de-emphasize an idea, such as bad news, try one of the following stylistic devices:

- **Use general words.**

De-emphasizes Harsh Statement	Emphasizes Harsh Statement
Our records indicate that *your employment status has recently changed.*	Our records indicate that *you were recently fired.*

- **Place the bad news in a dependent clause connected to an independent clause with something positive.** In sentences with dependent clauses, the main emphasis is always on the independent clause.

De-emphasizes Bad News	Emphasizes Bad News
Although credit cannot be issued at this time, you can fill your immediate needs on a cash basis with our special plan.	We cannot issue you credit at this time, but we have a special plan that will allow you to fill your immediate needs on a cash basis.

Using Active and Passive Voice

Active-voice sentences are preferred because the subject is the doer of the action.

In composing messages, you may use active or passive voice to express your meaning. In active voice, the subject is the doer of the action (*The manager hired Jim*). In passive voice, the subject is acted upon (*Jim was hired [by the manager]*). Notice that in the passive voice the attention shifts from the doer to the receiver of the action. You don't even have to reveal the doer if you choose not to. Writers generally prefer active voice because it is more direct, clear, and concise. Nevertheless, passive voice is useful in certain instances, such as the following:

- **To emphasize an action or the recipient of the action.** *An investigation was launched.*
- **To de-emphasize negative news.** *Cash refunds cannot be made.*
- **To conceal the doer of an action.** *An error was made in our sales figures.*

How can you tell whether a verb is active or passive? Identify the subject of the sentence and decide whether the subject is doing the acting or is being acted upon. For example, in the sentence *An appointment was made for January 1*, the subject is *appointment*. The subject is being acted upon; therefore, the verb (*was made*) is passive. Another clue in identifying passive-voice verbs is that they generally include a *to be* helping verb, such as *is, are, was, were, be, being,* or *been*. Figure 3.4 summarizes effective uses for active and passive voice.

Achieving Parallelism

Parallelism is a skillful writing technique that involves balanced writing. Sentences written so that their parts are balanced or parallel are easy to read and understand. To achieve

FIGURE 3.4 Using Active and Passive Voice Effectively

Use active voice for directness, vigor, and clarity.

Direct and Clear in Active Voice	Indirect and Less Clear in Passive Voice
The manager completed performance reviews for all employees.	Performance reviews were completed for all employees by the manager.
Evelyn initiated a customer service blog last year.	A customer service blog was initiated last year.
IBM will accept applications after January 1.	Applications will be accepted after January 1 by IBM.
Coca-Cola created a Sprite page in Facebook to advertise its beverage.	A Sprite page was created in Facebook by Coca-Cola to advertise its beverage.

Use passive voice to be tactful or to emphasize the action rather than the doer.

Less Tactful or Effective in Active Voice	More Tactful or Effective in Passive Voice
We cannot grant you credit.	Credit cannot be granted.
The CEO made a huge error in projecting profits.	A huge error was made in projecting profits.
I launched a successful fitness program for our company last year.	A successful fitness program was launched for our company last year.
We are studying the effects of the Sarbanes/Oxley Act on our accounting procedures.	The effects of the Sarbanes/Oxley Act on our accounting procedures are being studied.

parallel construction, use similar structures to express similar ideas. For example, the words *computing, coding, recording,* and *storing* are parallel because the words all end in *-ing*. To express the list as *computing, coding, recording,* and *storage* is disturbing because the last item is not what the reader expects. Try to match nouns with nouns, verbs with verbs, and clauses with clauses. Avoid mixing active-voice verbs with passive-voice verbs. Your goal is to keep the wording balanced when expressing similar ideas.

Balanced wording helps the reader anticipate and comprehend your meaning.

Lacks Parallelism	Improved
The policy affected all vendors, suppliers, and *those involved with consulting.*	The policy affected all vendors, suppliers, and *consultants.* (Matches nouns)
Our primary goals are to increase productivity, reduce costs, and *the improvement of product quality.*	Our primary goals are to increase productivity, reduce costs, and *improve product quality.* (Matches verbs)
We are scheduled to meet in Dallas on January 5, *we are meeting in Montreal on the 15th of March*, and in Chicago on June 3.	We are scheduled to meet in Dallas on January 5, *in Montreal on March 15*, and in Chicago on June 3. (Matches phrases)
Shelby audits all accounts lettered A through L; accounts lettered M through Z are audited by Andrew.	Shelby audits all accounts lettered A through L; Andrew audits accounts lettered M through Z. (Matches clauses)

Our Super Bowl ads have three objectives:

1. We want to increase product use.
2. Introduce complementary products.
3. Our corporate image will be enhanced.

Our Super Bowl ads have three objectives:

1. Increase product use
2. Introduce complementary products
3. Enhance our corporate image (Matches verbs in listed items)

"To make this easy to read, I have divided it into three parts: A, B, and 3."

Avoiding Dangling and Misplaced Modifiers

For clarity, modifiers must be close to the words they describe or limit. A modifier dangles when the word or phrase it describes is missing from its sentence (*After working overtime, the report was finally finished*). This sentence says the report was working overtime. Revised, the sentence contains a logical subject: *After working overtime, we finally finished the report.*

A modifier is misplaced when the word or phrase it describes is not close enough to be clear (*Firefighters rescued a dog from a burning car that had a broken leg*). Obviously, the car did not have a broken leg. The solution is to position the modifier closer to the word(s) it describes or limits: *Firefighters rescued a dog with a broken leg from a burning car.*

Introductory verbal phrases are particularly dangerous; be sure to follow them immediately with the words they logically describe or modify. Try this trick for detecting and remedying many dangling modifiers. Ask the question *Who?* or *What?* after any introductory phrase. The words immediately following should tell the reader who or what is performing the action. Try the *who?* test on the first three danglers here:

Dangling or Misplaced Modifier	Revision
Skilled at graphic design, the contract went to DesignOne.	Skilled at graphic design, DesignOne won the contract.
Working together as a team, the project was finally completed.	Working together as a team, we finally completed the project.
To meet the deadline, your Excel figures must be received by May 1.	To meet the deadline, you must send us your Excel figures by May 1.
The recruiter interviewed candidates who had excellent computer skills in the morning.	In the morning the recruiter interviewed candidates with excellent computer skills.
As an important customer to us, we invite you to our spring open house.	As you are an important customer to us, we invite you to our spring open house. *OR:* As an important customer to us, you are invited to our spring open house.

Drafting Powerful Paragraphs

A paragraph is a group of sentences about one idea. Paragraphs are most effective when they contain (a) a topic sentence, (b) support sentences that expand and explain only the main idea, and (c) techniques to build coherence.

Crafting Topic Sentences

A topic sentence states the main idea of the paragraph. Business writers generally place the topic sentence first in the paragraph. It tells readers what to expect and helps them understand the paragraph's central thought immediately. In the revision stage, you will check to be sure each paragraph has a topic sentence. Notice in the following examples how the topic sentence summarizes the main idea, which will be followed by support sentences explaining the topic sentence:

> Flexible work scheduling could immediately increase productivity and enhance employee satisfaction in our entire organization. [Support sentences explaining flex scheduling would expand the paragraph.]

The chat function at our main Web site is not functioning as well as we had expected. [Support sentences would describe existing problems in the Web chat function.]

Developing Support Sentences

Topic sentences summarize the main idea of a paragraph. Support sentences illustrate, explain, or strengthen the topic sentence. One of the hardest things for beginning writers to remember is that all support sentences in the paragraph must relate to the topic sentence. Any other topics should be treated separately. Support sentences provide specific details, explanations, and evidence:

> Flexible work scheduling could immediately increase productivity and enhance employee satisfaction in our entire organization. Managers would be required to maintain their regular hours. For many other employees, though, flexible scheduling permits extra time to manage family responsibilities. Feeling less stress, employees are able to focus their attention better at work; therefore, they become more relaxed and more productive.

Building Paragraph Coherence

Paragraphs are coherent when ideas are linked—that is, when one idea leads logically to the next. Well-written paragraphs take the reader through a number of steps. When the author skips from Step 1 to Step 3 and forgets Step 2, the reader is lost. Several techniques allow the reader to follow your ideas:

- **Repeat a key idea by using the same expression or a similar one:** *Employees treat guests as VIPs. These VIPs are never told what they can or cannot do.*
- **Use pronouns to refer to previous nouns:** *All new employees receive a two-week orientation. They learn that every staffer has a vital role.*
- **Show connections with transitional expressions:** *however, as a result, consequently,* and *meanwhile.* For a complete list, see Figure 3.5.

Controlling Paragraph Length

Although no rule regulates the length of paragraphs, business writers recognize the value of short paragraphs. Paragraphs with eight or fewer printed lines look inviting and readable. Long, solid chunks of print appear formidable. If a topic can't be covered in eight or fewer printed lines (not sentences), consider breaking it into smaller segments.

The most readable paragraphs contain eight or fewer printed lines.

FIGURE 3.5 Transitional Expressions to Build Coherence					
To Add or Strengthen	**To Show Time or Order**	**To Clarify**	**To Show Cause and Effect**	**To Contradict**	**To Contrast**
additionally	after	for example	accordingly	actually	as opposed to
accordingly	before	for instance	as a result	but	at the same time
again	earlier	I mean	consequently	however	by contrast
also	finally	in other words	for this reason	in fact	conversely
beside	first	put another way	hence	instead	on the contrary
indeed	meanwhile	that is	so	rather	on the other hand
likewise	next	this means	therefore	still	previously
moreover	now	thus	thus	yet	similarly

Composing the First Draft

Create a quiet place in which to write. Experts recommend freewriting for first drafts.

Once you have researched your topic, organized the data, and selected a pattern of organization, you are ready to begin composing. Communicators who haven't completed the preparatory work often suffer from "writer's block" and sit staring at a piece of paper or at the computer screen. Getting started is easier if you have organized your ideas and established a plan. Composition is also easier if you have a quiet environment in which to concentrate. Businesspeople with messages to compose set aside a given time and allow no calls, visitors, or other interruptions. This is a good technique for students as well.

As you begin composing, keep in mind that you are writing the first draft, not the final copy. Some experts suggest that you write quickly (*freewriting*). If you get your thoughts down quickly, you can refine them in later versions. Other writers, such as your author, prefer to polish sentences as they go. Different writers have different styles. Whether you are a freewriter or a polisher, learn to compose your thoughts at your keyboard. You might be tempted to write a first draft by hand and then transfer it to the computer. This wastes time and develops poor habits. Businesspeople must be able to compose at their keyboards, and now is the time to develop that confidence and skill.

Visit www.meguffey.com
- Chapter Review Quiz
- Flash Cards
- Grammar Practice
- PowerPoint Slides
- Personal Language Trainer
- Beat the Clock Quiz

Summing Up and Looking Forward

This chapter explained the second phase of the writing process, which includes researching, organizing, and composing. Before beginning a message, every writer collects data, either formally or informally. For most simple messages, you would look in the files, talk with your boss, interview the target audience, or possibly conduct an informal survey. Information for a message is then organized into a list or an outline. Depending on the expected reaction of the receiver, the message can be organized directly (for positive reactions) or indirectly (for negative reactions or when persuasion is necessary).

In composing the first draft, writers should use a variety of sentence types and avoid fragments, run-ons, and comma splices. Emphasis can be achieved through mechanics (underlining, italics, font changes, all caps, and so forth) or through style (using vivid words, labeling the main idea, and positioning the important ideas). Important writing techniques include skillfully using active- and passive-voice verbs, developing parallelism, and avoiding dangling or misplaced modifiers. Powerful paragraphs result from crafting a topic sentence, developing support sentences, and building coherence with the planned repetition of key ideas, proper use of pronouns, and inclusion of transitional expressions.

In the next chapter you will learn helpful techniques for the third phase of the writing process, which includes revising and proofreading.

Critical Thinking

1. "Writing is both a 'marker' of high-skill, high-wage, professional work and a 'gatekeeper' with clear equity implications," said Bob Kerry, chair of the Commission on Writing.[1] What does this statement mean in relation to your career field?

2. Why is audience analysis so important in choosing the direct or indirect pattern of organization for a business message?

3. How are speakers different from writers in the way they emphasize ideas?

4. Why are short sentences and short paragraphs appropriate for business communication?

5. When might it be unethical to use the indirect method of organizing a message?

6. Compare the first phase of the writing process with the second phase.

7. For routine writing tasks, what are some techniques for collecting informal data and generating ideas?

8. What is the difference between a list and an outline?

9. Why do many readers prefer the direct method for organizing messages?

10. When is the indirect method appropriate, and what are the benefits of using it?

11. List four techniques for achieving emphasis through style.

12. What is parallelism? Give an original example.

13. What are the four sentence types, and what do they consist of?

14. What is a topic sentence, and where is it usually found in business messages?

15. List three techniques for developing paragraph coherence.

Sentence Type

For each of the numbered sentences, select the letter that identifies its type:

a Simple   c Complex
b Compound   d Compound-complex

16. Many companies are now doing business in international circles.

17. If you travel abroad on business, you may bring gifts for business partners.

18. In Latin America a knife is not a proper gift; it signifies cutting off a relationship.

19. When Arabs, Middle Easterners, and Latin Americans talk, they stand close to each other.

20. Unless they are old friends, Europeans do not address each other by first names; consequently, businesspeople should not expect to do so.

21. In the Philippines men wear a long embroidered shirt called a *barong,* and women wear a dress called a *terno.*

Sentence Faults

In the following, identify the sentence fault (fragment, run-on, comma splice). Then revise to remedy the fault.

22. Because 90 percent of all business transactions involve written messages. Good writing skills are critical.

23. The recruiter requested a writing sample. Even though the candidate seemed to communicate well orally.

24. Major soft-drink companies considered a new pricing strategy, they tested vending machines that raise prices in hot weather.

25. Thirsty consumers may think that variable pricing is unfair they may also refuse to use the machine.

26. About half of Pizza Hut's 7,600 outlets make deliveries, the others concentrate on walk-in customers.

27. McDonald's sold its chain of Chipotle Mexican Grill restaurants the chain's share price doubled on the next day of trading.

Emphasis

For each of the following sentences, circle (a) or (b). Be prepared to justify your choice.

28. Which is more emphatic?

    a. Our dress code is good.

    b. Our dress code reflects common sense and good taste.

29. Which is more emphatic?

   a. A budget increase would certainly improve hiring.

   b. A budget increase of $70,000 would enable us to hire two new people.

30. Which is more emphatic?

   a. The committee was powerless to act.

   b. The committee was unable to take action.

31. Which de-emphasizes the refusal?

   a. Although our resources are committed to other projects this year, we hope to be able to contribute to your worthy cause next year.

   b. We can't contribute to your charity this year.

32. Which sentence places more emphasis on the date?

   a. The deadline is November 30 for health benefit changes.

   b. November 30 is the deadline for health benefit changes.

33. Which is *less* emphatic?

   a. One division's profits decreased last quarter.

   b. Profits in beauty care products dropped 15 percent last quarter.

34. Which sentence *de-emphasizes* the credit refusal?

   a. We are unable to grant you credit at this time, but we welcome your cash business and encourage you to reapply in the future.

   b. Although credit cannot be granted at this time, we welcome your cash business and encourage you to reapply in the future.

35. Which sentence gives more emphasis to *leadership*?

   a. Jason has many admirable qualities, but most important is his leadership skill.

   b. Jason has many admirable qualities, including leadership skill, good judgment, and patience.

36. Which is more emphatic?

   a. We notified three departments: (1) Marketing, (2) Accounting, and (3) Distribution.

   b. We notified three departments:

      1. Marketing

      2. Accounting

      3. Distribution

Active Voice

Business writing is more forceful if it uses active-voice verbs. Revise the following sentences so that verbs are in the active voice. Put the emphasis on the doer of the action.

Passive   Antivirus software was installed by Craig on his computer.
Active   Craig installed antivirus software on his computer.

37. Employees were given their checks at 4 P.M. every Friday by the manager.

38. New spices and cooking techniques were tried by McDonald's to improve its hamburgers.

39. Our new company logo was designed by my boss.

40. The managers with the most productive departments were commended by the CEO.

Passive Voice

Revise the following sentences so that they are in the passive voice.

41. The auditor discovered a computational error in the company's tax figures.

42. We cannot ship your order for ten monitors until June 15.

43. Stacy did not submit the accounting statement on time.

44. The Federal Trade Commission targeted deceptive diet advertisements by weight-loss marketers.

Parallelism

Revise the following sentences so that their parts are balanced.

45. (Hint: Match adjectives.) To be hired, an applicant must be reliable, creative, and show enthusiasm.

46. (Hint: Match active voice.) If you have decided to cancel our service, please cut your credit card in half and the pieces should be returned to us.

47. (Hint: Match verbs.) Guidelines for improving security at food facilities include inspecting incoming and outgoing vehicles, restriction of access to laboratories, preventing workers from bringing personal items into food-handling areas, and inspection of packaging for signs of tampering.

48. (Hint: Match adjective–noun expressions.) The committee will continue to monitor merchandise design, product quality, and check the feedback of customers.

49. (Hint: Match verb clauses.) To use the fax copier, insert your meter, the paper trays must be loaded, indicate the number of copies needed, and your original sheet should be inserted through the feeder.

50. (Hint: Match *ing* verbs.) Sending an e-mail establishes a more permanent record than to make a telephone call.

Dangling and Misplaced Modifiers

Revise the following to avoid dangling and misplaced modifiers.

51. After leaving the midtown meeting, Angela's car would not start.

52. Walking up the driveway, the Hummer parked in the garage was immediately spotted by the detectives.

53. To complete the project on time, a new deadline was established by the team.

54. Acting as manager, several new employees were hired by Mr. Lopez.

55. Michelle Mitchell presented a talk about workplace drug problems in our boardroom.

Organizing Paragraph Sentences

In a memo to the college president, the athletic director argues for a new stadium scoreboard. One paragraph will describe the old scoreboard and why it needs to be replaced. Study the following list of ideas for that paragraph.

1. *The old scoreboard is a tired warhorse that was originally constructed in the 1970s.*
2. *It is now hard to find replacement parts when something breaks.*
3. *The old scoreboard is not energy efficient.*
4. *Coca-Cola has offered to buy a new sports scoreboard in return for exclusive rights to sell soda pop on campus.*
5. *The old scoreboard should be replaced for many reasons.*
6. *It shows only scores for football games.*
7. *When we have soccer games or track meets, we are without any functioning scoreboard.*

56. Which sentence should be the topic sentence?

57. Which sentence(s) should be developed in a separate paragraph?

58. Which sentences should become support sentences?

Building Coherent Paragraphs

59. Use the information from the preceding sentences to write a coherent paragraph about replacing the sports scoreboard. Strive to use three devices to build coherence: (a) repetition of key words, (b) pronouns that clearly refer to previous nouns, and (c) transitional expressions.

60. Revise the following paragraph. Add a topic sentence and improve the organization. Correct problems with pronouns, parallelism, wordiness, and misplaced or dangling modifiers. Add transitional expressions if appropriate.

You may be interested in applying for a new position within the company. The Human Resources Department has a number of jobs available immediately. The positions are at a high level. Current employees may apply immediately for open positions in production, for some in marketing, and jobs in administrative support are also available. To make application, these positions require immediate action. Come to the Human Resources Department. We have a list showing the open positions, what the qualifications are, and job descriptions are shown. Many of the jobs are now open. That's why we are sending this now. To be hired, an interview must be scheduled within the next two weeks.

61. Revise the following paragraph. Add a topic sentence and improve the organization. Correct problems with pronouns, parallelism, wordiness, and misplaced or dangling modifiers.

As you probably already know, this company (Lasertronics) will be installing new computer software shortly. There will be a demonstration April 18, which is a Tuesday. You are invited. We felt this was necessary because this new software is so different from our previous software. It will be from 9 to 12 a.m. in the morning. This will show employees how the software programs work. They will learn about the operating system, and this should be helpful to nearly everyone. There will be information about the new word processing program, which should be helpful to administrative assistants and product managers. For all you people who work with payroll, there will be information about the new database program. We can't show everything the software will do at this one demo, but for these three areas there will be some help at the Tuesday demo. Presenting the software, the demo will feature Paula Roddy. She is the representative from Quantum Software.

Grammar/Mechanics Checkup 3

Verbs

Review Sections 1.10–1.15 in the Grammar Review section of the Grammar/Mechanics Handbook. Then study each of the following statements. Underline any verbs that are used incorrectly. In the space provided write the correct form (or *C* if correct) and the number of the G/M principle illustrated. When you finish, compare your responses with those provided near the end of the book. If your responses differ, study carefully the principles in parentheses.

has for *have*   (1.10c)   **Example** Not one of our customers <u>have</u> ever complained about lost e-mail messages.

1. A large group of our e-mail messages were recently blocked by spam filters.
2. Although Mark acts as if he was the manager, he doesn't know what to do about the e-mail disruption dilemma.
3. If even one of my e-mail messages are blocked by spam controls, I am unhappy.
4. Verizon, together with many other large ISPs, were singled out for using overzealous spam blockers.
5. Neither the sender nor the receiver of blocked messages know what has happened.
6. A typical e-mail user has wrote several messages that were never delivered.
7. Time and energy is required to follow up on e-mail messages.
8. Either the message or its attachment has triggered the spam-blocking software.
9. After many of its customers had began to complain about lost messages, one company sued.
10. If you could have saw the number of nondelivery error messages, you would have been upset also.
11. Ramon discovered that a lot of his legitimate e-mail had went to junk folders that he never checked.

In the space provided write the letter of the sentence that illustrates consistency in subject, voice, and verb form.

12. a. When Mason sent an e-mail message, its delivery was expected.
    b. When Mason sent an e-mail message, he expected it to be delivered.
13. a. All employees must wear photo identification; only then will you be admitted.
    b. All employees must wear photo identification; only then will they be admitted.
14. a. First, check all computers for viruses; then, install a firewall.
    b. First, check all computers for viruses; then, a firewall must be installed.
15. a. When Tina examined the computers, the spyware was discovered.
    b. When Tina examined the computers, she discovered the spyware.

The following letter has errors in spelling, proofreading, verbs, sentence structure, parallelism, and other writing techniques studied in this chapter. You may either (a) use standard proofreading marks (see Appendix B) to correct the errors here or (b) download the document from your companion Web site and revise at your computer. Study the guidelines in the Grammar/Mechanics Handbook to sharpen your skills.

Body Fitness
Training Massage Wellness
3392 Econlockhatchee Trail • Orlando, FL 32822 • (407) 551-8791

June 4, 200x

Mr. Allen C. Fineberg
3250 Ponciana Way
Palm Beach Gardens, FL 33410

Dear Mr. Fineburg:

You probably choose Body Fitness because it has became one of the top-rated gyms in the Palm Beach area. Making your work out enjoyable has always been our principal goal. To continue to provide you with the best equipment and programs, your feedback is needed by my partner and myself.

We have build an outstanding program with quality equipment, excellent training programs, and our support staff is very helpful. We feel, however, that we could have a more positive affect and give more individual attention if we could extend our peak usage time. You have probable noticed that attendance at the gym raises from 4 p.m. to 8 p.m. We wish it was possible to accommodate all our customers on their favorite equipment during those hours. Although we can't stretch an hour. We would like to make better use of the time between 8 p.m. and 11 p.m. With more members' coming later, we would have less crush from 4 to 8 p.m. Our exercise machines and strength-training equipment is lying idle later in the evening.

To encourage you to stay later, security cameras for our parking area are being considered by us. Cameras for some inside facilitys may also be added. We have gave this matter a great deal of thought. Although Body Fitness have never had an incident that endangered a member. We have went to considerable trouble to learn about security cameras. Because we think that you will feel more comfortable with them in action.

Please tell us what you think, fill out the enclosed questionnaire, and drop it the ballot box during your next visit at the desk. We are asking for your feed back about scheduling your workouts, selecting your equipment, and if you would consider coming later in the evening. If you have any other suggestions for reducing the crush at peak times. Please tell us on the enclosed form.

Cordially,

Nicolas Barajas, Manager

Enclosure

Communication Workshop: Ethics

Using Ethical Tools to Help You Do the Right Thing

In your career you will no doubt face times when you are torn by ethical dilemmas. Should you tell the truth and risk your job? Should you be loyal to your friends even if it means bending the rules? Should you be tactful or totally honest? Is it your duty to help your company make a profit, or should you be socially responsible?

Being ethical, according to the experts, means doing the right thing *given the circumstances*. Each set of circumstances requires analyzing issues, evaluating choices, and acting responsibly. Resolving ethical issues is never easy, but the task can be made less difficult if you know how to identify key issues. The following questions may be helpful.

- **Is the action you are considering legal?** No matter who asks you to do it or how important you feel the result will be, avoid anything that is prohibited by law. Giving a kickback to a buyer for a large order is illegal, even if you suspect that others in your field do it and you know that without the kickback you will lose the sale.
- **How would you see the problem if you were on the opposite side?** Looking at both sides of an issue helps you gain perspective. By weighing both sides of an issue, you can arrive at a more equitable solution.
- **What are the alternative solutions? Consider all dimensions of other options.** Would the alternative be more ethical? Under the circumstances, is the alternative feasible?
- **Can you discuss the problem with someone whose opinion you value?** Suppose you feel ethically bound to report accurate information to a client—even though your boss has ordered you not to do so. Talking about your dilemma with a coworker or with a colleague in your field might give you helpful insights and lead to possible alternatives.
- **How would you feel if your family, friends, employer, or coworkers learned of your action?** If the thought of revealing your action publicly produces cold sweats, your choice is probably not a wise one. Losing the faith of your friends or the confidence of your customers is not worth whatever short-term gains might be realized.

Career Application. One of the biggest accounting firms uses an ethical awareness survey that includes some of the following situations. You may face similar situations with ethical issues on the job or in employment testing.

Your Task

In teams or individually, decide whether each of the following ethical issues is (a) very important, (b) moderately important, or (c) unimportant. Then decide whether you (a) strongly approve, (b) are undecided, or (c) strongly disapprove of the action taken.[2] Apply the ethical tools presented here to determine whether the course of action is ethical. What alternatives might you suggest?

- **Recruiting.** You are a recruiter for your company. Although you know company morale is low, the turnover rate is high, and the work environment in many departments is deplorable, you tell job candidates that it is "a great place to work."
- **Training program.** Your company is offering an exciting training program in Hawaii. Although you haven't told anyone, you plan to get another job shortly. You decide to participate in the program anyway because you have never been to Hawaii. One of the program requirements is that participants must have "long-term career potential" with the firm.
- **Thievery.** As a supervisor, you suspect that one of your employees is stealing. You check with a company attorney and find that a lie detector test cannot be legally used. Then you decide to scrutinize the employee's records. Finally, you find an inconsistency in the employee's records. You decide to fire the employee, although this inconsistency would not normally have been discovered.
- **Downsizing.** As part of the management team of a company that makes potato chips, you are faced with the rising prices of potatoes. Rather than increase the cost of your chips, you decide to decrease slightly the size of the bag. Consumers are less likely to notice a smaller bag than a higher price.

CHAPTER 4

Revising Business Messages

OBJECTIVES
After studying this chapter, you should be able to

- Understand the revision phase of the writing process and employ techniques that enhance message conciseness such as eliminating flabby expressions, limiting long lead-ins, dropping fillers, and avoiding redundancies.

- Revise messages to improve clarity by dumping trite business phrases, using jargon judiciously, avoiding slang, and dropping clichés.

- Revise messages to improve vigor and directness by unburying verbs, controlling exuberance, and choosing precise words.

- Understand document design and be able to use white space, margins, typefaces, fonts, numbered and bulleted lists, and headings to improve readability.

- Apply effective techniques for proofreading routine and complex documents.

Understanding the Process of Revision

To be successful in the business world, you must be able to create messages and presentations that are concise, clear, and vigorous. This chapter focuses on writing techniques that achieve those qualities. These techniques are part of the third phase of the writing process, which centers on revising and proofreading. Revising means improving the content and sentence structure of your message. It may include adding, cutting, recasting, reformatting, and redesigning what you have written. Proofreading involves improving the grammar, spelling, punctuation, and mechanics of your messages.

> **Revision involves improving content, sentence structure, and design; proofreading involves improving grammar, spelling, punctuation, and mechanics.**

Both revising and proofreading require practice to develop your skills. Notice how the revised version of the memo in Figure 4.1 is clearer, more concise, and more vigorous because we removed much deadwood. Major ideas stand out when they are not lost in a forest of words.

Rarely is the first or even the second version of a message satisfactory. Experts say that only amateurs expect writing perfection on the first try. The revision stage is your chance to make sure your message is clear, forceful, and readable. This is the time when you will see how to draw out the major point and perhaps make a list so that the reader sees quickly what you mean.

Many professional writers compose the first draft quickly without worrying about language, precision, or correctness. Then they revise and polish extensively.

Other writers, however, prefer to revise as they go—particularly for shorter business documents. Whether you revise as you go or do it when you finish a document, you will want to focus on concise wording.

Revising for Conciseness

Main points are easier to understand in concise messages.

In business, time is indeed money. Translated into writing, this means that concise messages save reading time and, thus, money. In addition, messages that are written directly and efficiently are easier to read and comprehend. In the revision process look for shorter ways to say what you mean. Examine every sentence that you write. Could the thought be conveyed in fewer words? Your writing will be more concise if you eliminate flabby expressions, drop unnecessary introductory words, and get rid of redundancies.

Eliminating Flabby Expressions

As you revise, focus on eliminating flabby expressions. This takes conscious effort. As one expert copyeditor observed, "Trim sentences, like trim bodies, usually require far more effort than flabby ones."[1] Turning out slim sentences and lean messages means that you will strive to "trim the fat." For example, notice the flabbiness in this sentence: *Due to the fact that sales are booming, profits are good.* It could be said more concisely: *Because sales are booming, profits are good.* Many flabby expressions can be shortened to one concise word, as shown in Figure 4.2.

Limiting Long Lead-Ins

Another way to create concise sentences is to delete unnecessary introductory words. Consider this sentence: *I am sending you this e-mail to announce that a new*

FIGURE 4.1 Revising a Memo for Conciseness

NorthStar Telecommunication Services
Interoffice Memo

DATE: November 12, 200x

TO: Phillip Larios

FROM: Danika Freedman

SUBJECT: Investigation of Web Sites of Some of Our Competitors

This is just a short note to inform you that, as you requested, I have made an investigation of

several of our competitors' Web sites. Attached hereto is a summary of my findings.

of my investigation. I was really most interested in making a comparison of the employment of

strategies for marketing as well as the use of navigational graphics used to guide visitors

through the sites. In view of the fact that we will be revising our own Web site in the near future,

I was extremely intrigued by the organization, kind of marketing tactics, and navigation at

each and every site I visited.

In the event that you would like to discuss this information with me, feel free to call me at

Extension 219.

Attachment

FIGURE 4.2 Slimming Down Flabby Expressions

Wordy	Concise	Wordy	Concise
afford an opportunity	allow	in addition to the above	also
are of the opinion	believe, think	in all probability	probably
as a general rule	generally	in spite of the fact that	although
at a later date	later	in the event that	if
at this point in time	now, presently	in the amount of	for
despite the fact that	although	in the near future	soon
due to the fact that	because	in the normal course of events	normally
feel free to	please	in very few cases	seldom
for the period of	for	in view of the fact that	because
fully cognizant	aware	inasmuch as	since
in a careful manner	carefully	until such time as	until

manager has been hired. A more concise and more direct sentence deletes the long lead-in: *A new manager has been hired.* The meat of the sentence often follows the words *that* or *because,* as shown in the following:

Avoid long lead-ins that prevent the reader from reaching the meaning of the sentence.

Wordy	**Concise**
This e-mail message is being sent to all of you to let you know that new parking permits will be issued January 1	New parking permits will be issued January 1.
You will be interested to learn that you can now be served at our Web site.	You can now be served at our Web site.
I am writing this letter because Dr. Mara Evans suggested that your organization was hiring trainees.	Dr. Mara Evans suggested that your organization was hiring trainees.

Dropping Unnecessary *There is/are* and *It is/was* Fillers

In many sentences the expressions *there is/are* and *it is/was* function as unnecessary fillers. In addition to taking up space, these fillers delay getting to the point of the sentence. Eliminate them by recasting the sentence. Many—but not all—sentences can be revised so that fillers are unnecessary.

Wordy	**Concise**
There is only one candidate who passed the test.	Only one candidate passed the test.
There is an unused computer in the back office.	An unused computer is in the back office.
It was our auditor who discovered the theft.	Our auditor discovered the theft.

Getting Rid of Redundancies

The use of words whose meanings are clearly implied by other words is a writing fault called *redundancy.* For example, in the expression *final outcome,* the word

Redundancies convey a meaning more than once.

final is redundant and should be omitted because *outcome* implies finality. As you revise, look for redundant expressions such as the following:

Redundant	Concise
absolutely essential	essential
adequate enough	adequate
basic fundamentals	fundamentals *or* basics
big in size	big
combined together	combined
exactly identical	identical
each and every	each *or* every
necessary prerequisite	prerequisite
new beginning	beginning
refer back	refer
repeat again	repeat
true facts	facts

Revising for Clarity

Business writers appreciate clear messages that are immediately understandable. Techniques that improve clarity include dumping trite business phrases and avoiding slang, jargon, and clichés.

Dumping Trite Business Phrases

To sound "businesslike," many writers repeat the same stale expressions that other writers have used over the years. Your writing will sound fresher and more vigorous if you eliminate these phrases or find more original ways to convey the idea.

Trite Phrase	Improved Version
as per your request	as you request
pursuant to your request	at your request
enclosed please find	enclosed is
every effort will be made	we'll try
in accordance with your wishes	as you wish
in receipt of	have received
please do not hesitate to	please
thank you in advance	thank you
under separate cover	separately
with reference to	about

Train yourself not to use these trite business expressions.

Avoiding Jargon and Slang

Jargon, which is terminology unique to certain professions, should be reserved for individuals who understand it.

Except in certain specialized contexts, you should avoid jargon and unnecessary technical terms. Jargon is special terminology that is peculiar to particular activities or professions. For example, geologists speak knowingly of *exfoliation, calcareous ooze,* and *siliceous particles.* Engineers are familiar with phrases such as *infrared processing flags, output latches,* and *movable symbology.* Telecommunication experts use such words and phrases as *protocols, clickstream, neural networks,* and *asynchronous transmission.*

Every field has its own special vocabulary. Using that vocabulary within the field is acceptable and even necessary for accurate, efficient communication. Don't use specialized terms, however, if you think your audience may misunderstand them.

WORKPLACE IN FOCUS

Ask computer shoppers if they want a laptop with a microprocessor containing two or more cores that process multiple data streams into rich multimedia content fast, and you will encounter only blank stares. But ask if they want a laptop with multiple brains that can download songs, play videos, and allow the user to instant message with friends at the same time, and you have made a sale. *In what situations should communicators avoid using complex or technical language?*

Slang is composed of informal words with arbitrary and extravagantly changed meanings. Slang words quickly go out of fashion because they are no longer appealing when everyone begins to understand them. Consider the following statement of a government official who had been asked why his department was dropping a proposal to lease offshore oil lands: "The Administration has an awful lot of other things in the pipeline, and this has more wiggle room so they just moved it down the totem pole." He added, however, that the proposal might be offered again since "there is no pulling back because of hot-potato factors."

The meaning here, if the speaker really intended to impart any, is considerably obscured by the use of slang. Good communicators, of course, aim at clarity and avoid unintelligible slang. If you want to sound professional, avoid expressions such as *snarky, lousy, blowing the budget, bombed,* and *getting burned.*

> **Slang sounds fashionable, but it lacks precise meaning and should be avoided in business writing.**

Dropping Clichés

Clichés are expressions that have become exhausted by overuse. Many cannot be explained, especially to those who are new to our culture. Clichés lack not only freshness but also clarity. Instead of repeating clichés such as the following, try to find another way to say what you mean.

below the belt	easier said than done
better than new	exception to the rule
beyond a shadow of a doubt	fill the bill

DILBERT   **By Scott Adams**

first and foremost	quick as a flash
good to go	shoot from the hip
last but not least	stand your ground
make a bundle	think outside the box
pass with flying colors	true to form

Revising for Vigor and Directness

Clear, effective business writing reads well and is immediately understood. You have already studied techniques for improving clarity and conciseness. You can also strengthen the vigor and directness of your writing by unburying verbs, controlling exuberance, and choosing precise words.

Unburying Verbs

Burying verbs in wordy noun expressions weakens business writing.

Buried verbs are those that are needlessly converted to wordy noun expressions. This happens when verbs such as *acquire, establish,* and *develop* are made into nouns such as *acquisition, establishment,* and *development.* Such nouns often end in *-tion, -ment,* and *-ance.* Using these nouns increases sentence length, drains verb strength, slows the reader, and muddies the thought. Notice how you can make your writing cleaner and more forceful by avoiding wordy verb/noun conversions:

Buried Verbs	**Unburied Verbs**
conduct a discussion of	discuss
create a reduction in	reduce
engage in the preparation of	prepare
give consideration to	consider
make an assumption of	assume
make a discovery of	discover
perform an analysis of	analyze
reach a conclusion about	conclude
take action on	act

Controlling Exuberance

Avoid excessive use of adverb intensifiers.

Occasionally we show our exuberance with words such as *very, definitely, quite, completely, extremely, really, actually,* and *totally.* These intensifiers can emphasize and strengthen your meaning. Overuse, however, sounds unbusinesslike. Control your enthusiasm and guard against excessive use.

Excessive	**Businesslike**
We *totally* agree that we *actually* did not *really* give his proposal a *very* fair trial.	We agree that we did not give his proposal a fair trial.
The manufacturer was *extremely* upset to learn that its printers were *definitely* being counterfeited.	The manufacturer was upset to learn that its printers were being counterfeited.

Choosing Clear, Precise Words

As you revise, make sure your words are precise so that the audience knows exactly what you mean. Clear writing creates meaningful images in the mind of the reader. Such writing is sparked by specific verbs, concrete nouns, and vivid adjectives. Foggy messages are marked by sloppy references that may result in additional inquiries to clarify what was meant.

Unclear	More Precise
He asked everyone to help out.	Our manager begged each team member to volunteer.
They will consider the problem soon.	Our steering committee will consider the recruitment problem in one week.
We received many responses.	We received 28 job applications.
Someone called about the meeting.	Russell Vitello called about the June 12 sales meeting

Designing Documents for Readability

Well-designed documents improve your messages in two important ways. First, they enhance readability and comprehension. Second, they make readers think you are a well-organized and intelligent person. In the revision process, you have a chance to adjust formatting and make other changes so that readers grasp your main points quickly. Significant design techniques to improve readability include appropriate use of white space, margins, typefaces, numbered and bulleted lists, and headings for visual impact.

Successful document design improves readability, strengthens comprehension, and enhances your image.

Employing White Space

Empty space on a page is called *white space*. A page crammed full of text or graphics appears busy, cluttered, and unreadable. To increase white space, use headings, bulleted or numbered lists, short paragraphs, and effective margins. As discussed earlier, short sentences (20 or fewer words) and short paragraphs (eight or fewer printed lines) improve readability and comprehension. As you revise, think about shortening long sentences. Also consider breaking up long paragraphs into shorter chunks. Be sure, however, that each part of the divided paragraph has a topic sentence.

You can improve document readability with ample white (empty) space.

Understanding Margins and Text Alignment

Margins determine the white space on the left, right, top, and bottom of a block of type. They define the reading area and provide important visual relief. Business letters and memos usually have side margins of 1 to 1½ inches.

Your word processing program probably offers these forms of margin alignment: (a) lines aligned only at the left, (b) lines aligned only at the right, (c) lines aligned at both left and right (*justified*), and (d) centered lines. Nearly all text in Western cultures is aligned at the left and reads from left to right. The right margin may be *justified* or *ragged right*. The text in books, magazines, and other long works is often justified on both the left and right for a formal appearance.

Business documents are most readable with left-aligned text and ragged-right margins.

However, justified text may require more attention to word spacing and hyphenation to avoid awkward empty spaces or "rivers" of spaces running through a document. When right margins are "ragged"—that is, without alignment or justification—they provide more white space and improve readability. Therefore, you are best served by using left-justified text and ragged-right margins without justification. Centered text is appropriate for headings but not for complete messages.

Choosing Appropriate Typefaces

Business writers today may choose from a number of typefaces on their word processors. A typeface defines the shape of text characters. As shown in Figure 4.3, a wide range of typefaces is available for various purposes. Some are decorative and useful for special purposes. For most business messages, however, you should choose from *serif* or *sans serif* categories.

Serif typefaces have small features at the ends of strokes. The most common serif typeface is Times New Roman. Other popular serif typefaces are Century, Georgia, and Palatino. Serif typefaces suggest tradition, maturity, and formality. They are frequently used for body text in business messages and longer documents. Because books, newspapers, and magazines favor serif typefaces, readers are familiar with them.

Times New Roman is a typeface with serifs; Arial is a typeface without serifs (sans serif).

FIGURE 4.3	Typefaces With Different Personalities for Different Purposes			
All Purpose Sans Serif	Traditional Serif	Happy, Creative Script/Funny	Assertive, Bold Modern Display	Plain Monospaced
Arial	Century	*Brush Script*	**Britannic Bold**	Courier
Gothic	Garamond	Comic Sans	**Broadway**	Letter Gothic
Helvetica	Georgia	*Gigi*	**Elephant**	Monaco
Tahoma	Goudy	*Jokerman*	**Impact**	Prestige Elite
Univers	Palatino	*Lucinda*	**Bauhaus 93**	
Verdana	Times New Roman	Kristen	**SHOWCARD**	

Sans serif typefaces include Arial, Gothic, Tahoma, and Univers. These characters are cleaner and are widely used for headings, signs, and material where continuous reading is not required. Web designers often prefer sans serif typefaces for clean, pure pages. For longer documents, however, sans serif typefaces may seem colder and less accessible than familiar serif typefaces.

For less formal messages or special decorative effects, you might choose one of the happy fonts such as Comic Sans or a bold typeface such as Impact. You can simulate handwriting with a script typeface. Despite the wonderful possibilities available on your word processor, don't get carried away with fancy typefaces. All-purpose sans serif and traditional serif typefaces are most appropriate for your business messages. Generally, use no more than two typefaces within one document.

Capitalizing on Type Fonts and Sizes

Font refers to a specific typeface in a specific style, as shown in these examples:

Typeface: Time Roman   Font: *Times Roman italic*

Fonts include caps, boldface, italic, underline, outline, and shadow.

Within a typeface, you may choose from many font styles, such as italic, bold, and all caps. You may select CAPITALIZATION, SMALL CAPS, **boldface**, *italic*, and underline, as well as fancier fonts such as outline and shadow.

As discussed in Chapter 3, font styles are a mechanical means of adding emphasis to your words. All caps and small caps are useful for headings, subheadings, and single words or short phrases in the text. ALL CAPS, HOWEVER, SHOULD NEVER BE USED FOR LONG STRETCHES OF TEXT BECAUSE ALL THE LETTERS ARE THE SAME HEIGHT, MAKING IT DIFFICULT FOR READERS TO DIFFERENTIATE

DILBERT   By Scott Adams

WORDS. In addition, excessive use of all caps feels like shouting and irritates readers. **Boldface,** *italics,* and underlining are effective for calling attention to important points and terms. Be cautious, however, when using fancy or an excessive number of font styles. Don't use them if they will confuse, annoy, or delay readers.

During the revision process, think about type size. Readers are generally most comfortable with 10-point or 12-point type for body text. Small type enables you to fit more words into a space. Tiny type, however, makes text look dense and unappealing. Slightly larger type makes material more readable. Overly large type (14 points or more), however, looks amateurish and out of place for body text in business messages. It is appropriate for headings.

Numbering and Bulleting Lists for Quick Comprehension

One of the best ways to ensure rapid comprehension of ideas is through the use of numbered or bulleted lists. Lists provide high "skim value." This means that readers can browse quickly and grasp main ideas. By breaking up complex information into smaller chunks, lists improve readability, understanding, and retention. They also force the writer to organize ideas and write efficiently.

Improve the "skim" value of a message by adding high-visibility vertical lists.

In the revision process, look for items that could be converted to lists and follow these techniques to make your lists look professional:

- **Numbered lists:** Use for items that represent a sequence or reflect a numbering system.
- **Bulleted lists:** Use to highlight items that don't necessarily show a chronology.
- **Capitalization:** Capitalize the initial word of each line.
- **Punctuation:** Add end punctuation only if the listed items are complete sentences.
- **Parallelism:** Make all the lines consistent; for example, start each with a verb.

In the following examples, notice that the list on the left presents a sequence of steps with numbers. The bulleted list does not show a sequence of ideas; therefore, bullets are appropriate. Also notice the parallelism in each example. In the numbered list each item begins with a verb. In the bulleted list each item follows an adjective/noun sequence. Business readers appreciate lists because they focus attention. Be careful, however, not to use so many that your messages look like grocery lists.

Numbered lists represent sequences; bulleted lists highlight items that may not show a sequence.

Numbered List	Bulleted List
Our recruiters follow these steps when hiring applicants:	To attract upscale customers, we feature the following:
1. Examine the application.	• Quality fashions
2. Interview the applicant.	• Personalized service
3. Check the applicant's references.	• A generous return policy

Adding Headings for Visual Impact

Headings are an effective tool for highlighting information and improving readability. They encourage the writer to group similar material together. Headings help the reader separate major ideas from details. They enable a busy reader to skim familiar or less important information. They also provide a quick preview or review. Headings appear most often in reports, which you will study in greater detail in Chapters 9 and 10. However, main headings, subheadings, and category headings can also improve readability in e-mail messages, memos, and letters. In the following example they are used with bullets to summarize categories:

Headings help writers to organize information and enable readers to absorb important ideas.

Category Headings
Our company focuses on the following areas in the employment process:

- **Attracting applicants.** We advertise for qualified applicants, and we also encourage current employees to recommend good people.
- **Interviewing applicants.** Our specialized interviews include simulated customer encounters as well as scrutiny by supervisors.

- **Checking references.** We investigate every applicant thoroughly; we contact former employers and all listed references.

In Figure 4.4 the writer was able to convert a dense, unappealing e-mail message into an easier-to-read version by applying document design. Notice that the all-caps

FIGURE 4.4 Using Document Design to Improve Readability

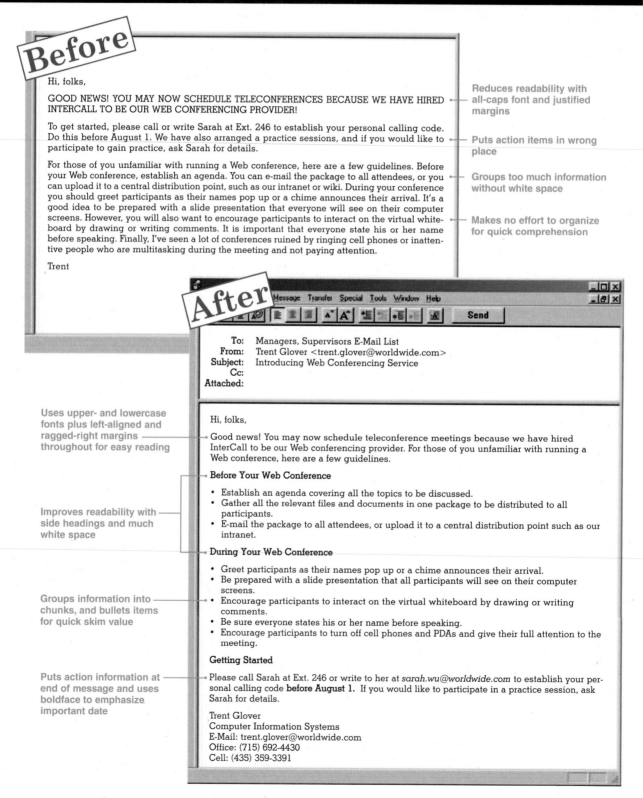

Before

Hi, folks,

GOOD NEWS! YOU MAY NOW SCHEDULE TELECONFERENCES BECAUSE WE HAVE HIRED INTERCALL TO BE OUR WEB CONFERENCING PROVIDER!

To get started, please call or write Sarah at Ext. 246 to establish your personal calling code. Do this before August 1. We have also arranged a practice sessions, and if you would like to participate to gain practice, ask Sarah for details.

For those of you unfamiliar with running a Web conference, here are a few guidelines. Before your Web conference, establish an agenda. You can e-mail the package to all attendees, or you can upload it to a central distribution point, such as our intranet or wiki. During your conference you should greet participants as their names pop up or a chime announces their arrival. It's a good idea to be prepared with a slide presentation that everyone will see on their computer screens. However, you will also want to encourage participants to interact on the virtual whiteboard by drawing or writing comments. It is important that everyone state his or her name before speaking. Finally, I've seen a lot of conferences ruined by ringing cell phones or inattentive people who are multitasking during the meeting and not paying attention.

Trent

Reduces readability with all-caps font and justified margins

Puts action items in wrong place

Groups too much information without white space

Makes no effort to organize for quick comprehension

After

Message Transfer Special Tools Window Help   Send

To: Managers, Supervisors E-Mail List
From: Trent Glover <trent.glover@worldwide.com>
Subject: Introducing Web Conferencing Service
Cc:
Attached:

Uses upper- and lowercase fonts plus left-aligned and ragged-right margins throughout for easy reading

Hi, folks,

Good news! You may now schedule teleconference meetings because we have hired InterCall to be our Web conferencing provider. For those of you unfamiliar with running a Web conference, here are a few guidelines.

Before Your Web Conference

- Establish an agenda covering all the topics to be discussed.
- Gather all the relevant files and documents in one package to be distributed to all participants.
- E-mail the package to all attendees, or upload it to a central distribution point such as our intranet.

Improves readability with side headings and much white space

During Your Web Conference

- Greet participants as their names pop up or a chime announces their arrival.
- Be prepared with a slide presentation that all participants will see on their computer screens.
- Encourage participants to interact on the virtual whiteboard by drawing or writing comments.
- Be sure everyone states his or her name before speaking.
- Encourage participants to turn off cell phones and PDAs and give their full attention to the meeting.

Groups information into chunks, and bullets items for quick skim value

Getting Started

Please call Sarah at Ext. 246 or write to her at *sarah.wu@worldwide.com* to establish your personal calling code **before August 1.** If you would like to participate in a practice session, ask Sarah for details.

Puts action information at end of message and uses boldface to emphasize important date

Trent Glover
Computer Information Systems
E-Mail: trent.glover@worldwide.com
Office: (715) 692-4430
Cell: (435) 359-3391

font in the first paragraph makes its meaning difficult to decipher. Justified margins and lack of white space further reduce readability. In the revised version, the writer changed the all-caps font to upper- and lowercase and also used ragged-right margins to enhance visual appeal. One of the best document design techniques in this message is the use of headings and bullets to help the reader see chunks of information in similar groups. All of these improvements are made in the revision process. You can make any message more readable by applying the document design techniques presented here.

Understanding the Process of Proofreading

Once your message is in its final form, set aside time to proofread. Don't proofread earlier because you may waste time checking items that eventually are changed or omitted.

Proofreading before a document is completed is generally a waste of time.

What to Watch for in Proofreading

Careful proofreaders check for problems in these areas:

- **Spelling.** Now is the time to consult the dictionary. Is *recommend* spelled with one or two *c*'s? Do you mean *affect* or *effect*? Use your computer spell checker, but don't rely on it totally.
- **Grammar.** Locate sentence subjects; do their verbs agree with them? Do pronouns agree with their antecedents? Review the principles in the Grammar/Mechanics Handbook if necessary. Use your computer's grammar checker, but don't let it replace careful manual proofreading.
- **Punctuation.** Make sure that introductory clauses are followed by commas. In compound sentences put commas before coordinating conjunctions *(and, or, but, nor)*. Double-check your use of semicolons and colons.
- **Names and numbers.** Compare all names and numbers with their sources because inaccuracies are not immediately visible. Especially verify the spelling of

"But there can't be any errors. My grammar and spell checkers found nothing wrong!"

WORKPLACE IN FOCUS

Editorial blunders are funny in Jay Leno's "Ridiculous Headlines" skit, but in the real world proofreading errors can be costly. Misprints, typos, and unfortunate turns of phrase lead to embarrassing situations that require corrections and retractions. Some high-profile flubs have made headline news, such as the marquee-sized misspelling of funnyman Will Ferrell's name at a recent Oscars ceremony. *The New York Times* has even admitted to misspelling "Neiman Marcus" in at least 195 articles since 1930. *What tips can help writers catch mistakes before they are published?*

the names of individuals receiving the message. Most of us are offended when someone misspells our name.

- **Format.** Be sure that letters, printed memos, and reports are balanced on the page. Compare their parts and formats with those of standard documents shown in Appendix A. If you indent paragraphs, be certain that all are indented.

How to Proofread Routine Documents

Routine documents need a light proofreading.

Most routine messages, including e-mails, require a light proofreading. Use the down arrow to reveal one line at a time, thus focusing your attention at the bottom of the screen. Read carefully for faults such as omitted or doubled words. Be sure to use your spell checker.

For routine messages such as printed letters or memos, a safer proofreading method is reading from a printed hard copy. You are more likely to find errors and to observe the tone. "Things really look different on paper," observed veteran writer Louise Lague at *People* magazine. "Don't just pull a letter out of the printer and stick it in an envelope. Read every sentence again. You will catch bad line endings, strange page breaks, and weird spacing. You can also get a totally different feeling about what you have said when you see it in print. Sometimes you can say something with a smile on your face; but if you put the same thing in print, it won't work."[2] Use standard proofreading marks, shown in Figure 4.5, to indicate changes.

How to Proofread Complex Documents

For both routine and complex documents, it is best to proofread from a printed copy, not on a computer screen.

Long, complex, or important documents demand more careful proofreading using the following techniques:

- Print a copy, preferably double-spaced, and set it aside for at least a day. You will be more alert after a breather.
- Allow adequate time to proofread carefully. A common excuse for sloppy proofreading is lack of time.

FIGURE 4.5 Proofreading Marks

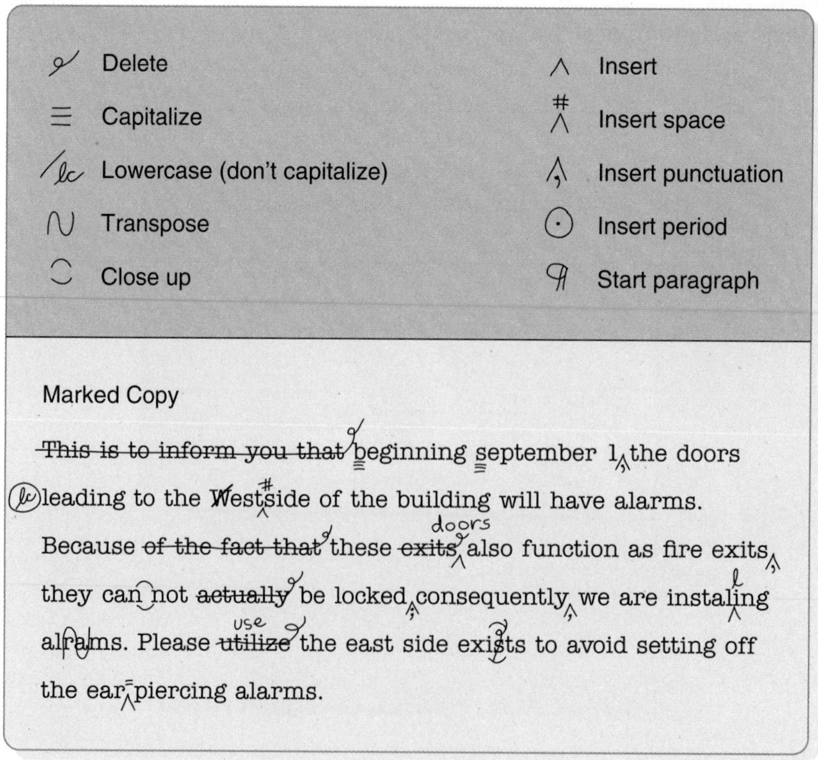

Most proofreaders use these standard marks to indicate revisions.

- Be prepared to find errors. One student confessed, "I can find other people's errors, but I can't seem to locate my own." Psychologically, we don't expect to find errors, and we don't want to find them. You can overcome this obstacle by anticipating errors and congratulating, not criticizing, yourself each time you find one.
- Read the message at least twice—once for word meanings and once for grammar/mechanics. For very long documents (book chapters and long articles or reports), read a third time to verify consistency in formatting.
- Reduce your reading speed. Concentrate on individual words rather than ideas.
- For documents that must be perfect, have someone read the message aloud. The reader should spell names and difficult words, note capitalization, and read punctuation.
- Use standard proofreading marks, shown in Figure 4.5, to indicate changes.

Your computer word processing program may include a style or grammar checker. These programs generally analyze aspects of your writing style, including readability level and the use of passive voice, trite expressions, split infinitives, and wordy expressions. To do so, they use sophisticated algorithms (step-by-step procedures) to identify significant errors. In addition to finding spelling and typographical errors, grammar checkers can find subject–verb lack of agreement problems, word misuse, spacing irregularities, punctuation problems, and many other faults. However, they won't find everything. Although grammar and spell checkers can help you a great deal, you are the final proofreader.

Visit www.meguffey.com
- Chapter Review Quiz
- Flash Cards
- Grammar Practice
- PowerPoint Slides
- Personal Language Trainer
- Beat the Clock Quiz

Summing Up and Looking Forward

Revision is the most important part of the writing process. To revise for conciseness, look for flabby phrases that can be shortened (such as *at this point in time*). Eliminate long lead-ins (*This is to inform you that*), fillers (*There are*), and redundancies (*combined together*). To revise for clarity, dump trite business phrases (*pursuant to your request*), confusing jargon, slang, and clichés (*think outside the box*). To revise for vigor and directness, unbury verbs (*make an examination*), control exuberance, and choose precise words.

To improve readability, employ document design principles. Use ample white space, ragged-right margins, and appropriate typefaces and fonts. Include numbered lists and bulleted lists as well as headings to help readers comprehend messages quickly.

After revising a message, you are ready for the last step in the writing process: proofreading. Watch for irregularities in spelling, grammar, punctuation, names and numbers, and format. Although routine messages may be proofread on the screen, you will have better results if you proofread from a printed copy. Complex documents should be printed, put away for a day or so, and then proofread several times.

In these opening chapters you have studied the writing process. You have also learned many practical techniques for becoming an effective business communicator. Now you can put these techniques to work. Chapter 5 introduces you to writing e-mail messages and memorandums, the most frequently used forms of communication for most business-people. Later chapters present letters and reports.

Critical Thinking

1. Your deadline is due, but your document needs proofreading. Should you spend the time necessary to proofread and miss the deadline?

2. Do you agree that good writers can sit down at a computer and turn out perfect documents on the first try? Why or why not?

3. Because clichés are familiar and have stood the test of time, do they help clarify writing?

4. Study the following sentence from an actual message: *Management was the driving farce behind the project.*[3] How could this proofreading error be costly?

5. Is it unethical to help a friend revise a report when you know that the friend will be turning that report in for a grade?

Chapter Review

6. What tasks are involved in revising a message?

7. Why is conciseness especially important in business?

8. What is a long lead-in? Give an original example.

9. What is wrong with this sentence: *There is no one who can do the job better than you.*

10. What is a redundancy? Give an example.

11. What happens when a verb (such as *describe*) is converted to a noun expression (*to make a description*)? Give an original example.

12. Name five design techniques that can improve readability of printed messages. Be prepared to explain each.

13. What is the difference between serif and sans serif typefaces? What is the most common use for each?

14. What five areas should you especially pay attention to when you proofread?

15. How does the proofreading of routine documents differ from that of complex documents?

Flabby Expressions

Revise the following sentences to eliminate flabby phrases.

16. Despite the fact that we lost the contract, we must at this time move forward.

17. Inasmuch as prices are falling, we will invest in the very near future.

18. We cannot fill the order until such time as payment is received for previous shipments.

19. Due to the fact that our manager is acquainted with your sales rep, we are fully cognizant of your price increases.

20. As a general rule, we would not accept the return; however, we will in all probability make an exception in this case.

Long Lead-Ins

Revise the following to eliminate long lead-ins.

21. This message is to let you know that I received your e-mail and its attachments.

22. This memo is to notify everyone that we will observe Monday as a holiday.

23. I am writing this letter to inform you that your homeowners' coverage expires soon.

24. This is to warn everyone that the loss of laptops endangers company security.

There is/It is Fillers

Revise the following to avoid unnecessary *there is/it is* fillers.

25. There are many businesses that are implementing strict e-mail policies.

26. It is the CEO who must give her approval to the plan.

27. There are several Web pages you must update.

28. The manager says that there are too many employees who are taking long breaks.

Redundancies

Revise the following to avoid redundancies.

29. Because the proposals are exactly identical, we need not check each and every item.

30. We will let you know the dollar amount of the remodeling charges.

31. The office walls were painted beige in color.

32. Our supervisor requested that all team members return back to the office.

Trite Business Phrases

Revise the following sentences to eliminate trite business phrases.

33. As per your request, we will no longer send e-mail offers.

34. Thank you in advance for considering our plea for community support.

35. Pursuant to your request, we are sending the original copies under separate cover.

36. Enclosed please find a check in the amount of $700.

Jargon, Slang, Clichés

Revise the following sentences to avoid confusing jargon, slang, clichés, and wordiness.

37. Although our last presentation bombed, we think that beyond the shadow of a doubt our new presentation will fly.

38. Our team must be willing to think outside the box in coming up with marketing ideas that pop.

39. True to form, our competitor has made a snarky claim that we think is way below the belt.

40. If you will refer back to the budget, you will see that there are provisions that prevent blowing the budget.

Buried Verbs

Revise the following to unbury the verbs.

41. Ms. Nelson gave an appraisal of the home's value.

42. The board of directors will give consideration to the contract at its next meeting.

43. Web-based customer service causes reduction in overall costs.

44. In preparing this proposal, we must make an application of new government regulations.

45. Management made a recommendation affirming abandonment of the pilot project.

46. The insurance investigator made a determination of the fire damages.

Precise, Direct Words

Revise the following sentences to improve clarity and precision. Use your imagination to add appropriate words.

Example They said it was a long way off.
Revision Management officials announced that the merger would not take place for two years.

47. Soon we will be in our new location.

48. An employee from that company notified us about the change in date.

49. Please contact us soon.

50. They said that the movie they saw was good.

51. The report was weak.

Lists, Bullets, and Headings

Revise the following sentences and paragraphs using techniques presented in this chapter. Improve parallel construction and reduce wordiness if necessary.

52. Revise the following by incorporating a bulleted list.
    Yellin Resources specializes in preemployment background reports. Among our background reports are ones that include professional reference interviews, criminal reports, driving records, and employment verification.

53. Revise the following by incorporating a numbered list.
    When writing to customers granting approval for loans, you should follow four steps that include announcing that loan approval has been granted. Then you should specify the terms and limits. Next you should remind the reader of the importance of making payments that are timely. Finally, a phone number should be provided for assistance.

54. Revise the following by incorporating a bulleted list.
The American Automobile Association makes a provision of the following tips for safe driving. You should start your drive well rested. You should wear sunglasses in bright sunshine. To provide exercise breaks, plan to stop every two hours. Be sure not to drink alcohol or take cold and allergy medications before you drive.

55. Revise the following by incorporating bulleted items with category headings.
Our attorney made a recommendation that we consider several things to avoid litigation in regard to sexual harassment. The first thing he suggested was that we should take steps regarding the establishment of an unequivocal written policy prohibiting sexual harassment within our organization. The second thing we should do is make sure training sessions are held for supervisors regarding a proper work environment. Finally, some kind of official procedure for employees to lodge complaints is necessary. This procedure should include investigation of complaints.

Grammar/Mechanics Checkup 4

Adjectives and Adverbs

Review Sections 1.16 and 1.17 of the Grammar/Mechanics Handbook. Then study each of the following statements. Underscore any inappropriate forms. In the space provided write the correct form (or *C* if correct) and the number of the G/M principle illustrated. You may need to consult your dictionary for current practice regarding some compound adjectives. When you finish, compare your responses with those provided at the end of the book. If your answers differ, carefully study the principles in parentheses.

seven-year-old (1.17e)   **Example** Most of our seven year old equipment is still working.

1. Our newly redecorated offices featured state of the art equipment.
2. Contractors may submit only work related expenses.
3. All applicants will be treated equal in the hiring process.
4. Many applicants submitted there résumés by e-mail.
5. Vice President Wilson said that we only had five days to finish the proposal.
6. We tried to make a point by point comparison of the programs.
7. Tyler and Joanna said that they're planning to start there own business next year.
8. Trevor made a spur of the moment decision regarding the equipment.
9. Not all decisions that are made on the spur of the moment turn out badly.
10. The committee offered a well thought out plan to revamp online registration.
11. You must complete a change of address form when you move.
12. Each decision will be made on a case by case basis.
13. I could be more efficient if my printer were more nearer my computer.
14. If you reject her offer to help, Kristen will feel badly.
15. The truck's engine is running smooth after its tune-up.

The following letter has errors in grammar, punctuation, conversational language, outdated expressions, sexist language, concise wording, long lead-ins, and other problems. You may either (a) use standard proofreading marks (see Appendix B) to correct the errors here or (b) download the document from your companion Web site and revise at your computer. Study the guidelines in the Grammar/Mechanics Handbook to sharpen your skills.

FIRST FINANCIAL SERVICES
3410 Willow Grove Boulevard
Philadelphia, PA 19137
215.593.4400
www.firstfinancial.com

June 9, 200x

Ms. Bonnie Jeffers
First Trust Guaranty, Inc.
1359 North Grand Avenue
Walnut, CA 91790

Dear Ms. Jeffer:

We are in appreciation of the fact that you have shown patience with us during the time of our merger with Capital One.

Pursuant to our telephone conversation this morning, this is to advise that two (2) agent's packages will be delivered to you next week. Due to the fact that new forms had to be printed; we do not have them immediately available.

Although we cannot offer a 50/50 commission split, we are able to offer new agents a 60/40 commission split. There are two new agreement forms that show this commission ratio. When you get ready to sign up a new agent have her fill in these up to date forms.

When you send me an executed agency agreement please make every effort to tell me what agency package was assigned to the agent. On the last form that you sent you overlooked this information. We need this information to distribute commissions in an expeditious manner.

If you have any questions, don't hesitate to call on me.

Yours very sincerely,

Brian Simpson
Senior Sales Manager

Using Word's *Track Changes* and *Comment* Features to Edit and Revise Documents

Collaborative writing and editing projects are challenging. Fortunately, Microsoft Word offers many useful tools to help team members edit and share documents electronically. Three simple but useful editing tools are **Highlight, Font Color**, and **Strikethrough**. These tools, included on the **Formatting** toolbar, enable reviewers to point out editing problems. For example, notice how you can use **Strikethrough** to delete a wordy lead-in or use yellow highlighting to call attention to a misspelled word:

~~This is just a note to let you know that~~ I would appreciate you're help in preparing the announcement about tornado safety tips.

Complex projects, however, may require more advanced editing tools such as **Track Changes** and **Insert Comments**.

Track Changes. To suggest specific editing changes to other team members, **Track Changes** is handy. The revised wording is visible on the screen, and deletions show up in callout balloons in the right-hand margin, as shown in the following document. Suggested revisions offered by different team members are identified and dated. The original writer may accept or reject these changes. In recent versions of Word, you will find **Track Changes** on the **Tools** menu.

Insert Comments. By using **Insert Comments,** you can point out problematic passages or errors, ask or answer questions, and share ideas without changing or adding text. When more than one person adds comments, the comments appear in different colors and are identified by the individual writer's name and a date/time stamp. To use this tool in Word 2003, each reviewer clicks **Tools, Options,** and fills in the **User Information** section. To facilitate adding, reviewing, editing, or deleting comments, Word provides a special toolbar. You can activate it by using the **View** pull-down menu (click **Toolbars** and **b.** On the **Reviewing** toolbar, click **New Comment.** Then type your comment, which can be seen in the Web or print layout view (click **View** and **Print Layout** or **Web Layout**).

If you would like to comment on a text in Word 2007, click the **Review** tab, and you will find the **New Comment** icon in the second panel from the left. See the figure on page 95 illustrating the Comment feature.

Career Application. On the job, you will likely be working with others on projects that require written documents. During employment interviews, employers may ask whether you have participated in team projects using collaborative software. To be able to answer that question favorably, take advantage of this opportunity to work on a collaborative document using some of the features described here.

Your Task

Divide into two-person teams. Each partner edits the Grammar/Mechanics Challenge letter. You may download the file from your companion Web site, or you may keyboard it from the textbook. Edit the letter, making all necessary corrections. Save the letter with a file name such as *YourName-GM4*. Send an e-mail message to your partner with the attached file. Ask your partner to make any further edits. The receiving partner uses font color, strikethrough, and the **Comment** feature to edit the partner's message. Print a copy of your partner's edited letter before you edit it. Submit that copy along with a copy of your partner's letter with your edits. Be sure to label each carefully.

Team-Written Document Showing MS Word Comment Feature

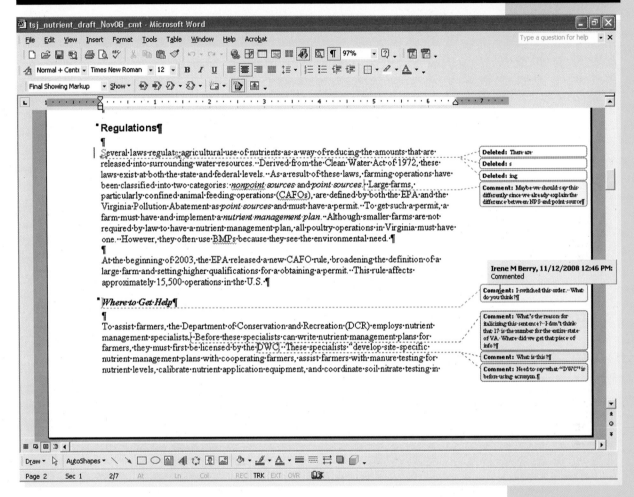

CHAPTER 5

Electronic Messages and Memorandums

OBJECTIVES
After studying this chapter, you should be able to

- Understand how organizations exchange paper-based and electronic messages.
- Know when to send and how to organize e-mail messages and memos.
- Describe appropriate formats of e-mail messages and memos.
- Analyze the writing process and explain how it helps you produce effective internal messages.
- Identify smart e-mail practices, including getting started; content, tone, and correctness; netiquette; reading and replying to e-mail; personal use; and other practices.
- Explain the pros and cons of instant messaging and how to use it professionally.
- Write information and procedure e-mail messages and memos.
- Write request and reply e-mail messages and memos.

How Organizations Exchange Messages and Information

People working in organizations exchange information both externally and internally. External messages go to customers, suppliers, other businesses, and government agencies. Internal messages go to fellow employees. These internal messages are increasing in number and importance because organizations are downsizing, flattening chains of command, forming work teams, and empowering rank-and-file employees. Given more power in making decisions, employees find that they need more information. In today's workplace you will be expected to collect, evaluate, and exchange information in clearly written messages.

Paper-based messages include business letters and memos. Electronic messages include e-mail, instant messaging, text messaging, podcasts, blogs, and wikis.

Written messages fall into two main categories: paper-based and electronic. Paper-based messages include business letters and memos. Electronic messages include e-mail, instant messaging, and text messaging. Electronic information may also be exchanged through podcasts, blogs, and wikis. Knowing what channel to use and how to prepare an effective message can save you time, reduce stress, and make you look professional.

When it comes to automobiles, it isn't easy being green. Despite winning the 2008 Green Car of the Year award for its Chevy Tahoe Hybrid, General Motors has been questioned about its dedication to green manufacturing. Critics gained ammunition when GM vice chairman Robert Lutz doubted publicly that humans cause climate change, calling global warming "a total crock." But when activists began using the comments to paint GM as environmentally irresponsible, Lutz quickly responded on the company's blog, stating that his views were personal and did not reflect GM policy. *In what situations might companies choose to communicate with the public using blogs?*

Communicating With Paper-Based Messages

Although the business world is quickly switching to electronic communication channels, paper-based documents still have definite functions.

- **Business letters.** Writers prepare business letters on letterhead stationery. This is the best channel when a permanent record is necessary, when confidentiality is important, when sensitivity and formality are essential, and when you need to make a persuasive, well-considered presentation. Chapters 6, 7, and 8 cover various business letters that you may write in today's workplace.
- **Interoffice memos.** Paper-based interoffice memos were once the chief form of internal communication. Today, employees use memos primarily to convey confidential information, emphasize ideas, deliver lengthy documents, or lend importance to a message. Memos are especially appropriate for explaining organizational procedures or policies that become permanent guidelines. Later in this chapter you will study various components in everyday interoffice memos.

Communicating With Electronic Messages

A number of electronic communication channels enable businesspeople to exchange information rapidly and efficiently. All of these new electronic channels display your writing skills.

- **E-mail.** E-mail involves the transmission of messages through computers and networks. Users can send messages to a single recipient or broadcast them to multiple recipients. When messages arrive in a simulated mailbox, recipients may read, print, forward, store, or delete them. E-mail is most appropriate for short messages that deliver routine requests and responses. It is inappropriate for sensitive, confidential, or lengthy documents. Used professionally, e-mail is a powerful business tool. You will learn more about safe and smart e-mail practices shortly.
- **Instant messaging.** More interactive than e-mail, instant messaging (IM) involves the exchange of text messages in real time between two or more people logged into an IM service. IM creates a form of private chat room so that individuals can carry on conversations similar to telephone calls. IM is especially useful for back-and-forth online conversations, such as a

Appropriate for brief comments, instant messaging is faster and more interactive than e-mail.

customer communicating with a tech support person to solve a problem. Like e-mail, instant messaging creates a permanent text record and must be used carefully.

- **Text messaging.** Sending really short messages (160 or fewer characters) from mobile phones and other wireless devices is called *text messaging*. This method uses Short Message Service (SMS) and is available on most digital mobile phones and some personal digital assistants with wireless telecommunications. SMS gateways exist to connect mobile phones with instant message services, the Web, desktop computers, and even landline telephones. Busy communicators use text messaging for short person-to-person inquiries and responses that keep them in touch while away from the office.

- **Podcasts.** A podcast is a digital media file that is distributed over the Internet and downloaded on portable media players and personal computers. Podcasts are distinguished by their ability to be syndicated, subscribed to, or downloaded automatically when new content is added. In business, podcasts are useful for improving customer relations, marketing, training, product launches, and "viral" marketing (creating online "buzz" about new products).

- **Blogs.** A blog is a Web site with journal entries usually written by one person with comments added by others. It may combine text, images, and links to other blogs or Web pages. Businesses use blogs to keep customers and employees informed and to receive feedback. Company news can be posted, updated, and categorized for easy cross-referencing. Blogs may be a useful tool for marketing and promotion as well as for showing a company's personal side.

- **Wikis.** A wiki is a Web site that enables multiple users to collaboratively create and edit pages. A wiki serves as a central location where shared documents can be viewed and revised by a large or dispersed team. Because a wiki can be used to manage and organize meeting notes, team agendas, and company calendars, it is a valuable project management tool.

Organizing E-Mail Messages and Memos

E-mail messages and memos are standard forms of communication within organizations. As such, they will probably become your most common business communication channel. These messages perform critical tasks such as informing employees, requesting data, supplying responses, confirming decisions, and giving directions. They generally follow a similar structure and formatting.

Knowing When to Send an E-Mail or a Memo

Before sending any message, you must choose a communication channel, as discussed in Chapter 2. Although both e-mail and memos deliver internal information, they are not interchangeable.

E-mail is appropriate for short, informal messages that request information and respond to inquiries. It is especially effective for messages to multiple receivers and messages that must be archived (saved). An e-mail is also appropriate as a cover document when sending longer attachments. E-mail, however, is not a substitute for face-to-face conversations, telephone calls, business letters, or memorandums. Face-to-face conversations or telephone calls are better channel choices if your goal is to convey enthusiasm or warmth, explain a complex situation, present a persuasive argument, or smooth over disagreements.

Interoffice memos are appropriate for a number of purposes. If you are delivering confidential data, such as salary or employee review information, a memo is suitable. If you are sending a lengthy report to others within your organization, memo formatting is proper. Memos are equally useful when you need to emphasize your ideas or send an internal message that is important or formal.

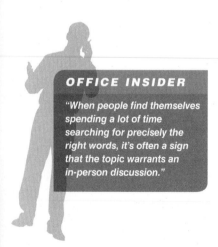

E-mail messages and memos inform employees, request data, give responses, confirm decisions, and provide directions.

OFFICE INSIDER

"When people find themselves spending a lot of time searching for precisely the right words, it's often a sign that the topic warrants an in-person discussion."

A final consideration in deciding whether to send an e-mail message or a memo is your receiver's preference and your organization's choice. Choose a channel that is comfortable to the receiver and appropriate for the organization.

Components of E-Mail Messages and Memos

Whether electronic or hard copy, direct internal messages generally contain four parts: (a) an informative subject line that summarizes the message, (b) an opening that reveals the main idea immediately, (c) a body that explains and justifies the main idea, and (d) an appropriate closing. Remember that direct messages deliver good news or standard information.

Writing the Subject Line.
In e-mails and memos an informative subject line is mandatory. It summarizes the central idea, thus providing quick identification for reading and for filing. In e-mail messages, a good subject line is critical. It often determines whether and when the message is read. Messages without subject lines may be automatically deleted.

What does it take to get your message read? For one thing, stay away from meaningless or dangerous words. A sure way to have your message deleted or ignored is to use a one-word heading such as *Issue, Problem, Important,* or *Help*. Including a word such as *Free* is dangerous because it may trigger spam filters. Try to make your subject line "talk" by including a verb. Explain the purpose of the message and how it relates to the reader. Remember that a subject line is usually written in an abbreviated style, often without articles *(a, an, the)*. It need not be a complete sentence, and it does not end with a period.

Subject lines summarize the purpose of the message in abbreviated form.

Poor Subject Line	Improved Subject Line
Trade Show	Need You to Showcase Two Items at Our Next Trade Show
Staff Meeting	Rescheduling Staff Meeting for 1 P.M. on May 12
Important!	Please Respond to Job Satisfaction Survey
Parking Permits	Obtain New Employee Parking Permits From HR

Opening With the Main Idea.
Most e-mails and memos cover nonsensitive information that can be handled in a straightforward manner. Begin by frontloading; that is, reveal the main idea immediately. Even though the purpose of the e-mail or memo is summarized in the subject line, that purpose should be restated—and amplified—in the first sentence. Busy readers want to know immediately why they are reading a message. As you learned in Chapter 3, most messages should begin directly. Notice how the following indirect opener can be improved by frontloading.

Direct e-mails and memos open by revealing the main idea immediately.

Indirect Opening	Direct Opening
For the past six months the Human Resources Development Department has been considering changes in our employee benefit plan.	Please review the following proposal regarding employee benefits, and let me know by May 20 if you approve these changes.

Explaining in the Body.
The body provides more information about the reason for writing. It explains and discusses the subject logically. Effective e-mail messages and memos generally discuss only one topic. Limiting the topic helps the receiver act on the subject and file it appropriately. A writer who, for example, describes a computer printer problem and also requests permission to attend a

Designed for easy comprehension, the body explains one topic.

conference runs a 50 percent failure risk. The reader may respond to the printer problem but delay or forget about the conference request.

The body of e-mail messages and memos should have high "skim value." This means that information should be easy to read and comprehend. As covered in the section on document design in Chapter 4, many techniques improve readability. You can use white space, bulleted lists, enumerated lists, appropriate typefaces and fonts, and headings. In the revision stage you will see many ways to improve the readability of the body of your message.

Messages should close with (a) action information including dates and deadlines, (b) a summary, or (c) a closing thought.

Closing With a Purpose. Generally close an e-mail message or a memo with (a) action information, dates, or deadlines; (b) a summary of the message; or (c) a closing thought. Here again the value of thinking through the message before actually writing it becomes apparent. The closing is where readers look for deadlines and action language. An effective memo or e-mail closing might be, *Please submit your written report to me by June 15 so that we can have your data before our July planning session.*

In more complex messages a summary of main points may be an appropriate closing. If no action request is made and a closing summary is unnecessary, you might end with a simple concluding thought *(I'm glad to answer your questions* or *This sounds like a useful project).* You need not close messages to coworkers with goodwill statements such as those found in letters to customers or clients. However, some closing thought is often necessary to prevent a feeling of abruptness. Closings can show gratitude or encourage feedback with remarks such as *I sincerely appreciate your help* or *What are your ideas on this proposal?* Other closings look forward to what's next, such as *How would you like to proceed?* Avoid closing with overused expressions such as *Please let me know if I may be of further assistance.* This ending sounds mechanical and insincere.

Putting It All Together. To see the development of a complete internal message, look at Figure 5.1. It shows the first draft and revision of an e-mail message that Madeleine Espinoza, senior marketing manager, wrote to her boss, Keith Milton. Although it contained solid information, the first draft was so wordy and dense that the main points were lost.

Revision helps you think through a problem, clarify a solution, and express it clearly.

In the revision stage Madeleine realized that she needed to reorganize her message into an opening, body, and closing. She desperately needed to improve the readability. In studying what she had written, she recognized that she was talking about two main problems. She discovered that she could present a three-part solution. These ideas didn't occur to her until she had written the first draft. Only in the revision stage was she able to see that she was talking about two separate problems as well as a three-part solution. The revision process can help you think through a problem and clarify a solution.

As she revised, Madeleine was more aware of the subject line, opening, body, and closing. She used an informative subject line and opened directly by explaining why she was writing. Her opening outlined the two main problems so that her reader understood the background of the following recommendations. In the body of the message, Madeleine identified three corrective actions, and she highlighted them for improved readability. Notice that she listed her three recommendations using numbers with boldface headings. Bullets don't always transmit well in e-mail messages. Madeleine closed her message with a deadline and a reference to the next action to be taken.

Applying E-Mail and Memo Formats

E-mail messages and hard-copy memos are similar in content and development, but their formats are slightly different.

FIGURE 5.1 Revising an Information E-Mail Message

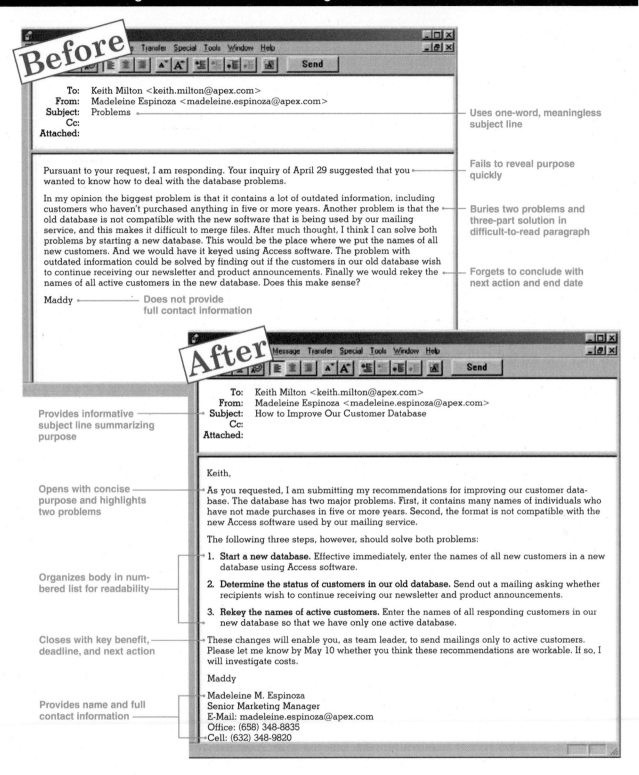

Formatting E-Mail Messages

Although e-mail is a relatively new communication channel, people are beginning to agree on specific formatting and usage conventions. The following suggestions identify current formatting standards. Always check with your organization, however, to observe its practices.

Guide Words. E-mail programs provide a set of guide words to help you create your message. Following the guide word *To*, some writers insert just the recipient's electronic address, such as *mphilly@accountpro.com*. Other writers prefer to include the receiver's full name plus the electronic address, as shown in Figure 5.2. By including full names in the *To* and *From* slots, both receivers and senders are better able to identify the message. By the way, the order of *Date*, *To*, *From*, *Subject*, and other guide words varies depending on your e-mail program and whether you are sending or receiving the message.

Most e-mail programs automatically add the current date after *Date*. On the *Cc* line (which stands for *carbon copy* or *courtesy copy*), you can type the address of anyone who is to receive a copy of the message. Remember, though, to send copies only to those people directly involved with the message. Most e-mail programs also include a line for *Bcc (blind carbon copy)*. This sends a copy without the addressee's

FIGURE 5.2 Formatting an E-Mail Request

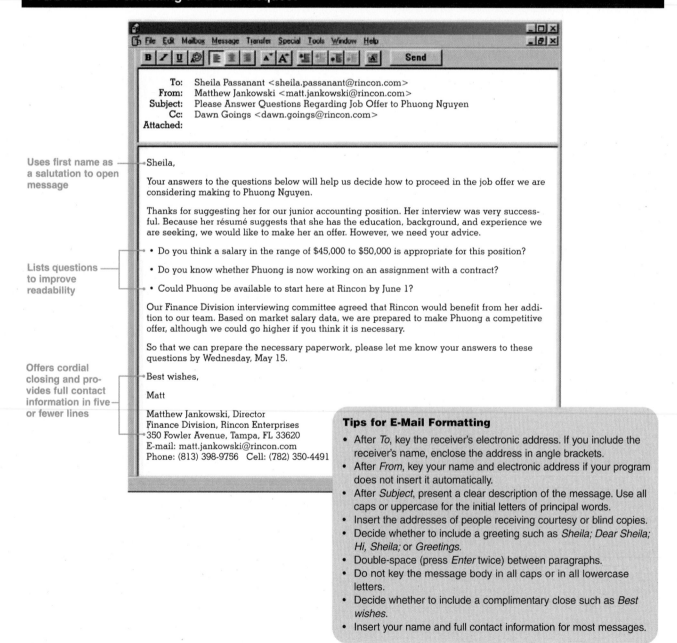

Uses first name as a salutation to open message

Lists questions to improve readability

Offers cordial closing and provides full contact information in five or fewer lines

To: Sheila Passanant <sheila.passanant@rincon.com>
From: Matthew Jankowski <matt.jankowski@rincon.com>
Subject: Please Answer Questions Regarding Job Offer to Phuong Nguyen
Cc: Dawn Goings <dawn.goings@rincon.com>
Attached:

Sheila,

Your answers to the questions below will help us decide how to proceed in the job offer we are considering making to Phuong Nguyen.

Thanks for suggesting her for our junior accounting position. Her interview was very successful. Because her résumé suggests that she has the education, background, and experience we are seeking, we would like to make her an offer. However, we need your advice.

• Do you think a salary in the range of $45,000 to $50,000 is appropriate for this position?

• Do you know whether Phuong is now working on an assignment with a contract?

• Could Phuong be available to start here at Rincon by June 1?

Our Finance Division interviewing committee agreed that Rincon would benefit from her addition to our team. Based on market salary data, we are prepared to make Phuong a competitive offer, although we could go higher if you think it is necessary.

So that we can prepare the necessary paperwork, please let me know your answers to these questions by Wednesday, May 15.

Best wishes,

Matt

Matthew Jankowski, Director
Finance Division, Rincon Enterprises
350 Fowler Avenue, Tampa, FL 33620
E-mail: matt.jankowski@rincon.com
Phone: (813) 398-9756 Cell: (782) 350-4491

Tips for E-Mail Formatting

• After *To*, key the receiver's electronic address. If you include the receiver's name, enclose the address in angle brackets.
• After *From*, key your name and electronic address if your program does not insert it automatically.
• After *Subject*, present a clear description of the message. Use all caps or uppercase for the initial letters of principal words.
• Insert the addresses of people receiving courtesy or blind copies.
• Decide whether to include a greeting such as *Sheila; Dear Sheila; Hi, Sheila;* or *Greetings*.
• Double-space (press *Enter* twice) between paragraphs.
• Do not key the message body in all caps or in all lowercase letters.
• Decide whether to include a complimentary close such as *Best wishes*.
• Insert your name and full contact information for most messages.

knowledge. Savvy writers today use *Bcc* for the names and addresses of a list of receivers, a technique that avoids revealing the addresses to the entire group. On the subject line, identify the subject of the memo. Be sure to include enough information to be clear and compelling.

Greeting. Begin your message with a greeting such as the following:

Hi, Kevin,   Thank you, Haley,

Greetings, Amy,   Dear Mr. Cotter,

Leslie,   Dear Leslie,

In addition to being friendly, a greeting provides a visual cue marking the beginning of the message. Many messages are transmitted or forwarded with such long headers that finding the beginning of the message can be difficult. A greeting helps, even if is just the receiver's name, as shown in Figures 5.1 and 5.2.

> An e-mail greeting shows friendliness and indicates the beginning of the message.

Body. When keying the body of an e-mail message, use standard caps and lower-case characters—never all uppercase or all lowercase characters. Cover just one topic, and try to keep the total message under three screens in length. Remember to double-space between paragraphs. For longer messages prepare a separate file to be attached. Use the e-mail message only as a cover document. To assist you in preparing your message, many e-mail programs have basic text-editing features, such as cut, copy, paste, and word-wrap. However, avoid graphics, font changes, bold-face, and italics unless your reader's system can handle them. As more and more programs offer HTML formatting options, writers are able to use all the graphics, colors, and fonts available in their word processing programs.

Closing Lines. Some people sign off their e-mail messages with a cordial expression such as *Cheers, All the best,* or *Warm Regards.* Regardless of the closing, be sure to sign your name. Messages without names become very confusing when forwarded or when they are part of a thread (string) of responses. To avoid further confusion, include a signature block with your contact information. This might include your name, title, organization, address, e-mail address, telephone number, cell phone number, and fax number. Decide what information is most important. Then prepare a signature block with five or fewer lines. Although you might be tempted to omit your e-mail address, it is wise to include it because some systems do not transmit your address automatically. When your message is forwarded, your e-mail address may be lost.

> E-mail messages are most helpful when they conclude with the writer's full contact information.

Formatting Interoffice Memorandums

In the past interoffice memorandums were the primary communication channel for delivering information within organizations. Although e-mail is more often used today, memos are still useful for important internal messages that require a permanent record or formality. For example, organizations use memos to deliver changes in procedures, official instructions, reports, and long internal documents.

> Hard-copy memos are useful for internal messages that require a permanent record or formality.

Memo Forms and Margins. Some organizations use printed interoffice memo forms. In addition to the name of the organization, these forms include the basic elements of *Date, To, From,* and *Subject.* Large organizations may include other identifying headings, such as *File Number, Floor, Extension, Location,* and *Distribution.* Because of the difficulty of aligning computer printers with preprinted forms, business writers may use default templates available on their word processors. Writers can customize these templates with their organization's name.

If you are preparing a memo on plain paper, set 1-inch top and bottom margins and left and right margins of 1.25 inches. Provide a heading that includes the name of the company plus "Memo" or "Memorandum." Begin the guide words a triple space (two blank lines) below the last line of the heading. Key in bold the guide words: **Date:, To:, From:,** and **Subject:** at the left margin. The guide words may appear in all caps or with only the initial letter capitalized. Triple-space (set two blank lines) after the last line of the heading. Do not justify the right margins. As discussed in the document design section of Chapter 4, ragged-right margins in printed messages are easier to read. Single-space the message, and double-space between paragraphs, as shown in Figure 5.3.

FIGURE 5.3 Interoffice Memo That Responds to Request

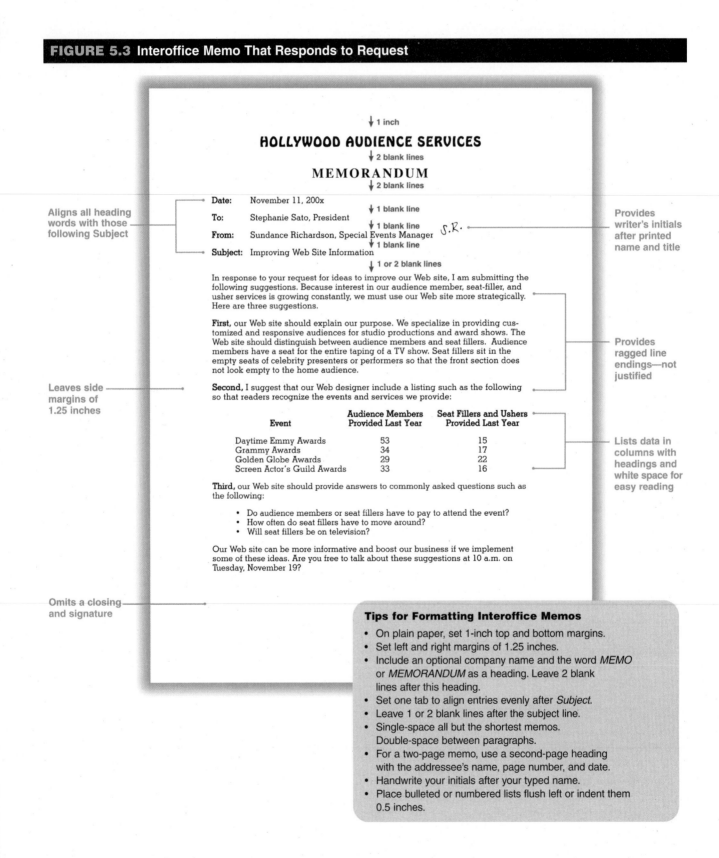

Aligns all heading words with those following Subject

Leaves side margins of 1.25 inches

Omits a closing and signature

Provides writer's initials after printed name and title

Provides ragged line endings—not justified

Lists data in columns with headings and white space for easy reading

↓ 1 inch

HOLLYWOOD AUDIENCE SERVICES
↓ 2 blank lines

MEMORANDUM
↓ 2 blank lines

Date: November 11, 200x
↓ 1 blank line
To: Stephanie Sato, President
↓ 1 blank line
From: Sundance Richardson, Special Events Manager   *S.R.*
↓ 1 blank line
Subject: Improving Web Site Information

↓ 1 or 2 blank lines

In response to your request for ideas to improve our Web site, I am submitting the following suggestions. Because interest in our audience member, seat-filler, and usher services is growing constantly, we must use our Web site more strategically. Here are three suggestions.

First, our Web site should explain our purpose. We specialize in providing customized and responsive audiences for studio productions and award shows. The Web site should distinguish between audience members and seat fillers. Audience members have a seat for the entire taping of a TV show. Seat fillers sit in the empty seats of celebrity presenters or performers so that the front section does not look empty to the home audience.

Second, I suggest that our Web designer include a listing such as the following so that readers recognize the events and services we provide:

Event	Audience Members Provided Last Year	Seat Fillers and Ushers Provided Last Year
Daytime Emmy Awards	53	15
Grammy Awards	34	17
Golden Globe Awards	29	22
Screen Actor's Guild Awards	33	16

Third, our Web site should provide answers to commonly asked questions such as the following:

- Do audience members or seat fillers have to pay to attend the event?
- How often do seat fillers have to move around?
- Will seat fillers be on television?

Our Web site can be more informative and boost our business if we implement some of these ideas. Are you free to talk about these suggestions at 10 a.m. on Tuesday, November 19?

Tips for Formatting Interoffice Memos
- On plain paper, set 1-inch top and bottom margins.
- Set left and right margins of 1.25 inches.
- Include an optional company name and the word *MEMO* or *MEMORANDUM* as a heading. Leave 2 blank lines after this heading.
- Set one tab to align entries evenly after *Subject*.
- Leave 1 or 2 blank lines after the subject line.
- Single-space all but the shortest memos. Double-space between paragraphs.
- For a two-page memo, use a second-page heading with the addressee's name, page number, and date.
- Handwrite your initials after your typed name.
- Place bulleted or numbered lists flush left or indent them 0.5 inches.

Preparing Memos as E-Mail Attachments. E-mail has become increasingly important for exchanging internal messages. However, it is inappropriate for long documents or for items that require formality or permanence. For such messages, writers may prepare the information in standard memo format and send it as an attachment to a cover e-mail.

In preparing e-mail attachments, be sure to include identifying information. Because the cover e-mail message may become separated from the attachment, the attachment must be fully identified. Preparing the e-mail attachment as a memo provides a handy format that identifies the date, sender, receiver, and subject.

To deliver a long or formal document, send a cover e-mail with an attachment.

Using the Writing Process to Create Effective Internal Messages

Internal electronic messages and hard-copy memos usually carry direct messages that are neither sensitive nor persuasive. Although these messages are straightforward, they require careful writing to be clearly and quickly understood. By following the three-phase writing process, you can speed up your efforts and greatly improve the product.

Analyzing, Anticipating, and Adapting

In the prewriting phase you will spend some time analyzing your task. It is amazing how many of us are ready to put our pens or computers into gear before engaging our minds. Before writing, ask yourself these important questions:

- **Do I really need to write this e-mail or memo?** A phone call or a quick visit to a nearby coworker might solve the problem—and save the time and expense of a written message. On the other hand, some written messages are needed to provide a permanent record.
- **Why am I writing?** Know why you are writing and what you hope to achieve. This will help you recognize what the important points are and where to place them.
- **How will the reader react?** Visualize the reader and the effect your message will have. In writing e-mail messages and memos, imagine that you are sitting and talking with your reader. Avoid speaking bluntly, failing to explain, or ignoring your reader's needs. Consider ways to shape the message to benefit the reader. Also be careful about what you say because your message may very well be forwarded to someone else—or may be read by your boss.
- **How can I save my reader's time?** Think of ways to make your message easier to comprehend at a glance. Use bullets, lists, headings, and white space to improve readability.

> **OFFICE INSIDER**
>
> In complaining about e-mail, one observer said, "Like bad advice, self-importance, and ugly carpeting, there's just too much of it in the office."

© RANDY GLASBERGEN. WWW.GLASBERGEN.COM

"Be careful what you write. My wonderful, charming, brilliant boss reads everyone's e-mail."

Researching, Organizing, and Composing

Phase 2, writing, involves gathering documentation, organizing, and actually composing the first draft. Although some of your electronic messages and memos will be short, you can ensure a more effective message by following these steps:

- **Conduct research.** Check the files, talk with your boss, and possibly consult the target audience to collect information before you begin to write. Gather any documentation necessary to support your message.

Gather background information; organize it into an outline; compose your message; and revise for clarity, correctness, and feedback

- **Organize your information.** Make a brief outline of the points you want to cover in your message. For short messages jot down notes on the document you are answering or make a scratch list at your computer.
- **Compose your first draft.** At your computer compose the message from your outline. As you compose, avoid amassing huge blocks of text. No one wants to read endless lines of type.

Revising, Proofreading, and Evaluating

Phase 3, revising, involves putting the final touches on your message. Careful and caring writers will ask a number of questions as they do the following:

- **Revise for clarity and conciseness.** Viewed from the receiver's perspective, are the ideas clear? Do they need more explanation? If the message is passed on to others, will they need further explanation? Consider having a colleague critique your message if it is an important one.
- **Revise for readability.** Did you group related information into paragraphs, preferably short ones? Paragraphs separated by white space look inviting. Does each paragraph begin with the main point, and is that point backed up by details? Can you add paragraph headings to improve readability? Can you form bullet points or lists to make the message easy to skim and comprehend?
- **Proofread for correctness.** Are the sentences complete and punctuated properly? Did you overlook any typos or misspelled words? Remember to use your spell checker and grammar checker to proofread your message before sending it.
- **Plan for feedback.** How will you know whether this message is successful? You can improve feedback by asking questions (such as *Are you comfortable with these suggestions?* or *What do you think?*). Remember to make it easy for the receiver to respond by providing your e-mail address or phone number.

Best Practices for Using E-Mail Smartly, Safely, and Professionally

E-mail is the preferred communication channel in most businesses today. Because its use grew so quickly, many people need help in using it smartly, safely, and professionally. Early users ignored stylistic and grammatical considerations. They thought that "words on the fly" required little editing or proofing. Correspondents used emoticons (such as sideways happy faces) to express their feelings.

Today, however, e-mail has grown up. It is a mainstream communication channel, with over 84 billion messages being sent each day worldwide.[1] E-mail is twice as likely as the telephone to be used to communicate at work. When asked what communication channel they preferred, 65 percent of senior executives chose e-mail.[2] We have become so dependent on e-mail that 53 percent of people using it at work say that their productivity drops when they are away from it.[3]

Wise e-mail business communicators are aware of the importance as well as the dangers of e-mail as a communication channel. They know that their messages can travel, intentionally or unintentionally, long distances. A quickly drafted note may end up in the boss's mailbox or be forwarded to an enemy's box. Making matters worse, computers—like elephants and spurned lovers—never forget. Even erased messages can remain on multiple servers that are backed up by companies or Internet service providers. Increasingly, e-mail has turned into the "smoking gun" uncovered by prosecutors to prove indelicate or even illegal intentions.

In addition, many users complain of poorly written messages and e-mail "ping-pong." Inboxes overflow with unnecessary back-and-forth exchanges seeking to clarify previous messages.[4]

> **Despite its popularity, e-mail may be dangerous because messages travel long distances, are difficult to erase, and may become evidence in court.**

MOTOROLA

SNAKESKIN FEEL. GOLDEN TOUCH.

Elegant 18k gold plating. Sensual snakeskin texture.
Lavish laser-etched detailing. Sharper than ever, hellomoto.

RAZR2
LUXURY EDITION

WORKPLACE IN FOCUS

When engineers at Motorola teamed up to design the fashionable ultra-thin Razr, confidentiality was a primary concern. To keep their cell phone project top-secret, group members prohibited the circulation of prototypes, digital photos, and drawings of the sleek device. In addition, team members kept their effort hidden from other Motorola colleagues and banned the use of e-mail during the Razr's development phase. *Why might e-mail be an inappropriate channel of communication for certain types of messages and documents?*

Best Practices—Getting Started

Despite its dangers and limitations, e-mail is the No. 1 channel of communication. To make your messages effective and to avoid e-mail ping-pong, take the time to organize your thoughts, compose carefully, and consider the receiver. The following best practices will help you get off to a good start in using e-mail smartly, safely, and professionally.

Because e-mail is now a mainstream communication channel, messages should be well organized, carefully composed, and grammatically correct.

- **Consider composing offline.** Especially for important messages, think about using your word processing program to write offline. Then upload your message to the e-mail network. This avoids "self-destructing" (losing all your writing through some glitch or pressing the wrong key) when working online.
- **Get the address right.** E-mail addresses are sometimes complex, often illogical, and always unforgiving. Omit one character or misread the letter *l* for the number 1, and your message bounces. Solution: Use your electronic address book for people you write to frequently. Double-check every address that you key in manually. Also be sure that you don't reply to a group of receivers when you intend to answer only one.
- **Avoid misleading subject lines.** As discussed earlier, make sure your subject line is relevant and helpful. Generic tags such as *Hi!* and *Important!* may cause your message to be deleted before it is opened.
- **Apply the top-of-screen test.** When readers open your message and look at the first screen, will they see what is most significant? Your subject line and first paragraph should convey your purpose.

Content, Tone, and Correctness

Although e-mail seems as casual as a telephone call, it definitely is not. Because it produces a permanent record, think carefully about what you say and how you say it.

- **Be concise.** Don't burden readers with unnecessary information. Remember that monitors are small and typefaces are often difficult to read. Organize your ideas tightly. If you must send a long message, prepare an attachment and use the e-mail as a cover message.
- **Don't send anything you wouldn't want published.** Because e-mail seems like a telephone call or a person-to-person conversation, writers sometimes send sensitive, confidential, inflammatory, or potentially embarrassing messages. Beware! E-mail creates a permanent record that does not go away even when deleted. Every message is a corporate communication that can be used against you or your employer. Don't write anything that you wouldn't want your boss, your family, or a judge to read.
- **Don't use e-mail to avoid contact.** E-mail is inappropriate for breaking bad news or for resolving arguments. For example, it is improper to fire a person by e-mail. It is also not a good channel for dealing with conflict with supervisors, subordinates, or others. If there is any possibility of hurt feelings, pick up the telephone or pay the person a visit.
- **Care about correctness.** People are still judged by their writing, whether electronic or paper-based. Sloppy e-mail messages (with missing apostrophes, haphazard spelling, and stream-of-consciousness writing) make readers work too hard. They resent not only the information but also the writer.
- **Care about tone.** Your words and writing style affect the reader. Avoid sounding curt, negative, or domineering.
- **Resist humor and tongue-in-cheek comments.** Without the nonverbal cues conveyed by your face and your voice, humor can easily be misunderstood.

Netiquette

Although e-mail is a relatively new communication channel, a number of rules of polite online interaction are emerging.

- **Limit any tendency to send blanket copies.** Send copies only to people who really need to see a message. It is unnecessary to document every business decision and action with an electronic paper trail.
- **Consider using identifying labels.** When appropriate, add one of the following labels to the subject line: *Action* (action required, please respond); *FYI* (for your information, no response needed); *Re* (this is a reply to another message); *Urgent* (please respond immediately); *REQ* (required).
- **Use capital letters only for emphasis or for titles.** Avoid writing entire messages in all caps, which is like SHOUTING.
- **Don't forward without permission and beware of long threads.** Obtain approval before forwarding a message. Also beware of forwarding e-mail consisting of a long thread (string) of messages. Some content in bottom screens may be inappropriate for the third receiver. Aside from the issue of clutter, leaving sensitive information in the thread can lead to serious trouble.

Reading and Replying to E-Mail

The following tips can save you time and frustration when reading and answering messages:

- **Scan all messages in your inbox before replying to each individually.** Because subsequent messages often affect the way you respond, scan all messages first (especially all those from the same individual).
- **Print only when necessary.** Generally, read and answer most messages online without saving or printing. Use folders to archive messages on special topics. Print only those messages that are complex, controversial, or involve significant decisions and follow-up.
- **Acknowledge receipt.** If you can't reply immediately, tell when you can (*Will respond Friday*).

Cathy

- **Don't automatically return the sender's message.** When replying, cut and paste the relevant parts. Avoid irritating your recipients by returning the entire thread (sequence of messages) on a topic.
- **Revise the subject line if the topic changes.** When replying or continuing an e-mail exchange, revise the subject line as the topic changes.
- **Provide a clear, complete first sentence.** Avoid fuzzy replies such as *That's fine with me* or *Sounds good!* Busy respondents forget what was said in earlier messages, so be sure to fill in the context and your perspective when responding.
- **Never respond when you are angry.** Always allow some time to cool off before shooting off a response to an upsetting message. You often come up with different and better alternatives after thinking about what was said. If possible, iron out differences in person.

Personal Use

Remember that office computers are meant for work-related communication.

- **Don't use company computers for personal matters.** Unless your company specifically allows it, never use your employer's computers for personal messages, personal shopping, or entertainment.
- **Assume that all e-mail is monitored.** Employers legally have the right to monitor e-mail, and many do.

Other Smart E-Mail Practices

Depending on your messages and audience, the following tips promote effective electronic communication.

- **Improve the readability of longer messages with graphic highlighting.** When a message requires several screens, help the reader with headings, bulleted listings, side headings, and perhaps an introductory summary that describes what will follow. Although these techniques lengthen a message, they shorten reading time.
- **Consider cultural differences.** Be especially clear and precise in your language in e-mail messages that travel across borders. Remember that figurative clichés (*pull up stakes, playing second fiddle,*) sports references (*hit a home run, play by the rules*), and slang (*cool, stoked*) cause confusion, especially for nonnative speakers.
- **Double-check before hitting the Send button.** Have you included everything? Did you attach the file you said you would? Avoid the necessity of sending a second message, which makes you look careless. Use spell-check and reread for fluency before sending. Checking your incoming messages before sending is also a good idea, especially if several people are involved in a rapid-fire exchange. This helps avoid "passing"—sending out a message that might be altered depending on an incoming note.

Design your messages to enhance readability, and double-check before sending.

Using Instant Messaging Professionally

Instant messaging (IM) enables you to use the Internet to communicate in real time in a private chat room with one or more individuals. It is like live e-mail or a text telephone call. More and more workers are using it as a speedy communication channel to exchange short messages.

How Instant Messaging Works

To send an instant message, you might use a client such as AOL's Instant Messenger, Yahoo! Messenger, Google Talk, Jabber, or Microsoft's Windows Live Messenger. These are public IM services. Once the client is installed, you would enter your name and password to log on. The software checks to see if any of the users in your contact list are currently logged in. If the server finds any of your contacts, it sends a message back to your computer. If the person you wish to contact is online, you can click that person's name and a window opens that you can enter text into. You enter a message, such as that shown in Figure 5.4, and click **Send**. Because your client has the Internet address and port number for the computer of the person you addressed, your message is sent directly to the client on that person's computer. All communication is directly between the two computers without the need of a server.

Unlike e-mail, IM provides no elaborate page layout options. The text box is short, and pressing the **Enter** key sends the message. Obviously, it is designed for brief but fast text interaction.

Weighing the Pros and Cons of Instant Messaging

Once primarily a consumer tool, instant messaging is increasingly being used by knowledge workers for many reasons. People like instant messaging because of its immediacy. Unlike e-mail, messages do not wait to be downloaded from a mail server. In addition, a user knows right away whether a message was delivered. Proponents of instant messaging say that it avoids phone tag and eliminates the

FIGURE 5.4 Instant Message for Brief, Fast Communication

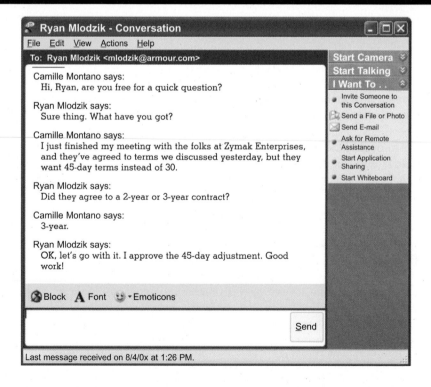

downtime associated with personal telephone conversations. Because it replaces expensive long-distance telephone and fax calls, instant messaging saves money. Another benefit of instant messaging includes "presence functionality." Coworkers can locate each other online, thus avoiding wild goose chases hunting someone who is out of the office. Many people consider instant messaging a productivity booster because it enables them to get answers quickly and helps them multitask.

Despite its popularity among workers, some organizations forbid employees to use instant messaging for a number of reasons. Employers consider instant messaging yet another distraction in addition to the interruptions caused by the telephone, e-mail, and the Web. Organizations also fear that privileged information and company records will be revealed through public instant messaging systems, which hackers can easily penetrate. Organizations worry about "phishing" schemes, viruses, malware, and *spim* (IM spam). Like e-mail, instant messages are subject to discovery (disclosure); that is, they can become evidence in lawsuits. Finally, companies fear instant messaging because it forces them to face the daunting task of tracking and storing messaging conversations to comply with legal requirements. The pros and cons of instant messaging are summarized in Figure 5.5.

For some organizations IM is not an essential business tool and not worth the risks involved. They simply block its use. Other companies, however, see instant messaging as a beneficial communication tool. They are investing in *enterprise-class IM systems*. Such systems enable workers to exchange instant messages within a closed-loop structure. These systems provide an audit trail and greater security. Organizations can selectively retain, archive, and destroy IM conversations to meet compliance laws.

> **Organizations may ban instant messaging because of productivity, security, litigation, and compliance fears.**

FIGURE 5.5 Pros and Cons of Instant Messaging

Pros	Cons
Speed: Connects people immediately.	**Security:** Imperils privileged information.
Cost savings: Reduces telephone bills.	**Litigation:** Endangers companies with possibility of disclosure in lawsuits.
Presence functionality: Locates people online.	**Control:** Requires companies to establish and enforce usage rules.
Convenience: Provides quick answers to short questions.	**Compliance:** Forces organizations to monitor and track conversations to meet legal requirements.
Productivity booster: Speeds project completion; enables multitasking.	**Productivity thief:** Distracts workers; encourages frivolous time wasting.

Best Practices for Instant Messaging

Instant messaging can definitely save time and simplify communications with coworkers and customers. Before using it on the job, however, be sure you have permission. Do not use public systems without checking with your supervisor. If your organization does allow instant messaging, you can use it efficiently and professionally by following a number of best practices.

- Learn about your organization's IM policies. Are you allowed to use instant messaging? With whom may you exchange messages?
- Make yourself unavailable when you need to complete a project or meet a deadline.
- Organize your contact lists to separate business contacts from family and friends.
- Keep your messages simple and to the point. Avoid unnecessary chitchat, and know when to say goodbye.
- Don't use IM to send confidential or sensitive information.
- Be aware that instant messages can be saved. Like e-mail, don't say anything that would damage your reputation or that of your organization.
- If personal messaging is allowed, keep it to a minimum. Your organization may prefer that personal chats be done during breaks or the lunch hour.
- Show patience by not blasting multiple messages to coworkers if a response is not immediate.
- Keep your presence status up-to-date so that people trying to reach you don't waste their time.
- Beware of jargon, slang, and abbreviations, which, although they may reduce keystrokes, may be confusing and appear unprofessional.
- Respect your receivers by employing proper grammar, spelling, and proofreading.

Writing Information and Procedure E-Mail Messages and Memos

Although you may exchange very short instant messages, most of your writing tasks on the job will probably involve preparing e-mail messages and interoffice memos. Some of the most frequent messages that you can expect to be writing as a business communicator are (a) information and procedure messages and (b) request and reply messages.

In this book we give you a number of writing plans appropriate for various messages. These plans provide a skeleton; they are the bones of a message. You will provide the flesh. Simply plugging in phrases or someone else's words won't work. Good writers provide details and link their ideas with transitions to create fluent and meaningful messages. However, a writing plan helps you get started and gives you ideas about what to include. At first, you will probably rely on these plans considerably. As you progress, these plans will become less important. Later in the book, no plans are provided.

Writing plans help beginners get started by providing an outline of what to include.

Writing Plan for Information and Procedure E-Mail Messages and Memos

- **Subject line:** Summarize the content of the message.
- **Opening:** Expand the subject line by stating the main idea concisely in a full sentence.
- **Body:** Provide background data and explain the main idea. Consider using lists, bullets, or headings to improve readability. In describing a procedure or giving instructions, use command language (*do this, don't do that*).
- **Closing:** Request a specific action, summarize the message, or present a closing thought. If appropriate, include a deadline and a reason.

Information and procedure messages distribute routine information, describe procedures, and deliver instructions. They typically flow downward from management to employees and relate to the daily operation of an organization. In writing these messages, you have one primary function: conveying your idea so clearly that no further explanation (return message, telephone call, or personal visit) is necessary.

You have already seen the development of a routine information message in Figure 5.1 on page 103. It follows the writing plan with an informative subject line, an opening that states the purpose directly, and a body that organizes the information for maximum readability. The closing in an information message depends on what was discussed. If the message involves an action request, it should appear in the closing—not in the opening or in the body. If no action is required, the closing can summarize the message or offer a closing thought.

Procedure messages must be especially clear and readable. Figure 5.6 shows the first draft of an interoffice memo written by Troy Bell. His memo was meant to

Information and procedure messages generally flow downward from management to employees.

FIGURE 5.6 Procedure Memo

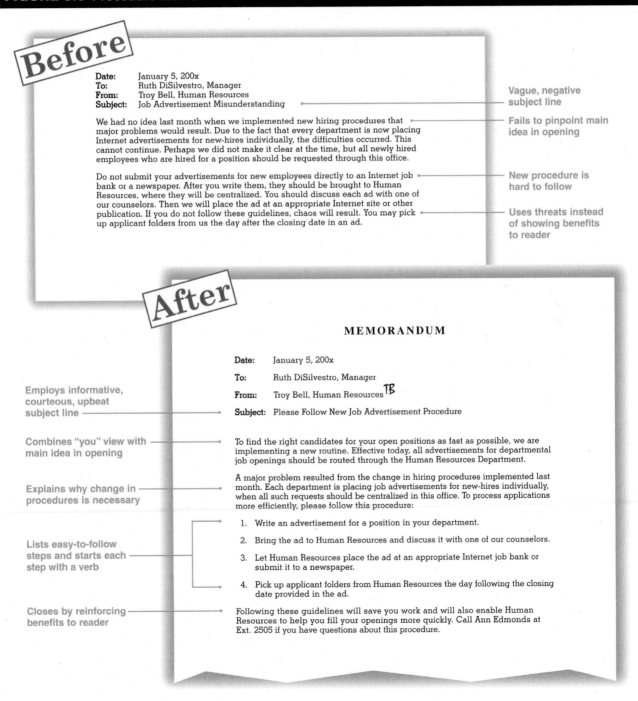

Before

Date:	January 5, 200x
To:	Ruth DiSilvestro, Manager
From:	Troy Bell, Human Resources
Subject:	Job Advertisement Misunderstanding

We had no idea last month when we implemented new hiring procedures that major problems would result. Due to the fact that every department is now placing Internet advertisements for new-hires individually, the difficulties occurred. This cannot continue. Perhaps we did not make it clear at the time, but all newly hired employees who are hired for a position should be requested through this office.

Do not submit your advertisements for new employees directly to an Internet job bank or a newspaper. After you write them, they should be brought to Human Resources, where they will be centralized. You should discuss each ad with one of our counselors. Then we will place the ad at an appropriate Internet site or other publication. If you do not follow these guidelines, chaos will result. You may pick up applicant folders from us the day after the closing date in an ad.

- Vague, negative subject line
- Fails to pinpoint main idea in opening
- New procedure is hard to follow
- Uses threats instead of showing benefits to reader

After

MEMORANDUM

Date:	January 5, 200x
To:	Ruth DiSilvestro, Manager
From:	Troy Bell, Human Resources TB
Subject:	Please Follow New Job Advertisement Procedure

To find the right candidates for your open positions as fast as possible, we are implementing a new routine. Effective today, all advertisements for departmental job openings should be routed through the Human Resources Department.

A major problem resulted from the change in hiring procedures implemented last month. Each department is placing job advertisements for new-hires individually, when all such requests should be centralized in this office. To process applications more efficiently, please follow this procedure:

1. Write an advertisement for a position in your department.
2. Bring the ad to Human Resources and discuss it with one of our counselors.
3. Let Human Resources place the ad at an appropriate Internet job bank or submit it to a newspaper.
4. Pick up applicant folders from Human Resources the day following the closing date provided in the ad.

Following these guidelines will save you work and will also enable Human Resources to help you fill your openings more quickly. Call Ann Edmonds at Ext. 2505 if you have questions about this procedure.

- Employs informative, courteous, upbeat subject line
- Combines "you" view with main idea in opening
- Explains why change in procedures is necessary
- Lists easy-to-follow steps and starts each step with a verb
- Closes by reinforcing benefits to reader

announce a new procedure for employees to follow in advertising open positions. However, the tone was negative, the explanation of the problem rambled, and the new procedure was unclear. Notice, too, that Troy's first draft told readers what they *shouldn't* do (*Do not submit advertisements for new employees directly to an Internet job bank or a newspaper*). It is more helpful to tell readers what they *should* do. Finally, Troy's first memo closed with a threat instead of showing readers how this new procedure will help them.

In the revision Troy improved the tone considerably. The subject line contains a *please,* which is always pleasant to see even if one is giving an order. The subject line also includes a verb and specifies the purpose of the memo. Instead of expressing his ideas with negative words and threats, Troy revised his message to explain objectively and concisely what went wrong.

Procedures and instructions are often written in numbered steps using command language (*Do this, don't do that*).

Troy realized that his original explanation of the new procedure was vague. Messages explaining procedures are most readable when the instructions are broken down into numbered steps listed chronologically. Each step should begin with an action verb in the command mode. Notice in Troy's revision in Figure 5.6 that numbered items begin with *Write, Bring, Let,* and *Pick up.* It is sometimes difficult to force all the steps in a procedure into this kind of command language. Troy struggled, but by trying different wording, he finally found verbs that worked.

Why should you go to so much trouble to make lists and achieve parallelism? Because readers can comprehend what you have said much more quickly, parallel language also makes you look professional and efficient.

In writing information and procedure messages, be careful of tone. Today's managers and team leaders seek employee participation and cooperation. These goals can't be achieved, though, if the writer sounds like a dictator or an autocrat. Avoid making accusations and fixing blame. Rather, explain changes, give reasons, and suggest benefits to the reader. Assume that employees want to contribute to the success of the organization and to their own achievement. Notice in the Figure 5.6 revision that Troy tells readers that they will save time and have their open positions filled more quickly if they follow the new procedures.

Visit www.meguffey.com for more information on *How to Write Instructions.*

The writing of instructions and procedures is so important that we have developed a special bonus online supplement called *How to Write Instructions.* It provides more examples and information. This online supplement at **www.meguffey.com** extends your textbook with in-depth material including links to real businesses to show you examples of well-written procedures and instructions.

Writing Request and Reply E-Mail Messages and Memos

Business organizations require information as their fuel. To make operations run smoothly, managers and employees request information from each other and then respond to those requests. Knowing how to write those requests and responses efficiently and effectively can save you time and make you look good.

Writing Plan for Request E-Mails and Memos

- **Subject line:** Summarize the request and note the action desired.
- **Opening:** Begin with the request or a brief statement introducing it.
- **Body:** Provide background, justification, and details. If asking questions, list them in parallel form.
- **Closing:** Request action by a specific date. If possible, provide a reason. Express appreciation, if appropriate.

Making Direct E-Mail and Memo Requests

If you are requesting routine information or action within an organization, the direct approach works best. Generally, this means asking for information or making the request without first providing elaborate explanations and justifications. Remember that readers are usually thinking, "Why me? Why am I receiving this?" They can understand the explanation better once they know what you are requesting.

If you are seeking answers to questions, you have three options for opening the message: (a) ask the most important question first, followed by an explanation and then the other questions, (b) use a polite command (*Please answer the following questions regarding*), or (c) introduce the questions with a brief statement (*Your answers to the following questions will help us . . .*).

In the body of the memo, explain and justify your request. When you must ask many questions, list them, being careful to phrase them similarly. Be courteous and friendly. In the closing include an end date (with a reason, if possible) to promote a quick response.

The e-mail message shown in Figure 5.7 requests information. The functional subject line uses a verb in noting the action desired (*Need Your Reactions to Our Casual-Dress Policy*). The reader knows immediately what is being requested. The message opens with a polite command followed by a brief explanation. Notice that the questions are highlighted with bullets to provide the high "skim value" that is important in business messages. The reader can quickly see what is being asked. The message concludes with an end date and a reason. Providing an end date helps the reader know how to plan a response so that action is completed by the date given. Expressions such as *do it whenever you can* or *complete it as soon as possible*

Use the direct approach in routine requests for information or action, opening with the most important question, a polite command, or a brief introductory statement.

FIGURE 5.7 Request E-Mail Message

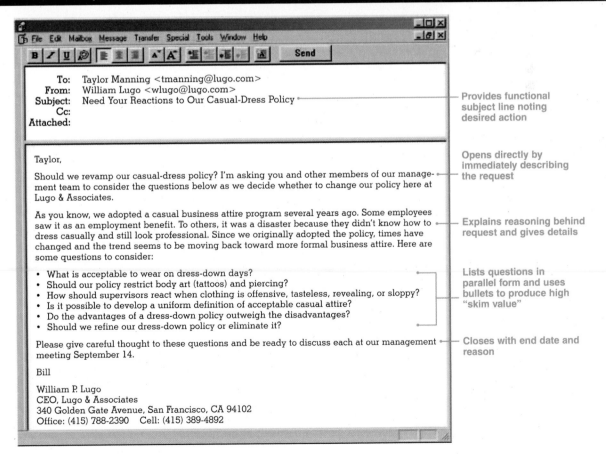

make little impression on procrastinators or very busy people. It is always wise to provide a specific date for completion. Dates can be entered on calendars to serve as reminders.

Replying to E-Mail and Memo Requests

Much business correspondence reacts or responds to previous messages. When replying to an e-mail, memo, or other document, be sure to follow the three-phase writing process. Analyze your purpose and audience, collect whatever information is necessary, and organize your thoughts. Make a brief outline of the points you plan to cover following this writing plan:

Writing Plan for E-Mail and Memo Replies

- **Subject line:** Summarize the main information from your reply.
- **Opening:** Start directly by responding to the request with a summary statement.
- **Body:** Provide additional information and details in a readable format.
- **Closing:** Add a concluding remark, summary, or offer of further assistance.

Writers sometimes fall into bad habits in replying to messages. Here are some trite and long-winded openers that are best avoided:

In response to your message of the 15th . . . (States the obvious.)

Thank you for your memo of the 15th in which you . . . (Suggests the writer can think of nothing more original.)

I have before me your memo of the 15th in which you . . . (Unnecessarily identifies the location of the previous message.)

Pursuant to your request of the 15th . . . (Sounds old-fashioned.)

This is to inform you that . . . (Delays getting to the point.)

Instead of falling into the trap of using one of the preceding shopworn openings, start directly by responding to the writer's request. If you agree to the request, show your cheerful compliance immediately. Consider these good-news openers:

Yes, we will be glad to . . . (Sends message of approval by opening with "Yes.")

Here are answers to the questions you asked about . . . (Sounds straightforward, businesslike, and professional.)

You are right in seeking advice about . . . (Opens with words that every reader enjoys seeing and hearing.)

We are happy to assist you in . . . (Shows writer's helpful nature and goodwill.)

As you requested, I am submitting . . . (Gets right to the point.)

After a direct and empathic opener, provide the information requested in a logical and coherent order. If you are answering a number of questions, arrange your answers in the order of the questions. In providing additional data, use familiar words, short sentences, short paragraphs, and active-voice verbs. Figure 5.3 on page 106 illustrates an interoffice memo that replies to a request. Notice that the writer organized her suggestions into separate paragraphs with the introductory words, *First, Second,* and *Third.* The writer also designed the document with columns, white space, and bullets to further improve readability. The message concludes with what is to happen next.

In responding to requests, your primary goal is to answer the request clearly and completely so that additional messages are unnecessary.

> **Overused and long-winded openers bore readers and waste their time.**

> **Direct opening statements can also be cheerful and empathic.**

Visit www.meguffey.com
- **Chapter Review Quiz**
- **Flash Cards**
- **Grammar Practice**
- **PowerPoint Slides**
- **Personal Language Trainer**
- **Beat the Clock Quiz**

Summing Up and Looking Forward

Organizations exchange messages externally and internally. Paper-based messages include business letters and interoffice memos. Electronic messages include e-mail, instant messaging, text messaging, podcasts, blogs, and wikis. Internal messages in today's workplace usually take the form of e-mail, interoffice memorandums, and, to a lesser extent, instant messaging. E-mails and memos use a standardized format to request and deliver information.

Because messages are increasingly being exchanged electronically, this chapter presented many techniques for sending and receiving safe and effective e-mail and instant messages. However, businesspeople are still using interoffice memos to convey confidential information, emphasize ideas, deliver lengthy documents, or lend importance to a message. In this chapter you learned to apply the direct strategy in writing internal messages that inform, describe procedures, request, and respond. In the next chapter you will extend the direct strategy to writing positive messages.

Critical Thinking

1. "E-mail is no longer a cutting edge tool," says *The New York Times*. "But it is clear that some people still do not know how to use it effectively."[5] What have you heard are the major complaints about the use of business e-mail?

2. What do you think this statement means? *Instant messaging could be the dial tone of the future.* Do you agree or disagree?

3. Why are lawyers and technology experts warning companies to store, organize, and manage computer data, including e-mail and instant messages, with sharper diligence?

4. Discuss the ramifications of the following statement: *Once a memo or any other document leaves your hands, you have essentially published it.*

5. **Ethical Issue:** Should managers have the right to monitor the e-mail messages and instant messages of employees? Why or why not? What if employees are warned that e-mail could be monitored? If a company establishes an e-mail policy, should only in-house transmissions be monitored? Only outside transmissions? See the Communication Workshop for this chapter for more on this topic.

Chapter Review

6. Name six forms of electronic communication and briefly describe each.

7. Are e-mail messages and interoffice memorandums interchangeable as communication channels? Explain.

8. How are the structure and formatting of e-mail messages and memos similar and different?

9. What are four questions you should ask yourself before writing an e-mail or memo?

10. Suggest at least ten pointers that you could give to a business e-mail user.

11. Name at least five rules of e-mail etiquette that show respect for others.

12. What do you think are the five most important practices for those sending instant messages at work?

13. What is the writing plan for an information or procedure message?
    Subject line:
    Opening:
    Body:

    Closing:

14. What is the writing plan for a request message?
    Subject line:
    Opening:
    Body:

    Closing:

15. What is the writing plan for a reply message?
    Subject line:
    Opening:
    Body:
    Closing:

Writing Improvement Exercises

Message Openers

Compare the following sets of message openers. Circle the letter of the opener that illustrates a direct opening. Be prepared to discuss the weaknesses and strengths of each.

16. An e-mail message inquiring about Web hosting:
    a. We are considering launching our own Web site because we feel it is the only way to keep up with our competition and make our product more visible in a crowded market. We have a lot of questions and need information about Web hosting.
    b. Please answer the following questions about hosting our new Web site, which we hope to launch to increase our product visibility in a crowded market.

17. An e-mail message announcing an in-service program:
    a. Employees interested in improving their writing and communication skills are invited to an in-service training program beginning October 4.
    b. For the past year we have been investigating the possibility of developing an in-service training program for some of our employees.

18. An e-mail message announcing a study:
    a. We have noticed recently a gradual but steady decline in the number of customer checking accounts. We are disturbed by this trend, and for this reason I am asking our Customer Relations Department to conduct a study and make recommendations regarding this important problem.
    b. Our Customer Relations Department will conduct a study and make recommendations regarding the gradual but steady decline of customer checking accounts.

19. A memo announcing a new procedure:
    a. It has come to our attention that increasing numbers of staff members are using instant messaging in sending business messages. We realize that IM often saves time and gets you fast responses, and we are prepared to continue to allow its use, but we have developed some specific procedures that we want you to use to make sure it is safe as well as efficient.
    b. The following new procedures for using instant messaging will enable staff members to continue to use it safely and efficiently.

Opening Paragraphs

The following opening paragraphs to memos are wordy and indirect. After reading each paragraph, identify the main idea. Then, write an opening sentence that illustrates a more direct opening.

20. Several staff members came to me and announced their interest in learning more about severance policies and separation benefits. As most of you know, these areas of concern are increasingly important for most Human Resources professionals. A seminar entitled "Severance & Separation Benefits" is being conducted February 11. I am allowing the following employees to attend the seminar: Terence Curran, Cindy Thompson, and Darlene McClure.

21. Your Intel Employees Association has secured for you discounts on auto repair, carpet purchases, travel arrangements, and many other services. These services are available to you if you have a Buying Power Card. All Intel employees are eligible for their own private Buying Power Cards.

Bulleted and Numbered Lists

22. Revise the following wordy paragraph into an introduction with a list. Should you use bullets or numbers?

    Producing excellent digital prints that equal what you see on your computer monitor is the most frustrating aspect of digital photography. You don't have to be frustrated, however. If you follow three steps, you can improve your prints immensely. I recommend that you first calibrate your screen. You should use the Pantone Spyder to do that. Next you should edit your photo so that your image looks natural and balanced. The final step involves configuring your printer. At the same time you should, of course, select the correct type of paper.

23. Use the following wordy instructions to compose a concise bulleted vertical list with an introductory statement:

    To write information for a Web site, there are three important tips to follow. For one thing, you should make the formatting as simple as possible. Another thing you must do is ensure the use of strong visual prompts. Last but not least, you should limit directions that are not needed.

24. The following information will appear in a business newsletter. Revise this wordy paragraph to include an introductory statement followed by a list. Should the list be bulleted or numbered?

    The National Crime Prevention Council made a statement about crime in the workplace. It also provided some tips for improving workplace safety and preventing crime at work. It says that crime prevention and safety measures are just as important at work as they are at home. Some of the ways you can improve safety and prevent crime include changing locks before you move into a new office. When doors, windows, and locks are broken or not working, someone should report this immediately. Lighting is another important factor. Many organizations leave some interior lights on even when the business may be closed. Dark places around a building should have lights, and shrubs can be a problem.[6]

Writing Improvement Cases

5.1 Request E-Mail: Dealing With Excessive E-Mail

The following e-mail from Stella Soto requests feedback from her managerial staff; however, her first draft suffers from many writing faults.

Your Task. Analyze the message. List its weaknesses and then outline an appropriate writing plan. If your instructor directs, revise the message. A copy of this message is provided at **www.meguffey.com** if you want to revise it online.

To: Amsoft Manager List
From: Stella Soto <stella.soto@amsoft.com>
Subject: E-Mail Problems
Cc:
Bcc:

Dear Managers,

As Amsoft vice president, I am troubled by a big problem. I am writing this note to ask for your help and advice to address an urgent problem—the problem of excessive e-mail. If you will do me the favor of answering the questions below, I'm sure your ideas will assist us in the development of a plan that should benefit your staff, yourself, and our organization will be improved. Your responses in writing to these questions (preferably by May 5) will help me prepare for our supervisory committee meeting on May 10.

Everyone had the expectation that e-mail would be a great big productivity tool. I'm afraid that its use is becoming extremely excessive. For our organization it is actually cutting into work time. Did you know that one study found that the average office worker is spending 2 hours a day on e-mail? In our organization we may be spending even more then this. Its exceedingly difficult to get any work done because of writing and answering an extraordinary number of e-mails coming in each and every day. Excessive e-mail is sapping the organization's strength and productivity. I would like to have your answers to some questions before the above referenced dates to help us focus on the problem.

Can you give a ballpark figure for how many e-mail messages you receive and answer on a personal basis each day? Think about how many hours the staff members in your department spend on e-mail each day. Approximately how many hours would you estimate? Do you have any ideas about how we can make a reduction in the volume of e-mail messages being sent and received within our own organization? Do you think that e-mail is being used by our employees in an excessive manner?

I'm wondering what you think about an e-mail-free day once a week. How about Fridays? I appreciate your suggestions and advice in developing a solution to the problem of controlling e-mail and making an improvement in productivity.

Stella

1. List at least five weaknesses of this message.

2. Outline a writing plan for this message.
   Subject line:
   Opening:
   Body:
   Closing:

5.2 Information Memo: Facts About Corporate Instant Messaging
The following interoffice memo reports information from a symposium, but it is poorly written.

Your Task. Analyze the message. List its weaknesses and then outline an appropriate writing plan. If your instructor directs, revise the message. A copy of this message is provided at **www.meguffey.com** if you want to revise it online.

Date: March 4, 200x
To: Trevor Kurtz, CEO
From: Emily Lopez-Rush
Subject: Instant Messaging

Thanks for asking me to attend the Instant Messaging Symposium. It was sponsored by Pixel Link and took place March 2. Do you think you will want me to expand on what I learned at the next management council meeting? I believe that meeting is March 25.

Anyway, here's my report. Jason Howard, the symposium leader told us that over 80 million workers are already using instant messaging and that it was definitely here to stay. But do the risks outweigh the advantages? He talked about benefits, providers, costs involved, and risks. The top advantages of IM are speed, documentation, and it saves costs. The major problems are spam, security, control, and disruptive. He said that the principal IM providers for consumers were AOL Instant Messenger, Windows Live Messenger, and Yahoo Messenger. Misuse of IM can result in reductions in productivity. However, positive results can be achieved with appropriate use. Although some employees are using consumer IM services, for maximum security many organizations are investing in enterprise-level IM systems, and they are adopting guidelines for employees. These enterprise-level IM systems range in cost from $30 to $100 per user license. The cost depends on the amount of functionality.

This is just a summary of what I learned. If you want to hear more, please do not hesitate to call.

1. List at least five weaknesses of this e-mail message.

2. Outline a writing plan for this message.
   Subject line:
   Opening:
   Body:

   Closing:

5.3 Request E-Mail: Planning a Charity Golf Event

The following e-mail from Seth Jackson requests information about planning a charity golf tournament. His first draft must be revised.

Your Task. Analyze the message. List its weaknesses and then outline an appropriate writing plan. If your instructor directs, revise the message. A copy of this message is provided at **www.meguffey.com** if you want to revise it online. Could this message benefit from category headings?

Date: February 1, 200x
To: Kaitlin Merek <kmerek@monarch.net>
From: Seth Jackson <seth.jackson@cox.net>
Subject: Need Help!

The Children's Resource Center badly needs funds. We have tried other things, but now we want to try a charity golf event. In view of the fact that you have expertise in this area and since you volunteered to offer your assistance, I am writing this e-mail to pick your brain, so to speak, in regard to questions that have to do with five basic fundamentals in the process of preparation. I'm going to need your answers these areas before February 15. Is that possible? Maybe you would rather talk to me. Should I contact you?

In regard to the budget, I have no idea how to estimate costs. For example, what about administrative costs. How about marketing? And there are salaries, cell-phone rentals, copiers, and a lot of other things.

I also need help in choosing a golf course. Should it be a public course? Or a private course? Resort? One big area that I worry about is sponsors. Should I go after one big sponsor? But let's say I get Pepsi to be a sponsor. Then do I have to ban Coke totally from the scene?

Another big headache is scoring. I will bet you can make some suggestions for tabulating the golf results. And posting them. By the way, did you see that Tiger Woods is back in the winner's circle?

I have noticed that other golf tournaments have extra events, such as a pairing party to introduce partners. Many also have an awards dinner to award prizes. Should I be planning extra events?

Seth Jackson
Philanthropy and Gifts Coordinator
Children's Resource Center

1. List at least five weaknesses of this request e-mail.

2. Outline a writing plan for this message.
   Subject line:
   Opening:
   Body:
   Closing:

5.4 Procedure E-Mail: New Process for Reporting Equipment Repairs

The following is a manager's first draft of an e-mail describing a new process for reporting equipment repairs. The message is addressed to one employee, but it will also be sent to others.

Your Task. Analyze the message. List its weaknesses and then outline an appropriate writing plan. If your instructor directs, revise the message. A copy of this message is provided at **www.meguffey.com** if you want to revise it online.

To: Faith Benoit <Faith.Benoit@stcc.edu>
From: Mia Murillo <Mia.Murillo@stcc.edu>
Subject: Repairs
Cc:
Bcc:

We have recently instituted a new procedure for all equipment repairs. Effective immediately, we are no longer using the "Equipment Repair Form" that we formerly used. We want to move everyone to an online database system. These new procedures will help us repair your equipment faster and keep track of it better. You will find the new procedure at http://www.BigWebDesk.net. That's where you log in. You should indicate the kind of repair you need. It may be for AudioVisual, Mac, PC, or Printer. Then you should begin the process of data entry for your specific problem by selecting **Create New Ticket**. The new ticket should be printed and attached securely to the equipment. Should you have questions or trouble, just call Sylvia at Extension 255. You can also write to her at *Sylvia.Freeman@stcc.edu*. The warehouse truck driver will pick up and deliver your equipment as we have always done in the past.

1. List at least five weaknesses of this e-mail message.

2. Outline a writing plan for this message.
   Subject line:
   Opening:
   Body:

   Closing:

Activities and Cases

E-MAIL

5.5 Request Memo: Redesigning the Company Web Site

You are part of the newly formed Committee on Web Site Redesign. Its function is to look into the possible redesign of your company Web site. Some managers think that the site is looking a bit dated. The committee delegates you to ask Cole Prewarski, Web master and manager, some questions. The committee wonders whether he has done any usability tests on the current site. The committee wants to know how much a total Web redesign might cost.

It also would like to know about the cost of a partial redesign. Someone wanted to know whether animation, sound, or video could be added and wondered if Cole would recommend doing so. Someone else thought that the timing of a redesign might be important. The committee asks you to add other questions to your memo. Invite Cole to a meeting April 6. Assume that he knows about the committee.

Your Task. Write an e-mail or an interoffice memo to Cole Prewarski requesting answers to several questions and inviting him to a meeting.

E-MAIL

5.6 Request E-Mail: Choosing a Holiday Plan

In the past your company offered all employees 11 holidays, starting with New Year's Day in January and proceeding through Christmas Day the following December. Other companies offer similar holiday schedules. In addition, your company has given all employees one floating holiday. That day was determined by a company-wide vote. As a result, all employees had the same day off. Now, however, management is considering a new plan that involves a floating holiday that each employee may choose. Selections, however, would be subject to staffing needs within individual departments. If two people wanted the same day, the employee with the most seniority would have the day off.

Your Task. As a member of the Human Resources staff, write an e-mail to employees asking them to choose between continuing the current company-wide uniform floating holiday or instituting a new plan for an individual floating holiday. Be sure to establish an end date.

E-MAIL

5.7 Request E-Mail or Memo: Smokers vs. Nonsmokers

The city of Milwaukee has mandated that employers "shall adopt, implement, and maintain a written smoking policy which shall contain a prohibition against smoking in restrooms and infirmaries." Employers must also "maintain a nonsmoking area of not less than two thirds of the seating capacity in cafeterias, lunchrooms, and employee lounges, and make efforts to work out disputes between smokers and nonsmokers."

Your Task. As Lindsay English, director of Human Resources, write an e-mail or interoffice memo to all department managers of Imperial Foods, a large food products company. Announce the new restriction, and tell the managers that you want them to set up departmental committees to mediate any smoking conflicts before complaints surface. Explain why this is a good policy.

E-MAIL

5.8 Response E-Mail or Memo: Enforcing Smoking Ban

As manager of Accounting Services for Imperial Foods, you must respond to Ms. English's memo in the preceding activity. You could have called Ms. English, but you prefer to have a permanent record of this message. You are having difficulty enforcing the smoking ban in restrooms. Only one men's room serves your floor, and 9 of your 27 male employees are smokers. You have already received complaints, and you see no way to enforce the ban in the restrooms. You have also noticed that smokers are taking longer breaks than other employees. Smokers complain that they need more time because they must walk to an outside area. Smokers are especially unhappy when the weather is cold, rainy, or snowy. Moreover, smokers huddle near the building entrances, creating a negative impression for customers and visitors. Your committee members can find no solutions; in fact, they have become polarized in their meetings to date. You need help from a higher authority.

Your Task. Write an e-mail or memo to Ms. English appealing for solutions. Perhaps she should visit your department.

E-MAIL **TEAM** **WEB**

5.9 Response E-Mail or Memo: Office Romance Off Limits?

Where can you find the hottest singles scene today? Some would say in your workplace. Because people are working long hours and have little time for outside contacts, relationships often develop at work. Estimates suggest that one third to one half of all romances start at work. Your boss is concerned about possible problems resulting from relationships at work. What happens if a relationship between a superior and subordinate results in perceived favoritism? What happens if a relationship ends in a nasty breakup? Your boss would like to simply ban all relationships between employees. However, that's not likely to work. He asks you, his assistant, to learn what guidelines could be established regarding office romances.

Your Task. Using professional databases or the Web, look for articles about workplace romance. From various articles, select four or five suggestions that you could make to your boss in regard to protecting an employer. Why is it necessary for a company to protect itself? Discuss your findings and reactions with your team. Individually or as a group, submit your findings and reactions in a well-organized, easy-to-read e-mail or memo to your boss (your instructor). You may list main points from the articles you research, but use your own words to write the message.

E-MAIL

5.10 Response E-Mail or Memo: Rescheduling Interviews to Accommodate a Traveling Boss

Your boss, Michael Kaufman, has scheduled three appointments to interview applicants for the position of project manager. All of these appointments are for Thursday, May 5. However, he now must travel to Atlanta that week. He asks you to reschedule all the appointments for one week later. He also wants a brief background summary for each candidate.

Although frustrated, you call each person and are lucky to arrange these times. Saul Salazar, who has been a project manager for nine years with Summit Enterprises, agrees to come at 10:30 A.M. Kaitlyn Grindell, who is a systems analyst and a consultant to many companies, will come at 11:30. Mary Montgomery, who has an MA degree and six years of experience as senior project coordinator at High Point Industries, will come at 9:30 A.M. You are wondering whether Mr. Kaufman forgot to include Bertha Ho, operations personnel officer, in these interviews. Ms. Ho usually is part of the selection process.

Your Task. Write an e-mail or memo to Mr. Kaufman including all the information he needs.

5.11 Response E-Mail or Memo: Proper Dress for Businesspeople in Saudi Arabia

The U.S. Air Force's highest ranking female fighter pilot, Lt. Col. Martha McSally, was unhappy about being required to wear neck-to-toe robes in Saudi Arabia when she was off base. She filed a federal lawsuit seeking to overturn the policy that requires female servicewomen to wear such conservative clothing when they are off base.

After seeing an article about this in the newspaper, your boss began to worry about sending female engineers to Saudi Arabia. Your company has been asked to submit a proposal to develop telecommunications within that country, and some of the company's best staff members are female. If your company wins the contract, it will undoubtedly need women to be in Saudi Arabia to complete the project. Because your boss knows little about the country, he asks you, his assistant, to do some research to find out what is appropriate business dress.

Your Task. Visit two or three Web sites and learn about dress expectations in Saudi Arabia. Is Western-style clothing acceptable for men? For women? Are there any clothing taboos? Should guest workers be expected to dress like natives? In teams discuss your findings. Individually or collectively, prepare a memo or e-mail addressed to LaDane Williams, your boss. Summarize your most significant findings.

5.12 Response E-Mail: Reaching Consensus Regarding Casual-Dress Policy

Casual dress in professional offices has been coming under attack. Your boss, Taylor Manning, received the e-mail shown in Figure 5.7 on page 117. He thinks it would be a good assignment for his group of management trainees to help him respond to that message. He asks your team to research answers to the first five questions in CEO William Lugo's message. He doesn't expect you to answer the final question, but any information you can supply to the first questions would help him shape a response.

Lugo & Associates is a public CPA firm with a staff of 120 CPAs, bookkeepers, managers, and support personnel. Located in downtown Pittsburgh, the plush offices in One Oxford Center overlook the Allegheny River and the North Shore. The firm performs general accounting and audit services as well as tax planning and preparation. Accountants visit clients in the field and also entertain them in the downtown office.

Your Task. Decide whether the entire team will research each question in Figure 5.7 or whether team members will be assigned certain questions. Collect information, discuss it, and reach consensus on what you will report to Mr. Manning. Write a concise, one-page response from your team addressed to <tmanning@lugo.com>. Your goal is to inform, not persuade. Remember that you represent management, not students or employees.

5.13 Procedure Memo: Standardizing Purchase Requests

The Purchasing Department handles purchases for a growing family company. Some purchase orders arrive on the proper forms, but others are memos or handwritten notes that are barely legible. The owner wants to establish a standard procedure for submitting purchase requests. The purchase requests must now be downloaded from the company intranet. To provide the fastest service, employees should fill out the purchase request. Employees must include the relevant information: date, quantities, catalog numbers, complete descriptions, complete vendor mailing address and contact information, delivery requirements, and shipping methods. The Purchasing Department should receive the original, and the sender should keep a copy. An important step in the new procedure is approval by the budget manager on the request form.

Your Task. As assistant manager in the Purchasing Department, write an interoffice memo to all employees informing them of the new procedure.

5.14 Procedure E-Mail or Memo: Rules for Cell Phone Use in Sales Reps' Cars

As one of the managers of Futura, a hair care and skin products company, you are alarmed at a newspaper article you just saw. A stockbroker for Smith Barney was making cold calls on his personal cell phone while driving. His car hit and killed a motorcyclist. The brokerage firm was sued and accused of contributing to an accident by encouraging employees to use cell phones while driving. To avoid the risk of paying huge damages awarded by an emotional jury, the brokerage firm offered the victim's family a $500,000 settlement.

You begin to worry, knowing that your company has provided its 75 sales representatives with mobile phones to help them keep in touch with the home base while they are in the field. At the next management meeting, other members agreed that you should draft a message detailing some mobile phone safety rules for your sales reps. On the Web you learned that anyone with a cell phone should get to know its features, including speed dial, automatic memory, and redial. Another suggestion involved using a hands-free device. Management members decided to purchase these for every sales rep and have the devices available within one month. When positioning cell phones in their cars, reps should make sure they are within easy reach. Cell phones should be where reps can grab them without removing their eyes from the road. If they get an incoming call at an inconvenient time, they should let their voice mail pick up the call. They should never talk, of course, during hazardous driving conditions, such as rain, sleet, snow, and ice.

Taking notes or looking up phone numbers is dangerous when driving. You want to warn sales reps not to get into dangerous situations by reading (such as an address book) or writing (such as taking notes) while driving.

The more you think about it, the more you think that sales reps should not use their cell phones in moving cars. They really should pull over. But you know that would be hard to enforce.

Your Task. Individually or in teams write a memo or e-mail to Futura sales reps outlining company suggestions (or should they be rules?) for safe wireless phone use in cars. You may wish to check the Web for additional safety ideas. Try to suggest reader benefits in this message. How is safety beneficial to the sales reps? The message is from you acting as operations manager.

`E-MAIL`   `WEB`

5.15 Procedure E-Mail or Memo: Revising a Rambling Security Memo

After a recent frightening experience, your boss, Olivia Solano-Hughes, realized that she must draft a memo about office security. Here is why she is concerned. A senior associate, Lucy Bonner, was working overtime cleaning up overdue reports. At about 9 p.m. she heard the office door open, but the intruder quickly left when he found that someone was in the office. Your boss hurriedly put together the following memo to be distributed to office managers in five branch offices. But she was on her way out of town, and she asked you to revise her draft and have it ready for her approval when she returns. One other thing—she wondered whether you would do online research to find other helpful suggestions. Your boss trusts you to totally revise, if necessary.

Your Task. Conduct a database or Web search to look for reasonable office security suggestions. Study the following memo. Then improve its organization, clarity, conciseness, correctness, and readability. Don't be afraid to do a total overhaul. Bulleted points are a must, and check the correctness, too. Your boss is no Ms. Grammar! Be sure to add an appropriate closing.

Date: Current
To: Branch Managers
From: Olivia Solano-Hughes, Vice President
Subject: Staying Safe in the Office

Office security is a topic we have not talked enough about. I was terrified recently when a senior associate, who was working late, told me she heard the front door of the branch office open and she thought she heard a person enter. When she called out, the person apparently left. This frightening experience reminded me there are several things that each branch can do to improve it's office security. The following are a few simple things, but we will talk more about this at our next quarterly meeting (June 8?). Please come with additional ideas.

If an office worker is here early or late, then it is your responsibility to talk with them about before and after hours security. When someone comes in early it is not smart to open the doors until most of the rest of the staff arrive. Needless to say, employees working overtime should make sure the door is locked and they should not open there office doors after hours to people they don't know, especially if you are in the office alone. Dark offices are especially attractive to thieves with valuable equipment.

Many branches are turning off lights at points of entry and parking areas to conserve energy. Consider changing this policy or installing lights connected to motion detectors, which is an inexpensive (and easy!) way to discourage burglars and intruders. I also think that "cash-free" decals are a good idea because they make thieves realize that not much is in this office to take. These signs may discourage breaking and entering. On the topic of lighting, we want to be sure that doors and windows that are secluded and not visible to neighbors or passersby is illuminated.

We should also beware of displaying any valuable equipment or other things. When people walk by, they should not be able to look in and see expensive equipment. Notebook computers and small portable equipment is particularly vulnerable at night. It should be locked up. In spite of the fact that most of our branches are guarded by FirstAlert, I'm not sure all branches are displaying the decals prominently—especially on windows and doors. We want people to know that our premises are electronically protected.

5.16 How to Write Clear Procedures and Instructions

At **www.meguffey.com,** you will find a supplement devoted to writing instructions. It includes colorful examples and links to Web sites with relevant examples of real sets of instructions from business Web sites.

Your Task. Locate "How to Write Instructions" and study all of its sections. Then choose one of the following application activities: A-5, "Revising the Instructions for an Imported Fax Machine," or A-6, "Evaluation: Instructions for Dealing With Car Emergencies." Complete the assignment and submit it to your instructor.

`WEB`

5.17 Procedure E-Mail or Memo: Instant Messaging in Your Office

A few members of your team are using instant messaging, but others are clueless. As assistant team director, you have been asked by your team leader, Jamila Tucker, to prepare a list of procedures for team members to follow in setting up an instant messaging service for their computers and mobile devices. She wants all team members to be able to exchange messages quickly.

Your Task. Prepare a set of procedures for signing up, installing, and using an instant messaging program. This procedure e-mail will go to team members. Use the Web to find information. You may choose any IM service. Outline the system requirements and the steps necessary to send an instant message so that even the slowest team members will understand what to do. Address the e-mail to *Team Members@lexcraft.com*. Be sure to end with an action request, a deadline, and a reason.

Video Resources

This important chapter offers two learning videos.

Video Library 1: *Smart E-Mail Messages and Memos Advance Your Career.* Watch this chapter-specific video for a demonstration of how to use e-mail skillfully and safely. You will better understand the writing process in relation to composing messages. You will also see tips for writing messages that advance your career instead of sinking it.

Video Library 2: *Innovation, Learning, and Communication: A Study of Yahoo.* This video familiarizes you with managers and inside operating strategies at the Internet company Yahoo. After watching the film, assume the role of assistant to John Briggs, senior producer, who appeared in the video. John has just received a letter asking for permission from another film company to use Yahoo offices and personnel in an educational video, similar to the one you just saw.

John wants you to draft a message for him to send to the operations manager, Ceci Lang, asking for permission for VX

Studios to film. VX says it needs about 15 hours of filming time and would like to interview four or five managers as well as founders David Filo and Jerry Yang. VX would need to set up its mobile studio van in the parking lot and would need permission to use advertising film clips. Although VX hopes to film in May, it is flexible about the date. John Briggs reminds you that Yahoo has participated in a number of films in the past two years, and some managers are complaining that they can't get their work done.

Your Task. After watching the video, write a memo or email request message to Ceci Lang, operations manager, asking her to allow VX Studios to film at Yahoo. Your message should probably emphasize the value of these projects in enhancing Yahoo's image among future users. Supply any details you think are necessary to create a convincing request memo that will win authorization from Ceci Lang to schedule this filming.

Grammar/Mechanics Checkup 5

Prepositions and Conjunctions

Review Sections 1.18 and 1.19 in the Grammar Review section of the Grammar/Mechanics Handbook. Then study each of the following statements. Write *a* or *b* to indicate the sentence in which the idea is expressed more effectively. Also record the number of the G/M principle illustrated. When you finish, compare your responses with those provided. If your answers differ, study carefully the principles shown in parentheses.

Example a. When do you expect to graduate college?   b   (1.18a)
          b. When do you expect to graduate from college?

1. a. No one knows where the meeting is.

    b. No one knows where the meeting is at.

2. a. I hate when we have to work overtime.

    b. I hate it when we have to work overtime.

3. a. Intel enjoyed greater profits this year then expected.

    b. Intel enjoyed greater profits this year than expected.

4. a. Gross profit is where you compute the difference between total sales and the cost of goods sold.

    b. Gross profit is computed by finding the difference between total sales and the cost of goods sold.

5. a. We advertise to increase sales, introduce complementary products, and enhance our corporate image.

    b. We advertise to have our products used more often, when we have complementary products to introduce, and we are interested in making our corporation look better to the public.

6. a. What type computer monitor do you prefer?

    b. What type of computer monitor do you prefer?

7. a. Your iPod was more expensive than mine.

   b. Your iPod was more expensive then mine.

8. a. Did you send an application to the headquarters in Cincinnati or to the branch in St. Louis?

   b. Did you apply to the Cincinnati headquarters or the St. Louis branch?

9. a. The most dangerous situation occurs when employees ignore the safety rules.

   b. The most dangerous situation is when employees ignore the safety rules.

10. a. She had a great interest, as well as a profound respect for, historical homes.

    b. She had a great interest in, as well as a profound respect for, historical homes.

11. a. Volunteers should wear long pants, bring gloves, and sunscreen should be applied.

    b. Volunteers should wear long pants, bring gloves, and apply sunscreen.

12. a. His PowerPoint presentation was short like we hoped it would be.

    b. His PowerPoint presentation was short as we hoped it would be.

13. a. An ethics code is where a set of rules spells out appropriate behavior standards.

    b. An ethics code is a set of rules spelling out appropriate behavior standards.

14. a. Please keep the paper near the printer.

    b. Please keep the paper near to the printer.

15. a. A behavioral interview question is when the recruiter says, "Tell me about a time . . . ."

    b. A behavioral interview question is one in which the recruiter says, "Tell me about a time . . . ."

The following memo has errors involving grammar, punctuation, wording, lead-ins, parallelism, language, listing techniques, and other problems. You may either (a) use standard proofreading marks (see Appendix B) to correct the errors here or (b) download the document from your companion Web site and revise at your computer. Study the guidelines in the Grammar/Mechanics Handbook to sharpen your skills.

MEMORANDUM

DATE: April 20, 200x

TO: Department Heads, Managers, and Supervisors .

FROM: Donna Cooper-Grey, Director, Human Resources

SUBJECT: Submitting Appraisals of Performance by June 1

This is to inform you that performance appraisals for all you employees must be submitted by June 1. These appraisal are especially important and essential this year because of job changes, new technologys and because of office reorganization.

To complete your performance appraisals in the most effective way, you should follow the procedures described in our employee handbook, let me briefly make a review of those procedures;

1. Be sure each and every employee has a performance plan with three or 4 main objective.
2. For each objective make an assessment of the employee on a scale of 5 (consistently exceeds requirements) to 0 (does not meet requirements.
3. You should identify three strengths that he brings to the job.
4. Name 3 skills that he can improve. These should pertain to skills such as Time Management rather then to behaviors such as habitual lateness.
5. You should meet with the employee to discuss his appraisal.
6. Then, be sure to obtain the employees signature on the form.

We look upon appraisals as a tool for helping each worker assess his performance. And enhance his output. Please submit and send each employees performance appraisal to my office by June 1. If you would like to discuss this farther, please do not hesitate to call me.

Communication Workshop: Ethics

Should Employers Restrict E-Mail, Instant Messaging, and Internet Use?

Most employees today work with computers and have Internet access. Should they be able to use their work computers for online shopping, personal messages, and personal work, as well as to listen to music and play games?

But It's Harmless. Office workers have discovered that it is far easier to shop online than to race to malls and wait in line. To justify her Web shopping at work, one employee, a recent graduate, said, "Instead of standing at the water cooler gossiping, I shop online." She went on to say, "I'm not sapping company resources by doing this."[7]

Those who use instant messaging say that what they are doing is similar to making personal phone calls. So long as they don't abuse the practice, they see no harm. One marketing director justified his occasional game playing and online shopping by explaining that his employer benefits because he is more productive when he takes minibreaks. "When I need a break, I pull up a Web page and just browse," he says. "Ten minutes later, I'm all refreshed, and I can go back to business-plan writing."[8]

Companies Cracking Down. Employers, however, see it differently. A recent survey reported that more than one fourth of employers have fired workers for misusing e-mail, and nearly one third have fired employees for misusing the Internet.[9] UPS discovered an employee running a personal business from his office computer. Lockheed Martin fired an employee who disabled its entire company network for six hours because of an e-mail message heralding a holiday event that the worker sent to 60,000 employees. Companies not only worry about lost productivity, but they fear litigation, security breaches, and other electronic disasters from accidental or intentional misuse of computer systems.

What's Reasonable? Some companies try to enforce a "zero tolerance" policy, prohibiting any personal use of company equipment. Ameritech Corporation specifically tells employees that computers and other company equipment are to be used only to provide service to customers and for other business purposes. Companies such as Boeing, however, allow employees to use faxes, e-mail, and the Internet for personal reasons. But Boeing sets guidelines. Use has to be of reasonable duration and frequency and can't cause embarrassment to the company. Strictly prohibited are chain letters, obscenity, and political and religious solicitation.

Career Application. As an administrative assistant at Texas Technologies in Fort Worth, you have just received an e-mail from your boss asking for your opinion. It seems that many employees have been shopping online and more are using instant messaging. One person actually received four personal packages from UPS in one morning. Although reluctant to do so, management is considering installing monitoring software that not only tracks Internet use but also blocks messaging, porn, hate, and game sites.

Your Task
- In teams or as a class, discuss the problem of workplace abuse of e-mail, instant messaging, and the Internet. Should full personal use be allowed?
- Are computers and their links to the Internet similar to other equipment such as telephones?
- Should employees be allowed to access the Internet for personal use if they use their own private e-mail accounts?
- Should management be allowed to monitor all Internet use?
- Should employees be warned if e-mail is to be monitored?
- What reasons can you give to support an Internet crackdown by management?
- What reasons can you give to oppose a crackdown?

Decide whether you support or oppose the crackdown. Explain your views in an e-mail or a memo to your boss, Arthur W. Rose, *awrose@txtech.com*.

CHAPTER 6

Positive Messages

OBJECTIVES
After studying this chapter, you should be able to

- Explain why business letters are important in delivering positive messages outside an organization.
- Write letters that make direct requests for information or action.
- Write letters that make direct claims.
- Write letters that reply to requests.
- Write adjustment letters to customers.
- Write goodwill messages that express thanks, recognition, and sympathy.

Sending Positive Written Messages Outside Your Organization

Most of the workplace messages you write will probably be positive. That is, they will deal with routine matters that require straightforward answers using the direct method. As communication channels continue to evolve, you will be using both electronic and paper-based channels to send positive, routine messages. Chapter 5 discussed electronic messages and memos dealing primarily with internal communication. This chapter focuses on positive external messages. The principal channel for external messages is business letters.

> The principal channel for delivering messages outside an organization is business letters.

Understanding the Power of Business Letters

Letters are a primary channel of communication for delivering messages *outside* an organization. Positive, straightforward letters help organizations conduct everyday business and convey goodwill to outsiders. Such letters go to suppliers, government agencies, other businesses, and, most important, customers. The letters to customers receive a high priority because these messages encourage product feedback, project a favorable image of the organization, and promote future business.

Even with the new media available today, a letter remains one of the most powerful and effective ways to get your message across. Although e-mail is incredibly successful for both internal and external communication, many important messages

When the Internal Revenue Service (IRS) sends letters emblazoned with the agency's official insignia and addressed "Dear Taxpayer," people get nervous. One IRS notice issued to millions of Americans, however, delivered positive news: "We are pleased to inform you that the United States Congress passed the Economic Stimulus Act of 2008, which provides for economic stimulus payments to be made to over 130 million American households." The body of the letter instructed qualifying taxpayers to file an annual tax return to receive the one-time cash payout. *Why does the IRS use letters in today's digital age?*

Business letters are important for messages that require a permanent record, confidentiality, formality, sensitivity, and a well-considered presentation.

still call for letters. Business letters are necessary when (a) a permanent record is required; (b) confidentiality is paramount; (c) formality and sensitivity are essential; and (d) a persuasive, well-considered presentation is important.

Business Letters Produce a Permanent Record.
Many business transactions require a permanent record. Business letters fulfill this function. For example, when a company enters into an agreement with another company, business letters introduce the agreement and record decisions and points of understanding. Although telephone conversations and e-mail messages may be exchanged, important details are generally recorded in business letters that are kept in company files. Business letters deliver contracts, explain terms, exchange ideas, negotiate agreements, answer vendor questions, and maintain customer relations. Business letters are important for any business transaction that requires a permanent written record.

Business Letters Can Be Confidential.
Carefree use of e-mail was once a sign of sophistication. Today, however, communicators know how dangerous it is to entrust confidential and sensitive information to digital channels. A writer in *The New York Times* recognized the unique value of letters when he said, "Despite the sneering term *snail mail,* plain old letters are the form of long-distance communication least likely to be intercepted, misdirected, forwarded, retrieved, or otherwise inspected by someone you didn't have in mind."[1]

Business Letters Convey Formality and Sensitivity.
Business letters presented on company stationery carry a sense of formality and importance not possible with e-mail. They look important. They carry a nonverbal message saying the writer considered the message to be so significant and the receiver so prestigious that the writer cared enough to write a real message. Business letters deliver more information than e-mail because they are written on stationery that usually is printed with company information such as logos, addresses, titles, and contact details.

Business Letters Deliver Persuasive, Well-Considered Messages.
When a business communicator must be persuasive and can't do it in person, a business letter is more effective than other communication channels. Letters

can persuade people to change their actions, adopt new beliefs, make donations, contribute their time, and try new products. Direct-mail letters remain a powerful tool to promote services and products, boost online and retail traffic, and solicit contributions. Business letters represent deliberate communication. They give you a chance to think through what you want to say, organize your thoughts, and write a well-considered argument. You will learn more about writing persuasive and marketing messages in Chapter 8.

Direct Requests for Information or Action

The majority of your business letters will involve routine messages organized directly. Before you write any letter, though, consider its costs in terms of your time and workload. Whenever possible, don't write! Instead of asking for information, could you find it yourself? Would a telephone call, e-mail message, instant message, or brief visit to a coworker solve the problem quickly? If not, use the direct pattern to present your request efficiently.

Because business letters are costly, avoid writing them unless absolutely necessary.

Many business messages are written to request information or action. Although the specific subjects of inquiries may differ, the similarity of purpose in routine requests enables writers to use the following writing plan:

Writing Plan for an Information or Action Request

- **Opening:** Ask the most important question first or express a polite command.
- **Body:** Explain the request logically and courteously. Ask other questions if necessary.
- **Closing:** Request a specific action with an end date, if appropriate, and show appreciation.

Open Your Request Directly

The most emphatic positions in a letter are the opening and closing. Readers tend to look at them first. The writer, then, should capitalize on this tendency by putting the most significant statement first. The first sentence of an information request is usually a question or a polite command. It should not be an explanation or justification, unless resistance to the request is expected. When the information requested is likely to be forthcoming, immediately tell the reader what you want. This saves the reader's time and may ensure that the message is read. A busy executive who skims the mail, quickly reading subject lines and first sentences only, may grasp your request rapidly and act on it. A request that follows a lengthy explanation, on the other hand, may never be found.

Readers find the openings and closings of letters most interesting and often read them first.

A letter inquiring about hotel accommodations, shown in Figure 6.1, begins immediately with the most important idea: Can the hotel provide meeting rooms and accommodations for 250 people? Instead of opening with an explanation of who the writer is or how the writer happens to be writing this letter, the letter begins more directly.

If several questions must be asked, you have two choices. You can ask the most important question first, as shown in Figure 6.1. An alternate opening begins with a summary statement, such as *Will you please answer the following questions about providing meeting rooms and accommodations for 250 people from March 20 through March 24.* Notice that the summarizing statement sounds like a question but has no question mark. That is because it is really a command disguised as a question. Rather than bluntly demanding information *(Answer the following questions)*, we often prefer to soften commands by posing them as questions. Such statements,

Begin an information request letter with the most important question or a summarizing statement.

FIGURE 6.1 Letter That Requests Information

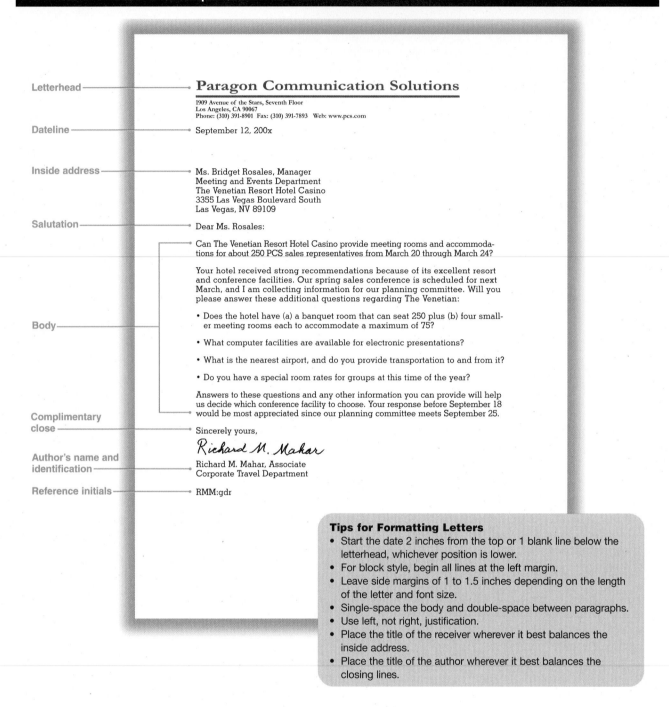

Letterhead

Paragon Communication Solutions

1909 Avenue of the Stars, Seventh Floor
Los Angeles, CA 90067
Phone: (310) 391-8901 Fax: (310) 391-7893 Web: www.pcs.com

Dateline

September 12, 200x

Inside address

Ms. Bridget Rosales, Manager
Meeting and Events Department
The Venetian Resort Hotel Casino
3355 Las Vegas Boulevard South
Las Vegas, NV 89109

Salutation

Dear Ms. Rosales:

Body

Can The Venetian Resort Hotel Casino provide meeting rooms and accommodations for about 250 PCS sales representatives from March 20 through March 24?

Your hotel received strong recommendations because of its excellent resort and conference facilities. Our spring sales conference is scheduled for next March, and I am collecting information for our planning committee. Will you please answer these additional questions regarding The Venetian:

• Does the hotel have (a) a banquet room that can seat 250 plus (b) four smaller meeting rooms each to accommodate a maximum of 75?

• What computer facilities are available for electronic presentations?

• What is the nearest airport, and do you provide transportation to and from it?

• Do you have a special room rates for groups at this time of the year?

Answers to these questions and any other information you can provide will help us decide which conference facility to choose. Your response before September 18 would be most appreciated since our planning committee meets September 25.

Complimentary close

Sincerely yours,

Richard M. Mahar

Author's name and identification

Richard M. Mahar, Associate
Corporate Travel Department

Reference initials

RMM:gdr

Tips for Formatting Letters
• Start the date 2 inches from the top or 1 blank line below the letterhead, whichever position is lower.
• For block style, begin all lines at the left margin.
• Leave side margins of 1 to 1.5 inches depending on the length of the letter and font size.
• Single-space the body and double-space between paragraphs.
• Use left, not right, justification.
• Place the title of the receiver wherever it best balances the inside address.
• Place the title of the author wherever it best balances the closing lines.

called rhetorical questions, should not be punctuated as questions because they do not require answers.

Put Details in the Body

The body of a request letter may contain an explanation or a list of questions.

The body of a letter that requests information should provide necessary details. Remember that the quality of the information obtained from a request letter depends on the clarity of the inquiry. If you analyze your needs, organize your ideas, and frame your request logically, you are likely to receive a meaningful answer that doesn't require a follow-up message. Whenever possible, itemize the information to improve readability. Notice that the questions in Figure 6.1 are bulleted, and they are parallel. That is, they use the same balanced construction.

Close With an Action Request

Use the final paragraph to ask for specific action, to set an end date if appropriate, and to express appreciation. As you learned in working with e-mail messages and memos, a request for action is most effective when an end date and reason for that date are supplied, as shown in Figure 6.1.

The ending of a request letter should tell the reader what you want done and when.

Ending a request letter with appreciation for the action taken is always appropriate. However, don't fall into a cliché trap, such as *Thanking you in advance, I remain . . .* or the familiar *Thank you for your cooperation.* Your appreciation will sound most sincere if you avoid mechanical, tired expressions.

Direct Claims

In business many things can go wrong—promised shipments are late, warranted goods fail, or service is disappointing. When you as a customer must write to identify or correct a wrong, the letter is called a *claim.* Straightforward claims are those to which you expect the receiver to agree readily. Even these claims, however, often require a letter. While your first action may be a telephone call or an e-mail message submitting your claim, you may not get the results you seek. Written claims are often taken more seriously, and they also establish a record of what happened. Claims that require persuasion are presented in Chapter 8. In this chapter you will learn to apply the following writing plan for a straightforward claim that uses a direct approach.

Claim letters register complaints and usually seek correction of a wrong.

Writing Plan for a Direct Claim

- **Opening:** Describe clearly the desired action.
- **Body:** Explain the nature of the claim, tell why the claim is justified, and provide details regarding the action requested.
- **Closing:** End pleasantly with a goodwill statement and include an end date and action request, if appropriate.

Open Your Claim With a Clear Statement of What You Want

If you have a legitimate claim, you can expect a positive response from a company. Smart businesses today want to hear from their customers. They know that retaining a customer is far less costly than recruiting a new customer. That is why you should open a claim letter with a clear statement of the problem or with the action you want the receiver to take. You might expect a replacement, a refund, a new order, credit to your account, correction of a billing error, free repairs, free inspection, or cancellation of an order.

The direct strategy is best for simple claims that require no persuasion.

When the remedy is obvious, state it immediately (*Please send us 24 Sanyo digital travel alarm clocks to replace the Sanyo analog travel alarm clocks sent in error with our order shipped January 8*). When the remedy is less obvious, you might ask for a change in policy or procedure or simply for an explanation (*Because three of our employees with confirmed reservations were refused rooms September 16 in your hotel, would you please clarify your policy regarding reservations and late arrivals*).

Explain and Justify Your Claim in the Body

In the body of a claim letter, explain the problem and justify your request. Provide the necessary details so that the difficulty can be corrected without further correspondence. Avoid becoming angry or trying to fix blame. Bear in mind that the person reading your letter is seldom responsible for the problem. Instead, state the facts logically, objectively, and unemotionally; let the reader decide on the causes.

Providing details without getting angry improves the effectiveness of a claim letter.

Include copies of all pertinent documents such as invoices, sales slips, catalog descriptions, and repair records. (By the way, be sure to send copies and *not* your originals, which could be lost.) When service is involved, cite names of individuals spoken to and dates of calls. Assume that a company honestly wants to satisfy its customers—because most do. When an alternative remedy exists, spell it out *(If you are unable to send 24 Sanyo digital travel alarm clocks immediately, please credit our account now and notify us when they become available).*

Close Your Claim With a Specific Action Request

Written claims submitted promptly are taken more seriously than delayed ones.

End a claim letter with a courteous statement that promotes goodwill and summarizes your action request. If appropriate, include an end date. *(We realize that mistakes in ordering and shipping sometimes occur. Because we have enjoyed your prompt service in the past, we hope that you will be able to send us the Sanyo digital travel alarm clocks by January 15.)* Finally, in making claims, act promptly. Delaying claims makes them appear less important. Delayed claims are also more difficult to verify. By taking the time to put your claim in writing, you indicate your seriousness. A written claim starts a record of the problem, should later action be necessary. Be sure to keep a copy of your letter.

Put It All Together and Revise

After completing your first draft, you are ready to revise as the last step in your writing plan. Figure 6.2 shows a first draft of a hostile claim that vents the writer's anger but accomplishes little else. Its tone is belligerent, and it assumes that the company intentionally mischarged the customer. Furthermore, it fails to tell the reader how to remedy the problem. The revision follows the three-step writing plan with a clear opening, body, and closing. Notice that the revision tempers the tone, describes the problem objectively, and provides facts and figures. Most important, it specifies exactly what the customer wants done. The letter in Figure 6.2 illustrates personal business style with the return address typed above the date. This style may be used when typing on paper without a printed letterhead.

Direct Replies

Before responding to requests, gather facts, check figures, and seek approval if necessary.

Often your messages will reply directly and favorably to requests for information or action. A customer wants information about a product. A supplier asks to arrange a meeting. Another business inquires about one of your procedures or about a former employee. In complying with such requests, you will want to apply the same direct pattern you used in making requests.

Writing Plan for Direct Replies

- **Subject line:** Identify previous correspondence or refer to the main idea.
- **Opening:** Deliver the most important information first.
- **Body:** Arrange information logically, explain and clarify it, provide additional information if appropriate, and build goodwill.
- **Closing:** End pleasantly.

Letters responding to requests may open with a subject line to identify the topic immediately.

A customer reply letter that starts with a subject line, as shown in Figure 6.3 on page 140, helps the reader recognize the topic immediately. Usually appearing one blank line below the salutation, the subject line refers in abbreviated form to previous correspondence and/or summarizes a message *(Subject: Your December 1 Letter Inquiring About Our Investigator 360 Program)*. It often omits articles *(a, an, the)*, is not a complete sentence, and does not end with a period. Knowledgeable business communicators use a subject line to refer to earlier correspondence so that in the first sentence, the most emphatic spot in a letter, they are free to emphasize the main idea.

FIGURE 6.2 Direct Claim Letter

Before

Dear Good Vibes:

You call yourself Good Vibes, but all I'm getting from your service is bad vibes! I'm furious that you have your salespeople slip in unwanted service warranties to boost your sales.

— Sounds angry; jumps to conclusions

When I bought my Panatronic DVR from Good Vibes, Inc., in August, I specifically told the salesperson that I did NOT want a three-year service warranty. But there it is on my Visa statement this month! You people have obviously billed me for a service I did not authorize. I refuse to pay this charge.

— Forgets that mistakes happen

How can you hope to stay in business with such fraudulent practices? I was expecting to return this month and look at HD TVs, but you can be sure I'll find an honest dealer this time.

— Fails to suggest a solution

Angrily,

After

Personal business letter style

325 Quail Ridge Road
Delray Beach, FL 33628
August 25, 200x

Ms. Ernestine Sanborn
Manager, Customer Satisfaction
Good Vibes, Inc.
2003 53rd Street
West Palm Beach, FL 33407

Dear Ms. Sanborn:

Please credit my Visa account to correct an erroneous charge of $299.

— States simply and clearly what to do

Explains objectively what went wrong

On August 1, 2009, I purchased a Panatronic DVR from Good Vibes, Inc. Although the salesperson discussed a three-year extended warranty with me, I decided against purchasing that service for $299. However, when my credit card statement arrived this month, I noticed an extra $299 charge from Good Vibes, Inc. I suspect that this charge represents the warranty I declined.

— Doesn't blame or accuse

Documents facts

Enclosed is a copy of my sales invoice along with my Visa statement on which I circled the charge.

Summarizes request and courteously suggests continued business once problem is resolved

Please authorize a credit immediately and send a copy of the transaction to me at the above address. I'm enjoying all the features of my Panatronic DVR and would like to be shopping at Good Vibes for an HD TV shortly.

Sincerely,

Christopher Kapper

Christopher A. Kapper

Enclosure

FIGURE 6.3 Direct Reply Letter

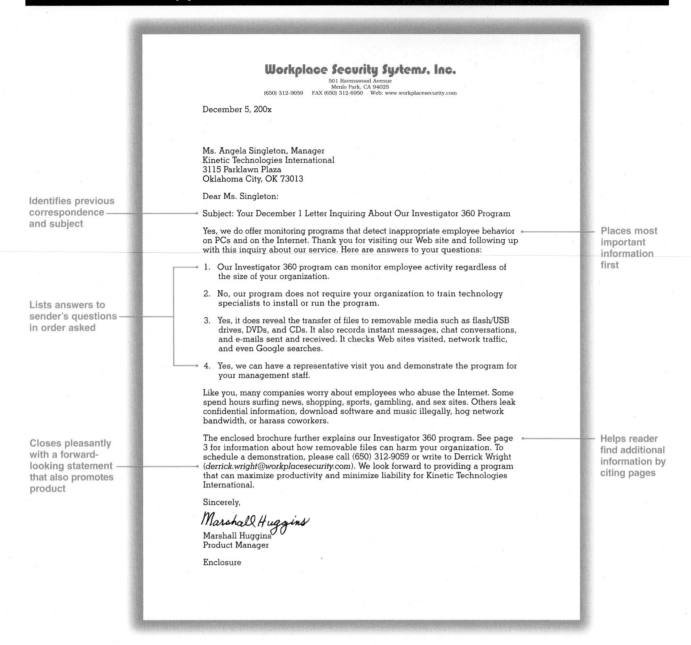

Identifies previous correspondence and subject

Lists answers to sender's questions in order asked

Closes pleasantly with a forward-looking statement that also promotes product

Places most important information first

Helps reader find additional information by citing pages

Workplace Security Systems, Inc.
501 Ravenswood Avenue
Menlo Park, CA 94025
(650) 312-9059   FAX (650) 312-6950   Web: www.workplacesecurity.com

December 5, 200x

Ms. Angela Singleton, Manager
Kinetic Technologies International
3115 Parklawn Plaza
Oklahoma City, OK 73013

Dear Ms. Singleton:

Subject: Your December 1 Letter Inquiring About Our Investigator 360 Program

Yes, we do offer monitoring programs that detect inappropriate employee behavior on PCs and on the Internet. Thank you for visiting our Web site and following up with this inquiry about our service. Here are answers to your questions:

1. Our Investigator 360 program can monitor employee activity regardless of the size of your organization.

2. No, our program does not require your organization to train technology specialists to install or run the program.

3. Yes, it does reveal the transfer of files to removable media such as flash/USB drives, DVDs, and CDs. It also records instant messages, chat conversations, and e-mails sent and received. It checks Web sites visited, network traffic, and even Google searches.

4. Yes, we can have a representative visit you and demonstrate the program for your management staff.

Like you, many companies worry about employees who abuse the Internet. Some spend hours surfing news, shopping, sports, gambling, and sex sites. Others leak confidential information, download software and music illegally, hog network bandwidth, or harass coworkers.

The enclosed brochure further explains our Investigator 360 program. See page 3 for information about how removable files can harm your organization. To schedule a demonstration, please call (650) 312-9059 or write to Derrick Wright (*derrick.wright@workplacesecurity.com*). We look forward to providing a program that can maximize productivity and minimize liability for Kinetic Technologies International.

Sincerely,

Marshall Huggins

Marshall Huggins
Product Manager

Enclosure

Announce the good news promptly.

Open Directly With Information the Reader Wants

In the first sentence of a direct reply letter, deliver the information the reader wants. Avoid wordy, drawn-out openings (*I have before me your letter of December 1, in which you request information about . . .*). More forceful and more efficient is an opener that answers the inquiry (*Here is the information you wanted about . . .*). When agreeing to a request for action, announce the good news promptly (*Yes, I will be happy to speak to your business communication class about . . .*).

Arrange Your Information Logically and Make It Readable

In the body of your reply, supply explanations and additional information. Because a letter written on company stationery is considered a legally binding contract, be sure to check facts and figures carefully. If a policy or procedure needs authorization, seek approval from a supervisor or executive before writing the letter.

When answering a group of questions or providing considerable data, arrange the information logically and make it readable by using lists, tables, headings, boldface, italics, or other graphic devices. When customers or prospective customers inquire about products or services, your response should do more than merely supply answers. Try to promote your organization and products. Often, companies have particular products and services they want to spotlight. Thus, when a customer writes about one product, provide helpful information that satisfies the inquiry, but consider using the opportunity to introduce another product as well. Be sure to present the promotional material with attention to the "you" view and to reader benefits *(You can use our standardized tests to free you from time-consuming employment screening)*. You will learn more about special techniques for developing marketing and persuasive messages in Chapter 8.

In concluding, make sure you are cordial and personal. Refer to the information provided or to its use. (*The enclosed list summarizes our recommendations. We wish you all the best in redesigning your Web site.*) If further action is required, describe the procedure and help the reader with specifics *(The Small Business Administration publishes a number of helpful booklets. Its Web address is . . .).*

Close Pleasantly and Personally

To avoid abruptness, include a pleasant closing remark that shows your willingness to help the reader. Provide extra information if appropriate. Tailor your remarks to fit this letter and this reader. Because everyone appreciates being recognized as an individual, avoid form-letter closings such as *If we may be of further assistance, ...*

Adjustment Letters

Even the best-run and best-loved businesses occasionally receive claims or complaints from consumers. When a company receives a claim and decides to respond favorably, the letter is called an *adjustment* letter. In these messages, you have three goals:

- To rectify the wrong, if one exists
- To regain the confidence of the customer
- To promote future business and goodwill

A positive adjustment letter represents good news to the reader. Therefore, use the direct strategy described in the following writing plan:

Writing Plan for Adjustment Letters

- **Subject line:** (optional) Identify the previous correspondence and refer to the main topic.
- **Opening:** Grant the request or announce the adjustment immediately.
- **Body:** Provide details about how you are complying with the request. Try to regain the customer's confidence. Apologize if appropriate, but don't admit negligence.
- **Closing:** End positively with a forward-looking thought; express confidence in future business relations. Include sales promotion, if appropriate. Avoid referring to unpleasantness.

HOW TO WIN AN ARGUMENT WITH A CUSTOMER:

YOU'RE RIGHT.

Reveal the Good News in the Opening

Readers want to learn the good news immediately.

Instead of beginning with a review of what went wrong, present the good news immediately. When Kimberly Patel responded to the claim of customer Yonkers Digital & Wireless about a missing shipment, her first draft, shown at the top of Figure 6.4, was angry. No wonder. Yonkers Digital apparently had provided the wrong shipping address, and the goods were returned. But once Kimberly and her company decided to send a second shipment and comply with the customer's claim, she had to give up the anger and strive to retain the goodwill and the business of this customer. The improved version of her letter announces that a new shipment will arrive shortly.

If you decide to comply with a customer's claim, let the receiver know immediately. Don't begin your letter with a negative statement (*We are very sorry to hear that you are having trouble with your dishwasher*). This approach reminds the reader of the problem and may rekindle the heated emotions or unhappy feelings experienced when the claim was written. Instead, focus on the good news. The following openings for various letters illustrate how to begin a message with good news.

> You're right! We agree that the warranty on your American Standard Model UC600 dishwasher should be extended for six months.

> You will be receiving shortly a new slim Nokia cell phone to replace the one that shattered when dropped recently.

> Please take your portable Admiral microwave oven to A-1 Appliance Service, 200 Orange Street, Pasadena, where it will be repaired at no cost to you.

> The enclosed check for $325 demonstrates our desire to satisfy our customers and earn their confidence.

Be enthusiastic, not grudging, when granting a claim.

In announcing that you will make an adjustment, try to do so without a grudging tone—even if you have reservations about whether the claim is legitimate. Once you decide to comply with the customer's request, do so happily. Avoid halfhearted or reluctant responses (*Although the American Standard dishwasher works well when used properly, we have decided to allow you to take yours to A-1 Appliance Service for repair at our expense*).

Explain How You Are Complying in the Body

In responding to claims, most organizations sincerely want to correct a wrong. They want to do more than just make the customer happy. They want to stand behind their products and services; they want to do what's right.

FIGURE 6.4 Customer Adjustment Letter

Before

Dear Sir:

I have before me your recent complaint about a missing shipment. First, let me say that it's very difficult to deliver merchandise when we have been given the wrong address.

After receiving your complaint, our investigators looked into your problem shipment and determined that it was sent immediately after we received the order. According to the shipper's records, it was delivered to the warehouse address given on your stationery: 451 Main Street, Yonkers, NY 10708. Unfortunately, no one at that address would accept delivery, so the shipment was returned to us. I see from your current stationery that your company has a new address. With the proper address, we probably could have delivered this shipment.

Although we feel that it is entirely appropriate to charge you shipping and restocking fees, as is our standard practice on returned goods, in this instance we will waive those fees. We hope this second shipment finally catches up with you at your current address.

Sincerely,

Fails to reveal good news immediately and blames customer

Creates ugly tone with negative words and sarcasm

Sounds grudging and reluctant in granting claim

After

DD

DIGITAL DEPOT
1405 Chambersburg Road
Trenton, NJ 08619-3590

Phone: (619) 839-2202
Fax: (619) 839-3320
Web: www.ddepot.com

April 24, 200x

Mr. Christopher Durante
Yonkers Digital & Wireless
359 South Broadway Avenue
Yonkers, NY 10705

Dear Mr. Durante:

Subject: Your April 19 Letter About Your Purchase Order

You should receive by April 26 a second shipment of the speakers, VCRs, headphones, and other digital equipment that you ordered April 2.

The first shipment of this order was delivered April 10 to 451 Main Street, Yonkers, NY. When no one at that address would accept the shipment, it was returned to us. Now that I have your letter, I see that the order should have been sent to 359 South Broadway Avenue, Yonkers, NY 10705. When an order is undeliverable, we usually try to verify the shipping address by telephoning the customer. Somehow the return of this shipment was not caught by our normally painstaking shipping clerks. You can be sure that I will investigate shipping and return procedures with our clerks immediately to see if we can improve existing methods.

Your respect is important to us, Mr. Durante. Although our rock-bottom discount prices have enabled us to build a volume business, we don't want to be so large that we lose touch with valued customers like you. Over the years our customers' respect has made us successful, and we hope that the prompt delivery of this shipment will retain yours.

Sincerely,

Kimberly Patel

Kimberly Patel
Distribution Manager

c Emanuel Chavez
  Shipping Department

Uses customer's name in salutation

Announces good news immediately

Regains confidence of customer by explaining what happened and by suggesting plans for improvement

Closes confidently with genuine appeal for customer's respect

In the body of the letter, explain how you are complying with the claim. In all but the most routine claims, you should also seek to regain the confidence of the customer. You might reasonably expect that a customer who has experienced difficulty with a product, with delivery, with billing, or with service has lost faith in your organization. Rebuilding that faith is important for future business.

How to rebuild lost confidence depends on the situation and the claim. If procedures need to be revised, explain what changes will be made. If a product has defective parts, tell how the product is being improved. If service is faulty, describe genuine efforts to improve it. Notice in Figure 6.4 on page 143 that the writer promises to investigate shipping procedures to see whether improvements might prevent future mishaps.

Sometimes the problem is not with the product but with the way it is being used. In other instances customers misunderstand warranties or inadvertently cause delivery and billing mix-ups by supplying incorrect information. Remember that rational and sincere explanations will do much to regain the confidence of unhappy customers.

In your explanation avoid emphasizing negative words such as *trouble, regret, misunderstanding, fault, defective, error, inconvenience,* and *unfortunately.* Keep your message positive and upbeat.

Decide Whether to Apologize

Whether to apologize is a debatable issue. Some writing experts argue that apologies remind customers of their complaints and are therefore negative. These writers avoid apologies; instead they concentrate on how they are satisfying the customer. Real letters that respond to customers' claims, however, often include apologies.[2] If you feel that your company is at fault and that an apology is an appropriate goodwill gesture, by all means include it. Be careful, though, not to admit negligence.

Show Confidence and Helpfulness in the Closing

End positively by expressing confidence that the problem has been resolved and that continued business relations will result. You might mention the product in a favorable light, suggest a new product, express your appreciation for the customer's business, or anticipate future business. It is often appropriate to refer to the desire to be of service and to satisfy customers. Notice how the following closings illustrate a positive, confident tone.

> You were most helpful in informing us of this situation and permitting us to correct it. We appreciate your thoughtfulness in writing to us.

> Thanks for writing. Your satisfaction is important to us. We hope that this refund check convinces you that service to our customers is our No. 1 priority. Our goals are to earn your confidence and continue to merit that confidence with quality products and excellent service.

CATHY

Your Inspiron 1420 HD widescreen laptop will come in handy whether you are working at home or on the road. What's more, if you desire an even bigger screen, you can upgrade to a 17-inch widescreen notebook for only $150. Take a look at the enclosed booklet detailing the big savings for essential technology on a budget. We value your business and look forward to your future orders.

Although the direct pattern works for many requests and replies, it obviously won't work for every situation. With more practice and experience, you will be able to alter the pattern and adapt your skills to other communication problems.

Goodwill Messages

Goodwill messages, which include thanks, recognition, and sympathy, seem to intimidate many communicators. Finding the right words to express feelings is sometimes more difficult than writing ordinary business documents. Writers tend to procrastinate when it comes to goodwill messages, or else they send a ready-made card or pick up the telephone. Remember, though, that the personal sentiments of the sender are always more expressive and more meaningful to readers than are printed cards or oral messages. Taking the time to write gives more importance to our well-wishing. Personal notes also provide a record that can be reread, savored, and treasured.

In expressing thanks, recognition, or sympathy, you should always do so promptly. These messages are easier to write when the situation is fresh in your mind, and they mean more to the recipient. Don't forget that a prompt thank-you note carries the hidden message that you care and that you consider the event to be important. You will learn to write various goodwill messages that deliver thanks, congratulations, praise, and sympathy. Instead of learning writing plans for each of them, we recommend that you concentrate on the five Ss. Goodwill messages should be:

Messages that express thanks, recognition, and sympathy should be written promptly.

- **Selfless.** Be sure to focus the message solely on the receiver not the sender. Don't talk about yourself; avoid such comments as *I remember when I . . . .*
- **Specific.** Personalize the message by mentioning specific incidents or characteristics of the receiver. Telling a colleague *Great speech* is much less effective than *Great story about McDonald's marketing in Moscow.* Take care to verify names and other facts.
- **Sincere.** Let your words show genuine feelings. Rehearse in your mind how you would express the message to the receiver orally. Then transform that conversational language to your written message. Avoid pretentious, formal, or flowery language *(It gives me great pleasure to extend felicitations on the occasion of your firm's twentieth anniversary).*
- **Spontaneous.** Keep the message fresh and enthusiastic. Avoid canned phrases *(Congratulations on your promotion, Good luck in the future).* Strive for directness and naturalness, not creative brilliance.
- **Short.** Although goodwill messages can be as long as needed, try to accomplish your purpose in only a few sentences. What is most important is remembering an individual. Such caring does not require documentation or wordiness. Individuals and business organizations often use special note cards or stationery for brief messages.

Goodwill messages are most effective when they are selfless, specific, sincere, spontaneous, and short.

Expressing Thanks

When someone has done you a favor or when an action merits praise, you need to extend thanks or show appreciation. Letters of appreciation may be written to customers for their orders, to hosts and hostesses for their hospitality, to individuals for kindnesses performed, and especially to customers who complain. After all, complainers are actually providing you with "free consulting reports from the field." Complainers who feel that they were listened to often become the greatest promoters of an organization.

Because the receiver will be pleased to hear from you, you can open directly with the purpose of your message. The letter in Figure 6.5 thanks a speaker who

Send letters of thanks to customers, hosts, and individuals who have performed kind acts.

FIGURE 6.5 Thank-You Letter for a Favor

1 Prewriting

Analyze: The purpose of this letter is to express appreciation to a business executive for presenting a talk before professionals.

Anticipate: The reader will be more interested in personalized comments than in general statements showing gratitude.

Adapt: Because the reader will be pleased, use the direct pattern.

2 Writing

Research: Consult notes taken during the talk.

Organize: Open directly by giving the reason for writing. Express enthusiastic and sincere thanks. In the body provide specifics. Refer to facts and highlights in the talk. Supply sufficient detail to support your sincere compliments. Conclude with appreciation. Be warm and friendly.

Compose: Write the first draft.

3 Revising

Revise: Revise for tone and warmth. Use the reader's name. Include concrete detail but do it concisely. Avoid sounding gushy or phony.

Proofread: Check the spelling of the receiver's name; verify facts. Check the spelling of *persistence*, *patience*, and *advice*.

Evaluate: Does this letter convey sincere thanks?

International Marketing Association

225 West 17th Street
New York, New York 10029
http://www.ima.com

February 26, 200x

Mr. Michael T. Reese
Marketing Manager
Toys "R" Us, Inc.
One Geoffrey Way
Wayne, NJ 07470-2030

Dear Michael:

Thank you for providing the Manhattan chapter of the IMA with one of the best presentations our group has ever heard.

Tells purpose and delivers praise

Your description of the battle Toys "R" Us waged to begin marketing products in Japan was a genuine eye-opener for many of us. Nine years of preparation establishing connections and securing permissions seems an eternity, but obviously such persistence and patience pay off. We now understand better the need to learn local customs and nurture relationships when dealing in Japan or other Asian countries.

Personalizes the message by using specifics rather than generalities

In addition to your good advice, we particularly enjoyed your sense of humor and jokes—as you must have recognized from the uproarious laughter. What a great routine you do on faulty translations!

Spotlights the reader's talents

We're grateful, Michael, for the entertaining and instructive evening you provided our marketing professionals.

Concludes with compliments and thanks

Cordially,

Rosetta H. Johnson

Rosetta H. Johnson
Program Chair, IMA

RHJ:mef

---

addressed a group of marketing professionals. Although such thank-you notes can be quite short, this one is a little longer because the writer wants to lend importance to the receiver's efforts. Notice that every sentence relates to the receiver and offers enthusiastic praise. By using the receiver's name along with contractions and positive words, the writer makes the letter sound warm and conversational.

Written notes that show appreciation and express thanks are significant to their receivers. In expressing thanks, you generally write a short note on special notepaper or heavy card stock. The following messages provide models for expressing thanks for a gift, for a favor, and for hospitality.

To Express Thanks for a Gift

Thanks, Laura, to you and the other members of the department for honoring me with the elegant Waterford crystal vase at the party celebrating my twentieth anniversary with the company.

The height and shape of the vase are perfect to hold roses and other bouquets from my garden. Each time I fill it, I will remember your thoughtfulness in choosing this lovely gift for me.

Identify the gift, tell why you appreciate it, and explain how you will use it.

To Send Thanks for a Favor

I sincerely appreciate your filling in for me last week when I was too ill to attend the planning committee meeting for the spring exhibition.

Without your participation much of my preparatory work would have been lost. It's comforting to know that competent and generous individuals like you are part of our team, Mark. Moreover, it's my very good fortune to be able to count you as a friend. I'm grateful to you.

Tell what the favor means using sincere, simple statements.

To Extend Thanks for Hospitality

Matt and I want you to know how much we enjoyed the dinner party for our department that you hosted Saturday evening. Your charming home and warm hospitality, along with the lovely dinner and sinfully delicious chocolate dessert, combined to create a truly memorable evening.

Most of all, though, we appreciate your kindness in cultivating togetherness in our department. Thanks, Lisa, for being such a special person.

Compliment the fine food, charming surroundings, warm hospitality, excellent host and hostess, and good company.

Responding to Goodwill Messages

Should you respond when you receive a congratulatory note or a written pat on the back? By all means! These messages are attempts to connect personally; they are efforts to reach out, to form professional and/or personal bonds. Failing to respond to notes of congratulations and most other goodwill messages is like failing to say "You're welcome" when someone says "Thank you." Responding to such messages is simply the right thing to do. Do avoid, though, minimizing your achievements with comments that suggest you don't really deserve the praise or that the sender is exaggerating your good qualities.

Take the time to respond to any goodwill message you may receive.

To Answer a Congratulatory Note

Thanks for your kind words regarding my award, and thanks, too, for sending me the newspaper clipping. I truly appreciate your thoughtfulness and warm wishes.

To Respond to a Pat on the Back

Your note about my work made me feel good. I'm grateful for your thoughtfulness.

Conveying Sympathy

Most of us can bear misfortune and grief more easily when we know that others care. Notes expressing sympathy, though, are probably more difficult to write than any other kind of message. Commercial "In sympathy" cards make the task easier—but they are far less meaningful. Grieving friends want to know what you think—not what

Sympathy notes should refer to the misfortune sensitively and offer assistance.

Hallmark's card writers think. To help you get started, you can always glance through cards expressing sympathy. They will supply ideas about the kinds of thoughts you might wish to convey in your own words. In writing a sympathy note, (a) refer to the death or misfortune sensitively, using words that show you understand what a crushing blow it is; (b) in the case of a death, praise the deceased in a personal way; (c) offer assistance without going into excessive detail; and (d) end on a reassuring, forward-looking note.

To Express Condolences

We are deeply saddened, Gayle, to learn of the death of your husband. Warren's kind nature and friendly spirit endeared him to all who knew him. He will be missed.

Although words seem empty in expressing our grief, we want you to know that your friends at QuadCom extend their profound sympathy to you. If we may help you or lighten your load in any way, you have but to call.

We know that the treasured memories of your many happy years together, along with the support of your family and many friends, will provide strength and comfort in the months ahead.

> **In condolence notes mention the loss tactfully and recognize the good qualities of the deceased.**

> **Conclude on a positive, reassuring note.**

Is E-Mail Appropriate for Goodwill Messages?

In expressing thanks or responding to goodwill messages, handwritten notes are most impressive. However, if you frequently communicate with the receiver by e-mail and if you are sure your note will not get lost, then sending an e-mail goodwill message is acceptable, according to the Emily Post Institute.[3] To express sympathy immediately after learning of a death or accident, you might precede a phone call or a written condolence message with an e-mail. E-mail is a fast and nonintrusive way to show your feelings. But, advises the Emily Post Institute, immediately follow with a handwritten note. Remember that e-mail messages are quickly gone and forgotten. Handwritten or printed messages remain and can be savored. Your thoughtfulness is more lasting if you take the time to prepare a handwritten or printed message on notepaper or personal stationery.

Visit www.meguffey.com

- **Chapter Review Quiz**
- **Flash Cards**
- **Grammar Practice**
- **PowerPoint Slides**
- **Personal Language Trainer**
- **Beat the Clock Quiz**

Summing Up and Looking Forward

Although e-mail is becoming an important communication channel for brief messages, business letters are still important. They are necessary for messages that must produce a permanent record, are confidential, convey formality and sensitivity, and deliver persuasive ideas. In this chapter you learned to write direct letters that request information or action. You also learned to write direct claims, direct replies, adjustment letters, and a variety of goodwill messages. All of these routine letters use the direct strategy. They open immediately with the main idea followed by details and explanations. But not all letters will carry good news. Occasionally, you must deny requests and deliver bad news. In the next chapter you will learn to use the indirect strategy in conveying negative news.

Critical Thinking

1. An article in a professional magazine carried this headline: "Is Letter Writing Dead?"[4] How would you respond to such a question?

2. In promoting the value of letter writing, a well-known columnist recently wrote, "To trust confidential information to e-mail is to be a rube."[5] What did he mean? Do you agree?

3. Which is more effective in claim letters—anger or objectivity? Why?

4. Why is it important to regain the confidence of a customer when you respond to a claim letter?

5. **Ethical Issue:** Should companies automatically grant adjustments? For example, some customers buy a video camera or a dress for a special event and return the product afterward. What safeguards could be implemented?

Chapter Review

6. Under what circumstances is it better for a businessperson to send a letter than to use another communication channel?

7. When should you *not* write a business letter?

8. What determines whether you write a letter directly or indirectly?

9. What are the two most important positions in a letter?

10. List two ways that you could begin an inquiry letter that asks many questions.

11. What three elements are appropriate in the closing of a request for information?

12. What is a claim letter? Give an original example of a situation that might require a claim letter.

13. What is an adjustment letter, and what three goals does it have?

14. The best goodwill messages include what five characteristics?

15. When is it appropriate to use e-mail to deliver goodwill messages?

Letter Openers

Your Task. Indicate which of the following entries represents an effective direct opening.

16. a. Please allow me to introduce myself. I am Marquis Jones, and I am assistant to the director of Employee Relations at United Anesthesia Associates. We place nurse anesthetists in hospitals. Each year we try to recognize outstanding staff members during Customer Service Week. I understand you provide an Idea Guide and that you sell special recognition gifts. I have a number of questions about them.

    b. Please answer the following questions about ideas and gifts to recognize outstanding staff members during our Customer Service Week.

17. a. We have on hand an ample supply of HON 500 Series lateral file cabinets.

    b. Thank you for your e-mail of June 13 in which you inquired about the availability of HON 500 Series lateral file cabinets.

18. a. Yes, we do offer "Get Away Today" discount vacations at Disneyland Resorts.

    b. This will acknowledge receipt of your May 15 inquiry in which you ask about our Disneyland Resort "Get Away Today" package with discount vacations.

19. a. Your letter of August 2 requesting a refund has been referred to me because Mr. Solano is away from the office. I am happy to respond to your inquiry requesting a refund of $175.

    b. Your refund check for $175 is enclosed.

20. a. We sincerely appreciate your recent order for Alpine Touring skis. Here at US Gear Shop, you will always find a wide range of skis, snowboards, and surfing equipment.

    b. The Alpine Touring skis you ordered were shipped today by Mountain Express and should reach you by October 12.

Direct Openings

Your Task. Revise the following openings so that they are more direct. Add information if necessary.

21. Hello! My name is Leeanne Gosbee, and I just saw the terrific Web site for your organization, Green Living Spaces, which I understand is one of the world's leading health and wellness companies. I have a number of questions about selling your products and earning commissions. At your Web site I learned about the possibility of gaining affiliate status, which I am definitely interested in, but I still have many questions not answered at your site.

22. Pursuant to your letter of November 19, I am writing in regard to your inquiry about whether we offer our Mediterranean-style patio umbrella in colors. This unique umbrella is a very popular item and receives a number of inquiries. Its 10-foot canopy protects you when the sun is directly overhead, but it also swivels and tilts to virtually any angle for continuous sun protection all day long. It comes in two colors: off-white and forest green.

23. Thank you for your letter inquiring about the possibility of my acting as a speaker at the final semester meeting of your business administration club on May 6. The topic of digital résumés and portfolios interests me and is one on which I think I could impart helpful information to your members. Therefore, I am responding in the affirmative to your kind invitation.

24. We have just received your letter of January 29 regarding the unfortunate troubles you are having with your Pilgrim DVD player. In your letter you ask whether you may send the flawed DVD player to us for inspection. Although we normally handle all service requests through our local dealers, in your circumstance we are willing to take a look at your unit here at our Atlanta plant. Therefore, please send it to us so that we may determine what's wrong.

25. Your message of June 18 has been given to me to answer. We regret that you were inconvenienced by receiving an incorrect invoice. We have used NetPost to transmit Visa invoices for eight years, and this is the first time that invoices were sent to the wrong recipients. We take what happened very seriously, and we are changing our procedures to avoid similar errors in the future. We can assure you that the revised invoice you will receive in two days is now correct. You may use your account again.

Closing Paragraph

Your Task. The following concluding paragraph to a claim letter response suffers from faults in strategy, tone, and emphasis. Revise and improve.

26. Although we do not feel that we are to blame for the delay in delivery of the hardwood floors about which you complained, we are willing to give you a 10 percent discount on the total cost of this shipment. This should offset your pain caused by the delay of 10 weeks due to the container cargo disruption of all imported goods from China. Your hardwood floors won't arrive for one more week, and once again, we apologize for the delay. Thank you for your business.

Writing Improvement Cases

6.1 Information Request: Workplace Security
The following letter requests information; however, the first draft suffers from many writing faults.

Your Task. Analyze the message. List its weaknesses and then outline an appropriate writing plan. If your instructor directs, revise the message. A copy of this message is provided at **www.meguffey.com** for revision online.

Current date

Mr. Kyle Gregory, Sales Manager
Micro Supplies and Software
830 North Meridian Street
Indianapolis, IN 46205

Dear Sir:

Our insurance rates will be increased in the near future due to the fact that we don't have security devices on our computer equipment. Local suppliers were considered, but at this point in time none had exactly what we wanted. That's why I am writing to see whether or not you can provide information and recommendations regarding equipment to prevent the possible theft of office computers and printers. In view of the fact that our insurance carrier has set a deadline of April 1, we need fast action.

Our office now has 18 computer workstations along with twelve printers. We need a device that can be used to secure separate computer components to desks or counters. Would you please recommend a device that can secure a workstation consisting of a computer, monitor, and keyboard. We wonder if professionals are needed to install your security devices and to remove them. We are a small company, and we don't have a staff of maintenance people.

One problem is whether the devices can be easily removed when we need to move equipment around. We are, of course, very interested in the price of each device. What about quantity discounts, if you offer them.

Until such time as we hear from you, thank you in advance for your attention to this matter.

Sincerely,

1. List at least five weaknesses of this letter.

2. Outline a writing plan for a direct request.
   Opening:
   Body:
   Closing:

6.2 Claim Request: Rental Car Gas Complaint

The following letter conveys a complaint and makes a claim. However, its poor tone and expression may prevent the receiver from getting what he wants.

Your Task. Analyze the message. List its weaknesses and then outline an appropriate writing plan. If your instructor directs, revise the message. A copy of this message is provided at **www.meguffey.com** for revision online.

Current date

Mr. Orion Murillo, Manager
Customer Response Center
Western Car Rentals
2259 Weatherford Boulevard
Dallas, TX 74091

Dear Manager Orion Murillo:

With the exorbitant cost of gasoline today, I am totally frustrated at my experience with Western Car Rentals! I'm ticked off because you can't seem to decide what to do about fill-ups. Either you provide customers with cars with full gas tanks or you don't. And if you don't, you shouldn't charge them when they return with empty tanks!

In view of the fact that I picked up a car at the Dallas-Ft. Worth International Airport on June 23 with an empty tank, I had to fill it immediately. Then I drove it until June 26. When I returned the car to Houston, as previously planned, I naturally let the tank go nearly empty, since that is the way I received the car in Dallas-Ft. Worth.

But your attendant in Houston charged me to fill the tank—$69.43 (premium gasoline at premium prices)! Although I explained to her that I had received it with an empty tank, she kept telling me that company policy required that she charge for a fill-up. My total bill came to $446.50, which, you must agree, is a lot of money for a rental period of only three days. I have the signed rental agreement and a receipt showing that I paid the full amount and that it included $69.43 for a gas fill-up when I returned the car. Those are the true facts! Any correspondence should be directed to the undersigned at Impact Group, 402 North Griffin Street, Dallas, TX 74105.

Inasmuch as my company is a new customer and inasmuch as we had hoped to use your agency for our future car rentals because of your competitive rates, I trust that you will give this matter your prompt attention.

Your unhappy customer,

1. List at least five weaknesses of this letter.

2. Outline a writing plan for a claim request.
   Opening:
   Body:
   Closing:

6.3 Adjustment Letter: Sagging Canvas Needs Restretching

When a company received an expensive office painting with sags in the canvas, it complained. The seller, Manhattan Galleries, responded with the following adjustment letter. How can it be improved?

Your Task. Analyze the message. List its weaknesses and then outline an appropriate writing plan. If your instructor directs, revise the message. A copy of this message is provided at **www.meguffey.com** for revision online.

Current date

Ms. Sharon Nickels
2459 Drew Street
Clearwater, FL 33765

Dear Ms. Nickels:

Your letter has been referred to me for reply. You claim that the painting recently sent by Manhattan Galleries arrived with sags in the canvas and that you are unwilling to hang it in your company's executive offices.

I have examined your complaint carefully, and, frankly, I find it difficult to believe because we are so careful about shipping, but if what you say is true, I suspect that the shipper may be the source of your problem. We give explicit instructions to our shippers that large paintings must be shipped standing up, not lying down. We also wrap every painting in two layers of convoluted foam and one layer of Perf-Pack foam, which we think should be sufficient to withstand any bumps and scrapes that negligent shipping may cause. We will certainly look into this.

Although it is against our policy, we will in this instance allow you to take this painting to a local framing shop for restretching. We are proud that we can offer fine works of original art at incredibly low prices, and you can be sure that we do not send out sagging canvases.

Sincerely,

1. List at least five weaknesses of this adjustment letter.

Activities and Cases

6.4 Information Request: Raising Puppies to Become Guide Dogs

As an assistant in the Community Involvement Program of your corporation, you have been given an unusual task. Your boss wants to expand the company's philanthropic and community relations mission and especially employee volunteerism. She heard about The Seeing Eye, a program in which volunteers raise puppies for 14 to 18 months for guide dog training. She thinks this would be an excellent outreach program for the company's employees. They could give back to the community in their role as puppy raisers. To pursue the idea, she asks you to request information about the program and ask questions about whether a company could sponsor a program encouraging employees to act as volunteers. She hasn't thought it through very carefully and relies on you to raise logical questions, especially about costs for volunteers.

Your Task. Write an information request to Susanna Odell, The Seeing Eye, 9002 East Chaparral Road, Scottsdale, AZ 85250. Include an end date and a reason.

6.5 Information Request: Brewing Coffee Shop Beverages in the Office

Workers in your office are big coffee drinkers. Some leave work to go to a nearby Starbucks, and others use instant coffee to brew their own. As manager, you realize that productivity and morale could be improved if your office supplied "coffee shop quality" in freshly brewed coffee. You saw a Maxima beverage system at another company, and you decide to look into purchasing such a system for your office. You have a number of questions about such a system.

The biggest problem is plumbing. If it requires plumbing, you can't use it. You do have cold water available, but not plumbing. You wonder whether a Maxima Brewing System offers drinks other than coffee, such as hot chocolate and tea. Because you are a cappuccino fan, you want to know whether it makes authentic milk foam. Naturally, you are concerned about cleaning, maintenance, supplies, and repairs. You also worry about how employees will pay for each cup of coffee or other beverage. Perhaps coin operation is available. A No. 1 concern, of course, is how much the system would cost and what kind of warranty is offered.

Your Task. Write a well-organized information request to Ms. Ann Pagnotta, Sales Manager, Maxima Brewing Systems, 1849 Alum Creek Drive, Columbus, OH 43207. Inquire about a Maxima Brewing System for your 25-person office staff. You need the information within two weeks for the next management council meeting.

6.6 Information Request: Meeting at Caesars Palace, Las Vegas

Your company, Software.com, wants to hold its next company-wide meeting in a resort location. The CEO has asked you, as marketing manager, to find a conference location for your 85 engineers, product managers, and marketing staff. He wants the company to host a four-day combination sales conference/vacation/retreat at some spectacular spot. He suggests that you start by inquiring at the amazing Caesars Palace Las Vegas. You check its Web site and discover interesting information. However, you decide to write a letter so that you can have a permanent, formal record of all the resorts you investigate.

You estimate that your company will require about 80 rooms. You will also need three conference rooms (to accommodate 25 or more) for one and a half days. You want to know room rates, conference facilities, and entertainment options for families. You have two periods that would be possible: April 20–24 or July 10–14. You know that one of these is at an off-peak time, and you wonder whether you can get a good room rate. You are interested in entertainment at Caesars during these times. One evening the CEO will want to host a banquet for about 125 people. The CEO wants a report from you by December 3.

Your Task. Write a well-organized information request to Ms. Isabella Cervantes, Manager, Convention Services, Caesars Palace, 257 Palace Drive, Las Vegas, NV 87551. You might like to take a look at the Caesars Web site at **http://www.caesars .com/palace.**

6.7 Direct Claim: "No Surprise" Policy

As marketing manager of Rochester Preferred Travel, you are upset with Premier Promos. Premier is a catalog company that provides imprinted promotional products for companies. Your travel company was looking for something special to offer in promoting its cruise ship travel packages. Premier offered free samples of its promotional merchandise under its "No Surprise" policy.

You figured, what could you lose? So on January 11 you placed a telephone order for a number of samples. These included three kinds of jumbo tote bags and a square-ended barrel bag with fanny pack, as well as a deluxe canvas attaché case and two colors of garment-dyed sweatshirts. All items were supposed to be free. You did think it odd that you were asked for your company's Master Card number, but Premier promised to bill you only if you kept the samples.

When the items arrived, you weren't pleased, and you returned them all on January 21 (you have a postal receipt showing the return). But your February credit statement showed a charge of $239.58 for the sample items. You called Premier in February and spoke to Diane, who assured you that a credit would be made on your next statement. However, your March statement showed no credit. You called again and received a similar promise. It is now April and no credit has been made. You decide to write and demand action.

Your Task. Write a claim letter that documents the problem and states the action you want taken. Add any information you feel is necessary. Address your letter to Mr. Kevin Chitwood, Customer Services, Premier Promos, 2445 Bermiss Road, Valdosta, GA 31602.

6.8 Direct Claim: Short Door for Tall Player

As the owner of Contempo Interiors, you recently worked on the custom Indiana home of an NBA basketball player. He requested an oversized 12-foot mahogany entry door. You ordered by telephone the solid mahogany door ("Provence") from American Custom Wood on May 17. When it arrived on June 28, your carpenter gave you the bad news. Magnificent as it was, the huge door was cut too small. Instead of measuring a total of 12 feet 2 inches, the door measured 11 feet 10 inches. In your carpenter's words, "No way can I stretch that door to fit this opening!" You waited four weeks for this hand-crafted custom door, and your client wanted it installed immediately. Your carpenter said, "I can rebuild this opening for you, but I'm going to have to charge you for my time." His extra charge came to $940.50.

You feel that the people at American Custom Wood should reimburse you for this amount since it was their error. In fact, you actually saved them a bundle of money by not returning the door. You decide to write to American Custom Wood and enclose a copy of your carpenter's bill. You wonder whether you should also include a copy of the invoice, even though it does not show the exact door measurements. You are a good customer of American Custom Wood, having used its quality doors and windows on many other jobs. You are confident that it will grant this claim.

Your Task. Write a claim letter to Michael Medina, Operations Manager, American Custom Wood, 140 NE 136 Avenue, Vancouver, WA 98654.

6.9 Direct Claim: The Real Thing

Have you ever bought a product that didn't work as promised? Have you been disappointed in service at a bank, video store, restaurant, department store, or discount house? Have you had ideas about how a company or organization could improve its image, service, or product? Remember that smart companies want to know what their customers think, especially if a product could be improved.

Your Task. Select a product or service that has disappointed you. Write a claim letter requesting a refund, replacement, explanation, or whatever seems reasonable. For claims about food products, be sure to include bar-code identification from the package, if possible. Your instructor may ask you to actually mail this letter. When you receive a response, share it with your class.

6.10 Direct Claim: Can't Attend Management Seminar

Ace Executive Training Institute offered a seminar titled "Enterprise Project Management Protocol" that sounded terrific. It promised to teach project managers how to estimate work, report status, write work packages, and cope with project conflicts. Because your company often is engaged in large cross-functional projects, it decided to send four key managers to the seminar to be held June 1–2 at the Ace headquarters in Pittsburgh. The fee was $2,200 each, and it was paid in advance. About six weeks before the seminar, you learned that three of the managers would be tied up in projects that would not be completed in time for them to attend.

Your Task. On your company letterhead, write a claim letter to Addison O'Neill, Registrar, Ace Executive Training Institute, 5000 Forbes Avenue, Pittsburgh, PA 15244. Ask that the seminar fees for three employees be returned because they cannot attend. Give yourself a title and supply any details necessary.

6.11 Direct Claim: Neglected Landscape

As project manager at Liberty Property Management, you are in charge of landscaping maintenance for many clients including Sycamore Business Park. Recently two tenants called to complain that their lawns had not been cut for two weeks and that weeds were growing in the parking lot. You drove out to see for yourself, and sure enough, Sycamore was looking a bit bedraggled. You also noticed that fallen tree branches from a recent windstorm were lying on the ground. Back in the office, you checked the files and saw that Stephen's Landscaping Service had been hired to mow lawns and service the grounds at Sycamore. You checked further and saw that the original contract called for a fee of $350 per month. However, the latest bill paid was $410. You can't understand why the price was increased without your knowledge. After leaving several telephone messages at Stephen's Landscaping and receiving no response, you know you must write a letter.

Your Task. Decide what you want to do in this situation. Send an appropriate letter explaining your claim or complaint to Stephen Hawasaki, Stephen's Landscaping Service, Box 11A, Elkhart, IN 46515. Add any necessary details.

WEB

6.12 Direct Reply: Going River Rafting

As the program chair for the SIU Ski Club, you have been asked by president Brian Krauss to investigate river rafting. The SIU Ski Club is an active organization, and its members want to schedule a summer activity. A majority favor rafting. Use a browser such as Google to search the Web for relevant information. Select five of the most promising Web sites offering rafting. If possible, print a copy of your findings.

Your Task. Summarize your findings in a response letter to SIU Ski Club president. The next meeting is May 8, but you think it would be a good idea if you could discuss your findings with Brian before the meeting. Address your letter to Brian Krauss, President, SIU Ski Club, 303 Founders Hall, Carbondale, IL 62901.

TEAM

6.13 Direct Reply: Telling Job Applicants How to Make a Résumé Scannable

As part of a team of interns at the catalog store Patagonia, you have been asked to write a form letter to send to job applicants who inquire about your résumé-scanning techniques. The following poorly written response to an inquiry was pulled from the file.

Dear Ms. Moscatelli:

Your letter of April 11 has been referred to me for a response. We are pleased to learn that you are considering employment here at Patagonia, and we look forward to receiving your résumé, should you decide to send same to us.

You ask if we scan incoming résumés. Yes, we certainly do. Actually, we use SmartTrack, an automated résumé-tracking system. We sometimes receive as many as 300 résumés a day, and SmartTrack helps us sort, screen, filter, and separate the résumés. It also processes them, helps us organize them, and keeps a record of all of these résumés. Some of the résumés, however, cannot be scanned, so we have to return those—if we have time.

The reasons that résumés won't scan may surprise you. Some applicants send photocopies or faxed copies, and these can cause misreading, so don't do it. The best plan is to send an original copy. Some people use colored paper. Big mistake!

White paper (8½ × 11-inch) printed on one side is the best bet. Another big problem is unusual type fonts, such as script or fancy gothic or antique fonts. They don't seem to realize that scanners do best with plain, readable fonts such as Helvetica or Arial in a 10- to 14-point size.

Other problems occur when applicants use graphics, shading, italics, underlining, horizontal and vertical lines, parentheses, and brackets. Scanners like plain, unadorned résumés. Oh yes, staples can cause misreading. And folding of a résumé can also cause the scanners to foul up. To be safe, don't staple or fold, and be sure to use wide margins and a quality printer.

When a hiring manager within Patagonia decides to look for an appropriate candidate, he is told to submit keywords to describe the candidate he has in mind for his opening. We tell him (or sometimes her) to zero in on nouns and phrases that best describe what they want. Thus, my advice to you is to try to include those words that highlight your technical and professional areas of expertise.

If you do decide to submit your résumé to us, be sure you don't make any of the mistakes described herein that would cause the scanner to misread it.

Sincerely,

Your Task. As a team, discuss how this letter could be improved. Decide what information is necessary to send to potential job applicants. Search for additional information that might be helpful. Then, submit an improved version to your instructor. Although the form letter should be written so that it can be sent to anyone who inquires, address this one to Carmela Moscatelli, 327 Avalon Way, Las Vegas, NV 89154.

6.14 Direct Reply: Describing Your Major
A friend in a distant city is considering moving to your area for more education and training in your field. Your friend has asked you for information about your program of study.

Your Task. Write a letter describing a program in your field (or any field you wish to describe). What courses must be taken? Toward what degree, certificate, or employment position does this program lead? Why did you choose it? Would you recommend this program to your friend? How long does it take? Add any information you feel would be helpful.

6.15 Adjustment: Responding to Door Claim
As Michael Medina, operations manager, American Custom Wood, you have a problem. Your firm manufactures quality pre-cut and custom-built doors and frames. You have received a letter from Erica Adams (described in Activity 6.8), an interior designer. Her letter explained that the custom mahogany door ("Provence") she received was cut to the wrong dimensions. She ordered an oversized door measuring 12 feet 2 inches. The door that arrived was 11 feet 10 inches.

Ms. Adams kept the door because her client, an NBA basketball player, insisted that the front of the house be closed up. Therefore, she had her carpenter resize the opening. He charged $940.50 for this corrective work. She claims that you should reimburse her for this amount, since your company was responsible for the error. You check her May 17 order and find that the order was filled correctly. In a telephone order, Ms. Adams requested the Provence double-entry door measuring 11 feet 10 inches, and that is what you sent. Now she says that the door should have been 12 feet 2 inches.

Your policy forbids refunds or returns on custom orders. Yet, you remember that around May 15 you had two new people working the phones taking orders. It is possible that they did not hear or record the measurements correctly. You don't know whether to grant this claim or refuse it. But you do know that you must look into the training of telephone order takers and be sure that they verify all custom order measurements. It might also be a good idea to have your craftspeople call a second time to confirm custom measurements.

Ms. Adams is a successful interior designer who has provided American Custom Wood with a number of orders. You value her business but aren't sure how to respond. You would like to remind her that American Custom Wood has earned a reputation as a premier manufacturer of wood doors and frames. Your doors feature prime woods, meticulous craftsmanship, and award-winning designs. What's more, the engineering is ingenious. You also have a wide range of classic designs.

Your Task. Decide how to treat this claim and then respond to Erica Adams, Contempo Interiors, 2304 River Ridge Road, Indianapolis, IN 46031. You might mention that you have a new line of greenhouse windows that are available in three sizes. Include a brochure describing these windows.

6.16 Adjustment: Winning Back a Dissatisfied Customer
As the marketing manager at Carolina Furniture Galleries, you handle customer claims, and today you must respond to Jill Hudson Owens. She is returning a North American white oak executive desk. This handsome desk, embellished with hand-inlaid walnut cross-banding, is made with full-suspension, silent ball-bearing drawer slides. She was disappointed in the wood grain, and she said that many of the drawers would not pull out easily. You find this hard to believe since the desk was in perfect condition when it was shipped. Not only does she want a full refund, as your catalog promises, but she wants you to pay the freight charges.

You are bothered that she is returning this executive desk (Invoice 2091), but your policy is to comply with customer wishes. If she doesn't want to keep the desk, you will certainly return the purchase price plus shipping charges. Desks are occasionally damaged in shipping, and this may explain the marred finish and sticking drawers.

You will try to persuade Ms. Owens to give Carolina Furniture Galleries another chance. After all, your office furniture and other wood products are made from the finest hand-selected woods by master artisans. Because she is apparently furnishing her office, send her another catalog and invite her to look at the traditional conference desk on page 9. This is available with a matching credenza, file cabinets, and accessories. She might be interested in your furniture-leasing plan, which can produce substantial savings.

Your Task. Write to Ms. Jill Hudson Owens, President, Estate Management Services, 3920 East Napier Avenue, Benton Harbor, MI 49021. In granting her claim, promise that you will personally examine any furniture she may order in the future. Supply any necessary details.

6.17 Claim Response: Pigeon Poisoning Must Stop

You didn't want to do it. But guests were complaining about the pigeons that roost on the Scottsdale Hilton's upper floors and tower. Pigeon droppings splattered sidewalks, furniture, and people. As manager, you had to take action. You called an exterminator who recommended Avitrol. This drug, he promised, would disorient the birds, preventing them from finding their way back to the Hilton. The drugging, however, produced a result you didn't expect: pigeons began dying.

After a story hit the local newspapers, you began to receive complaints. The most vocal came from the Avian Affairs Coalition, a local bird-advocacy group. It said that the pigeons are really Mediterranean rock doves, the original "Dove of Peace" in European history and the same species the Bible said Noah originally released from his ark during the great flood. Activists claimed that Avitrol is a lethal drug causing birds, animals, and even people who ingest as little as 1/600th of a teaspoon to convulse and die lingering deaths of up to two hours.

Repulsed at the pigeon deaths and the bad publicity, you stopped the use of Avitrol immediately. You are now considering installing wires that offer a mild, nonlethal electrical shock. These wires, installed at the Maricopa County Jail in downtown Phoenix for $50,000, keep thousands of pigeons from alighting and could save $1 million in extermination and cleanup costs over the life of the building. You are also considering installing netting that forms a transparent barrier, sealing areas against entry by birds.

Your Task. Respond to Mrs. Meredith Van Huss, 17168 Blackhawk Boulevard, Friendswood, TX 77546, a recent Scottsdale Hilton guest. She sent a letter condemning the pigeon poisoning and threatening to never return to the hotel unless it changed its policy. Try to regain the confidence of Mrs. Van Huss and promote further business.

6.18 Thanks for a Favor: Got the Job!

Congratulations! You completed your degree and got a terrific job in your field. One of your instructors was especially helpful to you when you were a student. This instructor also wrote an effective letter of recommendation that was instrumental in helping you obtain your job.

Your Task. Write a letter thanking your instructor. Remember to make your thanks specific so that your words are meaningful.

TEAM

6.19 Thanks for a Favor: The Century's Biggest Change in Job Finding

Your business communication class was fortunate to have author Joyce Lain Kennedy speak to you. She has written many books including *Electronic Job Search Revolution; Hook Up, Get Hired;* and *Electronic Résumé Revolution.* Ms. Kennedy talked about writing a scannable résumé, using keywords to help employers hire you, keeping yourself visible in databases on the Internet, and finding online classified ads. The class especially liked hearing the many examples of real people who had found jobs on the Internet. Ms. Kennedy shared many suggestions from human resources people, and she described how large and small employers are using computers to read résumés and track employees. You know that she did not come to plug her books, but when she left, most class members wanted to head straight for a bookstore to get some of them. Her talk was a big hit.

Your Task. Individually or in groups, draft a thank-you letter to Joyce Lain Kennedy, P.O. Box 3502, Carlsbad, CA 92009.

6.20 Thanks for the Hospitality: Holiday Entertaining

You and other members of your staff or organization were entertained at an elegant dinner during the winter holiday season.

Your Task. Write a thank-you letter to your boss (supervisor, manager, vice president, president, or chief executive officer) or to the head of an organization to which you belong. Include specific details that will make your letter personal and sincere.

6.21 Responding to Good Wishes: Saying Thank You

Your Task. Write a short note thanking a friend who sent you good wishes when you recently completed your degree.

6.22 Extending Sympathy: To a Spouse

Your Task. Imagine that a coworker was killed in an automobile accident. Write a letter of sympathy to his or her spouse.

Video Resources

Video Library 2: *Social Responsibility and Communication at Ben & Jerry's.*

In an exciting inside look, you will see managers discussing six factors that determine Ben & Jerry's continuing success. Toward the end of the video, you will hear a discussion of a new packaging material made with unbleached paper. The new packaging paper was chosen because chlorine is not used in its manufacture. What's wrong with chlorine? Although it makes paper white, chlorine contains dioxin, which is known to cause cancer, genetic and reproductive defects, and learning disabilities. In producing paper, pulp mills using chlorine are also adding to dioxin contamination of waterways. Finding a chlorine-free, unbleached paperboard for its packages delighted Ben & Jerry's. However, the new process resulted in packages whose inner surfaces are brown, rather than white.

You have been hired at Ben & Jerry's to help answer inquiries. Although you are fairly new, your boss gives you a letter from an unhappy customer. This customer opened a pint container of Ben & Jerry's "World's Best Vanilla" and then threw it out. He saw the brown inner lid and inner sides of the package, and he decided that his pint container must have been used for chocolate before it was used for vanilla. Or, he said, "The entire pint has gone bad and somehow turned the insides brown." Whatever the reason, he wasn't taking any chances. Although he is a longtime customer, he now wants his money back. The last comment in his letter was, "I like your stand on environmental and social issues, but I don't like getting my ice cream in used containers."

Your Task. Write an adjustment letter that explains the brown interior of the carton, justifies the use of the new packaging material, and retains the customer's business. How could you promote future business with this customer? Address your letter to Mr. Adam W. Johnson, 4030 West Griswold Road, Phoenix, AZ 85051.

Grammar/Mechanics Checkup 6

Commas 1

Review the Grammar Review section of the Grammar/Mechanics Handbook Sections 2.01–2.04. Then study each of the following statements and insert necessary commas. In the space provided write the number of commas that you add; write *0* if no commas are needed. Also record the number of the G/M principle illustrated. When you finish, compare your responses with those shown at the end of the book. If your answers differ, study carefully the principles shown in parentheses.

3 _____ (2.01)	**Example** In this class students learn to write clear and concise business letters, e-mail messages, memos, and reports.

1. We do not as a rule allow employees to take time off for dental appointments.
2. You may be sure Mr. Sanchez that your car will be ready by 4 p.m.
3. Anyone who is reliable conscientious and honest should be very successful.
4. A conference on sales motivation is scheduled for May 5 at the Anaheim Marriott Hotel beginning at 2 p.m.
5. As a matter of fact I just called your office this morning.
6. We are relocating our distribution center from Memphis Tennessee to Des Moines Iowa.
7. In the meantime please continue to send your orders to the regional office.
8. The last meeting recorded in the minutes was on February 4 2008 in Chicago.
9. Mr. Loh Mrs. Adams and Ms. Horne are our new representatives.
10. The package mailed to Ms. Leslie Holmes 3430 Larkspur Lane San Diego CA 92110 arrived three weeks after it was mailed.
11. The manager feels needless to say that the support of all employees is critical.
12. Eric was assigned three jobs: checking supplies replacing inventories and distributing delivered goods.
13. We will work diligently to retain your business Mr. Bell.
14. The vice president feels however that all sales representatives need training.
15. The name selected for a product should be right for that product and should emphasize its major attributes.

Document for Revision

The following memo has errors in grammar, punctuation, spelling, proofreading, and other problems. You may either (a) use standard proofreading marks (see Appendix B) to correct the errors here or (b) download the document from your companion Web site and revise at your computer. Study the guidelines in the Grammar/Mechanics Handbook to sharpen your skills.

May 25, 200x

Ms. Breanna Lee, Manager
White-Rather Enterprises
1349 Century Boulevard
Wichita Falls, TX 76308

Dear Mr. Lee:

Subject: Your May 20 Inquiry About WorkZone Software

Yes we do offer personel record-keeping software specially designed for small businesses like your's. Here's answers to your three questions about this software;

1. Our Work Zone software provide standard employee forms so you are all ways in compliance with current goverment regulations.
2. You receive an interviewer's guide for structured employee interviews and you also receive a scripted format for checking references by telephone.
3. Yes you can up date your employees records easy with out the need for additional software, hardware or training.

Our WorkZone software was specially designed to provide you with expert forms for interviewing, verifying references, recording attendance, evaluating performance and tracking the status of your employees. We even provide you with step by step instructions, and suggested procedures. You can treat your employees as if you had a Professional Human Resources Specialist on your staff.

On page 6 of the enclosed pamphlet you can read about our WorkZone software. to receive a preview copy, or to ask questions about it's use just call 1-800-354-5500. Our specialists are eager to help you week days from 8 to 5 PST. If you prefer visit our Web site at www.workzone.com for more information, or to place an order.

Sincerely,

Jacob Scott
Senior Marketing Representative

Enclosure

Communication Workshop: Career Skills

Dr. Guffey's Guide to Business Etiquette and Workplace Manners

Etiquette, civility, and goodwill efforts may seem out of place in today's fast-paced, high-tech offices. However, etiquette and courtesy are more important than ever if diverse employees want to work cooperatively and maximize productivity and workflow. Many organizations recognize that good manners are good for business. Some colleges and universities offer management programs that include a short course in manners. Companies are also conducting manners seminars for trainee and veteran managers. Why is politeness regaining legitimacy as a leadership tool? Primarily because courtesy works.

Good manners convey a positive image of an organization. We like to do business with people who show respect and treat others civilly. People also like to work in an environment that is pleasant. Considering how much time is spent at work, doesn't it make sense to prefer an agreeable environment to one in which people are rude and uncivil?

You can brush up your workplace etiquette skills online at "Dr. Guffey's Guide to Business Etiquette and Workplace Manners" (**www.meguffey.com**). Of interest to both workplace newcomers and veterans, this guide covers the following topics:

Professional Image	Business Cards
Introductions and Greetings	Dealing With Angry Customers
Networking Manners	Telephone Manners
General Workplace Manners	Cell Phone Etiquette
Coping With Cubicles	E-Mail Etiquette
Interacting With Superiors	Gender-Free Etiquette
Managers' Manners	Business Dining
Business Meetings	Avoiding Social Blunders When Abroad
Business Gifts	

To gauge your current level of knowledge of business etiquette, take the preview quiz at **www.meguffey.com**. Then, study all 17 business etiquette topics. These easy-to-read topics are arranged in bulleted lists of dos and don'ts. After you complete this etiquette module, your instructor may test your comprehension by giving a series of posttests.

Career Application. As manager at OfficeTemps, a company specializing in employment placement and human resources information, you received a request from a reporter. She is preparing an article for a national news organization about how workplace etiquette is changing in today's high-tech environment. The reporter asks for any other information you can share with her regarding her topic, "Information Age Etiquette." Her letter lists the following questions:

- Are etiquette and workplace manners still important in today's fast-paced Information Age work environment? Why or why not?
- Do workers need help in developing good business manners? Why or why not?
- Are the rules of office conduct changing? If so, how?
- What advice can you give about gender-free etiquette?
- What special manners do people working in shared workspaces need to observe?

Your Task
In teams or individually, prepare an information response letter addressed to Ms. Lindsey Ann Evans, National Press Association, 443 Riverside Drive, New York, NY 10024. Use the data you learned in this workshop. Conduct additional Web research if you wish. Remember that you will be quoted in her newspaper article, so make it interesting!

CHAPTER 7

Negative Messages

OBJECTIVES

After studying this chapter, you should be able to

● Describe the strategies and goals of business communicators in delivering bad news, including knowing when to use the direct and indirect patterns.

● Explain the writing process and how to avoid legal problems related to bad-news messages.

● Discuss and illustrate techniques for delivering bad news sensitively.

● Outline a plan for refusing direct requests and claims.

● Describe techniques for delivering bad news to customers.

● Describe techniques for announcing bad news within organizations.

● Distinguish between ethical and unethical use of the indirect strategy.

Strategies for Delivering Bad News

In all businesses, things sometimes go wrong. Goods are not delivered, products fail to perform as expected, service is poor, billing gets fouled up, or customers are misunderstood. You may have to write messages ending business relationships, declining proposals, announcing price increases, refusing requests for donations, terminating employees, turning down invitations, or responding to unhappy customers. You might have to apologize for mistakes in orders, errors in pricing, the rudeness of employees, overlooked appointments, substandard service, pricing errors, faulty accounting, defective products, or jumbled instructions.

Everyone occasionally must deliver bad news. Because bad news disappoints, irritates, and sometimes angers the receiver, such messages must be written carefully. The bad feelings associated with disappointing news can generally be reduced if the receiver (a) knows the reasons for the rejection, (b) feels that the news was revealed sensitively, (c) thinks the matter was treated seriously, and (d) believes that the decision was fair. You have probably heard people say, *It wasn't so much the bad news that I resented. It was the way I was told!*

In this chapter you will learn when to use the direct pattern and when to use the indirect pattern to deliver bad news. You will study the goals of business communicators in working with bad news, and you will examine three causes for legal concerns. The major focus of this chapter, however, is on developing the indirect

The sting of bad news can be reduced by giving reasons and communicating sensitively.

OFFICE INSIDER

"Delivering difficult messages is part of day-to-day life in all social groups, whether the organization is a family, a nation, or a business."

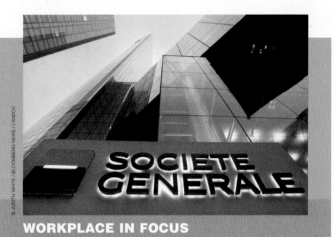

WORKPLACE IN FOCUS

Société Générale, situated here among the skyscrapers of Paris, suffered the worst loss in banking history when a junior employee liquidated more than $7 billion in a fraudulent trading scheme. In a letter to the bank's customers, CEO Daniel Bouton opened immediately with the bad news: "It is my duty to inform you that Société Générale has been a victim of a serious internal fraud committed by an imprudent employee in the Corporate and Investment Banking Division." Bouton went on to reveal a disaster-response plan and assured customers that lost funds would be replaced with emergency funding from the international banking community. *Should the bank have buffered this bad news by revealing it more gradually in the letter?*

strategy and applying it to situations in which you must refuse typical requests, reject claims, and deliver negative news to employees and customers.

Primary and Secondary Goals in Communicating Bad News

Delivering bad news is not the happiest writing task you may have, but it can be gratifying if you do it effectively. As a business communicator working with bad news, you will have many goals, the most important of which are these:

Primary Goals
- Make the receiver understand the bad news
- Help the receiver accept the bad news
- Maintain a positive image of you and your organization

Secondary Goals
- Reduce bad feelings
- Convey fairness
- Eliminate future correspondence
- Avoid creating legal liability or responsibility for you or your organization

These are ambitious goals, and we are not always successful in achieving them all. This chapter, however, provides the beginning communicator with strategies and tactics that many writers have found helpful in conveying disappointing news sensitively and safely. With experience, you will be able to vary these patterns and adapt them to your organization's specific writing tasks.

Using the Indirect Pattern to Prepare the Reader

The indirect pattern softens the impact of bad news by giving reasons and explanations first.

Whereas good news can be revealed quickly, bad news is generally easier to accept when broken gradually. Revealing bad news slowly and indirectly shows sensitivity to your reader. By preparing the reader, you tend to soften the impact. A blunt announcement of disappointing news might cause the receiver to stop reading and toss the message aside. The indirect strategy enables you to keep the reader's attention until you have been able to explain the reasons for the bad news. In fact, the most important part of a bad-news message is the explanation, which you will learn about shortly. The indirect plan consists of four parts, as shown in Figure 7.1:

FIGURE 7.1 Four-Part Indirect Pattern for Bad News

Buffer	Reasons	Bad News	Closing
Open with a neutral but meaningful statement that does not mention the bad news.	Explain the causes of the bad news before disclosing it.	Reveal the bad news without emphasizing it. Provide an alternative or compromise, if possible.	End with a personalized, forward-looking, pleasant statement. Avoid referring to the bad news.

- **Buffer.** Introduce the message with a neutral statement that makes the reader continue reading.
- **Reasons.** Explain why the bad news was necessary and that the matter was taken seriously.
- **Bad news.** Provide a clear but understated announcement of the bad news that might include an alternative or a compromise.
- **Closing.** End with a warm, forward-looking statement that might mention good wishes, gifts, or sales promotion.

When to Use the Direct Pattern

Many bad-news letters are best organized indirectly, beginning with a buffer and reasons. The direct pattern, with the bad news first, may be more effective, though, in situations such as the following:

- **When the receiver may overlook the bad news.** Rate increases, changes in service, new policy requirements—these critical messages may require directness to ensure attention.
- **When organization policy suggests directness.** Some companies expect all internal messages and announcements—even bad news—to be straightforward and presented without frills.
- **When the receiver prefers directness.** Busy managers may prefer directness. If you know that the reader prefers that the facts be presented straightaway, use the direct pattern.
- **When firmness is necessary.** Messages that must demonstrate determination and strength should not use delaying techniques. For example, the last in a series of collection letters that seek payment of overdue accounts may require a direct opener.
- **When the bad news is not damaging.** If the bad news is insignificant (such as a small increase in cost) and doesn't personally affect the receiver, then the direct strategy certainly makes sense.

The direct pattern is appropriate when the receiver might overlook the bad news, when directness is preferred, when firmness is necessary, and when the bad news is not damaging.

Applying the Writing Process

Thinking through the entire writing process is especially important in bad-news letters. Not only do you want the receiver to understand and accept the message, but also you want to be careful that your words say only what you intend. Therefore, you will want to apply the familiar 3-x-3 writing process to bad-news letters.

Following a writing process is especially important in crafting bad-news messages because of the potential consequences of poorly written messages.

Analysis, Anticipation, and Adaptation.
In Phase 1 (prewriting) you need to analyze the bad news so that you can anticipate its effect on the receiver. If the disappointment will be mild, announce it directly. If the bad news is serious or personal, consider techniques to reduce the pain. Adapt your words to protect the receiver's ego. Instead of *You neglected to change the oil, causing severe damage to the engine,* switch to the passive voice: *The oil wasn't changed, causing severe damage to the engine.* Choose words that show you respect the reader as a responsible, valuable person.

Research, Organization, and Composition.
In Phase 2 (writing) you can gather information and brainstorm for ideas. Jot down all the reasons you have that explain the bad news. If four or five reasons prompted your negative decision, concentrate on the strongest and safest ones. Avoid presenting any weak reasons; readers may seize on them to reject the entire message. After selecting your best reasons, outline the four parts of the bad-news pattern: buffer, reasons, bad news, and closing. Flesh out each section as you compose your first draft.

Revision, Proofreading, and Evaluation.
In Phase 3 (revising) you are ready to switch positions and put yourself into the receiver's shoes. Have you looked at the problem from the receiver's perspective? Is your message too blunt? Too subtle? Does the message make the refusal, denial, or bad-news announcement clear? Prepare the final version, and proofread for format, punctuation, and correctness.

Avoiding Three Causes of Legal Problems

Before we examine the components of a bad-news message, we must look more closely at how you can avoid exposing yourself and your employer to legal liability in writing negative messages. Although we can't always anticipate the consequences of our words, we should be alert to three causes of legal difficulties: (a) abusive language, (b) careless language, and (c) the "good-guy syndrome."

Abusive Language. Calling people names (such as *deadbeat*, *crook*, or *quack*) can get you into trouble. *Defamation* is the legal term for any false statement that harms an individual's reputation. When the abusive language is written, it is called *libel*; when spoken, it is *slander*.

Abusive language becomes legally actionable when it is false, harmful to the person's good name, and "published."

To be actionable (likely to result in a lawsuit), abusive language must be (a) false, (b) damaging to one's good name, and (c) "published"—that is, written or spoken within the presence of others. If you were alone with Jane Doe and you accused her of accepting bribes and selling company secrets to competitors, she could not sue because the defamation was not published. Her reputation was not damaged. However, if anyone heard the words or if they were written, you might be legally liable.

In a new wrinkle, you may now be prosecuted if you transmit a harassing or libelous message by e-mail or post it at a Web site. Such electronic transmissions are considered to be "published." Moreover, a company may incur liability for messages sent through its computer system by employees. That is one reason many companies are increasing their monitoring of both outgoing and internal messages. "Off-the-cuff, casual e-mail conversations among employees are exactly the type of messages that tend to trigger lawsuits and arm litigators with damaging evidence," says e-mail guru Nancy Flynn.[1] Instant messaging adds another danger for companies. Whether their messages are in print or sent electronically, competent communicators avoid making unproven charges and letting their emotions prompt abusive language.

Careless Language. As the marketplace becomes increasingly litigious, we must be certain that our words communicate only what we intend. Take the case of a factory worker injured on the job. His attorney subpoenaed company documents and discovered a seemingly harmless letter sent to a group regarding a plant tour. These words appeared in the letter: "Although we are honored at your interest in our company, we cannot give your group a tour of the plant operations as it would be too noisy and dangerous." The court found in favor of the worker, inferring from the letter that working conditions were indeed hazardous.[2] The letter writer did not intend to convey the impression of dangerous working conditions, but the court accepted that interpretation.

Careless language includes statements that could be damaging or misinterpreted.

Avoid statements that make you feel good but may be misleading or inaccurate.

The Good-Guy Syndrome. Most of us hate to have to reveal bad news— that is, to be the bad guy. To make ourselves look better, to make the receiver feel better, and to maintain good relations, we are tempted to make statements that are legally dangerous. Consider the case of a law firm interviewing job candidates. One of the firm's partners was asked to inform a candidate that she was not selected. The partner's letter said, "Although you were by far the most qualified candidate we interviewed, unfortunately, we have decided we do not have a position for a person of your talents at this time." To show that he personally had no reservations about this candidate and to bolster the candidate, the partner offered his own opinion. However, he differed from the majority of the recruiting committee. When the rejected interviewee learned later that the law firm had hired two male attorneys, she sued, charging sexual discrimination. The court found in favor of the rejected candidate. It agreed that a reasonable inference could be made from the partner's letter that she was the "most qualified candidate."[3]

Two important lessons emerge. First, business communicators act as agents of their organizations. Their words, decisions, and opinions are assumed to represent those of the organization. If you want to communicate your personal feelings or opinions, use your home computer or write on plain paper (rather than company letterhead) and sign your name without title or affiliation. Second, volunteering extra information can lead to trouble. Thus, avoid supplying data that could be misused, and avoid making promises that can't be fulfilled. Don't admit or imply responsibility for conditions that caused damage or injury. Even careless apologies *(We are sorry that a faulty bottle cap caused damage to your carpet)* may suggest liability.

Use organizational stationery for official business only, and beware of making promises that can't be fulfilled.

Techniques for Delivering Bad News Sensitively

Legal matters aside, let us now study specific techniques for using the indirect pattern in sending bad-news messages. In this pattern the bad news is delayed until after explanations have been given. The four components of the indirect pattern, shown in Figure 7.2, include buffer, reasons, bad news, and closing.

Buffering the Opening

A buffer is a device to reduce shock or pain. To buffer the pain of bad news, begin with a neutral but meaningful statement that makes the reader continue reading. The buffer should be relevant and concise and provide a natural transition to the explanation that follows. The individual situation, of course, will help determine what you should put in the buffer. Here are some possibilities for opening bad-news messages.

To reduce negative feelings, use a buffer opening for sensitive bad-news messages.

Best News. Start with the part of the message that represents the best news. For example, a message to workers announced new health plan rules limiting prescriptions to a 34-day supply and increasing co-payments. With home delivery, however, employees could save up to $24 on each prescription. To emphasize the good news, you might write, *You can now achieve significant savings and avoid trips to the drugstore by having your prescription drugs delivered to your home.*[4]

Compliment. Praise the receiver's accomplishments, organization, or efforts, but do so with honesty and sincerity. For instance, in a letter declining an invitation to speak, you could write, *The Thalians have my sincere admiration for their fundraising projects on behalf of hungry children. I am honored that you asked me to speak Friday, November 5.*

Openers can buffer the bad news with compliments, appreciation, agreement, relevant facts, and understanding.

FIGURE 7.2 Ideas for Delivering Bad News Sensitively

Buffer	Reasons	Bad News	Closing
• Best news • Compliment • Appreciation • Agreement • Facts • Understanding • Apology	• Cautious explanation • Reader or other benefits • Company policy explanation • Positive words • Evidence that matter was considered fairly and seriously	• Embedded placement • Passive voice • Implied refusal • Compromise • Alternative	• Forward look • Information about alternative • Good wishes • Freebies • Resale • Sales promotion

Appreciation. Convey thanks to the reader for doing business, for sending something, for conveying confidence in your organization, for expressing feelings, or simply for providing feedback. Suppose you had to draft a letter that refuses employment. You could say, *I appreciated learning about the hospitality management program at Cornell and about your qualifications in our interview last Friday.* Avoid thanking the reader, however, for something you are about to refuse.

Agreement. Make a relevant statement with which both reader and receiver can agree. A letter that rejects a loan application might read, *We both realize how much the export business has been affected by the relative weakness of the dollar in the past two years.*

Facts. Provide objective information that introduces the bad news. For example, in a memo announcing cutbacks in the hours of the employees' cafeteria, you might say, *During the past five years the number of employees eating breakfast in our cafeteria has dropped from 32 percent to 12 percent.*

Understanding. Show that you care about the reader. Notice how in this letter to customers announcing a product defect, the writer expresses concern: *We know that you expect superior performance from all the products you purchase from OfficeCity. That's why we are writing personally about the Exell printer cartridges you recently ordered.*

Apologizing

An apology is an admission of blameworthiness and regret for an undesirable event.

You learned about making apologies in adjustment letters discussed in Chapter 6. We expand that discussion here because apologies are often part of bad-news messages. The truth is that sincere apologies work. Peter Post, great grandson of famed etiquette expert Emily Post and director of the Emily Post Institute, said that Americans love apologies. They will forgive almost anything if presented with a sincere apology.[5] An apology is defined as an "admission of blameworthiness and regret for an undesirable event."[6] Here are some tips on how to apologize effectively in business messages:

- **Apologize to customers if you or your company erred.** Apologies cost nothing, and they go a long way in soothing hard feelings. Use good judgment, of course. Don't admit blame if it might prompt a lawsuit.
- **Apologize sincerely.** People dislike apologies that sound hollow (*We regret that you were inconvenienced* or *We regret that you are disturbed*). Focusing on your regret does not convey sincerity. Explaining what you will do to prevent recurrence of the problem projects sincerity in an apology.
- **Accept responsibility.** One CEO was criticized for the following weak apology: "I want our customers to know how much I personally regret any difficulties you may experience as a result of the unauthorized intrusion into our computer systems." Experts faulted this apology because it did not acknowledge responsibility.[7]

Consider these poor and improved apologies:

Poor apology: We regret that you are unhappy with the price of ice cream purchased at one of our scoop shops.

Improved apology: We are genuinely sorry that you were disappointed in the price of ice cream recently purchased at one of our scoop shops. Your opinion is important to us, and we appreciate your giving us the opportunity to look into the problem you describe.

Poor apology: We apologize if anyone was affected.

Improved apology: I apologize for the frustration our delay caused you. As soon as I received your message, I began looking into the cause of the delay and realized that our delivery tracking system must be improved.

Poor apology: We are sorry that mistakes were made in filling your order.

Improved apology: You are right to be concerned. We sincerely apologize for the mistakes we made in filling your order. To prevent recurrence of this problem, we are . . . .

Conveying Empathy

One of the hardest things to do in apologies is to convey sympathy and empathy. *Empathy* is the ability to understand and enter into the feelings of another. When ice storms trapped JetBlue Airways passengers on hot planes for hours, CEO Neeleman wrote a letter of apology that sounded as if it came from his heart. He said, "Dear JetBlue Customers: We are sorry and embarrassed. But most of all, we are deeply sorry." Later in his letter he said, "Words cannot express how truly sorry we are for the anxiety, frustration, and inconvenience that you, your family, friends, and colleagues experienced."[8] Neeleman put himself into the shoes of his customers and tried to experience their pain.

Here are other examples of ways to express empathy in written messages:

- In writing to an unhappy customer: *We did not intentionally delay the shipment, and we sincerely regret the disappointment and frustration you must have suffered.*
- In laying off employees: *It is with great regret that we must take this step. Rest assured that I will be more than happy to write letters of recommendation for anyone who asks.*
- In responding to a complaint: *I am deeply saddened that our service failure disrupted your sale, and we will do everything in our power to . . . .*
- In showing genuine feelings: *You have every right to be disappointed. I am truly sorry that . . . .*

Empathy involves understanding and entering into the feelings of someone else.

Presenting the Reasons

The most important part of a bad-news letter is the section that explains why a negative decision is necessary. Without sound reasons for denying a request or refusing a claim, a letter will fail, no matter how cleverly it is organized or written. As part of your planning before writing, you analyzed the problem and decided to refuse a request for specific reasons. Before disclosing the bad news, try to explain those reasons. Providing an explanation reduces feelings of ill will and improves the chances that readers will accept the bad news.

Bad-news messages should explain reasons before stating the negative news.

Explaining Clearly.
If the reasons are not confidential and if they will not create legal liability, you can be specific: *Growers supplied us with a limited number of patio roses, and our demand this year was twice that of last year.* In responding to a billing error, explain what happened: *After you informed us of an error on your January bill, we investigated the matter and admit the mistake was ours. Until our new automated system is fully online, we are still subject to human error. Rest assured that your account has been credited as you will see on your next bill.* In refusing a speaking engagement, tell why the date is impossible: *On January 17 we have a board of directors meeting that I must attend.* Don't, however, make unrealistic or dangerous statements in an effort to be the "good guy."

Citing Reader or Other Benefits if Plausible.
Readers are more open to bad news if in some way, even indirectly, it may help them. In refusing a customer's request for free hemming of skirts and slacks, Lands' End wrote: "We tested our ability to hem skirts a few months ago. This process proved to be very time-consuming. We have decided not to offer this service because the additional cost would have increased the selling price of our skirts substantially, and we did not want to impose that cost on all our customers."[9] Readers also accept bad news more readily if they recognize that someone or something else benefits, such as other workers or the environment: *Although we would like to consider your application, we prefer to fill managerial positions from within.* Avoid trying to show reader

Readers accept bad news more readily if they see that someone benefits.

benefits, though, if they appear insincere: *To improve our service to you, we are increasing our brokerage fees.*

Explaining Company Policy. Readers resent blanket policy statements prohibiting something: *Company policy prevents us from making cash refunds* or *Contract bids may be accepted from local companies only* or *Company policy requires us to promote from within.* Instead of hiding behind company policy, gently explain why the policy makes sense: *We prefer to promote from within because it rewards the loyalty of our*

employees. In addition, we have found that people familiar with our organization make the quickest contribution to our team effort. By offering explanations, you demonstrate that you care about readers and are treating them as important individuals.

Choosing Positive Words. Because the words you use can affect a reader's response, choose carefully. Remember that the objective of the indirect pattern is holding the reader's attention until you have had a chance to explain the reasons justifying the bad news. To keep the reader in a receptive mood, avoid expressions with punitive, demoralizing, or otherwise negative connotations. Stay away from such words as *cannot, claim, denied, error,*

"Dear Valued Customer: We're sorry, but company policy forbids apologies. Sincerely yours..."

failure, fault, impossible, mistaken, misunderstand, never, regret, rejected, unable, unwilling, unfortunately, and *violate.*

Showing That the Matter Was Treated Seriously and Fairly. In explaining reasons, demonstrate to the reader that you take the matter seriously, have investigated carefully, and are making an unbiased decision. Receivers are more accepting of disappointing news when they feel that their requests have been heard and that they have been treated fairly. In canceling funding for a program, board members provided this explanation: *As you know, the publication of* Urban Artist *was funded by a renewable annual grant from the National Endowment for the Arts. Recent cutbacks in federally sponsored city arts programs have left us with few funds. Because our grant has been discontinued, we have no alternative but to cease publication of* Urban Artist. *You have my assurance that the board has searched long and hard for some other viable funding, but every avenue of recourse has been closed before us. Accordingly, June's issue will be our last.*

WORKPLACE IN FOCUS

The ChicoBag Company knows that it is not what you say but how you say it that matters. While some environmental activists make strident calls to ban plastic bags that "hurt the earth," the California-based bag business takes a humorous approach to the issue. To illustrate the drawbacks of single-use plastic bags, ChicoBag dispatches Bag Monsters to roam the streets in high-visibility locations, such as on the streets at Mardi Gras or in front of the White House. The gimmicky-but-good-natured promotional effort helps the company sell its reusable nylon bags while muting the sometimes-negative tone taken by other eco-minded organizations. *Why is it important to accentuate the positive side of things?*

Cushioning the Bad News

Although you can't prevent the disappointment that bad news brings, you can reduce the pain somewhat by breaking the news sensitively. Be especially considerate when the reader will suffer personally from the bad news. A number of thoughtful techniques can cushion the blow.

Positioning the Bad News Strategically. Instead of spotlighting it, sandwich the bad news between other sentences, perhaps among your reasons. Don't let the refusal begin or end a paragraph—the reader's eye will linger on these high-visibility spots. Another technique that reduces shock is putting a painful idea in a subordinate clause: *Although another candidate was hired, we appreciate your interest in our organization and wish you every success in your job search.* Subordinate clauses often begin with words such as *although, as, because, if,* and *since.*

Using the Passive Voice. Passive-voice verbs enable you to depersonalize an action. Whereas the active voice focuses attention on a person *(We don't give cash refunds)*, the passive voice highlights the action *(Cash refunds are not given because . . .).* Use the passive voice for the bad news. In some instances you can combine passive-voice verbs and a subordinate clause: *Although franchise scoop shop owners cannot be required to lower their ice cream prices, we are happy to pass along your comments for their consideration.*

Accentuating the Positive. As you learned earlier, messages are far more effective when you describe what you can do instead of what you can't do. Rather than *We will no longer allow credit card purchases,* try a more positive appeal: *We are now selling gasoline at discount cash prices.*

Implying the Refusal. It is sometimes possible to avoid a direct statement of refusal. Often, your reasons and explanations leave no doubt that a request has been denied. Explicit refusals may be unnecessary and at times cruel. In this refusal to contribute to a charity, for example, the writer never actually says *no: Because we will soon be moving into new offices in Glendale, all our funds are earmarked for relocation costs. We hope that next year we will be able to support your worthwhile charity.* The danger of an implied refusal, of course, is that it is so subtle that the reader misses it. Be certain that you make the bad news clear, thus preventing the need for further correspondence.

Suggesting a Compromise or an Alternative. A refusal is not so depressing—for the sender or the receiver—if a suitable compromise, substitute, or alternative is available. In denying permission to a group of students to visit a historical private residence, for instance, this writer softens the bad news by proposing an alternative: *Although private tours of the grounds are not given, we do open the house and its gardens for one charitable event in the fall.* You can further reduce the impact of the bad news by refusing to dwell on it. Present it briefly (or imply it), and move on to your closing.

Closing Pleasantly

After explaining the bad news sensitively, close the message with a pleasant statement that promotes goodwill. The closing should be personalized and may include a forward look, an alternative, good wishes, freebies, resale information, or an off-the-subject remark.

Forward Look. Anticipate future relations or business. A letter that refuses a contract proposal might read: *Thanks for your bid. We look forward to working with your talented staff when future projects demand your special expertise.*

> Techniques for cushioning bad news include positioning it strategically, using the passive voice, implying the refusal, and suggesting alternatives or compromises.

"Send him our toughest refusal letter, threaten him with legal action, and don't pull the punches. But put XOXOXO under my signature to show that we still love him as a customer."

Alternative Follow-Up. If an alternative exists, end your letter with follow-through advice. For example, in a letter rejecting a customer's demand for replacement of landscaping plants, you might say: *I will be happy to give you a free inspection and consultation. Please call 746-8112 to arrange a date for my visit.* In a message to a prospective home buyer: *Although the lot you saw last week is now sold, we do have two lots with excellent views available at a slightly higher price.* In reacting to an Internet misprint: *Please note that our Web site contained an unfortunate misprint offering $850-per-night Bora Bora bungalows at $85. Although we cannot honor that rate, we are offering a special half-price rate of $425 to those who responded.*

Good Wishes. A letter rejecting a job candidate might read: *We appreciate your interest in our company, and we extend to you our best wishes in your search to find the perfect match between your skills and job requirements.*

Freebies. When customers complain—primarily about food products or small consumer items—companies often send coupons, samples, or gifts to restore confidence and to promote future business. In response to a customer's complaint about a frozen dinner, you could write: *Your loyalty and your concern about our frozen entrees are genuinely appreciated. Because we want you to continue enjoying our healthful and convenient dinners, we are enclosing a coupon that you can take to your local market to select your next Green Valley entree.*

Closings to bad-news messages might include a forward look, an alternative, good wishes, freebies, resale information, or sales promotion.

Resale or Sales Promotion. When the bad news is not devastating or personal, references to resale information or promotion may be appropriate: *The computer workstations you ordered are unusually popular because of their stain-, heat-, and scratch-resistant finishes. To help you locate hard-to-find accessories for these workstations, we invite you to visit our Web site where our online catalog provides a huge selection of surge suppressors, multiple outlet strips, security devices, and PC tool kits.*

Avoid endings that sound canned, insincere, inappropriate, or self-serving. Don't invite further correspondence *(If you have any questions, do not hesitate . . .),* and don't refer to the bad news. To review these suggestions for delivering bad news sensitively, take another look at Figure 7.2.

Refusing Direct Requests and Claims

Every business communicator will occasionally have to say *no* to a request. Depending on how you think the receiver will react to your refusal, you can use the direct or the indirect pattern. If you have any doubt, use the indirect pattern and the following writing plan:

Writing Plan for Refusing Routine Requests and Claims

- **Buffer:** Start with a neutral statement on which both reader and writer can agree, such as a compliment, appreciation, a quick review of the facts, or an apology. Try to include a key idea or word that acts as a transition to the reasons.
- **Reasons:** Present valid reasons for the refusal, avoiding words that create a negative tone. Include resale or sales promotion material if appropriate.
- **Bad news:** Soften the blow by de-emphasizing the bad news, using the passive voice, accentuating the positive, or implying a refusal. Suggest a compromise, alternative, or substitute if possible. The alternative may be part of the bad-news section or part of the closing.
- **Closing:** Renew good feelings with a positive statement. Avoid referring to the bad news. Look forward to continued business.

Rejecting Typical Requests

Most of us prefer to be let down gently when we are being refused something we want. That's why the reasons-before-refusal pattern works well when you must turn down requests for favors, money, information, action, and so forth.

The reasons-before-refusal pattern works well when turning down requests for favors, money, information, or action.

Saying *No* to Requests From Outsiders. Requests for contributions to charity are common. Many big and small companies receive requests for contributions of money, time, equipment, and support. Although the causes may be worthy, resources are usually limited. In a letter from Huron Architectural Services, shown in Figure 7.3, the company must refuse a request for a donation to a charity. Following the indirect strategy, the letter begins with a buffer acknowledging the request. It also praises the good works of the charity and uses those words as a transition to the second paragraph. In the second paragraph the writer explains why the company cannot donate. Notice that the writer reveals the refusal without actually

FIGURE 7.3 Refusing Donation Request

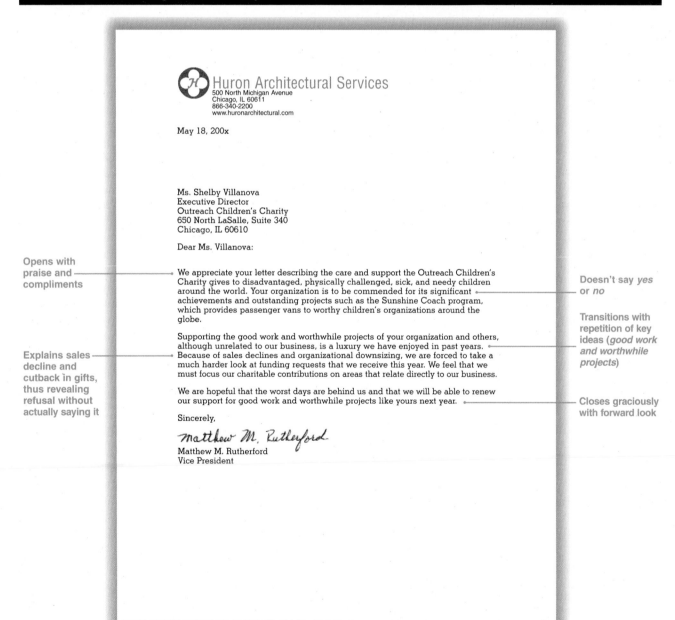

Opens with praise and compliments

Explains sales decline and cutback in gifts, thus revealing refusal without actually saying it

Doesn't say *yes* or *no*

Transitions with repetition of key ideas (*good work and worthwhile projects*)

Closes graciously with forward look

stating it (*Because of sales declines and organizational downsizing, we are forced to take a much harder look at funding requests that we receive this year*). This gentle refusal makes it unnecessary to be more blunt in stating the denial.

In some donation refusal letters, the reasons may not be fully explained: *Although we can't provide financial support at this time, we all unanimously agree that the symphony orchestra contributes much to the community*. The emphasis is on the symphony's attributes rather than on an explanation for the refusal. In the letter shown in Figure 7.3, the writer felt a connection to the charity. Thus, he wanted to give a fuller explanation.

Refusing Internal Requests.
Just as managers must refuse requests from outsiders, they must also occasionally refuse requests from employees. In Figure 7.4 you see the first draft and revision of a message responding to a request from a key specialist, Zachary Stapleton. He wants permission to attend a conference. However, he can't attend the conference because the timing is bad; he must be present at budget planning meetings scheduled for the same two weeks. Normally, this matter would be discussed in person. But Zach has been traveling among branch offices, and he hasn't been in the office recently.

The vice president's first inclination was to send a quickie memo, as shown in Figure 7.4, and "tell it like it is." In revising, the vice president realized that this message was going to hurt and that it had possible danger areas. Moreover, the memo misses a chance to give Zach positive feedback. An improved version of the memo starts with a buffer that delivers honest praise (*pleased with your exceptional leadership* and *your genuine professional commitment*). By the way, don't be stingy with compliments; they cost you nothing. As a philosopher once observed, "We don't live by bread alone. We need buttering up once in a while." The buffer also includes the date of the meeting, used strategically to connect the reasons that follow. You will recall from Chapter 3 that repetition of a key idea is an effective transitional device to provide smooth flow between components of a message.

The middle paragraph provides reasons for the refusal. Notice that these reasons focus on positive elements: Zach is the specialist; the company relies on his expertise; and everyone will benefit if he passes up the conference. In this section it becomes obvious that the request will be refused. The writer is not forced to say, *No, you may not attend*. Although the refusal is implied, the reader gets the message.

The closing suggests a qualified alternative (*if our workloads permit, we will try to send you then*). It also ends positively with gratitude for Zach's contributions to the organization and with another compliment (*you are our most valuable team player*). Notice that the improved version focuses on explanations and praise rather than on refusals and apologies.

The success of this message depends on attention to the entire writing process, not just on using a buffer or scattering a few compliments throughout.

Delivering Bad News to Customers

Businesses must occasionally respond to disappointed customers. In Chapter 6 you learned to use the direct strategy in granting claims and making adjustments because these are essentially good-news messages. In some situations, however, you have little good news to share. Sometimes your company is at fault, in which case an apology is generally in order. Other times the problem is with orders you can't fill, claims you must refuse, or credit you must deny. Messages with bad news for customers generally follow the same pattern as other negative messages. Customer letters, though, differ in one major way: they usually include resale or sales promotion information.

Damage Control: Dealing With Disappointed Customers

All companies occasionally disappoint their customers. Merchandise is not delivered on time, a product fails to perform as expected, service is deficient, charges

FIGURE 7.4 Refusing an Internal Request

Before

DATE: June 22, 200x

TO: Zachary Stapleton
           Chief Information Officer

FROM: Victoria M. Blaylock
           VP, Management Information Systems

SUBJECT: Request

This is to let you know that attending that conference in October, Zach, is out of
the question. Perhaps you didn't remember that budget-planning meetings are
scheduled for that month.

We really need your expertise to help keep the updating of our telecommunications
network on schedule. Without you, the entire system—which is shaky at best—
might fall apart. I'm really sorry to have to refuse your request to attend the conference. I know this is small thanks for the fine work you have done for us. Please
accept our humble apologies.

In the spring I'm sure your work schedule will be lighter, and we can release you
to attend a conference at that time.

*Announces the bad news too
quickly and painfully*

*Gives reasons, but includes a
potentially dangerous statement about the "shaky" system*

*Makes a promise that may be
difficult to keep*

After

MAGELLAN ENTERPRISES

MEMORANDUM

DATE: June 22, 200x

TO: Zachary Stapleton
           Chief Information Officer

FROM: Victoria M. Blaylock *VMB*
           VP, Management Information System

SUBJECT: Your Request to Attend October Conference

**Buffer: Includes sincere
praise**

The entire Management Council and I are pleased with the exceptional leadership
you have provided in setting up video transmission to our regional offices. Because
of your genuine professional commitment, Zach, I can understand your desire to
attend the conference of the Telecommunication Specialists of America from
October 23-27 in Phoenix.

**Reason: Tells why
refusal is necessary**

The last two weeks in October have been set aside for budget planning. As you
and I know, we have only scratched the surface of our teleconferencing projects
for the next five years. Because you are the specialist and we rely heavily on your
expertise, we need you here for these planning sessions.

**Bad news: Implies
refusal**

**Closing: Contains
realistic alternative**

If you are able to attend a similar conference in the spring and if our workloads
permit, we will try to send you then. You are our most valuable team member,
Zach, and we are grateful for the quality leadership you provide to the entire
Information Systems team.

---

are erroneous, or customers are misunderstood. All businesses offering products or
services must sometimes deal with troublesome situations that cause unhappiness to
customers. Whenever possible, these problems should be dealt with immediately and
personally. Many business professionals strive to control the damage and resolve
such problems in the following manner:[10]

- Call the individual involved.
- Describe the problem and apologize.

**When a customer problem
arises and the company is at
fault, many businesspeople
call and apologize, explain
what happened, and follow
up with a goodwill letter.**

- Explain why the problem occurred, what you are doing to resolve it, and how you will prevent it from happening again.
- Follow up with a letter that documents the phone call and promotes goodwill.

Dealing with problems immediately is very important in resolving conflict and retaining goodwill. Written correspondence is generally too slow for problems that demand immediate attention. But written messages are important (a) when personal contact is impossible, (b) to establish a record of the incident, (c) to formally confirm follow-up procedures, and (d) to promote good relations.

A bad-news follow-up letter is shown in Figure 7.5. Consultant Catherine Martinez found herself in the embarrassing position of explaining why she had given out the name of her client to a salesperson. The client, Alliance Resources International, had

FIGURE 7.5 Bad-News Follow-Up Message

PARAGON CONSULTING ASSOCIATES
4350 Camelback Blvd.
Scottsdale, AZ 85255
Voice: (480) 259-0971
Web: www.paragonassociates.com

May 7, 200x

Mr. Eric Nasserizad
Director, Administrative Operations
Alliance Resources International
538 Maricopa Plaza, Suite 1210
Phoenix, AZ 85008

Dear Mr. Nasserizad:

You have every right to expect complete confidentiality in your transactions with an independent consultant. As I explained in yesterday's telephone call, I am very distressed that you were called by a salesperson from Payroll Services, Inc. This should not have happened, and I apologize to you again for inadvertently mentioning your company's name in a conversation with a potential vendor, Payroll Services, Inc.

Opens with agreement and apology

All clients of Paragon Consulting are assured that their dealings with our firm are held in the strictest confidence. Because your company's payroll needs are so individual and because you have so many contract workers, I was forced to explain how your employees differed from those of other companies. Revealing your company name was my error, and I take full responsibility for the lapse. I can assure you that it will not happen again. I have informed Payroll Services that it had no authorization to call you directly and its actions have forced me to reconsider using its services for my future clients.

Explains what caused the problem and how it was resolved

Takes responsibility and promises to prevent recurrence

A number of other payroll services offer outstanding programs. I'm sure we can find the perfect partner to enable you to outsource your payroll responsibilities, thus allowing your company to focus its financial and human resources on its core business. I look forward to our next appointment when you may choose from a number of excellent payroll outsourcing firms.

Closes with forward look

Sincerely,

PARAGON CONSULTING ASSOCIATES

Catherine Martinez

Catherine Martinez
Partner

Tips for Resolving Problems and Following Up
- Whenever possible, call or see the individual involved.
- Describe the problem and apologize.
- Explain why the problem occurred.
- Take responsibility, if appropriate.
- Explain what you are doing to resolve the problem.
- Explain how it will not happen again.
- Follow up with a letter that documents the personal contact.
- Look forward to positive future relations.

hired her firm, Paragon Consulting Associates, to help find an appropriate service for outsourcing its payroll functions. Without realizing it, Catherine had mentioned to a potential vendor (Payroll Services, Inc.) that her client was considering hiring an outside service to handle its payroll. An overeager salesperson from Payroll Services immediately called on Alliance, thus angering the client. The client had hired the consultant to avoid this very kind of intrusion. Alliance did not want to be hounded by vendors selling their payroll services.

When she learned of the problem, the first thing consultant Catherine Martinez did was call her client to explain and apologize. She was careful to control her voice and rate of speaking. A low-pitched, deliberate pace gives the impression that you are thinking clearly, logically, and reasonably—not emotionally and certainly not irrationally. However, she also followed up with the letter shown in Figure 7.5. The letter not only confirms the telephone conversation but also adds the right touch of formality. It sends the nonverbal message that the writer takes the matter seriously and that it is important enough to warrant a written letter.

Denying Claims

Customers occasionally want something they are not entitled to or something you can't grant. They may misunderstand warranties or make unreasonable demands. Because these customers are often unhappy with a product or service, they are emotionally involved. Letters that say *no* to emotionally involved receivers will probably be your most challenging communication task. As publisher Malcolm Forbes observed, "To be agreeable while disagreeing—that's an art."[11]

Fortunately, the reasons-before-refusal plan helps you be empathic and artful in breaking bad news. Obviously, in denial letters you will need to adopt the proper tone. Don't blame customers, even if they are at fault. Avoid *you* statements that sound preachy *(You would have known that cash refunds are impossible if you had read your contract)*. Use neutral, objective language to explain why the claim must be refused. Consider offering resale information to rebuild the customer's confidence in your products or organization. In Figure 7.6 on page 176 the writer denies a customer's claim for the difference between the price the customer paid for speakers and the price he saw advertised locally (which would have resulted in a cash refund of $200). Although the catalog service does match any advertised lower price, the price-matching policy applies only to *identical* models. This claim must be rejected because the advertisement the customer submitted showed a different, older speaker model.

The letter to Cedrick Mandela opens with a buffer that agrees with a statement in the customer's letter. It repeats the key idea of product confidence as a transition to the second paragraph. Next comes an explanation of the price-matching policy. The writer does not assume that the customer is trying to pull a fast one. Nor does he suggest that the customer is a dummy who didn't read or understand the price-matching policy. The safest path is a neutral explanation of the policy along with precise distinctions between the customer's speakers and the older ones. The writer also gets a chance to resell the customer's speakers and demonstrate what a quality product they are. By the end of the third paragraph, it is evident to the reader that his claim is unjustified.

In denying claims, writers use the reasons-before-refusal pattern to set an empathic tone and buffer the bad news.

Refusing Credit

As much as companies want business, they can extend credit only when payment is likely to follow. Credit applications, from individuals or from businesses, are generally approved or disapproved on the basis of the applicant's credit history. This record is supplied by a credit-reporting agency, such as Experian, Equifax, or TransUnion. After reviewing the applicant's record, a credit manager applies the organization's guidelines and approves or disapproves the application.

If you must deny credit to prospective customers, you have four goals in conveying the refusal:

FIGURE 7.6 Denying a Claim

Digital Resources
4350 Dodge Street, Omaha, NE 68183   402-445-2300   www.digitalresources.com

September 24, 200x

Mr. Cedrick Mandela
430 Erie Avenue
Lansing, MI 48895

Dear Mr. Mandela:

Combines agreement with resale

You are right, Mr. Mandela. We do take pride in selling the finest products at rock-bottom prices. The Nautilus 800 speakers you purchased last month are premier concert hall speakers. They are the only ones we feature in our catalog because they are the best. — *Buffer*

Explains price-matching policy and how reader's purchase is different from lower-priced model

We have such confidence in our products and prices that we offer the price-matching policy you mention in your letter of September 15. That policy guarantees a refund of the price difference if you see one of your purchases offered at a lower price for 30 days after your purchase. To qualify for that refund, customers are asked to send us an advertisement or verifiable proof of the product price and model. As our catalog states, this price-matching policy applies only to exact models with USA warranties. — *Reasons*

Without actually saying no, shows why reader's claim can't be honored

Our Nautilus 800 speakers sell for $1,299. You sent us a local advertisement showing a price of $999 for Nautilus speakers. This advertisement, however, describes an earlier version, the Nautilus 600 series. The Nautilus 800 speakers you received have a wider dynamic range and smoother frequency response than the 600 model. Naturally, the improved model you purchased costs a little more than the older 600 model that the local advertisement describes. Your speakers have a new three-chamber bass module that virtually eliminates harmonic distortion. Finally, your speakers are 20 percent more compact than the 600 series. — *Implied refusal*

Uses resale in building confidence in wisdom of purchase; looks forward to future business

You bought the finest compact speakers on the market, Mr. Mandela. If you haven't installed them yet, you may be interested in ceiling mounts, shown in the enclosed catalog on page 32. For the most up-to-date prices and product information, please see our online catalog at our prize-winning Web site: www.digitalresources.com. We value your business and invite your continued comparison shopping. — *Positive closing*

Cordially,

Christine C. Guzik

Christine C. Guzik
Manager, Customer Service

Enclosure

Goals when refusing credit include maintaining customer goodwill and avoiding actionable language.

- Avoid language that causes hard feelings.
- Retain customers on a cash basis.
- Prepare for possible future credit without raising false expectations.
- Avoid disclosures that could cause a lawsuit.

Because credit applicants are likely to continue to do business with an organization even if they are denied credit, you will want to do everything possible to encourage that patronage. Thus, keep the refusal respectful, sensitive, and upbeat. A letter to a customer denying her credit application might begin as follows: *We genuinely appreciate your application of January 12 for a Mod Style credit account.* To avoid possible litigation, many companies offer no explanation of the reasons for a credit refusal. Instead, they provide the name of the credit-reporting agency and suggest that inquiries be directed to it. In the following example notice the use of passive voice (*credit cannot be extended*) and a long sentence to de-emphasize the bad news:

After we received a report of your current credit record from Experian, it is apparent that credit cannot be extended at this time. To learn more about your record, you may call an Experian credit counselor at (212) 356-0922.

A cordial closing looks forward to the possibility of a future reapplication:

Thanks, Ms. Love, for the confidence you have shown in Mod Style. We invite you to continue shopping at our stores, and we look forward to your reapplication in the future.

Some businesses do provide reasons explaining credit denials *(Credit cannot be granted because your firm's current and long-term credit obligations are nearly twice as great as your firm's total assets)*. They may also provide alternatives, such as deferred billing or cash discounts. When the letter denies a credit application that accompanies an order, the message may contain resale information. The writer tries to convert the order from credit to cash. For example, if a big order cannot be filled on a credit basis, perhaps part of the order could be filled on a cash basis. Whatever form the bad-news letter takes, it is a good idea to have the message reviewed by legal counsel because of the litigation land mines awaiting unwary communicators in this area.

Delivering Bad News Within Organizations

A tactful tone and a reasons-first approach help preserve friendly relations with customers. These same techniques are useful when delivering bad news within organizations. Interpersonal bad news might involve telling the boss that something went wrong or confronting an employee about poor performance. Organizational bad news might involve declining profits, lost contracts, harmful lawsuits, public relations controversies, and changes in policy. Whether you use a direct or an indirect pattern in delivering that news depends primarily on the anticipated reaction of the audience. Generally, bad news is better received when reasons are given first. Within organizations, you may find yourself giving bad news in person or in writing.

> **Bad news, whether delivered in person or in writing, is usually better received when reasons are given first.**

Giving Bad News Personally

Whether you are an employee or a supervisor, you may have the unhappy responsibility of delivering bad news. First, decide whether the negative information is newsworthy. For example, trivial, noncriminal mistakes or one-time bad behaviors are best left alone. However, fraudulent travel claims, consistent hostile behavior, or failing projects must be reported.[12] For example, you might have to tell the boss that the team's computer crashed with all its important files. As a team leader or supervisor, you might be required to confront an underperforming employee. If you know that the news will upset the receiver, the reasons-first strategy is most effective. When the bad news involves one person or a small group nearby, you should generally deliver that news in person. Here are pointers on how to do so tactfully, professionally, and safely:[13]

> **When you must deliver bad news in person, be sure to gather all the information, prepare, and rehearse.**

- **Gather all the information.** Cool down and have all the facts before marching in on the boss or confronting someone. Remember that every story has two sides.
- **Prepare and rehearse.** Outline what you plan to say so that you are confident, coherent, and dispassionate.
- **Explain: past, present, future.** If you are telling the boss about a problem such as the computer crash, explain what caused the crash, the current situation, and how and when you plan to fix it.
- **Consider taking a partner.** If you fear a "shoot the messenger" reaction, especially from your boss, bring a colleague with you. Each person should have a consistent and credible part in the presentation. If possible, take advantage of your organization's internal resources. To lend credibility to your view, call on auditors, inspectors, or human resources experts.

- **Think about timing.** Don't deliver bad news when someone is already stressed or grumpy. Experts also advise against giving bad news on Friday afternoon when people have the weekend to dwell on it.
- **Be patient with the reaction.** Give the receiver time to vent, think, recover, and act wisely.

Delivering Workplace Bad News

Organizations can sustain employee morale by communicating bad news openly and honestly.

Many of the same techniques used to deliver bad news personally are useful when organizations face a crisis or must deliver bad news in the workplace. Smart organizations involved in a crisis prefer to communicate the news openly to employees, customers, and stockholders. A crisis might involve serious performance problems, a major relocation, massive layoffs, a management shake-up, or public controversy. Instead of letting rumors distort the truth, they explain the organization's side of the story honestly and early. Morale can be destroyed when employees learn of major events affecting their jobs through the grapevine or from news accounts—rather than from management.

When bad news must be delivered to employees, management may want to deliver the news personally. With large groups, however, this is generally impossible. Instead, organizations may deliver bad news through interoffice memos. Organizations are experimenting with other delivery channels such as e-mail, videos, webcasts, and voice mail. Still, hard-copy interoffice memos seem to function most effectively because they are more formal and make a permanent record. The following writing plan outlines the content for such a message:

Writing Plan for Announcing Bad News to Employees

- **Buffer:** Open with a neutral or positive statement that transitions to the reasons for the bad news. Consider mentioning the best news, a compliment, appreciation, agreement, or solid facts. Show understanding.
- **Reasons:** Explain the logic behind the bad news. Provide a rational explanation using positive words and displaying empathy. If possible, mention reader benefits.
- **Bad News:** Position the bad news so that it does not stand out. Be positive but don't sugarcoat the bad news. Use objective language.
- **Closing:** Provide information about an alternative, if one exists. If appropriate, describe what will happen next. Look forward positively.

The draft of the memo shown in Figure 7.7 announces a substantial increase in the cost of employee health care benefits. However, the memo suffers from many problems. It announces jolting news bluntly in the first sentence. Worse, it offers little or no explanation for the steep increase in costs. It also sounds insincere (*We did everything possible . . .*) and arbitrary. In a final miscue, the writer fails to give credit to the company for absorbing previous health cost increases.

In the revision of this bad-news memo, the writer uses the indirect pattern and improves the tone considerably. Notice that it opens with a relevant, upbeat buffer regarding health care—but says nothing about increasing costs. For a smooth transition, the second paragraph begins with a key idea from the opening (*comprehensive package*). The reasons section discusses rising costs with explanations and figures. The bad news (*you will be paying $119 a month*) is clearly presented but embedded within the paragraph. Throughout, the writer strives to show the fairness of the company's position. The ending, which does not refer to the bad news, emphasizes how much the company is paying and what a wise investment it is. Notice that the entire memo demonstrates a kinder, gentler approach than that shown in the first draft. Of prime importance in breaking bad news to employees is providing clear, convincing reasons that explain the decision.

FIGURE 7.7 Announcing Bad News to Employees

Before

Beginning January 1 your monthly payment for health care benefits will be increased to $119 (up from $52 last year).

Every year health care costs go up. Although we considered dropping other benefits, Midland decided that the best plan was to keep the present comprehensive package. Unfortunately, we can't do that unless we pass along some of the extra cost to you. Last year the company was forced to absorb the total increase in health care premiums. However, such a plan this year is inadvisable.

We did everything possible to avoid the sharp increase in costs to you this year. A rate schedule describing the increases in payments for your family and dependents is enclosed.

— Hits readers with bad news without any preparation

— Offers no explanation

— Fails to take credit for absorbing previous increases

After

Northern, Inc.
MEMORANDUM

DATE: October 2, 200x

TO: Fellow Employees

FROM: Lawrence R. Romero, President *LRR*

SUBJECT: Maintaining Quality Health Care

Health care programs have always been an important part of our commitment to employees at Northern, Inc. We are proud that our total benefits package continues to rank among the best in the country.

Such a comprehensive package does not come cheaply. In the last decade health care costs alone have risen over 300 percent. We are told that several factors fuel the cost spiral: inflation, technology improvements, increased cost of outpatient services, and "defensive" medicine practiced by doctors to prevent lawsuits.

Just two years ago our monthly health care cost for each employee was $515. It rose to $569 last year. We were able to absorb that jump without increasing your contribution. But this year's hike to $639 forces us to ask you to share the increase. To maintain your current health care benefits, you will be paying $119 a month. The enclosed rate schedule describes the costs for families and dependents.

Northern continues to pay the major portion of your health care program ($520 each month). We think it's a wise investment.

Enclosure

Begins with positive buffer

Offers reasons costs are rising

Reveals bad news clearly but embeds it in paragraph

Ends positively by stressing the company's major share of the costs

Ethics and the Indirect Strategy

You may worry that the indirect organizational strategy is unethical or manipulative because the writer deliberately delays the main idea. But consider the alternative. Breaking bad news bluntly can cause pain and hard feelings. By delaying bad news, you soften the blow somewhat, as well as ensure that your reasoning will be read while the receiver is still receptive. One expert communicator recognized the significance of the indirect strategy when she said, "People must believe the reasons why before they will listen to the details of what and when."[14] In using the indirect

The indirect strategy is unethical only if the writer intends to deceive the reader.

strategy, your motives are not to deceive the reader or to hide the news. Rather, your goal is to be a compassionate, yet effective communicator.

The key to ethical communication lies in the motives of the sender. Unethical communicators *intend to deceive*. For example, Victoria's Secret, the clothing and lingerie chain, once offered free $10 gift certificates. However, when customers tried to cash the certificates, they found that they were required to make a minimum purchase of $50 worth of merchandise.[15] For this misleading, deceptive, and unethical offer, the chain paid a $100,000 fine. Although the indirect strategy provides a setting in which to announce bad news, it should not be used to avoid or misrepresent the truth.

Visit www.meguffey.com

- Chapter Review Quiz
- Flash Cards
- Grammar Practice
- PowerPoint Slides
- Personal Language Trainer
- Beat the Clock Quiz

Summing Up and Looking Forward

When faced with delivering bad news, you have a choice. You can announce it immediately, or you can delay it by presenting a buffer and reasons first. Many business communicators prefer the indirect strategy because it tends to preserve goodwill. In some instances, however, the direct strategy is effective in delivering bad news. In this chapter you learned the goals in communicating bad news and how to avoid creating legal problems. You studied many techniques for delivering bad news sensitively. Then, you learned to apply those techniques in refusing requests from outsiders (routine requests for favors, money, information, and action) as well as refusing internal requests. You studied techniques for breaking bad news to customers, denying claims, refusing credit, and delivering bad news to employees. Finally, you were taught to distinguish unethical applications of the indirect strategy.

Thus far you have studied electronic messages, memorandums, positive messages, and negative messages. In the next chapter you will learn to be persuasive, a powerful skill for any business communicator.

Critical Thinking

1. Does bad news travel faster and farther than good news? Why? What implications would this have for companies responding to unhappy customers?

2. Some people feel that all employee news, good or bad, should be announced directly. Do you agree or disagree? Why?

3. Consider times when you have been aware that others have used the indirect pattern in writing or speaking to you. How did you react?

4. When Boeing Aircraft reported that a laptop containing the names, salary information, and social security numbers of 382,000 employees had been stolen from an employee's car, CEO Jim McNerney wrote this e-mail to employees: "I've received many e-mails over the past 24 hours from employees expressing disappointment, frustration, and downright anger about yesterday's announcement of personal information belonging to thousands of employees and retirees being on a stolen computer. I'm just as disappointed as you are about it. I know that many of us feel that this data loss amounts to a betrayal of the trust we place in the company to safeguard our personal information. I certainly do." Critics have faulted this apology. With what did they find fault? Do you agree?

5. **Ethical Issue:** You work for a large corporation with headquarters in a small town. Recently you received shoddy repair work and a huge bill from a local garage. Your car's transmission has the same problems that it did before you took it in for repair. You know that a complaint letter written on your corporation's stationery would be much more authoritative than one written on plain stationery. Should you use corporation stationery?

6. What are the writer's primary and secondary goals in communicating bad news?

7. Describe the four parts of the indirect message pattern.

8. Name five situations in which the direct pattern should be used for bad news.

9. What is the difference between libel and slander?

10. What is a buffer? Name five or more techniques to buffer the opening of a bad-news message.

11. What is an apology? When should an apology be offered to customers?

12. Name four or more techniques that cushion the delivery of bad news.

13. Why is it a good idea to rehearse and also to take a partner when delivering bad news in person to a superior?

14. Identify a process used by a majority of business professionals in resolving problems with disappointed customers.

15. What are some channels that large organizations may use when delivering bad news to employees?

Writing Improvement Exercises

Passive-Voice Verbs

Passive-voice verbs may be preferable in breaking bad news because they enable you to emphasize actions rather than personalities. Compare these two refusals:

Example Active voice: I cannot authorize you to take three weeks of vacation in July.
Example Passive voice: Three weeks of vacation in July cannot be authorized.

Revise the following refusals so that they use passive-voice instead of active-voice verbs.

16. We will no longer be accepting credit cards for purchases under $5.

17. Our hospital policy forbids us from examining patients until we have verified their insurance coverage.

18. We cannot offer health and dental benefits until employees have been on the job for 12 months.

19. The manager and I have made arrangements for the investors to have lunch after the tour.

20. Your car rental insurance does not cover large SUVs.

21. Because management now requires more stringent security, we are postponing indefinitely requests for company tours.

Subordinate Clauses

You can further soften the effect of bad news by placing it in an introductory subordinate clause that begins with *although, since,* or *because.* The emphasis in a sentence is on the independent clause. Instead of saying *We cannot serve you on a credit basis,* try *Although we cannot serve you on a credit basis, we invite you to take advantage of our cash discounts and sale prices.* Revise the following so that the bad news is de-emphasized in a dependent clause that precedes an independent clause.

22. We are sorry to report that we are unable to ship your complete order at this point in time. However, we are able to send two corner workstations now; you should receive them within five days.

23. Unfortunately, we no longer print a complete catalog. However, we now offer all of our catalog choices at our Web site, which is always current.

24. We appreciate your interest in our organization, but we are unable to extend an employment offer to you at this time.

25. State law does not allow smoking within 5 feet of a state building. But the college has set aside 16 outdoor smoking areas.

Implying Bad News

Bad news can be de-emphasized by implying a refusal instead of stating it directly. Compare these refusals:

Example Direct refusal: We cannot send you a price list, nor can we sell our lawn mowers directly to customers. We sell only through dealers, and your dealer is HomeCo.

Example Implied refusal: Our lawn mowers are sold only through dealers, and your dealer is HomeCo.

Revise the following refusals so that the bad news is implied. If possible, use passive-voice verbs and subordinate clauses to further de-emphasize the bad news.

26. We cannot ship our fresh fruit baskets c.o.d. Your order was not accompanied by payment, so we are not shipping it. We have it ready, though, and will rush it to its destination as soon as you call us with your credit card number.

27. Unfortunately, we find it impossible to contribute to the fund-raising campaign this year. At present all the funds of my organization are needed to lease new equipment and offices for our latest branch in Richmond. We hope to be able to support this endeavor in the future.

28. Your team cannot schedule a retreat for the week of May 15. Too many staffers will be working on the Osgood Project, which will not be completed until June 1.

Writing Improvement Cases

7.1 Request Refusal: Shooting Down Request for Salary Stars

The following poorly written letter refuses a request from a reporter seeking salary information about top sales performers for an article.

Your Task. Analyze the message. List its weaknesses and then outline an appropriate writing plan. If your instructor directs, revise the message. A copy of this message is provided at **www.meguffey.com** for revision online.

Current date

Ms. Emily Decker
2415 Jefferson Road
Rochester, NY 14623

Dear Ms. Decker:

We cannot release salary information because such disclosure would violate our employees' privacy and lead to lawsuits. However, the article you are researching for *Business Management Weekly* sounds fascinating and will be most interesting to its readers. As a matter of fact, we are flattered that you wish to include LaserScope. You may be interested to know that we have many outstanding young salespeople—some are male and some are female—who command top salaries.

I cannot reveal private employee information because each of our salespeople operate under an individual salary contract. This is a result of salary negotiations several years ago. During those negotiations an agreement was reached that both sales staff members and management were in agreement to keep the terms of these individual contracts confidential. For obvious reasons, we cannot release specific salaries and commission rates. It has been suggested, however, that we can provide you with a list that is a ranking of our top salespeople for a period of the past five years. As a matter of fact, three of the top salespeople are currently under the age of thirty-five.

We are sorry that we cannot help you more with your fascinating research. Enclosed is a fact sheet in regard to our top salespeople, and we wish you every success with your article. It would be terrific to see LaserScope represented in it. Do not hesitate to call me if you have any questions.

Cordially,

1. List at least five weaknesses in this letter.

2. Outline a writing plan for a request refusal:
   Buffer:

   Reasons:

   Bad news:

   Closing:

7.2 Request Refusal: Diving Gear Warranty Rejection
The following letter refuses a consumer request for warranty service of a scuba diving computer used to monitor diving and decompression time.

Your Task. Analyze the message. List its weaknesses and then outline an appropriate writing plan. If your instructor directs, revise the message. A copy of this message is provided at **www.meguffey.com** for revision online.

Current date

Ms. Monica Soto
430 Bayou Vista Boulevard
Galveston, TX 77551

Dear Ms. Soto:

It is impossible for us to calibrate your Scuba Max XL diving computer, as requested in your letter which I have before me.

You acknowledge that you have used the product successfully off the Barrier Reefs in Australia and that you like its compact size and easy-to-read digits telling you exactly how much air time remains. Unfortunately, your letter does not include an important piece of information. We do not know whether you purchased this product from one of our authorized dealers. You can call 1-800-439-4509 to find out.

Our most popular products are the Scuba Max, Aqua Lung, and Atomic Aquatics. They come with 24-month warranties. However, we have a policy that states very clearly that these products must be sold through authorized dealers. This is the only way we can be sure that customers receive proper presale and postsale assistance. If our products are sold through authorized dealers, we can restrict their use to trained and certified divers.

We regret that we cannot approve your request to calibrate this product.

Sincerely,

1. List at least five weaknesses in this refusal letter.

2. Outline a plan for writing a refusal to a request.
   Buffer:

   Reasons:

   Bad news:

   Closing:

7.3 Claim Denial: Saying No to Free Repair

Following is a letter to a customer who demanded that a burned-out clothes dryer motor be replaced at no charge.

Your Task. Analyze the message. List its weaknesses and then outline an appropriate writing plan. If your instructor directs, revise the message. A copy of this message is provided at **www.meguffey.com** for revision online.

Current date

Ms. Kadence Larios
3591 Allen Avenue
Baton Rouge, LA 70809

Dear Ms. Larios:

This letter is being sent to you to inform you that warranty repairs are not available for damage caused by operator error. The motor on your clothes dryer burned out because the lint filter was full, thus clogging and overheating the motor.

After you called in your complaint, we had our service technician, Bryce Grindell, make an inspection. That's when he made the discovery that your lint filter was not being taken care of properly. Mr. Grindell said he had never seen such a clogged lint filter, and that without a doubt it caused the motor circuitry to overheat and then burn out. You are lucky it did not cause a house fire.

NewDay Harmony dryers get rave reviews from users. They talk about its large capacity, fast drying times, and antibacterial cycle. However, the warranty on your NewDay Harmony clothes dryer covers only these things: manufacturing defects or improper installation by us. As far as we can tell, the dryer had no defects and we know it was installed properly. We can't replace the motor at no charge. But we could install a reconditioned motor, at a cost of $99. Or we could bring you a new motor at $189. If you decide to go this route, we would only charge you as a continuing service call at $65 instead of the full rate of $130.

Let us know what you want to do.

Sincerely,

1. List at least five weaknesses in this letter.

2. Outline a plan for writing a refusal to a request.

Buffer:

Reasons:

Bad news:

Closing:

Activities and Cases

E-MAIL

7.4 Request Refusal: You Want Me to Do What?

As the manager of the Reprographics Department, you have been asked by two staff engineers for a copy of the latest version of Adobe Photoshop. This is an expensive licensed software program that your employees use. The engineers want it for home use. You know it is against the law to do this, and you understand why. Software companies would go out of business if they sold a program and it was copied by many others. Your Adobe software contract allowed you to install the updated version of Photoshop on one server and use it with up to five employees in this networked office. You would be breaking the contract and the law to let the program be copied. You wouldn't mind showing people how your department uses it, but you can't let the program be copied.

Your Task. Send an e-mail message to *robert.barnes@ecc.com* and *jose.lopez@ecc.com* refusing their requests and explaining why you cannot allow them to copy your updated version of Adobe Photoshop.

7.5 Request Refusal: Jamba Asks for Juicy Favor

In an aggressive expansion effort, Jamba Juice became a good customer of your software company. You have enjoyed the business it brought, and you are also quite fond of its products—especially Banana Berry and Mega Mango smoothies. Jamba Inc. is in the midst of expanding its menu with the goal of becoming the Starbucks of the smoothie. "Just as Starbucks defined the category of coffee, Jamba has the opportunity to define the category of the healthy snack," said analyst Brian Moore.[16] One goal of Jamba is to boost the frequency of customer visits by offering some products that are more filling. Then it could attract hungry customers as well as thirsty ones. It was experimenting with adding grains such as oatmeal or nuts such as almonds so that a smoothie packs more substance and could substitute for a meal.

You receive a letter from Joe Wong, your business friend and contact at Jamba Juice. He asks you to do him and Jamba Juice a favor. He wants to set up a juice tasting bar in your company cafeteria to test his new experimental drinks. All the drinks would be free, of course, but employees would have to fill out forms to evaluate each recipe. The details could be worked out later.

You definitely support healthy snacks, but you think this idea is terrible. First of all, your company doesn't even have a cafeteria. It has a small lunch room, and employees bring their own food. Secondly, you would be embarrassed to ask your boss to do this favor for Jamba Juice, despite the business it has brought your company.

Your Task. Write a letter that retains good customer relations with Jamba Juice but refuses this request. What reasons can you give, and what alternatives are available? Address your message to Joe Wong, Vice President, Product Development, Jamba Inc., 450 Golden Gate Avenue, San Francisco, 94102.

7.6 Request Refusal: Carnival Rejects Under-21 Crowd

The world's largest cruise line finds itself in a difficult position. Carnival climbed to the No. 1 spot by promoting fun at sea and pitching its appeal to younger customers who were drawn to on-board discos, swim-up bars, and hassle-free partying. But apparently the partying of high school and college students went too far. Roving bands of teens had virtually taken over some cruises in recent years. Travel agents complained of "drunken, loud behavior," as reported by Mike Driscall, editor of *Cruise Week.*

To crack down, Carnival raised the drinking age from 18 to 21 and required more chaperoning of school groups. Young individual travelers, however, were still unruly and disruptive. Thus, Carnival instituted a new policy, effective immediately. No one under 21 may travel unless accompanied by an adult over 25. Says Vicki Freed, Carnival's vice president for marketing, "We will turn them back at the docks, and they will not get refunds." As Eric Rivera, a Carnival marketing manager, you must respond to the inquiry of Sheryl Kiklas of All-World Travel, a New York travel agency that features special spring- and summer-break packages for college and high school students.

All-World Travel has been one of Carnival's best customers. However, Carnival no longer wants to encourage unaccompanied young people. You must refuse the request of Ms. Kiklas to help set up student tour packages. Carnival discourages even chaperoned tours. Its real market is now family packages. You must write to All-World Travel and break the bad news. Try to promote fun-filled, carefree cruises destined for sunny, exotic ports of call that remove guests from the stresses of everyday life. By the way, Carnival attracts more passengers than any other cruise line—over a million people a year from all over the world. Over 98 percent of Carnival's guests say that they were well satisfied. Tell her you will call during the week of January 5 to help her plan special family tour packages.[17]

Your Task. Write your letter to Sheryl Kiklas, All-World Travel Agency, 440 East Broadway, New York, NY 10014. Send her a schedule for spring and summer Caribbean cruises.

WEB

7.7 Request Refusal: Evict Loud Music Fan?

As the owner of Peachtree Business Plaza, you must respond to the request of Michael Vazquez, one of the tenants in your three-story office building. Mr. Vazquez, a CPA, demands that you immediately evict a neighboring tenant who plays loud music throughout the day, interfering with Mr. Vazquez's conversations with clients and with his concentration. The noisy tenant, Anthony Chomko, seems to operate an entertainment booking agency and spends long hours in his office. You know you can't evict Mr. Chomko because, as a legal commercial tenant, he is entitled to conduct his business. However, you might consider adding soundproofing, an expense that you would prefer to share with Mr. Chomko and Mr. Vazquez. You might also discuss limiting the time of day that Mr. Chomko could make noise.

Before responding to Mr. Vazquez, you decide to find out more about commercial tenancy. Use databases and the Web to search the keywords *commercial eviction*. Then develop a course of action.

Your Task. In writing to Mr. Vazquez, deny his request but retain his goodwill. Tell him how you plan to resolve the problem. Write to Michael Vazquez, CPA, Suite 230, Peachtree Business Plaza, 116 Krog Street, Atlanta, GA 30307. Your instructor may also ask you to write an appropriate message to Mr. Anthony Chomko, Suite 225.

7.8 Claim Denial: Airline Loses Passenger's Glasses

American Southern Airline (ASA) had an unhappy customer. Leticia Tomlinson flew from Atlanta to Seattle. The flight stopped briefly at Chicago O'Hare, where she got off the plane for half an hour. When she returned to her seat, her $400 prescription reading glasses were gone. She asked the flight attendant where the glasses were, and the attendant said they probably were thrown away since the cleaning crew had come in with big bags and tossed everything in them. Ms. Tomlinson tried to locate the glasses through the airline's lost-and-found service, but she failed. Then she wrote a strong letter to the airline demanding reimbursement for the loss. She felt that it was obvious that she was returning to her seat. The airline, however, knows that an overwhelming number of passengers arriving at hubs switch planes for their connecting flights. The airline does not know who is returning. What's more, flight attendants usually announce that the plane is continuing to another city and that passengers who are returning should take their belongings. Cabin-cleaning crews speed through planes removing newspapers, magazines, leftover foods, and trash. Airlines feel no responsibility for personal items left in cabins. The airline never refunds cash, but it might consider travel vouchers for the value of the glasses.[18]

Your Task. As a staff member of the customer relations department of American Southern Airline, deny the customer's claim but retain her goodwill using techniques learned in this chapter. Remember that apologies cost nothing. Write a claim denial to Mrs. Leticia Tomlinson, 1952 Kanako Lane, Mount Vernon, WA 98273.

7.9 Customer Bad News: J. Crew Goofs on Cashmere Turtleneck

Who wouldn't want a cashmere zip turtleneck sweater for $18? At the J. Crew Web site, many delighted shoppers scrambled to order the bargain cashmere. Unfortunately, the price should have been $218! Before J. Crew officials could correct the mistake, several hundred e-shoppers had bagged the bargain sweater for their digital shopping carts.

When the mistake was discovered, J. Crew immediately sent an e-mail message to the soon-to-be disappointed shoppers. The subject line shouted "Big Mistake!" The first line began with this statement: "I wish we could sell such an amazing sweater for only $18. Our price mistake on your new cashmere zip turtleneck probably went right by you, but rather than charge you such a large difference, I'm writing to alert you that this item has been removed from your recent order."

As an assistant in the communication department at J. Crew, you saw the e-mail message that was sent to customers and you tactfully suggested that the bad news might have been broken differently. Your boss says, "OK, hot stuff. Give it your best shot."

Your Task. Although you have only a portion of the message, analyze the customer bad-news message sent by J. Crew. Using the principles suggested in this chapter, write an improved e-mail message. In the end, J. Crew decided to allow customers who ordered the sweater at $18 to reorder it for $118.80 to $130.80, depending on the size. Customers were given a special Web site to reorder (make up an address). Remember that J. Crew customers are youthful and hip. Keep your message upbeat.[19]

WEB

7.10 Customer Bad News Follow-Up: Worms in Her PowerBars!

In a recent trip to her local grocery store, Kelly Keeler decided for the first time to stock up on PowerBars. These are low-fat, high-carbohydrate energy bars that are touted as a highly nutritious snack food specially formulated to deliver long-lasting energy. Since 1986, PowerBar (**http://www.powerbar.com**) has been dedicated to helping athletes and active people achieve peak performance. It claims to be "the fuel of choice" for top athletes around the world. Kelly is a serious runner and participates in many track meets every year.

On her way to a recent meet, Kelly grabbed a PowerBar and unwrapped it while driving. As she started to take her first bite, she noticed something white and shiny in the corner of the wrapping. An unexpected protein source wriggled out of her energy bar—a worm! Kelly's first inclination was to toss it out the window and never buy another PowerBar. On second thought, though, she decided to tell the company. When she called the toll-free number on the wrapper, Sophie, who answered the phone, was incredibly nice, extremely apologetic, and very informative about what happened. "I'm very sorry you experienced an infested product," said Sophie.

She explained that the infamous Indian meal moth is a pantry pest that causes millions of dollars in damage worldwide. It feeds on grains or grain-based products, such as cereal, flour, dry pasta, crackers, dried fruits, nuts, spices, and pet food. The tiny moth eggs lie dormant for some time or hatch quickly into tiny larvae (worms) that penetrate food wrappers and enter products.

At its manufacturing facilities, PowerBar takes stringent measures to protect against infestation. It inspects incoming grains, supplies proper ventilation, and shields all grain-storage areas with screens to prevent insects from entering. It also uses light traps and electrocuters; these devices eradicate moths with the least environmental impact. PowerBar President Brian Maxwell makes sure every complaint is followed up immediately with a personal letter. His letters generally tell customers that it is rare for infestations like this to occur. Entomologists say that the worms are not toxic and will not harm humans. Nevertheless, as President Maxwell says, "it is extremely disgusting to find these worms in food."

Your Task. For the signature of Brian Maxwell, PowerBar president, write a bad-news follow-up letter to Kelly Keeler, 932 Opperman Drive, Eagan, MN 55123. Keep the letter informal and personal. Explain how pests get into grain-based products and what you are doing to prevent infestation. You can learn more about the Indian meal moth by searching the Web. In your letter include a brochure titled "Notes About the Indian Meal Moth," along with a kit for Kelly to mail the culprit PowerBar to the company for analysis in Boise, Idaho. Also send a check reimbursing Kelly $36.85 for her purchase.[20]

7.11 Customer Bad News: Costly SUV Upgrade to a Ford Excursion

Steven Chan, a consultant from Oakland, California, was surprised when he picked up his rental car from Budget in Seattle over Easter weekend. He had reserved a full-size car, but the rental agent told him he could upgrade to a Ford Excursion for an additional $25 a day. "She told me it was easy to drive," Mr. Chan reported. "But when I saw it, I realized it was huge—like a tank. You could fit a full-size bed inside."

On his trip Mr. Chan managed to scratch the paint and damage the rear-door step. He didn't worry, though. He thought the damage would be covered because he had charged the rental on his American Express card. He knew that the company offered back-up car rental insurance coverage. To his dismay, he discovered that its car rental coverage excluded large SUVs. "I just assumed they'd cover it," he confessed. He wrote to Budget to complain about not being warned that certain credit cards may not cover damage to large SUVs or luxury cars.

Budget agents always encourage renters to sign up for Budget's own "risk product." They don't feel that it is their responsibility to study the policies of customers' insurance carriers and explain what may or may not be covered. Moreover, they try to move customers into their rental cars as quickly as possible and avoid lengthy discussions of insurance coverage. Customers who do not purchase insurance are at risk. Mr. Chan does not make any claim against Budget, but he is upset about being "pitched" to upgrade to the larger SUV, which he didn't really want.[21]

Your Task. As a member of the communication staff at Budget, respond to Mr. Chan's complaint. Budget obviously is not going to pay for the SUV repairs, but it does want to salvage his goodwill and future business. Offer him a coupon worth two days' free rental of any full-size sedan. Write to Steven Chan, 5300 Park Ridge, Apt. 4A, Oakland, CA 93578

TEAM

7.12 Damage Control for Disappointed Customers: Late Delivery of Printing Order

Kevin Kearns, a printing company sales manager, must tell one of his clients that the payroll checks his company ordered are not going to be ready by the date Kearns had promised. The printing company's job scheduler overlooked the job and didn't get the checks into production in time to meet the deadline. As a result, Kearns' client, a major insurance company, is going to miss its pay run.

Kearns meets with internal department heads. They decide on the following plan to remedy the situation: (a) move the check order to the front of the production line; (b) make up for the late production date by shipping some of the checks—enough to meet their client's immediate payroll needs—by air freight; (c) deliver the remaining checks by truck.

Your Task. Form groups of three or four students. Discuss the following issues about how to present the bad news to Andrew Tyra, Kearns' contact person at the insurance company.

a. Should Kearns call Tyra directly or delegate the task to his assistant?

b. When should Tyra be informed of the problem?

c. What is the best procedure for delivering the bad news?

d. What follow-up would you recommend to Kearns?

Be prepared to share your group's responses during a class discussion. Your instructor may ask two students to role-play the presentation of the bad news.

7.13 Credit Refusal: Cash Only at Gold's Gym and Fitness Center

As manager of Gold's Gym and Fitness Center, you must refuse the application of Monique Cooper for an Extended Membership. This is strictly a business decision. You liked Monique very much when she applied, and she seems genuinely interested in fitness and a healthful lifestyle. However, your Extended Membership plan qualifies the member for all your testing, exercise, recreation, yoga, and aerobics programs. This multiservice program is expensive for the club to maintain because of the huge staff required. Applicants must have a solid credit rating to join. To your disappointment, you learned that Monique's credit rating is decidedly negative. Her credit report indicates that she is delinquent in payments to four businesses, including Pros Athletic Club, your principal competitor.

You do have other programs, including your Drop In and Work Out plan, which offers the use of available facilities on a cash basis. This plan enables a member to reserve space on the racquetball and handball courts. The member can also sign up for yoga and exercise classes, space permitting. Because Monique is far in debt, you would feel guilty allowing her to plunge in any more deeply.

Your Task. Refuse Monique Cooper's credit application, but encourage her cash business. Suggest that she make an inquiry to the credit-reporting company Experian to learn about her credit report. She is eligible to receive a free credit report if she mentions this application. Write to Monique Cooper, 303 New Stine Road, Bakersfield, CA 93305.

E-MAIL **WEB**

7.14 Employee Bad News: Refusing the Use of Instant Messaging on the Job

As the vice president of the Green Group, an environmental firm, you had a request from team leader Emily Tsonga. She wants to know whether her team can use instant messaging on the job. Emily is working on the plans for an environmentally friendly shopping center, Westbury Mall. Her team project is moving ahead on schedule, and you have had excellent feedback from the shopping center developers.

Emily's team is probably already using instant messaging through public systems, and this worries you. You are concerned about security, viruses, and wasted time. However, the company has been considering a secured "enterprise-level" instant messaging system. The principal drawbacks are that such a system is expensive, requires administration, and limits use to organizational contacts only. You are not sure your company will ever adopt such a system.

You will have to refuse Emily's request, but you want her to know how much you value her excellent work on developing sustainability and green building techniques for the Westbury Mall project. You know you cannot get by with a quick refusal. You must give her solid reasons for rejecting her request.

Your Task. Send an e-mail to Emily Tsonga (*etsonga@greengroup.com*) refusing her request. See Chapter 5 for more information on the pros and cons of instant messaging. Also do research on the Web to understand better the risks of instant messaging.

7.15 Employee Bad News: No Go for Tuition Reimbursement

Ashley Arnett, a hardworking bank teller, has sent a request asking that the company create a program to reimburse the tuition and book expenses for employees taking college courses. Although some companies have such a program, First Federal has not felt that it could indulge in such an expensive employee perk. Moreover, CEO Richard Houston is not convinced that companies see any direct benefit from such programs. Employees improve their educational credentials and skills, but what is to keep them from moving that education and skill set to another employer? First Federal has over 200 employees. If even a fraction of them started classes, the company could see a huge bill for the cost of tuition and books. Because the bank is facing stiff competition and its profits are sinking, the expense of such a program is out of the question. In addition, it would involve administration—applications, monitoring, and record keeping. It is just too much of a hassle. When employees were hard to hire and retain, companies had to offer employment perks. But with a soft economy, such inducements are unnecessary.

Your Task. As director of Human Resources, send an individual response to Ashley Arnett. The answer is a definite *no*, but you want to soften the blow and retain the loyalty of this conscientious employee.

Video Resource

Video Library 2: *Bad News: BuyCostumes.* This video features BuyCostumes, the world's largest online costume and accessories retailer. After watching the video, play the part of a customer service representative.

BuyCostumes is proud of its extensive stock of costumes, its liberal return policy, and its many satisfied customers. But one day a letter arrived with a request that went beyond the company's ability to deliver. The customer said that he had ordered the Gorilla Blinky Eye with Chest costume. This popular gorilla costume comes with a unique gorilla mask, attractive suit with rubber chest, foot covers, and hands. The customer complained that the gorilla costume did not arrive until two days after his Halloween party. He planned an elaborate party with a gorilla theme, and he was extremely unhappy that he did not have his costume. He asks BuyCostumes to reimburse $300 that he spent on theme-related decorations, which he says were useless when he failed to receive his costume.

As a customer service representative, you checked his order and found that it was not received until five days before Halloween, the busiest time of the year for your company. The order was filled the next day, but standard shipping requires three to six business days for delivery. The customer did not order express or premium delivery; his shipping option was marked "Standard."

You showed the letter to the owner, Mr. Getz, who said that this request was ludicrous. However, he wanted to retain the customer's goodwill. Obviously, BuyCostumes was not going to shell out $300 for late delivery of a costume. But Mr. Getz suggested that the company would allow the customer to return the costume (in its original packaging) with a credit for the $134.99 charge. In addition, BuyCostumes would send a coupon for $20 off on the next costume purchase.

Your Task. Mr. Getz asks you to write a letter that retains the goodwill of this customer. Address your bad-news letter to Mr. Christopher King, 3579 Elm Street, Buffalo, NY 14202. Check **http://www.buycostumes.com** for more company information.

Grammar/Mechanics Checkup 7

Commas 2

Review the Grammar/Mechanics Handbook Sections 2.05–2.09. Then study each of the following statements and insert necessary commas. In the space provided write the number of commas that you add; write *0* if no commas are needed. Also record the number of the G/M principle(s) illustrated. When you finish, compare your responses with those provided at the end of the book. If your answers differ, study carefully the principles shown in parentheses.

1   (2.06a)   **Example** When U.S. organizations engage in overseas business, they must train their staffs accordingly.

1. If managers don't prepare for international business trips by learning about the culture they will be at a disadvantage when negotiating deals abroad.

2. One international support person works with time zones around the world and she keeps several clocks set to different zones.

3. Dealing with the unfamiliar is less challenging if you are patient and if you are able to avoid becoming irritated at misunderstandings.

4. The board of directors of Danube, Inc., appointed Elena Tolstaya who had served as the company's chief financial officer since 2007 to the position of president and CEO.

5. The imaginative promising software company opened its offices May 2 in Berlin.

6. Any sales associate who earns at least 1,000 recognition points this year will be honored with a bonus vacation trip to Tahiti.

7. James Manning the marketing manager for Chevron's Global Power Generation frequently engages in videoconferences that span time zones.

8. During the fourth quarter of the last fiscal year Rotor Company's earnings exceeded analysts' expectations.

9. When you are working with foreign clients for whom English is a second langauge you may have to speak slowly and repeat yourself.

10. To be most successful you must read between the lines and learn to pick up on various cultural vibes.

Review of Commas 1 and 2

11. Diamond Blade Company's new machine-tool facility showcases the latest advances in automation laser cutting and robotic bending in direct partnership with customers.

12. After she was hired she was told to report for work on Monday June 2 in Paris.

13. In the fall we expect to open a new branch in Sunnyvale which is an area of considerable growth.

14. As we discussed on the telephone the ceremony is scheduled for Thursday March 4 at 3 p.m.

15. The interviewer expected a firm handshake from the candidate but was greeted by a limp-fish clasp and she was uncomfortable touching the clammy hand.

The following letter has errors in spelling, proofreading, commas, parallelism, and other writing techniques studied in previous chapters. You may either (a) use standard proofreading marks (see Appendix B) to correct the errors here or (b) download the document from **www.meguffey.com** and revise at your computer. Study the guidelines in the Grammar/Mechanics Handbook to sharpen your skills.

Current date

Mr. John Brumfield
Human Resources Development
Gulfport Energy Enterprises
1400 Longhorn Blvd.
Houston, TX 76400

Dear Mr. Bumfield:

Did you know about the direct link between the health of your employes, and the health of your profits? Because we in the midst of tough economic times you are in all probability looking for benefits to offer your employees that help both you and them.

The benefits of healthyer employees includes lower health care costs, fewer medical claims, improved productivity, better morale and absenteeism is reduced. Here is how you can help your employees to have sound bodies, and also improve your companys profits:

* Provide them with Galaxy Fitness health club discounts.
* Bring our aerobics, massage, weight loss and educational programs on-site.
* You should have us manage your on-site fitness center.

Business Fortune magazine recently reported the following: "After a prevention and early intervention health program was implemented at L. L. Bean loss claims dropped by approximately 40 percent."

Please call (713) 839-2300 and speak to Jan Novak who is our corporate fitness expert to learn how you can add to the health of each and every employee and also to you are bottom line.

Sincerely,
GALAXY FITNESS

Missy Mischke
Senior Marketing Manager

Communication Workshop: Intercultural Issues

Presenting Bad News in Other Cultures

To minimize disappointment, Americans generally prefer to present negative messages indirectly. Other cultures may treat bad news differently, as illustrated in the following:

- In Germany business communicators occasionally use buffers but tend to present bad news directly.
- British writers tend to be straightforward with bad news, seeing no reason to soften its announcement.
- In Latin countries the question is not how to organize negative messages but whether to present them at all. It is considered disrespectful and impolite to report bad news to superiors. Therefore, reluctant employees may fail to report accurately any negative situations to their bosses.
- In Thailand the negativism represented by a refusal is completely alien; the word *no* does not exist. In many cultures negative news is offered with such subtleness or in such a positive light that it may be overlooked or misunderstood by literal-minded Americans.
- In many Asian and some Latin cultures, one must look beyond an individual's actual words to understand what is really being communicated. One must consider the communication style, the culture, and especially the context. Consider the following phrases and their possible meanings:

Phrase	Possible Meaning
I agree.	I agree with 15 percent of what you say.
We might be able to . . .	Not a chance!
We will consider . . .	*We* will consider, but the real decision maker will not.
That is a little too much . . .	That is outrageous!
Yes.	Yes, I'm listening. *OR:* Yes, you have a good point. *OR:* Yes, I understand, but I don't necessarily agree.

Career Application. Interview fellow students or work colleagues who are from other cultures. Collect information regarding the following questions:

- How is negative news handled in their cultures?
- How would typical business communicators refuse a request for a business favor (such as a contribution to a charity)?
- How would typical business communicators refuse a customer's claim?
- How would an individual be turned down for a job?

Your Task

Report the findings of your interviews in class discussion or in a memo report. In addition, collect samples of foreign business letters. You might ask foreign students, your campus admissions office, or local export/import companies whether they would be willing to share business letters from other countries. Compare letter styles, formats, tone, and writing strategies. How do these elements differ from those in typical North American business letters?

Persuasive Messages

OBJECTIVES
After studying this chapter, you should be able to

- Outline the opening, body, and closing of persuasive requests.
- Request favors and action convincingly.
- Write effective persuasive messages within organizations.
- Make reasonable claims and request adjustments credibly.
- Outline sales letters and their AIDA pattern: gaining attention, building interest, developing desire, and motivating action.
- Adapt the persuasive approach to online sales messages.

© ISTOCKPHOTO.COM / DMITRIY SHIRONOSOV

Making Persuasive Requests

Much of your success in business and in life depends on how skilled you are at persuading people to believe, accept, and act on what you are saying. Famous investor Warren Buffett, considered the richest person on earth by *Forbes,* was named by *Time* magazine as one of the world's 100 most influential people. Called "the Oracle of Omaha," Buffett commands respect when he speaks about stocks and the economy. He also had the public's ear when he announced plans to give away most of his fortune to charity.

Buffett's annual letters to shareholders feature more than facts and figures. The president and CEO of Berkshire Hathaway understands that he needs to connect to his audience's desires and needs. In addition to analyzing impressive numbers, Buffett sprinkles his prose with quotations and humor. Applying such persuasive techniques and many others can help you become a persuasive communicator. Because their ideas generally prevail, persuasive individuals become decision makers—managers, executives, and entrepreneurs. This chapter will examine techniques for presenting ideas persuasively, whether in your career or in your personal life.

Persuasion is necessary when you anticipate resistance or when you must prepare before you can present your ideas effectively. For example, let's say you bought a new car and the transmission repeatedly required servicing. When you finally got tired of taking it in for repair, you decided to write to the car manufacturer's district office asking that the company install a new transmission in your car. You knew that your request would be resisted. You had to convince the manufacturer that replacement, not repair, was needed. Direct claim letters, such as those you

The ability to persuade is a primary factor in personal and business success.

wrote in Chapter 6, are straightforward and direct. Persuasive requests, on the other hand, are generally more effective when they are indirect. Reasons and explanations should precede the main idea. To overcome possible resistance, the writer lays a logical foundation before delivering the request. A writing plan for a persuasive request requires deliberate development.

Writing Plan for a Persuasive Request

- **Opening:** Capture the reader's attention and interest. Describe a problem, state something unexpected, suggest reader benefits, offer praise or compliments, or ask a stimulating question.
- **Body:** Build interest. Explain logically and concisely the purpose of the request. Prove its merit. Use facts, statistics, expert opinion, examples, specific details, and direct and indirect benefits. Reduce resistance. Anticipate objections, offer counterarguments, establish credibility, demonstrate competence, and show the value of your proposal.
- **Closing:** Motivate action. Ask for a particular action. Make the action easy to take. Show courtesy, respect, and gratitude.

In this chapter you will learn to apply the preceding writing plan to messages that (a) request favors and action, (b) persuade subordinates and your superiors, and (c) make claims and request adjustments that may meet with opposition.

Requesting Favors and Action

Persuading someone to do something that largely benefits you is not easy. Fortunately, many individuals and companies are willing to grant requests for time, money, information, special privileges, and cooperation. They grant these favors for a variety of reasons. They may just happen to be interested in your project, or they may see goodwill potential for themselves. Often, though, they comply because they see that others will benefit from the request. Professionals sometimes feel obligated to contribute their time or expertise to "give back to the community."

You may find that you have few direct benefits to offer in your persuasion. Instead, you will be focusing on indirect benefits, as the writer does in Figure 8.1. In asking an individual to speak before a restaurant industry meeting, the writer has little to offer as a direct benefit other than a $300 honorarium. However, indirectly,

People are more likely to grant requests if they see direct or indirect benefits to themselves.

FIGURE 8.1 Persuasive Favor Request

Before

Dear Ms. Cunningham:

Would you be willing to speak to the members of the DC chapter of the National Restaurant Alliance? We hate to ask such a busy person, but we hoped you might be free on June 10 and would be able to come down from New York to join us in Washington.

Fails to pique interest; provides easy excuse

You would address our members on the topic of avoiding the seven cardinal sins in food service. This is a topic we understand you presented at your local chapter with some success. Although we can offer you only a $300 honorarium, we will also include dinner.

Does not promote direct and indirect benefits

Our group is informal, but I'm sure they would be interested in a 45-minute speech. Please let me know if you can join us at 7 p.m. at the CityZen restaurant in Washington.

Does not anticipate objections; fails to make it easy to respond

After

NATIONAL RESTAURANT ALLIANCE

1250 17th Street, Washington, DC 20034   www.restaurant.com   (202) 351-4300

February 23, 200x

Ms. Ann Cunningham, Manager
Max Hotels and Restaurants, Inc.
433 Madison Avenue
New York, NY 10022

Dear Ms. Cunningham:

Piques reader's interest with praise

News of the excellent presentation you made at your local chapter of the National Restaurant Alliance has reached us here in Washington, and we are very impressed.

Gains attention

Running a successful restaurant operation, as we all know, is tough even on a good day. The intense pace is frenzied, from scrubbing the vegetables early in the morning to latching the front door at day's end. In all this haste, it is easy to lapse into food service faults that can land an operation in big trouble. Your presentation focusing on seven cardinal sins in the food service industry certainly captured our attention.

Builds interest

Notes indirect benefit

The DC chapter of the National Restaurant Alliance asked me to invite you to be the featured speaker at our June 10 dinner on the topic of "Avoiding the Seven Cardinal Sins in Food Service." By sharing your expertise, you can help other restaurant operators recognize and prevent potential problems involving discrimination, workplace safety, hiring practices, and so forth. Although we can offer you only a small honorarium of $300 plus your travel expenses, we can promise you a big audience of enthusiastic restaurateurs eager to hear your presentation.

Notes direct benefit

Builds desire and reduces resistance

Offsets reluctance by making the talk informal and easy to organize

Our relaxed group doesn't expect a formal address; the members are most interested in hearing about best practices and solutions to prospective problems. To make your talk easy to organize, I have enclosed a list of questions our members submitted. Most talks are about 45 minutes long.

Motivates action

Can we count on you to join us for dinner at 7 p.m. June 10 at the CityZen restaurant in Washington? Just call me at (202) 351-1220 before March 15 to make arrangements.

Makes it easy to accept

Sincerely,

Lori McLaughlin

Lori McLaughlin
Program Chair, NRA

LM:grw

Enclosure

the writer offers enticements such as an enthusiastic audience and a chance to help other restaurant owners prevent food service problems.

The hurriedly written first version of the request suffers from many faults. It fails to pique the interest of the reader in the opening. It also provides an easy excuse for Ms. Cunningham to refuse (*hate to ask such a busy person*). The body fails to give her any incentive to accept the invitation. The letter also does not anticipate objections and fails to suggest counterarguments. Finally, the closing doesn't supply a telephone number or e-mail address for an easy response.

In the revised version, the writer gains attention with praise for a presentation Ms. Cunningham made. The letter builds interest with a number of appeals. The primary appeal is to the reader's desire to serve the restaurant industry, although a receptive audience and an opportunity to serve as an expert have a certain ego appeal as well. Together, these appeals—professional, self-serving, and monetary—make a persuasive argument rich and effective. The writer also anticipates objections and counters them by telling Ms. Cunningham that the talk is informal. The writer provides a list of questions so that the speaker can organize her talk more easily. The closing motivates action and makes acceptance as simple as a telephone call.

Persuading Within Organizations

When it comes to persuasion, the power relationships at work determine how we write—whether we choose a direct or indirect approach, for example. We may consider what type and amount of support we include, depending on whether we wish to persuade subordinates or superiors. The authority of our audience may also help us decide whether to adopt a formal or informal tone.

Persuading Subordinates. Instructions or directives moving downward from superiors to subordinates usually require little persuasion. Employees expect to be directed in how to perform their jobs. These messages (such as information about procedures, equipment, or customer service) follow the direct pattern, with the purpose immediately stated. However, employees are sometimes asked to perform in a capacity outside their work roles or to accept changes that are not in their best interests (such as pay cuts, job transfers, or reduced benefits). Occasionally, superiors need to address sensitive workplace issues such as smoking-cessation or exercise programs. Similarly, supervisors may want to create buy-in when introducing a healthier cafeteria menu. In these instances, a persuasive memo using the indirect pattern may be most effective.

The goal is not to manipulate employees or to seduce them with trickery. Rather, the goal is to present a strong but honest argument, emphasizing points that are important to the receiver or the organization. In business, honesty is not just the best policy—it is the only policy. People see right through puffery and misrepresentation. For this reason, the indirect pattern is effective only when supported by accurate, honest evidence.

Persuading the Boss. Another form of persuasion within organizations centers on suggestions made by subordinates. Convincing management to adopt a procedure or invest in a product or new equipment generally requires skillful communication. Managers are just as resistant to change as others are. Providing evidence is critical when subordinates submit recommendations to their bosses. "The key to making a request of a superior," advises communication consultant Patricia Buhler, "is to know your needs and have documentation [facts, figures, evidence]." Another important factor is moderation. "Going in and asking for the world [right] off the cuff is most likely going to elicit a negative response," she added.[1] Equally important is focusing on the receiver's needs. How can you make your suggestion appealing to the receiver?

Obviously, when you set out to persuade someone at work who has more clout than you, do so carefully. Use words like *suggest* and *recommend*, and craft sentences to begin with these words: *It might be a good idea if . . . .* That lets you offer suggestions without threatening the person's authority.

In Figure 8.2 you see a persuasive memo written by Marketing Manager Monique Hartung, who wants her boss to authorize the purchase of a multifunction color

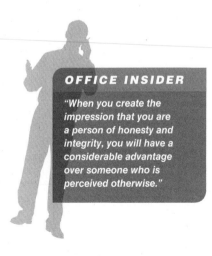

Internal persuasive messages present honest arguments detailing specific reader or company benefits.

FIGURE 8.2 E-Mail Cover Note With Attached Persuasive Memo

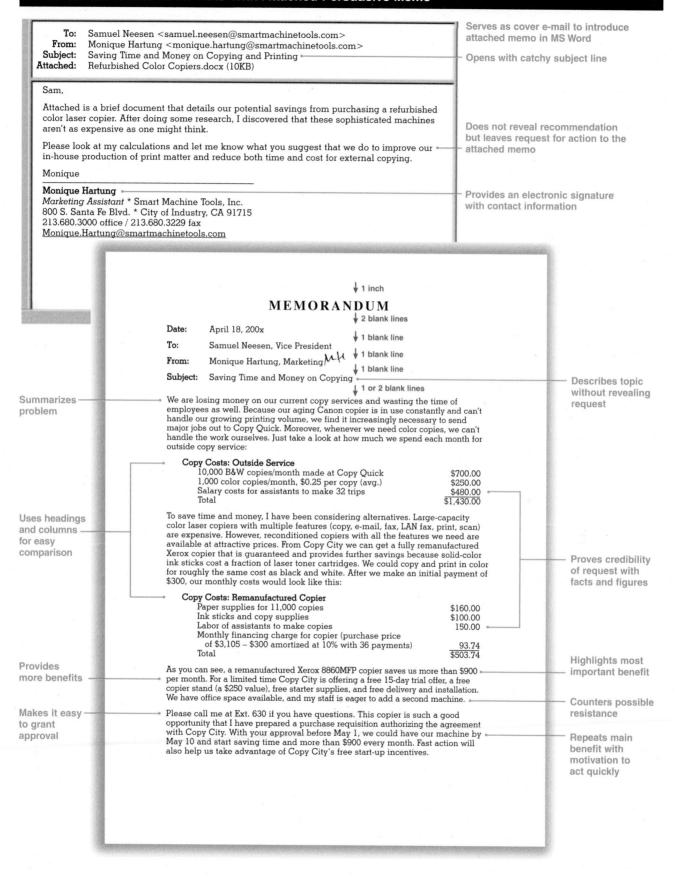

To: Samuel Neesen <samuel.neesen@smartmachinetools.com>
From: Monique Hartung <monique.hartung@smartmachinetools.com>
Subject: Saving Time and Money on Copying and Printing
Attached: Refurbished Color Copiers.docx (10KB)

Serves as cover e-mail to introduce attached memo in MS Word

Opens with catchy subject line

Sam,

Attached is a brief document that details our potential savings from purchasing a refurbished color laser copier. After doing some research, I discovered that these sophisticated machines aren't as expensive as one might think.

Please look at my calculations and let me know what you suggest that we do to improve our in-house production of print matter and reduce both time and cost for external copying.

Does not reveal recommendation but leaves request for action to the attached memo

Monique

Monique Hartung
Marketing Assistant * Smart Machine Tools, Inc.
800 S. Santa Fe Blvd. * City of Industry, CA 91715
213.680.3000 office / 213.680.3229 fax
Monique.Hartung@smartmachinetools.com

Provides an electronic signature with contact information

↓ 1 inch

MEMORANDUM

↓ 2 blank lines

Date: April 18, 200x
↓ 1 blank line
To: Samuel Neesen, Vice President
↓ 1 blank line
From: Monique Hartung, Marketing *MH*
↓ 1 blank line
Subject: Saving Time and Money on Copying

Describes topic without revealing request

↓ 1 or 2 blank lines

Summarizes problem

We are losing money on our current copy services and wasting the time of employees as well. Because our aging Canon copier is in use constantly and can't handle our growing printing volume, we find it increasingly necessary to send major jobs out to Copy Quick. Moreover, whenever we need color copies, we can't handle the work ourselves. Just take a look at how much we spend each month for outside copy service:

Uses headings and columns for easy comparison

Copy Costs: Outside Service
10,000 B&W copies/month made at Copy Quick	$700.00
1,000 color copies/month, $0.25 per copy (avg.)	$250.00
Salary costs for assistants to make 32 trips	$480.00
Total	$1,430.00

To save time and money, I have been considering alternatives. Large-capacity color laser copiers with multiple features (copy, e-mail, fax, LAN fax, print, scan) are expensive. However, reconditioned copiers with all the features we need are available at attractive prices. From Copy City we can get a fully remanufactured Xerox copier that is guaranteed and provides further savings because solid-color ink sticks cost a fraction of laser toner cartridges. We could copy and print in color for roughly the same cost as black and white. After we make an initial payment of $300, our monthly costs would look like this:

Proves credibility of request with facts and figures

Copy Costs: Remanufactured Copier
Paper supplies for 11,000 copies	$160.00
Ink sticks and copy supplies	$100.00
Labor of assistants to make copies	150.00
Monthly financing charge for copier (purchase price of $3,105 − $300 amortized at 10% with 36 payments)	93.74
Total	$503.74

Provides more benefits

As you can see, a remanufactured Xerox 8860MFP copier saves us more than $900 per month. For a limited time Copy City is offering a free 15-day trial offer, a free copier stand (a $250 value), free starter supplies, and free delivery and installation. We have office space available, and my staff is eager to add a second machine.

Highlights most important benefit

Counters possible resistance

Makes it easy to grant approval

Please call me at Ext. 630 if you have questions. This copier is such a good opportunity that I have prepared a purchase requisition authorizing the agreement with Copy City. With your approval before May 1, we could have our machine by May 10 and start saving time and more than $900 every month. Fast action will also help us take advantage of Copy City's free start-up incentives.

Repeats main benefit with motivation to act quickly

laser copier. She has researched the prices, features, and maintenance costs of the machines. They often serve as copiers, faxes, scanners, and printers and can cost several thousand dollars. Monique has found an outstanding deal offered by a local office supplier. Because Monique knows that her boss, Samuel Neesen, favors "cold, hard facts," she lists current monthly costs for copying at Copy Quick to increase her chances of gaining approval. Finally, she calculates the amortization of the purchase price and monthly costs of running the new color copier.

Notice that Monique's memo isn't short. A successful persuasive message will typically take more space than a direct message because proving a case requires evidence. In the end, Monique chose to send her memo as an e-mail attachment accompanied by a polite short e-mail message because she wanted to keep the document format in MS Word intact. She also felt that the message was too long to paste into her e-mail program. Monique's persuasive memo and her e-mail include a subject line that announces the purpose of the message without disclosing the actual request. By delaying the request until she has had a chance to describe the problem and discuss a solution, Monique prevents the reader's premature rejection.

The strength of this persuasive document, though, is in the clear presentation of comparison figures showing how much money the company can save by purchasing a remanufactured copier. Buying a copier that uses low-cost solid ink instead of expensive laser cartridges is another argument in this machine's favor. Although the organization pattern is not obvious, the memo begins with an attention-getter (a frank description of the problem), builds interest (with easy-to-read facts and figures), provides benefits, and reduces resistance. Notice that the conclusion tells what action is to be taken, makes it easy to respond, and repeats the main benefit to motivate action.

Composing Claim and Complaint Messages

Persuasive claim and complaint letters generally focus on damaged products, mistaken billing, inaccurate shipments, warranty problems, return policies, insurance snafus, faulty merchandise, and so on. The direct pattern is usually best for requesting straightforward adjustments (see Chapter 6). When you believe your request is justified and will be granted, the direct strategy is most efficient. However, if a past request has been refused or ignored or if you anticipate reluctance, then the indirect pattern is appropriate.

In a sense, a claim is a complaint letter. Someone is complaining about something that went wrong. Some complaint letters just vent anger; the writers are mad, and they want to tell someone about it. Conversely, if the goal is to change something (and why bother to write except to motivate change?), then persuasion is necessary. Effective claim letters make a reasonable claim, present a logical case with clear facts, and adopt a moderate tone. Anger and emotion are not effective persuaders.

Logical Development. Strive for logical development in a claim letter. You might open with sincere praise, an objective statement of the problem, a point of agreement, or a quick review of what you have done to resolve the problem. Then you can explain precisely what happened or why your claim is legitimate. Don't provide a blow-by-blow chronology of details; just hit the highlights. Be sure to enclose copies of relevant invoices, shipping orders, warranties, and payments. Close with a clear statement of what you want done: refund, replacement, credit to your account, or other action. Be sure to think through the possibilities and make your request reasonable.

Moderate Tone. The tone of your message is important. Don't suggest that the receiver intentionally deceived you or intentionally created the problem. Rather, appeal to the receiver's sense of responsibility and pride in the company's good name. Calmly express your disappointment in view of your high expectations of the product and of the company. Communicating your feelings, without rancor, is often your strongest appeal.

If at all possible, address your complaint letter or e-mail to a specific person. If you truly want a problem solved quickly, take the time to call the organization, search its Web site, or send an e-mail. Who should be informed about your issue? Who has the authority to act? Addressing a specific person is more likely to generate action than addressing a generic customer service department. Whether you approach an individual or a department, the tone of your message should, of course, be moderate.

Marilyn Easter's letter, shown in Figure 8.3, follows the persuasive pattern. She wants to return two voice over Internet protocol (VoIP) telephone systems. Notice her positive opening, her well-documented claims, and her request for specific action.

FIGURE 8.3 Claim Request (Complaint Letter)

ARTE INTERNATIONAL FURNISHINGS
3256 Riverton Avenue, North Hollywood, CA 91601   http://www.artedemexico.com

February 16, 200x

Customer Service
ZTech Electronics
1005 West McKinley Avenue
Mishawaka, IN 46545

Dear ZTech Customer Service:

Your VoIP Expandable Telephone System came highly recommended and seemed to be the answer to increasingly expensive telephone service. Here at Arte International Furnishings we were looking for a way to reduce our local and long-distance telephone charges. The VoIP system was particularly attractive to us because it offered Internet phone service with unlimited calling to the United States, Canada, and Puerto Rico. Our business in fine furnishings and unique objets d'art requires us to make and receive national and international calls.
Begins with compliment; keeps tone objective, rational, and unemotional

On February 8 we purchased two VoIP systems (SGU #IP7402-2) for our main office here in North Hollywood and for our Las Vegas showroom. Each system came with two cordless handsets and charging docks. Although we followed all the installation instructions, we discovered that an irritating static sound interfered with every incoming and outgoing telephone call.
Provides identifying data and justifies claim

This static is surprising and disappointing because the product description promised the following: "You will experience excellent signal clarity with Frequency Hopping Digital Spread Spectrum (FHDSS) transmission and a frequency of 5.8GHz. Ninety-five channel auto-search ensures a clear signal."
Explains why claim is valid and suggests responsibility of receiver

On February 10 we filled out a Return Merchandise Authorization form at your Web site. However, we are frustrated that we have had no response. We are confident that a manufacturer with your reputation for reliable products and superior customer service will want to resolve this matter quickly.
Expresses disappointment and appeals to receiver's reputation and customer service

Please authorize the return of these two systems and credit our account for $377.24, which represents the original cost plus taxes and shipping. Attached is a copy of the invoice with our credit card number.
Tells what action to take

Sincerely,

Marilyn Easter

Marilyn Easter
President

Enclosure

Tips for Making Complaints
- Begin with a compliment, point of agreement, statement of the problem, or brief review of action you have taken to resolve the problem.
- Provide identifying data.
- Prove that your claim is valid; explain why the receiver is responsible.
- Enclose document copies supporting your claim.
- Appeal to the receiver's fairness, ethical and legal responsibilities, and desire for customer satisfaction.
- Describe your feelings and your disappointment.
- Avoid sounding angry, emotional, or irrational.
- Close by telling exactly what you want done.

Writing Sales and Marketing Messages

Traditional direct-mail marketing uses snail mail; electronic marketing uses e-mail, Web documents, and fax.

Sales messages use persuasion to promote specific products and services. In our coverage we will be most concerned with sales messages delivered by mail. Many of the concepts you will learn about sales persuasion, however, can be applied to radio and TV advertising, as well as print, online, and wireless media. Smart companies strive to develop a balanced approach to their overall marketing strategy, including both online e-marketing and direct mail when appropriate.

Toward the end of this chapter, you will learn about preparing online sales messages. However, we will give most emphasis to traditional direct-mail campaigns featuring letters. Sellers feel that "even with all the new media we have available today, a letter remains one of the most powerful ways to make sales, generate leads, boost retail traffic, and solicit donations." Moreover, experts know that most recipients do look at their direct mail; in fact, about 80 percent of such promotional mail pieces are read.[2] Hard-copy sales letters are still recognized as the most "personal, one-to-one form of advertising there is."[3]

Sales letters are generally part of a package that may contain a brochure, price list, illustrations, testimonials, and other persuasive appeals. Professionals who specialize in traditional direct-mail services have made a science of analyzing a market, developing an effective mailing list, studying the product, preparing a sophisticated campaign aimed at a target audience, and motivating the reader to act. You have probably received many direct-mail packages, often called "junk mail."

Learning to write sales letters helps you sell yourself and your ideas as well as become a smarter consumer.

We are most concerned here with the sales letter: its strategy, organization, and evidence. Because sales letters are usually written by specialists, you may never write one on the job. Why, then, learn how to write a sales letter? In many ways, every letter we create is a form of sales letter. We sell our ideas, our organizations, and ourselves. When you apply for a job, you are both the seller and the product. Learning the techniques of sales writing will help you be more successful in any communication that requires persuasion and promotion. Furthermore, you will recognize sales strategies, thus enabling you to become a more perceptive consumer of ideas, products, and services.

Your primary goal in writing a sales message is to get someone to devote a few moments of attention to it.[4] You may be promoting a product, a service, an idea, or yourself. In each case the most effective messages will follow a writing plan. This is the same recipe we studied earlier, but the ingredients are different.

Writing Plan for a Sales Message: AIDA

The AIDA pattern (attention, interest, desire, and action) is used in selling because it is highly effective.

Professional marketers and salespeople follow the AIDA pattern (attention, interest, desire, and action) when persuading consumers. In addition to telemarketing and personal selling, this pattern works very well for written messages.

- **Opening:** Gain *attention*. Offer something valuable; promise a benefit to the reader; ask a question; or provide a quotation, fact, product feature, testimonial, startling statement, or personalized action setting.
- **Body:** Build *interest*. Describe central selling points and make rational and emotional appeals. Elicit *desire* in the reader and reduce resistance. Use testimonials, money-back guarantees, free samples, performance tests, or other techniques.
- **Closing:** Motivate *action*. Offer a gift, promise an incentive, limit the offer, set a deadline, or guarantee satisfaction.

Attention. One of the most critical elements of a sales letter is its opening paragraph, the attention-getter. This opener should be short (one to five lines), honest, relevant, and stimulating. Marketing pros have found that eye-catching typographical

© COURTESY OF DANA LOEWY

arrangements or provocative messages, such as the following, can hook a reader's attention:

- **Offer:** A free trip to Hawaii is just the beginning!
- **Benefit:** Now you can raise your sales income by 50 percent or even more with the proven techniques found in . . . .
- **Open-ended suggestive question:** Do you want your family to be safe?
- **Quotation or proverb:** Necessity is the mother of invention.
- **Compliment:** Life is full of milestones. You have reached one. You deserve . . . .
- **Fact:** The Greenland Eskimos ate more fat than anyone in the world, yet . . . they had virtually no heart disease.
- **Product feature:** Electronic stability control, ABS, and other active and passive safety features explain why the ultra-compact new Smart Fortwo has achieved a four-star crash rating in California.
- **Testimonial:** The most recent J.D. Power survey of "initial quality" shows that BMW ranks at the top of brands with the fewest defects and malfunctions, ahead of Chrysler, Hyundai, Lexus, Porsche, and Toyota.
- **Startling statement:** Let the poor and hungry feed themselves! For just $100 they can.
- **Personalized action setting:** It's 6:30 p.m. and you are working overtime to meet a pressing deadline. Suddenly your copier breaks down. The production of your color-laser brochures screeches to a halt. How you are wishing you had purchased the Worry-Free-Anytime service contract from Canon.

Other openings calculated to capture attention might include a solution to a problem, an anecdote, a personalized statement using the receiver's name, or a relevant current event.

Interest. In this phase of your sales message, you should describe clearly the product or service. Think of this part as a promise that the product or service will deliver to satisfy the audience's needs. In simple language emphasize the central selling points that you identified during your prewriting analysis. Those selling points can be developed using rational or emotional appeals.

Rational appeals are associated with reason and intellect. They translate selling points into references to making or saving money, increasing efficiency, or making the best use of resources. In general, rational appeals are appropriate when a product is expensive; long-lasting; or important to health, security, and financial success. Emotional appeals relate to status, ego, and sensual feelings. Appealing to

> Build interest by describing the benefits a product or service offers and by making rational or emotional appeals.

the emotions is sometimes effective when a product is inexpensive, short-lived, or nonessential. Many clever sales messages, however, combine emotional and rational strategies for a dual appeal. Consider these examples:

Rational Appeal
You can buy the things you need and want, pay household bills, pay off higher-cost loans and credit cards—as soon as you are approved and your Credit-Line account is opened.

Emotional Appeal
Leave the urban bustle behind and escape to sun-soaked Bermuda! To recharge your batteries with an injection of sun and surf, all you need is your bathing suit, a little suntan lotion, and your Credit-Line card.

Dual Appeal
New Credit-Line cardholders are immediately eligible for a $100 travel certificate and additional discounts at fun-filled resorts. Save up to 40 percent while lying on a beach in picturesque, sun-soaked Bermuda, the year-round resort island.

A physical description of your product is not enough, however. Zig Ziglar, thought by some to be America's greatest salesperson, pointed out that no matter how well you know your product, no one is persuaded by cold, hard facts alone. In the end, he contended, "People buy because of the product benefits."[5] Your job is to translate those cold facts into warm feelings and reader benefits. Let's say a sales letter promotes a hand cream made with aloe and cocoa butter extracts, along with Vitamin A. Those facts become, *Nature's hand helpers—including soothing aloe and cocoa extracts, along with firming Vitamin A—form invisible gloves that protect your sensitive skin against the hardships of work, harsh detergents, and constant environmental assaults.*

Desire. The goal at this stage in the sales message is to elicit desire in the reader and to overcome resistance. To make the audience want the product or service and to anticipate objections, focus strongly on reader benefits. Here the promises of the attention and interest sections are covered in great detail. Marketing pros use a number of techniques to elicit desire in their audience and to overcome resistance.

- **Testimonials:** *Thanks to your online selling workshop, I was able to increase the number of my sales leads from three per month to twelve per week!*—Carlton Strong, Phoenix, Arizona
- **Names of satisfied users (with permission, of course):** Enclosed is a partial list of private pilots who enthusiastically subscribe to our service.
- **Money-back guarantee or warranty:** We offer the longest warranties in the business—all parts and service on-site for two years!
- **Free trial or sample:** We are so confident that you will like our new accounting program that we want you to try it absolutely free.
- **Performance tests, polls, or awards:** Our Audi R8 supercar won World Design Car of the Year and World Performance Car of the Year awards—the first time a single car has received trophies in more than one category.

In addition, you need to anticipate objections and questions the receiver may have. When possible, translate these objections into selling points (*If you are worried about training your staff members on*

"A really great salesman convinced us we needed protection from stray asteroids."

© TED GOFF WWW.TEDGOFF.COM

Chapter 8: Persuasive Messages

the new software, remember that our offer includes $1,000 of on-site, one-on-one instruction). Be sure, of course, that your claims are accurate and do not stretch the truth.

When price is an obstacle, consider these suggestions:

- Delay mentioning price until after you have created a desire for the product.
- Show the price in small units, such as the price per issue of a magazine.
- Demonstrate how the reader saves money by, for instance, subscribing for two or three years.
- Compare your prices with those of a competitor.
- If applicable, offer advantageous financing terms.

Action. All the effort put into a sales message is wasted if the reader fails to act. To make it easy for readers to act, you can provide a reply card, a stamped and preaddressed envelope, a toll-free telephone number, a convenient Web address, or a promise of a follow-up call. Because readers often need an extra push, consider including additional motivators, such as the following:

Techniques for motivating action include offering a gift or incentive, limiting an offer, and guaranteeing satisfaction.

- **Offer a gift:** You will receive a free iPod nano with the purchase of any new car.
- **Promise an incentive:** With every new, paid subscription, we will plant a tree in one of America's Heritage Forests.
- **Limit the offer:** Only the first 100 customers receive free checks.
- **Set a deadline:** You must act before June 1 to get these low prices.
- **Guarantee satisfaction:** We will return your full payment if you are not entirely satisfied—no questions asked.

The final paragraph of the sales letter carries the punch line. This is where you tell readers what you want done and give them reasons for doing it. Most sales letters also include postscripts because they make irresistible reading. Even readers who might skim over or bypass paragraphs are drawn to a P.S. Therefore, use a postscript to reveal your strongest motivator, to add a special inducement for a quick response, or to reemphasize a central selling point.

© FROM THE WALL STREET JOURNAL-PERMISSION, CARTOON FEATURES SYNDICATE

"I find it hard to believe that we've actually won 20 million dollars when they send the letter bulk mail."

Putting It All Together

Sales letters are a preferred marketing medium because they can be personalized, directed to target audiences, and filled with a more complete message than other advertising media. However, direct mail is expensive. That is why the total sales message is crafted so painstakingly.

Figure 8.4 shows a sales letter addressed to a target group of small-business owners. To sell the new magazine *Small Business Monthly,* the letter incorporates all four components of an effective persuasive message. Notice that the personalized action-setting opener places the reader in a familiar situation (getting into an elevator) and draws an analogy between failing to reach the top floor and failing to achieve a business goal.

The writer develops a rational central selling point (a magazine that provides valuable information for a growing small business) and repeats this selling point in all the components of the letter. Notice, too, how a testimonial from a small-business executive lends support to the sales message, and how the closing pushes for action. Because the price of the magazine is not a selling feature, it is mentioned only on the reply card. This sales letter saves its strongest motivator—a free booklet—for the high-impact P.S. line.

In developing effective sales messages, some writers may be tempted to cross the line that separates legal from illegal sales tactics. Be sure to check out the

FIGURE 8.4 Sales Letter

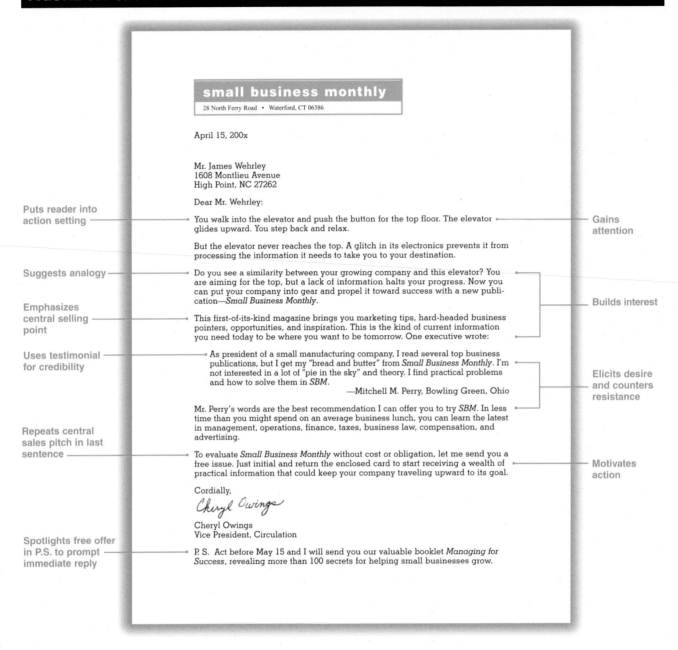

small business monthly

28 North Ferry Road • Waterford, CT 06386

April 15, 200x

Mr. James Wehrley
1608 Montlieu Avenue
High Point, NC 27262

Dear Mr. Wehrley:

You walk into the elevator and push the button for the top floor. The elevator glides upward. You step back and relax.

But the elevator never reaches the top. A glitch in its electronics prevents it from processing the information it needs to take you to your destination.

Do you see a similarity between your growing company and this elevator? You are aiming for the top, but a lack of information halts your progress. Now you can put your company into gear and propel it toward success with a new publication—*Small Business Monthly*.

This first-of-its-kind magazine brings you marketing tips, hard-headed business pointers, opportunities, and inspiration. This is the kind of current information you need today to be where you want to be tomorrow. One executive wrote:

> As president of a small manufacturing company, I read several top business publications, but I get my "bread and butter" from *Small Business Monthly*. I'm not interested in a lot of "pie in the sky" and theory. I find practical problems and how to solve them in *SBM*.
>
> —Mitchell M. Perry, Bowling Green, Ohio

Mr. Perry's words are the best recommendation I can offer you to try *SBM*. In less time than you might spend on an average business lunch, you can learn the latest in management, operations, finance, taxes, business law, compensation, and advertising.

To evaluate *Small Business Monthly* without cost or obligation, let me send you a free issue. Just initial and return the enclosed card to start receiving a wealth of practical information that could keep your company traveling upward to its goal.

Cordially,

Cheryl Owings

Cheryl Owings
Vice President, Circulation

P. S. Act before May 15 and I will send you our valuable booklet *Managing for Success*, revealing more than 100 secrets for helping small businesses grow.

Left margin annotations:
- Puts reader into action setting
- Suggests analogy
- Emphasizes central selling point
- Uses testimonial for credibility
- Repeats central sales pitch in last sentence
- Spotlights free offer in P.S. to prompt immediate reply

Right margin annotations:
- Gains attention
- Builds interest
- Elicits desire and counters resistance
- Motivates action

Communication Workshop for this chapter to see specific examples of what is legal and what is not.

Writing Successful Online Sales and Marketing Messages

To make the best use of limited advertising dollars while reaching a great number of potential customers, many businesses are turning to the Internet and to e-mail marketing campaigns in particular. Much like traditional direct mail, e-mail marketing can attract new customers, keep existing ones, encourage future sales, cross-sell, and cut costs. As consumers feel more comfortable and secure with online purchases, they will receive more e-mail sales messages.

Selling by E-Mail

If your organization requires an online sales message, try using the following techniques gleaned from the best-performing e-mails.

Communicate only with those who have given permission! By sending messages only to "opt-in" folks, you greatly increase your "open rate"—those e-mail messages that will be opened. E-mail users detest spam. However, receivers are surprisingly receptive to offers tailored specifically for them. Remember that today's customer is somebody—not anybody.

Today's promotional e-mail often comes with colorful and eye-catching graphics and a minimum of text. To allow for embedded images, sound, and even video, the e-mail is coded in HTML and can be viewed in an e-mail program or an Internet browser. Software programs make it easy to create e-newsletters for e-mail distribution. Figure 8.5 shows such a promotional message in HTML format by live music search engine Live Nation. It was sent by e-mail to customers who had bought tickets from Live Nation. They had to create an account and sign up to receive such periodic promotions or e-newsletters. Note that the marketers make it easy for the recipient to unsubscribe.

The principles you have learned to apply to traditional sales messages also work with electronic promotional tools. However, some fundamental differences are obvious when you study Figure 8.5. Online sales messages are much shorter than direct mail, feature colorful graphics, and occasionally even have sound or video clips. They offer a richer experience to readers who can click hyperlinks at will to access content that interests them. When such messages are sent out as ads or periodic e-newsletters, they may not have salutations or closings. Rather, they may resemble Web pages.

Here are a few guidelines that will help you create effective online sales messages:

- **Craft a catchy subject line.** Offer discounts or premiums: *Spring Sale: Buy now and save 20 percent!* Promise solutions to everyday work-related problems. Highlight hot new industry topics. Invite readers to scan a top-ten list of items such as issues, trends, or people.
- **Keep the main information "above the fold."** E-mail messages should be top heavy. Primary points should appear early in the message so that they capture the reader's attention.
- **Make the message short, conversational, and focused.** Because on-screen text is taxing to read, be brief. Focus on one or two central selling points only.
- **Convey urgency.** Top-performing e-mail messages state an offer deadline or demonstrate why the state of the industry demands action on the reader's part. Good messages also tie the product to relevant current events.
- **Sprinkle testimonials throughout the copy.** Consumers' own words are the best sales copy. These comments can serve as callouts or be integrated into the copy.
- **Provide a means for opting out.** It is polite and a good business tactic to include a statement that tells receivers how to be removed from the sender's mailing database.

Using Blogs, Wikis, and Other New Media to Convey Company and Product Information

Businesses increasingly look to blogs, wikis, and RSS feeds to convey their persuasive and promotional messages to partner firms and customers. These new tools can also be useful internally when communicating with employees.

Blogs. In the right hands blogs can be powerful marketing tools. Information technology giant Hewlett-Packard invites guest bloggers onto its site as advisors to small businesses, for example. Executives, HP employees, and outside experts discuss a wide range of technology- and company-related topics. Although not overtly pushing a marketing message, ultimately HP wants to generate goodwill; hence, the blogs serve as a public relations tool.[6] Nearly half of the CEOs questioned in one

FIGURE 8.5 E-Mail Sales Message to Opt-In Recipients

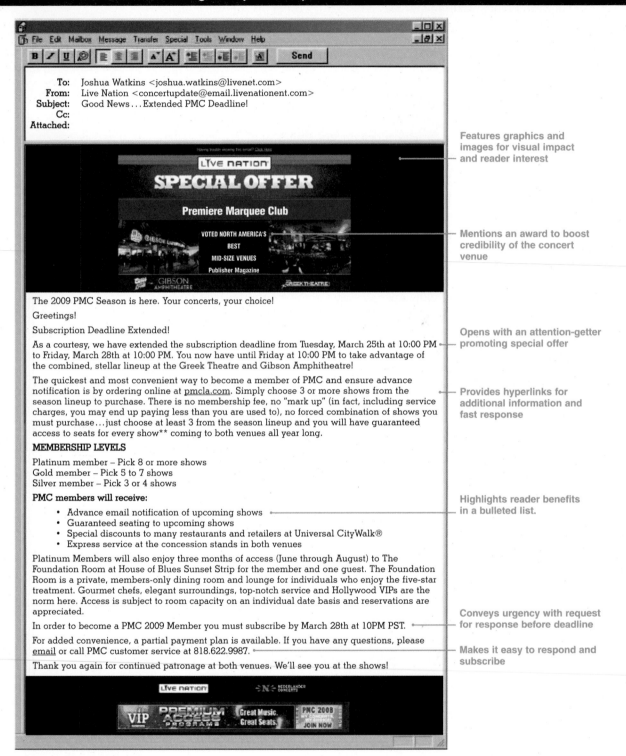

Features graphics and images for visual impact and reader interest

Mentions an award to boost credibility of the concert venue

Opens with an attention-getter promoting special offer

Provides hyperlinks for additional information and fast response

Highlights reader benefits in a bulleted list.

Conveys urgency with request for response before deadline

Makes it easy to respond and subscribe

survey said they believe blogs are useful for external public relations, and 59 percent said they find blogs valuable for internal communication.[7] Many companies now use blogs to subtly market their products and develop a brand image.

Wikis. Wikis generally facilitate collaboration inside organizations, but they also do so between companies, thus generating goodwill. A wiki contains digital information available on a Web portal or on a company's protected intranet where visitors can add or edit content. One big advantage of wikis is the ease of information and file sharing. Perhaps the best-known wiki is the online encyclopedia Wikipedia.

In business, wiki users can quickly document and publish a complex process to a group of recipients. Ziba Design of Portland, Oregon, launched what it calls "virtual studios," popular online meeting spots where the agency and its clients share files, exchange design ideas, and post news.[8] Ziba Design is providing a valuable service to its customers and, in turn, is learning about their needs. You will find out more about wikis as collaboration tools in Chapter 10.

RSS (really simple syndication). RSS (really simple syndication) is yet another tool for keeping customers and business partners up-to-date. Many companies now offer RSS feeds, a format for distributing news or information about recent changes on their Web sites, in wikis, or in blogs. Recipients subscribe to content they want using RSS reader software. Alternatively, they receive news items or articles in their e-mail.[9] The RSS feeds help users to keep up with their favorite Web magazines, Web sites, and blogs. As a promotional tool, this medium can create interest in a company and its products.

Podcasting. Podcasting is emerging as an important Internet marketing tool. Business podcasts are content-rich audio or video files featuring company representatives, business experts, or products and services. They can be distributed by RSS or downloaded from company Web sites and played back on a computer or an MP3 player.

Blogs, wikis, RSS, and podcasting are just a few new media available to companies for communicating with and persuading the public. Strategic use of these media can enable companies to increase their competitive profiles as well as their awareness of the needs and concerns of their customers.

Visit www.meguffey.com
- Chapter Review Quiz
- Flash Cards
- Grammar Practice
- PowerPoint Slides
- Personal Language Trainer
- Beat the Clock Quiz

Summing Up and Looking Forward

The ability to persuade is a powerful and versatile communication tool. In this chapter you learned to apply the indirect strategy in making favor and action requests, writing persuasive messages within organizations, making claims and requesting adjustments, and writing sales letters. You also learned techniques for developing successful online sales messages. In the Communication Workshop following this chapter, you can examine examples of what is legal and what is not in sales letters.

The techniques suggested in this chapter will be useful in many other contexts beyond the writing of business documents. They will come in handy when you apply for a position. Moreover, you will find that organizing your arguments logically is also extremely helpful when expressing ideas orally or any time you must overcome resistance to change.

In coming chapters you will learn how to modify and generalize the techniques of direct and indirect strategies in preparing and writing informal and formal reports and proposals. Nearly all businesspeople today find that they must write an occasional report.

Critical Thinking

1. Why do many writers prefer the indirect pattern for persuasive requests?

2. Describe the components of a persuasive request or a sales letter and explain what each part needs to accomplish.

3. Because of the burden that "junk mail" places on society (depleted landfills, declining timber supplies, an overburdened postal system), how can it be justified?

4. Why is it not a wise idea to "stretch the truth" when persuading?

5. Some individuals will never write an actual sales letter. Why is it nevertheless important for them to learn the techniques for doing so?

Chapter Review

6. What is the difference between direct and indirect benefits to individuals we may want to persuade?

7. How can a subordinate be effective in persuading a superior to adopt a new procedure or purchase new equipment?

8. Explain how you would decide whether to use the direct pattern or the indirect pattern.

9. List eight tips for making claims and complaints.

10. List at least ten ways to gain a reader's attention in the opening of a sales letter.

11. *Recline in your first-class seat and sip a freshly stirred drink while listening to 12 channels of superb audio, or snooze* is an example of what type of persuasive appeal? How does it compare to the following: *Take one of four daily direct flights to Europe on our modern Airbus aircraft, and enjoy the most legroom of any airline. If we are ever late, you will receive coupons for free trips.*

12. Name six writing techniques that reduce resistance in a sales message.

13. Name five techniques for motivating action in the closing of a sales message.

14. Describe the main purposes of using business podcasts, blogs, and wikis.

15. What techniques do writers of successful online sales messages use?

Writing Improvement Exercises

Strategies
For each of the following situations, check the appropriate writing strategy.

Direct Strategy	Indirect Strategy	
_____	_____	16. An invitation to a nationally known information technology expert to discuss the latest technology trends with the campus community
_____	_____	17. An announcement that must convince employees to stop smoking, start exercising, and opt for a healthy diet to lower health care expenses and reduce absenteeism
_____	_____	18. A request to another company for verification of employment regarding a job applicant
_____	_____	19. A letter to a cleaning service demanding a refund for sealing a dirty tiled floor and damaging a fresh paint job
_____	_____	20. A request for information about a wireless office network
_____	_____	21. A letter to a grocery store requesting permission to display posters advertising a school fund-raising car wash
_____	_____	22. A request for a refund of the cost of a computer program that does not perform the functions it was expected to perform
_____	_____	23. A request for correction of a routine billing error on your company credit card
_____	_____	24. An invitation to your boss or a business partner to join you for dinner
_____	_____	25. A memo to employees describing the schedule and menu selections of a new mobile catering service

8.1 Persuasive Letter: Favor Request

Your Task. Analyze the following message and list its weaknesses. If your instructor directs, revise the message. A copy of this message is provided at **www.meguffey.com** for revision online.

Current date

Ms. Lisa Gurchiek
590 Loudon Road
Loudonville, NY 12211

Dear Lisa:

Because we heard that you frequently travel to our fair city of Tampa, we thought it would not be too much trouble for you to be the keynote speaker at our UT Management Society banquet April 2. Your newspaper columns and many books on careers have been reliable sources of information and inspiration to readers across the country and especially to us business students here at the University of Tampa.

One of our professors said that you were the dean of career columnists. Maybe that is why you have been named the person that our students would most like to have as the keynote speaker at our UT Management Society banquet April 2. All of us will be seeking business careers when we graduate, so this is why we are interested in tips about résumés, cover letters and interviews. We were surprised, though, when our professor told us that you have written a number of "Dummies" books including *Résumés for Dummies, Cover Letters for Dummies,* and so on. We are not dummies, but we are especially interested in learning about Internet job searching, the topic of one of your recent columns.

We can't offer an honorarium; therefore, we have to rely on local speakers. But we can promise you a fine dinner at the UT Faculty Club.

We also know that you often stay in Crystal Beach, which is not too far from our campus, so we hoped you could work us into your schedule. Our banquet evening as a general rule begins at 6:30 with a social hour, followed by dinner at 7:30 P.M. and the speaker from 8:30 until 9 or 9:15 P.M. You won't have to worry about transportation; we can arrange a limousine for you and your husband if you need it.

We realize that you have a busy schedule, but we hope you will carve out a space for us. Please let our advisor, Professor Michael Eastman, have the favor of an early reply.

Cordially,

List at least five weaknesses of this letter.

8.2 Persuasive E-Mail: Importing T-Shirts From China

Your Task. Analyze the following message and list its weaknesses. If your instructor directs, revise the message. A copy of this message is provided at **www.meguffey.com** for revision online.

From: Donna Happich [dhappich@superfit.com]
To: Harry Lambrusco [hlambrusco@superfit.com]
Cc:
Subject: T-Shirts From China

Trade shows are a great way for us to meet customers and sell our Super Fit strength machines. But instead of expanding our visits to these trade shows, we continue to cut back the number that we attend. Lately we have been sending fewer staff members. I know that you have been asking us to find ways to reduce costs, but perhaps we are not going about it right.

With increased air fares and hotel charges, my staff has tried to find ways to live within our very tight budget. However, we are being asked to find additional ways to reduce our costs. I'm currently thinking ahead to the big Las Vegas trade show coming up in September.

One area where we could make a change is in the gift that we give away. In the past we have presented booth visitors with a nine-color T-shirt that is silk screened and gorgeous. But it comes at a cost of $15 for each and every one of these beauties from a top-name designer. To save money, I suggest that we try a $5 T-shirt made in China, which is reasonably present-able. It has got our name on it, and, after all, folks just use these shirts for workouts. Who cares if it is a fancy silk-screened T-shirt or a functional Chinese one that has "Super Fit" plastered on the chest? Since we give away 2,000 T-shirts at our largest show, we could save big bucks by dumping the designer shirt. But we have to act quickly. I put a cheap one in your mailbox, so you can take a look at it.

Let me know what you think.

List at least five weaknesses of this message.

8.3 Claim Request: Copier Ripoff!
The following letter makes a claim, but the message is not as effective as it could be.

Your Task. Analyze the message and list its weaknesses. If your instructor directs, revise the message. A copy of this message is provided at **www.meguffey.com** for revision online.

Current date

Mr. Carl Brownston
Leder Business Supplies
8933 Cribbins Road
Jeddo, MI 48032

Dear Sir:

Three months ago we purchased four of your Imager 500E photocopiers, and we have had nothing but trouble ever since.

Your salesperson, Judy Selles, assured us that the Imager 500E could easily handle our volume of 5,000 copies a day. This seemed strange since the sales brochure said that the Imager 500E was meant for 1,000 copies a day. But we believed Ms. Selles. Big mistake! Our four Imager 500E copiers are down constantly; we can't go on like this. Because they are still under warranty, they eventually get repaired. But we are losing considerable business in downtime.

Your Ms. Selles has been less than helpful, so I telephoned the district manager, Rick Jimenez. I suggested that we trade in our Imager 500E copiers (which we got for $2,500 each) on two Imager 1000E models (at $13,500 each). However, Mr. Jimenez said he would have to charge 50 percent depreciation on our Imager 500E copiers. What a ripoff! I think that 20 percent depre-ciation is more reasonable since we have had the machines only three months. Mr. Jimenez said he would get back to me, and I haven't heard from him since.

I'm writing to your headquarters because I have no faith in either Ms. Selles or Mr. Jimenez, and I need action on these machines. If you understood anything about business, you would see what a sweet deal I'm offering you. I'm willing to stick with your company and purchase your most expensive model—but I can't take such a steep loss on the Imager 500E copi-ers. The Imager 500E copiers are relatively new; you should be able to sell them with no trouble. And think of all the money you will save by not having your repair technicians making constant trips to service our 500E copiers! Please let me hear from you immediately.

Sincerely yours,

List at least five weaknesses of this letter.

8.4 Sales Letter Analysis

Your Task. Select a one- or two-page sales letter received by you or a friend. (If you are unable to find a sales letter, your instructor may have a collection.) Study the letter and then answer these questions:

a. What techniques capture the reader's attention?

b. Is the opening effective? Explain.

c. What are the central selling points?

d. Does the letter use rational, emotional, or a combination of appeals? Explain.

e. What reader benefits are suggested?

f. How does the letter build interest in the product or service?

g. How is price handled?

h. How does the letter anticipate reader resistance and offer counterarguments?

i. What action is the reader to take? How is the action made easy?

j. What motivators spur the reader to act quickly?

Activities and Cases

WEB

8.5 Persuasive Favor/Action Request: Financial Advice for the Young, Fabulous, and Broke

Despite spending countless hours in the classroom and writing stacks of meticulous research papers, many graduates who are about to enter the real world are clueless when it comes to basic personal finance, according to the experts. As program chair for the Associated Student Organization at the University of Nevada, Las Vegas, you suggest that the group invite financial celebrity Suze Orman to be its keynote speaker at a special graduation convocation. The ASO agreed and set aside $1,000 as an honorarium. This is not very much to entice the author of *The Money Book for the Young, Fabulous & Broke,* but Ms. Orman has been heavily promoting her book in cross-country tours to college campuses. The ASO group thinks it stands a fair chance of luring this financial celebrity to campus.[10]

Your Task. Write a convincing favor/action request to Suze Orman, P.O. Box 4502, New York, NY 10014. Learn more about her expertise and books by using the Web and electronic databases. Invite her to speak May 26. Provide direct and indirect benefits. Include an end date and make it easy to respond. Do not use the same wording as the model documents in this chapter.

TEAM

8.6 Persuasive Favor/Action Request: Celebrity Auction

Your professional or school organization (such as the Associated Students Organization) must find ways to raise money. The president of your group appoints a team and asks it to brainstorm for ways to meet your group's pledge to aid the United Way's battle against adult illiteracy in your community. The campaign against adult illiteracy has targeted an estimated 10,000 people in your community who cannot read or write. After considering and discarding a number of silly ideas, your team comes up with the brilliant idea of a celebrity auction. At a fall function, items or services from local and other celebrities would be auctioned. Your organization approves your idea and asks your team to persuade an important person in your professional organization (or your college president) to donate one hour of tutoring in a subject he or she chooses. If you have higher aspirations, write to a movie star or athlete of your choice—perhaps one who is part of your organization or who attended your school.

Your Task. As a team, discuss the situation and decide what action to take. Then write a persuasive letter to secure an item for the auction. You might wish to ask a star to donate a prop from a recent movie.

8.7 Persuasive Favor/Action Request: PDAs Lighten Realtors' Load in Orlando, Florida

Orlando, Florida, boasts warm weather year round. Its lack of income tax makes it a popular destination for retirees and others who want to stretch their dollar farther and soak up some sun. Orlando offers a lower cost of living and steadier home values than the rest of Florida and the nation. Orlando has been nicknamed "Hollywood East" for a growing movie industry and is an attractive destination for its theme parks and convention centers. The engineering and electronic gaming fields are booming and seem immune even to economic downturns.[11] All this is good news for the realtors in Orlando. However, agents have to grapple with telephone directory–size books of multiple listings—or run back and forth to their offices as they show home buyers what is on the market.

As a staffer at one of Orlando's top realty agencies, you recently attended a Association of Realtors meeting and talked with fellow agent Greg Sawicki. He showed you his new BlackBerry, a personal digital assistant (PDA), and said, "Watch this." He accessed listing after listing of homes for sale by his company and others. You couldn't believe your eyes. You saw island properties, historic homes, lakefront condos—all with pictures and complete listing information. In this little device, which could easily fit into a pocket (or purse), you could carry six months' worth of active, pending, and closed listings, along with contact details for agents and other valuable information.

You thought about the size of your multiple listing books and how often you had to trudge back to the office when a home buyer wanted to see a market listing. "Looks terrific," you said to Greg. "But what about new listings? And how much does this thing cost? I bet it has a steep learning curve." Eager to show off his new toy, Greg demonstrated its user-friendly interface that follows intuitive prompts such as price, area, and number of bedrooms. He explained that his agency bought the software for $129. For a monthly fee of $19, he downloads updates as often as he likes. In regard to ease of use, Greg said that even his fellow agent Annette, notoriously computer challenged, loved it. None of the staff found it confusing or difficult to operate.

You decide that the agency where you work should provide this service to all 18 full-time staff agents. Assume that multiple listing software is available for the greater Orlando area.

Your Task. With other staff members (your classmates), decide how to approach the agency owner, who is "old school" and shuns most technology. Decide what you want to request. Do you merely want the owner to talk with you about the service? Should you come right out and ask for PDAs and the service for all 18 staff members? Should you expect staff members to provide the hardware (a basic PDA at about $200) and the agency to purchase the service and individual updates for each full-time agent? Or should you ask for the service plus a top-of-the-line smartphone that provides PDA/phone, global positioning system (GPS), navigation, and other capabilities? Learn more about smartphones and PDAs such as BlackBerry, Treo, and iPhone on the Web. Explore this information with your team. Once you decide on a course of action, what appeals would be most persuasive? Discuss how to handle price in your persuasive argument. Individually or as a group, prepare a persuasive message to Michael J. Sawyer, President, Sawyer Orlando Realty. Decide whether you should deliver your persuasive message as a printed memo or an e-mail, possibly one with an attachment in MS Word.

8.8 Persuasive Favor/Action Request: Servers Want Recourse From Stingy Customers

Centered in the heart of a 650-acre Florida paradise, the Crescent Beach & Golf Resort offers gracious hospitality and beautiful accommodations. Its casually elegant restaurant, The Lido Beach Club, is the perfect stop after a day at the beach with infinite views of the Gulf of Mexico. As a server at the Lido, you enjoy working in this resort setting—except for one thing. You have occasionally been "stiffed" by a patron who left no tip. You know your service is excellent, but some customers just don't get it. They seem to think that tips are optional, a sign of appreciation. For servers, however, tips are 80 percent of their income.

In a recent *New York Times* article, you learned that some restaurants—like the famous Coach House Restaurant in New York—automatically add a 15 percent tip to the bill. In Santa Monica the Lula restaurant prints "gratuity guidelines" on checks, showing customers what a 15 or 20 percent tip would be. You also know that American Express recently developed a gratuity calculation feature on its terminals. This means that diners don't even have to do the math!

Your Task. Because they know you are studying business communication, your fellow servers have asked you to write a serious letter to Andrew Garcia, General Manager, Crescent Beach & Golf Resort, 9891 Gulf Shore Drive, Naples, FL 34108. Persuade him to adopt mandatory tipping guidelines in the restaurant. Talk with fellow servers (your classmates) to develop logical persuasive arguments.

8.9 Persuasive Favor/Action Request: Dictionary Definition of *McJobs* Angers McDonald's

The folks at McDonald's fumed when they heard about the latest edition of a highly regarded dictionary, *Merriam-Webster's Collegiate Dictionary,* defined the word *McJob* as "a low-paying job that requires little skill and provides little opportunity for advancement." Naturally, McDonald's was outraged. One executive said, "It's a slap in the face to the 12 million men and women who work hard every day in America's 900,000 restaurants."

The term *McJob* was coined by Canadian novelist Douglas Coupland in his 1991 novel *Generation X.* In this novel the term described a low-prestige, low-dignity, low-benefit, no-future job in the service sector. McDonald's strongly objects to this corruption of its name. For one thing, the company rejects the notion that its jobs are dead ends. Significant members of top management—including the president, chief operating officer, and CEO—began their McDonald's careers behind the counter. Moreover, when it comes to training, McDonald's trains more young people than the U.S. armed forces.

What is more, McDonald's is especially proud of its "MCJOBS" program for mentally and physically challenged people. Some officers even wonder whether the dictionary term *McJob* comes dangerously close to the trademarked name for its special program. Another point that rankles McDonald's is that, according to its records, over 1,000 people who now own McDonald's restaurants received their training while serving customers. Who says that its jobs have no future?

The CEO is burned up about Merriam-Webster's dictionary definition, and he wants to send a complaint letter. However, he is busy and asks you, a member of the communication staff, to draft a first version. He is so steamed that he is thinking of sending a copy of the letter to news agencies.

Your Task. Before writing this letter, decide what action, if any, to request. Think about an appropriate tone and also about the two possible audiences. Then write a persuasive letter for the signature of the CEO. Include the "a slap in the face" statement, which he insists on inserting. Address your letter to Frederick C. Mish, editor in chief, Merriam-Webster. Look for a street address on the Web.

WEB

8.10 Persuasive Favor/Action Request: Appealing to Your Congressional Representative to Listen and Act

Assume you are upset about an issue, and you want your representative or senator to know your position. Choose a national issue about which you feel strongly: student loans, social security depletion, human rights in other countries, federal safety regulations for employees, environmental protection, affirmative action, gun control, taxation of married couples, finding a cure for obesity, the federal deficit, or some other area regulated by Congress.

How does one write to a congressional representative? For best results, consider these tips:

a. Use the proper form of address (The Honorable John Smith, Dear Senator Smith or The Honorable Joan Doe, Dear Representative Doe).

b. Identify yourself as a member of his or her state or district.

c. Immediately state your position (*I urge you to support/oppose . . . because . . .*).

d. Present facts and illustrations and explain how they affect you personally. If legislation were enacted, how would you or your organization be better off or worse off? Avoid generalities.

e. Offer to provide further information.

f. Keep the message polite, constructive, and brief (one page tops).

Your Task. Use your favorite Web search engine such as Google to obtain your congressional representative's address. Try the search term *contacting Congress*. You should be able to find e-mail and land addresses, along with fax and telephone numbers. Remember that although e-mail and fax messages are fast, they don't carry as much influence as personal letters. Moreover, congressional representatives are having trouble responding to the overload of e-mail messages they receive. Decide whether it would be better to send an e-mail message or a letter.

TEAM

8.11 Persuasive Favor/Action Request: Vending Machines Are Cash Cows to Schools

"If I start to get huge, then, yeah, I'll cut out the chips and Coke," says seventeen-year-old Nicole O'Neill, as she munches sour-cream-and-onion potato chips and downs a cold can of soda fresh from the snack machine. Most days her lunch comes from a vending machine. The trim high school junior, however, isn't too concerned about how junk food affects her weight or overall health. Although she admits she would prefer a granola bar or fruit, few healthful selections are available from school vending machines.

Vending machines loaded with soft drinks and snacks are increasingly under attack in schools and lunchrooms. Some school boards, however, see them as cash cows. In Gresham, Oregon, the school district is considering a lucrative soft drink contract. If it signs an exclusive 12-year agreement with Coca-Cola to allow vending machines at Gresham High School, the school district will receive $75,000 up front. Then it will receive an additional $75,000 three years later. Commission sales on the 75-cent drinks will bring in an additional $322,000 over the 12-year contract, provided the school sells 67,000 cans and bottles every year. In the past the vending machine payments supported student body activities such as sending students to choir concerts and paying athletic participation fees. Vending machine funds also paid for an electronic reader board in front of the school and a sound system for the gym. The latest contract would bring in $150,000, which is already earmarked for new artificial turf on the school athletic field.

Coca-Cola's vending machines would dispense soft drinks, Fruitopia, Minute Maid juices, Powerade, and Dasani water. The hands-down student favorite, of course, is calorie-laden Coke. Because increasing childhood and adolescent obesity across the nation is a major health concern, the Gresham Parent–Teacher Association (PTA) decided to oppose the contract.

The PTA realizes that the school board is heavily influenced by the income generated from the Coca-Cola contract. It wonders what other school districts are doing about their vending machine contracts.

Your Task. As part of a PTA committee, you have been given the task of researching and composing a persuasive but concise (no more than one page) letter addressed to the school board. Use the Web to locate articles that might help you develop arguments, alternatives, and counterarguments. Meet with your team to discuss your findings. Then, individually or as a group, write a letter to the Board of Directors, Gresham-Barlow School District, P.O. Box 310, Gresham, OR 97033.

8.12 Personal Persuasive Memo or E-Mail: Dear Boss

In your own work or organization experience, identify a problem for which you have a solution. Should a procedure be altered to improve performance? Would a new or different piece of equipment help you perform your work better? Could some tasks be scheduled more efficiently? Are employees being used most effectively? Could customers be better served by changing something? Do you want to work other hours or perform other tasks?

Your Task. Once you have identified a situation requiring persuasion, decide whether to write an e-mail message or an interoffice memo (sent as an attachment to a short cover e-mail) to your boss or organization head. Use actual names and facts. Employ the concepts and techniques in this chapter to help you convince your boss that your idea should prevail. Include concrete examples, anticipate objections, emphasize reader benefits, and end with a specific action to be taken.

E-MAIL

8.13 Persuasive E-Mail: Scheduling Meetings More Strategically

The following message, with names changed, was actually sent.

Your Task. Based on what you have learned in this chapter, improve this e-mail. Expect the staff to be somewhat resistant because they have never before had meeting restrictions.

From: Dina Waterman [dwaterman@promosell.com]
To: All Managers
Cc:
Subject: Scheduling Meetings

Please be reminded that travel in the greater Los Angeles area is time consuming. In the future we are asking that you set up meetings that

1. Are of critical importance
2. Consider travel time for the participants
3. Consider phone conferences (or video or e-mail) in lieu of face-to-face meetings
4. Meetings should be at the location where most of the participants work and at the most opportune travel times
5. Traveling together is another way to save time and resources.

We all have our traffic horror stories. A recent one is that a certain manager was asked to attend a one-hour meeting in Burbank. This required one hour of travel in advance of the meeting, one hour for the meeting, and two and a half hours of travel through Los Angeles afterward. This meeting was scheduled for 4 P.M. Total time consumed by the manager for the one-hour meeting was four and a half hours.

Thank you for your consideration.

E-MAIL   **WEB**

8.14 Persuasive Internal E-Mail Request: Convincing Your Boss to Blog

You have just read Steve Rubel's *Micro Persuasion* blog, in which he cites an interesting study of chief executives and blogging.[12] It turns out that a majority of CEOs believe blogs to be useful for internal (59 percent) and external communication (47 percent). However, only 7 percent of the CEOs interviewed actually blog, although 18 percent expect to host a company blog within two years.

Your boss, Simon Dawkins, is a technophobe who is slow in adopting the latest information technology. You know that it will be a difficult sell, but you believe that corporate blogging is an opportunity not to be missed.

Your Task. Write a persuasive e-mail message to Simon Dawkins attempting to convince him that blogging is a useful public-relations and internal communication tool and that he or someone he officially designates should start a company weblog. Anticipate Dawkins' fears. Naturally, a blogger has to be prepared even for unflattering comments. If your instructor directs, visit the blogs of companies such as Google (**http://googleblog.blogspot.com/**), Microsoft (**http://blogs.msdn.com/**), or Chrysler (**http://www.chryslerweblog.com/**). You can search for company blogs in Google. Select the **More** tab on top of the screen and click **Blogs**.

8.15 Persuasive Internal Request: Can We Create Our Own Business Podcasts?

You are working for the small accounting firm, CPA Plus, and your boss, Bradford Trask, wonders whether your company could produce podcasts for its clients without professional help. He doesn't know how podcasting really works, nor what resources or costs would be required. However, he has read about the benefits of providing advice or sending promotional messages to customers who can download them from the company Web site or subscribe to them in a podcast directory.

Conduct some Web research to understand better how podcasting works and what hardware and software are needed. Visit podcast directories such as *Podcast Alley* (**http://www.podcastalley.com**) or *Podcast.net* (**http://www.podcast.net**) for some ideas, or search iTunes for business and investment podcasts. The Small Business Administration (**http://www.sba .gov/tools/resourcelibrary/Podcasts/**) also offers Web pages devoted to the topic.

Your Task. Consider your accounting firm's needs and its audience. Then write an e-mail or a memo addressed to Bradford Trask that you would send along with a brief e-mail cover message. In your memo argue for or against creating podcasts in house. For professional podcasts listen to *The Wall Street Journal's The Journal Report* or any number of business podcasts on iTunes.

8.16 Persuasive Claim: Legal Costs for Sharing a Slice of Heaven

Originally a shipbuilding village, the town of Mystic, Connecticut, captures the spirit of the nineteenth-century seafaring era. However, it is best known for Mystic Pizza, a bustling local pizzeria featured in a movie that launched the film career of Julia Roberts. Today, customers line the sidewalk waiting to taste its pizza, called by some "a slice of Heaven."

Assume that you are the business manager for Mystic Pizza's owners. They were approached by an independent vendor who wants to use the Mystic Pizza name and secret recipes to distribute frozen pizza through grocery and convenience stores. As business manager, you worked with a law firm, Santoro, Michaels, and Associates. This firm was to draw up contracts regarding the use of Mystic Pizza's name and quality standards for the product. When you received the bill from Tom Santoro, you were flabbergasted. It itemized 38 hours of attorney preparation, at $400 per hour, and 55 hours of paralegal assistance, at $100 per hour. The bill also showed $415 for telephone calls, which might be accurate because Mr. Santoro had to talk with the owners, who were vacationing in Italy at the time. You seriously doubt, however, that an experienced attorney would require 38 hours to draw up the contracts in question. When you began checking, you discovered that excellent legal advice could be obtained for $200 an hour.

Your Task. Decide what you want to request, and then write a persuasive request to Thomas E. Santoro, Attorney at Law, Santoro, Michaels, and Associates, 448 Asylum Street, Hartford, CT 06105. Include an end date and a reason for it.

8.17 Persuasive Claim: Champagne Breakfast Appears Only on Credit Card

As regional manager for an electronics parts manufacturer, you and two other employees attended a conference in Chicago. You stayed at the Hilton Chicago Lakeview because your company recommends that employees use this hotel chain. Generally, your employees have liked their accommodations, and the rates have been within your company's budget. The hotel's service has been excellent.

Now, however, you are unhappy with the charges you see on your company's credit statement from Hilton Chicago Lakeview. When your department's administrative assistant made the reservations, she was assured that you would receive the weekend rates and that a hot breakfast—in the hotel restaurant, The Pavilion—would be included in the rate. You hate those cold sweet-rolls-and-instant-coffee "continental" breakfasts, especially when you have to leave early and won't get another meal until afternoon. So you and the other two employees went to the restaurant and ordered a hot meal from the menu.

When you received the credit statement, though, you saw a charge for $81 for three champagne buffet breakfasts in the Atrium. You hit the ceiling! For one thing, you didn't have a buffet breakfast and certainly no champagne. The three of you got there so early that no buffet had been set up. You ordered pancakes and sausage, and for this you were billed $25 each. You are outraged! What is worse, your company may charge you personally for exceeding the expected rates.

In looking back at this event, you remembered that other guests on your floor were having a "continental" breakfast in a lounge on your floor. Perhaps that is where the hotel expected all guests on the weekend rate to eat. However, your administrative assistant had specifically asked about this matter when she made the reservations, and she was told that you could order breakfast from the menu at the hotel's restaurant.

Your Task. You want to straighten out this matter, and you can't do it by telephone because you suspect that you will need a written record of this entire mess. Write a claim request to Customer Service, Hilton Chicago Lakeview, 800 North Michigan Avenue, Chicago, IL 60604. Should you include a copy of the credit statement showing the charge?

8.18 E-Mail or Direct Mail Sales Message: Promoting Your Product or Service

Identify a situation in your current job or a previous one in which a sales letter is or was needed. Using suggestions from this chapter, write an appropriate sales message that promotes a product or service. Use actual names, information, and examples. If you have no work experience, imagine a business you would like to start: word processing, pet grooming, car detailing, tutoring, specialty knitting, balloon decorating, delivery service, child care, gardening, lawn care, or something else.

Your Task. Write a sales letter or an online e-mail message selling your product or service to be distributed to your prospective customers. Be sure to tell them how to respond.

You don't need to know HTML to craft a concise and eye-catching online sales message. Try designing it in MS Word and saving it as a Web page (in Word 2003, go to **File**, click **Save as**, and select **Web Page** in the **Save as type** pull-down window; in Word 2007 you reach the same window by clicking the MS logo, then **Save as**). Consider adding graphics or photos—either your own or samples borrowed from the Internet. As long as you use them for this assignment and don't publish them online, you are not violating copyright laws.

Video Resources

This chapter has one video with a writing assignment.

Video Library 2: *Persuasive Request: Hard Rock Café.* This video takes you inside the Hard Rock Cafe where you learn about changes it has undergone in surviving over 30 years in the rough-and-tumble world of hospitality. One problem involves difficulty in maintaining its well-known logo around the world. While watching the video, look for references to the changes taking place and the discussion of brand control.

Your Task. As an assistant in the Hard Rock Corporate Identity Division, you have been asked to draft a persuasive message to be sent to the Edinburgh International Comedy Festival. In doing research, you learned that this festival is one of the three largest comedy festivals in the world, alongside Melbourne Madness Festival and Montreal's Just for Laughs Festival. An annual event, the Edinburgh International Comedy Festival takes over this Scotland city each autumn with stand-up comedy, cabaret, theater, street performance,

film, television, radio, and visual arts programs. Some of the programs raise funds for charity.

The problem is that the festival is staging some of its events at the Hard Rock Cafe, and the festival is using outdated Hard Rock logos at their Web site and in print announcements. Your task is to persuade the Edinburgh International Comedy Festival organizers to stop using the old logos. Explain why it is necessary to use the official Hard Rock logo. Make it easy for them to obtain the official logo at **http://www.hardrock.net .official.logo**. Organizers must also sign the logo usage agreement. Organizers may be resistant because they have invested in announcements and Web designs with the old logo. If they don't comply by June 1, Hard Rock attorneys may begin legal actions. However, you need to present this date without making it sound like a threat. Your boss wants this message to develop goodwill, not motivate antagonism. Write a persuasive e-mail message to Edinburgh International Comedy Festival organizer Barry Cook at *bcook@edinburghfestival.com*. Add any reasonable details.

Grammar/Mechanics Checkup 8

Commas 3
Review the Grammar/Mechanics Handbook Sections 2.10–2.15. Then study each of the following statements and insert necessary commas. In the space provided write the number of commas that you add; write *0* if no commas are needed. Also record the number of the G/M principle(s) illustrated. When you finish, compare your responses with those provided at the end of the book. If your answers differ, study carefully the principles shown in parentheses.

Example Management selected Meredith Jones, not Ronald Lee, to be the next manager. 2 (2.12)

1. "There are no gains" said Benjamin Franklin "without pains."

2. The featured speakers are Keiko Krahnke PhD and Reggie Kostiz MBA.

3. You inspected their Web site didn't you?

4. Research shows that talking on a cell phone distracts drivers and quadruples their chances of getting into accidents such as rear-ending a car ahead of them.

5. The bigger the monitor the clearer the picture.

Review Commas 1, 2, 3

6. As you may know information chips are already encoded in the visas of people who need them for work travel or study in this country.

7. We think however that the new passports will be issued only to diplomats and other government employees beginning in August.

8. To fill the vacant position we hope to hire Wilma Robinson who is currently working in Virginia Beach.

9. All things considered our conference will attract more participants if it is held in a resort setting such as Las Vegas Scottsdale or Orlando.

10. If you examine the log closely you will see that we shipped 15 orders on Thursday; on Friday only 4.

11. In the past ten years we have promoted over 30 well-qualified individuals many of whom started in accounting.

12. Nancy Rubey who spoke to our class last week is the author of a book titled *The Digital Workplace.*

13. A recent study of productivity that was conducted by authoritative researchers revealed that workers in the United States are more productive than workers in Europe or Japan.

14. America's secret productivity weapons according to the report were not bigger companies more robots or even brainier managers.

15. As a matter of fact the report said that America's productivity resulted from a capitalistic system of unprotected hands-off competition.

The following letter has errors in grammar, punctuation, spelling, proofreading, and other problems. You may either (a) use standard proofreading marks (see Appendix B) to correct the errors here or (b) download the document from **www.meguffey.com** and revise at your computer. Study the guidelines in the Grammar/Mechanics Handbook to sharpen your skills.

Current date
Mrs. E. R. Churchill
224 Oak Grove Avenue
Chapel Hill, NC 27514

Dear Mrs. Churchell:

This message is to inform you that we appreciate receiving your recent letter requesting that a curve in Highway 35 be rebuilt. The Department of Transportation shares your concern about the safety of the stretch between Mount Vernon and Pittsboro which is near your home.

Highway 35 as you mentioned has many hills curves and blind spots. However it's accident rate which is 4.05 per million vehicle miles is far from the worse in the state. In fact at least 49 other state highways have worse safety records.

At this point in time I want you to know that we do have studies under way that will result in the relocation of sections of highway 35 to terrain that will provide safer driving conditions. As you are aware such changes take time. We must coordinate our plans with town county state and federal authorities. Money is assigned to these projects by priority and Highway 35 does not have top priority. In addition accidents along Highway 35 are not concentrated at any one curve, they are spread out over the entire highway.

For all of the above reasons we do not anticipate immediately rebuilding any curves on Highway 35. In the near future we plan to install guardrails and we will be certain to place a guardrail at the curve that concerns you.

We appreciate your concern for safety Mrs. Churchill. Please write to us again if you have other ideas for reducing accidents.

Sincerely,

Mitchell M. Overton

Mitchell M. Overton
Office of Safety and Speed Management

What Is Legal and What Is Not in Sales Letters

In promoting products and writing sales letters, be careful about the words you choose and the claims you make. How far can you go in praising and selling your product?

- **Puffery.** In a sales letter, you can write, *Hey, we've got something fantastic! It's the very best product on the market!* Called "puffery," such promotional claims are not taken literally by reasonable consumers.
- **Proving your claims.** If you write that a gadget or additive you sell will help consumers save gasoline, you had better have competent and reliable scientific evidence to support the claim. Such a claim goes beyond puffery and requires proof. The Federal Trade Commission warned companies about making misleading claims regarding the benefits of gas-saving and other energy-related devices without scientifically proving their assertions.[13] In a litigious society, marketers who exaggerate are often taken to court.
- **Celebrities.** The unauthorized use of a celebrity's name, likeness, or nickname is not permitted in sales messages. For example, actor, writer, and director Woody Allen successfully sued a video store chain that used a model who looked enough like Allen to cause confusion in consumers; they may have been led to believe that Allen endorsed the business. Similarly, film star Dustin Hoffman won millions of dollars for the unauthorized use of a digitally altered photo showing him in an evening gown and Ralph Lauren heels. Even a commercial showing the image of a celebrity such as Tiger Woods on a camera phone is risky without permission.
- **Misleading statements.** You cannot tell people that they are winners or finalists in a sweepstake unless they actually are. American Family Publishers was found guilty of sending letters tricking people into buying magazine subscription in the belief that they had won $1.1 million. Similarly, it is deceptive to invite unsuspecting consumers to cash a check that will then hook them into entering a legal contract or a subscription. Finally, companies may not misrepresent the nature, characteristics, qualities, or geographic origin of goods or services they are promoting.
- **Unwanted merchandise.** If you enclose unsolicited merchandise with a letter, don't require the receiver to pay for it or return it. Express Publishing, for example, sent a copy of its *Food & Wine Magazine's Cookbook* with a letter inviting recipients to preview the book. "If you don't want to preview the book, simply return the advance notice card within 14 days." Courts, however, have ruled that recipients are allowed to retain, use, or discard any unsolicited merchandise without paying for it or returning it.

Career Application. Bring to class at least three sales letters or advertisements that may represent issues described here. What examples of puffery can you identify? Are claims substantiated by reliable evidence? What proof is offered? Do any of your examples include names, images, or nicknames of celebrities? How likely is it that the celebrity authorized this use? Have you ever received unwanted merchandise as part of a sales campaign? What were you expected to do with it?

Reporting Workplace Data

Chapter 9
Informal Reports

Chapter 10
Proposals and Formal Reports

CHAPTER 9

Informal Reports

OBJECTIVES

After studying this chapter, you should be able to

- Describe business report basics, including functions, organizational patterns, formats, and delivery methods.

- Develop informal reports, including determining the problem and purpose, and gathering data.

- Select an appropriate writing style, be objective, and compose effective headings.

- Describe six kinds of informal reports.

- Write information and progress reports.

- Write justification/recommendation reports.

- Write feasibility reports.

- Write minutes of meetings and summaries of longer publications.

Understanding Report Basics

> **The ultimate goal of a written report is to get your ideas across to your readers.**

Why do you need to learn how to write reports? As a business and professional communicator, you will probably have your share of reports to write. Reports are a fact of life in business today. With increasing emphasis on performance and profits, businesspeople analyze the pros and cons of problems, studying alternatives and assessing facts, figures, and details. This analysis results in reports.

Management decisions in many organizations are based on information submitted in the form of reports. Reports may be submitted in writing, orally, or digitally. Increasingly, workplace information is presented in a PowerPoint talk accompanied by a written report or a series of digital slides called a *deck*. You will learn about making oral presentations in Chapter 12.

In this chapter we will concentrate on informal reports, the most common type of report in the workplace. These reports tend to be short (usually eight or fewer pages), use memo or letter format, and are personal in tone. You will learn about the functions, patterns, formats, and writing styles of typical business reports. You will also learn to write good reports by examining basic techniques and by analyzing appropriate models.

Because of their abundance and diversity, business reports are difficult to define. They may range from informal half-page trip reports to formal 200-page financial forecasts. Reports may be presented orally in front of a group or electronically by e-mail or a Web site. Some reports appear as words on paper in the form of memos and letters. Others are primarily numerical data, such as tax reports or profit-and-loss statements. Some reports provide information only; others analyze and make recommendations. Although reports vary greatly in length, content, form, and formality level, they all have one common purpose: *to answer questions and solve problems.*

Functions of Reports

In terms of what they do, most reports fit into two broad categories: informative reports and analytical reports.

Informative Reports. Reports that present data without analysis or recommendations are primarily informative. Although writers collect and organize facts, they are not expected to analyze the facts for readers. A trip report describing an employee's visit to a conference, for example, simply presents information. Other reports that present information without analysis involve routine operations, compliance with regulations, and company policies and procedures.

"Your report was a bit unfocused, so I trimmed it down from 300 pages to one strong paragraph."

Analytical Reports. Reports that provide data, analyses, and conclusions are analytical. If requested, writers also supply recommendations. Analytical reports may intend to persuade readers to act or to change their beliefs. Assume you are writing a feasibility report that compares several potential locations for a skateboard arena. After analyzing and discussing alternatives, you might recommend one site, thus attempting to persuade readers to accept this choice.

Organizational Patterns for Reports

Like letters and memos, reports may be organized directly or indirectly. The reader's expectations and the content of a report determine its pattern of development, as illustrated in Figure 9.1.

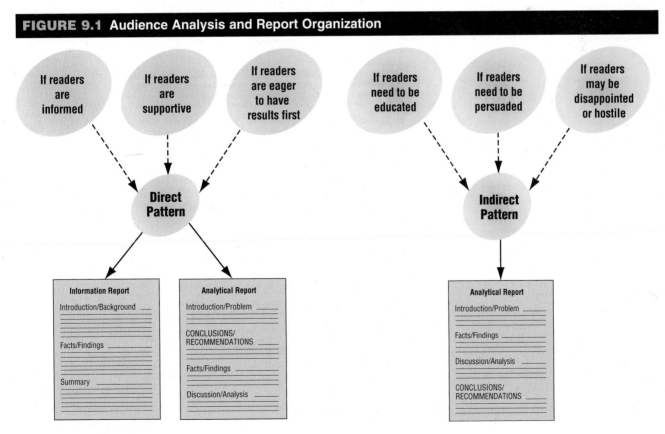

FIGURE 9.1 Audience Analysis and Report Organization

Direct Pattern. When the purpose for writing is presented close to the beginning, the organizational pattern is direct. Information reports, such as the letter report shown in Figure 9.2, are usually arranged directly. They open with an introduction,

---

FIGURE 9.2 Information Report—Letter Format With E-Mail Transmittal

Dear Ms. Burgess:

As you requested, I am sending you information that discusses how your homeowners' association can provide a free legal services plan for its members.

Should you have any questions that the attached report does not answer, please let me know. My contact information is listed below.

Sincerely,

Richard M. Ramos

Richard M. Ramos, Esq., Executive Director
Center for Consumers of Legal Services
Richmond, VA 23234 • (804) 248-8931
rramos@cclegalservices.com
www.cclegalservices.com

Uses formal salutation in an e-mail to a customer

Announces attachment

Provides complimentary close and signature block with contact information

---

Center for Consumers of Legal Services
P.O. Box 260   (804) 248-8931
Richmond, VA 23234   www.cclegalservices.com

September 17, 200x

Ms. Lisa Burgess, Secretary
Lake Austin Homeowners
3902 Oak Hill Drive
Austin, TX 78134

Dear Ms. Burgess:

As executive director of the Center for Consumers of Legal Services, I'm pleased to send you this information describing how your homeowners' association can sponsor a legal services plan for its members. After an introduction with background data, this report will discuss three steps necessary for your group to start its plan.

Introduction

A legal services plan promotes preventive law by letting members talk to attorneys whenever problems arise. Prompt legal advice often avoids or prevents expensive litigation. Because groups can supply a flow of business to the plan's attorneys, groups can negotiate free consultation, follow-up, and discounts.

Two kinds of plans are commonly available. The first, a free plan, offers free legal consultation along with discounts for services when the participating groups are sufficiently large to generate business for the plan's attorneys. These plans actually act as a substitute for advertising for the attorneys. The second common type is the prepaid plan. Prepaid plans provide more benefits, but members must pay annual fees, usually of $200 or more a year. More than 30 million people are covered by legal services plans today, and a majority belong to free plans.

Because you inquired about a free plan for your homeowners' association, the following information describes how to set up such a program.

Determine the Benefits Your Group Needs

The first step in establishing a free legal services plan is to meet with the members of your group to decide what benefits they want. Typical benefits include the following:

Free consultation. Members may consult a participating attorney—by phone or in the attorney's office—to discuss any matter. The number of consultations is unlimited, provided each is about a separate matter. Consultations are generally limited to 30 minutes, but they include substantive analysis and advice.

Free document review. Important papers—such as leases, insurance policies, and installment sales contracts—may be reviewed with legal counsel. Members may ask questions and receive an explanation of terms.

Uses letterhead stationery for an informal report addressed to an outsider

Presents introduction and facts without analysis or recommendations

Arranges facts of report into section with descriptive headings

Emphasizes benefits in paragraph headings with boldface type

---

followed by the facts and a summary. In Figure 9.2 the writer explains a legal services plan. The letter report begins with an introduction. Then it presents the facts, which are divided into three subtopics identified by descriptive headings. The letter ends with a summary and a complimentary close. Note that the report was sent as an attachment by e-mail.

Analytical reports may also be organized directly, especially when readers are supportive or are familiar with the topic. Many busy executives prefer this pattern because it gives them the results of the report immediately. They don't have to spend time wading through the facts, findings, discussion, and analyses to get to the two items they are most interested in—the conclusions and recommendations. You

> **The direct pattern places conclusions and recommendations near the beginning of a report.**

FIGURE 9.2 Continued

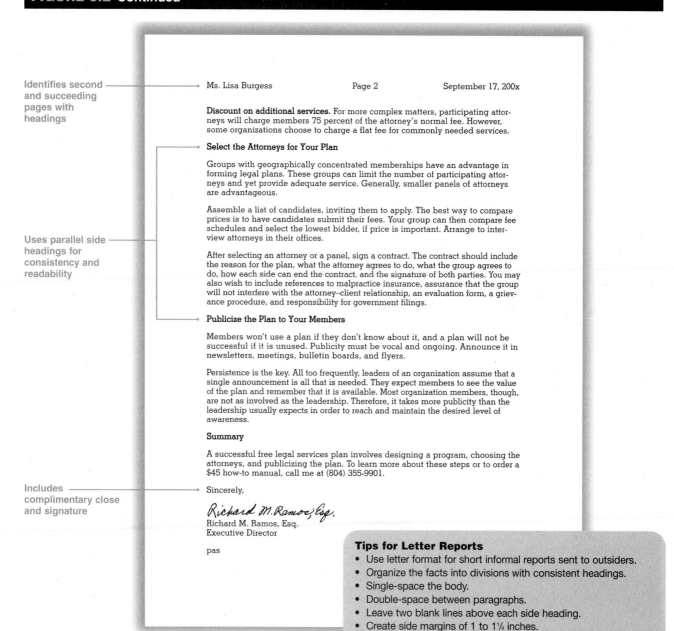

Identifies second and succeeding pages with headings

Uses parallel side headings for consistency and readability

Includes complimentary close and signature

Ms. Lisa Burgess   Page 2   September 17, 200x

Discount on additional services. For more complex matters, participating attorneys will charge members 75 percent of the attorney's normal fee. However, some organizations choose to charge a flat fee for commonly needed services.

Select the Attorneys for Your Plan

Groups with geographically concentrated memberships have an advantage in forming legal plans. These groups can limit the number of participating attorneys and yet provide adequate service. Generally, smaller panels of attorneys are advantageous.

Assemble a list of candidates, inviting them to apply. The best way to compare prices is to have candidates submit their fees. Your group can then compare fee schedules and select the lowest bidder, if price is important. Arrange to interview attorneys in their offices.

After selecting an attorney or a panel, sign a contract. The contract should include the reason for the plan, what the attorney agrees to do, what the group agrees to do, how each side can end the contract, and the signature of both parties. You may also wish to include references to malpractice insurance, assurance that the group will not interfere with the attorney–client relationship, an evaluation form, a grievance procedure, and responsibility for government filings.

Publicize the Plan to Your Members

Members won't use a plan if they don't know about it, and a plan will not be successful if it is unused. Publicity must be vocal and ongoing. Announce it in newsletters, meetings, bulletin boards, and flyers.

Persistence is the key. All too frequently, leaders of an organization assume that a single announcement is all that is needed. They expect members to see the value of the plan and remember that it is available. Most organization members, though, are not as involved as the leadership. Therefore, it takes more publicity than the leadership usually expects in order to reach and maintain the desired level of awareness.

Summary

A successful free legal services plan involves designing a program, choosing the attorneys, and publicizing the plan. To learn more about these steps or to order a $45 how-to manual, call me at (804) 355-9901.

Sincerely,

Richard M. Ramos, Esq.

Richard M. Ramos, Esq.
Executive Director

pas

> **Tips for Letter Reports**
> - Use letter format for short informal reports sent to outsiders.
> - Organize the facts into divisions with consistent headings.
> - Single-space the body.
> - Double-space between paragraphs.
> - Leave two blank lines above each side heading.
> - Create side margins of 1 to 1¼ inches.
> - Start the date 2 inches from the top or one blank line below the last line of the letterhead.
> - Add a second-page heading, if necessary, consisting of the addressee's name, the page number, and the date.

should be aware, though, that unless readers are familiar with the topic, they may find the direct pattern confusing. Some readers prefer the indirect pattern because it seems logical and mirrors the way we solve problems.

Indirect Pattern. When the conclusions and recommendations, if requested, appear at the end of the report, the organizational pattern is indirect. Such reports usually begin with an introduction or description of the problem, followed by facts and interpretation from the writer. They end with conclusions and recommendations. This pattern is helpful when readers are unfamiliar with the problem. It is also useful when readers must be persuaded or when they may be disappointed in or hostile toward the report's findings. The writer is more likely to retain the reader's interest by first explaining, justifying, and analyzing the facts and then making recommendations. This pattern also seems most rational to readers because it follows the normal thought process: problem, alternatives (facts), solution.

The indirect pattern is appropriate for analytical reports that seek to persuade or that convey bad news.

Report Formats

The format of a report is governed by its length, topic, audience, and purpose. After considering these elements, you will probably choose from among the following five formats.

How you format a report depends on its length, topic, audience, and purpose.

Letter Format. Use letter format for short (usually eight or fewer pages) informal reports addressed outside an organization. Prepared on a company's letterhead stationery, a letter report contains a date, inside address, salutation, and complimentary close, as shown in Figure 9.2. Although they may carry information similar to that found in correspondence, letter reports usually are longer and show more careful organization than most letters. They also include headings.

Memo Format. For short informal reports that stay within organizations, memo format is appropriate. Memo reports begin with essential background information, using standard headings: *Date, To, From,* and *Subject.* Like letter reports, memo reports differ from regular memos in length, use of headings, and deliberate organization. The trip report in Figure 9.3 illustrates the format of an internal memo report. Note that the writer attaches the report to an e-mail message, which introduces the attachment.

OFFICE INSIDER

A nonprofit organization polled 120 businesses to find out what type of writing they required of their employees. More than half of the business leaders responded that they "frequently" or "almost always" produce technical reports (59 percent), formal reports (62 percent), and memos and correspondence (70 percent).

Manuscript Format. For longer, more formal reports, use manuscript format. These reports are usually printed on plain paper instead of letterhead stationery or memo forms. They begin with a title followed by systematically displayed headings and subheadings. You will see examples of proposals and formal reports using manuscript formats in Chapter 10.

Printed Forms. Prepared forms are often used for repetitive data, such as monthly sales reports, performance appraisals, merchandise inventories, expense claims, and personnel and financial reports. Standardized headings on these forms save time for the writer. Preprinted forms also make similar information easy to locate and ensure that all necessary information is provided.

Digital Format. Some reports are not primarily meant to be printed but will be projected or viewed and edited digitally. Increasingly, businesses encourage employees to upload reports to the company intranet. Firms provide software enabling workers to update information about their activities, progress on a project, and other information about their on-the-job performance.

FIGURE 9.3 Information Memo Report—Trip Report With E-Mail Transmittal

Hi, Mark!

As you requested, I am sending you the attached trip report describing my amazing experiences at the largest IT trade show in the world, the CeBIT.

Thank you for the opportunity. I networked with lots of people and, yes, I had a blast.

Cheers,

Grant

Grant Snow, Developer
Idea Networking Solutions, Inc.
408.599.3434 Ext. 598
gsnow@ideaNTSolutions.com
www.idea-networking-solutions.com

Uses informal form of address in e-mail cover note announcing attached memo

Uses informal yet professional language

Includes complimentary close and signature block

IDEA NETWORKING SOLUTIONS, INC.
MEMORANDUM

Date: March 16, 200x

To: Mark Roach, IT Director

From: Grant Snow, Developer *GS*

Subject: Trip Report from the CeBIT Trade Show in Hannover, Germany

For the first time, I attended the huge CeBIT computer show in Hannover on March 4–9. CeBIT runs for six days and attracts almost 500,000 visitors from Germany, Europe, and all over the world to the famed Hannover fairgrounds. It features 27 halls full of technology and people. If you have been to Comdex Las Vegas in the fall, think of a show that is easily five times larger. Let me describe our booth, overall trends, and the contacts I made in Hannover.

Identifies the event

Focuses on three main points

Our Presence at the Fair

Our Idea Networking Solutions booth spanned two floors. The ground floor had a theater with large screen, demonstration stations, and partners showing their products and services. Upstairs we had tables and chairs for business meetings, press interviews, food, and drinks—along with a kitchen with a cooking area and a dishwasher. Because no one has time to get food elsewhere, we ate in the booth.

Current Trends

What was the big news from this year's CeBIT? The top story was "Green IT." The expo management decided to spotlight a range of topics dealing with Green IT, showcasing many approaches in the "Green IT Village" in Hall 9. The main focus centered on highly energy-efficient solutions and power-saving technologies and their contribution to climate protection. Green IT is the big buzzword now and was even dubbed the "Megatrend of this expo" by the organizer. Only the future will tell whether Green IT will be able to spawn attractive new business areas.

Summarizes key information

Meeting Customers and Prospects

Like any major trade show, CeBIT is a great way to connect with customers and prospects. Sometimes it is a way of meeting people you only knew virtually. In this case, we had three fans of our Internetpakt.com podcast visit us at the booth: Jürgen Schmidt, Karin Richter, and Peter Jahn of MEGAFunk. All three came in our white INS T-Shirts, which could only be rewarded with new black Internetpakt.com T-Shirts. All in all, we made about 600 contacts and have 50 solid leads. The visit was definitely worthwhile and will pay off very soon.

Highlights the value of the trip

In closing, this was probably one of the best conference experiences I've ever had. Customers and partners like INS; they are excited about our technology, and they want more. Some know us because of our software solutions and were surprised to learn that we sell hardware, too (this is a good sign). All want us to grow and gain in influence.

Check out my CeBIT photo gallery on Flickr for more impressions of our booth at CeBIT with comments. Thank you for giving me the opportunity to network and to experience one of the biggest trade shows in the business. My itemized expenses and receipts are attached.

Shows appreciation and mentions expenses

> **Tips for Trip Reports**
> - Use memo format for short informal reports sent within the organization.
> - Identify the event (exact date, name, and location) and preview the topics to be discussed.
> - Summarize in the body three to five main points that might benefit the reader.
> - Itemize your expenses, if requested, on a separate sheet. Mention this in the report.
> - Close by expressing appreciation, suggesting action to be taken, or synthesizing the value of the trip or event.

Report Delivery

Once reports are written, you must decide what channel to use to deliver them to your readers. Written business reports can be delivered in the following ways:

In Person. If you are located close to the reader, deliver your report in person. This delivery method works especially well when you would like to comment on the report or clarify its purpose. Delivering a report in person also makes the report seem more important or urgent.

By Mail. Many reports are delivered by mail. You can send your reports by interoffice mail, U.S. Postal Service delivery, or commercial delivery service such as UPS or FedEx.

By Fax. You can fax your report to your reader, but be sure to seek the recipient's permission. Very long reports can overwhelm most fax machines. Be sure to include a cover page that identifies the sender and introduces the report.

By E-Mail. Reports in any format can be attached to an e-mail message. When using this channel, you will introduce the report and refer clearly to the attachment in the body of your e-mail message. Figure 9.2 on page 224 shows an example of an e-mail transmittal or cover that announces the enclosed letter report and goes to a recipient outside the organization. In Figure 9.3 the writer is sending an internal memo report by e-mail as an attachment within the organization.

Online. You might choose to make your report available online. Many report writers today are making their reports available to their readers on the Web. One common method for doing this involves saving the report in Portable Document Format (PDF) and then uploading it to the company's Web site or its intranet. This is an inexpensive method of delivery and allows an unlimited number of readers access to the report. If the report contains sensitive or confidential information, access to the document can be password protected.

Defining the Purpose and Gathering Data

Your natural tendency in preparing a report is to sit down and begin writing immediately. If you follow this urge, however, you will very likely have to backtrack and start again. Reports take planning, beginning with defining the project and gathering data. The following guidelines will help you plan your project.

Determining the Problem and Purpose of Your Report

The first step in writing a report is understanding the problem or assignment clearly. This includes coming up with a statement of purpose. Ask yourself: Am I writing this report to inform, to analyze, to solve a problem, or to persuade? The answer to this question should be a clear, accurate statement identifying your purpose. In informal reports the statement of purpose may be only one sentence; that sentence usually becomes part of the introduction. Notice how the following introductory statement describes the purpose of the report:

> This report analyzes the feasibility and costs of operating an on-site recreation center for use by employees.

After writing a statement of purpose, analyze who will read your report. If your report is intended for your immediate supervisors and they are supportive of your project, you need not include extensive details, historical development, definition of terms, or persuasion. Other readers, however, may require background data and persuasive strategies.

WORKPLACE IN FOCUS

Though new to the international tourism scene, the Ritz-Carlton, Moscow, has quickly become a hotel hot spot for five-star travelers. Located within walking distance of Red Square and the Kremlin, the 11-story luxury hotel features marble bathrooms, regal amenities, a dedicated concierge staff, and a panoramic view of one of the world's most historic cities. The traditional-styled guest rooms and suites, along with the hotel's ultra-mod rooftop lounge, offer unparalleled comfort with a touch of contemporary ambiance. *What data sources might an architectural firm use when developing plans for an upscale hotel?*

The expected audience for your report influences your writing style, research methods, vocabulary, areas of emphasis, and communication strategy. Remember, too, that your audience may consist of more than one set of readers. Reports are often distributed to secondary readers who may need more details than the primary readers.

Gathering Data

One of the most important steps in the process of writing a report is that of researching and gathering data. A good report is based on solid, accurate, verifiable facts. Typical sources of factual information for informal reports include (a) company records; (b) observation; (c) surveys, questionnaires, and inventories; (d) interviews; (e) printed material; and (f) electronic resources.

> The facts for reports are often obtained from company records, observation, surveys, interviews, printed material, and electronic resources.

Company Records. Many business reports begin with an analysis of company records and files. From these records you can observe past performance and methods used to solve previous problems. You can collect pertinent facts that will help determine a course of action.

Observation. Another logical source of data for many problems lies in personal observation and experience. For example, if you were writing a report on the need for a comprehensive policy on the use of digital media, you might observe how employees are using e-mail and the Web for personal errands or whether they spread potentially damaging company information in their blogs.

Surveys, Questionnaires, and Inventories. Data from groups of people can be collected most efficiently and economically by using surveys, questionnaires, and inventories. For example, if you were part of a committee investigating the success of an employee carpooling program, you might begin by using a questionnaire.

Interviews. Talking with individuals directly concerned with the problem produces excellent firsthand information. For example, if you are researching whether your company should install wireless technology, you could interview an expert in wireless technology about the pros and cons. Interviews also allow for one-on-one communication, thus giving you an opportunity to explain your questions and ideas to elicit the most accurate information.

> Interviews provide rich, accurate firsthand information because questions can be explained.

Printed Material. Although we are seeing a steady movement away from print to electronic data, print sources are still the most visible part of most libraries. Much information is available only in print. Print sources include books, newspapers, and periodicals, such as magazines and journals.

Electronic Resources. An extensive source of current and historical information is available electronically by using a computer to connect to the Web, electronic databases, and other online resources. From a personal or office computer you can access storehouses of information provided by the government, newspapers, magazines, nonprofit organizations, and businesses. Business researchers are also using such electronic tools as mailing lists, discussion boards, and blogs to conduct research. For short, informal reports you will probably find the most usable data in online resources. Chapter 10 gives you more detailed suggestions about online research and electronic research tools.

Choosing a Report Writing Style and Creating Headings

In previous chapters you have learned that the tone and style we adopt in business documents matter as much as the message we convey. Not surprisingly, reports require an appropriate writing style. They also benefit from objectivity and effective headings.

Adopting an Appropriate Writing Style

Like other business messages, reports can range from informal to formal, depending on their purpose, audience, and setting. Research reports from consultants to their clients tend to be rather formal. Such reports must project an impression of objectivity, authority, and impartiality.

In this chapter we are most concerned with an informal writing style. Your short reports will probably be written for familiar audiences and involve noncontroversial topics. You may use first-person pronouns (*I, we, me, my, us, our*) and contractions (*I'm, it's, let's, can't, didn't*). You will emphasize active-voice verbs and strive for shorter sentences using familiar words. Figure 9.4 will help you distinguish between formal and informal report writing styles.

Whether you choose a formal or informal writing style, remember to apply the writing techniques you have learned in earlier chapters. The same techniques you have been using to compose effective memos, letters, and e-mail messages apply to developing outstanding reports. Like all business documents, business reports must be clear and concise. They should be written using topic sentences, support sentences, and transitional expressions to build coherence. Avoid wordiness, outdated expressions, slang, jargon, and clichés in your reports. Finally, proofread all business reports carefully to make sure that they contain no errors in spelling, grammar, punctuation, names and numbers, or format.

Being Objective

Reports are convincing only when the facts are believable and the writer is credible. You can build credibility in a number of ways:

- **Present both sides of an issue.** Even if you favor one possibility, discuss both sides and show through logical reasoning why your position is superior. Remain impartial, letting the facts prove your point.
- **Separate fact from opinion.** Suppose a supervisor wrote, *Our department works harder and gets less credit than any other department in the company.* This opinion is difficult to prove, and it damages the credibility of the writer. A more convincing statement might be, *Our productivity has increased 6 percent over the past year, and I'm proud of the extra effort my employees are making.* After you have made a claim or presented an important statement in a report,

An informal writing style includes first-person pronouns, contractions, active-voice verbs, short sentences, and familiar words.

Reports are more believable if the author is impartial, separates fact from opinion, uses moderate language, and cites sources.

FIGURE 9.4 Report Writing Styles

	Informal Writing Style	Formal Writing Style
Use	Short, routine reports	Theses
	Reports for familiar audiences	Research studies
	Noncontroversial reports	Controversial or complex reports (especially to outsiders)
	Most reports to company insiders	
Effect	Feeling or warmth, personal involvement, closeness	Impression of objectivity, accuracy, professionalism, fairness
		Distance created between writer and reader
Characteristics	Use of first-person pronouns (*I, we, me, my, us, our*)	Absence of first-person pronouns; use of third person (*the researcher, the writer*); increasingly, however, the informal style is acceptable
	Use of contractions (*can't, don't*)	Absence of contractions (*cannot, do not*)
	Emphasis on active-voice verbs (*I conducted the study*)	Use of passive-voice verbs (*the study was conducted*)
	Shorter sentences; familiar words	Complex sentences; long words
	Occasional use of humor, metaphors	Absence of humor and figures of speech
	Occasional use of colorful speech	Reduced use of colorful adjectives and verbs
	Acceptance of author's opinions and ideas	Elimination of "editorializing" (author's opinions, perceptions)

ask yourself, *Is this a verifiable fact?* If the answer is *no*, rephrase your statement to make it sound more reasonable.

- **Be sensitive and moderate in your choice of language.** Don't exaggerate. Instead of saying *most people think . . .,* it might be more accurate to say *Some people think . . . .* Better yet, use specific figures such as *Sixty percent of employees agree . . . .* Also avoid using labels and slanted expressions. Calling someone a *loser,* a *control freak,* or an *elitist* demonstrates bias. If readers suspect that a writer is prejudiced, they may discount the entire argument.

- **Cite sources.** Tell your readers where the information came from. For example, *In a telephone interview with Blake Spence, director of transportation, October 15, he said . . .* OR: *The Wall Street Journal (August 10, p. 40) reports that . . . .* By referring to respected sources, you lend authority and credibility to your statements. Your words become more believable and your argument, more convincing. In Chapter 10 you will learn how to document your sources properly.

"He says our report is objective. However, quoting Winston Churchill, he writes that the report, by its very length, defends itself against the risk of being read."

Using Effective Report Headings

Good headings are helpful to both the report reader and the writer. For the reader they serve as an outline of the text, highlighting major ideas and categories. They also act as guides for locating facts and pointing the way through the text. Moreover, headings provide resting points for the mind and for the eye, breaking up large chunks of text into manageable and inviting segments. For the writer headings require that the report author organize the data into meaningful blocks. To learn more about designing readable headings, as well as to pick up other tips on designing documents, see Figure 9.5.

FIGURE 9.5 Ten Tips for Designing Better Documents

Desktop publishing packages, high-level word processing programs, and advanced printers now make it possible for you to turn out professional-looking documents. The temptation, though, is to overdo it by incorporating too many features in one document. Here are ten tips for applying good sense and sound design principles in "publishing" your documents:

1. **Analyze your audience.** Avoid overly flashy type, colors, and borders for conservative business documents. Also consider whether your readers will be reading painstakingly or merely browsing. Lists and headings help readers who are in a hurry.

2. **Choose an appropriate type size.** For most business memos, letters, and reports, the body text should be 10 to 12 points tall (a point is 1/72 of an inch). Larger type looks amateurish, and smaller type is hard to read.

3. **Use a consistent typeface.** Although your software may provide a variety of fonts, stay with a single family of type within one document. In Word 2003, Times New Roman and Arial were the default typefaces and, therefore, became the most popular choices. Word 2007 offers many potential style variations, but the default typefaces are Cambria and Calibri. For emphasis and contrast, you may vary the font size and weight with **bold,** *italic,* ***bold italic,*** and other selections.

4. **Generally, don't justify right margins.** Textbooks, novels, newspapers, magazines, and other long works are usually set with justified (even) right margins. However, for shorter works ragged-right margins are recommended because such margins add white space and help readers locate the beginnings of new lines. Slower readers find ragged-right copy more legible.

5. **Separate paragraphs and sentences appropriately.** The first line of a paragraph should be indented or preceded by a blank line. To separate sentences, typists have traditionally left two spaces. This spacing is still acceptable, but most writers now follow printers' standards and leave only one space.

6. **Design readable headlines.** Presenting headlines and headings in all caps is generally discouraged because solid blocks of capital letters interfere with the recognition of word patterns. To further improve readability, select a sans serif typeface (one without cross strokes or embellishment), such as Arial.

7. **Strive for an attractive page layout.** In designing title pages or graphics, provide for a balance between print and white space. Also consider placing the focal point (something that draws the reader's eye) at the optical center of a page—about three lines above the actual center. Moreover, remember that the average reader scans a page from left to right and top to bottom in a Z pattern. Plan your visuals accordingly.

8. **Use graphics and clip art with restraint.** Charts, original drawings, and photographs can be scanned into documents. Ready-made clip art and graphics can also be inserted into documents. Use such images, however, only when they are well drawn, relevant, purposeful, and appropriately sized.

9. **Avoid amateurish results.** Many beginning writers, eager to display every graphic device a program offers, produce busy, cluttered documents. Too many typefaces, ruled lines, images, and oversized headlines will overwhelm readers. Strive for simple, clean, and forceful effects.

10. **Develop expertise.** Learn to use the desktop publishing features of your current word processing software, or investigate one of the special programs, such as Quark's QuarkXPress; Adobe's PageMaker, InDesign, and FrameMaker; and Corel's Ventura. Although the learning curve for these popular programs is steep, such effort is well spent if you will be producing newsletters, brochures, announcements, visual aids, and promotional literature.

Functional headings show the outline of a report; talking headings describe the content.

You may choose functional or talking headings. Functional headings (such as *Background, Findings, Staffing,* and *Projected Costs*) describe functions or general topics. They show the outline of a report but provide little insight for readers. Functional headings are useful for routine reports. They are also appropriate for sensitive or controversial topics that might provoke emotional reactions. Functional headings are used in the progress report shown in Figure 9.6 on page 235.

Talking headings (such as *Employees Struggle With Lack of Day-Care Options*) describe content and provide more information to the reader. Many of the examples in this chapter use talking headings, including the information reports in Figures 9.2 and 9.3. To provide even greater clarity, you can make headings both functional and descriptive, such as *Recommendations: Saving Costs With Off-Site Care.* Whether your headings are talking or functional, keep them brief and clear. To create the most effective headings, follow a few basic guidelines:

- **Use appropriate heading levels.** The position and format of a heading indicate its level of importance and relationship to other points.
- **Strive for parallel construction within levels.** All headings at a given level should be grammatically similar. Use balanced expressions such as *Current Quarterly Budget* and *Next Quarterly Budget* rather than *Current Quarterly Budget* and *Budget Projected in the Next Quarter.*

- **For short reports use first- and second-level headings.** Many business reports contain only one or two levels of headings. For such reports use first-level headings (centered, bolded) and/or second-level headings (flush left, bolded).
- **Capitalize and underline carefully.** Most writers use all capital letters (without underlines) for main titles, such as the report, chapter, and unit titles. For first- and second-level headings, they capitalize only the first letter of main words. For additional emphasis, they use a bold font. Don't enclose headings in quotation marks.
- **Keep headings short but clear.** Try to make your headings brief (no more than eight words) but understandable. Experiment with headings that concisely tell who, what, when, where, and why.
- **Don't use headings as antecedents for pronouns.** Don't follow headings with pronouns, such as *this, that, these,* and *those.* For example, when the heading reads *Mobile Devices,* don't begin the next sentence with *These are increasingly multifunctional and capable.*
- **Include at least one heading per report page.** Headings increase the readability and attractiveness of report pages. If used correctly, headings help the reader grasp the report structure quickly. Use at least one per page to break up blocks of text.

Preparing Typical Informal Reports

Informal business reports generally fall into one of six categories. In many instances the boundaries of the categories overlap; distinctions are not always clear-cut. Individual situations, goals, and needs may make one report take on some characteristics of a report in another category. Still, these general categories, presented here in a brief overview, are helpful to beginning writers. Later you will learn how to fully develop each of these reports.

- **Information reports.** Reports that collect and organize information are informative or investigative. They may record routine activities such as daily, weekly, and monthly reports of sales or profits. They may investigate options, performance, or equipment. Although they provide information, they do not analyze that information.

  One distinct type of information report is the trip report. In it business travelers identify the event they attended or the company they visited, objectively summarize three to five main points and, if requested, itemize their expenses on a separate sheet. Trip reports inform management about new procedures, equipment, trends, and laws or regulations. They may supply information affecting products, operations, and service.
- **Progress reports.** Progress reports monitor the headway of unusual or nonroutine activities. For example, progress reports would keep management informed about a committee's preparations for a trade show 14 months from now. Such reports usually answer three questions: (a) Is the project on schedule? (b) Are corrective measures needed? and (c) What activities are next?
- **Justification/recommendation reports.** Justification and recommendation reports are similar to information reports in that they present information. However, they offer analysis in addition to data. They attempt to solve problems by evaluating options and offering recommendations. These reports are often solicited; that is, the writer has been asked to investigate and report.
- **Feasibility reports.** When a company must decide whether to proceed with a plan of action, it may require a feasibility report. For example, should a company invest thousands of dollars to expand its Web site? A feasibility report would examine the practicality of implementing the proposal.

Justification/recommendation and feasibility reports attempt to solve problems by presenting data, drawing conclusions, and making recommendations.

Minutes of meetings and summaries organize and condense information for quick reading and reference.

- **Minutes of meetings.** A record of the proceedings of a meeting is called "the minutes." This record is generally kept by a secretary or recorder. Minutes may be kept for groups that convene regularly, such as clubs, committees, and boards of directors.
- **Summaries.** A summary condenses the primary ideas, conclusions, and recommendations of a longer report or publication. Employees may be asked to write summaries of technical reports. Students may be asked to write summaries of periodical articles or books to sharpen their writing skills. Executive summaries condense long reports such as business plans and proposals.

Information Reports

Writers of information reports provide information without drawing conclusions or making recommendations. Some information reports are highly standardized, such as police reports, hospital admittance reports, monthly sales reports, or government regulatory reports. Other information reports are more personalized, as illustrated in the letter report shown in Figure 9.2 on pages 224–225 and the memo report in 9.3 on page 227. Information reports generally contain three parts: introduction, body (findings), and conclusion. The body may have many subsections. Consider these suggestions for writing information reports:

- Explain why you are writing in the introduction.
- Describe what methods and sources were used to gather information and why they are credible.
- Provide any special background information that may be necessary. Preview what is to follow.
- Organize the facts/findings in a logical sequence.

Organize information chronologically, alphabetically, topically, geographically, journalistically, from simple to complex, or from most to least important.

- Consider grouping the facts/findings in one of these patterns: (a) chronological, (b) alphabetical, (c) topical, (d) geographical, (e) journalism style (*who, what, when, where, why,* and *how*), (f) simple-to-complex, or (g) most to least important. Organizational strategies will be explained in detail in Chapter 10.
- Summarize your findings, synthesize your reactions, suggest action to be taken, or express appreciation in the conclusion.

In the two-page information report shown in Figure 9.2 on pages 224–225, Richard Ramos responds to an inquiry about prepaid legal services. In the introduction he explains the purpose of the report and previews the organization of the report. In the findings/facts section, he arranges the information topically. He uses the summary to emphasize the three main topics previously discussed.

As the trip report in Figure 9.3 demonstrates, internal memo reports can be informal and still be professional, informational, and effective. In this report the writer Grant Snow organizes his general impressions from the CeBIT trade show by focusing on contacts he established and the main trends that emerged during the annual gathering. You will find that communication in the information technology sector tends to be informal.

Progress Reports

Progress reports tell management whether projects are on schedule.

Continuing projects often require progress reports to describe their status. These reports may be external (telling customers how their projects are advancing) or internal (informing management of the status of activities). Progress reports typically follow this pattern of development:

- Specify in the opening the purpose and nature of the project.
- Provide background information if the audience requires filling in.
- Describe the work completed.
- Explain the work currently in progress, including personnel, activities, methods, and locations.
- Anticipate problems and possible remedies.
- Discuss future activities and provide the expected completion date.

As a location manager in the film industry, Robin Ellsworth frequently writes progress reports, such as the one shown in Figure 9.6. Producers want to be informed of what she is doing, and a phone call does not provide a permanent record. Notice that her progress report identifies the project and provides brief background information. She then explains what has been completed, what is yet to be completed, and what problems she expects.

Justification/Recommendation Reports

Both managers and employees must occasionally write reports that justify or recommend something, such as buying equipment, changing a procedure, hiring an

FIGURE 9.6 Progress Report—Memo Format

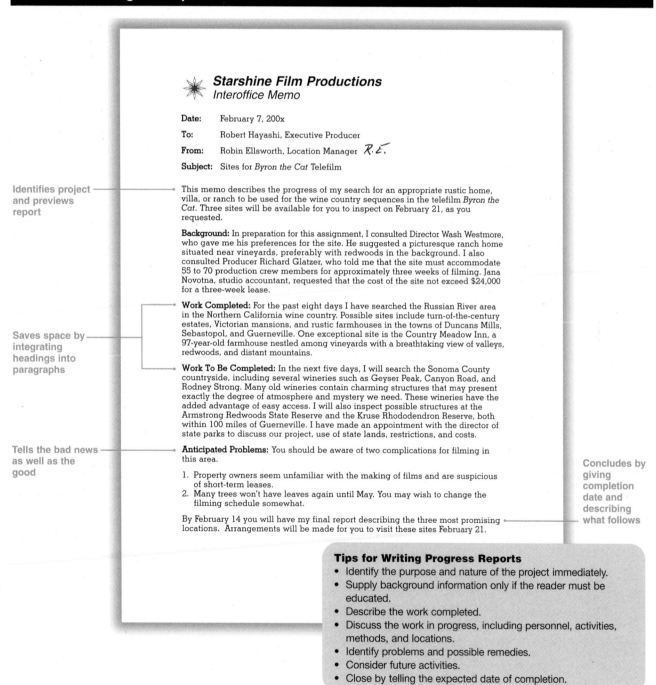

Starshine Film Productions
Interoffice Memo

Date: February 7, 200x
To: Robert Hayashi, Executive Producer
From: Robin Ellsworth, Location Manager *R.E.*
Subject: Sites for *Byron the Cat* Telefilm

Identifies project and previews report

This memo describes the progress of my search for an appropriate rustic home, villa, or ranch to be used for the wine country sequences in the telefilm *Byron the Cat*. Three sites will be available for you to inspect on February 21, as you requested.

Background: In preparation for this assignment, I consulted Director Wash Westmore, who gave me his preferences for the site. He suggested a picturesque ranch home situated near vineyards, preferably with redwoods in the background. I also consulted Producer Richard Glatzer, who told me that the site must accommodate 55 to 70 production crew members for approximately three weeks of filming. Jana Novotna, studio accountant, requested that the cost of the site not exceed $24,000 for a three-week lease.

Saves space by integrating headings into paragraphs

Work Completed: For the past eight days I have searched the Russian River area in the Northern California wine country. Possible sites include turn-of-the-century estates, Victorian mansions, and rustic farmhouses in the towns of Duncans Mills, Sebastopol, and Guerneville. One exceptional site is the Country Meadow Inn, a 97-year-old farmhouse nestled among vineyards with a breathtaking view of valleys, redwoods, and distant mountains.

Work To Be Completed: In the next five days, I will search the Sonoma County countryside, including several wineries such as Geyser Peak, Canyon Road, and Rodney Strong. Many old wineries contain charming structures that may present exactly the degree of atmosphere and mystery we need. These wineries have the added advantage of easy access. I will also inspect possible structures at the Armstrong Redwoods State Reserve and the Kruse Rhododendron Reserve, both within 100 miles of Guerneville. I have made an appointment with the director of state parks to discuss our project, use of state lands, restrictions, and costs.

Tells the bad news as well as the good

Anticipated Problems: You should be aware of two complications for filming in this area.

1. Property owners seem unfamiliar with the making of films and are suspicious of short-term leases.
2. Many trees won't have leaves again until May. You may wish to change the filming schedule somewhat.

By February 14 you will have my final report describing the three most promising locations. Arrangements will be made for you to visit these sites February 21.

Concludes by giving completion date and describing what follows

Tips for Writing Progress Reports
- Identify the purpose and nature of the project immediately.
- Supply background information only if the reader must be educated.
- Describe the work completed.
- Discuss the work in progress, including personnel, activities, methods, and locations.
- Identify problems and possible remedies.
- Consider future activities.
- Close by telling the expected date of completion.

employee, consolidating departments, or investing funds. Large organizations sometimes prescribe how these reports should be organized; they use forms with conventional headings. When you are free to select an organizational plan yourself, however, let your audience and topic determine your choice of direct or indirect structure.

Direct Pattern. For nonsensitive topics and recommendations that will be agreeable to readers, you can organize directly according to the following sequence:

- In the introduction identify the problem or need briefly.
- Announce the recommendation, solution, or action concisely and with action verbs.
- Explain more fully the benefits of the recommendation or steps to be taken to solve the problem.
- Discuss pros, cons, and costs.
- Conclude with a summary specifying the recommendation and necessary action.

Troy Barnwell applied the preceding process in writing the recommendation report shown in Figure 9.7. Troy is operations manager in charge of a fleet of trucks for a large parcel delivery company in Charleston, South Carolina. When he heard about a new Goodyear smart tire with an electronic chip, Troy thought his company should give the new tire a try. His recommendation report begins with a short introduction to the problem followed by his two recommendations. Then he explains the product and how it would benefit his company. He concludes by highlighting his recommendation and specifying the action to be taken.

Indirect Pattern. When a reader may oppose a recommendation or when circumstances suggest caution, don't be in a hurry to reveal your recommendation. Consider using the following sequence for an indirect approach to your recommendations:

- Make a general reference to the problem, not to your recommendation, in the subject line.
- Describe the problem or need your recommendation addresses. Use specific examples, supporting statistics, and authoritative quotes to lend credibility to the seriousness of the problem.
- Discuss alternative solutions, beginning with the least likely to succeed.
- Present the most promising alternative (your recommendation) last.
- Show how the advantages of your recommendation outweigh its disadvantages.
- Summarize your recommendation. If appropriate, specify the action it requires.
- Ask for authorization to proceed if necessary.

Feasibility Reports

Feasibility reports analyze whether a proposal or plan will work.

Feasibility reports examine the practicality and advisability of following a course of action. They answer this question: Will this plan or proposal work? Feasibility reports typically are internal reports written to advise on matters such as consolidating departments, offering a wellness program to employees, or hiring an outside firm to handle a company's accounting or computing operations. These reports may also be written by consultants called in to investigate a problem. The focus in these reports is on the decision of whether to stop or proceed with the proposal. Since your role is not to persuade the reader to accept the decision, you will want to present the decision immediately. In writing feasibility reports, consider these suggestions:

- Announce your decision immediately.
- Describe the background and problem necessitating the proposal.
- Discuss the benefits of the proposal.
- Describe any problems that may result.
- Calculate the costs associated with the proposal, if appropriate.
- Show the time frame necessary for implementing the proposal.

FIGURE 9.7 Justification/Recommendation Report—Memo Format

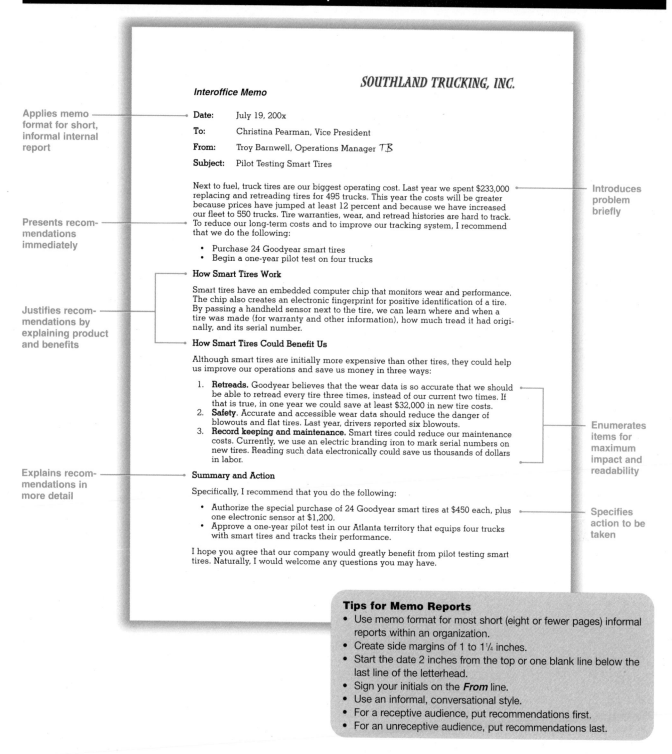

Applies memo format for short, informal internal report

Presents recommendations immediately

Justifies recommendations by explaining product and benefits

Explains recommendations in more detail

SOUTHLAND TRUCKING, INC.

Interoffice Memo

Date: July 19, 200x

To: Christina Pearman, Vice President

From: Troy Barnwell, Operations Manager T.B.

Subject: Pilot Testing Smart Tires

Next to fuel, truck tires are our biggest operating cost. Last year we spent $233,000 replacing and retreading tires for 495 trucks. This year the costs will be greater because prices have jumped at least 12 percent and because we have increased our fleet to 550 trucks. Tire warranties, wear, and retread histories are hard to track. To reduce our long-term costs and to improve our tracking system, I recommend that we do the following:

- Purchase 24 Goodyear smart tires
- Begin a one-year pilot test on four trucks

How Smart Tires Work

Smart tires have an embedded computer chip that monitors wear and performance. The chip also creates an electronic fingerprint for positive identification of a tire. By passing a handheld sensor next to the tire, we can learn where and when a tire was made (for warranty and other information), how much tread it had originally, and its serial number.

How Smart Tires Could Benefit Us

Although smart tires are initially more expensive than other tires, they could help us improve our operations and save us money in three ways:

1. **Retreads.** Goodyear believes that the wear data is so accurate that we should be able to retread every tire three times, instead of our current two times. If that is true, in one year we could save at least $32,000 in new tire costs.
2. **Safety.** Accurate and accessible wear data should reduce the danger of blowouts and flat tires. Last year, drivers reported six blowouts.
3. **Record keeping and maintenance.** Smart tires could reduce our maintenance costs. Currently, we use an electric branding iron to mark serial numbers on new tires. Reading such data electronically could save us thousands of dollars in labor.

Summary and Action

Specifically, I recommend that you do the following:

- Authorize the special purchase of 24 Goodyear smart tires at $450 each, plus one electronic sensor at $1,200.
- Approve a one-year pilot test in our Atlanta territory that equips four trucks with smart tires and tracks their performance.

I hope you agree that our company would greatly benefit from pilot testing smart tires. Naturally, I would welcome any questions you may have.

Introduces problem briefly

Enumerates items for maximum impact and readability

Specifies action to be taken

Tips for Memo Reports
- Use memo format for most short (eight or fewer pages) informal reports within an organization.
- Create side margins of 1 to 1¼ inches.
- Start the date 2 inches from the top or one blank line below the last line of the letterhead.
- Sign your initials on the *From* line.
- Use an informal, conversational style.
- For a receptive audience, put recommendations first.
- For an unreceptive audience, put recommendations last.

Ashley Denton-Tait, human resources manager for a large public accounting firm in San Antonio, Texas, wrote the feasibility report shown in Figure 9.8. Because she discovered that the company was losing time and money as a result of personal e-mail and Internet use by employees, she talked with the vice president about the problem. The vice president didn't want Ashley to take time away from her job to investigate what other companies were doing to prevent this type of problem. Instead, she suggested that they hire a consultant to investigate what other companies

FIGURE 9.8 Feasibility Report—Memo Format

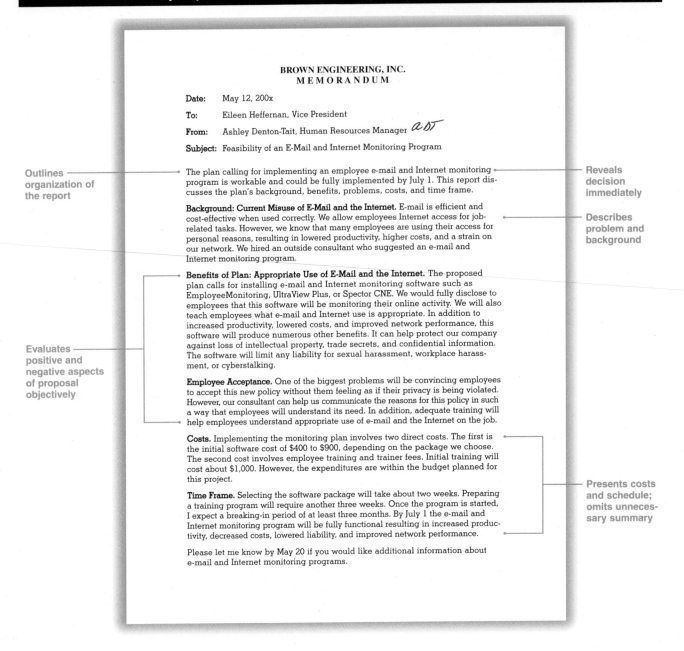

Outlines organization of the report

Reveals decision immediately

Describes problem and background

Evaluates positive and negative aspects of proposal objectively

Presents costs and schedule; omits unnecessary summary

BROWN ENGINEERING, INC.
MEMORANDUM

Date: May 12, 200x

To: Eileen Heffernan, Vice President

From: Ashley Denton-Tait, Human Resources Manager *ADT*

Subject: Feasibility of an E-Mail and Internet Monitoring Program

The plan calling for implementing an employee e-mail and Internet monitoring program is workable and could be fully implemented by July 1. This report discusses the plan's background, benefits, problems, costs, and time frame.

Background: Current Misuse of E-Mail and the Internet. E-mail is efficient and cost-effective when used correctly. We allow employees Internet access for job-related tasks. However, we know that many employees are using their access for personal reasons, resulting in lowered productivity, higher costs, and a strain on our network. We hired an outside consultant who suggested an e-mail and Internet monitoring program.

Benefits of Plan: Appropriate Use of E-Mail and the Internet. The proposed plan calls for installing e-mail and Internet monitoring software such as EmployeeMonitoring, UltraView Plus, or Spector CNE. We would fully disclose to employees that this software will be monitoring their online activity. We will also teach employees what e-mail and Internet use is appropriate. In addition to increased productivity, lowered costs, and improved network performance, this software will produce numerous other benefits. It can help protect our company against loss of intellectual property, trade secrets, and confidential information. The software will limit any liability for sexual harassment, workplace harassment, or cyberstalking.

Employee Acceptance. One of the biggest problems will be convincing employees to accept this new policy without them feeling as if their privacy is being violated. However, our consultant can help us communicate the reasons for this policy in such a way that employees will understand its need. In addition, adequate training will help employees understand appropriate use of e-mail and the Internet on the job.

Costs. Implementing the monitoring plan involves two direct costs. The first is the initial software cost of $400 to $900, depending on the package we choose. The second cost involves employee training and trainer fees. Initial training will cost about $1,000. However, the expenditures are within the budget planned for this project.

Time Frame. Selecting the software package will take about two weeks. Preparing a training program will require another three weeks. Once the program is started, I expect a breaking-in period of at least three months. By July 1 the e-mail and Internet monitoring program will be fully functional resulting in increased productivity, decreased costs, lowered liability, and improved network performance.

Please let me know by May 20 if you would like additional information about e-mail and Internet monitoring programs.

---

were doing to prevent or limit personal e-mail and Internet use. The vice president then wanted to know whether the consultant's plan was feasible. Although Ashley's report is only one page long, it provides all the necessary information: background, benefits, problems, costs, and time frame.

Minutes of Meetings

Meeting minutes record summaries of old business, new business, announcements, and reports as well as the precise wording of motions.

Minutes summarize the proceedings of meetings. Formal, traditional minutes, illustrated in Figure 9.9, are written for large groups and legislative bodies. If you are the secretary or recorder of a meeting, you will want to write minutes that do the following:

- Provide the name of the group, as well as the date, time, and place of the meeting.
- Identify the names of attendees and absentees, if appropriate.
- State whether the previous minutes were approved or revised.
- Record old business, new business, announcements, and reports.

FIGURE 9.9 Minutes of Meeting—Report Format

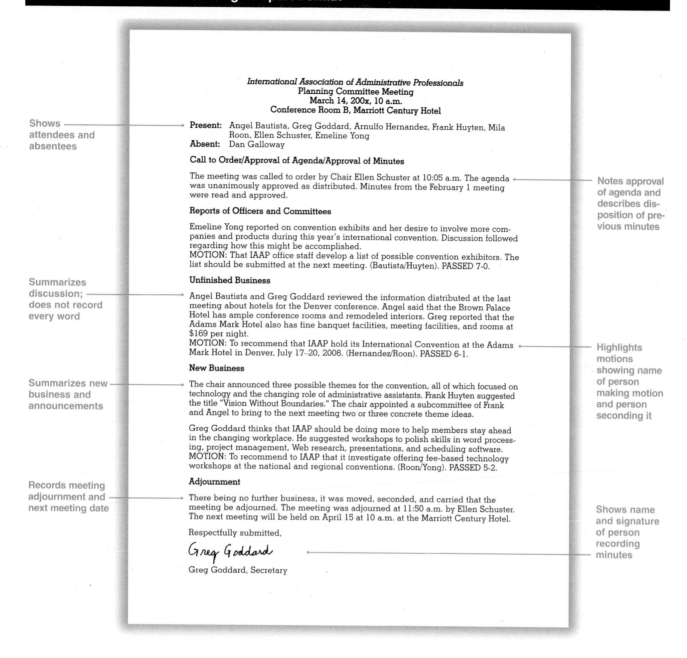

International Association of Administrative Professionals
Planning Committee Meeting
March 14, 200x, 10 a.m.
Conference Room B, Marriott Century Hotel

Shows attendees and absentees →

Present: Angel Bautista, Greg Goddard, Arnulfo Hernandez, Frank Huyten, Mila Roon, Ellen Schuster, Emeline Yong
Absent: Dan Galloway

Call to Order/Approval of Agenda/Approval of Minutes

The meeting was called to order by Chair Ellen Schuster at 10:05 a.m. The agenda was unanimously approved as distributed. Minutes from the February 1 meeting were read and approved.

← **Notes approval of agenda and describes disposition of previous minutes**

Reports of Officers and Committees

Emeline Yong reported on convention exhibits and her desire to involve more companies and products during this year's international convention. Discussion followed regarding how this might be accomplished.
MOTION: That IAAP office staff develop a list of possible convention exhibitors. The list should be submitted at the next meeting. (Bautista/Huyten). PASSED 7-0.

Summarizes discussion; does not record every word →

Unfinished Business

Angel Bautista and Greg Goddard reviewed the information distributed at the last meeting about hotels for the Denver conference. Angel said that the Brown Palace Hotel has ample conference rooms and remodeled interiors. Greg reported that the Adams Mark Hotel also has fine banquet facilities, meeting facilities, and rooms at $169 per night.
MOTION: To recommend that IAAP hold its International Convention at the Adams Mark Hotel in Denver, July 17–20, 2008. (Hernandez/Roon). PASSED 6-1.

← **Highlights motions showing name of person making motion and person seconding it**

New Business

Summarizes new business and announcements →

The chair announced three possible themes for the convention, all of which focused on technology and the changing role of administrative assistants. Frank Huyten suggested the title "Vision Without Boundaries." The chair appointed a subcommittee of Frank and Angel to bring to the next meeting two or three concrete theme ideas.

Greg Goddard thinks that IAAP should be doing more to help members stay ahead in the changing workplace. He suggested workshops to polish skills in word processing, project management, Web research, presentations, and scheduling software.
MOTION: To recommend to IAAP that it investigate offering fee-based technology workshops at the national and regional conventions. (Roon/Yong). PASSED 5-2.

Adjournment

Records meeting adjournment and next meeting date →

There being no further business, it was moved, seconded, and carried that the meeting be adjourned. The meeting was adjourned at 11:50 a.m. by Ellen Schuster. The next meeting will be held on April 15 at 10 a.m. at the Marriott Century Hotel.

← **Shows name and signature of person recording minutes**

Respectfully submitted,

Greg Goddard

Greg Goddard, Secretary

- Include the precise wording of motions; record the vote and action taken.
- Conclude with your name and signature.

Notice in Figure 9.9 that Secretary Goddard tries to summarize discussions rather than capture every comment. However, when a motion is made, he records it verbatim. He also shows in parentheses the name of the individual making the motion and the person who seconded it. By using all capital letters for *MOTION* and *PASSED*, he makes these important items stand out for easy reference.

Informal minutes are usually shorter and easier to read than formal minutes. They may be formatted with three categories: summaries of topics discussed,

"Here are the minutes of our last meeting. Some events have been fictionalized for dramatic purposes."

decisions reached, and action items (showing the action item, the person responsible, and the due date).

Although the format of informal minutes and lists of action items varies, spreadsheets or tables work well for readability, as Figure 9.10 indicates. The executives of a property management company worried about the cost, effectiveness, and environmental impact of pest control measures for a large number of condominiums and apartment buildings. Fairway Property Management held a meeting, and several attendees assumed research tasks as outlined in Figure 9.10.

Summaries

A summary compresses the main points from a book, report, article, Web site, meeting, or convention. A summary saves time because it can reduce a report or article 85 to 95 percent. Employees are sometimes asked to write summaries that condense technical reports, periodical articles, or books so that their staffs or superiors may grasp the main ideas quickly. Students may be asked to write summaries of articles, chapters, or books to sharpen their writing skills and to confirm their knowledge of reading assignments. In writing a summary, you will follow these general guidelines:

- Present the goal or purpose of the document being summarized. Why was it written?

FIGURE 9.10 Action Item List for Meeting Minutes

Organizations may include a list of action items as part of their minutes so that individuals know what task has been assigned to whom. This list can later be used to track task completion. Fairway Property Management is investigating pest control methods for a large group of apartments and condominiums. The table below was generated in MS Excel to allow easy sorting by due date or other variables.

FAIRWAY PROPERTY MANAGEMENT TERMITE ABATEMENT ACTION ITEMS/OPEN ISSUES					
Sorted by due date				Last Update 6/14/09 6:00 p.m. Hassan	
No.	**Item**	**Date**	**Who**	**Status**	**Date completed**
1	Review traditional methods of termite abatement, their pros/cons	6/15/09	Erin to summarize findings	Done Will be distributed at meeting on 6/20	6/4/09
2	Investigate alternative pest control methods and their efficacy in large apartment complexes	6/15/09	Bob	Done Will report on 6/20	6/14/09
3	Contact at least two independent research chemists about Vikane residue	6/15/09	Erin	Waiting for callback	
4	Research consumer information and resources	6/15/09	Hassan		
5	Search for government sources and information	6/15/09	Chris	CLOSED: none found	6/10/09
6	Call at least five termite control companies for bids; request large-volume discounts, long term	7/2/09	Chris		

Shows numbered action items with descriptions

Lists names of members responsible for tasks

Indicates dates when tasks were assigned

Identifies dates when tasks were completed

- Highlight the research methods (if appropriate), findings, conclusions, and recommendations.
- Omit illustrations, examples, and references.
- Organize for readability by including headings and bulleted or enumerated lists.
- Include your reactions or an overall evaluation of the document if asked to do so.

An *executive summary* summarizes a long report, proposal, or business plan. It concentrates on what management needs to know from a longer report. The executive summary shown in Figure 9.11 summarizes main points from a business plan prepared by Bluewater Koi fish farm. This company wants to expand, and it needs $72,000 to acquire additional land for three fish ponds. To secure financial backing, Bluewater wrote a business plan explaining its operation, service, product, marketing, and finances. Part of that business plan is an executive summary, which you see in Figure 9.11.

FIGURE 9.11 Executive Summary (excerpt from business plan)

EXECUTIVE SUMMARY

Bluewater Koi Expansion Plan

Summarizes purpose of longer report

The purpose of this business plan is to acquaint venture capitalists with Bluewater Koi fish farm and to solicit support for an expansion plan to be undertaken over the next two years. This report will do the following:

- Profile the current Bluewater Koi operation
- Explain the need for expansion to meet market demands
- Summarize expansion costs and expected payback

Uses headings to improve readability

Business Profile

Bluewater Creek is a 45-acre ornamental fish farm located in South Alabama. Bluewater specializes in breeding and selling koi, which are exotic and beautifully colored carp developed in Japan. Koi are collected by hobbyists and usually live in lushly landscaped fish ponds indoors or outside. Although a grand champion koi in Asia has sold for over a million dollars, the koi sold at Bluewater Creek range in price from $2.20 to $90 each. Bluewater had total sales of $347,000 last year in its retail and wholesale operations. The fish at Bluewater are grown in five surface ponds, and the operation ranges from breeding to shipping.

Provides overview of main points

Expansion to Meet Market Demands

Follows sequence of longer report

Bluewater has enjoyed increasing sales and profits since its inception as a fish hatchery in 1981. It has developed a large clientele, selling to retailers and wholesalers through its print catalog and its Web site. Fish quality and health are of utmost importance at Bluewater. Because koi are susceptible to viruses, Bluewater has adopted a policy of not buying or reselling fish from other U.S. growers. As a result, all Bluewater koi are bred and grown on-site. This policy, coupled with constantly increasing sales, makes it necessary to acquire a 9-acre farm to accommodate three additional growing ponds.

Financial Needs and Payback

Acquiring the 9-acre farm is expected to cost $38,000. An additional $12,000 is needed to move 60,000 cubic yards of earth to enable the ponds to reach the natural water table necessary for maintaining water levels in the ponds. Other expenses include $22,000 to expand the breeding operation, which involves matching high-quality male and female brood fish imported from Japan. Artificial spawning yields high hatching rates. But this practice is labor intensive. Equally laborious is the following culling process in which only the best colored, patterned, and conformed fish are kept. A total investment of $72,000 will enable Bluewater to complete its needed expansion. Projected annual sales and costs indicate that Bluewater should be able to repay the loan in five years.

Focuses on most important parts of business plan, including marketing, finances, and payback

WORKPLACE IN FOCUS

Breeding beautifully colored koi for collectors is a profitable but hazardous and costly business. Commercial growers need acreage to build breeding and growing ponds, expensive equipment to monitor water quality and prevent diseases, and caring personnel to oversee the intricate breeding program. To secure financial backing, businesses such as Bluewater Koi submit proposals that often include executive summaries, such as that shown in Figure 9.11. *How do business communicators decide what information to include in summaries of long reports?*

Visit www.meguffey.com

- **Chapter Review Quiz**
- **Flash Cards**
- **Grammar Practice**
- **PowerPoint Slides**
- **Personal Language Trainer**
- **Beat the Clock Quiz**

Summing Up and Looking Forward

This chapter presented six common types of informal business reports: information reports, progress reports, justification/recommendation reports, feasibility reports, minutes of meetings, and summaries. Information reports generally provide data only. Justification/recommendation and feasibility reports are more analytical in that they also evaluate the information, draw conclusions, and make recommendations. This chapter also discussed five formats for reports. Letter format is used for reports sent outside an organization; memo format is used for internal reports. More formal reports are formatted on plain paper with a manuscript design, whereas routine reports may be formatted on prepared forms. Some companies enable workers to file reports online. The chapter presented numerous model documents illustrating the many kinds of reports and their formats.

All of the examples in this chapter are considered relatively informal. Longer, more formal reports are necessary for major investigations and research. These reports and proposals, along with suggestions for research methods, are presented in Chapter 10.

Critical Thinking

1. What are the main differences between formal and informal reports?

2. How do business reports differ from business letters?

3. How are informative reports different from analytical reports? Give an original example of each.

4. Of the reports presented in this chapter, discuss those that require indirect development versus those that require direct development.

5. How are the reports that you write for your courses similar to those presented here? How are they different?

6. Why do you need to know how to write reports?

7. List six kinds of informal reports. Be prepared to describe each.

8. List five formats suitable for reports. Be prepared to discuss each.

9. From the lists you made in Questions 7 and 8, select a report category and appropriate format for each of the following situations.
   a. Your supervisor asks you to review the Apple iPhone to determine if the gadget would work with your corporate e-mail system.

   b. You want to tell management about an idea you have for consolidating two departments in order to eliminate redundancy and lower expenses.

   c. You are in charge of developing a new procedure for processing payroll. Your boss wants to know what you have done thus far.

   d. You were selected to record the meeting of a project team where new tasks were assigned to each member.

   e. As Accounting Department manager, you have been asked to describe for all employees your procedure for processing expense claims.

   f. As a security officer, you are writing a report of an office break-in.

   g. At a Web-based retail company, your supervisor asks you to investigate ways to reduce the number of steps that customers must go through to place an online order. She wants your report to examine the problem and offer solutions.

10. If you were about to write the following reports, where would you gather information? Be prepared to discuss the specifics of each choice.
   a. You are a peer promoter of a free Sony camera that the company gave you to use and talk about to fellow students to create buzz and increase sales. Your instructor wants you to write a report about your experiences and sketch the digital camera market.

   b. As department manager, you must write job descriptions for several new positions you wish to establish in your department.

   c. You are proposing a new company Internet-use policy to management.

   d. You must produce a document that will survey the past fiscal year and recommend steps to turn around your employer, a struggling clothing retailer.

11. List and explain four ways you can build credibility in a business report.

12. What one factor distinguishes reports developed directly from those developed indirectly?

13. What is the difference between a functional heading and a talking heading? Give an example of each for a report about employee reactions to a proposed reduction in health benefits.

14. What should the minutes of a meeting include?

15. What should a summary of a long article or report contain?

Writing Improvement Exercises

Evaluating Headings and Titles
Identify the following report headings and titles as *talking* or *functional/descriptive*. Discuss the usefulness and effectiveness of each.

16. Overview

17. Suggestions for Energy Savings and Recycling

Activities and Cases

9.1 Information Report: Describing Your Job

Your instructor wants to learn about your employment. Select a position you now hold or one that you have held in the past. If you have not been employed, choose a campus, professional, or community organization to which you belong. You may also select an internship or volunteer activity.

Your Task. Write an information report describing your employment or involvement. In the introduction describe the company and its products or services, its ownership, and its location. In the main part of the report, describe your position, including its tasks and the skills required to perform these tasks. Summarize by describing the experience you gained. Your memo report should be single-spaced and 1½ to 2 pages long and should be addressed to your instructor.

> **WEB**

9.2 Information Report: Searching for Career Information

Gather information about a career or position in which you might be interested. Learn about the nature of the job. Discover whether certification, a license, or experience is required. One of the best places to search is the latest *Occupational Outlook Handbook*. Use a search engine such as Google to locate the handbook, sponsored by the U.S. Bureau of Labor Statistics. Click the *OOH Search/A-Z Index* link; then search for a specific job title or search the alphabetic list for an occupation.

Your Task. Write an information report to your instructor that describes your target career area. Discuss the nature of the work, working conditions, necessary qualifications, and the future job outlook for the occupation. Include information about typical salary ranges and career paths. If your instructor wants an extended report, collect information about two companies where you might apply. Investigate each company's history, products and/or services, size, earnings, reputation, and number of employees. Describe the functions of an employee working in the position you have investigated. To do this, interview one or more individuals who are working in that position. Devote several sections of your report to the specific tasks, functions, duties, and opinions of these individuals. You can make this into a recommendation report by drawing conclusions and making recommendations. One conclusion that you could draw relates to success in this career area. Who might be successful in this field?

> **WEB**

9.3 Information Report: Exploring a Possible Place to Work

You are thinking about taking a job with a Fortune 500 company, and you want to learn as much as possible about the company. Select a Fortune 500 company (or any other company that interests you), and collect information about it on the Web. Visit **http://www.hoovers.com** for basic facts. Then take a look at the company's Web site; check its background, news releases, and annual report. Learn about its major product, service, or emphasis. Find its Fortune 500 ranking (if applicable), its current stock price (if listed), and its high and low range for the year. Look up its profit-to-earnings ratio. Track its latest marketing plan, promotion, or product. Identify its home office, major officers, and number of employees. Study the company's future plans.

Your Task. In a memo report to your instructor, summarize your research findings. Explain why this company would be a good or bad employment choice.

9.4 Information Report: Briefing Your Boss

Your boss wants to know more about intercultural and international business etiquette. Today most managers recognize that they need to be polished and professional if they wish to earn the respect of diverse audiences. Assume that your boss will assign various countries to several interns and recent hires. Choose a country that interests you and conduct a Web search. For example, in Google, search with terms such as *business etiquette, business etiquette abroad,* or *intercultural communication.* You could visit Web sites such as the popular, informative etiquette and business guides for specific countries by Kwintessential Ltd. (**http://www.kwintessential.co.uk**).

Your Task. As an intern or a new-hire, write a short memo report about one country that is a lot different from the United States and that offers new business opportunities. Address your report to Clifford Danielson, CEO. Summarize your research into what U.S. managers need to know about business etiquette in that culture. You should investigate social customs such as greetings, attire, gift giving, formality, business meals, attitudes toward time, communication styles, and so forth, to help your CEO avoid etiquette blunders.

9.5 Progress Report: Making Headway Toward Your Degree

You made an agreement with your parents (or spouse, partner, relative, or friend) that you would submit a progress report at this time describing the progress you have made toward your educational goal (employment, certificate, or degree).

Your Task. In memo format write a progress report that fulfills your promise to describe your progress toward your educational goal. Address your progress report to your parents, spouse, partner, relative, or friend. In your memo (a) describe your goal; (b) summarize the work you have completed thus far; (c) discuss thoroughly the work currently in progress, including your successes and anticipated obstacles; and (d) forecast your future activities in relation to your scheduled completion date.

9.6 Progress Report: Keeping Your Supervisor Updated

As office manager for the Animal Rescue Foundation (**http://www.arf.net**), a nonprofit organization that rescues and finds homes for abandoned and abused animals, you have been asked to come up with ways to increase community awareness of your organization. For the past month you have been meeting with business and community leaders, conducting Web research, and visiting with representatives from other nonprofit organizations. Your supervisor has just asked you to prepare a written report to outline what you have accomplished so far.

Your Task. In memo format write a progress report to your supervisor. In your memo (a) state whether the project is on schedule; (b) summarize the activities you have completed thus far; (c) discuss thoroughly the work currently in progress; and (d) describe your future activities. Also let your supervisor know of any obstacles you have encountered and whether the project is on schedule.

9.7 Progress Report: Connecting With E-Mail

If you are working on a long report for either this chapter or Chapter 10, keep your instructor informed of your progress.

Your Task. Send your instructor a report by e-mail detailing the progress you are making on your long report assignment. Discuss (a) the purpose of the report, (b) the work already completed, (c) the work currently in progress, and (d) your schedule for completing the report.

9.8 Justification/Recommendation Report: Expanding the Company Library

Despite the interest in online publications, managers and employees at your company still like to browse through magazines in the company library. Andy Kivel, the company librarian, wants to add business periodicals to the library subscription list and has requested help from various company divisions.

Your Task. You have been asked to recommend four periodicals in your particular specialty (accounting, marketing, etc.). Visit your library and use appropriate indexes and guides to select four periodicals to recommend. Write a memo report to Mr. Kivel describing the particular readership, usual contents, and scope of each periodical. To judge each adequately, you should examine several issues. Explain why you think each periodical should be ordered and who would read it. Convince the librarian that your choices would be beneficial to your department.

9.9 Justification/Recommendation Report: Solving a Campus Problem

In any organization, room for improvement always exists. Your college campus is no different. You are the member of a student task force that has been asked to identify problems and suggest solutions.

In groups of two to five, investigate a problem on your campus, such as inadequate parking, slow registration, poor class schedules, an inefficient bookstore, a weak job-placement program, unrealistic degree requirements, or a lack of internship programs. Within your group develop a solution to the problem. If possible, consult the officials involved to ask for their input in arriving at a feasible solution. Do not attack existing programs; instead, strive for constructive discussion and harmonious improvements.

Your Task. After reviewing persuasive techniques discussed in Chapter 8, write a justification/recommendation report in memo or letter format. Address your report to the college president.

TEAM **WEB**

9.10 Justification/Recommendation Report: Developing a Company E-Mail and Web-Use Policy

As a manager in a midsized financial services firm, you are aware that members of your department frequently use e-mail and the Internet for private messages, shopping, games, and other personal activities. In addition to the strain on your company's computer network, you worry about declining productivity, security problems, and liability issues. When you walked by one worker's computer and saw what looked like pornography on the screen, you knew you had to do something. Although workplace privacy is a controversial issue for unions and employee-rights groups, employers have legitimate reasons for wanting to know what is happening on their computers. A high percentage of lawsuits involve the use and abuse of e-mail. You think that the executive council should establish some kind of e-mail and Web-use policy. The council is generally receptive to sound suggestions, especially if they are inexpensive. You decide to talk with other managers about the problem and write a justification/recommendation report.

In teams of two to five, discuss the need for an e-mail and Web-use policy. Using the Web, find sample policies used by other firms. Look for examples of companies struggling with lawsuits over e-mail abuse. Find information about employers' rights to monitor employees' e-mail and Web use. Use this research to determine what your company's e-mail and Web-use policy should cover. Each member of the team should present and support his or her ideas regarding what should be included in the policy and how to best present your ideas to the executive council.

Your Task. Write a convincing justification/recommendation report in memo or letter format to the executive council based on the conclusions you draw from your research and discussion. Decide whether you should be direct or indirect.

TEAM

9.11 Justification/Recommendation Report: Diversity Training—Does It Work?

Employers recognize the importance of diversity awareness and intercultural sensitivity in the workplace because both are directly related to productivity. It is assumed that greater harmony also minimizes the threat of lawsuits. An interest in employee diversity training has spawned numerous corporate trainers and consultants, but after many years of such training, some recent studies seem to suggest that they may be ineffective or indicate mixed results at best. An article in *Time* magazine concluded that diversity training does not necessarily change biases in executives or increase the number of minorities in the workplace.[1]

Search the Web or electronic databases for information about diversity training. Examine articles favorable to diversity training and those that exhibit a more pessimistic view of such efforts.

Your Task. As a group of two to five members, write a memo report to your boss (address it to your instructor) and define diversity training. Explain which measures companies take to make their managers and workers culturally aware and respectful of differences. If you have personally encountered such a training, draw on your experience in addition to your research. Your report should answer the question, Does diversity training work? If yes, recommend steps your company should take to become more sensitive to minorities. If not, suggest how current practices could be improved to be more effective.

9.12 Feasibility Report: Professional Business Organization

To fulfill a student project in your department, you have been asked to submit a letter report to the dean evaluating the feasibility of starting a Phi Beta Lambda (**http://www.fbla-pbl.org/**) chapter on campus. Find out how many business students are on your campus, the benefits Phi Beta Lambda would provide for students, how one goes about starting a chapter, and whether a faculty sponsor is needed. Assume that you conducted an informal survey of business students. Of the 39 who filled out the survey, 31 said they would be interested in joining.

Your Task. Write a report in memo or letter format to the dean outlining the practicality and advisability of starting a Phi Beta Lambda chapter on your college campus.

9.13 Feasibility Report: Improving Employee Fitness

Your company is considering ways to promote employee fitness and morale. Select a possible fitness program that seems reasonable for your company. Consider a softball league, bowling teams, a basketball league, lunchtime walks, lunchtime fitness speakers and demos, company-sponsored health club memberships, a workout room, a fitness center, nutrition programs, and so on.

Your Task. Assume that your supervisor has tentatively agreed to one of the programs and has asked you to write a memo report investigating its feasibility.

9.14 Minutes: Recording the Proceedings of a Meeting

Attend an open meeting of an organization at your school, in your community, or elsewhere. Assume that you are asked to record the proceedings.

Your Task. Record the meeting proceedings in formal or informal minutes. Review the chapter to be sure you include all the data necessary for minutes. Focus on motions, votes, decisions reached, and action taken.

TEAM

9.15 Minutes and Action Items: Assigning Report Writing Tasks

When writing a formal report or proposal with a team, take notes at a team meeting about your research, especially one you may schedule with your instructor. Divide research, writing, editing, and formatting responsibilities among the group members.

Your Task. Write minutes recording the meeting. Include a list or table of action items that clearly show how tasks were divided along with names and deadlines. See Figure 9.10 on page 240 for a sample action item list.

WEB

9.16 Summary: Using Blogs for Research

Your supervisor has just learned about the popularity of using blogs (or weblogs) as research tools. This is the first he has heard of this new communication tool, and he wants to learn more. He asks you to conduct Internet research to see what has been written on the subject.

Your Task. Using an electronic database or the Web, find an article that discusses the use of blogs in the workplace for research purposes. In a memo report addressed to your boss, David Wong, summarize the primary ideas, conclusions, and recommendations presented in the article. Be sure to identify the author, article name, journal, and date of publication in your summary.

WEB

9.17 Executive Summary: Keeping the Boss Informed

Like many executives, your boss is too rushed to read long journal articles. But she is eager to keep up with developments in her field. Assume she has asked you to help her stay abreast of research in her field. She asks you to submit to her one executive summary every month on an article of interest.

Your Task. In your field of study, select a professional journal, such as the *Journal of Management*. Using an electronic database search or a Web search, look for articles in your target journal. Select an article that is at least five pages long and is interesting to you. Write an executive summary in memo format. Include an introduction that might begin with *As you requested, I am submitting this executive summary of . . . .* Identify the author, article name, journal, and date of publication. Explain what the author intended to do in the study or article. Summarize three or four of the most important findings of the study or article. Use descriptive rather than functional headings. Summarize any recommendations you make. Your boss would also like a concluding statement indicating your reaction to the article. Address your memo to Susan Wright.

9.18 Report Topics

A list of over 90 report topics is available at **www.meguffey.com**. The topics are divided into the following categories: accounting, finance, human resources, marketing, information systems, management, and general business/education/campus issues. You can collect information for many of these reports by using electronic databases and the Web. Your instructor may assign them as individual or team projects. All involve critical thinking in collecting and organizing information into logical reports.

Semicolons and Colons

Review Sections 2.16–2.19 in the Grammar/Mechanics Handbook. Then study each of the following statements. Insert any necessary punctuation. Use the delete sign to omit unnecessary punctuation. In the space provided indicate the number of changes you made and record the number of the G/M principle(s) illustrated. (When you replace one punctuation mark with another, count it as one change.) If you make no changes, write *0*. This exercise concentrates on semicolon and colon use, but you will also be responsible for correct comma use. When you finish, compare your responses with those shown at the end of the book. If your responses differ, study carefully the specific principles shown in parentheses.

Example Nino Rota's job is to make sure that his company has enough cash to meet its obligations, moreover, he is responsible for finding ways to reduce operating expenses.

2   (2.16a)

1. Informal reports tend to be short and informational formal reports on the other hand are mostly delivered in manuscript format and are usually analytical.

2. Our supplier has experienced labor shortages causing delays however we will do our best to deliver your order as soon as we can.

3. Business slows down to a crawl in Europe because of extensive vacations during the following months June July and August.

4. Large American corporations that offer a variety of financial services are: Bank of America and Citibank.

5. As long as you observe the ethics guidelines in your company's employee handbook you have nothing to fear from your next employee performance appraisal.

6. A supermarket probably requires no short-term credit a seasonal company such as a ski resort however typically would need considerable short-term credit.

7. We offer three basic types of short-term lines of credit commercial paper and single-payer credit.

8. Speakers at the conference on credit include the following businesspeople Lynne Krause financial manager American International Investments Patrick Coughlin comptroller NationsBank and Shannon Daly legal counsel Fidelity National Financial.

9. Users must first establish an account on the company's e-commerce site and then they can order from the online catalog.

10. Many methods are used to calculate finance charges for example average daily balance adjusted balance two-cycle average daily balance and previous balance.

11. Hot Topic, which is a small clothing retailer with a solid credit rating recently applied for a loan however Union Bank refused the loan application because the bank was short on cash.

12. When Hot Topic was refused by Union Bank its financial managers submitted applications to: Chemical Bank, Washington Mutual, and Wells Fargo.

13. The cost of financing capital investments at the present time is very high therefore Hot Topic's managers elected to postpone certain expansion projects.

14. If interest rates reach as high as 18 percent the cost of borrowing becomes prohibitive and many businesses are forced to reconsider or abandon projects that require financing.

15. Many small stockholders invested in stocks when the markets were riding high then they lost a lot of money after the markets declined.

The following progress report has faults in grammar, punctuation, spelling, number form, wordiness, and word use. Use standard proofreading marks (see Appendix B) to correct the errors. When you finish, your instructor can show you the revised version of this report.

Date: November 9, 200x
To: Eric Sternlicht, President
From: Durene Washington, Development Officer
Subject: Progress Report on Construction of Seattle Branch Office

Construction of Apex Realtys Portland Branch Office has entered Phase three. Although we are 1 week behind the contractors original schedule the building should be already for occupancie on March 10.

Past Progress

Phaze one involved development of the architects plans, this process was completed onJune 5. Phaze two involved submission of the plan's for county building department approval. Each of the plans were then given to the following 2 contractors for the purpose of eliciting estimates, Steven Duffy Construction, and Titan Builders. The lowest bidder was Steven Duffy Construction, consequently this firm began construction on July 15.

Present Status

Phase three includes initial construction processes. We have completed the following steps as of November 9:

- Demolition of existing building at 11485 North 27 Avenue
- Excavation of foundation footings for the building and for the surrounding wall
- Steel reinforcing rods installed in building pad and wall
- Pouring of concrete foundation

Steven Duffy Construction indicated that he was 1 week behind schedule for these reasons. The building inspectors required more steel reinforcement then was showed on the architects blueprints. In addition excavation of the footings required more time then the contractor anticipated because the 18 inch footings were all below grade.

Future Schedule

In spite of the fact that we lost time in Phase 3 we are substantially on target for the completion of this office building by March 1. Phase 4 include the following activities, framing drywalling and installation of plumbing.

Communication Workshop: Collaboration

Laying the Groundwork for Team Writing Projects

The chances are that you can look forward to some kind of team writing in your future career. You may collaborate voluntarily (seeking advice and differing perspectives) or involuntarily (through necessity or by assignment). Working with other people can be frustrating, particularly when some team members don't carry their weight or when conflict breaks out. Team projects, though, can be harmonious, productive, and rewarding when members establish ground rules at the outset and adhere to guidelines such as those presented here.

Collaboration tools, such as wikis, allow team members to contribute to and edit a text online. Many businesses today turn to wikis to facilitate teamwork. Your instructor may have access to wiki software or to the wiki function in Blackboard.

Preparing to Work Together. Before you discuss the project, talk about how your group will function.

- Limit the size of your team, if possible, to two to five members. Larger groups have more difficulties. An odd number is usually preferable to avoid ties in voting.
- Name a team leader (to plan and conduct meetings), a recorder (to keep a record of group decisions), and an evaluator (to determine whether the group is on target and meeting its goals).
- Decide whether your team will be governed by consensus (everyone must agree) or by majority rule.
- Compare schedules of team members, and set up the best meeting times. Plan to meet often. Avoid other responsibilities during meetings. Team meetings can take place face-to-face or virtually.
- Discuss the value of conflict. By bringing conflict into the open and encouraging confrontation, your team can prevent personal resentment and group dysfunction. Conflict can actually create better final documents by promoting new ideas and avoiding groupthink.
- Discuss how you will deal with members who are not pulling their share of the load.

Planning the Document. Once you have established ground rules, you are ready to discuss the project and resulting document. Be sure to keep a record of the decisions your team makes.

- Establish the document's specific purpose and identify the main issues involved.
- Decide on the final form of the document. What parts will it have?
- Discuss the audience(s) for the document and what appeal would help it achieve its purpose.
- Develop a work plan. Assign jobs. Set deadlines.
- Decide how the final document will be written: individuals working separately on assigned portions, one person writing the first draft, the entire group writing the complete document together, or some other method.

Collecting Information. The following suggestions help teams gather accurate information:

- Brainstorm for ideas as a group.
- Decide who will be responsible for gathering what information.
- Establish deadlines for collecting information.
- Discuss ways to ensure the accuracy and currency of the information collected.

Organizing, Writing, and Revising. As the project progresses, your team may wish to modify some of its earlier decisions.

- Review the proposed organization of your final document, and adjust it if necessary.
- Write the first draft. If separate team members are writing segments, they should use the same word processing program to facilitate combining files.
- Meet to discuss and revise the draft(s).
- If individuals are working on separate parts, appoint one person (probably the best writer) to coordinate all the parts, striving for consistent style and format.

Editing and Evaluating. Before the document is submitted, complete these steps:

- Give one person responsibility for finding and correcting grammatical and mechanical errors.
- Meet as a group to evaluate the final document. Does it fulfill its purpose and meet the needs of the audience?

Option: Using a Wiki to Collaborate. Hosting companies such as PBwiki (**http://pbwiki .com/education.wiki**) offer easy-to-use, free wiki accounts to educators to run in their classes without the need of involving the IT department. Blackboard supports a wiki option as long as a college or university selects it with its subscription. A wiki within Blackboard is a page, or multiple pages, that students enrolled in the class can edit and change. They may add other content such as images and hyperlinks. A log allows instructors to track changes and the students' contributions. Ask you instructor about these options.

Career Application. Select a report topic from this chapter or Chapter 10. Assume that you must prepare the report as a team project. If you are working on a long report, your instructor may ask you to prepare individual progress reports as you develop your topic.

Your Task

- Form teams of two to five members.
- Prepare to work together by using the suggestions provided here.
- Plan your report by establishing its purpose, analyzing the audience, identifying the main issues, developing a work plan, and assigning tasks.
- Collect information, organize the data, and write the first draft.
- Decide how the document will be revised, edited, and evaluated.

Tip: For revising and editing, consider using the tools in MS Word introduced in Chapter 4 to track changes and make comments.

Your instructor may assign grades not only on the final report but also on your team effectiveness and your individual contribution, as determined by fellow team members and, potentially, by tracking your activities if you are using a wiki.

Proposals and Formal Reports

OBJECTIVES

After studying this chapter, you should be able to

- Identify and explain the parts of informal and formal proposals.
- Describe the preparatory steps for writing a formal report.
- Learn to collect data from secondary sources including print and electronic sources.
- Understand how to use Web browsers, search tools, blogs, and other online communication tools to locate reliable data.
- Discuss how to generate primary data from surveys, interviews, observation, and experimentation.
- Understand the need for the accurate documentation of data.
- Describe how to organize report data, create an outline, and make effective headings.
- Illustrate data using tables, charts, and graphs.
- Describe and sequence the parts of a formal report.

Understanding Business Proposals

You may wonder what proposals are and why you are learning to write them. For example, a business plan, a type of proposal, is necessary to obtain financing if you wish to start your own business. Similarly, if you apply for a grant or a graduate fellowship, you will need to provide a written plan or sketch a worthy project. The goal when writing business proposals and formal reports is to make them accessible and useful to your readers. In this chapter you will learn how to achieve this goal. Our discussion will start with proposals.

Proposals are written offers to solve problems, provide services, or sell equipment. Some proposals are internal, often taking the form of justification and recommendation reports. You learned about these reports in Chapter 9. Most proposals, however, are external and are a critical means of selling equipment and services that generate income for many companies.

External proposals may be divided into two categories: solicited and unsolicited. Enterprising companies looking for work might submit unsolicited proposals, but most proposals are solicited. When a firm knows exactly what it wants, it prepares

> **Proposals are persuasive offers to solve problems, provide services, or sell equipment.**

a request for proposal (RFP) specifying its requirements. Government agencies as well as private businesses use RFPs to solicit competitive bids from vendors.

For example, let's say that apparel merchandiser Abercrombie & Fitch wants to upgrade the computers and software in its home office in New Albany, Ohio. If the company knows exactly what it wants, it would prepare a request for proposals (RFP) specifying its requirements. It then publicizes this RFP, and companies interested in bidding on the job submit proposals. Both large and small companies are increasingly likely to use RFPs to solicit competitive bids on their projects. This enables them to compare "apples to apples." That is, they can compare prices from different companies on their projects. They also want the legal protection offered by proposals, which are legal contracts.

Many companies earn a sizable portion of their income from sales resulting from proposals. That is why creating effective proposals is especially important today. In writing proposals, the most important thing to remember is that proposals are sales presentations. They must be persuasive, not merely mechanical descriptions of what you can do. You may recall from Chapter 8 that effective persuasive sales messages (a) emphasize benefits for the reader, (b) "toot your horn" by detailing your expertise and accomplishments, and (c) make it easy for the reader to understand and respond.

Both large and small companies today often use requests for proposals (RFPs) to solicit competitive bids on projects.

"I have no objection to creative problem solving as long as it's not too creative and it's not a real problem."

Informal Proposals

Informal proposals may contain an introduction, background information, the proposal, staffing requirements, a budget, and an authorization request.

Proposals may be informal or formal; they differ primarily in length and format. Informal proposals are often presented in short (two- to four-page) letters. Sometimes called *letter proposals,* they contain six principal parts: introduction, background, proposal, staffing, budget, and authorization request. The informal letter proposal shown in Figure 10.1 on page 256 illustrates all six parts of a letter proposal. This proposal is addressed to a Cambridge, Massachusetts dentist who wants to improve patient satisfaction.

Introduction

Effective proposal openers "hook" readers by promising extraordinary results or resources or by identifying key benefits, issues, or outcomes.

Most proposals begin by explaining briefly the reasons for the proposal and by highlighting the writer's qualifications. To make your introduction more persuasive, you need to provide a "hook" to capture the reader's interest. One proposal expert suggests these possibilities:[1]

- Hint at extraordinary results, with details to be revealed shortly.
- Promise low costs or speedy results.
- Mention a remarkable resource (well-known authority, new computer program, well-trained staff) available exclusively to you.
- Identify a serious problem (worry item) and promise a solution, to be explained later.
- Specify a key issue or benefit that you feel is the heart of the proposal.

For example, in the introduction of the proposal shown in Figure 10.1, Allen Ward focused on what the customer was looking for. He analyzed the request of the Cambridge dentist, Dr. Diane Corbett, and decided that she was most interested in specific recommendations for improving service to her patients. But Ward did not hit on this hook until he had written a first draft and had come back to it later. Indeed, it is often a good idea to put off writing

WORKPLACE IN FOCUS

In a move reminiscent of suburban bomb shelters of the Cold War era, urban planners are preparing "lilypad cities" to house survivors if climate-disaster fears ever materialize. Should the planet become inundated by rising sea levels, these zero-emission ships could literally bob around the globe as self-sustaining habitats, complete with energy supplied from solar panels and wind turbines. Designed by award-winning Belgian architect Vincent Callebaut, and inspired by the shape of lilypads, the giant floating metropolises are both stylish and loaded with the comforts of modern living. *What organizations might submit proposals in the development of lily-pad cities?*

the introduction to a proposal until after you have completed other parts. For longer proposals the introduction also outlines the organization of the material to come.

Although writers may know what goes into the proposal introduction, many face writer's block before they get started. It doesn't help that most proposals and reports must be completed under the pressure of tight deadlines. To get the creative juices flowing, former Raytheon proposal specialist Dr. Mark Grinyer suggests studying the RFP closely to understand what the client really wants. Based on that analysis, he would look for persuasive themes until a proposal outline emerged.[2] Addressing the client's needs may be the ticket to getting off to a good start.

Background, Problem, Purpose

The background section identifies the problem and discusses the goals or purposes of the project. In an unsolicited proposal your goal is to convince the reader that a problem exists. As a result, you must present the problem in detail, discussing such factors as monetary losses, failure to comply with government regulations, and loss of customers. In a solicited proposal your aim is to persuade the reader that you understand the problem completely. Therefore, if you are responding to an RFP, this means repeating its language. For example, if the RFP asks for the *design of a company Web site that can handle multiuser access with differential permissions to view data,*[3] you would use the same language in explaining the purpose of your proposal. This section might include segments titled *Basic Requirements, Most Critical Tasks,* and *Most Important Secondary Problems.*

Proposal, Plan, Schedule

In the proposal section itself, you should discuss your plan for solving the problem. In some proposals this is tricky because you want to disclose enough of your plan to secure the contract without giving away so much information that your services aren't needed. Without specifics, though, your proposal has little chance, so you must decide how much to reveal. Tell what you propose to do and how it will benefit the reader. Remember, too, that a proposal is a sales presentation. Sell your methods, product, and "deliverables"—items that will be left with the client. In this section some writers specify how the project will be managed and how its progress

The proposal section must give enough information to secure the contract but not so much detail that the services aren't needed.

FIGURE 10.1 Informal Proposal

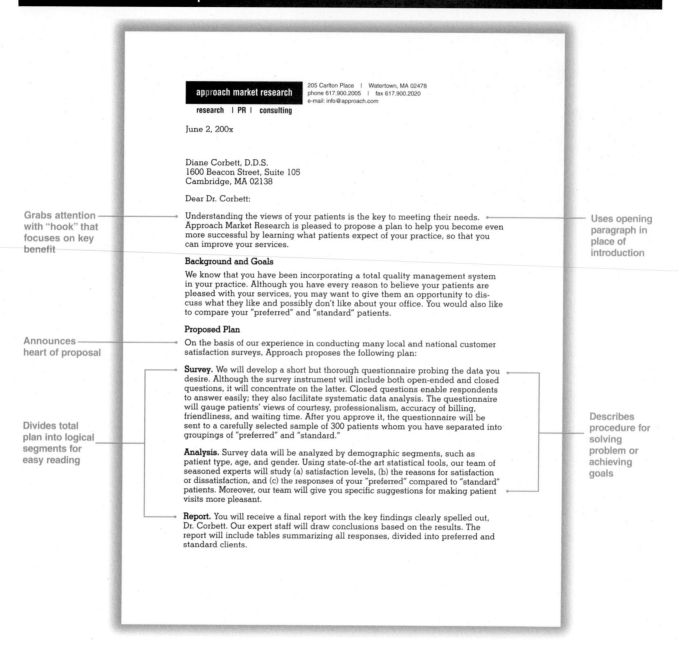

Grabs attention with "hook" that focuses on key benefit

Announces heart of proposal

Divides total plan into logical segments for easy reading

Uses opening paragraph in place of introduction

Describes procedure for solving problem or achieving goals

---

will be audited. Most writers also include a schedule of activities or timetable showing when events will take place.

Staffing

The staffing section promotes the credentials and expertise of the project leaders and support staff.

The staffing section of a proposal describes the credentials and expertise of the project leaders. It may also identify the size and qualifications of the support staff, along with other resources such as computer facilities and special programs for analyzing statistics. The staffing section is a good place to endorse and promote your staff. In longer proposals some firms follow industry standards and include staff qualifications and generic résumés of key people in an appendix. Using generic rather than actual résumés ensures privacy for individuals and also protects the company in case the staff changes after a proposal has been submitted to a client.

FIGURE 10.1 Continued

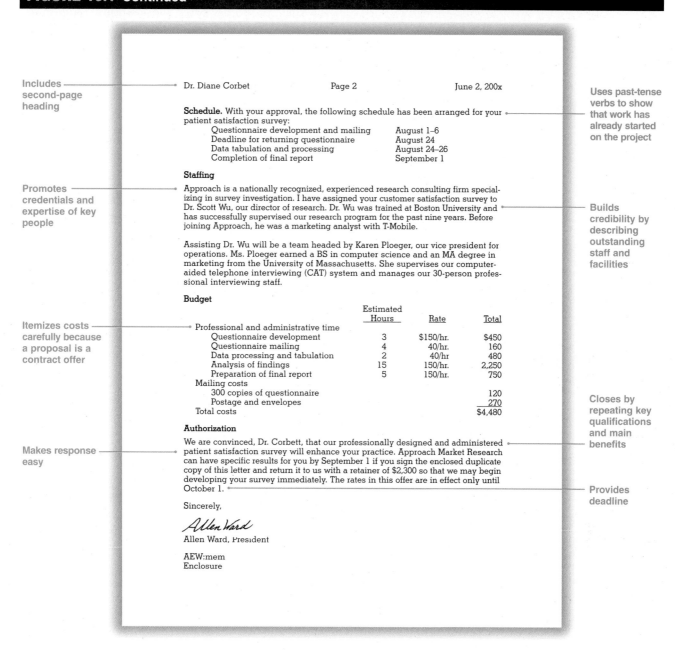

Includes second-page heading

Uses past-tense verbs to show that work has already started on the project

Promotes credentials and expertise of key people

Builds credibility by describing outstanding staff and facilities

Itemizes costs carefully because a proposal is a contract offer

Closes by repeating key qualifications and main benefits

Makes response easy

Provides deadline

Dr. Diane Corbet   Page 2   June 2, 200x

Schedule. With your approval, the following schedule has been arranged for your patient satisfaction survey:

Questionnaire development and mailing	August 1–6
Deadline for returning questionnaire	August 24
Data tabulation and processing	August 24–26
Completion of final report	September 1

Staffing

Approach is a nationally recognized, experienced research consulting firm specializing in survey investigation. I have assigned your customer satisfaction survey to Dr. Scott Wu, our director of research. Dr. Wu was trained at Boston University and has successfully supervised our research program for the past nine years. Before joining Approach, he was a marketing analyst with T-Mobile.

Assisting Dr. Wu will be a team headed by Karen Ploeger, our vice president for operations. Ms. Ploeger earned a BS in computer science and an MA degree in marketing from the University of Massachusetts. She supervises our computer-aided telephone interviewing (CAT) system and manages our 30-person professional interviewing staff.

Budget

Professional and administrative time	Estimated Hours	Rate	Total
Questionnaire development	3	$150/hr.	$450
Questionnaire mailing	4	40/hr.	160
Data processing and tabulation	2	40/hr.	480
Analysis of findings	15	150/hr.	2,250
Preparation of final report	5	150/hr.	750
Mailing costs			
300 copies of questionnaire			120
Postage and envelopes			270
Total costs			$4,480

Authorization

We are convinced, Dr. Corbett, that our professionally designed and administered patient satisfaction survey will enhance your practice. Approach Market Research can have specific results for you by September 1 if you sign the enclosed duplicate copy of this letter and return it to us with a retainer of $2,300 so that we may begin developing your survey immediately. The rates in this offer are in effect only until October 1.

Sincerely,

Allen Ward

Allen Ward, President

AEW:mem
Enclosure

Budget

A central item in most proposals is the budget, a list of project costs. You need to prepare this section carefully because it represents a contract; you can't raise the price later—even if your costs increase. You can—and should—protect yourself with a deadline for acceptance. In the budget section some writers itemize hours and costs; others present a total sum only. A proposal to design and build a complex e-commerce Web site might, for example, contain a detailed line-by-line budget. In the proposal shown in Figure 10.1, Allen Ward felt that he needed to justify the budget for his firm's patient satisfaction survey, so he itemized the costs. But the budget included for a proposal to conduct a one-day diversity awareness seminar for employees might be presented as a lump sum only. Your analysis of the project will help you decide what kind of budget to prepare.

Because a proposal is a legal contract, the budget must be carefully researched.

"I haven't read your proposal yet, Bob, but I already have some great ideas on how to improve it."

Authorization Request

Informal proposals often close with a request for approval or authorization. In addition, the closing should remind the reader of key benefits and motivate action. It might also include a deadline date beyond which the offer is invalid. At some companies, such as Hewlett-Packard, authorization to proceed isn't part of the proposal. Instead, it is usually discussed after the customer has received the proposal. In this way the customer and the sales account manager are able to negotiate terms before a formal agreement is drawn.

Formal Proposals

> **Formal proposals respond to big projects and may contain 200 or more pages.**

Formal proposals differ from informal proposals not in style but in tone, structure, format, and length. Formal proposals respond to big projects and may range from 5 to 200 or more pages. To facilitate comprehension and reference, they are organized into many parts. In addition to the six basic parts just described, formal proposals contain some or all of the following additional parts: copy of the RFP, letter or memo of transmittal, abstract and/or executive summary, title page, table of contents, list of figures, and appendix. In addition, the tone used in formal proposals is often more formal than the tone used in informal proposals.

Well-written proposals win contracts and business for companies and individuals. In fact, many companies depend entirely on proposals to generate their income. Companies such as Microsoft, KPMG, and Boeing employ staffs of people who do nothing but prepare proposals to compete for new business. For more information about industry standards and resources, visit the Web site of the Association of Proposal Management Professionals at **http://www.apmp.org**.

Preparing to Write Formal Reports

> **Formal reports discuss the results of a process of thorough investigation and analysis.**

Formal reports are similar to formal proposals in length, organization, and serious tone. Instead of making an offer, however, formal reports represent the product of thorough investigation and analysis. They present organized information to decision makers in business, industry, government, and education. Although formal reports in business are seen infrequently, they serve an important function. They provide management with vital data for decision making. In this section we will consider the entire process of writing a formal report: preparing to write, researching secondary data, generating primary data, documenting data, organizing and outlining data, illustrating data, and presenting the final report.

Like proposals and informal reports, formal reports begin with a definition of the project. Probably the most difficult part of this definition is limiting the scope of the report. Every project has limitations. If you are writing a formal report, decide at the outset what constraints influence the range of your project and how you will achieve your purpose. How much time do you have for completing your report? How much space will you be allowed for reporting on your topic? How accessible are the data you need? How thorough should your research be?

If you are writing about low morale among swing-shift employees, for example, how many of your 475 employees should you interview? Should you limit your research to company-related morale factors, or should you consider external factors over which the company has no control? In investigating the relationship between work and students' graduation rate, should you focus on a particular groups, such as seniors and transfer students, or should you consider all students, including graduate students? The first step in writing a report, then, is determining the precise boundaries of the topic.

Once you have defined the project and limited its scope, write a statement of purpose. Preparing a written statement of purpose is a good idea because it defines the focus of the report and provides a standard that keeps the project on target. The statement of purpose should describe the goal, significance, and limitations of the report. In writing useful statements of purpose, choose action verbs telling what you intend to do: *analyze, choose, investigate, compare, justify, evaluate, explain, establish, determine,* and so on. Notice how the following statement pinpoints the research and report and uses action verbs:

> The purpose of this report is to explore employment possibilities for entry-level paralegal workers in the city of Phoenix. It will consider typical salaries, skills required, opportunities, and working conditions. This research is significant because of the increasing number of job openings in the paralegal field. This report won't consider legal secretarial employment, which represents a different employment focus.

The planning of every report begins with a statement of purpose explaining the goal, significance, and limitations of the report.

Researching Secondary Data

One of the most important steps in the process of writing a report is that of gathering information (research). Because a report is only as good as its data, you will want to spend considerable time collecting data before you begin writing.

Data fall into two broad categories, primary and secondary. Primary data result from firsthand experience and observation. Secondary data come from reading what others have experienced and observed. Coca-Cola and Pepsi-Cola, for example, produce primary data when they stage taste tests and record the reactions of consumers. These same sets of data become secondary after they have been published and, let's say, a newspaper reporter uses them in an article about soft drinks. Secondary data are easier and cheaper to develop than primary data, which might involve interviewing large groups or sending out questionnaires.

Primary data come from firsthand experience and observation; secondary data, from reading.

You are going to learn first about secondary data because that is where nearly every research project should begin. Often, something has already been written about your topic. Reviewing secondary sources can save time and effort and prevent you from "reinventing the wheel." Most secondary material is available either in print or electronically.

Print Resources

Although we are seeing a steady movement away from print to electronic data, print sources are still the most visible parts of most libraries. Because some information is available only in print, you may want to use some of the following print resources.

If you are an infrequent library user, begin your research by talking with a reference librarian about your project. These librarians won't do your research for you, but they will steer you in the right direction. What is more, they are very accommodating. Several years ago a *Wall Street Journal* poll revealed that librarians are thought to be among the friendliest, most approachable people in the working world. Many libraries help you understand their computer, cataloging, and retrieval systems by providing brochures, handouts, and workshops.

Books. Although quickly outdated, books provide excellent historical, in-depth data on a large variety of subjects. Books can be located through print catalogs or online catalogs. Most automated systems today enable you to learn not only whether a book is in the library but also whether it is currently available.

Books provide historical, in-depth data; periodicals provide limited but current coverage.

Periodicals. Magazines, pamphlets, and journals are called *periodicals* because of their recurrent, or periodic, publication. Journals are compilations of scholarly articles. Articles in journals and other periodicals will be extremely useful to you because they are concise, limited in scope, and current, and can supplement information in books.

Bibliographic Indexes. *The Readers' Guide to Periodical Literature* is a valuable index of general-interest magazine article titles. It includes such magazines as *Time, Newsweek, The New Yorker,* and *U.S. News & World Report.* More useful to business writers, though, will be the titles of articles appearing in business and industrial magazines and newspapers (such as *Forbes, Fortune, The Economist, BusinessWeek, Barron's,* and *The Wall Street Journal*). For an index of these publications, consult the *Business Periodicals Index.* Most indexes today are available in print, CD-ROM, and Web versions for easy searching.

Electronic Databases

Most researchers today begin by looking in electronic databases.

As a writer of business reports today, you will probably begin your secondary research with electronic resources. Although some databases are still presented on CD-ROM, information is increasingly available in online databases. These online databases have become a staple of secondary research. Most writers turn to them first because they are fast and easy to use. College and public libraries and some employers offer free access to several commercial databases, sparing you the high cost of individual subscriptions. With an Internet connection, you can conduct detailed searches without ever leaving your office, home, or dorm room.

A database is a collection of information stored electronically so that it is accessible by computer and digitally searchable. Databases provide both bibliographic (titles of documents and brief abstracts) as well as full-text documents. Most researchers prefer full-text documents. Various databases contain a rich array of magazine, newspaper, and journal articles, as well as newsletters, business reports, company profiles, government data, reviews, and directories. Well-known databases are EBSCO Business Source Premier, Factiva, ABI/Inform, and LexisNexis.

The Web

The World Wide Web is a collection of hypertext pages that offer information and links on trillions of pages.

The best-known area of the Internet is the World Wide Web. Growing at a dizzying pace, the Web includes an enormous collection of Web sites around the world. With trillions of pages of information available on the Web, chances are that if you have a question, an answer exists online. Web offerings include online databases, magazines, newspapers, library resources, sound and video files, and many other information resources. You can expect to find such items as product and service facts, public relations material, mission statements, staff directories, press releases, current company news, government information, selected article reprints, collaborative scientific project reports, stock research, financial information, and employment information. The Web is indeed a vast network of resources at your fingertips.

The Web is unquestionably one of the greatest sources of information now available to anyone needing simple facts quickly and inexpensively. But finding relevant, credible information can be frustrating and time consuming. The constantly changing contents of the Web and its lack of organization irritate budding researchers. Moreover, content isn't always reliable. Anyone posting a Web site is a publisher without any quality control or guarantee. Check out the Communication Workshop at the end of this chapter to learn more about what questions to ask in assessing the quality of a Web document. The problem of gathering information is complicated by the fact that the total number of Web sites recently surpassed 100 million, growing at a rate of about 4 million new addresses each month.[4] Therefore, to succeed in your search for information and answers, you need to understand how to browse the Web and use search tools. You also need to understand how to evaluate the information you find.

Web Browsers and URLs. Searching the Web requires a Web browser, such as Microsoft Internet Explorer, Safari, or Firefox. Browsers are software programs that enable you to view the graphics and text of, as well as access links to, Web pages. To locate the Web page of a specific organization, you need its Web site address, or URL (Uniform Resource Locator). URLs are case and space sensitive, so be sure to type the address exactly as it is printed. For most companies, the URL is **http://www.xyzcompany.com**. Your goal is to locate the top-level Web page (called *home page* and, in certain cases, *portal*) of an organization's site. On this page you will generally find an overview of the site contents or a link to a site map. If you can't guess a company's URL, you can usually find it quickly using Google (**http://www.google.com**).

Web access has gone mobile in the last few years, as increasingly sophisticated smartphones and PDAs (personal digital assistants) now offer nearly the same functions as desktop and laptop computers do. Mobile browsers, also called minibrowsers, are small versions of their bigger cousins, Internet Explorer or Firefox. Businesspeople can surf Web pages and write e-mail on the go with devices such as the popular BlackBerry and iPhone, which fit into their pockets. Similarly, users can listen to podcasts, digital recordings of radio programs, and other audio and video files on demand. Podcasts are distributed for downloading to a computer or an MP3 audio player such as the iPod and can be enjoyed anywhere you choose.

> Web browsers are software programs that access Web pages and their links. Increasingly users access the Web on the go with smartphones and PDAs.

Search Tools. The Web is packed with amazing information. Instead of visiting libraries or searching reference books when you need to find something, you can now turn to the Web for all kinds of facts. However, you will need a good search tool, such as Google, Yahoo, or MSN. A search tool is a service that indexes, organizes, and often rates and reviews Web pages. Some search tools rely on people to maintain a catalog of Web sites or pages. Others use software to identify key information. They all begin a search based on the keywords you enter. The most-used search tool at this writing is Google. It has developed a cultlike following with its "uncanny ability to sort through millions of Web pages and put the sites you really want at the top of its results pages."[5]

> A search tool is a service that indexes, organizes, and often rates and reviews Web pages.

Web Search Tips and Techniques. To conduct a thorough Web search for the information you need, use these tips and techniques:

> You must know how to use search tools to make them most effective.

- **Use two or three search tools.** Different Internet search engines turn up different results. However, at this writing, Google consistently turns up more reliable "hits" than other search tools.
- **Know your search tool.** When connecting to a search service for the first time, always read the description of its service, including its FAQs (Frequently Asked Questions), Help, and How to Search sections.
- **Understand case sensitivity.** Generally use lowercase for your searches, unless you are searching for a term that is typically written in upper- and lowercase, such as a person's name.
- **Use nouns as search words and as many as eight words in a query.** The right key words—and more of them—can narrow your search considerably.
- **Use quotation marks.** When searching for a phrase, such as *cost-benefit analysis*, most search tools will retrieve documents having all or some of the terms. This AND/OR strategy is the default of most search tools. To locate occurrences of a specific phrase, enclose it in quotation marks.
- **Omit articles and prepositions.** Known as "stop words," articles and prepositions don't add value to a search. Instead of *request for proposal*, use *proposal request*.
- **Proofread your search words.** Make sure you are searching for the right thing by proofreading your search words carefully. For example, searching for *sock market* will come up with substantially different results than searching for *stock market*.
- **Save the best.** To keep better track of your favorite Web sites, save them as bookmarks or favorites.

- **Keep trying.** If a search produces no results, check your spelling. Try synonyms and variations on words. Try to be less specific in your search term. If your search produces too many hits, try to be more specific. Think of words that uniquely identify what you are looking for, and use as many relevant keywords as possible. Use a variety of search tools, and repeat your search a few days later.

Blogs (Weblogs), Wikis, and Social Networks

The Web continues to grow and expand, offering a great variety of virtual communities and collaboration tools. Mentioned most frequently are blogs, wikis, and social networking sites. Far from being mere entertainment for "wired" teens, these resources are affecting the way we do business today.

One of the newest ways to locate secondary information on the Web is through the use of *weblogs*, more commonly referred to as *blogs*. A Google search yields dozens of definitions. A Cornell University glossary defines the term as a "journal on the web, which may be public or private, individual or collaborative."[6] An individual's opinions or news are posted regularly in reverse chronological order, allowing visitors to comment.

Blogs are used by business researchers, students, politicians, the media, and many others to share and gather information. Marketing firms and their clients are looking closely at blogs because blogs can produce unbiased consumer feedback faster and more cheaply than such staples of consumer research as focus groups and surveys.[7] Employees and executives at companies such as Google, Sun Microsystems, IBM, and Hewlett-Packard maintain blogs. They use blogs to communicate internally with employees and externally with clients.[8]

A blog is basically an online diary or journal that allows visitors to leave public comments. At this time, writers have posted 70 million blogs, up nearly 30 percent in one year.[9] However, only about half of these blogs are active, meaning that posts were published within three months. A recent Forrester Research study suggests that 25 percent of the U.S. population read a blog once a month.[10] Although blogs may have been overrated in their importance, they do represent an amazing new information stream if used wisely. Be sure to evaluate all blog content using the checklist provided in the Communication Workshop at the end of this chapter.

At least as important to business as blogs are new communication tools such as wikis and social networking sites. A wiki is collaborative software, typically a collection of Web pages, that can be edited by a group of users tapping into the same technology that runs the well-known online encyclopedia Wikipedia. Large companies, such as British Telecom (BT), encourage their employees to team up to author software, launch branding campaigns, and map cell phone stations. Most projects are facilitated with the help of wikis, a tool that is especially valuable across vast geographic distances and multiple time zones.[11]

Far from being only entertaining leisure sites, social networks such as Facebook and Twitter are used by businesses to enable teams to form spontaneously and naturally and then to assign targeted projects to them. Idea generators are easy to spot. A BT executive considers these contributors invaluable, adding that "a new class of supercommunicators has emerged."[12] However, these exciting new online tools require sound judgment when researchers wish to use them. The Communication Workshop at the end of this chapter will help you establish reliable evaluation criteria.

Generating Primary Data

Although you will begin a business report by probing for secondary data, you will probably need primary data to give a complete picture. Business reports that solve specific current problems typically rely on primary, firsthand data. If, for example, management wants to discover the cause of increased employee turnover in its Las Vegas office, it must investigate conditions in Las Vegas by collecting recent information. Providing answers to business problems often means generating primary data

> **Blogs, wikis, and informal online networks can be used to generate primary or secondary data.**

> **Business reports often rely on primary data from firsthand experience.**

through surveys, interviews, observation, or experimentation. In addition to generating secondary data, blogs can also be used to generate primary data. Similarly, wikis can be harnessed by teams to discuss a project and solicit feedback that may produce primary data.

Surveys

Surveys collect data from groups of people. When companies develop new products, for example, they often survey consumers to learn their needs. The advantages of surveys are that they gather data economically and efficiently. Surveys can be mailed to participants, or they can be administered online. Both mailed and online surveys reach big groups nearby or at great distances. Moreover, people responding to mailed and online surveys have time to consider their answers, thus improving the accuracy of the data.

Surveys yield efficient and economical primary data for reports.

Mailed surveys, of course, have disadvantages. Most of us rank them with junk mail, so response rates may be no higher than 2 percent. Online surveys also have disadvantages, although response rates tend to be higher. Furthermore, those who do respond to either mailed or online surveys may not represent an accurate sample of the overall population, thus invalidating generalizations from the group. Let's say, for example, that an e-commerce site sends out a survey questionnaire asking about online shopping preferences. If only young Internet users respond, the survey data can't be used to generalize what people in other age groups might think. A final problem with surveys has to do with truthfulness. Some respondents exaggerate their incomes or distort other facts, thus causing the results to be unreliable. Nevertheless, surveys may be the best way to generate data for business and student reports.

Interviews

Some of the best report information, particularly on topics about which little has been written, comes from individuals. These individuals are usually experts or veterans in their fields. Consider both in-house and outside experts for business reports. Tapping these sources will call for in-person, telephone, or online interviews. To elicit the most useful data, try these techniques:

Interviews with experts produce useful report data, especially when little has been written about a topic.

- **Locate an expert.** Ask managers and individuals working in an area whom they consider to be most knowledgeable. Check membership lists of professional organizations, and consult articles about the topic or related topics. Search business-related blogs to find out who the experts are in your area of interest. You could also post an inquiry to an Internet *newsgroup*. An easy way to search newsgroups in a topic area is through the browse groups now indexed by the popular search tool Google (**http://groups.google.com**). Most people enjoy being experts or at least recommending them.
- **Prepare for the interview.** Learn about the individual you are interviewing, and make sure you can pronounce the interviewee's name correctly. Research the background and terminology of the topic. Let's say you are interviewing a corporate communication expert about producing an in-house newsletter. You ought to be familiar with terms such as *font* and software such as QuarkXpress and Adobe InDesign. In addition, be prepared by making a list of questions that pinpoint your focus on the topic. Ask the interviewee if you may record the talk.
- **Maintain a professional attitude.** Call before the interview to confirm the arrangements, and then arrive on time. Bring what you need to take notes, and dress professionally. Use your body language to convey respect.
- **Make your questions objective and friendly.** Adopt a courteous and respectful attitude. Don't get into a debating match with the interviewee. Remember that you are there to listen, not to talk! Use open-ended questions (*What are your predictions for the future of the telecommunications industry?*), rather than yes-or-no questions (*Do you think we will see more video e-mail in the future?*) to draw experts out.

- **Watch the time.** Tell interviewees in advance how much time you expect to need for the interview. Don't overstay your appointment.
- **End graciously.** Conclude the interview with a general question, such as *Is there anything you would like to add?* Express your appreciation, and ask permission to telephone later if you need to verify points. Send a thank-you note within a day or two after the interview.

Observation and Experimentation

Some of the best report data come from firsthand observation and experimentation.

Some kinds of primary data can be obtained only through firsthand observation and experimentation. If you determine that the questions you have require observational data, then you need to plan the observations carefully. One of the most important questions to ask is what or whom you are observing and how often those observations are necessary to provide reliable data. For example, if you want to learn more about an organization's customer-service phone service, you probably need to use observation techniques, along with interviews and perhaps even surveys. You will want to answer questions such as, *How long does a typical caller wait before a customer-service rep answers the call?* and *Is the service consistent?*

Observation produces rich data, but that information is especially prone to charges of subjectivity. One can interpret an observation in many ways. Thus, to make observations more objective, try to quantify them. For example, record customer telephone wait-time for 60-minute periods at different times throughout a week. This will give you a better picture than just observing for an hour on a Friday before a holiday.

Experimentation produces data suggesting causes and effects. Informal experimentation might be as simple as a pretest and posttest in a college course. Did students expand their knowledge as a result of the course? More formal experimentation is undertaken by scientists and professional researchers who control variables to test their effects. Assume, for example, that the Hershey Company wants to test the hypothesis (which is a tentative assumption) that chocolate lifts people out of the doldrums. An experiment testing the hypothesis would separate depressed individuals into two groups: those who ate chocolate (the experimental group) and those who did not (the control group). What effect did chocolate have? Such experiments aren't done haphazardly, however. Valid experiments require sophisticated research designs and careful attention to matching the experimental and control groups.

Documenting Data

Report writers document their sources to strengthen an argument, protect themselves from charges of plagiarism, and help readers locate data.

Whether you collect data from primary or secondary sources, the data must be documented; that is, you must indicate where the data originated. Using the ideas of someone else without giving credit is called *plagiarism* and is unethical. Even if you *paraphrase* (put the information in your own words), the ideas must be documented. You will learn more about paraphrasing in this section.

Purposes of Documentation

As a careful writer, you should properly document your data for the following reasons:

- **To strengthen your argument.** Including good data from reputable sources will convince readers of your credibility and the logic of your reasoning.
- **To instruct the reader.** Citing references enables readers to pursue a topic further and make use of the information themselves.
- **To protect yourself against charges of plagiarism.** Acknowledging your sources keeps you honest. Plagiarism, which is illegal and unethical, is the act of using others' ideas without proper documentation or paraphrasing poorly.

Plagiarism of words or ideas is a serious charge and can lead to loss of a job. The career-ending missteps of journalists such as Jayson Blair of *The New York*

WORKPLACE IN FOCUS

Hailed as the largest science experiment in history, the Large Hadron Collider is a multibillion-dollar atom-smasher out to uncover the origins of the universe. Buried 330 feet below Meyrin, Switzerland, the massive particle accelerator uses barrel-shaped solenoids and supercooled magnets to recreate conditions believed to have existed during the Big Bang. Physicists at CERN built the collider to investigate the existence of extra dimensions and "dark matter"—an invisible mass that may comprise much of the universe. Despite public fears that the atomic project could unleash an Earth-swallowing black hole, scientists backing the collider have issued formal reports affirming its safety. *Why is it important for CERN to provide accurate documentation in its safety reports?*

Times and, more recently, of *Baltimore Sun* columnist Michael Olesker, illustrate that plagiarism is serious business.[13] You can avoid charges of plagiarism as well as add clarity to your work by knowing what to document and by developing good research habits.

Learning What to Document

When you write business or academic reports, you are continually dealing with other people's ideas. You are expected to conduct research, synthesize ideas, and build on the work of others. But you are also expected to give proper credit for borrowed material. To avoid plagiarism, you must give credit whenever you use the following:[14]

- Another person's ideas, opinions, examples, or theory
- Any facts, statistics, graphs, and drawings that aren't common knowledge
- Quotations of another person's actual spoken or written words
- Paraphrases of another person's spoken or written words

Information that is common knowledge requires no documentation. For example, the following statement needs no documentation: *The Wall Street Journal is a popular business newspaper.* Statements that aren't common knowledge, however, must be documented. For example, *Eight of the nation's top ten fastest-growing large cities (100,000 or more population) since Census 2000 lie in the Western states of Arizona, Nevada, and California* would require a citation because most people don't know this fact. Cite sources for proprietary information such as statistics organized and reported by a newspaper or magazine. You probably know to use citations to document direct quotations, but you must also cite ideas that you summarize in your own words.

Developing Good Research Habits

Report writers who are gathering information should record documentation data immediately after locating the information. This information can then be used in footnotes, endnotes, or in-text citations; and it can be listed in a bibliography or works-cited list at the end of the report. Here are some tips for gathering the documentation data you need from some of the most popular types of resources:

> Give credit when you use another's ideas, when you borrow facts that aren't common knowledge, and when you quote or paraphrase another's words.

- For a book, record the title, author(s), publisher, place of publication, year of publication, and pages cited.
- For newspaper, magazine, and journal articles, record the publication title, article title, author(s), issue/volume number, date, and pages cited.
- For online newspaper and magazine articles, record the author(s), article title, publication title, date the article was written, the exact URL, and the date you retrieved the article.
- For an entire Web site, record the name of the company or organization sponsoring the site, the URL, and the date you retrieved the page.

Report writers who are gathering information have two methods available for recording the information they find. The time-honored manual method of notetaking works well because information is recorded on separate cards, which can then be arranged in the order needed to develop a thesis or argument. Today, though, writers rely heavily on electronic researching. Instead of recording facts on note cards, savvy researchers manage their data by saving sources to memory sticks and disks, e-mailing documents, bookmarking favorites, and copying and pasting information from the Web into word processing software for easy storage and retrieval. Be careful, though, not to cut-and-paste your way into plagiarism.

You can learn more about what types of documentation information to record during your research by studying the formal report in Figure 10.17 and by consulting Appendix C.

Practicing the Fine Art of Paraphrasing

Paraphrasing involves putting an original passage into your own words.

In writing business or academic reports and using the ideas of others, you will probably rely heavily on paraphrasing, which means restating an original passage in your own words and in your own style. To do a good job of paraphrasing, follow these steps:

- Read the original material carefully to comprehend its full meaning.
- Write your own version without looking at the original.
- Don't repeat the grammatical structure of the original, and don't merely replace words with synonyms.
- Reread the original to be sure you covered the main points but did not borrow specific language.

To better understand the difference between plagiarizing and paraphrasing, study the following passages. Notice that the writer of the plagiarized version uses the same grammatical construction as the source and often merely replaces words with synonyms. Even the acceptable version, however, requires a reference to the source author.

Source
While the BlackBerry has become standard armor for executives, a few maverick leaders are taking action to reduce e-mail use. . . . The concern, say academics and management thinkers, is misinterpreted messages, as well as the degree to which e-mail has become a substitute for the nuanced conversations that are critical in the workplace.[15]

The plagiarized version copies sentence structure and merely replaces some words.

Plagiarized version
Although smartphones are standard among business executives, some pioneering bosses are acting to lower e-mail usage. Business professors and management experts are concerned that messages are misinterpreted and e-mail substitutes for nuances in conversations that are crucial on the job (Brady, 2006).

The acceptable paraphrase changes sentence structure and perspective.

Acceptable paraphrase
E-mail on the go may be the rage in business. However, some executives are rethinking its use, as communication experts warn that e-mail triggers misunderstandings. These specialists believe that e-mail should not replace the more subtle face-to-face interaction needed on the job (Brady, 2006).

Knowing When and How to Quote

On occasion you will want to use the exact words of a source. Anytime you use the exact words from a source, you must enclose the words in quotation marks. Be careful when doing this that you don't change the wording of the quoted material in any way.

Also beware of overusing quotations. Documents that contain pages of spliced-together quotations suggest that writers have few ideas of their own. Wise writers and speakers use direct quotations for three purposes only:

- To provide objective background data and establish the severity of a problem as seen by experts
- To repeat identical phrasing because of its precision, clarity, or aptness
- To duplicate exact wording before criticizing

When you must use an exact quotation, try to summarize and introduce it in your own words. Readers want to know the gist of a quotation before they tackle it. For example, to introduce a quotation discussing the shrinking staffs of large companies, you could precede it with your words: *In predicting employment trends, Charles Waller believes the corporation of the future will depend on a small core of full-time employees*. To introduce quotations or paraphrases, use wording such as the following:

According to Waller, ...

Waller argues that . . . .

In his recent study, Waller reported . . . .

Use quotation marks to enclose exact quotations, as shown in the following: "The current image," says Charles Waller, "of a big glass-and-steel corporate head-quarters on landscaped grounds directing a worldwide army of tens of thousands of employees may soon be a thing of the past."

> **Use quotations only to provide background data, to cite experts, to repeat precise phrasing, or to duplicate exact wording before criticizing.**

> **OFFICE INSIDER**
>
> Changing the words of an original source is not sufficient to prevent plagiarism. If you have retained the essential idea of an original source, and have not cited it, then no matter how drastically you may have altered its context or presentation, you have still plagiarized.

Using Citation Formats

You can direct readers to your sources with parenthetical notes inserted into the text and with bibliographies or works-cited lists. The most common citation formats are those presented by the Modern Language Association (MLA) and the American Psychological Association (APA). Learn more about how to use these formats in Appendix C. Guidelines for the most up-do-date citation formats for electronic references are at **www.guffey.com**. You will find model citation formats for online magazine, newspaper, and journal articles, as well as for Web references.

Organizing and Outlining Data

Once you have collected the data for a report and recorded that information on notes or printouts, you are ready to organize it into a coherent plan of presentation. First, you should decide on an organizational strategy, and then, following your plan, you will want to outline the report. Poorly organized reports lead to frustration; therefore, it is important to organize your report carefully so that readers will understand, remember, or be persuaded.

Organizational Strategies

The readability and effectiveness of a report are greatly enhanced by skillful organization of the information presented. As you begin the process of organization, ask yourself two important questions: (a) Where should I place the conclusions/recommendations? and (b) How should I organize the findings?

In the direct strategy, conclusions and recommendations come first; in the indirect strategy, they are last.

Where to Place the Conclusions and Recommendations.

As you recall from earlier instruction, the direct strategy requires that we present main ideas first. In formal reports that would mean beginning with your conclusions and recommendations. For example, if you were studying five possible locations for a proposed shopping center, you would begin with the recommendation of the best site. Use this strategy when the reader is supportive and knowledgeable. However, if the reader isn't supportive or needs to be informed, the indirect strategy may be better. This strategy involves presenting facts and discussion first, followed by conclusions and recommendations. Since formal reports often seek to educate the reader, this order of presentation is often most effective. Following this sequence, a study of possible locations for a shopping center would begin with data regarding all proposed sites followed by an analysis of the information and conclusions drawn from that analysis.

Organize report findings chronologically, geographically, topically, or by one of the other methods shown in Figure 10.2.

How to Organize the Findings.

After collecting your facts, you need a coherent plan for presenting them. We describe here three principal organizational patterns: chronological, geographical, and topical. You will find these and other patterns summarized in Figure 10.2. The pattern you choose depends on the material collected and the purpose of your report.

- **Chronological order.** Information sequenced along a time frame is arranged chronologically. This plan is effective for presenting historical data or for

FIGURE 10.2 Organizational Patterns for Report Findings

Pattern	Development	Use
Chronology	Arrange information in a time sequence to show history or development of topic.	Useful in showing time relationships, such as five-year profit figures or a series or events leading to a problem
Geography/Space	Organize information by regions or areas.	Appropriate for topics that are easily divided into locations, such as East Coast and West Coast, etc.
Topic/Function	Arrange by topics or functions.	Works well for topics with established categories, such as a report about categories of company expenses
Compare/Contrast	Present problem and show alternative solutions. Use consistent criteria. Show how the solutions are similar and different.	Best used for "before and after" scenarios or for problems with clear alternatives
Journalism Pattern	Arrange information in paragraphs devoted to *who, what, when, where, why,* and *how.* May conclude with recommendations.	Useful with audiences that need to be educated or persuaded
Value/Size	Start with the most valuable, biggest, or most important item. Discuss other items in descending order.	Useful for classifying information in, for example, a realtor's report on home values
Importance	Arrange from most important to least importance or build from least to most important.	Appropriate when persuading the audience to take a specific action or change a belief
Simple/Complex	Begin with simple concept; proceed to more complex idea.	Useful for technical or abstract topics
Best Case/Worst Case	Describe the best and possibly the worst possible outcomes.	Useful when dramatic effect is needed to achieve results; helpful when audience is uninterested or uninformed
Convention	Organize the report using a prescribed plan that all readers understand.	Useful for many operational and recurring reports such as weekly sales reports

describing a procedure. Agendas, minutes of meetings, progress reports, and procedures are usually organized by time. A description of the development of a multinational company, for example, would be chronological. A report explaining how to obtain federal funding for a project might be organized chronologically. Often topics are arranged in a past-to-present or present-to-past sequence.

- **Geographical or spatial arrangement.** Information arranged geographically or spatially is organized by physical location. For instance, a report analyzing a company's national sales might be divided into sections representing geographical areas such as the East, South, Midwest, West, and Northwest.
- **Topical or functional arrangement.** Some subjects lend themselves to arrangement by topic or function. A report analyzing changes in the management hierarchy of an organization might be arranged in this manner. First, the report would consider the duties of the CEO followed by the functions of the general manager, business manager, marketing manager, and so forth.

Outlines and Headings

Most writers agree that the clearest way to show the organization of a report topic is by recording its divisions in an outline. Although the outline isn't part of the final report, it is a valuable tool of the writer. It reveals at a glance the overall organization of the report. As you learned in Chapter 3, outlining involves dividing a topic into major sections and supporting those with details. Figure 10.3 shows an abbreviated outline of a report about forms of business ownership. Rarely is a real outline so perfectly balanced; some sections are usually longer than others. Remember, though, not to put a single topic under a major component. If you have only one subpoint, integrate it with the main item above it or reorganize. Use details, illustrations, and evidence to support subpoints.

The main points used to outline a report often become the main headings of the written report. In Chapter 9 you studied tips for writing talking and functional headings. Formatting those headings depends on what level they represent. Major headings, as you can see in Figure 10.4, are centered and typed in bold font. Second-level headings start at the left margin, and third-level headings are indented and become part of a paragraph.

Outlines show the organization and divisions of a report.

FIGURE 10.3 Outline Format

> **FORMS OF BUSINESS OWNERSHIP**
>
> **I. Sole proprietorship (*first main topic*)**
>   A. Advantages of sole proprietorship (*first subdivision of Topic I*)
>   1. Minimal capital requirements (*first subdivision of Topic A*)
>   2. Control by owner (*second subdivision of Topic A*)
>   B. Disadvantages of sole proprietorship (*second subdivision of Topic I*)
>   1. Unlimited liability (*first subdivision of Topic B*)
>   2. Limited management talent (*second subdivision of Topic B*)
> **II. Partnership (*second main topic*)**
>   A. Advantages of partnership (*first subdivision of Topic II*)
>   1. Access to capital (*first subdivision of Topic A*)
>   2. Management talent (*second subdivision of Topic A*)
>   3. Ease of formation (*third subdivision of Topic A*)
>   B. Disadvantages of partnership (*second subdivision of Topic II*)
>   1. Unlimited liability (*first subdivision of Topic B*)
>   2. Personality conflicts (*second subdivision of Topic B*)

FIGURE 10.4 Levels of Headings in Reports

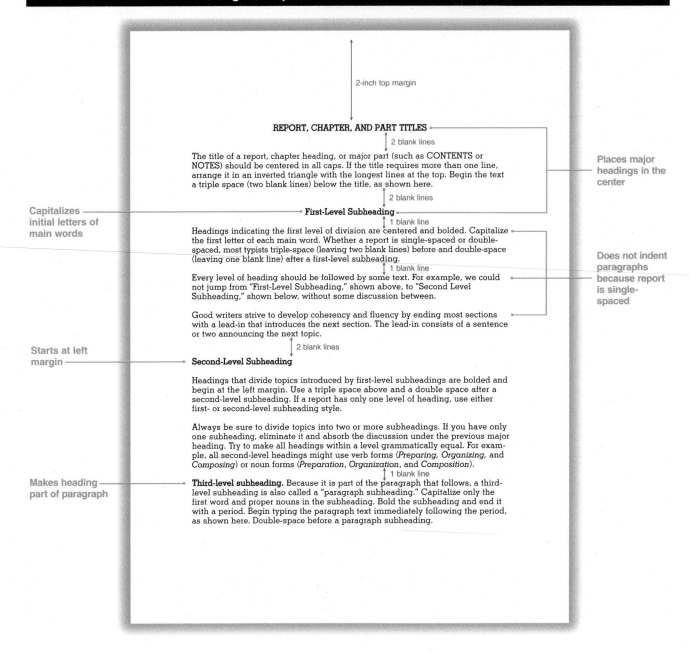

Illustrating Data

Effective graphics clarify numerical data and simplify complex ideas.

After collecting information and interpreting it, you need to consider how best to present it to your audience. If your report contains complex data and numbers, you may want to consider using graphics such as tables and charts. Appropriate graphics clarify data, create visual interest, and make numerical data meaningful. By simplifying complex ideas and emphasizing key data, well-constructed graphics make key information more understandable and easier to remember. In contrast, readers tend to be bored and confused by text paragraphs packed with complex data and numbers. The same information summarized in a table or chart becomes clear.

Because data can be shown in many forms (for example, in a chart, table, or graph), you need to recognize how to match the appropriate graphic with your objective. In addition, you need to know how to incorporate graphics into your reports.

Matching Graphics and Objectives

In developing the best graphics, you should first decide what data you want to highlight. Chances are you will have many points you would like to show in a table or chart. But which graphics are most appropriate for your objectives? Tables? Bar charts? Pie charts? Line charts? Surface charts? Flowcharts? Organization charts? Pictures?

Figure 10.5 summarizes appropriate uses for each type of graphic. Notice that tables are appropriate when you must report exact figures and values. However, if you want to compare one item with others or demonstrate changes in quantitative data over time, bar and line charts are better. To show the parts of a whole and the proportions of all the parts, you might draw a pie chart. If you must show a process such as how a product is made, a flowchart works well. An organization chart defines elements in a hierarchy such as the line of command in business management. Photographs, maps, and illustrations are most useful to create authenticity, to spotlight a location, and to show an item in use.

Let's look at each kind of graphic in greater detail so that you can use it effectively.

Tables

Probably the most frequently used visual aid in reports is the table. Because a table presents quantitative or verbal information in systematic columns and rows, it can clarify large quantities of data in small spaces. The disadvantage is that tables don't readily display trends. In making tables, you will be constructing rows and columns. A row is a list of items presented straight across a table. Each row must have a row heading. In Figure 10.6, the row headings are years. Columns are lists of items presented vertically.

> **Tables permit the systematic presentation of large amounts of data, whereas charts enhance visual comparisons.**

FIGURE 10.5 Matching Graphics to Objectives

Graphic		Objective
Table		To show exact figures and values
Bar Chart		To compare one item with others
Line Chart		To demonstrate changes in quantitative data over time
Pie Chart		To visualize a whole unit and the proportions of its components
Flowchart		To display a process or procedure
Organization Chart		To define a hierarchy of elements
Photograph, Map, Illustration		To create authenticity, to spotlight a location, and to show an item in use

> **Selecting an appropriate graphic form depends on the purpose that it serves.**

FIGURE 10.6 Table Summarizing Precise Data

		Figure 1 MPM Entertainment Company Income by Division (in millions of dollars)		
	Theme Parks	**Motion Pictures**	**DVDs and Videos**	**Total**
2006	$15.8	$39.3	$11.2	$66.3
2007	18.1	17.5	15.3	50.9
2008	23.8	21.1	22.7	67.6
2009	32.2	22.0	24.3	78.5
2010 (projected)	35.1	21.0	26.1	82.2

Source: *Industry Profiles* (New York: DataPro, 2009), 225.

Here are specific tips for designing good tables:

- Provide a descriptive title at the top of the table.
- Arrange items in a logical order (alphabetical, chronological, geographical, highest to lowest), depending on what you want to emphasize.
- Provide clear headings for the rows and columns.
- Identify the units in which figures are given (percentages, dollars, units per worker hour, and so forth) in the table title, in the column or row head, with the first item in a column, or in a note at the bottom.
- Use *N/A* (not available) for missing data.
- Make long tables easier to read by shading alternate lines or by leaving a blank line after groups of five.
- Place tables as close as possible to the place where they are mentioned in the text.

Bar Charts

Bar charts enable readers to compare related items, see changes over time, and understand how parts relate to a whole.

Although they lack the precision of tables, bar charts enable you to make emphatic visual comparisons by using horizontal or vertical bars of varying lengths. Bar charts can be used to compare related items, illustrate changes in data over time, and show segments as part of a whole. Figures 10.7 through 10.10 show vertical (also called column charts), horizontal, grouped, and segmented bar charts that highlight some of the data shown in the MPM Entertainment Company table (Figure 10.6). Note how the varied bar charts present information in different ways.

FIGURE 10.7 Vertical Bar Chart

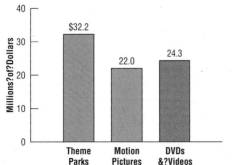

Figure 1
2009 MPM INCOME BY DIVISION

Source: *Industry Profiles* (New York: DataPro, 2009), 225.

FIGURE 10.8 Horizontal Bar Chart

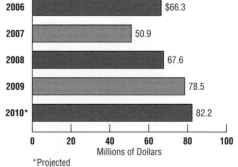

Figure 2
TOTAL MPM INCOME, 2006 TO 2010

*Projected
Source: *Industry Profiles.*

FIGURE 10.9 Grouped Bar Chart

Figure 3

MPM INCOME BY DIVISION
2006, 2008, AND 2010

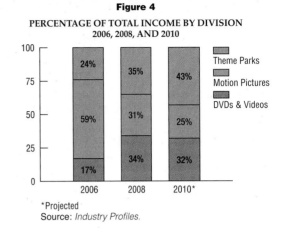

Source: *Industry Profiles.*

FIGURE 10.10 Segmented 100% Bar Chart

Figure 4

PERCENTAGE OF TOTAL INCOME BY DIVISION
2006, 2008, AND 2010

*Projected
Source: *Industry Profiles.*

Many suggestions for tables also hold true for bar charts. Here are a few additional tips:

- Keep the length and width of each bar and segment proportional.
- Include a total figure in the middle of a bar or at its end if the figure helps the reader and doesn't clutter the chart.
- Start dollar or percentage amounts at zero.
- Avoid showing too much information, which produces clutter and confusion.
- Place each bar chart as close as possible to the place where it is mentioned in the text.

Line Charts

The major advantage of line charts is that they show changes over time, thus indicating trends. The vertical axis is typically the dependent variable (such as dollars), and the horizontal axis is the independent one (such as years). Figures 10.11 through 10.13 show line charts that reflect income trends for the three divisions of MPM. Notice that line charts don't provide precise data, such as the 2009 MPM DVD and video income. Instead, they give an overview or impression of the data. Experienced report writers use tables to list exact data; they use line charts or bar charts to spotlight important points or trends.

Line charts illustrate trends and changes in data over time.

FIGURE 10.11 Simple Line Chart

Figure 5

MOTION PICTURE REVENUES
2005 TO 2010

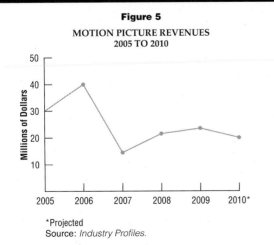

*Projected
Source: *Industry Profiles.*

FIGURE 10.12 Multiple Line Chart

Figure 6

COMPARISON OF DIVISION REVENUES
2005 TO 2010

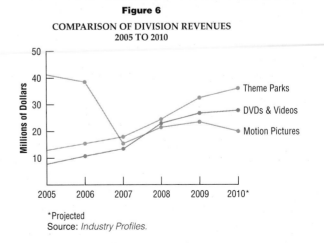

*Projected
Source: *Industry Profiles.*

Simple line charts (Figure 10.11) show just one variable. Multiple line charts compare items, such as two or more data sets, using the same variable (Figure 10.12). Segmented line charts (Figure 10.13), also called *surface charts,* illustrate how the components of a whole change over time.

Here are tips for preparing line charts:

- Begin with a grid divided into squares.
- Arrange the time component (usually years) horizontally across the bottom; arrange values for the other variable vertically.
- Draw small dots at the intersections to indicate each value at a given year.
- Connect the dots and add color if desired.
- To prepare a segmented (surface) chart, plot the first value (say, DVD and video income) across the bottom; add the next item (say, motion picture income) to the first figures for every increment; for the third item (say, theme park income) add its value to the total of the first two items. The top line indicates the total of the three values.
- Place each line chart as close as possible to the place where it is mentioned in the text.

Pie Charts

Pie, or circle, charts enable readers to see a whole and the proportion of its components, or wedges. Although less flexible than bar or line charts, pie charts are useful in showing percentages, as Figure 10.14 illustrates. Notice that a wedge can be "exploded," or popped out, for special emphasis, as seen in Figure 10.14. For the most effective pie charts, follow these suggestions:

- Begin at the 12 o'clock position, drawing the largest wedge first. (Computer software programs don't always observe this advice, but if you are drawing your own charts, you can.)
- Include, if possible, the actual percentage or absolute value for each wedge.
- Use four to eight segments for best results; if necessary, group small portions into one wedge called "Other."
- Distinguish wedges with color, shading, or cross-hatching.
- Keep all labels horizontal.
- Place each pie chart as close as possible to the place where it is mentioned in the text.

FIGURE 10.13 Segmented Line (Surface) Chart

Figure 7

COMPARISON OF DIVISION REVENUES
2005 TO 2010

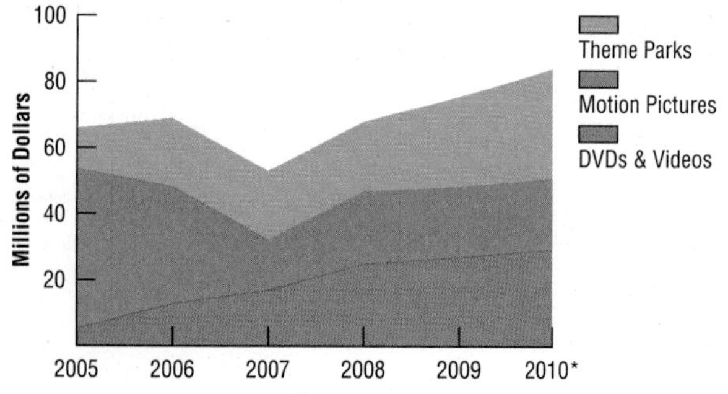

Theme Parks

Motion Pictures

DVDs & Videos

*Projected

Source: *Industry Profiles.*

FIGURE 10.14 Pie Chart

Figure 8

2009 MPM INCOME BY DIVISION

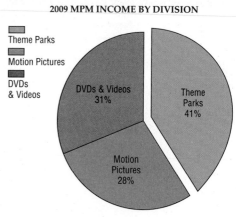

Theme Parks

Motion Pictures

DVDs & Videos

Source: *Industry Profiles.*

Flowcharts use standard
symbols to illustrate a
process or procedure.

Flowcharts

Procedures are simplified and clarified by diagramming them in a flowchart, as shown in Figure 10.15. Whether you need to describe the procedure for handling a customer's purchase order or outline steps in solving a problem, flowcharts help the reader visualize the process. Traditional flowcharts use the following symbols:

- **Ovals:** to designate the beginning and end of a process
- **Diamonds:** to denote decision points
- **Rectangles:** to represent major activities or steps

Software programs such as SmartDraw!, EasyDraw, and ConceptDraw can be used to create professional-quality flowcharts.

Organization Charts

Many large organizations are so complex that they need charts to show the chain of command, from the boss down to the line managers and employees. Organization charts like the one in Figure 10.16 provide such information as who reports to whom, how many subordinates work for each manager (the span of control), and what channels of official communication exist. These charts may illustrate a company's structure, for example, by function, customer, or product. They may also be organized by the work being performed in each job or by the hierarchy of decision making.

Photographs, Maps, and Illustrations

Some business reports include photographs, maps, illustrations, and other graphics to serve specific purposes. Photos, for example, add authenticity and provide a visual record. An environmental engineer may use photos to document hazardous waste sites. Maps enable report writers to depict activities or concentrations geographically, such as dots indicating sales reps in states across the country. Illustrations and diagrams are useful in indicating how an object looks or operates. A drawing showing the parts of a printer with labels describing their functions, for example, is more instructive than a photograph or verbal description. With today's computer technology, photographs, maps,

FIGURE 10.15 Flowchart

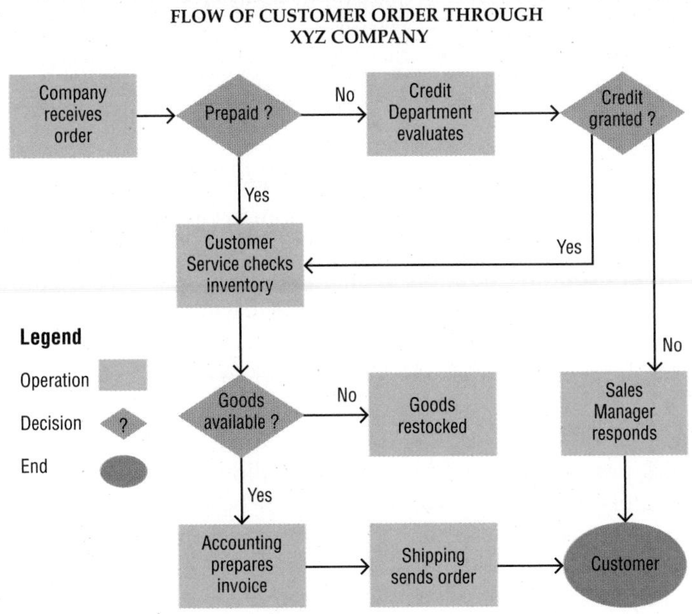

FLOW OF CUSTOMER ORDER THROUGH XYZ COMPANY

FIGURE 10.16 Organization Chart

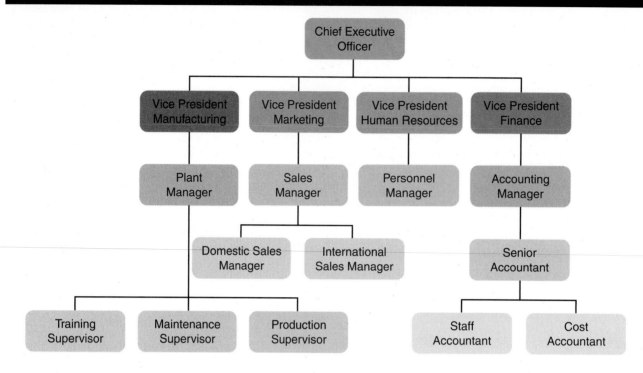

illustrations, and other graphics can be scanned and inserted directly into business reports.

Incorporating Graphics in Reports

Used appropriately, graphics make reports more interesting and easier to understand. In putting graphics into your reports, follow these suggestions for best effects:

- **Evaluate the audience.** Consider the reader, the content, your schedule, and your budget.
- **Use restraint.** Don't overuse color or decorations. Too much color can be distracting and confusing.
- **Be accurate and ethical.** Double-check all graphics for accuracy of figures and calculations. Be certain that your visuals aren't misleading—either accidentally or intentionally. Also be sure to cite sources when you use someone else's facts.
- **Introduce a graph meaningfully.** Refer to every graphic in the text, and place the graphic close to the point where it is mentioned. Most important, though, help the reader understand the significance of the graphic.
- **Choose an appropriate caption or heading style.** Like reports, graphics may use functional or talking heads. These headings were discussed in Chapter 9.

Using Your Computer to Produce Charts

Designing effective, accurate bar charts, pie charts, figures, and other graphics is easy with today's software. Spreadsheet programs such as Excel, as well as presentation graphics programs such as PowerPoint, allow even nontechnical people to design high-quality graphics. These graphics can be printed directly on paper for written reports or used for transparency masters and slides for oral presentations. The benefits of preparing visual aids on a computer are near-professional quality, shorter preparation time, and substantial cost savings.

> Computer software programs enable you to produce top-quality graphics quickly and cheaply.

Presenting the Final Report

Long reports are generally organized into three major divisions: (a) prefatory parts, (b) body, and (c) supplementary parts. Following is a description of the order and content of each part. Refer to the model formal report in Figure 10.17 for illustrations of most of these parts.

Prefatory Parts (Preceding the Body of Report)

Title Page. A report title page, as illustrated in Figure 10.17, begins with the name of the report typed in uppercase letters (no underscore and no quotation marks). Next comes *Prepared for* (or *Submitted to*) and the name, title, and organization of the individual receiving the report. Lower on the page is *Prepared by* (or *Submitted by*) and the author's name plus any necessary identification. The last item on the title page is the date of submission. All items after the title appear in a combination of upper- and lowercase letters. The information on the title page should be evenly spaced and balanced on the page for a professional look.

Letter or Memo of Transmittal. Generally written on organization letterhead stationery, a letter or memo of transmittal introduces a formal report. You will recall that letters are sent to outsiders and memos to insiders. A transmittal letter or memo follows the direct pattern and is usually less formal than the report itself. For example, the letter or memo may use contractions and first-person pronouns such as *I* and *we*. The transmittal letter or memo typically (a) announces the topic of the report and tells how it was authorized; (b) briefly describes the project; (c) highlights the report's findings, conclusions, and recommendations, if the reader is expected to be supportive; and (d) closes with appreciation for the assignment, instructions for the reader's follow-up actions, acknowledgment of help from others, or offers of assistance in answering questions. If a report is going to different readers, a special transmittal letter or memo should be prepared for each, anticipating what each reader needs to know in using the report.

> A letter or memo of transmittal presents an overview of the report, suggests how to read it, describes limitations, acknowledges assistance, and expresses appreciation.

Table of Contents. The table of contents shows the headings in a report and their page numbers. It gives an overview of the report topics and helps readers locate them. You should wait to prepare the table of contents until after you have completed the report. For short reports include all headings. For longer reports you might want to list only first- and second-level headings. Leaders (spaced or unspaced dots) help guide the eye from the heading to the page number. Items may be indented in outline form or typed flush with the left margin.

List of Figures. For reports with several figures or illustrations, you may wish to include a list of figures to help readers locate them. This list may appear on the same page as the table of contents, space permitting. For each figure or illustration, include a title and page number.

Executive Summary. As you learned in Chapter 9, the purpose of an executive summary is to present an overview of a longer report to people who may not have time to read the entire document. This timesaving device summarizes the purpose, key points, findings, and conclusions. An executive summary is usually no longer than 10 percent of the original document. Therefore, a 20-page report might require a 2-page executive summary. Chapter 9 discussed how to write an executive summary and included an example in Figure 9.11. You can see another executive summary in Figure 10.17.

FIGURE 10.17 Model Formal Report

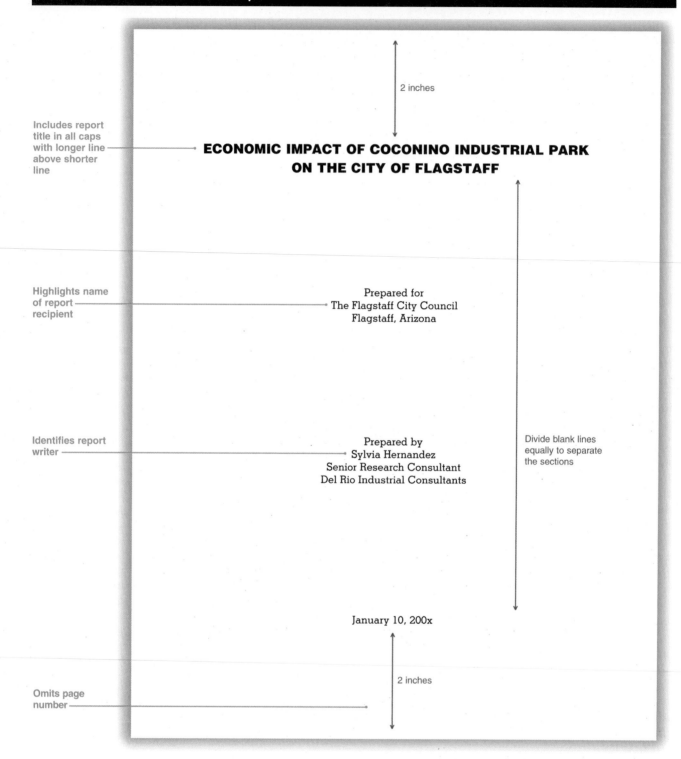

Includes report title in all caps with longer line above shorter line

2 inches

ECONOMIC IMPACT OF COCONINO INDUSTRIAL PARK ON THE CITY OF FLAGSTAFF

Highlights name of report recipient

Prepared for
The Flagstaff City Council
Flagstaff, Arizona

Identifies report writer

Prepared by
Sylvia Hernandez
Senior Research Consultant
Del Rio Industrial Consultants

Divide blank lines equally to separate the sections

January 10, 200x

2 inches

Omits page number

The title page is usually arranged in four evenly balanced areas. If the report is to be bound on the left, move the left margin and center point ¼ inch to the right. Notice that no page number appears on the title page, although it is counted as page i. In designing the title page, be careful to avoid anything unprofessional—such as too many type fonts, italics, oversized print, and inappropriate graphics. Keep the title page simple and professional. This model report uses MLA documentation style. However, it doesn't illustrate double-spacing, the recommended format for research papers using MLA style. Instead, this model uses single-spacing, which saves space and is more appropriate for business reports.

FIGURE 10.17 (Continued) Letter of Transmittal

DEL RIO INDUSTRIAL CONSULTANTS

110 West Route 66
Flagstaff, Arizona 86001

www.delrio.com
(928) 774-1101

January 12, 200x

City Council
City of Flagstaff
211 West Aspen Avenue
Flagstaff, AZ 86001

Dear Council Members:

The attached report, requested by the Flagstaff City Council in a letter to Goldman-Lyon & Associates dated October 20, describes the economic impact of Coconino Industrial Park on the city of Flagstaff. We believe you will find the results of this study useful in evaluating future development of industrial parks within the city limits.

This study was designed to examine economic impact in three areas:

- Current and projected tax and other revenues accruing to the city from Coconino Industrial Park
- Current and projected employment generated by the park
- Indirect effects on local employment, income, and economic growth

Primary research consisted of interviews with 15 Coconino Industrial Park tenants and managers, in addition to a 2009 survey of over 5,000 CIP employees. Secondary research sources included the Annual Budget of the City of Flagstaff, county and state tax records, government publications, periodicals, books, and online resources. Results of this research, discussed more fully in this report, indicate that Coconino Industrial Park exerts a significant beneficial influence on the Flagstaff metropolitan economy.

We would be pleased to discuss this report and its conclusions with you at your request. My firm and I thank you for your confidence in selecting our company to prepare this comprehensive report.

Sincerely,

Sylvia Hernandez

Sylvia Hernandez
Senior Research Consultant

SMH:mef
Attachment

ii

Annotations (left margin):
- Announces report and identifies authorization
- Gives broad overview of report purposes
- Uses a bulleted list for clarity and ease of reading
- Describes primary and secondary research
- Offers to discuss report; expresses appreciation
- Uses Roman numerals for prefatory pages

A letter or memo of transmittal announces the report topic and explains who authorized it. It briefly describes the project and previews the conclusions, if the reader is supportive. Such messages generally close by expressing appreciation for the assignment, suggesting follow-up actions, acknowledging the help of others, or offering to answer questions. The margins for the transmittal should be the same as for the report, about 1 to 1¼ inches for side margins. The dateline is placed 2 inches from the top, and the margins should be left-justified. A page number is optional.

FIGURE 10.17 (Continued) Table of Contents and List of Figures

Uses leaders to
guide eye from
heading to
page number

Indents
secondary
headings to
show levels
of outline

Includes tables
and figures in
one list for
simplified
numbering

TABLE OF CONTENTS

LIST OF FIGURES

Figure

iii

Because the table of contents and the list of figures for this report are small, they are combined on one page. Notice that the titles of major report parts are in all caps, whereas other headings are a combination of upper- and lowercase letters. This duplicates the style within the report. Advanced word processing capabilities enable you to generate a contents page automatically, including leaders and accurate page numbering—no matter how many times you revise. Notice that the page numbers are right-justified.

FIGURE 10.17 (Continued) Executive Summary

EXECUTIVE SUMMARY

The city of Flagstaff can benefit from the development of industrial parks like the Coconino Industrial Park. Both direct and indirect economic benefits result, as shown by this in-depth study conducted by Del Rio Industrial Consultants. The study was authorized by the Flagstaff City Council when Goldman-Lyon & Associates sought the City Council's approval for the proposed construction of a G-L industrial park. The City Council requested evidence demonstrating that an existing development could actually benefit the city.

Our conclusion that the city of Flagstaff benefits from industrial parks is based on data supplied by a survey of 5,000 Coconino Industrial Park employees, personal interviews with managers and tenants of CIP, city and state documents, and professional literature.

Analysis of the data revealed benefits in three areas:

- **Revenues.** The city of Flagstaff earned nearly $2 million in tax and other revenues from the Coconino Industrial Park in 2009. By 2015 this income is expected to reach $3.4 million (in constant 2009 dollars).

- **Employment.** In 2009, CIP businesses employed a total of 7,035 workers, who earned an average wage of $56,579. By 2015, CIP businesses are expected to employ directly nearly 15,000 employees who will earn salaries totaling over $998 million.

- **Indirect benefits.** Because of the multiplier effect, by 2015 Coconino Industrial Park will directly and indirectly generate a total of 38,362 jobs in the Flagstaff metropolitan area.

On the basis of these findings, it is recommended that development of additional industrial parks be encouraged to stimulate local economic growth.

Opens directly with major research findings

Identifies data sources

Summarizes organization of report

Condenses recommendations

iv

For readers who want a quick overview of the report, the executive summary presents its most important elements. Executive summaries focus on the information the reader requires for making a decision related to the issues discussed in the report. The summary may include some or all of the following elements: purpose, scope, research methods, findings, conclusions, and recommendations. Its length depends on the report it summarizes. A 100-page report might require a 10-page summary. Shorter reports may contain 1-page summaries, as shown here. Unlike letters of transmittal (which may contain personal pronouns and references to the writer), the executive summary of a long report is formal and impersonal. It uses the same margins as the body of the report. See Chapter 9 for additional discussion of executive summaries.

FIGURE 10.17 (Continued) Page 1

Uses a bulleted list for clarity and ease of reading

Lists three problem questions

Describes authorization for report and back-ground of study

PROBLEM

This study was designed to analyze the direct and indirect economic impact of Coconino Industrial Park on the city of Flagstaff. Specifically, the study seeks answers to these questions:

- What current tax and other revenues result directly from this park? What tax and other revenues may be expected in the future?

- How many and what kind of jobs are directly attributable to the park? What is the employment picture for the future?

- What indirect effects has Coconino Industrial Park had on local employment, incomes, and economic growth?

BACKGROUND

The development firm of Goldman-Lyon & Associates commissioned this study of Coconino Industrial Park at the request of the Flagstaff City Council. Before authorizing the development of a proposed Goldman-Lyon industrial park, the City Council requested a study examining the economic effects of an existing park. Members of the City Council wanted to determine to what extent industrial parks benefit the local community, and they chose Coconino Industrial Park as an example.

For those who are unfamiliar with it, Coconino Industrial Park is a 400-acre industrial park located in the city of Flagstaff about 4 miles from the center of the city. Most of the area lies within a specially designated area known as Redevelopment Project No. 2, which is under the jurisdiction of the Flagstaff Redevelopment Agency. Planning for the park began in 1997; construction started in 1999.

The original goal for Coconino Industrial Park was development for light industrial users. Land in this area was zoned for uses such as warehousing, research and development, and distribution. Like other communities, Flagstaff was eager to attract light industrial users because such businesses tend to employ a highly educated workforce, are quieter, and do not pollute the environment. The city of Flagstaff recognized the need for light industrial users and widened an adjacent highway to accommodate trucks and facilitate travel by workers and customers coming from Flagstaff.

1

The first page of a formal report generally contains the title printed 2 inches from the top edge. Titles for major parts of a report are centered in all caps. In this model document we show functional heads, such as *PROBLEM, BACKGROUND, FINDINGS,* and *CONCLUSIONS.* However, most business reports would use talking heads or a combination such as *FINDINGS REVEAL REVENUE AND EMPLOYMENT BENEFITS.* First-level headings (such as *Revenues* on page 2) are printed with bold upper- and lowercase letters. Second-level headings (such as *Distribution* on page 3) begin at the side, are bolded, and are written in upper- and lowercase letters. See Figure 10.4 for an illustration of heading formats. This business report is shown with single-spacing, although some research reports might be double-spaced. Always check with your organization to learn its preferred style.

FIGURE 10.17 (Continued) Page 2

The park now contains 14 building complexes with over 1.25 million square feet of completed building space. The majority of the buildings are used for office, research and development, marketing and distribution, or manufacturing uses. Approximately 50 acres of the original area are yet to be developed.

Data for this report came from a 2009 survey of over 5,000 Coconino Industrial Park employees; interviews with 15 CIP tenants and managers; the annual budget of the city of Flagstaff; county and state tax records; and current books, articles, journals, and online resources. Projections for future revenues resulted from analysis of past trends and "Estimates of Revenues for Debt Service Coverage, Redevelopment Project Area 2" (Miller 79).

DISCUSSION OF FINDINGS

The results of this research indicate that major direct and indirect benefits have accrued to the city of Flagstaff and surrounding metropolitan areas as a result of the development of Coconino Industrial Park. The research findings presented here fall into two categories: revenues and employment.

Revenues

Coconino Industrial Park contributes a variety of tax and other revenues to the city of Flagstaff, as summarized in Figure 1. Current revenues are shown, along with projections to the year 2015. At a time when the economy is unstable, revenues from an industrial park such as Coconino can become a reliable income stream for the city of Flagstaff.

Figure 1

REVENUES RECEIVED BY THE CITY OF FLAGSTAFF
FROM COCONINO INDUSTRIAL PARK

Current Revenues and Projections to 2015

	2009	2015
Sales and use taxes	$ 904,140	$1,335,390
Revenues from licenses	426,265	516,396
Franchise taxes	175,518	229,424
State gas tax receipts	83,768	112,134
Licenses and permits	78,331	112,831
Other revenues	94,039	141,987
Total	$1,762,061	$2,448,162

Source: Arizona State Board of Equalization Bulletin. Phoenix: State Printing Office, 2009, 103.

2

Annotations (left margin):

Provides specifics for data sources

Uses functional heads

Previews organization of report

Places figure close to textual reference

Notice that this formal report is single-spaced. Many businesses prefer this space-saving format. However, some organizations prefer double-spacing, especially for preliminary drafts. If you single-space, don't indent paragraphs. If you double-space, do indent the paragraphs. Page numbers may be centered 1 inch from the bottom of the page or placed 1 inch from the upper right corner at the margin. Your word processor can insert page numbers automatically. Strive to leave a minimum of 1 inch for top, bottom, and side margins. References follow the parenthetical citation style (or in-text citation style) of the Modern Language Association (MLA). Notice that the author's name and a page reference are shown in parentheses. The complete bibliographic entry for any in-text citation appears at the end of report in the works-cited section.

FIGURE 10.17 (Continued) Page 3

Sales and Use Revenues

As shown in Figure 1, the city's largest source of revenues from CIP is the sales and use tax. Revenues from this source totaled $904,140 in 2009, according to figures provided by the Arizona State Board of Equalization (28). Sales and use taxes accounted for more than half of the park's total contribution to the city of $1,762,061.

Other Revenues

Other major sources of city revenues from CIP in 2009 include alcohol licenses, motor vehicle in lieu fees, trailer coach licenses ($426,265), franchise taxes ($175,518), and state gas tax receipts ($83,768). Although not shown in Figure 1, other revenues may be expected from the development of recently acquired property. The U.S. Economic Development Administration has approved a grant worth $975,000 to assist in expanding the current park eastward on an undeveloped parcel purchased last year. Revenues from leasing this property may be sizable.

Projections

Total city revenues from CIP will nearly double by 2015, producing an income of $2.45 million. This estimate is based on an annual growth rate of 0.65 percent, as projected by the Bureau of Labor Statistics and reported at the Web site of Infoplease.com ("Economic Outlook Through 2015").

Employment

One of the most important factors to consider in the overall effect of an industrial park is employment. In Coconino Industrial Park the distribution, number, and wages of people employed will change considerably in the next six years.

Distribution

A total of 7,035 employees currently work in various industry groups at Coconino Industrial Park. The distribution of employees is shown in Figure 2. The largest number of workers (58 percent) is employed in manufacturing and assembly operations. In the next largest category, the computer and electronics industry employs 24 percent of the workers. Some overlap probably exists because electronics assembly could be included in either group. Employees also work in publishing (9 percent), warehousing and storage (5 percent), and other industries (4 percent).

Although the distribution of employees at Coconino Industrial Park shows a wide range of employment categories, it must be noted that other industrial parks would likely generate an entirely different range of job categories.

3

FIGURE 10.17 (Continued) Page 4

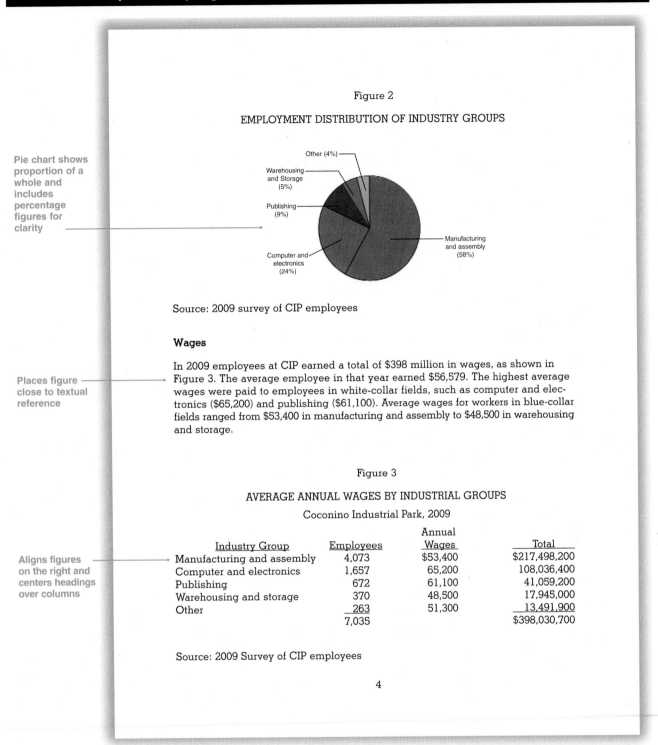

Pie chart shows proportion of a whole and includes percentage figures for clarity

Figure 2

EMPLOYMENT DISTRIBUTION OF INDUSTRY GROUPS

Other (4%)

Warehousing and Storage (5%)

Publishing (9%)

Computer and electronics (24%)

Manufacturing and assembly (58%)

Source: 2009 survey of CIP employees

Wages

Places figure close to textual reference

In 2009 employees at CIP earned a total of $398 million in wages, as shown in Figure 3. The average employee in that year earned $56,579. The highest average wages were paid to employees in white-collar fields, such as computer and electronics ($65,200) and publishing ($61,100). Average wages for workers in blue-collar fields ranged from $53,400 in manufacturing and assembly to $48,500 in warehousing and storage.

Figure 3

AVERAGE ANNUAL WAGES BY INDUSTRIAL GROUPS

Coconino Industrial Park, 2009

Aligns figures on the right and centers headings over columns

Industry Group	Employees	Annual Wages	Total
Manufacturing and assembly	4,073	$53,400	$217,498,200
Computer and electronics	1,657	65,200	108,036,400
Publishing	672	61,100	41,059,200
Warehousing and storage	370	48,500	17,945,000
Other	263	51,300	13,491,900
	7,035		$398,030,700

Source: 2009 Survey of CIP employees

4

If you use figures or tables, be sure to introduce them in the text (for example, *as shown in Figure 3*). Although it isn't always possible, try to place them close to the spot where they are first mentioned. To save space, you can print the title of a figure at its side. Because this report contains few tables and figures, the writer named them all "Figures" and numbered them consecutively.

FIGURE 10.17 (Continued) Page 5

Projections

By 2015 Coconino Industrial Park is expected to more than double its number of employees, bringing the total to over 15,000 workers. The total payroll in 2015 will also more than double, producing over $998 million (using constant 2009 dollars) in salaries to CIP employees. These projections are based on an 8 percent growth rate (Miller 78), along with anticipated increased employment as the park reaches its capacity.

Future development in the park will influence employment and payrolls. One CIP project manager stated in an interview that much of the remaining 50 acres is planned for medium-rise office buildings, garden offices, and other structures for commercial, professional, and personal services (Novak). Average wages for employees are expected to increase because of an anticipated shift to higher-paying white-collar jobs. Industrial parks often follow a similar pattern of evolution (Badri 41). Like many industrial parks, CIP evolved from a warehousing center into a manufacturing complex.

Clarifies information and tells what it means in relation to original research questions

CONCLUSIONS AND RECOMMENDATIONS

Summarizes conclusions and recommendations

Analysis of tax revenues, employment data, personal interviews, and professional literature leads to the following conclusions and recommendations about the economic impact of Coconino Industrial Park on the city of Flagstaff:

Uses a numbered list for clarity and ease of reading

1. Sales tax and other revenues produced nearly $1.8 million in income to the city of Flagstaff in 2009. By 2015 sales tax and other revenues are expected to produce $2.5 million in city income.

2. CIP currently employs 7,035 employees, the majority of whom are working in manufacturing and assembly. The average employee in 2009 earned $56,579.

3. By 2015 CIP is expected to employ more than 15,000 workers producing a total payroll of over $998 million.

4. Employment trends indicate that by 2015 more CIP employees will be engaged in higher-paying white-collar positions.

On the basis of these findings, we recommend that the City Council of Flagstaff authorize the development of additional industrial parks to stimulate local economic growth.

5

After discussing and interpreting the research findings, the writer articulates what she considers the most important conclusions and recommendations. Longer, more complex reports may have separate sections for conclusions and resulting recommendations. In this report they are combined. Notice that it is unnecessary to start a new page for the conclusions.

FIGURE 10.17 (Continued) Works Cited

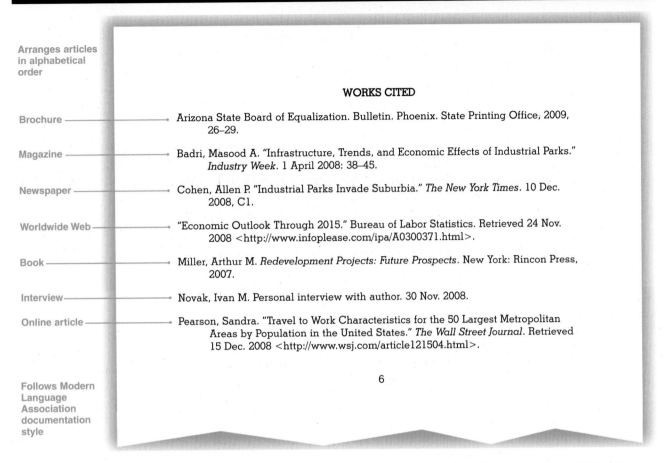

Arranges articles in alphabetical order

Brochure

Magazine

Newspaper

Worldwide Web

Book

Interview

Online article

Follows Modern Language Association documentation style

WORKS CITED

Arizona State Board of Equalization. Bulletin. Phoenix. State Printing Office, 2009, 26–29.

Badri, Masood A. "Infrastructure, Trends, and Economic Effects of Industrial Parks." *Industry Week.* 1 April 2008: 38–45.

Cohen, Allen P. "Industrial Parks Invade Suburbia." *The New York Times.* 10 Dec. 2008, C1.

"Economic Outlook Through 2015." Bureau of Labor Statistics. Retrieved 24 Nov. 2008 <http://www.infoplease.com/ipa/A0300371.html>.

Miller, Arthur M. *Redevelopment Projects: Future Prospects.* New York: Rincon Press, 2007.

Novak, Ivan M. Personal interview with author. 30 Nov. 2008.

Pearson, Sandra. "Travel to Work Characteristics for the 50 Largest Metropolitan Areas by Population in the United States." *The Wall Street Journal.* Retrieved 15 Dec. 2008 <http://www.wsj.com/article121504.html>.

6

On this page the writer lists all references cited in the text as well as others that she examined during her research. The writer lists these citations following the MLA referencing style. Notice that all entries are arranged alphabetically. Book and periodical titles are italicized, but they could be underlined. When referring to online items, she shows the full name of the citation and then identifies the URL as well as the date on which she accessed the electronic reference. This works-cited page is shown with single-spacing, which is preferable for business reports. However, MLA style recommends double-spacing for research reports, including the works-cited page.

Body of Report

The main section of a report is the body. It generally begins with an introduction, includes a discussion of findings, and concludes with a summary and possibly recommendations.

The body of a report includes an introduction; discussion of findings; and summary, conclusions, or recommendations.

Introduction. The body of a formal report starts with an introduction that sets the scene and announces the subject. Because they contain many parts serving different purposes, formal reports have a degree of repetition. The same information may be included in the letter or memo of transmittal, executive summary, and introduction. To avoid sounding repetitious, try to present the information slightly differently in each section.

A good report introduction typically covers the following elements, although not necessarily in this order:

- **Background.** Describe the events leading up to the problem or need.
- **Problem or purpose.** Explain the report topic and specify the problem or need that motivated the report.
- **Significance.** Tell why the topic is important. You may wish to quote experts or cite secondary sources to establish the importance of the topic.

- **Scope.** Clarify the boundaries of the report, defining what will be included or excluded.
- **Sources and methods.** Describe your secondary sources. Also explain how you collected primary data.
- **Summary.** Include a summary of findings, if the report is written directly.
- **Organization.** Preview the major sections of the report to follow, thus providing coherence and transition for the reader.

Discussion of Findings. This is the main section of the report and contains numerous headings and subheadings. This section discusses, analyzes, interprets, and evaluates the research findings or solution to the initial problem. This is where you show the evidence that justifies your conclusions. It is unnecessary to use the title *Discussion of Findings;* many business report writers prefer to begin immediately with the major headings into which the body of the report is divided. As summarized in Figure 10.2, you may organize the findings chronologically, geographically, topically, or by some other method. Regardless of the organizational pattern, present your findings logically and objectively. In most cases you will want to avoid the use of first-person pronouns *(I, we)*, unless you are certain that your audience prefers informal language. Include tables, charts, and graphs if necessary to illustrate findings. Analytic and scientific reports may include another section titled *Implications of Findings,* in which the findings are analyzed and related to the problem. Less formal reports contain the author's analysis of the research findings within the *Discussion* section.

Summary, Conclusions, Recommendations. The conclusion to a report tells what the findings mean, particularly in terms of solving the original problem. If the report has been largely informational, it ends with a summary of the data presented. If the report analyzes research findings, then it ends with conclusions drawn from the analyses. An analytic report frequently poses research questions. The conclusion to such a report reviews the major findings and answers the research questions. If a report seeks to determine a course of action, it may end with conclusions and recommendations. Recommendations regarding a course of action may be placed in a separate section or incorporated with the conclusions.

Supplementary Parts of Report

Works Cited, References, or Bibliography. Readers look in the bibliography section to locate the sources of ideas mentioned in a report. Your method of report documentation determines how this section is developed. If you use the Modern Language Association (MLA) referencing format, all citations would be listed alphabetically in the "Works Cited." If you use the American Psychological Association (APA) format, your list would be called "References." Regardless of the format, you must include the author, title, publication, date of publication, page number, and other significant data for all sources used in your report. For electronic references include the URL and the date you accessed the information online. To see electronic and other citations, examine the list of references at the end of Figure 10.17, which follows the MLA documentation style. See Appendix C for more information on documentation formats.

Appendix. The appendix contains any supplementary or supporting information needed to clarify the report. This information is relevant to some readers but not to all. Extra information that might be included in an appendix are such items as survey forms, a survey cover letter, correspondence relating to the report, maps, other reports, and optional tables. Items in the appendix are labeled Appendix A, Appendix B, and so forth; and these items should be referenced in the body of the report.

Endnotes, a bibliography, and appendixes may appear after the body of the report.

Visit www.meguffey.com
- Chapter Review Quiz
- Flash Cards
- Grammar Practice
- PowerPoint Slides
- Personal Language Trainer
- Beat the Clock Quiz

Summing Up and Looking Forward

Proposals are written offers to solve problems, provide services, or sell equipment. Both large and small businesses today write proposals to generate income. Informal proposals may be as short as 2 pages; formal proposals may run 200 pages or more. Regardless of the size, proposals contain standard parts that must be developed persuasively.

Formal reports present well-organized information systematically. The information may be collected from primary or secondary sources. All ideas borrowed from others must be documented. Good reports contain appropriate headings to help guide readers through the report. In addition, formal reports often contain tables, charts, and graphs to illustrate data.

Written reports are vital to decision makers. But oral reports can be equally important. In Chapter 12 you will learn how to organize and make professional oral presentations. Before learning about oral reports, however, in Chapter 11 you will learn how to become an ethical, polished business professional. In addition to business ethics and etiquette, you will also study how to communicate effectively in person, by telephone, in teams, and in meetings.

Critical Thinking

1. Consider personal and business uses of proposals. How might you benefit if you know how to write proposals?

2. Who is hurt by plagiarism? Discuss.

3. Are charts and graphs objective, unbiased presentations of data? Explain.

4. Is information obtained on the Web as reliable as information obtained from journals, newspapers, and magazines? Explain.

5. Should all reports be written so that they follow the sequence of investigation—that is, description of the initial problem, analysis of issues, data collection, data analysis, and conclusions? Why or why not?

Chapter Review

6. Why are many large companies encouraging their employees to participate in social networking sites such as Facebook and LinkedIn or to create their own formal or informal networks?

7. What is the difference between a solicited and an unsolicited proposal. Give an example of when each would be written.

8. What are the six principal parts of an informal proposal? Be prepared to explain each.

9. How are formal proposals different from informal proposals?

10. How can business writers overcome writer's block when setting out to write a proposal or report?

11. Explain when documentation is required and when it is not required.

12. List four sources of secondary information, and be prepared to discuss how valuable each might be in writing a formal report about outsourcing your company's payroll function.

13. Name at least four commercial electronic databases useful to business writers and researchers.

14. What are blogs and how can they be used for research?

15. Pie charts are most helpful in showing what? Line charts are most effective in showing what?

Activities and Cases

10.1 Researching Secondary and Primary Data

In teams, discuss how you would collect information for each of the following report topics. Would your research be primary, secondary, or a combination of methods? What resources would be most useful—books, articles, the Web, interviewing, surveys?

a. Comparing the health care systems in France and the United Kingdom

b. Which public relations firm will best improve the image of a company so that its stock price increases

c. Investigating high turnover and apparent employee dissatisfaction at a large retailer

d. The latest Occupational Safety and Health Administration (OSHA) rulings that might affect your small business

e. The traffic count at a possible location for a new coffee shop

f. Planning to introduce healthier food in the company cafeteria and investigating how workers would feel about the new choices

g. The costs and features of a new network system for your company

h. How users are reacting to a new digital imaging software that was recently released

i. How to meet international quality standards (ISO certification) so that you can sell your products in Europe

10.2 Gathering and Documenting Data: Biotechnology Alters Foods

California is home to the nation's most diverse and valuable agricultural industry. Many of its crops are sold in Japanese and European markets where customers are extremely wary of genetically modified foods. Despite that fact, sources in the state capital are reporting that the biotech industry is actively seeking sponsors for a bill in the state legislature that would preempt the right of counties to ban genetically engineered crops. As an intern working for the Organic Consumers Association, the nation's largest public interest group dedicated to a healthy and sustainable food system, you have been asked to gather data about the dangers of genetically engineered crops. The organization plans to write a report to the state government about this issue.

Your Task. Conduct a keyword search using three different search tools on the Web. Select three articles you think would be most pertinent to the organization's argument. Save them using the strategies for managing data, and create a bibliography. Conduct the same keyword search in an electronic database. Save the three most pertinent articles, and add these items to your bibliography. In a short memo to your instructor, summarize what you have found and describe its value. Attach the bibliography.

10.3 Writing a Survey: Studying Employee Use of Instant Messaging

Instant messaging (IM) is a popular way to exchange messages in real time. It offers the convenience of telephone conversations and e-mail. Best of all, it allows employees to contact anyone in the world while retaining a written copy of the conversation—without a whopping telephone bill! But instant messaging is risky for companies. They may lose trade secrets or confidential information over insecure lines. They also may be liable if inappropriate material is exchanged. Moreover, IM opens the door to viruses that can infect a company's entire computer system.

Your boss just read an article stating that 40 percent of companies now use IM for business, and up to 90 percent of employees use IM *without* their managers' knowledge or authorization. He asks you to prepare a survey of your 48-member staff to learn how many are using IM. He wants to know what type of IM software they have downloaded, how many hours a day they spend on IM, what are the advantages of IM, and so forth. The goal isn't to identify those using or abusing IM. Instead, the goal is to learn when, how, and why it is being used so that appropriate policies can be designed.

Your Task. Use an electronic database or the Web to learn more about instant messaging. Then prepare a short employee survey. Include an appropriate introduction that explains the survey and encourages a response. Should you ask for names on the survey? How can you encourage employees to return the forms? Your instructor may wish to expand this survey into a report by having you produce fictitious survey results, analyze the findings, draw conclusions, and make recommendations.

10.4 Outlining: Explaining Blogs

Your boss has been hearing a lot about blogs (weblogs) lately and wonders if this is something your company should start using for research and communication. He has asked you to write a short report on how blogs can be used in a business environment. He also wonders whether a blogging policy would be needed. Here are some ideas you gathered from your Internet research:

Although some companies worry that blogs could be used to expose company secrets or violate securities laws, many companies are encouraging their employees to take part in blogging. The corporate world has found that blogging is an effective way to communicate with customers and clients, to encourage internal interaction, and to make them look more approachable and "human" to the outside world. Blogs can also be used by employees for research, for data collection, and for keeping up with what competitors are doing. Some companies have both external and internal blogs, and some even allow employees to set up personal blogs.

Companies that use blogs should probably have policies or guidelines governing their use. Companies might adopt guidelines that require employees to use first-person pronouns and to be honest. Microsoft tells employees to avoid writing blog entries when they are upset or emotional. Other companies provide lists of topics that should be avoided in blogs, such as anything that should remain confidential, private, or secret or anything that is embarrassing, libelous, or illegal. Above all, any policy should state that employees are responsible for their own posts.

Various tools can be used to set up blogs. Some of the most popular include Google's Blogger.com, Microsoft's MSN Spaces, and Yahoo's 360° service. These tools make setting up blogs easy to do. They help users publish text entries, add photos, publish links to other blogs and Web pages, and establish privacy if desired. They also provide themes and various editing tools that can help corporate blogs look professional.

Your Task. Select the most important information and organize it into an outline such as that shown in Figure 10.3. You should have three main topics with three subdivisions under each. Assume that you will gather more information later. Add a title.

10.5 Selecting Graphics

In teams identify the best graphic (table, bar chart, line chart, pie chart, flowchart, organization chart, illustration, map) to illustrate the following data:

a. Figure showing the process of making paper

b. Figures showing what proportion of every state tax dollar is spent on education, social services, transportation, debt, and other expenses

c. Data showing the newly formed divisions of a major multinational company after several mergers and leveraged buyouts

d. Figures showing the operating revenue of a company for the past five years

e. Figures comparing the sales of PDAs (personal digital assistants), cell phones, and laptop computers over the past five years

f. Percentages showing the causes of forest fires (lightning, 73 percent; arson, 5 percent; campfires, 9 percent; and so on) in the Rocky Mountains

g. Figure comparing the costs of cable, DSL, and satellite Internet service in ten major metropolitan areas of the United States for the past ten years (the boss wants to see exact figures)

h. Figure showing the locations of a popular family-owned fast-food franchise operating in California and the Southwest.

10.6 Evaluating Graphics in Publications
From *U.S. News & World Report, USA Today, BusinessWeek,* a textbook, or some other publication, locate one example each of a table, a pie chart, a line chart, a bar chart, and an organization chart. Bring copies of these visual aids to class. How effectively could the data have been expressed in words, without the graphics? Is the appropriate graphic form used? How is the graphic introduced in the text? Do you think the graphic is misleading or unethical in any way? Your instructor may ask you to submit a memo discussing visual aids.

10.7 Studying Graphics in Annual Reports
In a memo to your instructor, evaluate the effectiveness of graphics in three to five corporation annual reports. Critique their readability, clarity, and success in visualizing data. How were they introduced in the text? What suggestions would you make to improve them? Do you feel the graphics presented the data accurately and ethically?

10.8 Developing Bibliography Skills
Select a business topic that interests you. Prepare a bibliography of at least five current magazine or newspaper articles, three books, and five online references that contain relevant information regarding the topic. Your instructor may ask you to divide your bibliography into sections: *Books, Periodicals, Online Resources.* You may also be asked to annotate your bibliography, that is, to compose a brief description of each reference, such as this:

McManus, Reed. "Hybrid Helpers." *Sierra,* Mar/Apr 2007, 16.

McManus writes that U.S. cities are promoting new gas-electric hybrids with large rechargeable batteries to combat air pollution, over half of which comes from motor vehicles. The new vehicles will travel up to 60 miles without needing their gasoline engines. Many electric utilities have expressed interest in this cause. Toyota, Ford, and GM have agreed to manufacture hybrid cars although they are skeptical of electric vehicles and worry about the cost of large batteries.

10.9 Creating an Annotated Works-Cited List
Being a quick learner and smart researcher will serve you well in college and in the workplace. Savvy businesspeople are lifelong learners who often must become knowledgeable fast in a subject they initially know very little about. To become a well-informed citizen and businessperson, you will need to be able to make sense of controversies and public discussions. Here are a few topic suggestions:

a. Should the government and airlines allow in-flight cell phone calls?

b. Should something be done about high gas prices (affordable housing, tax reform, health care, and so forth), and what are some of the proposals being discussed?

c. What are the security risks of e-commerce? How do fraud, identify theft, and invasions of privacy affect online business?

d. Should the government grant more H-1B visas to foreign nationals in specialty occupations such as computer technology, as Microsoft and other tech companies demand?
   Your instructor may suggest other topics or ask you to find a current business controversy on your own.

Your Task. Consider one current hot-button business topic and gather several—up to ten—highly relevant and informative sources, preferably articles reflecting a wide spectrum of opinions. List them in the MLA works-cited format and provide each with a brief (60 words maximum) summary, as shown in Activity 10.8.

10.10 Setting Up a Wiki to Complete a Group Project

Younger workers who grew up with digital technology are spearheading a new trend in business. They are bringing their tech savvy to the table, and as a result, wikis, blogs, and other new communication channels are being used in the workplace to manage projects and exchange information. When writing a team paper, for example, you could share graphics and other data along with report drafts or the articles you found.

If you would like to try collaborating online, you can set up a free wiki virtually in seconds. Two very popular free sites are PBwiki.com (**http://pbwiki.com**) and Wetpaint (**http://www.wetpaint.com**). At PBwiki.com be sure to select *Education* as your purpose or you will be charged about $10 per month for premium membership.

As you register, you can select a variety of features—for example, to make your wiki accessible to anyone or only to invitees whom you choose. Templates and intuitive menus make creating a wiki simple and easy.

Your Task. Whether you create a wiki to share common interests online with friends or whether you use it to collaborate on a team project, becoming an experienced user of wikis will prepare you for the workplace. Visit either PBwiki.com or Wetpaint and set up a wiki for yourself and your team. Be sure to invite your instructor as well, so that he or she can observe your online collaboration.

10.11 Proposals: Comparing Real Proposals

Many new companies with services or products to offer would like to land corporate or government contracts. But they are intimidated by the proposal (RFP process). You have been asked for help by your friend Chloe, who has started her own designer uniform company. Her goal is to offer her colorful yet functional uniforms to hospitals and clinics. Before writing a proposal, however, she wants to see examples and learn more about the process.

Your Task. Use the Web to find at least two examples of business proposals. Don't waste time on sites that want to sell templates or books. Find actual examples. Then prepare a memo to Chloe in which you do the following:

a. Identify two sites with sample business proposals.

b. Outline the parts of each proposal.

c. Compare the strengths and weaknesses of each proposal.

d. Draw conclusions. What can Chloe learn from these examples?

10.12 Proposal: Solving a Workplace Problem in an Unsolicited Informal Proposal

The ability to spot problems before they turn into serious risks is prized by most managers. Draw on your internship and work experience. Can you identify a problem that could be solved with a small to moderate financial investment? Look for issues such as missing lunch or break rooms for staff; badly needed health initiatives such as gyms or sports club memberships; switching to high-gas-mileage, low-emission company vehicles; or encouraging recycling efforts.

Your Task. Discuss with your instructor the workplace problem that you have identified. Make sure you choose a relatively weighty problem that can nevertheless be lessened or eliminated with a minor expenditure. Be sure to include a cost-benefit analysis. Address your unsolicited letter or memo proposal to your current or former boss and copy your instructor.

10.13 Unsolicited Proposal: Working From Home

You have been working as an administrative/virtual assistant for your company since its inception in 2001. Every day you commute from your home, almost two hours round trip. Most of your work is done at a computer terminal with little or no human contact. You would prefer to eliminate the commute time, which could be better spent working on your programming. You believe your job would be perfect for telecommuting. With a small investment in the proper equipment, you could do all of your work at home, perhaps reporting to the office once a week for meetings and other activities.

Your Task. Research the costs and logistics of telecommuting, and present your proposal to your supervisor, Sidney Greene. Because this is an unsolicited proposal, you will need to be even more persuasive. Convince your supervisor that the company will benefit from this telecommuting arrangement.

10.14 Unsolicited Proposal: Thwarting Dorm Room Thievery

As an enterprising college student, you recognized a problem as soon as you arrived on campus. Dorm rooms filled with pricey digital doodads were very attractive to thieves. Some students move in with more than $3,000 in gear, including laptop computers, flat-screen TVs, digital cameras, MP3 players, video game consoles, PDAs, and DVD players. You solved the problem by buying an extra-large steel footlocker to lock away your valuables. However, shipping the footlocker was expensive (nearly $100), and you had to wait for it to arrive from a catalog company. Your bright idea is to propose to the Associated Student Organization that it allow you to offer these steel footlockers to students at a reduced price and with campus delivery. Your footlocker, which you found by searching the Web, is extremely durable and works great as a coffee table, nightstand, or card table. It comes with a smooth interior liner and two compartments.

Your Task. Working individually or with a team, imagine that you have made arrangements with a manufacturer to act as a middleman selling footlockers on your campus at a reduced price. Consult the Web for manufacturers and make up your own figures. However, how can you get the ASO's permission to proceed? Give that organization a cut? Use your imagination in deciding how this plan might work on a college campus. Then prepare an unsolicited proposal to your ASO. Outline the problem and your goals of protecting students' valuables and providing convenience. Check the Web for statistics regarding on-campus burglaries. Such figures should help you develop one or more persuasive "hooks." Then explain your proposal, project possible sales, discuss a timetable, and describe your staffing. Submit your proposal to Billie White, president, Associated Student Organization.

TEAM

10.15 Proposal: Starting Your Own Business

You and your buddies have a terrific idea for a new business in your town. For example, you might want to propose to Starbucks the concept of converting some of its coffee shops into Internet cafes. Or you might propose to the city or another organization a better Web site, which you and your team would design and maintain. You might want to start a word processing business that offers production, editing, and printing services. Often businesses, medical centers, attorneys, and other professionals have overload transcribing or word processing to farm out to a service.

Your Task. Working in teams, explore entrepreneurial ventures based on your experience and expertise. Write a proposal to secure approval and funding. Your report should include a transmittal letter, as well as a description of your proposed company, its product or service, a market analysis, an operations and management plan, and a financial plan.

TEAM

10.16 Formal Report: Intercultural Communication

U.S. businesses are expanding into foreign markets with manufacturing plants, sales offices, and branch offices abroad. Unfortunately, most Americans have little knowledge of or experience with people from other cultures. To prepare for participation in the global marketplace, you are to collect information for a report focused on an Asian, Latin American, African, or European country where English isn't regularly spoken. Before selecting the country, though, consider consulting your campus international student program for volunteers who are willing to be interviewed. Your instructor may make advance arrangements seeking international student volunteers.

Your Task. In teams of two to four, collect information about your target country from the library, the Web, and other sources. If possible, invite an international student representing your target country to be interviewed by your group. As you conduct primary and secondary research, investigate the topics listed in Figure 10.18.[16] Confirm what you learn in your secondary research by talking with your interviewee. When you complete your research, write a report for the CEO of your company (make up a name and company). Assume that your company plans to expand its operations abroad. Your report should advise the company's executives of social customs, family life, attitudes, appropriate business attire, religions, economic institutions, and values in the target country. Remember that your company's interests are business oriented; don't dwell on tourist information. Write your report individually or in teams.

10.17 Formal Report: Is Vinyl Back?

Although you and fellow students were probably born long after the introduction of the CD in the early 1980s and download MP3 tracks from iTunes to an iPod, something strange is afoot. Lately, sales of turntables and vinyl long-playing records (LPs) have been picking up. "Classic" bands such as the Beatles and Pink Floyd are not the only ones on vinyl. Contemporary artists such as R.E.M., the White Stripes, the Foo Fighters, and Metallica, have released their music on vinyl to enthusiastic audiences. Listeners even claim that music sounds better on vinyl than it does on a CD.[17] Perhaps most surprising, many vinyl fans are not nostalgic baby boomer parents but their teenage or twenty-something children.

Major music retailers caught on to the trend. Although Amazon.com has been selling vinyl records since its founding in 1994, it has recently begun to offer a vinyl-only section on its site. Now, your employer, Best Buy Company, is eager to test vinyl sales at some of its stores. Your manager, José Martinez, was asked by headquarters to explore the feasibility of offering a vinyl selection in his store, and he left this research job to you.

Your Task. This assignment calls for establishing primary data using a survey. Devise a questionnaire and poll young music consumers in your area to find out whether they enjoy and, more important, purchase vinyl records. Examine attitudes toward LPs in the populations and age groups most likely to find them intriguing. After collecting your data, determine whether your Best Buy store could establish a profitable vinyl business. Support your recommendation with conclusions you draw from your survey but also from secondary research detailing the new trend. To illustrate your findings, use pie charts for percentages (e.g., how many LPs are sold in comparison to CDs and other media), line graphs to indicate trends over time (e.g., sales figures in various consumer segments), and other graphics. Prepare a formal report for José Martinez, who will share your report with upper management.

FIGURE 10.18 Intercultural Interview Topics and Questions

Social Customs

1. How do people react to strangers? Are they friendly? Hostile? Reserved?
2. How do people greet each other?
3. What are the appropriate manners when you enter a room? Bow? Nod? Shake hands with everyone?
4. How are names used for introductions? Is it appropriate to inquire about one's occupation or family?
5. What are the attitudes toward touching?
6. How does one express appreciation for an invitation to another's home? Bring a gift? Send flowers? Write a thank-you note? Are any gifts taboo?
7. Are there any customs related to how or where one sits?
8. Are any facial expressions or gestures considered rude?
9. How close do people stand when talking?
10. What is the attitude toward punctuality in social situations? In business situations?
11. What are acceptable eye contact patterns?
12. What gestures indicate agreement? Disagreement?

Family Life

1. What is the basic unit of social organization? Basic family? Extended family?
2. Do women work outside of the home? In what occupations?

Housing, Clothing, and Food

1. Are there differences in the kind of housing used by different social groups? Differences in location? Differences in furnishings?
2. What occasions require special clothing?
3. Are some types of clothing considered taboo?
4. What is appropriate business attire for men? For women?
5. How many times a day do people eat?
6. What types of places, food, and drink are appropriate for business entertainment? Where is the seat of honor at a table?

Class Structure

1. Into what classes is society organized?
2. Do racial, religious, or economic factors determine social status?
3. Are there any minority groups? What is their social standing?

Political Patterns

1. Are there any immediate threats to the political survival of the country?
2. How is political power manifested?
3. What channels are used for expression of popular opinion?
4. What information media are important?
5. Is it appropriate to talk politics in social situations?

Religion and Folk Beliefs

1. To which religious groups do people belong? Is one predominant?
2. Do religious beliefs influence daily activities?
3. Which places have sacred value? Which objects? Which events?
4. How do religious holidays affect business activities?

Economic Institutions

1. What are the country's principal products?
2. Are workers organized in unions?
3. How are businesses owned? By family units? By large public corporations? By the government?
4. What is the standard work schedule?
5. Is it appropriate to do business by telephone?
6. How has technology affected business procedures?
7. Is participatory management used?
8. Are there any customs related to exchanging business cards?
9. How is status shown in an organization? Private office? Secretary? Furniture?
10. Are businesspeople expected to socialize before conducting business?

Value Systems

1. Is competitiveness or cooperation more prized?
2. Is thrift or enjoyment of the moment more valued?
3. Is politeness more important than factual honesty?
4. What are the attitudes toward education?
5. Do women own or manage businesses? If so, how are they treated?
6. What are your people's perceptions of Americans? Do Americans offend you? What has been hardest for you to adjust to in America? How could Americans make this adjustment easier for you?

10.18 Formal Report: Fast-Food Checkup

The national franchising headquarters for a fast-food chain has received complaints about the service, quality, and cleanliness of one of its restaurants in your area. You have been sent to inspect and to report on what you see.

Your Task. Select a nearby fast-food restaurant. Visit on two or more occasions. Make notes about how many customers were served, how quickly they received their food, and how courteously they were treated. Observe the number of employees and supervisors working. Note the cleanliness of observable parts of the restaurant. Inspect the restroom as well as the exterior and surrounding grounds. Sample the food. Your boss is a stickler for details; she has no use for general statements such as *The restroom was not clean.* Be specific. Draw conclusions. Are the complaints justified? If improvements are necessary, make recommendations. Address your report to Sandra M. Ross, President.

10.19 Formal Report: Consumer Product Investigation

Study a consumer product that you might consider buying. Are you, or is your family or your business, interested in purchasing a flat-screen TV, DVD player, computer, digital camera, espresso machine, car, SUV, hot tub, or some other product?

Your Task. Use at least five primary and five secondary sources in researching your topic. Your primary research will be in the form of interviews with individuals (owners, users, salespeople, technicians) in a position to comment on attributes of your product. Secondary research will be in the form of print or electronic sources, such as magazine articles, owner manuals, and Web sites. Be sure to use electronic databases and the Web to find appropriate articles. Your report should analyze and discuss at least three comparable models or versions of the target product. Decide what criteria you will use to compare the models, such as price, features, warranty, service, and so forth. The report should include these components: letter of transmittal, table of contents, executive summary, introduction (including background, purpose, scope of the study, and research methods), findings (organized by comparison criteria), summary of findings, conclusions, recommendations, and bibliography. Address the report to your instructor. You may work individually, in pairs, or in teams.

10.20 Formal Report: Communication Skills on the Job

Collect information regarding communication skills used by individuals in a particular career field (accounting, management, marketing, office administration, paralegal, and so forth). Interview three or more individuals in a specific occupation in that field. Determine how much and what kind of writing they do. Do they make oral presentations? How much time do they spend in telephone communication? Do they use e-mail? If so, how much and for what? What other technology do they use for communication? What recommendations do they have for training for this position?

Your Task. Write a report that discusses the findings from your interviews. What conclusions can you draw regarding communication skills in this field? What recommendations would you make for individuals entering this field? Your instructor may ask you to research the perception of businesspeople over the past ten years regarding the communication skills of employees. To gather such data, conduct library or online research.

10.21 Formal Report: All About Wikis

As discussed in this chapter on p. 262, wikis are becoming increasingly important to businesses that rely on teamwork across time zones and national borders. Some educators also use wikis for collaboration in their college-level classes. You are part of a group of interns from your college working at a large financial institution, Home Bank. Your intern team has collaborated on your finance-related research using a wiki. Your informal wiki has also been helpful when you worked together on a team project for college credit. Your internship supervisor is impressed and would like you to collect more hard data so he can pilot wikis for wider application in collaborative settings at the bank. Your preliminary research suggests that quite a few companies are using wikis, such as Best Buy's Geek Squad, Xerox, and IBM. In fact, IBM conducted a massive online brainstorming session that took two 72-hour sessions and involved 100,000 employees, customers, and business partners in over 160 countries.[18] Your boss is interested in reading about such cases to decide whether to pilot a wiki, and if so, what kind would work for Home Bank. Your team of three to five will investigate.

Your Task. Keep in mind that your boss, Irving E. Pound, will share your report with other managers who may be computer-literate users but no tech heads. Start with the brief definition of wikis earlier in this chapter. Expand the definition by searching the Web and electronic database articles. First explain what wikis are and how they work, which resources (cost, software, hardware) are needed, how much training is required, and so forth. Examine the use of wikis in business today. How are large and small companies benefiting from collaboration facilitated by wikis? If your instructor directs, the report (or a section thereof) could discuss wikis in education and how instructors harness this new tool. After collecting a sufficient amount of information and data, outline and then write a formal report with a recommendation at the end suggesting whether and how Home Bank would benefit from investing in wiki software.

10.22 More Proposal and Report Topics

A list with over 90 report topics is available at **www.guffey.com**. The topics are divided into the following categories: accounting, finance, human resources, marketing, information systems, management, and general business/education/campus issues. You can collect information for many of these reports by using electronic databases and the Web. Your instructor may assign them as individual or team projects. All involve critical thinking in organizing information, drawing conclusions, and making recommendations. The topics include assignments appropriate for proposals, business plans, and formal reports.

Apostrophes

Review Sections 2.20–2.22 in the Grammar/Mechanics Handbook. Then study each of the following statements. Underscore any inappropriate form. Write a correction in the space provided and record the number of the G/M principle(s) illustrated. If a sentence is correct, write *C*. When you finish, compare your responses with those at the back of the book. If your answers differ, study carefully the principles shown in parentheses.

| years' (2.20b) | **Example** In just two <u>years</u> time, Marti earned her MBA degree. |

1. Mark Hanleys PDA was found in the conference room.
2. The severance package includes two weeks salary for each year worked.
3. In only one years time, her school loans totaled $5,000.
4. The board of directors strongly believed that John Petersons tenure as CEO was exceptionally successful.
5. Several employees records were accidentally removed from the files.
6. The last witness testimony was the most convincing to the jury members.
7. Outstanding performance, efficiency, and superior communication skills led to Robins promotion.
8. I always get my moneys worth at my favorite restaurant.
9. Three local companies went out of business last month.
10. In one months time we hope to have our new Web site up and running.
11. I need my boss signature on this expense claim.
12. Only one legal secretaries document was error-free.
13. In certain aerospace departments new applicants must apply for security clearance.
14. My companys stock price rose dramatically last month.
15. In three months several businesses opening hours will change.

The following executive summary has faults in grammar, punctuation, spelling, wordiness, parallelism, and possessives. You may either (a) use standard proofreading marks (see Appendix B) to correct the errors here or (b) download the document from **www.guffey.com** and revise at your computer. Study the guidelines in the Grammar/Mechanics Handbook to sharpen your skills.

HOW PURE IS BOTTLED WATER?

EXECUTIVE SUMMARY

Problem

Bottled water has become a $4 billion-a-year business in the United states. Millions of consumer's use bottled water as there primary source of drinking water. Although most bottled water is of good quality some bottled water contains bacterial contaminants. Reassurances from the water industrys executives that bottled water is totally safe is false.

Summary of Findings

Commissioned by the National Resource's Defense Commission, this report analyzes tests of bottled water. The tests showed that most bottled water is not contaminated, however, after testing more then 1,000 bottles, we found that about one fourth were contaminated at levels violating many states limits. Bottled water contaminated with microbes may raise public health issues, and todays consumers are rightfully concerned.

There are government bottled water regulations and programs that have serious deficiencys. Under the FDAs control, the regulation of most bottled water is left to ill-equipped and understaffed state governments. In spite of the fact that voluntary bottled water industry controls are commendable. They are an inadequate substitute for strong government rules. FDA officials has stated that bottled water regulation carries a low priority. In addition the marketing of bottled water can be misleading. However, the long term solution to drinking water problems are to fix tap water rather than switching to bottled water.

Recommendations

Based on our tests and analysis we submit the following reccomendations:

1. Fix tap water quality so that consumers' will not resort to bottled water.
2. Establish the publics right to know about the contents of bottled water.
3. Require FDA inspections of all bottling facilities and thier water sources.
4. Institute a penny per bottle fee to ensure bottled water safety.
5. Bottled water certification should be established.

Communication Workshop: Technology

Trash or Treasure: Assessing the Quality of Web Documents

Many users think that documents found by a World Wide Web search tool have somehow been previously validated by a trustworthy authority. Others think that, because the Web is the most current and most accessible source of information, its documents must be the most reliable available. Wrong on both counts! Almost anyone with a computer and an Internet connection can publish almost anything on the Web. In every Web domain, reliable sites and unreliable ones compete for your attention.

Unlike the contents of the journals, magazines, and newspapers found in research-oriented libraries, the contents of most Web sites haven't been carefully scrutinized by experienced editors and peer writers. To put it another way, print journals, magazines, and newspapers have traditionally featured reasonably unbiased, trustworthy articles; all too many Web sites, however, have another goal in mind. They are above all else interested in promoting a cause or in selling a product.

To use the Web meaningfully, you must learn to scrutinize carefully what you find in the documents it offers. The following checklist will help you distinguish Web trash from Web treasure.

Checklist for Assessing the Quality of a Web Page

Authority

- Who publishes or sponsors this Web page?
- Is the author or sponsor clearly identified?
- What makes the author or sponsor of the page an authority?
- Is information about the author or creator available?
- If the author is an individual, is he or she affiliated with a reputable organization?
- Is contact information, such as an e-mail address, available?
- To what domain (.com, .org, .edu, .gov, .net, .biz, .tv) does the site containing it belong?
- Is the site based in the United States or abroad (usually indicated by .uk, .ca, ru, or other designation in the URL)?
- Is the site "personal" (often indicated by "~" or "%" in the site's URL)?

Currency

- What is the date of the Web page?
- When was the last time the Web page was updated?
- Is some of the information obviously out of date?

Content

- Is the purpose of the page to entertain, inform, convince, or sell?
- How would you classify this page (e.g., news, personal, advocacy, reference)?
- Is the objective or purpose of the Web page clear?
- Who is the intended audience of the page, based on its content, tone, and style?
- Can you judge the overall value of the content as compared with other resources on this topic?
- Does the content seem to be comprehensive (does it cover everything about the topic)?
- Is the site easy to navigate?
- What other sites does the Web page link to? These may give you a clue to the credibility of the target page.
- Does the page contain distracting graphics or fill your screen with unwanted pop-ups?

Accuracy

- Do the facts that are presented seem reliable to you?
- Do you find spelling, grammar, or usage errors?
- Does the page have broken links or graphics that don't load?
- Do you see any evidence of bias?
- Are footnotes or other documentation necessary? If so, have they been provided?
- If the site contains statistics or other data, are the source, date, and other pertinent information disclosed?
- Are advertisements clearly distinguished from content?

Career Application. As interns at a news-gathering service, you have been asked to assess the quality of the following Web sites. Which of these could you recommend as sources of valid information?

- Beef Nutrition (**http://www.beefnutrition.org**)
- Edmunds—Where Smart Car Buyers Start (**http://www.edmunds.com**)
- I Hate Windows (**http://www.ihatewindowsxp.com**)
- EarthSave International (**http://www.earthsave.org**)
- The Vegetarian Resource Group (**http://www.vrg.org/nutshell/nutshell.htm**)
- The White House (**http://www.whitehouse.org**)
- The White House (**http://www.whitehouse.gov**)
- The White House (**http://www.whitehouse.com**)
- The Anaheim White House (**http://www.anaheimwhitehouse.com**)
- National Anti-Vivisection Society (**http://www.navs.org**)
- Dow Chemical Company (**http://www.dow.com**)
- Dow: A Chemical Company on the Global Playground (**http://www.dowethics.com**)
- Smithsonian Institution (**http://www.si.edu**)
- Drudge Report (**http://www.drudgereport.com**)
- American Cancer Society (**http://www.cancer.org**)
- CraigsList (**http://www.craigslist.com**)

Your Task

If you are working with a team, divide the preceding list among team members. If you are working individually, select four of the sites. Answer the questions in the preceding checklist as you evaluate each site. Summarize your evaluation of each site in a memo report to your instructor or in team or class discussion.

Professionalism, Teamwork, Meetings, and Speaking Skills

Chapter 11
Professionalism at Work: Business Etiquette, Ethics, Teamwork, and Meetings

Chapter 12
Business Presentations

© ISTOCKPHOTO.COM / JACOB WACKERHAUSEN

Professionalism at Work: Business Etiquette, Ethics, Teamwork, and Meetings

OBJECTIVES

After studying this chapter, you should be able to

- Show that you understand the importance of professional behavior, business etiquette, and ethics and know what employers want.

- Discuss improving face-to-face workplace communication including using your voice as a communication tool.

- Specify procedures for promoting positive workplace relations through conversation.

- Review techniques for responding professionally to workplace criticism and for offering constructive criticism on the job.

- Explain ways to polish your professional telephone skills and practice proper cell phone and voice mail etiquette.

- Describe the role of conventional and virtual teams, explain positive and negative team behavior, and identify the characteristics of successful teams.

- Outline procedures for planning, leading, and participating in productive business meetings, including using professional etiquette techniques, resolving conflict, and handling dysfunctional group members.

Recognizing the Importance of Professionalism, Business Etiquette, and Ethical Behavior

Whether we call it professionalism, business etiquette, ethical conduct, social intelligence, or soft skills, we are referring to a whole range of desirable workplace behaviors.

You have probably been told that being *professional* is important. When you search for definitions, however, you will find a wide range of meanings. Related terms and synonyms, such as *business etiquette* or *protocol, soft skills, social intelligence, polish,* and *civility,* may add to the confusion. However, they all have one thing in common: They describe desirable workplace behavior. Businesses have an interest in a workforce that gets along and delivers positive results that enhance profits and boost a company's image. As a budding business professional, you have a stake in acquiring skills that will make you a strong job applicant and a valuable, successful employee.

In this section you will learn which professional characteristics most businesspeople value in workplace relationships and will expect of you. Next you will be asked to consider the link between professional and ethical behavior on the job.

Finally, by knowing what recruiters want, you will have the power to shape yourself into the kind of professional they are looking to hire.

Defining Professional Behavior

Smooth relations in the workplace and when interacting with business partners or the public are crucial for the bottom line. Therefore, many businesses have established protocol procedures or policies to encourage civility. They are responding to increasing incidents of "desk rage" in American workplaces. Here are a few synonyms that attempt to define professional behavior to foster positive workplace relations:

Civility. Management consultant Patricia M. Buhler defines rising incivility at work "as behavior that is considered disrespectful and inconsiderate of others."[1] For an example of a policy encouraging civility, view Wikipedia's guidelines to its editors (**http://en.wikipedia.org/wiki/Wikipedia:CIV**), which offer principles to prevent rudeness and hateful responses on the Internet. The largest wiki ever created, the free encyclopedia must ensure that its more than 75,000 active collaborators get along and respect each other. Interestingly, Wikipedia admits that it is easier to define civility by its opposite: "[I]ncivility . . . consists of personally-targeted, belligerent behavior and persistent rudeness that result in an atmosphere of conflict and stress."[2] Surely such actions would not be acceptable in most businesses.

Polish. You may hear businesspeople refer to someone as being *polished* or displaying *polish* when dealing with others. In her book with the telling title *Buff and Polish: A Practical Guide to Enhance Your Professional Image and Communication Style,* Kathryn J. Volin focuses on nonverbal techniques and etiquette guidelines that are linked to career success. For example, she addresses making first impressions, shaking hands, improving one's voice quality, listening, and presentation skills. You will find many of these valuable traits of a polished business professional in this textbook and on the Web (see **www.meguffey.com**).

Business and Dining Etiquette. Proper business attire, dining etiquette, and other aspects of your professional presentation can make or break your interview, as you will see in Chapter 14. Even a seemingly harmless act such as sharing a business meal can have a huge impact on your career. In the words of a Fortune 500 executive, "Eating is not an executive skill . . . but it is especially hard to imagine why anyone negotiating a rise to the top would consider it possible to skip mastering the very simple requirements . . . what else did they skip learning?"[3] This means that you will be judged on more than your college-bred expertise. You will need to hone your etiquette skills as a well-rounded future business professional.

Social Intelligence. Occasionally you may encounter the expression *social intelligence.* In the words of one of its modern proponents, it is "The ability to get along well with others and to get them to cooperate with you."[4] Social intelligence points to a deep understanding of culture and life that helps us negotiate interpersonal and social situations. This type of intelligence can be much harder to acquire than simple etiquette. Social intelligence requires us to interact well, be perceptive, show sensitivity toward others, and grasp a situation quickly and accurately.

Soft Skills. Perhaps the most common term for important interpersonal habits is *soft skills*, as opposed to *hard skills,* a term for the technical knowledge in your field. Soft skills are a whole cluster of personal qualities, habits, attitudes (for example, optimism and friendliness), communication skills, and social graces. Employers want managers and employees who are comfortable with diverse coworkers, who can listen actively to customers and colleagues, who can make eye contact, who display good workplace manners, and who possess a host of other interpersonal

© MARC ROMANELLI / WORKBOOK STOCK / JUPITERIMAGES

skills. *Dress for Success* guru John T. Molloy says that 99 out of 100 executives view social skills as prerequisites to success, whether over cocktails, during dinner, or in the boardroom. These skills are immensely important not only to be hired but also to be promoted.

Simply put, all attempts to explain proper behavior at work aim at identifying traits that make someone a good employee and a compatible coworker. You will want to achieve a positive image on the job and to maintain a solid reputation. For the sake of simplicity, in the discussion that follows, the terms *professionalism, business etiquette*, and *soft skills* will be used largely synonymously.

Understanding the Relationship Between Ethics and Professional Behavior

The wide definition of professionalism also encompasses another crucial quality in a businessperson: *ethics* or *integrity*. Perhaps you subscribe to a negative view of business after learning about companies such as Enron, WorldCom, and Global Crossing. The collapse of these businesses along with fraud charges against their executives has reinforced the cynical perception of business as unethical and greedy. However, for every company that captures the limelight for misconduct, hundreds or even thousands of others operate honestly and serve their customers and the public well. The overwhelming majority of businesses wish to recruit ethical and polished graduates.

The difference between ethics and etiquette is minimal in the workplace. Ethics professor Douglas Chismar—and Harvard professor Stephen L. Carter before him—suggest that no sharp distinction between ethics and etiquette exists. How we approach the seemingly trivial events of work life reflects our character and attitudes when we handle larger issues. Our conduct should be consistently ethical and professional. Professor Chismar believes that "[w]e each have a moral obligation to treat each other with respect and sensitivity every day."[5] He calls on all of us to make a difference in the quality of life, morale, and even productivity at work. When employed appropriately in business, he says, professionalism brings greater good to society and makes for a better workplace.

Figure 11.1 summarizes the many components of professional workplace behavior[6] and identifies six main dimensions that will ease your entry into the world of work. Follow these guidelines to ensure your success on the job and increase the likelihood of promotion.

Business etiquette is closely related to everyday ethical behavior.

FIGURE 11.1 The Six Dimensions of Professional Behavior

Professional Dimension	What Professionalism Means on the Job
Courtesy and respect	• Be punctual. • Speak and write clearly and in language others can understand. • Apologize for errors or misunderstandings. • Notify the other person promptly when running late. • Accept constructive criticism. • Provide fair and gentle feedback. • Practice active listening.
Appearance and appeal	• Present yourself pleasantly with good hygiene and grooming. • Choose attractive, yet not distracting business attire. • Understand that appropriate dress and behavior are the first indication of professionalism and create lasting impressions. • Display proper business and dining etiquette.
Tolerance and tact	• Demonstrate self-control. • Stay away from public arguments and disagreements, including in written documents and e-mail. • Eliminate biases and prejudices in all business dealings. • Keep personal opinions of people private. • Avoid snap judgments especially when collaborating with others.
Honesty and ethics	• Avoid even the smallest lies at all cost. • Steer clear of conflicts of interest. • Pay for services and products promptly. • Keep confidential information confidential. • Pass up opportunities to badmouth competitors—emphasize your company's benefits, not your competitors' flaws. • Take positive, appropriate actions; avoid resorting to vengeful behavior when you feel wronged.
Reliability and responsibility	• Be dependable. • Follow through on commitments. • Keep promises and deadlines. • Perform work consistently and deliver effective results. • Make realistic promises about the quantity and quality of work output in a projected time frame.
Diligence and collegiality	• Deliver only work you can be proud of. • Strive for excellence at all times. • Give to customers more than they expect. • Be prepared before meetings and when presenting reports. • Do what needs to be done; do not leave work for others to do. • Show a willingness to share expertise. • Volunteer services to a worthy community or charity group. • Join networking groups and help their members.

Anticipating What Employers Want

Professional polish is increasingly valuable in our knowledge-based economy and will set you apart in competition with others. Hiring managers expect you to have technical expertise in your field. A good résumé and interview may get you in the door. However, soft skills and professional polish will ensure your long-term success. Advancement and promotions will depend on your grasp of workplace etiquette and

In the workplace we are judged to a great extent on our soft skills and professionalism.

the ability to communicate with your boss, coworkers, and customers. You will also earn recognition on the job if you prove yourself as an effective and contributing team member—and as a well-rounded professional overall.

Even in technical fields such as accounting and finance, employers are looking for professionalism and soft skills. Based on a survey of international accounting executives, *CA Magazine* concluded that "the future is bright for the next generation of accounting and finance professionals provided they are armed with such soft skills as the ability to communicate, deal with change, and work in a team setting."[7] A survey of chief financial officers revealed that a majority believed that communication skills carry a greater importance today than in the past.[8] Increasingly, finance professionals must be able to interact with the entire organization and explain terms without using financial jargon.

Employment advertisements frequently mention team, communication, and people skills.

Employers want team players who can work together productively. If you look at current online or newspaper want ads, chances are you will find requirements such as the following examples:

- Proven team skills to help deliver on-time, on-budget results
- Strong verbal and written communication skills as well as excellent presentation skills
- Excellent interpersonal, organizational, and teamwork skills
- Interpersonal and team skills plus well-developed communication skills
- Good people skills and superior teamwork abilities

In addition, most hiring managers are looking for new-hires who show enthusiasm, are eager to learn, volunteer to tackle even difficult tasks, and exhibit a positive attitude. You will not be hired to warm a seat.

This chapter focuses on developing interpersonal skills, telephone and voice mail etiquette, teamwork proficiency, and meeting management skills. These are some of the soft skills that employers seek in today's increasingly interconnected and competitive environments. You will learn many tips and techniques for becoming a professional communicator, valuable team player, and polished meeting participant.

Becoming a Professional Communicator in Face-to-Face Settings

One-dimensional communication technologies cannot replace the richness or effectiveness of face-to-face communication.

Because today's technologies provide many alternate communication channels, you may think that face-to-face communication is no longer essential or even important in business and professional transactions. You have already learned that e-mail is now the preferred communication channel because it is faster, cheaper, and easier than telephone, mail, or fax. However, despite their popularity and acceptance, alternate communication technologies can't replace the richness or effectiveness of face-to-face communication.[9] Imagine that you want to tell your boss how you solved a problem. Would you settle for a one-dimensional phone call, a fax, or an e-mail when you could step into her office and explain in person?

Face-to-face conversation has many advantages. It allows you to be persuasive and expressive because you can use your voice and body language to make a point. You are less likely to be misunderstood because you can read feedback and make needed adjustments. In conflict resolution, you can reach a solution more efficiently and cooperate to create greater levels of mutual benefit when communicating face-to-face.[10] Moreover, people want to see each other to satisfy a deep human need for social interaction. For numerous reasons communicating in person remains the most effective of all communication channels. In this chapter you will explore helpful business and professional interpersonal speaking techniques, starting with viewing your voice as a communication tool.

Using Your Voice as a Communication Tool

It has been said that language provides the words, but your voice is the music that makes words meaningful.[11] You may believe that a beautiful or powerful voice is unattainable. After all, this is the voice you were born with and it can't be changed. Actually, the voice is a flexible instrument. Actors hire coaches to help them eliminate or acquire accents or proper inflection for challenging roles. For example, Nicole Kidman, who speaks with an Australian accent, often takes on other accents, including American Southern and South African, for film roles. Celebrities, business executives, and everyday people consult voice and speech therapists to help them shake bad habits or just help them speak so that they can be understood and not sound less intelligent than they are. Rather than consult a high-paid specialist, you can pick up useful tips for using your voice most effectively by learning how to control such elements as pronunciation, voice quality, pitch, volume, rate, and emphasis.

Like an actor, you can change your voice to make it a more powerful communication tool.

Pronunciation. Proper pronunciation involves saying words correctly and clearly with the accepted sounds and accented syllables. You will have a distinct advantage in your job if, through training and practice, you learn to pronounce words correctly. How can you improve your pronunciation skills? The best ways are to listen carefully to educated people, to look words up in the dictionary, and to practice. Online dictionaries frequently allow you to play back the pronunciation when you have found your desired word.

Proper pronunciation means saying words correctly and clearly with the accepted sounds and accented syllables.

Voice Quality. The quality of your voice sends a nonverbal message to listeners. It identifies your personality and your mood. Some voices sound enthusiastic and friendly, conveying the impression of an upbeat person who is happy to be with the listener. But voices can also sound controlling, patronizing, slow-witted, angry, bored, or childish. This doesn't mean that the speaker necessarily has that attribute. It may mean that the speaker is merely carrying on a family tradition or pattern learned in childhood. To check your voice quality, record your voice and listen to it critically. Is it projecting a positive quality about you? Do you sound professional?

Pitch. Effective speakers use a relaxed, controlled, well-pitched voice to attract listeners to their message. *Pitch* refers to sound vibration frequency; that is, the highness or lowness of a sound. Voices are most engaging when they rise and fall in conversational tones. Flat, monotone voices are considered boring and ineffectual.

Volume and Rate. The volume of your voice is the degree of loudness or the intensity of sound. Just as you adjust the volume on your radio or television set, you should adjust the volume of your speaking to the occasion and your listeners. *Rate* refers to the pace of your speech. If you speak too slowly, listeners are bored and their attention wanders. If you speak too quickly, listeners may not be able to understand you. Most people normally talk at about 125 words a minute. Monitor the nonverbal signs of your listeners and adjust your volume and rate as needed.

Speaking in a moderately low-pitched voice at about 125 words a minute makes you sound pleasing and professional.

Emphasis. By emphasizing or stressing certain words, you can change the meaning you are expressing. To make your message interesting and natural, use emphasis appropriately.

Some speakers today are prone to *uptalk*. This is a habit of using a rising inflection at the end of a sentence resulting in a singsong pattern that makes statements sound like questions. Once used exclusively by teenagers, uptalk is increasingly found in the workplace with negative results. When statements sound like questions, speakers seem weak and tentative. Their messages lack conviction and authority. On the job, managers afflicted by uptalk may have difficulty convincing staff members to follow directions because their voice inflection implies that other valid options are available. If you want to sound confident and competent, avoid uptalk.

"Uptalk," in which sentences sound like questions, makes speakers seem weak and tentative.

You will be most effective in workplace conversations if you use correct names and titles, choose appropriate topics, avoid negative and judgmental remarks, and give sincere and specific praise.

Promoting Positive Workplace Relations Through Conversation

In the workplace, conversations may involve giving and taking instructions, providing feedback, exchanging ideas on products and services, participating in performance appraisals, or engaging in small talk about such things as families and sports. Face-to-face conversation helps people work together harmoniously and feel that they are part of the larger organization. Our goal here is to provide you with several business etiquette guidelines that promote positive workplace conversations, both in the office and at work-related social functions.

Use Correct Names and Titles. Although the world seems increasingly informal, it is still wise to use titles and last names when addressing professional adults (*Ms. O'Malley, Mr. Santiago*). In some organizations senior staff members speak to junior employees on a first-name basis, but the reverse may not be encouraged. Probably the safest plan is to ask your superiors how they want to be addressed. Customers and others outside the organization should always be addressed initially by title and last name. Wait for an invitation to use first names.

When you meet strangers, do you have trouble remembering their names? You can improve your memory considerably if you associate the person with an object, place, color, animal, job, adjective, or some other memory hook. For example, *technology pro Gina, L.A. Matt, silver-haired Mr. Elliott, baseball fan John, programmer Tanya, traveler Ms. Choi*. The person's name will also be more deeply imbedded in your memory if you use it immediately after being introduced, in subsequent conversation, and when you part.

Choose Appropriate Topics. In some workplace activities, such as social gatherings or interviews, you will be expected to engage in small talk. Be sure to stay away from controversial topics with someone you don't know very well. Avoid politics, religion, or controversial current event items that can start heated arguments. To initiate appropriate conversations, read newspapers and listen to radio and TV shows discussing current events. Subscribe to e-newsletters that deliver relevant news to you via e-mail, or visit news portals such as Google News or Yahoo on the Web. Make a mental note of items that you can use in conversation, taking care to remember where you saw or heard the news items so that you can report accurately and authoritatively. Try not to be defensive or annoyed if others present information that upsets you.

Avoid Negative Remarks. Workplace conversations are not the place to complain about your colleagues, your friends, the organization, or your job. No one enjoys listening to whiners. What's more, your criticism of others may come back to haunt you. A snipe at your boss or a complaint about a fellow worker may reach him or her, sometimes embellished or distorted with meanings you did not intend. Be circumspect in all negative judgments. Remember, some people love to repeat statements that will stir up trouble or set off internal workplace wars. Don't give them the ammunition!

Listen to Learn. In conversations with managers, colleagues, subordinates, and customers, train yourself to expect to learn something from what you are hearing. Being attentive is not only instructive but also courteous. Beyond displaying good manners, you will probably find that your conversation partner has information that you don't have. Being receptive and listening with an open mind means not interrupting or prejudging. Let's say you want very much to be able to work at home for part of your workweek. You try to explain your ideas to your boss, but he cuts you off shortly after you start. He says, *It is out of the question; we need you here every day.* Suppose instead he had said, *I have strong reservations about your telecommuting, but maybe you will change my mind;* and he settles in to listen to your presentation. Even if your boss decides against your request, you will feel that your ideas were heard and respected.

Give Sincere and Specific Praise. The Greek philosopher Xenophon once said, "The sweetest of all sounds is praise." Probably nothing promotes positive workplace relationships better than sincere and specific praise. Whether the compliments and appreciation are traveling upward to management, downward to workers, or horizontally to colleagues, everyone responds well to recognition. Organizations run more smoothly and morale is higher when people feel appreciated. In your workplace conversations, look for ways to recognize good work and good people. Try to be specific. Instead of saying, *You did a good job in leading that meeting,* say something more specific, such as, *Your excellent leadership skills certainly kept that meeting short, focused, and productive.*

Act Professionally in Social Situations. You will likely attend many work-related social functions during your career, including dinners, picnics, holiday parties, and other events. It is important to remember that your actions at these events can help or harm your career. Dress appropriately, and avoid or limit alcohol consumption. Choose appropriate conversation topics, and make sure that your voice and mannerisms communicate that you are glad to be there.

Responding Professionally to Workplace Criticism

Most of us hate giving criticism, but we dislike receiving it even more. However, it is normal to both give and receive criticism on the job. The criticism may be given informally, for example, during a casual conversation with a supervisor or coworker. Or the criticism may be given formally, for example, during a performance evaluation. The important thing is that you are able to accept and respond professionally when receiving criticism.

When being criticized, you may feel that you are being attacked. You can't just sit back and relax. Your heart beats faster, your temperature shoots up, your face reddens, and you respond with the classic fight-or-flight response. You want to instantly retaliate or escape from the attacker. But focusing on your feelings distracts you from hearing the content of what is being said, and it prevents you from responding professionally. Some or all of the following suggestions will guide you in reacting positively to criticism so that you can benefit from it:

- **Listen without interrupting.** Even though you might want to protest, make yourself hear the speaker out.
- **Determine the speaker's intent.** Unskilled communicators may throw "verbal bricks" with unintended negative-sounding expressions. If you think the intent is positive, focus on what is being said rather than reacting to poorly chosen words.
- **Acknowledge what you are hearing.** Respond with a pause, a nod, or a neutral statement such as, *I understand you have a concern.* This buys you time. Do not disagree, counterattack, or blame, which may escalate the situation and harden the speaker's position.
- **Paraphrase what was said.** In your own words restate objectively what you are hearing.
- **Ask for more information, if necessary.** Clarify what is being said. Stay focused on the main idea rather than interjecting side issues.
- **Agree—if the comments are accurate.** If an apology is in order, give it. Explain what you plan to do differently. If the criticism is on target, the sooner you agree, the more likely you will be to engender respect from the other person.
- **Disagree respectfully and constructively—if you feel the comments are unfair.** After hearing the criticism, you might say, *May I tell you my perspective?* Or you could try to solve the problem by saying, *How can we improve this situation in a way you believe we can both accept?* If the other person continues to criticize, say, *I want to find a way to resolve your concern. When do you want to talk about it next?*
- **Look for a middle position.** Search for a middle position or a compromise. Be genial even if you don't like the person or the situation.

When being criticized, you should listen, paraphrase, and clarify what is said; if you agree, apologize or explain what you will do differently.

If you feel you are being criticized unfairly, disagree respectfully and constructively; look for a middle position.

- **Learn from criticism.** Most work-related criticism is given with the best of intentions. You should welcome the opportunity to correct your mistakes and to learn from them. Responding positively and professionally to workplace criticism can help improve your job performance. As Winston Churchill said, "All men make mistakes, but only wise men learn from their mistakes."[12]

Offering Constructive Criticism on the Job

No one likes to receive criticism, and most of us don't like to give it either. But in the workplace cooperative endeavors demand feedback and evaluation. How are we doing on a project? What went well? What failed? How can we improve our efforts? Today's workplace often involves team projects. As a team member, you will be called on to judge the work of others. In addition to working on teams, you can also expect to become a supervisor or manager one day. As such, you will need to evaluate subordinates. Good employees seek good feedback from their supervisors. They want and need timely, detailed observations about their work to reinforce what they do well and help them overcome weak spots. But making that feedback palatable and constructive is not always easy. Depending on your situation, you may find some or all of the following suggestions helpful when you must deliver constructive criticism:

- **Mentally outline your conversation.** Think carefully about what you want to accomplish and what you will say. Find the right words and deliver them at the right time and in the right setting.
- **Generally, use face-to-face communication.** Most constructive criticism is better delivered in person rather than in e-mail messages or memos. Personal feedback offers an opportunity for the listener to ask questions and give explanations. Occasionally, however, complex situations may require a different strategy. You might prefer to write out your opinions and deliver them by telephone or in writing. A written document enables you to organize your thoughts, include all the details, and be sure of keeping your cool. Remember, though, that written documents create permanent records—for better or worse.
- **Focus on improvement.** Instead of attacking, use language that offers alternative behavior. Use phrases such as *Next time, you could . . . .*
- **Offer to help.** Criticism is accepted more readily if you volunteer to help in eliminating or solving the problem.
- **Be specific.** Instead of a vague assertion such as, *Your work is often late*, be more specific: *The specs on the Riverside job were due Thursday at 5 p.m., and you didn't hand them in until Friday.* Explain how the person's performance jeopardized the entire project.
- **Avoid broad generalizations.** Don't use words such as *should, never, always,* and other encompassing expressions as they may cause the listener to shut down and become defensive.
- **Discuss the behavior, not the person.** Instead of saying, *You seem to think you can come to work any time you want*, focus on the behavior: *Coming to work late means that we have to fill in with someone else until you arrive.*
- **Use the word *we* rather than *you*.** Saying, *We need to meet project deadlines*, is better than saying, *You need to meet project deadlines.* Emphasize organizational expectations rather than personal ones. Avoid sounding accusatory.
- **Encourage two-way communication.** Even if well planned, criticism is still hard to deliver. It may surprise or hurt the feelings of the employee. Consider ending your message with, *It can be hard to hear this type of feedback. If you would like to share your thoughts, I'm listening.*
- **Avoid anger, sarcasm, and a raised voice.** Criticism is rarely constructive when tempers flare. Plan in advance what you will say and deliver it in low, controlled, and sincere tones.
- **Keep it private.** Offer praise in public; offer criticism in private. "Setting an example" through public criticism is never a wise management policy.

Practicing Professional Telephone, Cell Phone, and Voice Mail Etiquette

Despite the heavy reliance on e-mail, the telephone is still an extremely important piece of equipment in offices. With the addition of today's wireless technology, it doesn't matter whether you are in or out of the office. You can always be reached by phone. As a business communicator, you can be more productive, efficient, and professional by following some simple suggestions. In this chapter we will focus on traditional telephone etiquette as well as cell phone use and voice mail techniques.

For most businesses, telephones—both traditional and wireless—are a primary contact with the outside world.

Making Telephone Calls Professionally

Before making a telephone call, decide whether the intended call is really necessary. Could you find the information yourself? If you wait a while, would the problem resolve itself? Perhaps your message could be delivered more efficiently by some other means. Some companies have found that telephone calls are often less important than the work they interrupt. Alternatives to telephone calls include instant messaging, e-mail, memos, or calls to voice mail systems. If you must make a telephone call, consider using the following suggestions to make it fully productive:

You can make productive telephone calls by planning an agenda, identifying the purpose, being cheerful and accurate, being professional and courteous, and avoiding rambling.

- **Plan a mini-agenda.** Have you ever been embarrassed when you had to make a second telephone call because you forgot an important item the first time? Before placing a call, jot down notes regarding all the topics you need to discuss. Following an agenda guarantees not only a complete call but also a quick one. You will be less likely to wander from the business at hand while rummaging through your mind trying to remember everything.

- **Use a three-point introduction.** When placing a call, immediately (a) name the person you are calling, (b) identify yourself and your affiliation, and (c) give a brief explanation of your reason for calling. For example: *May I speak to Jeremy Johnson? This is Paula Soltani of Coughlin and Associates, and I'm seeking information about a software program called ZoneAlarm Internet Security.* This kind of introduction enables the receiving individual to respond immediately without asking further questions.

- **Be brisk if you are rushed.** For business calls when your time is limited, avoid questions such as *How are you?* Instead, say, *Lauren, I knew you'd be the only one who could answer these two questions for me.* Another efficient strategy is to set a "contract" with the caller: *Look, Lauren, I have only ten minutes, but I really wanted to get back to you.*

- **Be cheerful and accurate.** Let your voice show the same kind of animation that you radiate when you greet people in person. In your mind try to envision the individual answering the telephone. A smile can certainly affect the tone of your voice; therefore, even though the individual can't see you, smile at that person. Speak with a tone that is enthusiastic, respectful, and attentive. Moreover, be accurate about what you say. *Hang on a second; I'll be right back* rarely is true. It is better to say, *It may take me two or three minutes to get that information. Would you prefer to hold or have me call you back?*

- **Be professional and courteous.** Remember that you are representing yourself and your company when you make phone calls. Use professional vocabulary and courteous language. Say *thank you* and *please* during your conversations. Don't eat, drink, or chew gum while talking on the phone, which can often be heard on the other end. Articulate your words clearly so that the receiver can understand you. Avoid doing other work during the phone call so that you can focus entirely on the conversation.

- **Bring it to a close.** The responsibility for ending a call lies with the caller. This is sometimes difficult to do if the other person rambles on. You may need to use suggestive closing language, such as the following: (a) *I have certainly enjoyed talking with you,* (b) *I have learned what I needed to know, and now I can proceed with* *my work*, (c) *Thanks for your help*, (d) *I must go now, but may I call you again in the future if I need . . . ?* or (e) *Should we talk again in a few weeks?*

- **Avoid telephone tag.** If you call someone who is not in, ask when it would be best for you to call again. State that you will call at a specific time—and do it. If you ask a person to call you, give a time when you can be reached—and then be sure you are in at that time.

- **Leave complete voice mail messages.** Remember that there is no rush when you leave a voice mail message. Always enunciate clearly. And be sure to provide a complete message, including your name, telephone number, and the time and date of your call. Explain your purpose so that the receiver can be ready with the required information when returning your call.

Receiving Telephone Calls Professionally

With a little forethought you can project a professional image and make your telephone a productive, efficient work tool. Developing good telephone manners also reflects well on you and on your organization. You will be most successful on the job if you practice the following etiquette guidelines:

- **Answer promptly and courteously.** Try to answer the phone on the first or second ring if possible. Smile as you pick up the phone.

- **Identify yourself immediately.** In answering your telephone or someone else's, provide your name, title or affiliation, and a greeting. For example, *Juan Salinas, Digital Imaging Corporation. How may I help you?* Force yourself to speak clearly and slowly. Remember that the caller may be unfamiliar with what you are saying and fail to recognize slurred syllables.

- **Be responsive and helpful.** If you are in a support role, be sympathetic to callers' needs and show that you understand their situations. Instead of *I don't know*, try *That is a good question; let me investigate*. Instead of *We can't do that*, try *That is a tough one; let's see what we can do*. Avoid *No* at the beginning of a sentence. It sounds especially abrasive and displeasing because it suggests total rejection.

- **Be cautious when answering calls for others.** Be courteous and helpful, but don't give out confidential information. It is better to say, *She is away from her desk* or *He is out of the office* than to report a colleague's exact whereabouts. Also be tight lipped about sharing company information with strangers. Security experts insist that employees answering telephones must become guardians of company information.[13]

- **Take messages carefully.** Few things are as frustrating as receiving a potentially important phone message that is illegible. Repeat the spelling of names and verify telephone numbers. Write messages legibly and record their time and date. Promise to give the messages to intended recipients, but don't guarantee return calls.

- **Leave the line respectfully.** If you must put a call on hold, let the caller know and give an estimate of how long you expect the call to be on hold. Give the caller the option of holding. Say *Would you prefer to hold, or would you like me to call you back?* If the caller is on hold for a long time, check back periodically so that the caller doesn't think that he or she has been forgotten or that the call has been disconnected.

- **Explain what you are doing when transferring calls.** Give a reason for transferring, and identify the extension to which you are directing the call in case the caller is disconnected.

Using Cell Phones for Business

Cell phones enable you to conduct business from virtually anywhere at any time. More than a plaything or a mere convenience, the cell phone has become an essential part of communication in today's workplace. A few years ago, for the first time, the number of U.S. cell phone users surpassed the number of landline telephone users, and the number of cell phone users has continued to grow.[14] More than 80 percent of Americans own a cell phone,[15] and a third of wireless customers rarely use a landline.[16] Today's highly capable smartphones are used for much more than making and receiving calls.

High-end cell phones and personal digital assistants (PDAs) can be used to store contact information, make to-do lists, keep track of appointments and important dates, send and receive e-mail, send and receive text and multimedia messages, search the Web, get news and stock quotes from the Internet, take pictures and videos, synchronize with Outlook and other software applications, and many other functions.

With so many people depending on their cell phones, it is important to understand proper use and etiquette. How are they best used? When is it acceptable to take calls? Where should calls be made? Most of us have experienced thoughtless and rude cell phone behavior. To avoid offending, smart business communicators practice cell phone etiquette, as outlined in Figure 11.2. In projecting a professional image, they are careful about location, time, and volume in relation to their cell phone calls.

> Cell phones are essential workplace communication tools, but they must be used without offending others.

Location. Use good judgment in placing or accepting cell phone calls. Some places are dangerous or inappropriate for cell phone use. Turn off your cell phone when entering a conference room, interview venue, theater, place of worship, or any other place where it could be distracting or disruptive to others. Taking a call in a crowded room or bar makes it difficult to hear and reflects poorly on you as a professional. Taking a call while driving can be dangerous, leading some states to ban cell phone use while driving. A bad connection also makes a bad impression. Static or dropped signals create frustration and miscommunication. Don't sacrifice professionalism for the sake of a quick phone call. It is smarter to turn off your phone in an area where the signal is weak and when you are likely to have interference. Use voice mail and return the call when conditions are better. Also, be careful about using your cell phone to discuss private or confidential company information.

Time. Often what you are doing is more important than whatever may come over the air waves to you on your phone. For example, when you are having an important discussion with a business partner, customer, or superior, it is rude to allow yourself to be interrupted by an incoming call. It is also poor manners to practice multitasking while on the phone. What's more, it is dangerous. Although you might be able to read and print out e-mail messages, deal with a customer at the counter, and talk on your cell phone simultaneously, it is impolite and risky. Lack of attention results in errors. If a phone call is important enough to accept, then it is important enough to stop what you are doing and attend to the conversation.

FIGURE 11.2 Practicing Courteous and Responsible Cell Phone Use

Business communicators find cell phones to be enormously convenient and real time-savers. But rude users have generated a backlash against inconsiderate callers. Here are specific suggestions for using cell phones safely and responsibly:

- **Be courteous to those around you.** Don't force those near you to hear your business. Don't step up to a service counter, such as at a restaurant, bank, or post office, while talking on your cell phone. Don't carry on a cell phone conversation while someone is waiting on you. Think first of those in close proximity instead of those on the other end of the phone. Apologize and make amends gracefully for occasional cell phone blunders.
- **Observe wireless-free quiet areas.** Don't allow your cell phone to ring in theaters, restaurants, museums, classrooms, important meetings, and similar places. Use the cell phone's silent/vibrating ring option. A majority of travelers prefer that cell phone conversations *not* be held on most forms of public transportation.
- **Speak in low, conversational tones.** Microphones on cell phones are quite sensitive, thus making it unnecessary to talk loudly. Avoid "cell yell."
- **Take only urgent calls.** Make full use of your cell phone's caller ID feature to screen incoming calls. Let voice mail take those calls that are not pressing.
- **Drive now, talk later.** Pull over if you must make a call. Talking while driving increases the chance of accidents fourfold, about the same as driving while intoxicated. Some companies are implementing cell phone policies that prohibit employees from using cell phones while driving for company business.
- **Choose a professional ringtone.** These days you can download a variety of ringtones, from classical to rap to the *Star Wars* theme. Choose a ringtone that will sound professional.

Volume. Many people raise their voices when using their cell phones because the small devices offer little aural feedback. "Cell yell" results, much to the annoyance of anyone nearby. Raising your voice is unnecessary since most phones have excellent microphones that can pick up even a whisper. If the connection is bad, louder volume will not improve the sound quality. As in face-to-face conversations, a low, modulated voice sounds professional and projects the proper image.

Making the Best Use of Voice Mail

Because telephone calls can be disruptive, most businesspeople are making extensive use of voice mail to intercept and screen incoming calls. Voice mail links a telephone system to a computer that digitizes and stores incoming messages. Some systems also provide functions such as automated attendant menus, allowing callers to reach any associated extension by pushing specific buttons on a touch-tone telephone.

Voice mail is quite efficient for message storage. Because as many as half of all business calls require no discussion or feedback, the messaging capabilities of voice mail can mean huge savings for businesses. Incoming information is delivered without interrupting potential receivers and without all the niceties that most two-way conversations require. Stripped of superfluous chitchat, voice mail messages allow communicators to focus on essentials. Voice mail also eliminates telephone tag, inaccurate message taking, and time-zone barriers.

However, voice mail should not be overused. Individuals who screen all incoming calls cause irritation, resentment, and needless telephone tag. Both receivers and callers can use etiquette guidelines to make voice mail work most effectively for them.

> Voice mail eliminates telephone tag, inaccurate message taking, and time-zone barriers; it also allows communicators to focus on essentials.

On the Receiver's End. Your voice mail should project professionalism and should provide an efficient mechanism for your callers to leave messages for you. Here are some voice mail etiquette tips to follow:

"Thank you for calling. Please leave a message. In case I forget to check my messages, please send your message as an audio file to my e-mail, then send me a fax to remind me to check my e-mail, then call back to remind me to check my fax."

- **Don't overuse voice mail.** Don't use voice mail as a means to avoid taking phone calls. It is better to answer calls yourself than to let voice mail messages build up.
- **Set the number of rings appropriately.** Set your voice mail to ring as few times as possible before picking up. This shows respect for your callers' time.
- **Prepare a professional, concise, friendly greeting.** Make your mechanical greeting sound warm and inviting, both in tone and content. Your greeting should be in your own voice, not a computer-generated voice. Identify yourself and your organization so that callers know they have reached the right number. Thank the caller and briefly explain that you are unavailable. Invite the caller to leave a message or, if appropriate, call back. Here's a typical voice mail greeting: *Hi! This is Larry Lopez of Proteus Software, and I appreciate your call. You have reached my voice mailbox because I'm either working with customers or talking on another line at the moment. Please leave your name, number, and reason for calling so that I can be prepared when I return your call.* Give callers an idea of when you will be available, such as *I'll be back at 2:30* or *I'll be out of my office until Wednesday, May 20.* If you screen your calls as a time-management technique, try this message: *I'm not near my phone right now, but I should be able to return calls after 3:30.*
- **Test your message.** Call your number and assess your message. Does it sound inviting? Sincere? Professional? Understandable? Are you pleased with your tone? If not, record your message again until it conveys the professional image you want.

- **Change your message.** Update your message regularly, especially if you travel for your job.
- **Respond to messages promptly.** Check your messages regularly, and try to return all voice mail messages within one business day.
- **Plan for vacations and other extended absences.** If you will not be picking up voice mail messages for an extended period, let callers know how they can reach someone else if needed.

On the Caller's End. When leaving a voice mail message, you should follow these tips:

- **Be prepared to leave a message.** Before calling someone, be prepared for voice mail. Decide what you are going to say and what information you are going to include in your message. If necessary, write your message down before calling.
- **Leave a concise, thorough message.** When leaving a message, always identify yourself using your complete name and affiliation. Mention the date and time you called and a brief explanation of your reason for calling. Always leave a complete phone number, including the area code, even if you think the receiver already has it. Tell the receiver the best time to return your call. Don't ramble.
- **Use a professional and courteous tone.** When leaving a message, make sure that your tone is professional, enthusiastic, and respectful. Smile when leaving a message to add warmth to your voice.
- **Speak slowly and articulate.** You want to make sure that your receiver will be able to understand your message. Speak slowly and pronounce your words carefully, especially when providing your phone number. The receiver should be able to write information down without having to replay your message.
- **Be careful with confidential information.** Don't leave confidential or private information in a voice mail message. Remember that anyone could gain access to this information.
- **Don't make assumptions.** If you don't receive a call back within a day or two after leaving a message, don't get angry or frustrated. Assume that the message wasn't delivered or that it couldn't be understood. Call back and leave another message, or send the person an e-mail message.

Becoming a Team Player in Professional Groups and Teams

As we discussed in Chapter 1, the workplace and economy are changing. Responding to fierce global competition, businesses are being forced to operate ever more efficiently. One significant recent change is the emphasis on teamwork. You might find yourself a part of a work team, project team, customer support team, supplier team, design team, planning team, functional team, cross-functional team, or some other group. All of these teams are being formed to accomplish specific goals, and your career success will depend on your ability to function well in a team-driven professional environment.

Teams can be effective in solving problems and in developing new products. Take, for example, the creation of Red Baron's "Stuffed Pizza Slices." Featuring a one-of-a-kind triangular, vented design, the product delivers taste, convenience, and style. But coming up with an innovative new hit required a cross-functional team with representatives from product development, packaging, purchasing, and operations. The entire team worked to shape an idea into a hit product using existing machinery.[17]

German auto manufacturer BMW likes to "throw together" designers, engineers, and marketing experts to work intensively on a team project. Ten team members, for example, working in an old bank building in London, collaborated on the redesign of the Rolls-Royce Phantom. The result was a best-selling superluxury automobile that remained true to the Rolls heritage. The new model had twenty-first-century lines with BMW's technological muscle under the hood.[18] Perhaps you can now imagine why forming teams is important.

The Importance of Conventional and Virtual Teams in the Workplace

Businesses are constantly looking for ways to do jobs better at less cost. They are forming teams for the following reasons:

- **Better decisions.** Decisions are generally more accurate and effective because group and team members contribute different expertise and perspectives.
- **Faster response.** When action is necessary to respond to competition or to solve a problem, small groups and teams can act rapidly.
- **Increased productivity.** Because they are often closer to the action and to the customer, team members can see opportunities for improving efficiency.
- **Greater buy-in.** Decisions arrived at jointly are usually better received because members are committed to the solution and are more willing to support it.
- **Less resistance to change.** People who have input into decisions are less hostile, aggressive, and resistant to change.
- **Improved employee morale.** Personal satisfaction and job morale increase when teams are successful.
- **Reduced risks.** Responsibility for a decision is diffused, thus carrying less risk for any individual.

Organizations are forming teams for better decisions, faster response, increased productivity, greater buy-in, less resistance to change, improved morale, and reduced risks.

To connect with distant team members across borders and time zones, many organizations are creating *virtual teams*. These are groups of people who work interdependently with a shared purpose across space, time, and organization boundaries using technology.[19] The author of this textbook, for example, works in her office in Santa Barbara, California. Her developmental editor is located in Kentucky, the production editor is in Minnesota, and the publisher is in Ohio. Important parts of the marketing team are in Singapore and Canada. Although they work in different time zones and rarely see each other, team members use e-mail and teleconferencing to exchange ideas, make decisions, and stay connected.

Virtual teams are groups of people who work interdependently with a shared purpose across space, time, and organization boundaries using technology.

Virtual teams may be local or global. At Best Buy's corporate headquarters in Richfield, Minnesota, certain employees are allowed to work anywhere and anytime—as long as they successfully complete their assignments on time. They can decide how, when, and where they work.[20] Although few other organizations are engaging in such a radical restructuring of work, many workers today complete their tasks from remote locations, thus creating local virtual teams. Hyundai Motors exemplifies virtual teaming at the global level. For its vehicles, Hyundai completes engineering in Korea, research in Tokyo and Germany, styling in California, engine calibration and testing in Michigan, and heat testing in the California desert.[21] Members of its virtual teams coordinate their work and complete their tasks across time and geographic zones. Work is increasingly viewed as what you do rather than a place you go.

In some organizations, remote coworkers may be permanent employees of the same company or may be specialists called together for temporary projects. Regardless of the assignment, virtual teams can benefit from shared views and skills.

Positive and Negative Team Behavior

Team members who are committed to achieving the group's purpose contribute by displaying positive behavior. How can you be a professional team member? The most effective groups have members who are willing to establish rules and abide by those rules. Effective team members are able to analyze tasks and define problems so that they can work toward solutions. They offer information and try out their ideas on the group to stimulate discussion. They show interest in others' ideas by listening actively. Helpful team members also seek to involve silent members.

Professional team members follow team rules, analyze tasks, define problems, share information, listen actively to others, and try to involve quiet members.

They help to resolve differences, and they encourage a warm, supportive climate by praising and agreeing with others. When they sense that agreement is near, they review significant points and move the group toward its goal by synthesizing points of understanding.

Not all groups, however, have members who contribute positively. Negative behavior is shown by those who constantly put down the ideas and suggestions of others. They insult, criticize, and aggress against others. They waste the group's time with unnecessary recounting of personal achievements or irrelevant topics. The team joker distracts the group with excessive joke telling, inappropriate comments, and disruptive antics. Also disturbing are team members who withdraw and refuse to be drawn out. They have nothing to say, either for or against ideas being considered. To be a productive and welcome member of a group, be prepared to perform the positive tasks described in Figure 11.3. Avoid the negative behaviors.

Negative team behavior includes insulting, criticizing, aggressing against others, wasting time, and refusing to participate.

Characteristics of Successful Professional Teams

The use of teams has been called the solution to many ills in the current workplace.[22] Someone even observed that as an acronym TEAM means "Together, Everyone Achieves More."[23] Yet, many teams do not work well together. In fact, some teams can actually increase frustration, lower productivity, and create employee dissatisfaction. Experts who have studied team workings and decisions have discovered that effective teams share some or all of the following characteristics.

"Isn't this what teamwork is all about? You doing all my work for me?"

Small Size, Diverse Makeup. Teams may range from 2 to 25 members, although 4 or 5 is optimum for many projects. Larger groups have trouble interacting constructively, much less agreeing on actions.[24] For the most creative decisions, teams generally have male and female members who differ in age, ethnicity, social background, training, and experience. Members should bring complementary skills to a team. Fred Adair, a partner at executive search firm Heidrick & Struggles, had this to say about diverse teams when asked about his recent study of nearly 700 top business leaders: "Yes, diverse teams are generally better. There is a more balanced consideration of different perspectives, and I'm using the word 'diversity' in the broadest sense—diversity of personality, of opinion, of decision-making style."[25] The key business advantage of diversity is the ability to view a project and its context from multiple perspectives. Many of us tend to think that everyone in the world

Small, diverse teams often produce more creative solutions with broader applications than homogeneous teams do.

FIGURE 11.3 Positive and Negative Team Behaviors

Positive Team Behaviors	Negative Team Behaviors
Setting rules and abiding by them	Blocking the ideas and suggestions of others
Analyzing tasks and defining problems	Insulting and criticizing others
Contributing information and ideas	Wasting the group's time
Showing interest by listening actively	Making inappropriate jokes and comments
Encouraging members to participate	Failing to stay on task
Synthesizing points of agreement	Withdrawing, failing to participate

is like us because we know only our own experience.[26] Teams with members from a variety of ethnicities and cultures can look at projects beyond the limited view of one culture. Many organizations are finding that diverse teams can produce innovative solutions with broader applications than homogeneous teams can.

Agreement on Purpose. An effective team begins with a purpose. For example, when Magic Johnson Theatres was developing its first theater, it hired a team whose sole purpose was to help the company move rapidly through the arduous state permit application process. Even the task of obtaining a license for the site's popcorn machine was surprisingly difficult.[27] Xerox scientists who invented personal computing developed their team purpose after the chairman of Xerox called for an "architecture of information." A team at Sealed Air Corporation developed its purpose when management instructed it to cut waste and reduce downtime.[28] Working from a general purpose to specific goals typically requires a huge investment of time and effort. Meaningful discussions, however, motivate team members to "buy into" the project.

Agreement on Procedures. The best teams develop procedures to guide them. They set up intermediate goals with deadlines. They assign roles and tasks, requiring all members to contribute equivalent amounts of real work. They decide how they will reach decisions using one of the strategies discussed earlier. Procedures are continually evaluated to ensure movement toward the attainment of the team's goals.

Ability to Confront Conflict. Poorly functioning teams avoid conflict, preferring sulking, gossiping, or backstabbing. A better plan is to acknowledge conflict and address the root of the problem openly. Although it may feel emotionally risky, direct confrontation saves time and enhances team commitment in the long run. To be constructive, however, confrontation must be task oriented, not person oriented. An open airing of differences, in which all team members have a chance to speak their minds, should center on the strengths and weaknesses of the different positions and ideas—not on personalities. After hearing all sides, team members must negotiate a fair settlement, no matter how long it takes. Good decisions are based on consensus: most members must agree.

Use of Good Communication Techniques. The best teams exchange information and contribute ideas freely in an informal environment. Team members speak clearly and concisely, avoiding generalities. They encourage feedback. Listeners become actively involved, read body language, and ask clarifying questions before responding. Tactful, constructive disagreement is encouraged. Although a team's task is taken seriously, successful teams are able to inject humor into their interactions.

Ability to Collaborate Rather Than Compete. Effective team members are genuinely interested in achieving team goals instead of receiving individual recognition. They contribute ideas and feedback unselfishly. They monitor team progress, including what is going right, what is going wrong, and what to do about it. They celebrate individual and team accomplishments.

Shared Leadership. Effective teams often have no formal leader. Instead, leadership rotates to those with the appropriate expertise as the team evolves and moves from one phase to another. Many teams operate under a democratic approach. This approach can achieve buy-in to team decisions, boost morale, and create fewer hurt feelings and less resentment. But in times of crisis, a strong team member may need to step up as leader.

Acceptance of Ethical Responsibilities. Teams as a whole have ethical responsibilities to their members, to their larger organizations, and to society. Members have a number of specific responsibilities to each other, as shown in Figure 11.4. As a whole, teams have a responsibility to represent the organization's view

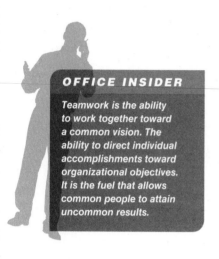

Effective teams exchange information freely and collaborate rather than compete.

FIGURE 11.4 Ethical Responsibilities of Group Members and Leaders

When people form a group or a team to achieve a purpose, they agree to give up some of their individual sovereignty for the good of the group. They become interdependent and assume responsibilities to one another and to the group. Here are important ethical responsibilities for members to follow:

- **Determine to do your best.** When you commit to the group process, you are obligated to offer your skills freely. Don't hold back, perhaps fearing that you will be repeatedly targeted because you have skills to offer. If the group project is worth doing, it is worth your best effort.
- **Decide to behave with the group's good in mind.** You may find it necessary to set aside your personal goals in favor of the group's goals. Decide to keep an open mind and to listen to evidence and arguments objectively. Strive to evaluate information carefully, even though it may contradict your own views or thwart your personal agendas.
- **Make a commitment to fair play.** Group problem solving is a cooperative, not a competitive, event. Decide that you cannot grind your private ax at the expense of the group project.
- **Expect to give and receive a fair hearing.** When you speak, others should give you a fair hearing. You have a right to expect them to listen carefully, provide you with candid feedback, strive to understand what you say, and treat your ideas seriously. Listeners do not have to agree with you, of course. However, all speakers have a right to a fair hearing.

© DMITRY SHIRONOSOV / SHUTTERSTOCK

- **Be willing to take on a participant/analyst role.** As a group member, it is your responsibility to pay attention, evaluate what is happening, analyze what you learn, and help make decisions.
- **As a leader, be ready to model appropriate team behavior.** It is a leader's responsibility to coach team members in skills and teamwork, to acknowledge achievement and effort, to share knowledge, and to periodically remind members of the team's missions and goals.

and respect its privileged information. They should not discuss with outsiders any sensitive issues without permission. In addition, teams have a broader obligation to avoid advocating actions that would endanger members of society at large.

The skills that make you a valuable and ethical team player will serve you well when you run or participate in professional meetings.

Conducting Productive Business and Professional Meetings

As businesses become more team oriented and management becomes more participatory, people are attending more meetings than ever. Despite heavy reliance on e-mail and the growing use of wireless devices to stay connected, meetings are still the most comfortable way to exchange information. However, many meetings are a waste of time. One survey showed that a quarter of U.S. workers would rather go to the dentist than attend a boring meeting.[29] Regardless, meetings are here to stay. Our task, then, is to make them efficient, satisfying, and productive.

Meetings consist of three or more individuals who gather to pool information, solicit feedback, clarify policy, seek consensus, and solve problems. For you, however, meetings have another important purpose. They represent opportunities. Because they are a prime tool for developing staff, they are career-critical. The inability to run an effective meeting can sink a career, warns *The Wall Street Journal*.[30] The head of a leadership training firm echoed this warning when he said, "If you can't orchestrate a meeting, you are of little use to the corporation."[31] At meetings, judgments are formed and careers are made. Therefore, instead of treating meetings as thieves of your valuable time, try to see them as golden opportunities

> Because you can expect to attend many workplace meetings, learn to make them efficient, satisfying, and productive.

to demonstrate your leadership, communication, and problem-solving skills. So that you can make the most of these opportunities, here are techniques for planning and conducting successful meetings. You will also learn how to be a valuable meeting participant.

Before the Meeting

Benjamin Franklin once said, "By failing to prepare, you are preparing to fail."[32] If you are in charge of a meeting, give yourself plenty of preparation time to guarantee the meeting's success. Before the meeting, determine your purpose, decide how and where to meet, organize an agenda, decide who to invite, and prepare the meeting location and materials.

Determining Your Purpose. Before you do anything else, you must decide the purpose of your meeting and whether a meeting is even necessary. No meeting should be called unless the topic is important, can't wait, and requires an exchange of ideas. If the flow of information is strictly one way and no immediate feedback will result, then don't schedule a meeting. For example, if people are merely being advised or informed, send an e-mail, memo, or letter. Leave a telephone or voice mail message, but don't call a costly meeting. Remember, the real expense of a meeting is the lost productivity of all the people attending. To decide whether the purpose of the meeting is valid, it is a good idea to consult the key people who will be attending. Ask them what outcomes are desired and how to achieve them. This consultation also sets a collaborative tone and encourages full participation.

Deciding How and Where to Meet. Once you have determined that a meeting is necessary, you must decide whether to meet face-to-face or virtually. If you decide to meet face-to-face, reserve a meeting room. If you decide to meet virtually, make any necessary advance arrangements for your voice conference, videoconference, or Web conference. These electronic tools were discussed in Chapter 1.

Organizing an Agenda. Prepare an agenda of topics to be discussed during the meeting. Also include any reports or materials that participants should read in advance. For continuing groups, you might also include a copy of the minutes of the previous meeting. To keep meetings productive, limit the number of agenda items. Remember, the narrower the focus, the greater the chances for success. Consider putting items that will be completed quickly near the beginning of the agenda to give the group a sense of accomplishment. Save emotional topics for the end. You should distribute the agenda at least two days in advance of the meeting. A good agenda, as illustrated in Figure 11.5, covers the following information:

- Date and place of meeting
- Start time and end time
- Brief description of each topic, in order of priority, including names of individuals who are responsible for performing some action
- Proposed allotment of time for each topic
- Any premeeting preparation expected of participants

Inviting Participants. The number of meeting participants is determined by the purpose of the meeting, as shown in Figure 11.6. If the meeting purpose is motivational, such as an awards ceremony for sales reps of Mary Kay Cosmetics, then the number of participants is unlimited. But to make decisions, according to studies at 3M Corporation, the best number is five or fewer participants.[33] Ideally, those attending should be people who will make the decision and people with information necessary to make the decision. Also attending should be people who will be responsible for implementing the decision and representatives of groups who will

Call meetings only when necessary, and invite only key people.

OFFICE INSIDER

Effective meetings don't happen by accident; they happen by design.

Before a meeting, pass out a meeting agenda showing topics to be discussed and other information.

Problem-solving meetings should involve five or fewer people.

FIGURE 11.5 Typical Meeting Agenda

AGENDA
Atlantis Global Travel
Staff Meeting
October 13, 200x
1 to 2 p.m.
Conference Room, Fifth Floor

		Person	Proposed Time
I.	Call to order; roll call		
II.	Approval of agenda		
III.	Approval of minutes from previous meeting		
IV.	Committee reports		
	A. Web site update	Kelly	5 minutes
	B. Tour packages	John	10 minutes
V.	Old business		
	A. Equipment maintenance	Doris	5 minutes
	B. Client escrow accounts	Rolla	5 minutes
	C. Internal newsletter	Tasha	5 minutes
VI.	New business		
	A. New accounts	Hung Wei	5 minutes
	B. Pricing policy for trips	Mark	15 minutes
VII.	Announcements		
VIII.	Chair's summary, adjournment		

benefit from the decision. Let's say, for example, that the CEO of rugged sportswear manufacturer Timberland is strongly committed to community service. He wants his company to participate more fully in community service. So he might meet with managers, employee representatives, and community leaders to decide how his employees could volunteer to refurbish a school, build affordable housing, or volunteer at a clinic.[34]

Preparing the Meeting Location and Materials. If you are meeting face-to-face, decide the layout of the room. To maximize collaboration and participation, try to arrange tables and chairs in a circle or a square so that all participants can see one another. Moreover, where you sit at the table or stand in the room signals whether you wish to be in charge or are willing to share leadership.[35] Set up any presentation equipment that will be needed. Make copies of documents that will be handed out during the meeting. Arrange for refreshments.

FIGURE 11.6 Meeting Purpose and Number of Participants

Purpose	Ideal Size
Intensive problem solving	5 or fewer
Problem identification	10 or fewer
Information reviews and presentations	30 or fewer
Motivational	Unlimited

During the Meeting

Meetings can be less boring, more efficient, and more productive if leaders and participants recognize how to get the meeting started, move it along, handle conflict, and deal with dysfunctional participants. Whether you are the meeting leader or a participant, it is important to act professionally during the meeting. Figure 11.7 outlines etiquette tips for both meeting leaders and participants. Following are additional guidelines to adhere to during the meeting to guarantee its success.

Start meetings on time and open with a brief introduction.

Getting the Meeting Started. To avoid wasting time and irritating attendees, always start meetings on time—even if some participants are missing. Waiting for latecomers causes resentment and sets a bad precedent. For the same reasons, don't give a quick recap to anyone who arrives late. At the appointed time, open the meeting by having all participants introduce themselves if necessary. Then continue with a three- to five-minute introduction that includes the following:

- Goal and length of the meeting
- Background of topics or problems
- Possible solutions and constraints
- Tentative agenda
- Ground rules to be followed

Meeting leaders and participants should follow professional meeting etiquette at all times.

A typical set of ground rules might include arriving on time, communicating openly, being supportive, listening carefully, participating fully, confronting conflict frankly, turning off cell phones and pagers, and following the agenda. Participants should also determine how decisions will be made. More formal groups follow parliamentary procedures based on Robert's Rules of Order. After establishing basic ground rules, the leader should ask whether participants agree thus far. The next step is to assign one attendee to take minutes and one to act as a recorder. The recorder stands at a flipchart or whiteboard and lists the main ideas being discussed and agreements reached.

FIGURE 11.7 Etiquette Checklist for Meeting Leaders and Participants

Meeting Participants

✓ Arrive on time and stay until the meeting ends, unless you have made prior arrangements to arrive late or leave early.
✓ Leave the meeting only for breaks and emergencies.
✓ Come to the meeting prepared.
✓ Turn off cell phones and pagers.
✓ Follow the ground rules.
✓ If you are on the agenda as a presenter, do not go over your allotted time.
✓ Do not exhibit nonverbal behavior that suggests you are bored, frustrated, angry, or negative in any way.
✓ Do not interrupt others or cut anyone off.
✓ Make sure your comments, especially negative comments, are about ideas, not people.
✓ Listen carefully to what other meeting participants are saying.
✓ Participate fully.
✓ Do not go off on tangents; be sure that you stick to the topic being discussed.
✓ Do not engage in side conversations.
✓ Clean up after yourself when leaving the meeting.
✓ Complete in a timely manner any follow-up work that you are assigned.

Meeting Leader

✓ Start and end the meeting on time.
✓ Introduce yourself and urge participants to introduce themselves.
✓ Make everyone feel welcome and valued.
✓ Maintain control of the group members and discussion.
✓ Make sure that everyone participates.
✓ Stick to the agenda.
✓ Encourage everyone to follow the ground rules.
✓ Schedule breaks for longer meetings.

While most people know to turn off cell phones at company meetings, some employees show little hesitation in sending text messages during group presentations. Whether one is tapping away sneakily under the table or ripping off full e-mails in plain view, texting during meetings is an inappropriate practice that distracts others and sends a message that the gathering is unimportant. The behavior has reached epidemic proportions, especially among young college graduates. *What can team leaders do to prevent unwanted texting at meetings?*

Moving the Meeting Along.

After the preliminaries, the leader should say as little as possible. Like a talk show host, an effective leader makes "sure that each panel member gets some air time while no one member steals the show."[36] Remember that the purpose of a meeting is to exchange views, not to hear one person, even the leader, do all the talking. If the group has one member who monopolizes, the leader might say, *Thanks, Gary, for that perspective, but please hold your next point while we hear how Rachel would respond to that.* This technique also encourages quieter participants to speak up.

To avoid allowing digressions to sidetrack the group, try generating a "Parking Lot" list. This is a list of important but divergent issues that should be discussed at a later time. Another way to handle digressions is to say, *Look, folks, we're veering off track here. Let's get back to the central issue of ....* It is important to adhere to the agenda and the time schedule. Equally important, when the group seems to have reached a consensus, is to summarize the group's position and check to see whether everyone agrees.

Dealing With Conflict.

Conflict is a normal part of every workplace. Although conflict may cause you to feel awkward and uneasy, conflict is not always negative. In fact, conflict in the workplace can even be desirable. When managed properly, conflict can improve decision making, clarify values, increase group cohesiveness, stimulate creativity, decrease tensions, and reduce dissatisfaction. Unresolved conflict, however, can destroy productivity and seriously reduce morale.

In meetings, conflict typically develops when people feel unheard or misunderstood. If two people are in conflict, the best approach is to encourage each to make a complete case while group members give their full attention. Let each one question the other. Then, the leader should summarize what was said, and the group should offer comments. The group may modify a recommendation or suggest alternatives before reaching consensus on a direction to follow. You will find more suggestions for dealing with conflict in the Communication Workshop, "Five Rules for Resolving Workplace Conflicts," at the end of this chapter.

Keep the meeting moving by avoiding issues that sidetrack the group.

"Wow! This meeting lasted longer than I thought. It appears the year is now 2053."

When a conflict develops between two members, allow each to make a complete case before the group.

Handling Difficult Group Members. When individuals are performing in a dysfunctional role (such as blocking discussion, monopolizing the conversation, attacking other speakers, joking excessively, not paying attention, or withdrawing), they should be handled with care and tact. The following specific techniques can help a meeting leader control some group members and draw others out.[37]

To control dysfunctional behavior, team leaders should establish rules and seat problem people strategically.

- **Lay down the rules in an opening statement.** Give a specific overall summary of topics, time allotment, and expected behavior. Warn that speakers who digress will be interrupted.
- **Seat potentially dysfunctional members strategically.** Experts suggest seating a difficult group member immediately next to the leader. It is easier to control a person in this position. Make sure the person with dysfunctional behavior is not seated in a power point, such as at the end of the table or across from the leader.
- **Avoid direct eye contact.** In American society direct eye contact is a nonverbal signal that encourages talking. Thus, when asking a question of the group, look only at those whom you wish to answer.
- **Assign dysfunctional members specific tasks.** Ask a potentially disruptive person, for example, to be the group recorder.
- **Ask members to speak in a specific order.** Ordering comments creates an artificial, rigid climate and should be done only when absolutely necessary. But such a regimen ensures that everyone gets a chance to participate.
- **Interrupt monopolizers.** If a difficult member dominates a discussion, wait for a pause and then break in. Summarize briefly the previous comments or ask someone else for an opinion.
- **Encourage nontalkers.** Give only positive feedback to the comments of reticent members. Ask them direct questions about which you know they have information or opinions.
- **Give praise and encouragement** to those who seem to need it, including the distracters, the monopolizers, the blockers, and the withdrawn.

Ending the Meeting and Following Up

How do you know when to stop a meeting? Many factors determine when a meeting should be adjourned, including (a) when the original objectives have been accomplished, (b) when the group has reached an impasse, or (c) when the agreed-upon ending time arrives. To show respect for participants, the leader should be sure the meeting stops at the promised time. It may be necessary to table (postpone for another meeting) some unfinished agenda items. Concluding a meeting effectively helps participants recognize what was accomplished so that they feel that the meeting was worthwhile. Effective leaders perform a number of activities in ending a meeting and following up.

End the meeting with a summary of accomplishments and a review of action items; follow up by distributing meeting minutes and reminding participants of their assigned tasks.

Concluding the Meeting. When the agreed-upon stopping time arrives or when the objectives have been met, discussion should stop. The leader should summarize what has been decided and who is going to do what. Deadlines for action items should also be established. It may be necessary to ask people to volunteer to take responsibility for completing action items agreed to in the meeting. No one should leave the meeting without a full understanding of what was accomplished. One effective technique that encourages full participation is "once around the table." Everyone is asked to summarize briefly his or her interpretation of what was decided and what happens next. Of course, this closure technique works best with smaller groups.

An effective leader concludes by asking the group to set a time for the next meeting. The leader should also assure the group that a report will follow and thank participants for attending. Participants should vacate the meeting room once the meeting is over, especially if another group is waiting to enter. The room should be returned to a neat and orderly appearance.

Distributing Minutes. If minutes were taken during the meeting, they should be keyed in an appropriate format. You will find guidelines for preparing meeting minutes in Chapter 9. Minutes should be distributed within a couple of days after the meeting. Send the minutes to all meeting participants and to anyone else who needs to know what was accomplished and discussed during the meeting.

Completing Assigned Tasks. It is the leader's responsibility to see that what was decided at the meeting is accomplished. The leader may need to call people to remind them of their assignments and also to volunteer to help them if necessary. Meeting participants should complete any assigned tasks by the agreed-upon deadline.

Visit www.meguffey.com

- Chapter Review Quiz
- Flash Cards
- Grammar Practice
- PowerPoint Slides
- Personal Language Trainer
- Beat the Clock Quiz

Summing Up and Looking Forward

In this chapter you studied how to practice professional behavior in individual face-to-face settings, on the phone, as well as in teams and meetings. You learned how to use your voice as a communication tool, how to promote positive workplace relations through conversation, and how to give and take constructive criticism on the job. You were given tips on professional telephone, cell phone, and voice mail etiquette, including making and receiving productive telephone calls. You learned about a variety of tools enabling you to participate constructively in professional teams.

Finally, the chapter presented techniques for planning and participating in productive business and professional meetings, both face-to-face and virtual.

The next chapter covers an additional facet of oral communication, that of making business presentations. Learning to speak before groups is important to your career success because you will probably be expected to do so occasionally. You will learn helpful techniques and get practice applying them so that you can control stage fright in making polished presentations.

Critical Thinking

1. Why does ethics professor Douglas Chismar argue that no difference between everyday ethics and etiquette exists in the workplace?

2. Why are professionalism, business etiquette, or soft skills so important in the workplace?

3. Is face-to-face communication always preferable to one-dimensional channels of communication such as e-mail and fax? Why or why not?

4. In what ways can conflict be a positive force in meetings and how should it be addressed?

5. How can business meetings help you advance your career?

Chapter Review

6. Define *soft skills* and the qualities the term describes.

7. Name as many synonyms for professionalism on the job as you can recall after reading this chapter:

8. Name five elements that you control in using your voice as a communication tool.

9. If you are criticized at work, what are nine ways you can respond and benefit professionally?

10. How can business professionals create and maintain positive workplace relations in face-to-face contact?

11. Name six ways callers can practice courteous and responsible cell phone use.

12. Name several reasons companies are using teams.

13. What are some characteristics of effective teams?

14. List ten etiquette guidelines for meeting participants that you feel are most important.

15. List eight tactics that a meeting leader can use in dealing with difficult participants.

Activities and Cases

TEAM

11.1 Researching Definitions and Compiling an Annotated Works-Cited List

The ability to scan articles quickly, summarize them efficiently, and list sources in the correct MLA format will be very useful to you. In your classes and as you continue learning throughout your life, you will need to be a quick study who demonstrates attention to detail. Moreover, frequently you will need to grasp a new subject area or field in a relatively short amount of time. Naturally, research typically starts with definitions of key terms. You have seen that many definitions for *professionalism* exist. Recently, an opportunity to practice your research skills has arisen when your boss was invited to make a presentation to a group of human relations officers. He asked you and a small group of fellow interns to help him find articles about professionalism, soft skills, and other interpersonal qualities.

Your Task. Review activities 10.8 and 10.9 in Chapter 10 and as a team divide your research in such a way that each intern is responsible for one or two search terms, depending on the size of your group. Look for articles with definitions of *professionalism, business etiquette, civility, business ethics, social skills, soft skills,* and *social intelligence.* Find at least three useful articles for each search term. If you get bogged down in your research, consult with a business librarian on campus or report to your instructor. After compiling your findings, as a team present your annotated works cited list in an informational memo report to your boss, Henry Franks.

11.2 Soft Skills: Checking Job Ads
What soft skills do employers request when they list job openings in your field?

Your Task. Check job listings in your field at an online job board. Visit a job board such as Monster, College Recruiter, Career Builder, or Yahoo Top Jobs. Follow the instructions to search job categories and locations. Study many job listings in your field. Then prepare a list of the most frequently requested soft skills in your field. Next to each item on the list, indicate the degree to which you have the skill or trait mentioned. Your instructor may ask you to submit your findings or report to the class. If you are not satisfied with the job selection at any job site, choose another job board.

11.3 Voice Quality
Recording your voice gives you a chance to learn how your voice sounds to others and provides an opportunity to improve its effectiveness. Don't be surprised if you fail to recognize your own voice.

Your Task. Record yourself reading a newspaper or magazine article.

a. If you think your voice sounds a bit high, practice speaking slightly lower.

b. If your voice is low or expressionless, practice speaking slightly louder and with more inflection.

c. Ask a colleague, teacher, or friend to provide feedback on your pronunciation, pitch, volume, rate, and professional tone.

11.4 Surviving a Social Business Function
The idea of attending a social business function provokes anxiety in many businesspeople. What should you talk about? What should you wear? How can you make sure you maintain your professionalism?

Your Task. In groups of two to four, discuss appropriate behavior in four social situations. Decide appropriate attire, suitable topics of conversation, and other etiquette guidelines that you should follow. Present your decisions regarding the following social functions to your instructor in a memo or e-mail message:

a. Company picnic

b. Holiday party

c. Formal dinner

d. Business luncheon

11.5 Delivering and Responding to Criticism
Develop your skills in handling criticism by joining with a partner to role-play critical messages you might deliver and receive on the job.

Your Task. Designate one person "A" and the other "B." A describes the kinds of critical messages she or he is likely to receive on the job and identifies who might deliver them. In Scenario 1, B takes the role of the critic and delivers the criticism in an unskilled manner. A responds using techniques described in this chapter. In Scenario 2, B again is the critic but delivers the criticism using techniques described in this chapter. A responds again. Then A and B reverse roles and repeat Scenarios 1 and 2.

11.6 Discussing Workplace Criticism
In the workplace, criticism is often delivered thoughtlessly.

Your Task. In teams of two or three, describe a time when you were criticized by an untrained superior or colleague. What made the criticism painful? What goal do you think the critic had in mind? How did you feel? How did you respond? Considering techniques discussed in this chapter, how could the critic have improved his or her delivery? How does the delivery technique affect the way a receiver responds to criticism? Your instructor may ask you to submit a memo or e-mail analyzing an experience in which you were criticized.

11.7 Going It Alone or Making It a Team Effort at Timberland
He introduces himself as a New Hampshire bootmaker, but Timberland CEO Jeffrey B. Swartz is much more. Although he heads a fast-rising company that produces boots and sportswear, he is strongly committed to civic responsibility and employee involvement. *Fortune* magazine consistently ranks Timberland as one of the 100 best companies to work for in America. With the zeal of a missionary, the enthusiastic, fast-talking Swartz travels extensively, preaching the power of volunteerism among the 200 Timberland stores and factories.[38]

Your Task. Let's say that you work for Timberland, and Swartz asks you to organize an extensive volunteer program using Timberland employees. The program involves much planning and cooperation to be successful. You are flattered that he respects you and thinks that you are capable of completing the task. But you think that a team could do a better job than an individual. What arguments would you use to convince him that a team could work better than a single person?

11.8 Analyzing a Meeting
You have learned a number of techniques in this chapter for planning and participating in meetings. Here's your chance to put your knowledge to work.

Your Task. Attend a structured meeting of a college, social, business, community, or other organization. Compare the manner in which the meeting is conducted with the suggestions presented in this chapter. Why did the meeting succeed or fail? Prepare a memo for your instructor or be ready to discuss your findings in class.

11.9 Planning a Meeting
Assume that the next meeting of your Associated Students Organization (ASO) will discuss preparations for a job fair in the spring. The group will hear reports from committees working on speakers, business recruiters, publicity, reservations of campus space, setup of booths, and any other matters you can think of.

Your Task. As president of your ASO, prepare an agenda for the meeting. Compose your introductory remarks to open the meeting. Your instructor may ask you to submit these two documents or use them in staging an actual meeting in class.

11.10 Leading a Meeting
Your boss is unhappy at the way some employees lead meetings. Because he knows that you have studied this topic, he asks you to send him a memo or e-mail listing specific points that he can use in an in-house training session in which he plans to present ideas on how to conduct business meetings.

Your Task. Using an electronic database, locate articles providing tips on leading meetings. Three particularly good articles are listed below. Prepare a memo to your boss, Mark Shields, outlining eight or more points on how to lead a meeting. Include at least five tips that are not found in this chapter.

Krattemnaker, T. (2007, December). Make every meeting matter. *Harvard Management Update,* pp. 3–5. Retrieved June 18, 2008, from EBCO database.

Motley, A. (2005, January). Minding your meeting manners. *Association Management,* pp. 39–40. Retrieved June 18, 2008, from ProQuest database.

Olsztynski, J. (2004, October 1). Productive meetings vs. bull sessions. *Roofing Contractor,* p. 14. Retrieved June 18, 2008, from http://www.roofingcontractor.com/CDA/Archives/3437189ac3c58010VgnVCM100000f932a8c0

11.11 Improving Telephone Skills by Role-Playing
Acting out the roles of telephone caller and receiver is an effective technique for improving skills. To give you such practice, your instructor will divide the class into pairs.

Your Task. For each scenario take a moment to read and rehearse your role silently. Then play the role with your partner. If time permits, repeat the scenarios, changing roles.

Partner 1

A. You are the personnel manager of Wireless World, Inc. Call Susan Campbell, office manager at Digitron Corporation. Inquire about a job applicant, Lisa Chung, who listed Ms. Campbell as a reference.

B. Call Ms. Campbell again the following day to inquire about the same job applicant, Lisa Chung. Ms. Campbell answers today, but she talks on and on, describing the applicant in great detail. Tactfully close the conversation.

C. You are now the receptionist for Cyrus Artemis, of Artemis Imports. Answer a call for Mr. Artemis, who is working in another office, at Ext. 2219, where he will accept calls.

D. You are now Cyrus Artemis, owner of Artemis Imports. Call your attorney, Maria Solomon-Williams, about a legal problem. Leave a brief, incomplete message.

E. Call Ms. Solomon-Williams again. Leave a message that will prevent telephone tag.

Partner 2

A. You are the receptionist for Digitron Corporation. The caller asks for Susan Campbell, who is home sick today. You don't know when she will be able to return. Answer the call appropriately.

B. You are now Ms. Campbell, office manager. Describe Lisa Chung, an imaginary employee. Think of someone with whom you have worked. Include many details, such as her ability to work with others, her appearance, her skills at computing, her schooling, her ambition, and so forth.

C. You are now an administrative assistant for attorney Maria Solomon-Williams. Call Cyrus Artemis to verify a meeting date Ms. Solomon-Williams has with Mr. Artemis. Use your own name in identifying yourself.

D. You are now the receptionist for attorney Maria Solomon-Williams. Ms. Solomon-Williams is skiing in Aspen and will return in two days, but she doesn't want her clients to know where she is. Take a message.

E. Reverse roles and take a message again.

11.12 Leaving a Professional Voice Mail Message

Voice mail messages can be very effective communication tools as long as they are professional and easy to respond to.

Your Task. If your instructor allows, call his or her office number after hours or within a specified time frame. Plan what you will say; if needed, jot down a few notes. Leave a professional voice mail message as described in this chapter. Start by introducing yourself by name, then give your telephone number, and finally leave a brief message about something you discussed in class, read in the chapter, or want the instructor know about yourself. Speak slowly, loudly enough, and clearly, so that your instructor won't need to replay your message.

Grammar/Mechanics Checkup 11

Other Punctuation

Although this checkup concentrates on Sections 2.23–2.29 in the Grammar/Mechanics Handbook, you may also refer to other punctuation principles. Insert any necessary punctuation. In the space provided, indicate the number of changes you make and record the number of the G/M principle(s) illustrated. Count each mark separately; for example, a set of parentheses counts as 2. If you make no changes, write *O*. When you finish, compare your responses with those provided at the end of the book. If your responses differ, study carefully the specific principles shown in parentheses.

2   (2.27)   **Example** (De-emphasize.) Several cities chosen by *CNN/Money* as the best places to live in the United States (Alexandria, Chesapeake, Chantilly, and Reston) are in Virginia.

1. (Emphasize.) Employers will typically want to know about four key areas education, experience, hard skills, and soft skills before making you an offer.

2. Will you please Eddie put the report on my desk by five o'clock

3. (De-emphasize.) Sales of durable goods in the first quarter of the year see Figure 5.1 are down sharply.

4. To determine whether to spell Web site as one word or two consult our company style book.

5. Cargill, Koch Industries, and Mars these enterprises are the top three largest private US companies.

6. Warren Buffet said, "Why not invest your assets in companies you really like

7. Have you read The Wall Street Journal article titled Oracle's Ellison Gives $115 Million to Harvard Study

8. (Emphasize.) The biggest wine-producing states California, Washington, and Oregon are all located on the Pacific Coast.

9. Have you received reservations and membership dues from Ms Alice Theodor, Mr Ron P Gill, and Dr Wei Li Chin

10. I enjoyed the chapter titled The Almost Perfect Meeting that appeared in Emily Post's book called The Etiquette Advantage in Business.

11. Donald Trump said, "Generally I like other people to fire, because it is always a lousy task" however he has fired many people himself.

12. Devon described the filthy factory floor as gross.

13. Is the vice president coming in today at 9 a m

14. Wow You have picked up some awesome sales techniques haven't you

15. In business the word speculator may be defined as one who attempts to profit by anticipating price changes.

The following report of meeting minutes has faults in grammar, punctuation, spelling, number form, wordiness, and word use. Use standard proofreading marks (see Appendix B) to correct the errors. When you finish, your instructor can show you the revised version of this summary.

Honolulu-Pacific Federal Interagency Board
Policy Board Committee
Room 25, 310 Ala Moana Boulevard, Honolulu
February 4, 200x

Present: Debra Chinnapongse, Tweet Jackson, Irene Kishita, Barry Knaggs, Kevin Poepoe, and Ralph Mason

Absent: Alex Watanabe

The meeting was call to order by Chair Kevin Poepo at 9:02 a.m. in the morning. Minutes from the January 6th meeting was read and approve.

Old Business

Debra Chinnapongse discussed the cost of the annual awards luncheon. That honors outstanding employees. The ticket price ticket does not cover all the expenses incured. Major expenses include: awards, leis, and complementary lunches for the judges, VIP guests and volunteers. Honolulu-Pacific Federal Interagency Board can not continue to make up the difference between income from tickets and costs for the luncheon. Ms. Chinnapongse reported that it had come to her attention that other interagency boards relied on members contributions for their awards' programs.

MOTION: To send a Letter to board members asking for there contributions to support the annual awards luncheon. (Chinapongse/Kishita). PASSED 6-0.

Reports

Barry Knaggs reported that the homeland defense committee sponsored a get acquainted meeting in November. More than eighty people from various agencys attended.

The Outreach Committee reports that they have been asked to assist the Partnership for Public Service, a non profit main land organization in establishing a speakers bureau of Hawaiian Federal employees. It would be available to speak at schools and colleges about Federal jobs and employment.

New Business

The chair announced a Planning Meeting to be held in March regarding revising the emergency dismissal plan. In other New Business Ralph Mason reported that the staff had purchased fifty tickets for members, and our committees to attend the Zig Ziglar seminar in the month of March.

Next Meeting

The next meeting of the Policy Boare Committee will be held in early Aprl at the Fleet and Industrial Supply Center, Pearl harbor. At that time the meeting will include a tour of the Red Hill under ground fuel storage facility.

The meeting adjourned at 10:25 am by Keven Poepoe.

Respectfully submitted,

Communication Workshop: Career Skills

Five Rules for Resolving Workplace Conflicts

"Conflict is inevitable in a team . . . in fact, to achieve synergistic solutions, a variety of ideas and approaches is needed. These are the ingredients for conflict," says consultant Susan Gerke.[39] Although all workplaces experience conflict from time to time, some people think that workplace conflict is escalating.

Several factors may be tied to increasing problems at work. One factor is our increasingly diverse workforce. Sharing ideas that stem from a variety of backgrounds, experiences, and personalities may lead to better problem solving, but it can also lead to conflict. Another factor related to increased conflict is the trend toward participatory management. In the past only bosses had to resolve problems, but now more employees are making decisions and facing conflict. This is particularly true of teams. Working together harmoniously involves a great deal of give and take, and conflict may result if some people feel that they are being taken advantage of.

Not all conflict is negative or dysfunctional. In fact, conflict can serve a number of healthy functions. In groups, conflict can increase involvement and cohesiveness. When people clash over differing views, they can become more committed to their purpose and to each other. Handled properly, conflict can provide an outlet for hostility and can increase group productivity.[40] The famous piano manufacturer Theodore E. Steinway used the following metaphor to illustrate the benefit of conflict: "In one of our concert grand pianos, 243 taut strings exert a pull of 40,000 pounds on an iron frame. It is proof that out of great tension may come great harmony."[41]

When problems arise in the workplace, it is important for everyone to recognize that conflict is a normal occurrence[42] and that it should be confronted and resolved. Effective conflict resolution requires good listening skills, flexibility, and a willingness to change. Individuals must be willing to truly listen and seek to understand rather than immediately challenge the adversary. In many workplace conflicts, involving a third party to act as a mediator is necessary. Although problems vary greatly, the following five rules offer a good basic process for resolving conflicts.[43]

Five Rules for Resolving Conflict

1. **Set the scene.** Make sure that good relationships are the first priority. Treat the parties involved calmly and try to build mutual respect. Be courteous and remain constructive. Use active listening skills—restate, paraphrase, and summarize—to ensure that you hear and understand other's positions and perceptions.

2. **Keep people and problems separate. Agree on the problem.** Recognize that often the other person is not just "being difficult." Real and valid differences may lurk behind conflicts. Separate the problem from the person to debate real issues without damaging working relationships. Often people perceive problems very differently. You will need to agree on the problem that you are trying to solve before you can find a mutually acceptable solution.

3. **Pay attention to the interests that are being presented.** Try to get to the underlying interests, needs, and concerns. Explore hidden motivations and goals. Is work performance affected? Listen with empathy, use "I" statements, and clarify feelings.

4. **Listen first, talk second.** If you listen carefully, you will most likely understand why the person is adopting his or her position. To solve a problem effectively, you have to understand the other person's position before defending your own.

5. **Explore options together. Brainstorm and negotiate solutions.** Be open to the idea that a third position may exist, and that you can get to this idea jointly. To feel satisfied with the resolution, everyone needs to have fair input in generating solutions.

At this stage, you may better understand the position of the other and a mutually satisfactory solution may be clear to all. However, sometimes you may uncover real and valid differences among the positions. This is where the win–win technique of negotiation can be helpful.

Career Application. As leader of your work team, you were recently confronted by an angry fellow team member. Linda, a story editor on your film production team, is upset because, for the third time in as many weeks, she was forced to give up part of her weekend for work. This time it was for a black-tie affair that everyone in the office tried to duck. Linda is particularly angry with Robert, who should have represented the team at this awards dinner. But he uttered the magic word: *family*. "Robert says he has plans with his family, and it is like a get-out-of-jail-free card," Linda complains to you. "I don't resent him or his devotion to his family. But I do resent it when my team constantly expects me to give up my personal time because I don't have kids. That is my choice, and I don't think I should be punished for it."[44]

Your Task

Using the principles outlined here, work out a conflict resolution plan for Linda and Robert. Your instructor may wish to divide your class into three-person teams to role-play Linda, Robert, and the team leader. Add any details to make a realistic scenario.

- What are the first steps in resolving this conflict?
- What arguments might each side present?
- What alternatives might be offered?
- What do you think is the best solution?
- How could the solution be implemented with the least friction?

Business Presentations

OBJECTIVES

After studying this chapter, you should be able to

● Discuss two important first steps in preparing effective oral presentations.

● Explain the major elements in organizing the content of a presentation, including the introduction, body, and conclusion.

● Identify techniques for gaining audience rapport, including (a) using effective imagery, (b) providing verbal signposts, and (c) sending appropriate nonverbal messages.

● Discuss types of visual aids, including multimedia slides, handouts, overhead transparencies, and speaker's notes.

● Explain how to design an impressive multimedia presentation, including adapting text and color schemes; organizing, composing, and editing your slideshow; rehearsing your talk; and keeping audiences engaged.

● Specify delivery techniques for use before, during, and after a presentation.

Organizations today are increasingly interested in hiring people with good presentation skills. Why? The business world is changing. As you have seen in Chapter 11, technical skills aren't enough to guarantee success. You also need to be able to communicate ideas effectively in presentations to customers, vendors, members of your team, and management. Your presentations will probably be made to inform, influence, or motivate action.

Speaking skills are useful at every career stage. An AT&T and Stanford University study found that the No. 1 predictor of success and upward mobility is how much you enjoy public speaking and how effective you are at it.[1] You might, for example, have to make a sales pitch before customers or speak to a professional gathering. You might need to describe your company's expansion plans to your banker, or you might need to persuade management to support your proposed marketing strategy. Speaking skills rank very high on recruiters' wish lists. As reported in an employer study, 70 percent of executives considered oral communication skills very important for high school graduates entering the job market; 82 percent for two-year college graduates, and a whopping 95 percent for four-year college graduates.[2]

This chapter prepares you to use speaking skills in making effective and professional oral presentations. You will learn what to do before, during, and after your presentation; and how to design effective visual aids and multimedia presentations.

Getting Ready for an Oral Presentation

In getting ready for an oral presentation, you probably feel a great deal of anxiety. For many people the dread of speaking before a group is irrational and paralyzing. Executive coach Aileen Pincus writes that "fear of public speaking ranks No. 1 on the list of people's worst fears, far ahead of even fear of death!"[3]

The good news is that for any presentation, you can reduce your fears and lay the foundation for a professional performance by focusing on five areas: preparation, organization, audience rapport, visual aids, and delivery.

Knowing Your Purpose

The most important part of your preparation is deciding your purpose. What do you want to accomplish? Do you want to sell a health care program to a prospective client? Do you want to persuade management to increase the marketing budget? Do you want to inform customer service reps of three important ways to prevent miscommunication? Do you want to give advice to graduating high school seniors? Whether your goal is to persuade, to inform, or to entertain, you must have a clear idea of where you are going. At the end of your presentation, what do you want your listeners to believe, remember, or do?

Mark Miller, a loan officer at First Fidelity Trust, faced such questions as he planned a talk for a class in small business management. (You can see the outline for his talk in Figure 12.3.) Mark's former business professor had asked him to return to campus and give the class advice about borrowing money from banks in order to start new businesses. Because Mark knew so much about this topic, he found it difficult to extract a specific purpose statement for his presentation. After much thought he narrowed his purpose to this: *To inform potential entrepreneurs about three important factors that loan officers consider before granting start-up loans to launch small businesses.* His entire presentation focused on ensuring that the class members understood and remembered three principal ideas.

Understanding Your Audience

A second key element in preparation is analyzing your audience, anticipating its reactions, and making appropriate adaptations. Audiences may fall into four categories, as summarized in Figure 12.1. By anticipating your audience, you have a better idea of how to organize your presentation. A friendly audience, for example, will respond to humor and personal experiences. A neutral audience requires an even, controlled delivery style. The talk would probably be filled with facts, statistics, and expert opinions. An uninterested audience that is forced to attend requires a brief presentation. Such an audience might respond best to humor, cartoons, colorful visuals, and startling statistics. A hostile audience demands a calm, controlled delivery style with objective data and expert opinion. Whatever type of audience you will have, remember that the most important thing to do is to plan your presentation so that it focuses on audience benefits. The members of your audience will want to know what's in it for them.

Other elements, such as age, gender, education, experience, professional background, and audience size will affect your style and message content. Analyze the following questions to help you determine your organizational pattern, delivery style, and supporting material.

- *How will this topic appeal to this audience?*
- *How can I relate this information to my listeners' needs?*
- *How can I gain credibility and earn respect so that they accept my message?*
- *What would be most effective in making my point? Facts? Statistics? Personal experiences? Expert opinion? Humor? Cartoons? Graphic illustrations? Demonstrations? Case histories? Analogies?*
- *What measures must I take to ensure that this audience remembers my main points?*

Preparing for an oral presentation means identifying your purpose and understanding the audience.

Audience analysis issues include size, age, gender, experience, attitude, and expectations.

FIGURE 12.1 Succeeding With Four Audience Types

Audience Members	Organizational Pattern	Delivery Style	Supporting Material
Friendly			
They like you and your topic.	Use any pattern. Try something new. Involve the audience.	Be warm, pleasant, and open. Use lots of eye contact and smiles.	Include humor, personal examples, and experiences.
Neutral			
They are calm, rational; their minds are made up, but they think they are objective.	Present both sides of the issue. Use pro/con or problem/solution patterns. Save time for audience questions.	Be controlled. Do nothing showy. Use confident, small gestures.	Use facts, statistics, expert opinion, and comparison and contrast. Avoid humor, personal stories, and flashy visuals.
Uninterested			
They have short attention spans; they may be there against their will.	Be brief—no more than three points. Avoid topical and pro/con patterns that seem lengthy to the audience.	Be dynamic and entertaining. Move around. Use large gestures.	Use humor, cartoons, colorful visuals, powerful quotations, and startling statistics.
	Avoid darkening the room, standing motionless, passing out handouts, using boring visuals, or expecting the audience to participate.		
Hostile			
They want to take charge or to ridicule the speaker; they may be defensive, emotional.	Organize using a noncontroversial pattern, such as a topical, chronological, or geographical strategy.	Be calm and controlled. Speak evenly and slowly.	Include objective data and expert opinion. Avoid anecdotes and humor.
	Avoid a question-and-answer period, if possible; otherwise, use a moderator or accept only written questions.		

Organizing Content for a Powerful Impact

Good organization and intentional repetition help your audience understand and retain what you say.

Once you have determined your purpose and analyzed the audience, you are ready to collect information and organize it logically. Good organization and conscious repetition are the two most powerful keys to audience comprehension and retention. In fact, many speech experts recommend the following admittedly repetitious, but effective, plan:

Step 1: Tell them what you are going to say.
Step 2: Say it.
Step 3: Tell them what you have just said.

In other words, repeat your main points in the introduction, body, and conclusion of your presentation. Although it sounds deadly, this strategy works surprisingly well. You will want to keep this strategy in mind as you construct the three parts of a presentation: introduction, body, and conclusion.

Capturing Attention in the Introduction

Attention-grabbing openers include questions, startling facts, jokes, anecdotes, and quotations.

How many times have you heard a speaker begin with, *It is a pleasure to be here, I'm honored to be asked to speak,* or *I'm going to do my presentation on . . . .* Boring openings such as these get speakers off to a dull start. Avoid such banalities by striving to accomplish three goals in the introduction to your presentation:

- Capture listeners' attention and get them involved.
- Identify yourself and establish your credibility.
- Preview your main points.

When the Detroit Symphony Orchestra (DSO) wanted to tout its acclaimed music program for disadvantaged youth, organizers hosted a concert by renowned cellist Yo-Yo Ma and opened the event with a surprise. As the lights dimmed and the audience grew silent, a 4-foot-tall robot named ASIMO took to the stage. The Honda-built humanoid promptly strutted to the conductor's rostrum and led the orchestra in a beautiful rendition of "Impossible Dream," thrilling the crowd while drawing attention to Honda's support of the program. *What attention-grabbing techniques can professional speakers use to captivate audiences and gain their involvement?*

If you are able to appeal to listeners and involve them in your presentation right from the start, you are more likely to hold their attention until the finish. Consider some of the same techniques that you used to open sales letters: a question, a startling fact, a joke, a story, or a quotation. Some speakers achieve involvement by opening with a question or command that requires audience members to raise their hands or stand up. Ten techniques for effectively capturing and maintaining your audience's attention are described in Figure 12.2.

To establish your credibility, you need to describe your position, knowledge, education, or experience—whatever qualifies you to speak. Try also to connect with your audience. Listeners are particularly drawn to speakers who reveal something of themselves and identify with them. A consultant addressing office workers might explain how he started as a temporary worker; a CEO might tell a funny story in which the joke is on herself. Use humor if you can pull it off (not everyone can); self-effacing humor may work best for you.

"Always start your presentation with a joke, but be careful not to offend anyone! Don't mention religion, politics, race, age, money, technology, men, women, children, plants, animals, food...."

The opening scene of Al Gore's film about global warming, *An Inconvenient Truth*, shows the former presidential candidate on stage, slide remote in hand, a giant screen behind him. Thousands of college students in the audience cheer and then wait in silence for the presentation to begin. Al Gore then introduces himself: "Hello, my name is Al Gore, and I used to be the next president of the United States." The audience responds with roaring laughter and applause. The speaker has instantly won his viewers over. He has become likeable and funny by poking fun at himself for ultimately losing the presidency in 2000.[4]

After capturing attention, introducing yourself, and establishing your credibility, you will want to preview the main points of your topic, perhaps with a visual aid. You may wish to put off actually writing your introduction, however, until after you have organized the rest of the presentation and crystallized your principal ideas.

Take a look at Mark Miller's introduction, shown in Figure 12.3, to see how he integrated all the elements necessary for a good opening.

OFFICE INSIDER

Stories and punch lines pack power. Humor anchors key points. Humor makes your message memorable.

Experienced speakers know how to capture the attention of an audience and how to maintain that attention during a presentation. You can give your presentations a boost by trying these proven techniques.

- **A promise.** Begin with a promise that keeps the audience expectant (for example, *By the end of this presentation, you will know how you can increase your sales by 50 percent!*).
- **Drama.** Open by telling an emotionally moving story or by describing a serious problem that involves the audience. Throughout your talk include other dramatic elements, such as a long pause after a key statement. Change your vocal tone or pitch. Professionals use high-intensity emotions such as anger, joy, sadness, and excitement.
- **Eye contact.** As you begin, command attention by surveying the entire audience to take in all listeners. Give yourself two to five seconds to linger on individuals to avoid fleeting, unconvincing eye contact. Don't just sweep the room and the crowd.
- **Movement.** Leave the lectern area whenever possible. Walk around the conference table or down the aisles of your audience. Try to move toward your audience, especially at the beginning and end of your talk.
- **Questions.** Keep listeners active and involved with rhetorical questions. Ask for a show of hands to get each listener thinking. The response will also give you a quick gauge of audience attention.
- **Demonstrations.** Include a member of the audience in a demonstration (for example, *I'm going to show you exactly how to implement our four-step customer courtesy process, but I need a volunteer from the audience to help me*).
- **Samples/props.** If you are promoting a product, consider using items to toss out to the audience or to award as prizes to volunteer participants. You can also pass around product samples or promotional literature. Be careful, though, to maintain control.
- **Visuals.** Give your audience something to look at besides yourself. Use a variety of visual aids in a single session. Also consider writing the concerns expressed by your audience on a flipchart or on the board as you go along.
- **Dress.** Enhance your credibility with your audience by dressing professionally for your presentation. Professional attire will help you look more competent and qualified, which will make your audience more likely to listen to you and take you seriously.
- **Self-interest.** Review your entire presentation to ensure that it meets the critical *What's-in-it-for-me* audience test. Remember that people are most interested in things that benefit them.

Organizing the Body

The best oral presentations focus on a few key ideas.

The biggest problem with most oral presentations is a failure to focus on a few principal ideas. Therefore, the body of your short presentation (20 or fewer minutes) should include a limited number of main points, say, two to four. Develop each main point with adequate, but not excessive, explanation and details. Too many details can obscure the main message, so keep your presentation simple and logical. Remember, listeners have no pages to review should they become confused.

When Mark Miller began planning his presentation, he realized immediately that he could talk for hours on his topic. He also knew that listeners are not good at separating major and minor points. Therefore, instead of drowning his listeners in a sea of information, he sorted out a few main ideas. In the banking industry, loan officers generally ask the following three questions of each applicant for a small business loan: (a) Are you ready to "hit the ground running" in starting your business? (b) Have you done your homework? and (c) Have you made realistic projections of potential sales, cash flow, and equity investment? These questions would become his main points, but Mark wanted to streamline them further so that his audience would be sure to remember them. He capsulized the questions in three words: *experience, preparation*, and *projection*. As you can see in Figure 12.3, Mark prepared a sentence outline showing these three main ideas. Each is supported by examples and explanations.

FIGURE 12.3 Oral Presentation Outline

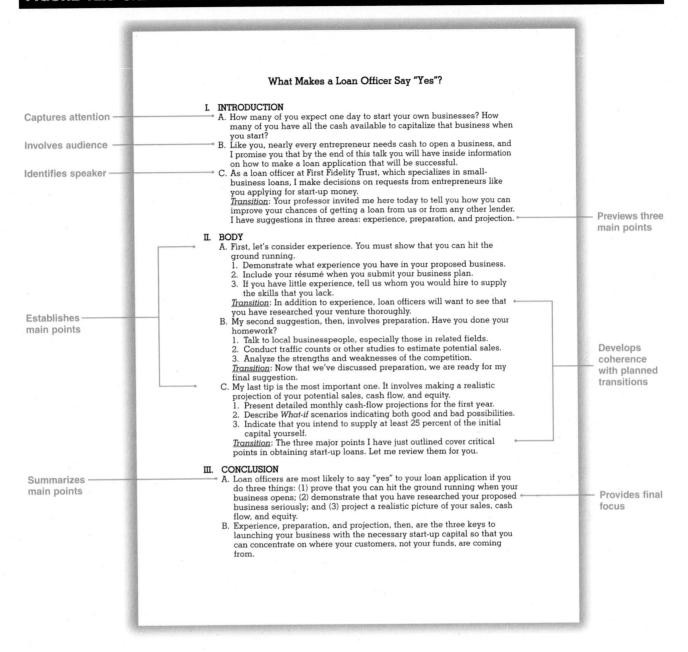

How to organize and sequence main ideas may not be immediately obvious when you begin working on a presentation. The following patterns, which review and amplify the patterns discussed in Chapter 10 (Figure 10.2), provide many possible strategies and examples to help you organize a presentation:

- **Chronology.** Example: A presentation describing the history of a problem, organized from the first sign of trouble to the present.
- **Geography/space.** Example: A presentation about the changing diversity of the workforce, organized by regions in the country (East Coast, West Coast, and so forth).
- **Topic/function/conventional grouping.** Example: A report discussing mishandled airline baggage, organized by names of airlines.
- **Comparison/contrast (pro/con).** Example: A presentation comparing organic farming methods with those of modern industrial farming.

Organize your report by time, geography, function, importance, or some other method that is logical to the receiver.

- **Journalism pattern (the six Ws).** Example: A presentation describing how identity thieves can steal your money and ruin your good name. Organized by *who, what, when, where, why,* and *how.*
- **Value/size.** Example: A presentation describing fluctuations in housing costs, organized by prices of homes.
- **Importance.** Example: A report describing five reasons that a company should move its headquarters to a specific city, organized from the most important reason to the least important.
- **Problem/solution.** Example: A company faces a problem such as declining sales. A solution such as reducing staff is offered.
- **Simple/complex.** Example: A report explaining genetic modification of plants such as corn, organized from simple seed production to complex gene introduction.
- **Best case/worst case.** Example: A report analyzing whether two companies should merge, organized by the best-case results (improved market share, profitability, employee morale) opposed to the worst-case results (devalued stock, lost market share, employee malaise).

In the presentation shown in Figure 12.3, Mark arranged the main points by importance, placing the most important point last where it had maximum effect. When organizing any presentation, prepare a little more material than you think you will actually need. Savvy speakers always have something useful in reserve such as an extra handout, transparency, or idea—just in case they finish early. At the same time, most speakers go about 25 percent over the allotted time as opposed to their practice runs at home in front of the mirror. If your speaking time is limited, as it usually is in your classes, aim for less than the limit when rehearsing, so that you don't take time away from the next presenters.

Summarizing in the Conclusion

Effective conclusions summarize main points and allow the speaker to exit gracefully.

Nervous speakers often rush to wrap up their presentations because they can't wait to flee the stage. But listeners will remember the conclusion more than any part of a speech. That is why you should spend some time to make it most effective. Strive to achieve three goals:

- Summarize the main themes of the presentation.
- Leave the audience with a specific and memorable "take-away."
- Include a statement that allows you to leave the podium gracefully.

When it is time to end your presentation, be careful not to introduce any new material. Anything important should have been included in the body of your presentation. The conclusion is the time to summarize that information, not to bring up new details.

Some speakers end blandly with comments such as *I guess that is about all I have to say* or *That's it.* Such lame statements show little enthusiasm and are not the culmination of the talk that listeners expect. Skilled speakers alert the audience that they are finishing. They use phrases such as, *In conclusion, As I end this presentation,* or, *It is time for me to sum up.* Then they proceed immediately to the conclusion. Audiences become justly irritated with a speaker who announces the conclusion but then talks on for ten more minutes.

A straightforward summary should review major points and focus on what you want the listeners to do, think, or remember. You might say, *In bringing my presentation to a close, I will restate my major purpose . . . ,* or, *In summary, my major purpose has been to . . . . In support of my purpose, I have presented three major points. They are (a) . . . , (b) . . . , and (c) . . . .* Notice how Mark Miller, in the conclusion shown in Figure 12.3, summarized his three main points and provided a final focus to listeners.

If you are promoting a recommendation, you might end as follows: *In order to increase our sales by at least 25 percent, I recommend that we retain Matrixx Marketing to conduct a telemarketing campaign beginning September 1 at a cost* of X dollars. *To complete this recommendation, I suggest that we (a) finance this campaign from our operations budget, (b) develop a persuasive message describing our new product, and (c) name Lisa Beck to oversee the project.* Avoid using phrases such as *I think, I believe,* or *I feel,* which state the obvious and will weaken your presentation.

A conclusion is like a punch line and must be memorable. Think of it as the high point of your presentation, a valuable nugget of information to take away. The valuable nugget of information, or take-away, should tie in with the opening and present a forward-looking idea. Avoid merely rehashing, in the same words, what you said before. Instead, ensure that the audience will take away very specific information or benefits and a positive impression of you and your company. The so-called take-away is the value of the presentation to the audience and the benefit it believes to have received. The tension that you built in the early parts of the talk now culminates in the close.

In your conclusion you might want to use an anecdote, an inspiring quotation, or a statement that ties in the opener and offers a new insight. Whatever you choose, be sure to include a closing thought that indicates you are finished. For example, *This concludes my presentation. After investigating many marketing firms, we are convinced that Matrixx is the best for our purposes. Your authorization of my recommendations will mark the beginning of a very successful campaign for our new product. Thank you.*

Building Rapport Like a Pro

Good speakers are adept at building audience rapport. They form a bond with the audience; they entertain as well as inform. They keep their audience involved throughout the presentation. How do they do it? From observations of successful and unsuccessful speakers, we learn that the good ones use a number of verbal and nonverbal techniques to connect with the audience. Some of their helpful techniques include providing effective imagery, supplying verbal signposts, and using body language strategically.

Effective Imagery
You will lose your audience quickly if your talk is filled with abstractions, generalities, and dry facts. To enliven your presentation and enhance comprehension, try using some of the following techniques. However, beware of exaggeration or distortion. Keep your imagery realistic and credible.

- **Analogies.** A comparison of similar traits between dissimilar things can be effective in explaining and drawing connections. For example, *Product development is similar to the process of conceiving, carrying, and delivering a baby.* Or, *Downsizing or restructuring is similar to an overweight person undergoing a regimen of dieting, habit changing, and exercise.*
- **Metaphors.** A comparison between otherwise dissimilar things without using the words *like* or *as* results in a metaphor. For example, *Our competitor's CEO is a snake when it comes to negotiating,* or, *My desk is a garbage dump.*
- **Similes.** A comparison that includes the words *like* or *as* is a simile. For example, *Our CEO was as angry as a bear with a sore foot when he read the government report.* Or, *The microwave in our lunch room sparked and smoked like Fourth of July fireworks.*
- **Personal anecdotes.** Nothing connects you faster or better with your audience than a good personal story. In a talk about e-mail techniques, you could reveal your own blunders that became painful learning experiences. In a talk to potential investors, the founder of a new ethnic magazine might tell a story about growing up without positive ethnic role models.

> Use analogies, metaphors, similes, personal anecdotes, personalized statistics, and worst- and best-case scenarios instead of dry facts.

- **Personalized statistics.** Although often misused, statistics stay with people—particularly when they relate directly to the audience. A speaker discussing job searching might say, *Look around the room. Only three out of five graduates will find a job immediately after graduation.* If possible, simplify and personalize facts. For example, *The sales of Coca-Cola totaled 2 billion cases last year. That means that every man, woman, and child in the United States consumed six full cases of Coke.*
- **Worst- and best-case scenarios.** Hearing the worst that could happen can be effective in driving home a point. For example, *If we do nothing about our computer backup system now, it is just a matter of time before the entire system crashes and we lose all of our customer contact information. Can you imagine starting from scratch in building all of your customer files again? However, if we fix the system now, we can expand our customer files and actually increase sales at the same time.*

Verbal Signposts

Knowledgeable speakers provide verbal signposts to indicate when they are previewing, summarizing, or switching directions.

Speakers must remember that listeners, unlike readers of a report, cannot control the rate of presentation or flip back through pages to review main points. As a result, listeners get lost easily. Knowledgeable speakers help the audience recognize the organization and main points in an oral message with verbal signposts. They keep listeners on track by including helpful previews, summaries, and transitions, such as these:

- **Previewing**
  The next segment of my talk presents three reasons for . . . .
  Let's now consider two causes of . . . .
- **Summarizing**
  Let me review with you the major problems I have just discussed.
  You see, then, that the most significant factors are . . . .
- **Switching directions**
  Thus far we have talked solely about . . . ; now let's move to . . . .
  I have argued that . . . and . . . , but an alternate view holds that . . . .

You can further improve any oral presentation by including appropriate transitional expressions such as *first, second, next, then, therefore, moreover, on the other hand, on the contrary,* and *in conclusion.* These transitional expressions build coherence, lend emphasis, and tell listeners where you are headed. Notice in Mark Miller's outline, in Figure 12.3 on page 341, the specific transitional elements designed to help listeners recognize each new principal point.

Nonverbal Messages

Your appearance, movement, and speech affect the success of your presentation.

Although what you say is most important, the nonverbal messages you send can also have a powerful effect on how well your message is received. How you look, how you move, and how you speak can make or break your presentation. The following suggestions focus on nonverbal tips to ensure that your verbal message is well received.

- **Look terrific!** Like it or not, you will be judged by your appearance. For everything but small in-house presentations, be sure to dress professionally. The rule of thumb is that you should dress at least as well as the best-dressed person in the audience. However, even if you know that your audience will be dressed casually, showing up in professional attire will help you build credibility. You will feel better about yourself too!
- **Animate your body.** Be enthusiastic and let your body show it. Stand with good posture to show confidence. Emphasize ideas to enhance points about size, number, and direction. Use a variety of gestures, but don't consciously plan them in advance.

- **Speak extemporaneously.** Do not read from notes or a manuscript, but speak freely. Use your presentation slides to guide your talk. You will come across as more competent and enthusiastic if you are not glued to your notes or manuscript. Use note cards or a paper outline only when presenting without an electronic slideshow.
- **Punctuate your words.** You can keep your audience interested by varying your tone, volume, pitch, and pace. Use pauses before and after important points. Allow the audience to take in your ideas.
- **Use appropriate eye contact.** Maintaining eye contact with your audience shows that you are confident and prepared. In addition, looking at audience members, rather than looking at your notes or your computer screen, helps them feel more involved.
- **Get out from behind the podium.** Avoid being planted behind the podium. Movement makes you look natural and comfortable and helps you connect more with your audience. You might pick a few places in the room to walk to. Even if you must stay close to your visual aids, make a point of leaving them occasionally so that the audience can see your whole body.
- **Vary your facial expression.** Begin with a smile, but change your expressions to correspond with the thoughts you are voicing. You can shake your head to show disagreement, roll your eyes to show disdain, look heavenward for guidance, or wrinkle your brow to show concern or dismay. To see how speakers convey meaning without words, mute the sound on your TV and watch the facial expressions of a talk show personality, newscaster, or politician.

Whenever possible, beginning presenters should have an experienced speaker watch them and give them tips as they rehearse. Your instructor is an important coach who can provide invaluable feedback. In the absence of helpers, try to tape yourself and watch for your nonverbal behavior on camera.

Planning Visual Aids

Before you make a business presentation, consider this wise Chinese proverb: "Tell me, I forget. Show me, I remember. Involve me, I understand." Your goals as a speaker are to make listeners understand, remember, and act on your ideas. To get them interested and involved, include effective visual aids. Some experts say that we acquire as much as 85 percent of all our knowledge visually. Therefore, an oral presentation that incorporates visual aids is far more likely to be understood and retained than one lacking visual enhancement.

Good visual aids have many purposes. They emphasize and clarify main points, thus improving comprehension and retention. They increase audience interest, and they make the presenter appear more professional, better prepared, and more persuasive. Furthermore, research shows that the use of visual aids may shorten meetings.[5] Visual aids are particularly helpful for inexperienced speakers because the audience concentrates on the aid rather than on the speaker. However, experienced speakers work hard at not being eclipsed or upstaged by their slideshows. Good visuals also serve to jog the memory of a speaker, thus improving self-confidence, poise, and delivery.

Visual aids clarify points, improve comprehension, and aid retention.

Types of Visual Aids

Fortunately for today's speakers, many forms of visual media are available to enhance a presentation. When deciding what types of visual aids to include in your presentation, you should consider the cost, the ease of preparation, the degree of formality desired, and the potential effectiveness. Figure 12.4 describes the pros and cons of a number of visual aids and can guide you in selecting the best visual aid for any speaking occasion. Four popular visuals are multimedia slides, overhead transparencies, handouts, and speaker's notes.

FIGURE 12.4 Pros and Cons of Visual Aid Options

Medium	Pros	Cons
Multimedia slides	Create professional appearance with many color, art, graphic, and font options. Easy to use and transport via removable storage media, Web download, or e-mail attachment. Inexpensive to update.	Present potential incompatibility issues. Require costly projection equipment and practice for smooth delivery. Tempt user to include razzle-dazzle features that may fail to add value.
Transparencies	Give professional appearance with little practice. Easy to (a) prepare, (b) update and maintain, (c) locate reliable equipment, and (d) limit information shown at one time.	Appear to some as an outdated presentation method. Hold speaker captive to the machine. Provide poor reproduction of photos and some graphics.
Handouts or speaker's notes	Encourage audience participation. Easy to maintain and update. Enhance recall because audience keeps reference material.	Increase risk of unauthorized duplication of speaker's material. Can be difficult to transport. May cause speaker to lose audience's attention.
Flipcharts or whiteboards	Provide inexpensive option available at most sites. Easy to (a) create, (b) modify or customize on the spot, (c) record comments from the audience, and (d) combine with more high-tech visuals in the same presentation.	Require graphics talent. Difficult for larger audiences to see. Prepared flipcharts are cumbersome to transport and easily worn with use.
Video	Gives an accurate representation of the content; strong indication of forethought and preparation.	Creates potential for compatibility issues related to computer video formats. Expensive to create and update.
Props	Offer a realistic reinforcement of message content. Increase audience participation with close observation.	Lead to extra work and expense in transporting and replacing worn objects. Limited use with larger audiences.

Multimedia Slides. With today's excellent software programs—such as Microsoft PowerPoint, Apple Keynote, Lotus Freelance Graphics, Corel Presentations, and Adobe Presenter or Adobe Ovation—you can create dynamic, colorful presentations with your PC or Mac. The output from these programs is generally shown on a computer monitor, a TV monitor, an LCD (liquid crystal display) panel, or a screen. With a little expertise and advanced equipment, you can create a multimedia presentation that includes stereo sound, videos, and hyperlinks, as described shortly in the discussion of multimedia presentations. Multimedia slides can also be uploaded to a Web site or broadcast live over the Internet.

Overhead Transparencies. Student and professional speakers alike still rely on the overhead projector for many reasons. Most meeting areas are equipped with projectors and screens. Moreover, acetate transparencies for the overhead are cheap, effortlessly prepared on a computer or copier, and simple to use. What's more, because rooms need not be darkened, a speaker using transparencies can maintain eye contact with the audience. Many experienced speakers create overhead slides in addition to their electronic slideshows to have a backup plan in the case of malfunctioning presentation technology. A word of caution, though: stand to the side of the projector so that you don't obstruct the audience's view. Also make sure that the information on your transparencies can be seen by all audience members.

Handouts. You can enhance and complement your presentations by distributing pictures, outlines, brochures, articles, charts, summaries, or other supplements. Speakers who use multimedia presentation software often prepare handouts that have images of their slides along with notes to distribute to viewers. Timing the distribution of any handout, though, is tricky. If given out during a presentation, your handouts tend to distract the audience, causing you to lose control. Therefore, you should discuss handouts during the presentation but delay distributing them until after you finish. If you plan to give your audience handouts at the end, tell them near the beginning of the presentation.

To maintain control, distribute handouts after you finish speaking.

Speaker's Notes. You have a variety of options for printing hard-copy versions of your presentation. You can, for example, make speaker's notes that are a wonderful aid for practicing your talk. Beneath the miniature image of each slide is space for you to key in your supporting comments for the abbreviated material in your slides. You can also include up to nine miniature versions of your slides per printed page. These miniatures are handy if you want to preview your talk to a sponsoring organization or if you want to supply the audience with a summary of your presentation. However, resist the temptation to read from your notes during the slide presentation. It might turn off your audience and make you appear insecure and incompetent.

Designing an Impressive Multimedia Presentation

Few businesspeople would want to live without the razzle-dazzle of colorful images to make their point. Electronic slideshows, PowerPoint in particular, have become a staple of business presentations. However, overuse or misuse may be the downside of the ever-present multimedia slideshow. Over the two decades of the software program's existence, millions of poorly created and badly delivered PowerPoint presentations have tarnished PowerPoint's reputation as an effective communication tool. Tools are helpful only when used properly.

Microsoft PowerPoint has become the business standard for presenting, defending, and selling ideas.

Imagine those who sit through the more than 30 million PowerPoint presentations that Microsoft estimates are made each day.[6] No doubt, many of them would say this "disease" has reached epidemic proportions. PowerPoint, say its detractors, dictates the way information is structured and presented. They say that the program is turning the nation's businesspeople into a "mindless gaggle of bullet-pointed morons."[7] If you looked up *death by PowerPoint* in your favorite search engine, you would score about 120,000 hits. However, text-laden, amateurish slides that distract and bore audiences are the fault of their creator and not the software program itself.

Critics say that PowerPoint is too rigid and produces "bullet-pointed morons."

In the sections that follow, you will learn to create an impressive multimedia presentation using the most widely used presentation software program, PowerPoint. With any software program, of course, gaining expertise requires your investment

Although videoconferencing, Web seminars, and other virtual-meeting platforms can make business presentations more stimulating and cost-effective, failure to manage these tools may lead to embarrassing career blunders. In one instance, a business executive delivering a virtual presentation became flummoxed when the words "I love you teddy bear" appeared unexpectedly on the computer screen. The instant message, which a love interest had transmitted during the meeting, was visible to all attendees, earning the executive the nickname Teddy Bear. *What precautions should communicators take to ensure the smooth delivery of multimedia presentations?*

of time and effort. You could take a course or you could teach yourself through an online tutorial such as that at **http://office.microsoft.com/en-us/training/default.aspx**. Another way to master PowerPoint is to read a book such as Faithe Wempen's *PowerPoint 2007 Bible*. If operated by a proficient slide preparer and a skillful presenter, PowerPoint can add a distinct visual impact to any presentation.

Preparing a Visually Appealing PowerPoint Presentation

Some presenters prefer to create their slides first and then develop the narrative around their slides. Others prepare their content first and then create the visual component. The risk associated with the first approach is that you may be tempted to spend too much time making your slides look good and not enough time preparing your content. Remember that great-looking slides never compensate for thin content. In the following discussion, you will learn how to adjust the content and design of your slides to the situation or purpose and your audience. You will also receive detailed how-to instructions for composing a PowerPoint slideshow.

Analyzing the Situation and Purpose. Making the best content and design choices for your slides depends greatly on your analysis of the presentation situation and the purpose of your slideshow. Will your slides be used during a live presentation? Will they be part of a self-running presentation such as in a store kiosk? Will they be saved on a server so that those with Internet access can watch the presentation at their convenience? Will they be sent as a PowerPoint slideshow or a PDF document—also sometimes called a *deck*—to a client instead of a hardcopy report? Are you converting PowerPoint slideshows for viewing on video iPods or BlackBerry devices?

If you are e-mailing the presentation or posting it online as a self-contained file, the slides will typically feature more text than if they were delivered orally. If, on the other hand, you are creating slides for a live presentation, your analysis will include answering questions such as these: *Should I prepare speaker's notes pages for my own use during the presentation? Should I distribute hard copies of my slides to my audience?*

GLASBERGEN

"My presentation lacks power and it has no point. I assumed the software would take care of that!"

Anticipating Your Audience. Think about how you can design your presentation to get the most positive response from your audience. Audiences respond, for example, to the colors you use. Slide backgrounds for business presentations should be in bold colors such as blue, green, and purple. Because the messages that colors convey can vary from culture to culture, colors must be chosen carefully. In the United States blue is the color of credibility, tranquility, conservatism, and trust. Therefore, it is the background color of choice for many business presentations. Green relates to interaction, growth, money, and stability. It can work well as a background or an accent color. Purple can be used as a background or accent color. It conveys spirituality, royalty, dreams, and humor.[8] As for slide text, adjust the color so it provides high contrast and is readable. White or yellow, for example, usually works well on dark backgrounds.

Just as you anticipate audience members' reactions to color, you can usually anticipate their reactions to special effects. Using animation and sound effects—flying objects, swirling text, clashing cymbals, and the like—only because they are available is not a good idea. Special effects distract your audience, drawing attention away from your main points. Add animation features only if doing so helps convey your message or adds interest to the content. When your audience members leave, they should be commenting on the ideas you conveyed—not the cool swivels and sound effects.

Adapting Text and Color Selections. Adapt the amount of text on your slide to how your audience will use the slides. As a general guideline, most graphic designers encourage the 6-x-6 rule: "Six bullets per screen, max; six words per bullet, max."[9] You may find, however, that breaking this rule is sometimes necessary, particularly when your users will be viewing the presentation on their own with no speaker assistance.

Adjust the colors based on where the presentation will be given. Use light text on a dark background for presentations in darkened rooms. Use dark text on a light background for presentations in lighted rooms. Avoid using a dark font on a dark background, such as red text on a dark blue background. In the same way, avoid using a light font on a light background, such as white text on a pale blue background. Dark on dark or light on light results in low contrast, making the slides difficult to read.

> Follow the 6-x-6 rule and select background and text colors based on the lightness of the room.

Organizing Your Slides. When you prepare your slides, translate the major headings in your presentation outline into titles for slides. Then build bullet points using short phrases. In Chapter 4 you learned to improve readability by using graphic highlighting techniques, including bullets, numbers, and headings. In preparing a PowerPoint presentation, you will use those same techniques.

The slides you create to accompany your spoken ideas can be organized with visual elements that will help your audience understand and remember what you want to communicate. Let's say, for example, that you have three points in your presentation. You can create a blueprint slide that captures the three points in a visually appealing way, and then you can use that slide several times throughout your presentation. Near the beginning, the blueprint slide provides an overview of your points. Later, it will provide transitions as you move from point to point. For transitions, you can direct your audience's attention by highlighting the next point you will be talking about. Finally, the blueprint slide can be used near the end to provide a review of your key points.

Composing Your Slideshow. All presentation programs require you to (a) select or create a template that will serve as the background for your presentation and (b) make each individual slide by selecting a layout that best conveys your message. You can use one of the templates provided with your presentation software program, download one from many Web sites, or create one from scratch.

Novice and even advanced users choose existing templates because they are designed by professionals who know how to combine harmonious colors, borders, bullet styles, and fonts for pleasing visual effects. If you prefer, you can alter existing templates so they better suit your needs. Adding a corporate logo, adjusting the color scheme to better match the colors used on your organization's Web site, and selecting a different font are just some of the ways you can customize existing templates.

Be careful, though, of what one expert labels "visual clichés."[10] Overused templates and even clip art that ship with PowerPoint can weary viewers who have seen them repeatedly in presentations. Instead of using a standard template, search for *PowerPoint template* in your favorite search engine. You will see hundreds of template options available as free downloads. Unless your employer requires that presentations all have the same look, your audience will most likely appreciate fresh templates that complement the purpose of your presentation and provide visual variety.

Figure 12.5 illustrates some of the many layout and design options for creating your slides. You can alter layouts by repositioning, resizing, or changing the fonts for the placeholders in which your title, bulleted list, organization chart, video clip, photograph, or other elements appear. As Figure 12.5 shows, you can experiment with graphic elements that will enhance your presentation by making your slides visually more appealing and memorable. Try to avoid long, boring bulleted lists.

If you look more closely at Figure 12.5, you will notice that the bulleted items on the first slide are not parallel. The slide looks as if the author had been brainstorming or freewriting a first draft. The second and sixth bullet points express the same thought, that shopping online is convenient and easy for customers. Some bullet points are too long. As opposed to that, the bullets on the improved slide are very short, well within the 6-x-6 rule, although they are complete sentences. The photograph in the revised slide adds interest and illustrates the point. You may use stock photos that you can download from the Web for personal or school use without penalty, or consider taking your own pictures if you own a digital camera.

Figure 12.6 shows how to add variety and pizzazz to your slides. Notice that the same information that appeared as bullet points in Figure 12.5 now appears as exciting spokes radiating from the central idea: *Why you should sell online*. This spoke

FIGURE 12.5 Revising and Enhancing Slides for Greater Impact

Before Revision

After Revision

Reasons for Selling Online

- Your online business can grow globally.
- Customer convenience.
- Conduct business 24/7.
- No need for renting a retail store or hiring employees.
- Reduce inquiries by providing policies and a privacy statement.
- Customers can buy quickly and easily.

Why You Should Sell Online

- Grow your business globally.
- Provide convenience for customers.
- Conduct business 24/7.
- Save on rent and hiring.
- Provide policies to reduce inquiries.

The slide on the left contains bullet points that are not parallel and that overlap meaning. The second and sixth bullet points say the same thing. Moreover, some bullet points are too long. After revision, the slide on the right has a more convincing title illustrating the "you" view. The bullet points are shorter, and each begins with a verb for parallelism. The photo adds interest. Note that the revised slide features a more lively and readable color scheme, starting with the title.

Chapter 12: Business Presentations

FIGURE 12.6 Converting a Bulleted Slide into an Animated Diagram

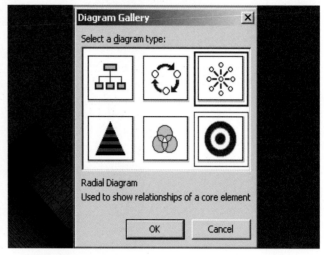

The same content that appears in the Figure 12.5 slides takes on a totally different look when arranged as spokes radiating from a central idea. When presenting this slide, you can animate each item and control its appearance, further enlivening your presentation. PowerPoint provides a Diagram Gallery with six choices for arranging information.

diagram is just one of six common diagram possibilities available in PowerPoint's **Diagram Gallery**. You can also animate each item in the diagram. Occasionally, try to convert pure text and bullet points to diagrams, charts, and other images to add punch to your slideshow. You will keep your audiences interested and help them retain the information you are presenting.

Numeric information is more easily grasped in charts or graphs than in a listing of numbers. Moreover, in most programs, you can animate your graphs and charts. Say, for instance, you have four columns in your bar chart. You can control the entry of each column by determining in what order and how each column appears on the screen. The goal is to use animation strategically to introduce elements of the presentation as they unfold in your spoken remarks. Figure 12.7 shows how a chart can be used to illustrate a concept discussed in the presentation about selling online.

> **Use animation to introduce elements of a presentation as they unfold in your spoken remarks.**

During this composition stage many users fall into the trap of excessive formatting and programming. They fritter away precious time fine-tuning their slides and don't spend enough time on what they are going to say and how they will say it. To avoid this trap, set a limit for how much time you will spend making your slides visually appealing. Your time limit will be based on how many "bells and whistles" (a) your audience expects and (b) your content requires to make it understandable. Remember that not every point nor every thought requires a visual. In fact, it is smart to switch off the slides occasionally and direct the focus to yourself. Darkening the screen while you discuss a point, tell a story, give an example, or involve the audience will add variety to your presentation.

Create a slide only if the slide accomplishes at least one of the following purposes:

- Generates interest in what you are saying and helps the audience follow your ideas
- Highlights points you want your audience to remember
- Introduces or reviews your key points
- Provides a transition from one major point to the next
- Illustrates and simplifies complex ideas

In a later section of this chapter you will find very specific steps to follow as you create your presentation.

FIGURE 12.7 Using a Bar Chart (Column Chart) to Illustrate a Concept

This slide was created using PowerPoint's *Insert, Chart* function. The information presented here is more exciting and easier to comprehend than if it had been presented in a bulleted list.

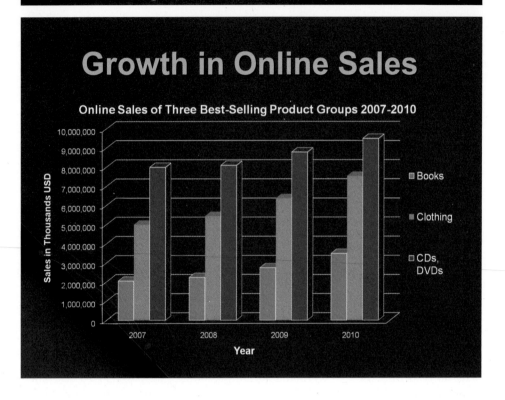

Growth in Online Sales

Online Sales of Three Best-Selling Product Groups 2007-2010

Revising, Proofreading, and Evaluating Your Slideshow. Use PowerPoint's **Slide Sorter View** to rearrange, insert, and delete slides during the revision process. This is the time when you will focus on making your presentation as clear and concise as possible. If you are listing items, be sure that all items use parallel grammatical form. Figure 12.8 shows how to revise a slide to improve it for conciseness, parallelism, and other features. Study the design tips described in

FIGURE 12.8 Designing More Effective Slides

Before Revision

DESIGN TIPS FOR SLIDE TEXT

1. STRIVE TO HAVE NO MORE THAN SIX BULLETS PER SLIDE AND NO MORE THAN SIX WORDS PER BULLET.
2. IF YOU USE UPPER- AND LOWERCASE TYPE, IT IS EASIER TO READ
3. IT IS BETTER TO USE PHRASES RATHER THAN SENTENCES.
4. USING A SIMPLE, HIGH-CONTRAST TYPE FACE IS EASIER TO READ AND DOES NOT DETRACT FROM YOUR PRESENTATION
5. BE CONSISTENT IN YOUR SPACING, CAPITALIZATION, AND PUNCTUATION.

After Revision

Design Tips for Slide Text

- Limit: 6 bullets per slide
- Limit: 6 words per bullet
- Upper- and lowercase type
- Concise phrases, not sentences
- Simple type face
- Consistent spacing, capitalization, and punctuation

The slide on the left is difficult to read and understand because it violates many slide-making rules. How many violations can you detect? The slide on the right illustrates an improved version of the same information. Which slide do you think viewers would rather read?

the first slide and determine which suggestions were not followed. Then compare it with the revised slide.

Notice that both slides in Figure 12.8 feature a blue background. This calming color is the color of choice for most business presentations. However, the background swirls on the first slide look distracting. In addition, the uppercase white font is hard to read and contributes to making the image look busy. Inserting a transparent overlay and choosing a dark font to mute the distracting waves create a cleaner-looking slide.

As you are revising, check carefully to find spelling, grammar, punctuation, and other errors. Use the PowerPoint spell check, but don't rely on it without careful proofing, preferably from a printed copy of the slideshow. Nothing is as embarrassing as projecting errors on a huge screen in front of your audience. Also check for consistency in how you capitalize and punctuate points throughout the presentation.

Finally, critically evaluate your slideshow. Consider whether you have done all you can to use the tools PowerPoint provides to communicate your message in a visually appealing way. In addition, test your slides on the equipment and in the room you will be using during your presentation. Do the colors you selected work in this new setting? Are the font styles and sizes readable from the back of the room? Figure 12.9 shows examples of slides that incorporate what you have learned in this discussion.

FIGURE 12.9 PowerPoint Slides That Summarize and Illustrate Multimedia Presentations

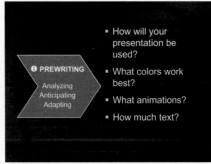

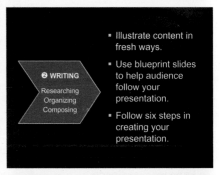

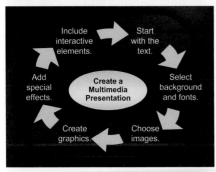

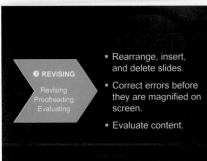

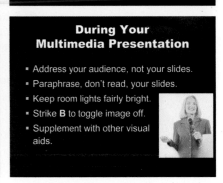

The dark purple background and the green and blue hues in the slideshow shown in Figure 12.9 are standard choices for many business presentations. With an unobtrusive dark background, white fonts are a good option for maximum contrast and, hence, readability. The creator of the presentation varied the slide design to break the monotony of bulleted or numbered lists. Images and animated diagrams add interest and zing to the slides.

Using PowerPoint Effectively With Your Audience

Many promising presentations have been sabotaged by technology glitches or by the presenter's unfamiliarity with the equipment. Fabulous slides are of value only if you can manage the technology expertly. Apple CEO Steve Jobs is famous for his ability to wow his audiences during his keynote addresses. A *BusinessWeek* cover story described his approach: "Jobs unveils Apple's latest products as if he were a particularly hip and plugged-in friend showing off inventions in your living room. Truth is, the sense of informality comes only after grueling hours of practice."[11] At one of his recent Macworld rehearsals, for example, he spent more than four hours on stage practicing and reviewing every technical and performance aspect of his product launch.

Practicing and Preparing

Allow plenty of time before your presentation to set up and test your equipment.[12] Confirm that the places you plan to stand are not in the line of the projected image. Audience members don't appreciate having part of the slide displayed on your body. Make sure that all video or Web links are working and that you know how to operate all features the first time you try. No matter how much time you put into preshow setup and testing, you still have no guarantee that all will go smoothly. Therefore, you should always bring backups of your presentation. Overhead transparencies or handouts of your presentation provide good substitutes. Transferring your presentation to a CD or a USB flash drive that could run from any available notebook might prove useful as well.

Keeping Your Audience Engaged

In addition to using the technology to enhance and enrich your message, here are additional tips for performing like a professional and keeping the audience engaged:

- Know your material, so you are free to look at your audience and to gaze at the screen, not your practice notes. Maintain genuine eye contact to connect with individuals in the room.
- As you show new elements on a slide, allow the audience time to absorb the information. Then paraphrase and elaborate on what the listeners have seen. Don't insult your audience's intelligence by reading verbatim from a slide.
- Leave the lights as bright as you can. Make sure the audience can see your face and eyes.
- Use a radio remote control (not infrared) so you can move freely rather than remain tethered to your computer. Radio remotes will allow you to be up to 50 feet away from your laptop.
- Maintain a connection with the audience by using a laser pointer to highlight slide items to discuss. Be aware, however, that a dancing laser point in a shaky hand may make you appear nervous. Steady your hand.
- Don't leave a slide on the screen when you are no longer discussing it. In **Slide Show, View Show** mode, strike *B* on the keyboard to turn on or off the screen image by blackening it. Pressing *W* will turn the screen white.

Some presenters allow their PowerPoint slides to steal their thunder. One expert urges speakers to "use their PowerPresence in preference to their PowerPoint."[13] Although multimedia presentations supply terrific sizzle, they cannot replace the steak. In developing a presentation, don't expect your slides to carry the show. You can avoid being upstaged by not relying totally on your slides. Help the audience visualize your points by using other techniques. For example, drawing a diagram on a whiteboard or flipchart can be more engaging than showing slide after slide of static drawings. Demonstrating or displaying real objects or props is a welcome relief from slides. Remember that slides should be used only to help your audience understand the message and to add interest. You are still the main attraction!

Eight Steps to Making a Powerful Multimedia Presentation

We have now discussed many suggestions for making effective PowerPoint presentations, but you may still be wondering how to put it all together. Here is a step-by-step process for creating a powerful multimedia presentation:

1. **Start with the text.** The text is the foundation of your presentation. Express your ideas using words that are clear, concise, and understandable. Once the entire content of your presentation is in place, you are ready to begin adding color and all the other elements that will make your slides visually appealing.

2. **Select background and fonts.** Select a template that will provide consistent font styles, font sizes, and a background for your slides. You can create your own template or use one included with PowerPoint. You can also download free templates or pay for templates from many online sites. You can't go wrong selecting a basic template design with an easy-to-read font, such as Times New Roman or Arial. As a general rule, use no more than two font styles in your presentation. The point size should be between 24 and 36. Title fonts should be larger than text font. The more you use PowerPoint and find out what works and doesn't work, the more you can experiment with bolder, more innovative background and font options that effectively convey your message.

3. **Choose images that help communicate your message.** Images, such as clip art, photographs, and maps, should complement the text. Never use an image that is not immediately relevant. Microsoft Office Online is accessed in PowerPoint and contains thousands of clip art images and photographs, most of which are in the public domain and require no copyright permissions. Before using images from other sources, determine whether permission from the copyright holder is required. Bear in mind that some people consider clip art amateurish, so photographs are usually preferable. In addition, clip art is available to any user, so it tends to become stale fast.

4. **Create graphics.** PowerPoint includes a variety of tools to help you simplify complex information or to transform a boring bulleted list into a visually appealing graphic. You can use PowerPoint's **Draw** and **AutoShapes** tools to create a time line or a flowchart. The **Diagram Gallery** will help you create an organization chart or a cycle, radial, pyramid, Venn, or target diagram as well as over a dozen chart types including line, pie, and bar charts. All of these tools require practice before you can create effective graphics. Remember that graphics should be easy to understand without overloading your audience with unnecessary details or too much text. In fact, consider putting such details in handouts rather than cluttering your slides with them.

5. **Add special effects.** To keep your audience focused on what you are discussing, use PowerPoint's **Custom Animation** feature to control when objects or text appear on the screen. Animate points in a bulleted list to appear one at a time, for example, or the boxes in a radial diagram to appear as each is discussed. Keep in mind that the first thing your audience sees on every slide should describe the slide's content. With motion paths and other animation options, you can move objects to various positions on the slide; or to minimize clutter, you can dim or remove them once they have served their purpose.

   In addition, as you move from slide to slide in a presentation, you can select transition effects, such as *wipe down*. The animation and transition options range from subtle to flashy—choose them with care so that the visual delivery of

For a powerful presentation, first write the text, and then work on templates, font styles, and colors.

Learn to simplify complex information in visually appealing graphics.

your presentation doesn't distract from the content of your message. An option at this step is to purchase a PowerPoint add-in product, such as *Ovation*, that can add professional-looking special effects to your presentation with very little effort.[14]

6. **Create hyperlinks to approximate the Web browsing experience.** Make your presentation more interactive and intriguing by connecting your PowerPoint presentation, via hyperlinks, to other sources that provide content that will enhance your presentation. You can hyperlink to (a) other slides within the presentation or in other PowerPoint files; (b) other programs that will open a second window that displays items such as spreadsheets, documents or videos; and (c) if you have an Internet connection, Web sites.

   Once you have finished discussing the hyperlinked source or watching the video that opened in a second window, close that window and your hyperlinked PowerPoint slide is in view. In this way, you can break up the monotony of typical linear PowerPoint presentations. Instead, your hyperlinked show approximates the viewing experience of a Web user who enters a site through a main page or portal and then navigates at will to reach second- and third-level pages.

7. **Engage your audience by asking for interaction.** When audience response and feedback are needed, interactive tools are useful. Audience response systems may be familiar to you from game shows, but they are also used for surveys and opinion polls, group decision making, voting, quizzes and tests, and many other applications. To interact with your audience, present polling questions. Audience members submit their individual or team responses using handheld devices read by a PowerPoint add-in program. The audience immediately sees a bar chart that displays the response results. If you would like to know more about audience response systems, visit one of the many Web sites devoted to them, for example, **http://www.audienceresponse.com** or **http://www.turningtechnologies.com**.

8. **Move your presentation to the Internet.** You have a range of alternatives, from simple to complex, for moving your multimedia presentation to the Internet or your company's intranet. The simplest option is posting your slides online for others to access. Even if you are giving a face-to-face presentation, attendees appreciate these *electronic handouts* because they don't have to lug them home. The most complex option for moving your multimedia presentation to the Internet involves a Web conference or broadcast.

   Web presentations with slides, narration, and speaker control have emerged as a way for anyone who has access to the Internet to attend your presentation without leaving the office. For example, you could initiate a meeting via a conference call, narrate using a telephone, and have participants see your slides from the browsers on their computers. If you prefer, you could skip the narration and provide a prerecorded presentation. Web-based presentations have many applications, including providing access to updated training or sales data whenever needed.[15]

   Some businesses convert their PowerPoint presentations to PDF documents or send PowerPoint shows (file extension *.PPS), which open directly in **Slide Show View**, ready to run. Both types of documents are highly suitable for e-mailing. For one thing, they start immediately, can't be easily changed, and typically result in smaller, less memory-hogging files.

Internet options for slide presentations range from posting slides online to conducting a live Web conference with slides, narration, and speaker control.

Polishing Your Delivery and Following Up

Once you have organized your presentation and prepared visuals, you are ready to practice delivering it. You will feel more confident and appear more professional if you know more about various delivery methods and techniques to use before, during, and after your presentation.

Delivery Method

Inexperienced speakers often feel that they must memorize an entire presentation to be effective. Unless you are an experienced performer, however, you will sound wooden and unnatural. What's more, forgetting your place can be disastrous! That is why we don't recommend memorizing an entire oral presentation. However, memorizing significant parts—the introduction, the conclusion, and perhaps a meaningful quotation—can be dramatic and impressive.

If memorizing your business presentation won't work, is reading from a manuscript the best plan? Definitely not! Reading to an audience is boring and ineffective. Because reading suggests that you don't know your topic well, the audience loses confidence in your expertise. Reading also prevents you from maintaining eye contact. You can't see audience reactions; consequently, you can't benefit from feedback.

Neither memorizing nor reading creates very convincing business presentations. The best plan, by far, is to present *extemporaneously*, especially when you are displaying an electronic slideshow such as PowerPoint. Extemporaneous delivery means speaking freely, generally without notes, after preparation and rehearsing. It means that in your talk you comment on the electronic slideshow you have prepared and rehearsed several times. Remember, PowerPoint and other presentation software have replaced traditional outlines and notes. Reading notes or a manuscript in addition to PowerPoint slides will damage your credibility.

Extemporaneous delivery results in more convincing presentations than those that are memorized or read.

If you give a talk without PowerPoint, however, you may use note cards or an outline containing key sentences and major ideas. In any case, beware of reading from a script. By preparing and then practicing with your notes, you can talk to your audience in a conversational manner. Your notes should be neither entire paragraphs nor single words. Instead, they should contain a complete sentence or two to introduce each major idea. Below the topic sentence(s), outline subpoints and illustrations. Note cards will keep you on track and prompt your memory, but only if you have rehearsed the presentation thoroughly.

© SPANDY GLASBERGEN WWW.GLASBERGEN.COM

"Fear of public speaking is quite common. If dressing up as Speaker Man makes you feel more confident, then so be it."

Combating Stage Fright

Nearly everyone experiences some degree of stage fright when speaking before a group. "If you hear someone say he or she isn't nervous before a speech, you are talking either to a liar or a very boring speaker," says corporate speech consultant Dianna Booher.[16] Being afraid is quite natural and results from actual physiological changes occurring in your body. Faced with a frightening situation, your body responds with the fight-or-flight response, discussed more fully in Figure 12.10. You can learn to control and reduce stage fright, as well as to incorporate techniques for effective speaking, by using the following strategies and techniques before, during, and after your presentation.

Stage fright is both natural and controllable.

Before Your Presentation

Speaking in front of a group will become less daunting if you allow for adequate preparation, sufficient practice, and rehearsals. Interacting with the audience and limiting surprises such as malfunctioning equipment will also add to your peace of mind. Review the following tips for a smooth start:

- **Prepare thoroughly.** One of the most effective strategies for reducing stage fright is knowing your subject thoroughly. Research your topic diligently and prepare a careful sentence outline. Those who try to "wing it" usually suffer the worst butterflies—and make the worst presentations.

Thorough preparation, extensive rehearsal, and stress-reduction techniques can lessen stage fright.

FIGURE 12.10 Techniques for Conquering Stage Fright

Ever get nervous before giving a speech? Everyone does! And it is not all in your head, either. When you face something threatening or challenging, your body reacts in what psychologists call the *fight-or-flight response*. This physical reflex provides your body with increased energy to deal with threatening situations. It also creates those sensations—dry mouth, sweaty hands, increased heartbeat, and stomach butterflies—that we associate with stage fright. The fight-or-flight response arouses your body for action—in this case, making a presentation.

Because everyone feels some form of apprehension before speaking, it is impossible to eliminate the physiological symptoms altogether. However, you can reduce their effects with the following techniques:

- **Breathe deeply.** Use deep breathing to ease your fight-or-flight symptoms. Inhale to a count of ten, hold this breath to a count of ten, and exhale to a count of ten. Concentrate on your counting and your breathing; both activities reduce your stress.
- **Convert your fear.** Don't view your sweaty palms and dry mouth as evidence of fear. Interpret them as symptoms of exuberance, excitement, and enthusiasm to share your ideas.
- **Know your topic and come prepared.** Feel confident about your topic. Select a topic that you know well and that is relevant to your audience. Test your equipment and arrive with time to spare.
- **Use positive self-talk.** Remind yourself that you know your topic and are prepared. Tell yourself that the audience is on your side—because it is! Moreover, most speakers appear to be more confident than they feel. Make this apparent confidence work for you.

- **Take a sip of water.** Drink some water to alleviate your dry mouth and constricted voice box, especially if you are talking for more than 15 minutes.
- **Shift the spotlight to your visuals.** At least some of the time the audience will be focusing on your slides, transparencies, handouts, or whatever you have prepared—and not totally on you.
- **Ignore any stumbles.** Don't apologize or confess your nervousness. If you keep going, the audience will forget any mistakes quickly.
- **Don't admit you are nervous.** Never tell your audience that you are nervous. They will probably never notice!
- **Feel proud when you finish.** You will be surprised at how good you feel when you finish. Take pride in what you have accomplished, and your audience will reward you with applause and congratulations. Your body, of course, will call off the fight-or-flight response and return to normal!

- **Rehearse repeatedly.** When you rehearse, practice your entire presentation, not just the first half. In PowerPoint you may print out speaker's notes, an outline, or a handout featuring miniature slides, which are excellent for practice. If you don't use an electronic slideshow, place your outline sentences on separate note cards. You may also wish to include transitional sentences to help you move to the next topic as you practice. Rehearse alone or before friends and family. Also try an audio or video recording so that you can evaluate your effectiveness.
- **Time yourself.** Most audiences tend to get restless during longer talks. Therefore, try to complete your presentation in no more than 20 minutes. If you have a time limit, don't go over it. Set a simple kitchen timer during your rehearsal to keep track of time. Better yet, PowerPoint offers a function, **Rehearse Timings**, that can measure the length of your talk as you practice.
- **Dress professionally.** Dressing professionally for a presentation will make you look more credible to your audience. You will also feel more confident.
- **Request a lectern.** Every beginning speaker needs the security of a high desk or lectern from which to deliver a presentation. It serves as a note holder and a convenient place to rest wandering hands and arms. Don't, however, lean on it. Eventually you will want to interact with the audience without any physical barriers.
- **Check the room.** If you are using a computer, a projector, or sound equipment, be certain they are operational. Before you start, check electrical outlets and the position of the viewing screen. Ensure that the seating arrangement is appropriate to your needs.
- **Greet members of the audience.** Try to make contact with a few members of the audience when you enter the room, while you are waiting to be introduced, or when you walk to the podium. Your body language should convey friendliness, confidence, and enjoyment.
- **Practice stress reduction.** If you feel tension and fear while you are waiting your turn to speak, use stress-reduction techniques, such as deep breathing. Additional techniques to help you conquer stage fright are presented in Figure 12.10.

During Your Presentation

Now that you have rehearsed and completed your preparation, you are ready to meet your audience. By following these suggestions during your presentation, you can apply techniques used by professionals to win over the audience, feel comfortable, and look polished:

- **Begin with a pause.** When you first approach the audience, take a moment to adjust your notes and make yourself comfortable. Establish your control of the situation.

- **Present your first sentence from memory.** By memorizing your opening, you can immediately establish rapport with the audience through eye contact. You will also sound confident and knowledgeable.

- **Maintain eye contact.** If the size of the audience overwhelms you, pick out two individuals on the right and two on the left. Talk directly to these people. Don't ignore listeners in the back of the room. If you are presenting to a smaller audience, try to make eye contact with everyone in the room at least once during your presentation.

> Eye contact, a moderate tone of voice, and natural movements enhance a presentation.

- **Control your voice and vocabulary.** This means speaking in moderated tones but loudly enough to be heard. Eliminate verbal static, such as *ah, er, like, you know,* and *um.* Silence is preferable to meaningless fillers when you are thinking of your next idea.

- **Skip the apologies.** Don't begin with a weak opening, such as *I will not take much time. I know you are busy.* Or: *I know you have heard this before, but we need to review it anyway.* Or: *I had trouble with my computer and the slides, so bear with me.* Unless the issue is blatant, such as not being able to load the presentation or make the projector work, apologies are counterproductive. Focus on your presentation. Dynamic speakers never say they are sorry.

- **Incorporate pauses when appropriate.** Silence can be effective especially when you are transitioning from one point to another. Pauses are also effective in giving the audience time to absorb an important point.

"This is where you all went wrong, causing my plan to fail."

- **Show enthusiasm.** If you are not excited about your topic, how can you expect your audience to be? Show passion for your topic through your tone, facial expressions, and gestures. Adding variety to your voice also helps to keep your audience alert and interested.

- **Put the brakes on.** Many novice speakers talk too rapidly, displaying their nervousness and making it difficult for audience members to understand their ideas. Slow down and listen to what you are saying.

- **Move naturally.** If you have a lectern, don't remain glued to it. Move about casually and naturally. Avoid fidgeting with your clothing, your hair, or items in your pockets. Do not roll up your sleeves or put your hands in your pockets. Learn to use your body to express a point.

- **Use visual aids effectively.** Discuss and interpret each visual aid for the audience. Move aside as you describe it so that it can be seen fully. Use a laser pointer if necessary, but steady your hand if it is shaking.

- **Avoid digressions.** Stick to your outline and notes. Don't suddenly include clever little anecdotes or digressions that occur to you on the spot. If it is not part of your rehearsed material, leave it out so that you can finish on time.

- **Summarize your main points and arrive at the high point of your talk.** Conclude your presentation by reiterating your main points or by emphasizing what you want the audience to think, do, or remember. Once you have announced your conclusion, proceed to it directly.

After Your Presentation

As you are concluding you presentation, handle questions and answers competently and provide handouts if appropriate. Try the following techniques:

The time to answer questions, distribute handouts, and reiterate main points is after a presentation.

- **Distribute handouts.** If you prepared handouts with data the audience will not need during the presentation, pass them out when you finish.
- **Encourage questions.** If the situation permits a question-and-answer period, announce it at the beginning of your presentation. Then, when you finish, ask for questions. Set a time limit for questions and answers. If you don't know the answer to a question, don't make one up. Instead, offer to find the answer within a day or two. If you make such a promise to your audience, be sure to follow through.
- **Repeat questions.** Although the speaker may hear the question, audience members often do not. Begin each answer with a repetition of the question. This also gives you thinking time. Then, direct your answer to the entire audience.
- **Reinforce your main points.** You can use your answers to restate your primary ideas (*I'm glad you brought that up because it gives me a chance to elaborate on ...*). In answering questions, avoid becoming defensive or debating the questioner.
- **Keep control.** Don't allow one individual to take over. Keep the entire audience involved.
- **Avoid Yes, *but* answers.** The word *but* immediately cancels any preceding message. Try replacing it with *and*. For example, *Yes, X has been tried. And Y works even better because* ....
- **End with a summary and appreciation.** To signal the end of the session before you take the last question, say something like *We have time for just one more question*. As you answer the last question, try to work it into a summary of your main points. Then, express appreciation to the audience for the opportunity to talk with them.

Visit www.meguffey.com
- Chapter Review Quiz
- Flash Cards
- Grammar Practice
- PowerPoint Slides
- Personal Language Trainer
- Beat the Clock Quiz

Summing Up and Looking Forward

This chapter presented techniques for making effective oral presentations. Good presentations begin with analyses of your audience and your purpose. Organizing the content involves preparing an effective introduction, body, and closing. The introduction should capture the listener's attention, identify the speaker, establish credibility, and preview the main points. The body should discuss two to four main points, with appropriate explanations, details, and verbal signposts to guide listeners. The conclusion should review the main points, provide a final focus, or take-away, and allow the speaker to leave the podium gracefully. You can improve audience rapport by using effective imagery including analogies, metaphors, similes, personal anecdotes, statistics, and worst-/best-case scenarios. In illustrating a presentation, use simple, easily understood visual aids to emphasize and clarify main points. If you employ PowerPoint, you can enhance the presentation by using templates, layout designs, bullet points, and multimedia elements. Don't allow your PowerPoint slides, however, to steal your thunder.

Before delivering your presentation, rehearse repeatedly. Check your equipment before the talk. During the presentation consider beginning with a pause and presenting your first sentence from memory. Dress professionally, make eye contact, control your voice, show enthusiasm for your topic, speak and move naturally, and avoid digressions. After your talk distribute handouts and answer questions. End gracefully and express appreciation.

The final two chapters of this book focus on your ultimate goal—getting a job or advancing in your career. In Chapter 13 you will learn how to write a persuasive résumé and other employment documents. In Chapter 14 you will discover how to ace an employment interview.

1. What are some of the differences between conventional presentations and multimedia presentations with presentation software such as PowerPoint? How would you prepare for each?

2. Discuss the advantages and disadvantages of your various visual aid options—multimedia slides, transparencies, handouts, flipcharts or whiteboards, videos, and props.

3. If PowerPoint is so effective, why are people speaking out against using it in presentations?

4. How can speakers prevent electronic presentation software from upstaging them?

5. What techniques are most effective for reducing stage fright?

Chapter Review

6. What are the two key elements you need to clarify before you can begin creating your presentation?

7. Why is it important to analyze your audience when preparing your presentation?

8. Name three goals to be achieved in the introduction of an oral presentation.

9. Name at least five of the ten techniques for gaining and keeping audience attention.

10. Focusing on effective imagery, list the specific techniques that have the power to enliven your presentation and help you connect with the audience.

11. Name three ways for a speaker to use verbal signposts in a presentation. Illustrate each.

12. What should you consider when deciding what types of visual aids to use during your presentation?

13. How is the 6-x-6 rule applied in preparing bulleted points?

14. List six techniques that you think would be most helpful to you in overcoming stage fright.

15. Name at least five things savvy speakers do after their presentations.

Activities and Cases

12.1 Critiquing a Speech

Your Task. Visit your library and select a speech from *Vital Speeches of Our Day*. You can also listen to a variety of famous speeches online at **http://www.historychannel.com/speeches/archive1.html**. (**Note:** If this link doesn't work, use a search tool such as Google to search for *speech transcripts*.) For tips on speech critiques and to learn how the pros review speeches, visit Andrew Dlugan's blog at **http://sixminutes.dlugan.com/2008/** or search Google for *speech critiques*. Write a memo report to your instructor critiquing the speech in terms of the following:

a. Effectiveness of the introduction, body, and conclusion

b. Evidence of effective overall organization

c. Use of verbal signposts to create coherence

d. Emphasis of two to four main points

e. Effectiveness of supporting facts (use of examples, statistics, quotations, and so forth)

f. Focus on audience benefits

g. Enthusiasm for the topic

12.2 Knowing Your Audience

Your Task. Select a recent issue of *Fortune, The Wall Street Journal, Fast Company, BusinessWeek, The Economist*, or another business periodical approved by your instructor. Based on your analysis of your classmates, select an article that will appeal to them and that you can relate to their needs. Submit to your instructor a one-page summary that includes the following: (a) the author, article title, source, issue date, and page reference; (b) a one-paragraph article summary; (c) a description of why you believe the article will appeal to your classmates; and (d) a summary of how you can relate the article to their needs.

12.3 Preparing an Oral Presentation From an Article

Your Task. Select a business-related newspaper or magazine article and prepare an oral report based on it. Submit your outline, introduction, and conclusion to your instructor, or present the report to your class. You might use the same article you used for Activity 12.2. If you are required to present the report to your class, your instructor will set criteria such as length of time.

12.4 Overcoming Stage Fright

What are you most afraid of about making a presentation before a class? Being tongue-tied? Having all eyes on you? Messing up? Forgetting your ideas and looking silly?

Your Task. Discuss the previous questions as a class. Then, in groups of three or four, talk about ways to overcome these fears. Your instructor may ask you to write a memo (individual or collective) summarizing your suggestions, or you may break out of your small groups and report your best ideas to the entire class.

12.5 Investigating Oral Communication in Your Field

One of the best sources of career information is someone in your field.

Your Task. Interview one or two individuals in your professional field. How is oral communication important in this profession? Does the need for oral skills change as one advances? What suggestions can these people make to newcomers to the field for developing proficient oral communication skills? Present your findings to your class.

12.6 Outlining an Oral Presentation

One of the hardest parts of preparing an oral presentation is developing the outline.

Your Task. Select an oral presentation topic from the list in Activity 12.11 or suggest an original topic. Prepare an outline for your presentation using the following format.

Title
Purpose

	I. INTRODUCTION
State your name	A.
Gain attention and involve audience	B.
Establish credibility	C.
Preview main points	D.
Transition	
	II. BODY
Main point	A.
Illustrate, clarify, contrast	1.
	2.
	3.
Transition	
Main point	B.
Illustrate, clarify, contrast	1.
	2.
	3.
Transition	
Main point	C.
Illustrate, clarify, contrast	1.
	2.
	3.
Transition	
	III. CONCLUSION
Summarize main points	A.
Provide final focus or "take-away"	B.
Encourage questions	C.

12.7 Creating an Oral Presentation: Outline Your Job Duties

What if you had to create a presentation for your classmates and instructor, or perhaps a potential recruiter, that describes the multiple tasks you fulfill at work? Could you do it in a five-minute PowerPoint presentation?

Your instructors, for example, may wear many hats. Most academics (a) teach; (b) conduct research to publish; and (c) provide service to the department, college, university, and community. Can you see how those aspects of their profession lend themselves to an outline of primary slides (teaching, publishing, service) and second-level slides (instructing undergraduate and graduate classes, presenting workshops, and giving lectures under the *teaching* label)?

Your Task. Now it is your turn to introduce the duties of a current position or a past job, volunteer activity, or internship, in a brief, simple, yet well-designed PowerPoint presentation. Your goal is to inform your audience of your job duties in a three- to five-minute talk. Use animation features and graphics where appropriate. Your instructor may show you a completed example of this project.

12.8 Discovering New Presentation Tips

Your Task. Using an electronic database or the Web, search for business presentations. Read at least three articles that provide suggestions for giving business presentations. If possible, print the most relevant findings. Select at least eight good tips or techniques that you did not learn from this chapter. Your instructor may ask you to bring them to class for discussion or to submit a short memo report outlining your tips.

12.9 Exploring the New World of Web Conferencing

Your boss at the Home Realty Company is interested in learning more about Web conferencing but doesn't have time to do the research herself. She asks you to find out the following:

a. In terms of revenue, how big is the Web conferencing industry?

b. Who are the leading providers of Web conferencing tools?

c. What are the typical costs associated with holding a Web conference?

d. How are other realtors using Web conferencing?

Your Task. Using electronic databases and the Internet, locate articles and Web sites that provide the information your boss has requested. Be prepared to role-play an informal presentation to your boss in which you begin with an introduction, answer the four questions in the body, and present a conclusion.

12.10 Researching *Fortune* List Information

Your Task. Using electronic databases, perform a search to learn how *Fortune* magazine determines which companies make its annual lists. Research the following lists. Then organize and present a five- to ten-minute informative talk to your class.

a. Fortune 500

b. Global 500

c. 100 Best Companies to Work For

d. America's Most Admired Companies

e. Global Most Admired Companies

12.11 Choosing a Topic for an Oral Presentation

Your Task. Select a topic from the following list or from the report topics at the end of Chapter 10. For an expanded list of report topics, go to **www.meguffey.com**. Prepare a five-to ten-minute oral presentation. Consider yourself an expert who has been called in to explain some aspect of the topic before a group of interested people. Because your time is limited, prepare a concise yet forceful presentation with effective visual aids.

a. How can students and other citizens contribute to conserving gasoline and other resources in order to save money and help slow global warming?

b. What is the career outlook in a field of your choice? Consider job growth, compensation, and benefits. What kind of academic or other experience is typically required in your field?

c. How could students in the United States be motivated to learn languages and study abroad in greater numbers?

d. What simple network security tips can your company use to avoid problems?

e. What is telecommuting, and for what kinds of workers is it an appropriate work alternative?

f. What criteria should parents use in deciding whether their young child should attend public, private, parochial, or home school?

g. What travel location would you recommend for college students during the holidays or in the summer?

h. What is the economic outlook for a given product, such as hybrid cars, laptop computers, digital cameras, fitness equipment, or a product of your choice?

i. How can your company or educational institution improve its image?

j. What are the Webby Awards, and what criteria do the judges use to evaluate Web sites?

k. What brand and model of computer and printer represent the best buy for college students today?

l. What franchise would offer the best investment opportunity for an entrepreneur in your area?

m. How should a job candidate dress for an interview?

n. What should a guide to proper cell phone use include?

o. Are internships worth the effort?

p. Why should a company have a written e-mail and Internet use policy?

q. Where should your organization hold its next convention?

r. What is your opinion of the statement "Advertising steals our time, defaces the landscape, and degrades the dignity of public institutions"?[17]

s. How can businesspeople reduce the amount of e-mail spam they receive?

t. What is the outlook for real estate (commercial or residential) investment in your area?

u. What are the pros and cons of videoconferencing for [name an organization]?

v. What do the personal assistants for celebrities do, and how does one become a personal assistant? (Investigate the Association of Celebrity Personal Assistants.)

w. What kinds of gifts are appropriate for businesses to give clients and customers during the holiday season?

x. What scams are on the Federal Trade Commission's List of Top 10 Consumer Scams, and how can consumers avoid falling for them?

y. How are businesses and conservationists working together to protect the world's dwindling tropical forests?

z. Should employees be able to use computers in a work environment for anything other than work-related business?

WEB

12.12 Will Maxing Out My Credit Cards Improve My Credit Rating?

The program chair for the campus business club has asked you to present a talk to the group about consumer credit. He saw a newspaper article saying that only 10 percent of Americans know their credit scores. Many consumers, including students, have dangerous misconceptions about their scores. Not knowing your score could result in denial of credit as well as difficulty obtaining needed services and even a job.

Your Task. Using electronic databases and the Web, learn more about credit scores and typical misconceptions. For example, is a higher or lower credit score better? Can you improve your credit score by marrying well? If you earn more money, will you improve your score? If you have a low score, is it impossible to raise it? Can you raise your score by maxing out all your credit cards? (One survey reported that 28 percent of consumers believed the latter statement was true!) Prepare an oral presentation appropriate for a student audience. Conclude with appropriate recommendations.

12.13 Self-Contained Multimedia Activity: Creating a PowerPoint Presentation (No additional research required)

You are a consultant who has been hired to improve the effectiveness of corporate trainers. These trainers frequently make presentations to employees on topics such as conflict management, teamwork, time management, problem solving, performance appraisals, and employment interviewing. Your goal is to teach these trainers how to make better presentations.

Your Task. Create six visually appealing slides. Base the slides on the following content, which will be spoken during the presentation titled "Effective Employee Training." The comments shown here are only a portion of a longer presentation.

Trainers have two options when they make presentations. The first option is to use one-way communication where the trainer basically dumps the information on the employees and leaves. The second option is to use a two-way audience involvement approach. The two-way approach can accomplish many purposes, such as helping the trainer connect with the employees, helping the trainer reinforce key points, increasing the employees' retention rates, and changing the pace and adding variety. The two-way approach also encourages employees to get to know each other better. Because today's employees demand more than just a "talking head," trainers must engage their audiences by involving them in a two-way dialogue.

When you include interactivity in your training sessions, choose approaches that suit your delivery style. Also, think about which options your employees would be likely to respond to most positively. Let's consider some interactivity approaches now. Realize, though, that these ideas are presented to help you get your creative juices flowing. After I present the list, we will think about situations in which these options might be effective. We will also brainstorm to come up with creative ideas we can add to this list.

- Ask employees to guess at statistics before revealing them.
- Ask an employee to share examples or experiences.
- Ask a volunteer to help you demonstrate something.
- Ask the audience to complete a questionnaire or worksheet.
- Ask the audience to brainstorm or list something as fast as possible.
- Ask a variety of question types to achieve different purposes.
- Invite the audience to work through a process or examine an object.
- Survey the audience.
- Pause to let the audience members read something to themselves.
- Divide the audience into small groups to discuss an issue.

12.14 Improving the Design and Content of PowerPoint Slides

Your Task. Identify ways to improve the design and content of the three slides presented in Figure 12.11. Classify your comments under the following categories: (a) color choices, (b) font choice including style and point size, (c) 6-x-6 rule, (d) listings in parallel grammatical form, (e) consistent capitalization and punctuation, and (f) graphics and images. Identify what needs to be improved and exactly how you would improve it. For example, if you identify category (d) as an area needing improvement, your answer would include a revision of the listing. When you finish, your instructor may show you a revised set of slides.

FIGURE 12.11 PowerPoint Slides Needing Revision

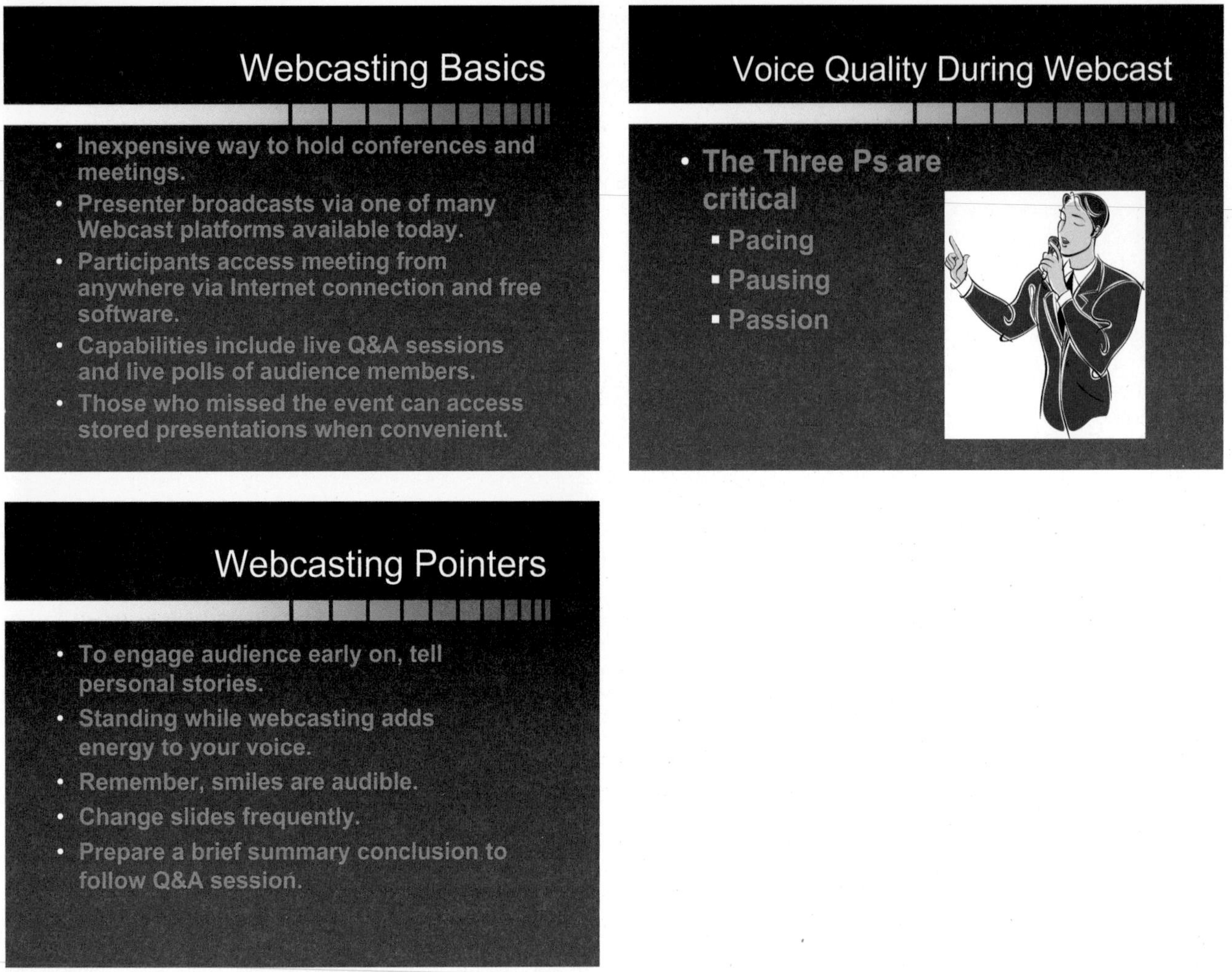

Webcasting Basics
- Inexpensive way to hold conferences and meetings.
- Presenter broadcasts via one of many Webcast platforms available today.
- Participants access meeting from anywhere via Internet connection and free software.
- Capabilities include live Q&A sessions and live polls of audience members.
- Those who missed the event can access stored presentations when convenient.

Voice Quality During Webcast
- The Three Ps are critical
  - Pacing
  - Pausing
  - Passion

Webcasting Pointers
- To engage audience early on, tell personal stories.
- Standing while webcasting adds energy to your voice.
- Remember, smiles are audible.
- Change slides frequently.
- Prepare a brief summary conclusion to follow Q&A session.

Video Resource

Video Library 1: *Building Workplace Skills: Effective On-the-Job Oral Presentations.* Watch this video to see how businesspeople apply a writing process in developing a persuasive oral presentation.

Capitalization

Review Sections 3.01–3.16 in the Grammar/Mechanics Handbook. Then study each of the following statements. Draw three underlines below any letter that should be capitalized. Draw a slash (/) through any capital letter that you wish to change to lowercase. Indicate in the space provided the number of changes you made in each sentence and record the number of the G/M principle(s) illustrated. If you made no changes, write *0*. When you finish, compare your responses with those provided at the back of the book. If your responses differ, study carefully the principles in parentheses.

5   (3.01, 3.06a) **Example** Once the M̲anagement T̲eam and the U̶nion members finally agreed, m̲ayor Johnson signed the A̶greement.

1. The suzuki employees had to evacuate their Branch office in suite 500 after the yorba linda fire department units arrived.

2. Travel to europe is down because of the weak Dollar; trips to the U.S. by french citizens, however, have increased, says Pierre Rostand, an Accounting Director at Hilton hotels.

3. Annan, part-time Chauffeur to Hollywood stars, wants to start his own Limo Service after college.

4. Patricia was disappointed when she read that the University of New England eliminated german from its curriculum; she now must take History, Geography, and Political Science classes to learn about Germany.

5. Did you see the *BusinessWeek* article entitled "harry potter and the endless cash"?

6. Although I recommend the dell inspiron 2200, you may purchase any Notebook Computer you choose.

7. According to a Federal Government report, any regulation of State and County banking must receive local approval.

8. The vice president of the united states said, "we continue to look for Foreign investment opportunities."

9. The Comptroller of Zarconi Industries reported to the President and the Board of Directors that the securities and exchange commission was beginning an investigation of their Company.

10. My Father, who lives near death valley, says that the Moon and Stars are especially brilliant on a cold, clear night.

11. Our Marketing Director met with Karin Bloedorn, Manager of the Advertising Sales Department, to plan an Ad Campaign for our newly redesigned Wireless Phone.

12. During the Summer semester our Faculty Advisor explored new exchange and semester-abroad opportunities in japan, korea, and china to find new Sponsors.

13. To reach Belle Isle park, which is located on an Island in the Detroit river, tourists pass over the Douglas MacArthur bridge.

14. On page 8 of the report, you will find a list of all employees in our accounting department with Master's degrees.

15. Please consult figure 3.2 in chapter 5 for U.S. census bureau figures regarding non-english-speaking residents.

The following executive summary of a report has faults in grammar, punctuation, spelling, number form, wordiness, and word use. Correct the errors with standard proofreading marks (see Appendix B) or revise the message online at **www.meguffey.com**.

EXECUTIVE SUMMARY

Purpose of Report

The purposes of this report is (1) To determine the Sun coast university campus communitys awareness of the campus recycling program and (2) To recommend ways to increase participation. Sun Coasts recycling program was intended to respond to the increasing problem of waste disposal, to fulfil it's social responsibility as an educational institution, and to meet the demands of legislation that made it a requirement for individuals and organizations to recycle.

A Survey was conducted in an effort to learn about the campus communities recycling habits and to make an assessment of the participation in the recycling program that is current. 220 individuals responded to the Survey but twenty-seven Surveys could not be used. Since Sun coast universitys recycling program include only aluminum, glass, paper and plastic at this point in time these were the only materials considered in this Study.

Recycling at Sun coast

Most Survey respondants recognized the importance of recycling, they stated that they do recycle aluminum, glass, paper and plastic on a regular basis either at home or at work. However most respondants displayed a low-level of awareness, and use of the on campus program. Many of the respondants was unfamilar with the location of the bins around campus; and therefore had not participated in the Recycling Program. Other responses indicated that the bins were not located in convenent locations.

Reccommendations for increasing recycling participation

Recommendations for increasing participation in the Program include the following;

1. relocating the recycling bins for greater visability
2. development of incentive programs to gain the participation of on campus groups
3. training student volunteers to give on campus presentations that give an explanation of the need for recycling, and the benefits of using the Recycling Program
4. we should increase Advertising in regard to the Program

Communication Workshop: Collaboration

Techniques for Taking Part in Effective and Professional Team Presentations

You may find that you are assigned to a team that must prepare and deliver an oral presentation. This can happen in the classroom and on the job. If you have been part of any team before, you also know that such projects can be very frustrating—particularly when some team members don't carry their weight or when members cannot resolve conflict. On the other hand, team projects can be harmonious and productive when members establish ground rules and follow guidelines related to preparing, planning, collecting information for, organizing, rehearsing, and evaluating team projects. Here are steps to take to ensure that your team presentation is a success.

- **Prepare to work together.** Before you begin working on the presentation, you should (a) compare schedules of team members in order to set up the best meetings times, (b) plan to meet often, and (c) discuss how you will deal with team members who are not contributing to the project.
- **Plan the presentation.** You need to make a number of decisions in the beginning about the presentation. These include agreeing on (a) the specific purpose of the presentation; (b) who your audience is, (c) how long the presentation will be; (d) what types of visuals will be included, and (e) the basic structure and content of the presentation.
- **Make assignments.** Once you have a clear understanding of what your presentation will cover, give each team member a written assignment that details his or her responsibilities for researching content, producing visuals, developing handouts, building transitions between segments, and showing up for team meetings and rehearsals.
- **Collect information.** To gather or generate information, teams can brainstorm together, conduct interviews, or search the Web for information. The team should decide on deadlines for collecting information and should discuss how to ensure the accuracy and currency of the information collected. Team members should exchange periodic progress reports on how their research is coming along.
- **Organize and develop the presentation.** Once all the research has been gathered, it is time for the team to start working on the presentation. Decide on the organization of the presentation, compose a draft of the presentation in writing, and prepare PowerPoint slides and other visual aids. The team should meet often to discuss and revise the presentation and to determine which team member will be responsible for delivering what parts of the presentation. Be sure each member builds a transition to the next presenter's topic and launches it smoothly. Strive for logical connections between segments.
- **Edit, rehearse, and evaluate.** Before you deliver the presentation, rehearse several times as a team. Make sure that transitions from speaker to speaker are smooth. For example, you might say, *Now that I have discussed how to prepare for the meeting, Renee is going to discuss how to get the meeting started.* Decide who will be responsible for advancing slides during the presentation. Practice fielding questions if you plan to have a question-and-answer session. Decide how you are going to dress so that you look professional and competent. Run a spell check and look over your PowerPoint slides to make sure that the design, format, and vocabulary are consistent.
- **Deliver the presentation.** On the day of the presentation, show up on time and in appropriate attire. Deliver your part of the presentation with professionalism and enthusiasm. Remember that your audience is judging the team on its performance, not the individuals. Do what you can to make your team shine!

Career Application. You have just been named to a team that is to produce an organizational five-year plan for your company. You know this assignment will end with an oral presentation to management and stockholders. Your first reaction is dismay. You have been on teams before in the classroom, and you know how frustrating they can be. But you decide that if you must take on this task, you want to make sure you know what you are doing and that you will contribute positively to this team effort.

Your Task

In small groups or with the entire class, discuss what traits and actions make effective and ineffective team members. How can one contribute positively to a team? How should teams deal with members who are not contributing or who have negative attitudes? What should team members do to ensure that the final presentation is professional, well coordinated, and effective?

Employment Communication

Chapter 13
The Job Search, Résumés, and Cover Letters

Chapter 14
Interviewing and Following Up

The Job Search, Résumés, and Cover Letters

OBJECTIVES

After studying this chapter, you should be able to

- Prepare for employment by identifying your interests, evaluating your assets, recognizing the changing nature of jobs, and choosing a career path.

- Apply both electronic and traditional techniques in a successful job search.

- Compare and contrast chronological and functional résumés.

- Organize and format the parts of a résumé to produce a persuasive product.

- Identify techniques that prepare a résumé for today's technologies, including preparing a scannable résumé, a plain-text résumé, and an e-portfolio.

- Write a persuasive cover letter to accompany your résumé.

The Internet has changed the way we look for jobs today. Workplace experts point out that the Internet has made job searching easier but also more challenging.[1] Because hundreds and perhaps thousands of candidates may be applying for an advertised position, you must do everything possible to be noticed and to outshine the competition. You must also look beyond the Internet.

The better prepared you are, the more confident you will feel during your search. This chapter provides expert current advice in preparing for employment, searching the job market, writing a persuasive résumé, and developing an effective cover letter. What you learn here can lead to a successful job search and maybe even your dream job.

Preparing for Employment

Finding a satisfying career requires learning about yourself, the job market, and the employment process.

You may think that the first step in finding a job is writing a résumé. Wrong! The job-search process actually begins long before you are ready to prepare your résumé. Regardless of the kind of employment you seek, you must invest time and effort getting ready. You can't hope to find the position of your dreams without (a) knowing yourself, (b) knowing the job market, and (c) knowing the employment process.

One of the first things you should do is obtain career information and choose a specific job objective. At the same time, you should be studying the job market and becoming aware of substantial changes in the nature of work. You will want to understand how to use the latest Web resources in your job search. Finally, you will

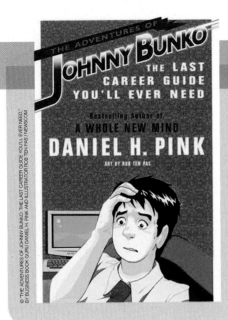

WORKPLACE IN FOCUS

Given the box-office success of comic book heroes such as Batman and Spider Man, it is not surprising that the hottest career hero of the new generation is also a fictional character—Johnny Bunko. In the Japanese magna book *The Adventures of Johnny Bunko: The Last Career Guide You'll Ever Need*, anime character Johnny Bunko is a disillusioned office worker who longs to escape his dead-end job and find true occupational happiness. Aided by the spellbinding avatar Diana and a pair of magic chopsticks, Bunko embarks on an action-packed career journey that gives readers valuable insights into their own career paths. *Why should job seekers consult career guides when preparing for employment?*

need to design a persuasive résumé and cover letter appropriate for small businesses as well as for larger organizations that may be using résumé-scanning programs. Following these steps, summarized in Figure 13.1 and described in this chapter, gives you a master plan for landing a job you really want.

Identifying Your Interests

The employment process begins with introspection. This means looking inside yourself to analyze what you like and dislike so that you can make good employment choices. Off-campus career counselors charge large sums for helping individuals

Analyzing your likes and dislikes helps you make wise employment decisions.

FIGURE 13.1 The Employment Search

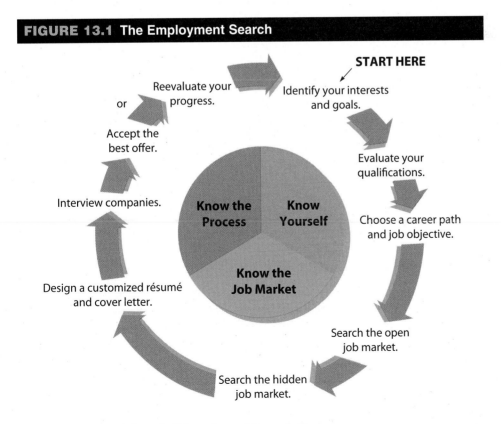

learn about themselves. You can do the same kind of self-examination—without spending a dime. For guidance in choosing a field that eventually proves to be satisfying, answer the following questions. If you have already chosen a field, think carefully about how your answers relate to that choice.

- Do you enjoy working with people, data, or things?
- Would you like to work for someone else or be your own boss?
- How important are salary, benefits, technology support, and job stability?
- How important are working environment, colleagues, and job stimulation?
- Would you rather work for a large or a small company?
- Must you work in a specific city, geographical area, or climate?
- Are you looking for security, travel opportunities, money, power, or prestige?
- How would you describe the perfect job, boss, and coworkers?

Answering specific questions can help you choose a career.

To aid you with appraising your abilities, many college career centers offer skills assessment and personality type testing. Be sure to explore resources available on campus, including one-on-one sessions with career counselors, job-search and etiquette workshops, local employer job postings, internships, and more.

Evaluating Your Qualifications

Decide what qualifications you possess and how you can prove them.

In addition to your interests, assess your qualifications. Employers today want to know what assets you have to offer them. Your responses to the following questions will target your thinking as well as prepare a foundation for your résumé. Remember, though, that employers seek more than empty assurances; they will want proof of your qualifications.

- *What technology skills can you offer?* Employers are often interested in specific computer software programs and your level of expertise.
- *What other skills have you acquired in school, on the job, or through activities?* How can you demonstrate these skills?
- *Do you work well with people? Do you enjoy teamwork?* What proof can you offer? Consider extracurricular activities, clubs, class projects, and jobs.
- *Are you a leader, self-starter, or manager?* What evidence can you offer?
- *Do you speak, write, or understand another language?*
- *Do you learn quickly? Are you creative? Do you take initiative? Are you flexible?* How can you demonstrate these characteristics?
- *Do you communicate well in speech and in writing?* How can you verify these talents?

Recognizing the Changing Nature of Jobs

People feel less job security after downsizing, outsourcing, and offshoring of jobs.

As you learned in Chapter 1, the workplace is changing. One of the most significant changes involves the concept of the "job." Following the downsizing of corporations and the outsourcing and offshoring of jobs in recent years, companies are employing fewer people in permanent positions.

Other forms of employment are replacing traditional jobs. In many companies teams complete special projects and then disband. Work may also be outsourced to a group that is not even part of an organization. Because new technologies can spring up overnight making today's skills obsolete, employers are less willing to hire people into jobs with narrow descriptions. Instead, they are hiring contingency employees who work temporarily and then leave. What's more, big companies are no longer the main employers. People work for smaller companies, or they are starting their own businesses. By 2020 small, privately owned companies are expected to comprise 25 percent of U.S. businesses.[2]

What do these changes mean for you? For one thing, you should probably forget about a lifelong career with a single

"We found someone overseas who can drink coffee and talk about sports all day for a fraction of what we're paying you."

GLASBERGEN

© RANDY GLASBERGEN. WWW.GLASBERGEN.COM

company. Don't count on regular pay raises, promotions, and a comfortable retirement income. You should also become keenly aware that a career that relies on yesterday's skills is headed for trouble. You are going to need updated, marketable skills that serve you well as you move from job to job. Upgrading your skills through constant retraining is the best career strategy for the twenty-first century. People who learn quickly and adapt to change will always be in demand even in a climate of surging change.[3]

Jobs are becoming more flexible and less permanent.

Choosing a Career Path

The job picture today is extraordinarily dynamic and flexible. On average, workers between ages eighteen and thirty-eight in the United States will have ten different employers, and job tenure currently averages 6.6 years.[4] Although you may be frequently changing jobs in the future (especially before you reach forty), you still need to train for a specific career area now. In choosing an area, you will make the best decisions when you can match your interests and qualifications with the requirements and rewards in specific career fields. Where can you find the best career data? Here are some suggestions:

- **Visit your campus career center.** Most have literature, inventories, career-related software programs, and employment or internship databases that allow you to search such fields as accounting, finance, office technology, information systems, hotel management, and so forth.
- **Search the Web.** Many job-search sites on the Web offer career-planning information and resources. You will learn about some of the best sites in the next section.
- **Use your library.** Many print and online resources are especially helpful. Consult *O*NET Occupational Information Network*, *Dictionary of Occupational Titles*, *Occupational Outlook Handbook*, and *The Jobs Rated Almanac* for information about job duties, qualifications, salaries, and employment trends.
- **Take a summer job, internship, or part-time position in your field.** Nothing is better than trying out a career by actually working in it or in a related area. Many companies offer internships and temporary or part-time jobs to begin training college students and to develop relationships with them. Experts commonly believe that at least 60 percent of these relationships blossom into permanent positions.
- **Interview someone in your chosen field.** People are usually flattered when asked to describe their careers. Inquire about needed skills, required courses, financial and other rewards, benefits, working conditions, future trends, and entry requirements.
- **Volunteer with a nonprofit organization.** Many colleges and universities encourage service learning opportunities. In volunteering their services, students gain valuable experience, and nonprofits appreciate the expertise and fresh ideas that students bring.
- **Monitor the classified ads.** Early in your college career, begin monitoring want ads and Web sites of companies in your career area. Check job availability, qualifications sought, duties, and salary range. Don't wait until you are about to graduate to see how the job market looks.
- **Join professional organizations in your field.** Frequently, professional organizations offer student membership status and reduced rates. You will receive inside information on issues, career news, and possibly jobs. Campus business clubs and associations help with career tips and networking opportunities.

Career information can be obtained at campus career centers and libraries, from the Web, in classified ads, and from professional organizations.

Summer jobs, part-time employment, and internships are good opportunities to learn about various careers and to establish a professional network.

Searching for a Job Electronically

Another significant change in the workplace involves the way we find jobs. Just ten years ago, a job seeker browsed the local classified ads, found a likely sounding job listing, prepared an elegant résumé on bond paper, and sent it out by U.S. mail. All that has changed with the advent of the Internet. Searching for a job electronically has become a common, but not always fruitful, approach. With all the publicity

Employment Web sites list many jobs, but finding a job electronically requires more work than simply clicking a mouse.

given to Internet job boards, you might think that electronic job searching has totally replaced traditional methods. Not so! Although Web sites such as *Yahoo HotJobs.com* and *CareerBuilder.com*, shown in Figure 13.2, list millions of jobs, actually landing a job is much harder than just clicking a mouse. In addition, these job boards are facing recent competition from social networking sites such as LinkedIn and Facebook.[5]

Both recruiters and job seekers complain about online job boards. Corporate recruiters say that the big job boards bring a flood of candidates, many of whom are not suited for the listed jobs. Workplace experts estimate that the average Fortune 500 company is inundated with 2,000 résumés a day.[6] Job candidates grumble that listings are frequently out-of-date and fail to produce leads. Some career advisors call these sites *black holes*,[7] into which résumés vanish without a trace. Applicants worry about the privacy of information posted at big boards. Most important, an independent study has shown that the percentage of hires resulting from job boards is astonishingly low—3.6 percent at *Monster.com*, 1.5 percent at *CareerBuilder.com*, and 0.5 percent at *HotJobs.com*.[8] Workplace expert Liz Ryan advises job seekers not to count on finding a job by devoting all their energy to searching online job boards.[9]

Using the Big Job Boards. Despite these gloomy prospects, many job seekers use job boards to gather job-search information, such as résumé, interviewing, and salary tips. Job boards also serve as a jumping-off point in most searches. They can inform you about the kinds of jobs that are available and the skill sets required. With over 40,000 job boards and employment Web sites deluging the

---

FIGURE 13.2 Using the Web to Search for a Job

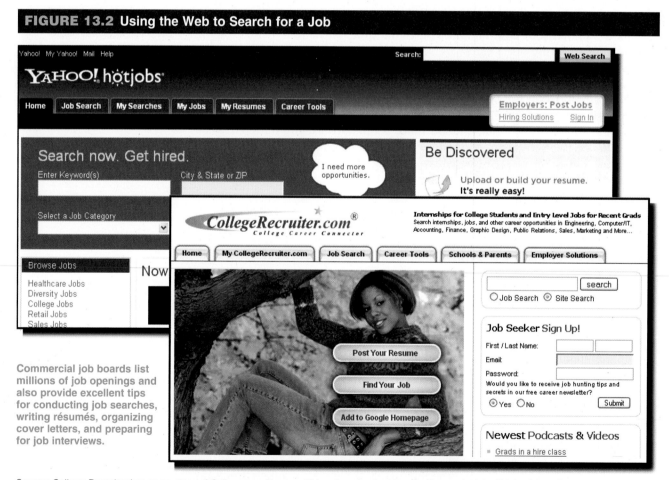

Commercial job boards list millions of job openings and also provide excellent tips for conducting job searches, writing résumés, organizing cover letters, and preparing for job interviews.

Source: College Recruiter image courtesy of Collegerecruiter.com. Yahoo image reproduced with permission of Yahoo! Inc. © 2007. YAHOO! and the Yahoo! logo are trademarks of Yahoo Inc.

Internet, it is hard to know where to start. We have listed a few of the best-known online job sites here:[10]

- **CareerBuilder (http://www.careerbuilder.com)** claims to be the nation's largest employment network. At this writing it lists 1.5 million jobs and has over 250,000 client companies posting jobs. Users can search for these jobs by keyword, geographic location, and job type.
- **Monster (http://www.monster.com)** offers access to information on more than 1.1 million jobs worldwide with 275,000 client companies posting jobs. You may search for jobs by keyword, company name, geographic location, and job category. Many consider it to be the Web's premier job site.
- **College Recruiter (http://www.CollegeRecruiter.com)** claims to be the "highest traffic entry-level job site" for students and graduates. It lists over 250,000 jobs from more than 12,500 client companies.
- **CareerJournal (http://www.CareerJournal.com)**, sponsored by *The Wall Street Journal*, lists over 125,000 executive positions from over 4,000 companies.
- **Yahoo HotJobs (http://hotjobs.yahoo.com)** lists over 150,000 job openings.[11] It says that job seekers voted it the "Best General Purpose Job Board for Job Seekers."

Beyond the Big Job Boards. Disillusioned job seekers increasingly turn their backs on the big online job boards but not on electronic job-searching tactics. Savvy candidates know how to use their computers to search for jobs at Web sites such as the following:

- **Corporate Web sites.** Probably the best way to find a job online is at a company's own Web site. One poll found that 70 percent of job seekers felt they were more likely to obtain an interview if they posted their résumés on corporate sites. In addition to finding a more direct route to decision makers, job seekers thought that they could keep their job searches more private at corporate Web sites than at big job board sites.[12]
- **Association Web sites.** Online job listings have proved to be the single-most popular feature of many professional organizations such as the International Association of Administrative Professionals, the American Institute of Certified Public Accountants, the National Association of Sales Professionals, the National Association of Legal Assistants, and the Association of Information Technology Professionals. Although you pay a fee, the benefits of joining a professional association in your career field are enormous. Networking starts on campus. If you join an accounting, finance, or marketing association, you will jumpstart your professional connections.
- **JobCentral National Labor Exchange.** JobCentral is a public service Web site provided by the DirectEmployers Association, a nonprofit consortium of Fortune 500 and other leading U.S. corporations. Several hundred companies now use **http://www.jobcentral.com** as a gateway to job listing at their own Web sites, advertising an estimated five million jobs. Best of all, this service is free, bypassing the big commercial job boards. You can enter a job description or job title, and a list of openings pops up. When you click one, you are taken straight to the company's Web site, where you can apply.
- **Local employment Web sites.** Workplace expert Liz Ryan encourages candidates to focus on smaller, locals sites, such as a local *Jobing.com* site—for example, for Colorado (**http://colorado.jobing.com/**)—and JobStar (**http://jobstar.org**).[13]
- **Niche Web sites.** If you want a job in a specialized field, look for a niche Web site, such as *HealthCareerWeb.com, CareerWomen.com, SixFigureJobs.com*, and so on. Already, niche sites control well over half of the job-search market.[14]
- **Professional networking sites.** Perhaps you use MySpace to chat with friends. However, users are increasingly tapping into social networking sites to prospect for jobs. Facebook and other sites have started professional offshoots. LinkedIn boasts more than 13 million active users, but smaller sites, such as invite-only

Job prospects may be more promising at the Web sites of corporations, professional organizations, employers' organizations, niche fields, and, most recently, professional networking sites.

Doostang, may have an edge in specialized fields.[15] Finally, international networking sites—Chinese Wealink and German Xing—can help candidates who seek a global reach.

Thousands of job boards listing millions of jobs now flood the Internet. The harsh reality, however, is that landing a job still depends largely on personal contacts. Stanford sociologist Mark Granovetter found that 70 percent of jobs are discovered through networking.[16] One employment expert believes that overreliance on technology may have made job seekers lazy: "At the end of the day, the job hunt is largely about people and it is about networking—looking at who you know and where they work."[17] Job-search consultant Debra Feldman concurs: "More important than what you know is who knows what you know. Make sure you are on the radar of people who have access to the kind of job leads you want."[18]

Searching for a Job Using Traditional Techniques

Finding the perfect job requires an early start and a determined effort. A research study of college graduates revealed that those with proactive personalities were the most successful in securing interviews and jobs. Successful candidates were not passive; they were driven to "make things happen."[19]

Whether you use traditional or online job-search techniques, you should be prepared to launch an aggressive campaign. What's more, you can't start too early. Some universities now require first- and second-year students to take an employment seminar called "Reality 101." Students are told early on that a college degree alone doesn't guarantee a job. They are cautioned that grade point averages make a difference to employers.[20] They are also advised of the importance of experience, such as internships. Traditional job-search techniques, such as those described here, continue to be critical in landing jobs.

- **Check classified ads in local and national newspapers.** Be aware, though, that classified ads are only one small source of jobs.
- **Check announcements in publications of professional organizations.** If you do not have a student membership, ask your professors to share current copies of professional journals, newsletters, and so on. Your college library is another good source.
- **Contact companies in which you are interested, even if you know of no current opening.** Write an unsolicited letter and include your résumé. Follow up with a telephone call. Check the company's Web site for employment possibilities and procedures.
- **Sign up for campus interviews with visiting company representatives.** Campus recruiters may open your eyes to exciting jobs and locations. They may also help you prepare by offering mock interviews.
- **Attend career fairs.** Job fairs are invaluable in your quest to learn about specific companies and your future career options. Recruiters say that the more you know about the company and its representatives, the more comfortable you will be in an interview.[21]
- **Ask for advice from your instructors.** They often have contacts and ideas for expanding your job search.
- **Develop your own network of contacts.** Networking accounts for almost two thirds of the jobs found by candidates. Therefore, plan to spend a considerable portion of your job-search time developing a personal network. The Communication Workshop at the end of this chapter gives you step-by-step instructions for traditional networking as well as some ideas for online networking.

Creating a Customized Résumé

After using both traditional and online resources to learn about the employment market and to develop job leads, you will focus on writing a customized résumé. This means you will prepare a special résumé for every position you want. The competition is so stiff today that you cannot get by with a generic, all-purpose résumé. Although you can start with a basic résumé, you should customize it to fit each company and position if you want your résumé to stand out from the crowd. Include many keywords that describe the skills, traits, tasks, and job titles associated with your targeted job. You will learn more about keywords shortly.

The Internet has made it so easy to apply that recruiters are swamped with applications. As a job seeker, you have about five seconds to catch the recruiter's eye—if your résumé is even read by a person. Many companies use computer scanning technologies to weed out unqualified candidates.[22] Your goal is to make your résumé fit the targeted position and be noticed. Such a résumé does more than merely list your qualifications. It packages your assets into a convincing advertisement that sells you for a specific job.

In the scramble to get noticed, some job seekers—particularly in creative professions—occasionally resort to unusual job-hunting tactics; for example, sending a recruiter a shoe "to get a foot in the door" or a bowling pin to suggest "I'll bowl you over."[23] The survey of hiring managers revealed that more than half of marketing and a quarter of advertising executives view such unconventional approaches as unprofessional. Whereas in advertising gimmicky applications may be acceptable to almost half of the executives polled, in most business disciplines they would be a huge gamble. Perhaps you should think twice before drawing attention to yourself the way one applicant did by putting up posters of himself in the garage where the executives parked.

The purpose of a résumé is winning an interview. Even if you are not in the job market at this moment, preparing a résumé now has advantages. Having a current résumé makes you look well organized and professional should an unexpected employment opportunity arise. Moreover, preparing a résumé early can help you recognize weak areas and give you time to bolster them. Even after you have accepted a position, it is a good idea to keep your résumé up-to-date. You never know when an opportunity might come along!

> Winning an interview is the purpose of a customized résumé.

Choosing a Résumé Style

Résumés usually fall into two categories: chronological and functional. In this section we present basic information as well as inside tips on how to choose an appropriate résumé style, how to determine its length, and how to arrange its parts. You will also learn about adding a summary of qualifications, which busy recruiters increasingly want to see. Models of the résumés in the following discussion are shown in our comprehensive résumé section beginning on page 386.

> See our comprehensive collection of résumé styles beginning on page 386.

Chronological. The most popular résumé format is the chronological résumé, shown in Figures 13.6 through 13.9 in our résumé collection. It lists work history job by job, starting with the most recent position. Recruiters favor the chronological format because such résumés quickly reveal a candidate's education and experience record. Recruiters are familiar with the chronological résumé, and as many as 84 percent of employers prefer to see a candidate's résumé in this format.[24] The chronological style works well for candidates who have experience in their field of employment and for those who show steady career growth, but it is less appropriate for people who have changed jobs frequently or who have gaps in their employment records. For college students and others who lack extensive experience, the functional résumé format may be preferable.

> Chronological résumés focus on job history with the most recent positions listed first.

Functional. The functional résumé, shown in Figure 13.10, focuses attention on a candidate's skills rather than on past employment. Like a chronological résumé, the functional résumé begins with the candidate's name, address, telephone number, job objective, and education. Instead of listing jobs, though, the functional résumé groups skills and accomplishments in special categories, such as *Supervisory and Management Skills* or *Retailing and Marketing Experience*. This résumé style highlights accomplishments and can de-emphasize a negative employment history.

> Because functional résumés focus on skills, they may be more advisable for graduates with little experience.

People who have changed jobs frequently, who have gaps in their employment records, or who are entering an entirely different field may prefer the functional résumé. Recent graduates with little or no related employment experience often find the functional résumé useful. Older job seekers who want to de-emphasize a long job history and job hunters who are afraid of appearing overqualified may also prefer the functional format. Be aware, though, that online job boards may insist on chronological format. In addition, some recruiters are suspicious of functional résumés, thinking the candidate is hiding something.

Deciding on Length

Recruiters may say they prefer one-page résumés, but many choose to interview those with longer résumés.

Experts simply do not agree on how long a résumé should be. Conventional wisdom has always held that recruiters prefer one-page résumés. A carefully controlled study of 570 recruiters, however, revealed that they *claimed* they preferred one-page résumés. The recruiters actually *chose* to interview the applicants with two-page résumés.[25] Recruiters who are serious about candidates often prefer a full picture with the kind of details that can be provided in a two-page résumé. On the other hand, recruiters are said to be extremely busy and prefer concise résumés.

Perhaps the best advice is to make your résumé as long as needed to sell your skills to recruiters and hiring managers. Individuals with more experience will naturally have longer résumés. Those with fewer than ten years of experience, those making a major career change, and those who have had only one or two employers will likely have a one-page résumé. Those with ten years or more of related experience may have a two-page résumé. Finally, some senior-level managers and executives with a lengthy history of major accomplishments might have a résumé that is three pages or longer.[26] A recent survey by a global staffing firm found that 61 percent of hiring managers now prefer to receive two-page résumés from experienced candidates for management jobs; 31 percent stated that they would accept three pages. Even applicants for low-level staff jobs may opt for two pages, 44 percent of recruiters said.[27]

Arranging the Parts

The parts of résumés should be arranged with the most important qualifications first.

Although résumés have standard parts, their arrangement and content should be strategically planned. A customized résumé emphasizes skills and achievements aimed at a particular job or company. It shows a candidate's most important qualifications first, and it de-emphasizes any weaknesses. In arranging your information and qualifications, try to create as few headings as possible; more than six generally looks cluttered. No two résumés are ever exactly alike, but most writers consider including all or some of these items: main heading, career objective, summary of qualifications, education, experience, capabilities and skills, awards and activities, personal information, and references.

Main Heading. Your résumé, whether it is chronological or functional, should begin with your name; add your middle initial for an even more professional look. Following your name, list your contact information, including your complete address, area code and phone number, and e-mail address. If possible, include a telephone number where messages may be left for you. The outgoing message at this number should be in your voice, it should mention your full name, and it should be concise and professional. If you are expecting an important recruiting call on your cell phone, pick up only when you are in a quiet environment and can concentrate. Keep the main heading as uncluttered

"That's my resume, my autobiography, and six of my last projects."

© TED GOFF WWW.TEDGOFF.COM

and simple as possible. Format your name so that it stands out on the page. Don't include the word *résumé*; it is like putting the word *letter* above correspondence.

For your e-mail address, be sure it sounds professional instead of something like *1foxylady@yahoo.com* or *hotdaddy@hotmail.com*. Also be sure that you are using a personal e-mail address. Putting your work e-mail address on your résumé announces to prospective employers that you are using your current employer's resources to look for another job.

Career Objective.

Opinion is divided about the effect of including a career objective on a résumé. Recruiters think such statements indicate that a candidate has made a commitment to a career and is sure about what he or she wants to do. Career objectives, of course, make the recruiter's life easier by quickly classifying the résumé. But such declarations can also disqualify a candidate if the stated objective doesn't match a company's job description.[28] A well-written objective customized for the job opening can add value to a chronological or functional résumé.

Career objectives are most appropriate for specific, targeted positions, but they may limit a broader job search.

A person applying for an auditor position might include the following objective: *Seeking an auditor position in an internal corporate accounting department where my accounting skills, computer experience, knowledge of GAAP, and attention to detail will help the company run efficiently and ensure that its records are kept accurately.*

Your objective should also focus on the employer's needs. Therefore, it should be written from the employer's perspective, not your own. Focus on how you can contribute to the organization, not on what the organization can do for you. A typical self-serving objective is *To obtain a meaningful and rewarding position that enables me to learn more about the graphic design field and allows for advancement.* Instead, show how you will add value to the organization with an objective such as *Position with advertising firm designing Web sites, publications, logos, and promotional displays for clients, where creativity, software knowledge, and proven communication skills can be used to build client base and expand operations.*

Also be careful that your career objective doesn't downplay your talents. For example, some consultants warn against using the words *entry-level* in your objective, as these words emphasize lack of experience or show poor self-confidence. Finally, your objective should be concise. Try to limit your objective to no more than two or three lines. Avoid using complete sentences and the pronoun *I*.

If you choose to omit the career objective, be sure to discuss your objectives and goals in your cover letter. Savvy job seekers are also incorporating their objectives into a summary of qualifications, which is discussed next.

Summary of Qualifications.

"The biggest change in résumés over the last decade has been a switch from an objective to a summary at the top," says career expert Wendy Enelow.[29] Recruiters are busy, and smart job seekers add a summary of qualifications to their résumés to save the time of recruiters and hiring managers. Once a job is advertised, a hiring manager may get hundreds or even thousands of résumés in response. A summary at the top of your résumé makes it easier to read and ensures that your most impressive qualifications are not overlooked by a recruiter, who may be skimming résumés quickly. A well-written summary motivates the recruiter to read further.

A summary of qualifications section lists your most impressive accomplishments and qualifications in one concise bulleted list.

A summary of qualifications will include three to eight bulleted statements that prove you are the ideal candidate for the position. When formulating these statements, consider your experience in the field, your education, your unique skills, awards you have won, certifications, and any other accomplishments that you want to highlight. Include numbers wherever possible. Target the most important qualifications an employer will be looking for in the person hired for this position. Examples of summaries of qualifications appear in Figures 13.6, 13.7, 13.9, and 13.11 in the résumé models found in our collection.

Education. The next component in a chronological résumé is your education—if it is more noteworthy than your work experience. In this section you should include the name and location of schools, dates of attendance, major fields of study, and degrees received. By the way, once you have attended college, you don't need to list high school information on your résumé.

Your grade point average and/or class ranking may be important to prospective employers. Sixty-six percent of employers screen candidates by GPA, a recent survey found, and 58 percent of survey respondents stated that they would be less likely to hire candidates with GPAs below 3.0. One way to enhance your GPA is to calculate it in your major courses only (for example, *3.6/4.0 in major*). It is not unethical to showcase your GPA in your major—as long as you clearly indicate what you are doing. Although some hiring managers may think that applicants are hiding something if they omit a poor record of grades, consultant Terese Corey Blanck suggests leaving out a poor GPA. Instead, she advises that students try to excel in internships, show extracurricular leadership, and target smaller, lesser-known companies to offset low grades.[30]

Under *Education* you might be tempted to list all the courses you took, but such a list makes for very dull reading. Refer to courses only if you can relate them to the position sought. When relevant, include certificates earned, seminars attended, workshops completed, and honors earned. If your education is incomplete, include such statements as *B.S. degree expected 5/10* or *80 units completed in 120-unit program*. Title this section *Education, Academic Preparation,* or *Professional Training.* If you are preparing a functional résumé, you will probably put the education section below your skills summaries, as Kevin Touhy has done in Figure 13.10.

Work Experience or Employment History. If your work experience is significant and relevant to the position sought, this information should appear before your education information. List your most recent employment first and work backward, including only those jobs that you think will help you win the targeted position. A job application form may demand a full employment history, but your résumé may be selective. Be aware, though, that time gaps in your employment history will probably be questioned in the interview. For each position show the following:

- Employer's name, city, and state
- Dates of employment (month and year)
- Most important job title
- Significant duties, activities, accomplishments, and promotions

Describe your employment achievements concisely but concretely to make what resume consultants call "a strong value proposition."[31] Avoid generalities such as *Worked with customers.* Be more specific, with statements such as *Served 40 or more retail customers a day; Successfully resolved problems about custom stationery orders;* or *Acted as intermediary among customers, printers, and suppliers.* If possible, quantify your accomplishments, such as *Conducted study of equipment needs of 100 small businesses in Houston; Personally generated orders for sales of $90,000 annually;* or *Keyed all the production models for a 250-page employee procedures manual.* One professional recruiter said, "I spend a half hour every day screening 50 résumés or more, and if I don't spot some [quantifiable] results in the first 10 seconds, the résumé is history."[32]

Your employment achievements and job duties will be easier to read if you place them in a bulleted list. When writing these bullet points, don't try to list every single thing you have done on the job; instead, customize your information so that it relates to the target job. Make sure your list of job duties shows what you have to contribute and how you are qualified for the position you are applying for. Do not make your bullet points complete sentences, and avoid using personal pronouns (*I, me, my*) in them. If you have performed a lot of the same duties for multiple employers, you don't have to repeat them.

FIGURE 13.3 Strengthen Your Résumé With Action Verbs

accelerated	enabled	introduced	reviewed
achieved	encouraged	managed	revitalized
analyzed	engineered	organized	screened
collaborated	established	originated	served
conceptualized	expanded	overhauled	spearheaded
constructed	expedited	pioneered	spurred
converted	facilitated	reduced	strengthened
designed	improved	resolved	targeted
directed	increased	restructured	transformed

In addition to technical skills, employers seek individuals with communication, management, and interpersonal capabilities. This means you will want to select work experiences and achievements that illustrate your initiative, dependability, responsibility, resourcefulness, flexibility, and leadership. Employers also want people who can work together in teams. Therefore, include statements such as *Collaborated with interdepartmental task force in developing ten-page handbook for temporary workers* and *Headed student government team that conducted most successful voter registration in campus history.*

Statements describing your work experience can be made forceful and persuasive by using action verbs, such as those listed in Figure 13.3 and illustrated in Figure 13.4. Starting each of your bullet points with an action verb will help ensure that your bulleted lists are parallel.

Capabilities and Skills. Recruiters want to know specifically what you can do for their companies. Therefore, list your special skills, such as *Proficient in preparing federal, state, and local payroll tax returns as well as franchise and personal property tax returns.* Include your ability to use the Internet, software programs, office equipment, and communication technology tools. If you speak a foreign language or use sign language, include it on your résumé. Describe proficiencies you have acquired through training and experience, such as *Certified in computer graphics and Web design through an intensive 350-hour classroom program.* Use expressions such as *competent in, skilled in, proficient with, experienced in,* and *ability to;* for example, *Competent in*

> Emphasize the skills and aptitudes that prove you are qualified for a specific position.

FIGURE 13.4 Use Action Verbs in Statements That Quantify Achievements

Identified weaknesses in internships and **researched** five alternate programs
Reduced delivery delays by an average of three days per order
Streamlined filing system, thus reducing 400-item backlog to zero
Organized holiday awards program for 1,200 attendees and 140 workers
Designed three pages in HTML for company Web site
Represented 2,500 students on committee involving university policies and procedures
Calculated shipping charges for overseas deliveries and **recommended** most economical rates
Managed 24-station computer network linking data in three departments
Distributed and **explained** voter registration forms to over 500 prospective voters
Praised by top management for enthusiastic teamwork and achievement
Secured national recognition from National Arbor Foundation for tree project

writing, editing, and proofreading reports, tables, letters, memos, manuscripts, and business forms.

You will also want to highlight exceptional aptitudes, such as working well under stress, learning computer programs quickly, and interacting with customers. If possible, provide details and evidence that back up your assertions; for example, *Mastered PhotoShop in 25 hours with little instruction*. Search for examples of your writing, speaking, management, organizational, and interpersonal skills—particularly those talents that are relevant to your targeted job. For recent graduates, this section can be used to give recruiters evidence of your potential. Instead of *Capabilities*, the section might be called *Skills and Abilities*.

Those job hunters preparing a functional résumé will place more focus on skills than on any other section. A well-written functional résumé groups skills into categories such as *Accounting/Finance Skills*, *Management/Leadership Skills*, *Communication/Teamwork Skills*, and *Computer/Technology Skills*. Each skills category includes a bulleted list of achievements and experience that demonstrate the skill, including specific numbers whenever possible. These skills categories should be placed in the beginning of the résumé, where they will be highlighted, followed by education and work experience. The action verbs shown in Figures 13.3 and 13.4 can also be used when constructing a functional résumé.

Awards, honors, and activities are appropriate for the résumé.

Awards, Honors, and Activities. If you have three or more awards or honors, highlight them by listing them under a separate heading. If not, put them with activities or in the education or work experience section if appropriate. Include awards, scholarships (financial and other), fellowships, dean's list, honors, recognition, commendations, and certificates. Be sure to identify items clearly. Your reader may be unfamiliar, for example, with Greek organizations, honors, and awards; tell what they mean. Instead of saying *Recipient of Star award*, give more details: *Recipient of Star award given by Pepperdine University to outstanding graduates who combine academic excellence and extracurricular activities*.

It is also appropriate to include school, community, volunteer, and professional activities. Employers are interested in evidence that you are a well-rounded person. This section provides an opportunity to demonstrate leadership and interpersonal skills. Strive to use action statements. For example, instead of saying *Treasurer of business club*, explain more fully: *Collected dues, kept financial records, and paid bills while serving as treasurer of 35-member business management club*.

Omit personal data not related to job qualifications.

Personal Data. Today's résumés omit personal data, such as birth date, marital status, height, weight, national origin, health, and religious affiliation. Such information doesn't relate to genuine occupational qualifications, and recruiters are legally barred from asking for such information. Some job seekers do, however, include hobbies or interests (such as skiing or photography) that might grab the recruiter's attention or serve as conversation starters. For example, let's say you learn that your hiring manager enjoys distance running. In that case you may want to mention that you have run a marathon if you share that interest. Many executives practice tennis or golf, two sports highly suitable for networking. Naturally, you shouldn't mention time-consuming interests or dangerous pastimes (such as rock climbing, scuba diving, caving, bungee jumping, or motorcycle racing). You could also indicate your willingness to travel or to relocate since many companies will be interested.

References are unnecessary for the résumé, but they should be available for the interview.

References. Listing references directly on a résumé takes up valuable space. Moreover, references are not normally instrumental in securing an interview—few companies check them before the interview. Instead, recruiters prefer that you bring to the interview a list of individuals willing to discuss your qualifications. Therefore, you should prepare a separate list, such as that in Figure 13.5, when you begin your job search. Ask three to five instructors, your current employer or previous employers, colleagues or subordinates, and other professional contacts whether they would

FIGURE 13.5 Sample Reference List

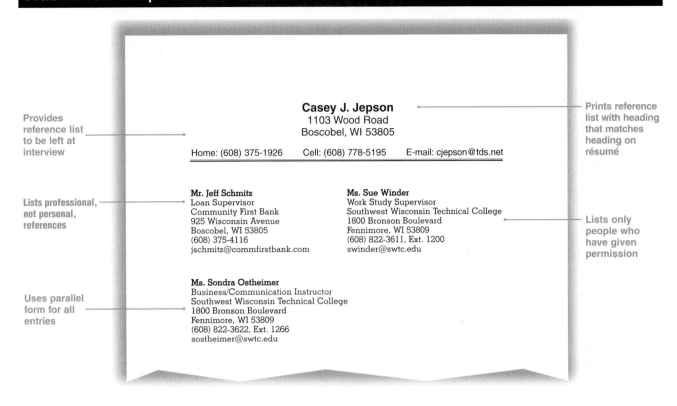

Provides reference list to be left at interview

Lists professional, not personal, references

Uses parallel form for all entries

Casey J. Jepson
1103 Wood Road
Boscobel, WI 53805

Home: (608) 375-1926   Cell: (608) 778-5195   E-mail: cjepson@tds.net

Mr. Jeff Schmitz
Loan Supervisor
Community First Bank
925 Wisconsin Avenue
Boscobel, WI 53805
(608) 375-4116
jschmitz@commfirstbank.com

Ms. Sue Winder
Work Study Supervisor
Southwest Wisconsin Technical College
1800 Bronson Boulevard
Fennimore, WI 53809
(608) 822-3611, Ext. 1200
swinder@swtc.edu

Ms. Sondra Ostheimer
Business/Communication Instructor
Southwest Wisconsin Technical College
1800 Bronson Boulevard
Fennimore, WI 53809
(608) 822-3622, Ext. 1266
sostheimer@swtc.edu

Prints reference list with heading that matches heading on résumé

Lists only people who have given permission

be willing to answer inquiries regarding your qualifications for employment. Be sure, however, to provide them with an opportunity to refuse. No reference is better than a negative one. Better yet, to avoid rejection and embarrassment, ask only those contacts who will give you a glowing endorsement.

Do not include personal or character references, such as friends, family, or neighbors, because recruiters rarely consult them. Companies are more interested in the opinions of objective individuals who know how you perform professionally and academically. One final note: most recruiters see little reason for including the statement *References furnished upon request*. It is unnecessary and takes up precious space.

In Figures 13.6 through 13.10, you will find a collection of models for chronological and functional résumés. Use these models to help you organize the content and format of your own persuasive résumé.

"I don't have any references, but 4 out of 5 phone psychics say I'm destined for greatness."

Optimizing Your Résumé for Today's Technologies

Thus far we have aimed our résumé advice at human readers. However, the first reader of your résumé may well be a computer. Hiring organizations today use a variety of methods to process incoming résumés. Some organizations still welcome traditional print-based résumés that may include attractive formatting.

To highlight her skills and capabilities, Casey placed them in the summary of qualifications at the top of her resume. She used the tables feature of her word processing program to create neat, invisible columns and to fit more information on one page, the length favored by most recruiters.

Omits objective to keep all options open

Focuses on skills and aptitudes that employers seek

Uses present-tense verbs for current jobs

Arranges employment by job title for easy recognition

Combines activities and awards to show extracurricular involvement

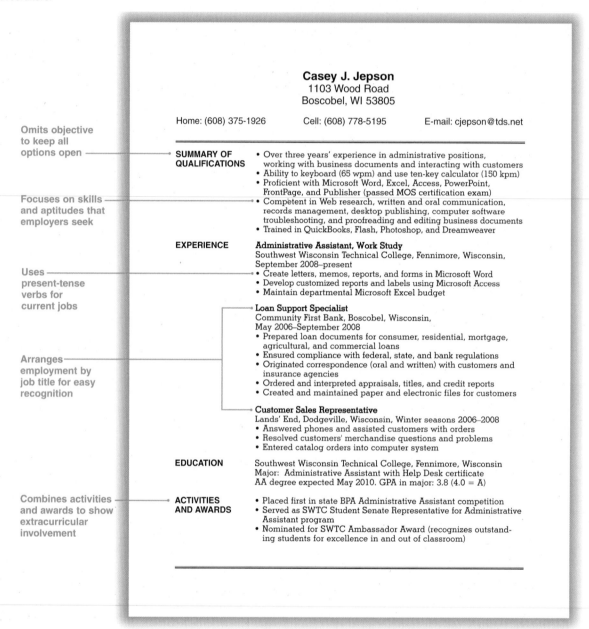

Casey J. Jepson
1103 Wood Road
Boscobel, WI 53805

Home: (608) 375-1926   Cell: (608) 778-5195   E-mail: cjepson@tds.net

SUMMARY OF QUALIFICATIONS
- Over three years' experience in administrative positions, working with business documents and interacting with customers
- Ability to keyboard (65 wpm) and use ten-key calculator (150 kpm)
- Proficient with Microsoft Word, Excel, Access, PowerPoint, FrontPage, and Publisher (passed MOS certification exam)
- Competent in Web research, written and oral communication, records management, desktop publishing, computer software troubleshooting, and proofreading and editing business documents
- Trained in QuickBooks, Flash, Photoshop, and Dreamweaver

EXPERIENCE

Administrative Assistant, Work Study
Southwest Wisconsin Technical College, Fennimore, Wisconsin, September 2008–present
- Create letters, memos, reports, and forms in Microsoft Word
- Develop customized reports and labels using Microsoft Access
- Maintain departmental Microsoft Excel budget

Loan Support Specialist
Community First Bank, Boscobel, Wisconsin, May 2006–September 2008
- Prepared loan documents for consumer, residential, mortgage, agricultural, and commercial loans
- Ensured compliance with federal, state, and bank regulations
- Originated correspondence (oral and written) with customers and insurance agencies
- Ordered and interpreted appraisals, titles, and credit reports
- Created and maintained paper and electronic files for customers

Customer Sales Representative
Lands' End, Dodgeville, Wisconsin, Winter seasons 2006–2008
- Answered phones and assisted customers with orders
- Resolved customers' merchandise questions and problems
- Entered catalog orders into computer system

EDUCATION
Southwest Wisconsin Technical College, Fennimore, Wisconsin
Major: Administrative Assistant with Help Desk certificate
AA degree expected May 2010. GPA in major: 3.8 (4.0 = A)

ACTIVITIES AND AWARDS
- Placed first in state BPA Administrative Assistant competition
- Served as SWTC Student Senate Representative for Administrative Assistant program
- Nominated for SWTC Ambassador Award (recognizes outstanding students for excellence in and out of classroom)

Because résumés are increasingly becoming part of searchable databases, you may need three versions.

Larger organizations, however, must deal with thousands of incoming résumés. Increasingly, they are placing those résumés directly into searchable databases. So that you can optimize your chances, you may need three versions of your résumé: (1) a traditional print-based résumé, (2) a scannable résumé, and (3) a plain-text résumé for e-mailing or online posting. This does not mean that you have to write different résumés. You are merely preparing different versions of your traditional résumé. With all versions, you should also be aware of the significant role of résumé keywords. Finally, you may decide to create an e-portfolio to showcase your qualifications.

Courtney Castro used a chronological resume to highlight her work experience, most of which was related directly to the position she seeks. Although she is a recent graduate, she has accumulated experience in two part-time jobs and one full-time job. She included a summary of qualifications to highlight her skills, experience, and interpersonal traits aimed at a specific position. Notice that Courtney designed her résumé in two columns with five major categories listed in the left column. In the right column she included bulleted items for each of the five categories. Conciseness and parallelism are important in writing an effective résumé. In the *Experience* category, she started each item with an active verb, which improved readability and parallel form.

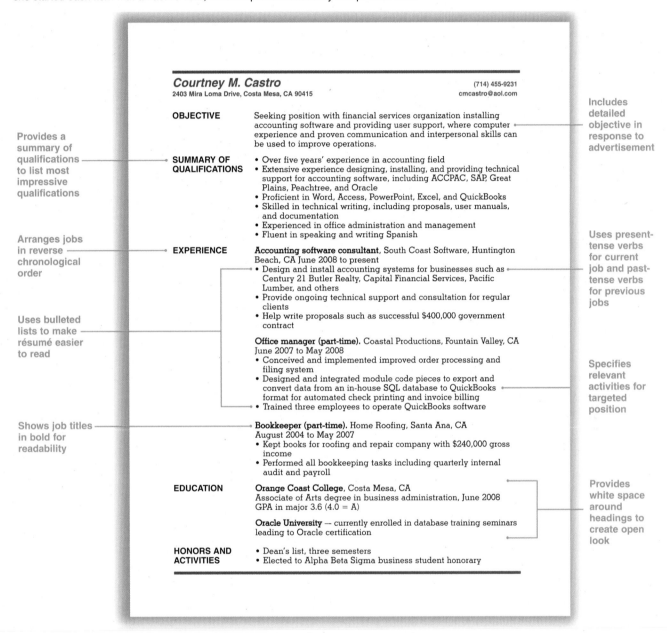

Designing a Print-Based Résumé

Print-based résumés (also called *presentation résumés*) are attractively formatted to maximize readability. You can create a professional-looking résumé by using your word processing program to highlight your qualifications. The examples in this chapter provide ideas for simple layouts that are easily duplicated. You can also examine résumé templates for design and format ideas. Their inflexibility, however, leads to frustration as you try to force your skills and experience into a

Eric used MS Word to design a traditional chronological print-based résumé that he plans to give to recruiters at the campus job fair or during an interview. Although Eric has work experience not related to his future employment, his résumé looks impressive because he has transferable skills. His internship is related to his future career, and his language skills and study abroad experience will help him score points in competition with applicants. Eric's volunteer experience is also attractive because it shows him as a well-rounded, compassionate individual. Because his experience in his future field is limited, he omitted a summary of qualifications.

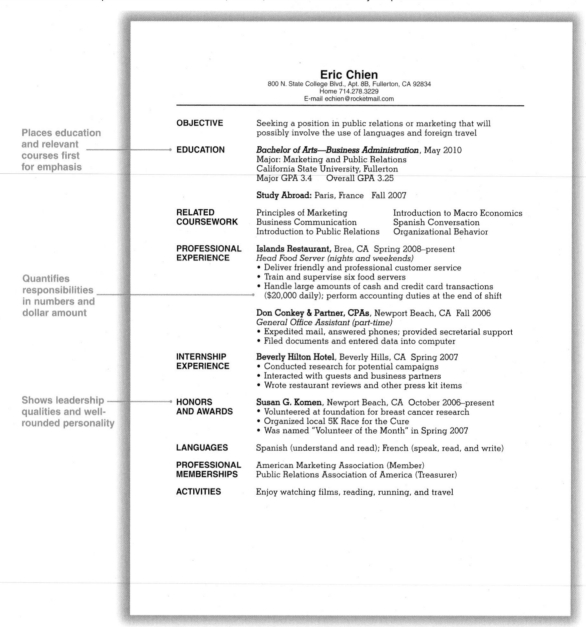

Places education and relevant courses first for emphasis

Quantifies responsibilities in numbers and dollar amount

Shows leadership qualities and well-rounded personality

Eric Chien
800 N. State College Blvd., Apt. 8B, Fullerton, CA 92834
Home 714.278.3229
E-mail echien@rocketmail.com

OBJECTIVE
Seeking a position in public relations or marketing that will possibly involve the use of languages and foreign travel

EDUCATION
Bachelor of Arts—Business Administration, May 2010
Major: Marketing and Public Relations
California State University, Fullerton
Major GPA 3.4   Overall GPA 3.25

Study Abroad: Paris, France   Fall 2007

RELATED COURSEWORK
Principles of Marketing   Introduction to Macro Economics
Business Communication   Spanish Conversation
Introduction to Public Relations   Organizational Behavior

PROFESSIONAL EXPERIENCE
Islands Restaurant, Brea, CA Spring 2008–present
Head Food Server (nights and weekends)
• Deliver friendly and professional customer service
• Train and supervise six food servers
• Handle large amounts of cash and credit card transactions ($20,000 daily); perform accounting duties at the end of shift

Don Conkey & Partner, CPAs, Newport Beach, CA Fall 2006
General Office Assistant (part-time)
• Expedited mail, answered phones; provided secretarial support
• Filed documents and entered data into computer

INTERNSHIP EXPERIENCE
Beverly Hilton Hotel, Beverly Hills, CA Spring 2007
• Conducted research for potential campaigns
• Interacted with guests and business partners
• Wrote restaurant reviews and other press kit items

HONORS AND AWARDS
Susan G. Komen, Newport Beach, CA October 2006–present
• Volunteered at foundation for breast cancer research
• Organized local 5K Race for the Cure
• Was named "Volunteer of the Month" in Spring 2007

LANGUAGES
Spanish (understand and read); French (speak, read, and write)

PROFESSIONAL MEMBERSHIPS
American Marketing Association (Member)
Public Relations Association of America (Treasurer)

ACTIVITIES
Enjoy watching films, reading, running, and travel

predetermined template sequence. What's more, recruiters who read hundreds of résumés can usually spot a template-based résumé. Instead, create your own original résumé that fits your unique qualifications.

Your print-based résumé should use an outline format with headings and bullet points to present information in an orderly, uncluttered, easy-to-read format. An attractive print-based résumé is necessary (a) when you are competing for a job that does not require electronic submission, (b) to present in addition to an electronic submission, and (c) to bring with you to job interviews. Even if a résumé is submitted

Because Rachel has many years of experience and seeks executive-level employment, she highlighted her experience by placing it before her education. Her summary of qualifications highlighted her most impressive experience and skills. This chronological two-page résumé shows the steady progression of her career to executive positions, a movement that impresses and reassures recruiters.

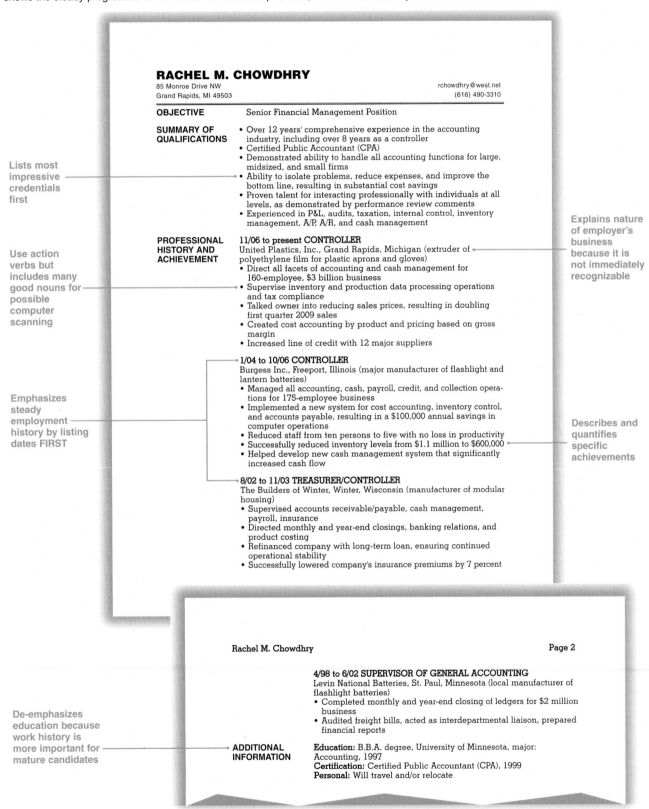

Lists most impressive credentials first

Use action verbs but includes many good nouns for possible computer scanning

Emphasizes steady employment history by listing dates FIRST

Explains nature of employer's business because it is not immediately recognizable

Describes and quantifies specific achievements

De-emphasizes education because work history is more important for mature candidates

RACHEL M. CHOWDHRY
85 Monroe Drive NW
Grand Rapids, MI 49503

rchowdhry@west.net
(616) 490-3310

OBJECTIVE   Senior Financial Management Position

SUMMARY OF QUALIFICATIONS
- Over 12 years' comprehensive experience in the accounting industry, including over 8 years as a controller
- Certified Public Accountant (CPA)
- Demonstrated ability to handle all accounting functions for large, midsized, and small firms
- Ability to isolate problems, reduce expenses, and improve the bottom line, resulting in substantial cost savings
- Proven talent for interacting professionally with individuals at all levels, as demonstrated by performance review comments
- Experienced in P&L, audits, taxation, internal control, inventory management, A/P, A/R, and cash management

PROFESSIONAL HISTORY AND ACHIEVEMENT

11/06 to present CONTROLLER
United Plastics, Inc., Grand Rapids, Michigan (extruder of polyethylene film for plastic aprons and gloves)
- Direct all facets of accounting and cash management for 160-employee, $3 billion business
- Supervise inventory and production data processing operations and tax compliance
- Talked owner into reducing sales prices, resulting in doubling first quarter 2009 sales
- Created cost accounting by product and pricing based on gross margin
- Increased line of credit with 12 major suppliers

1/04 to 10/06 CONTROLLER
Burgess Inc., Freeport, Illinois (major manufacturer of flashlight and lantern batteries)
- Managed all accounting, cash, payroll, credit, and collection operations for 175-employee business
- Implemented a new system for cost accounting, inventory control, and accounts payable, resulting in a $100,000 annual savings in computer operations
- Reduced staff from ten persons to five with no loss in productivity
- Successfully reduced inventory levels from $1.1 million to $600,000
- Helped develop new cash management system that significantly increased cash flow

8/02 to 11/03 TREASURER/CONTROLLER
The Builders of Winter, Winter, Wisconsin (manufacturer of modular housing)
- Supervised accounts receivable/payable, cash management, payroll, insurance
- Directed monthly and year-end closings, banking relations, and product costing
- Refinanced company with long-term loan, ensuring continued operational stability
- Successfully lowered company's insurance premiums by 7 percent

Rachel M. Chowdhry   Page 2

4/98 to 6/02 SUPERVISOR OF GENERAL ACCOUNTING
Levin National Batteries, St. Paul, Minnesota (local manufacturer of flashlight batteries)
- Completed monthly and year-end closing of ledgers for $2 million business
- Audited freight bills, acted as interdepartmental liaison, prepared financial reports

ADDITIONAL INFORMATION
Education: B.B.A. degree, University of Minnesota, major: Accounting, 1997
Certification: Certified Public Accountant (CPA), 1999
Personal: Will travel and/or relocate

Recent graduate Kevin Touhy chose this functional format to de-emphasize his meager work experience and emphasize his potential in sales and marketing. This version of his résumé is more generic than one targeted for a specific position. Nevertheless, it emphasizes his strong points with specific achievements and includes an employment section to satisfy recruiters. The functional format presents ability-focused topics. It illustrates what the job seeker can do for the employer instead of narrating a history of previous jobs. Although recruiters prefer chronological résumés, the functional format is a good choice for new graduates, career changers, and those with employment gaps.

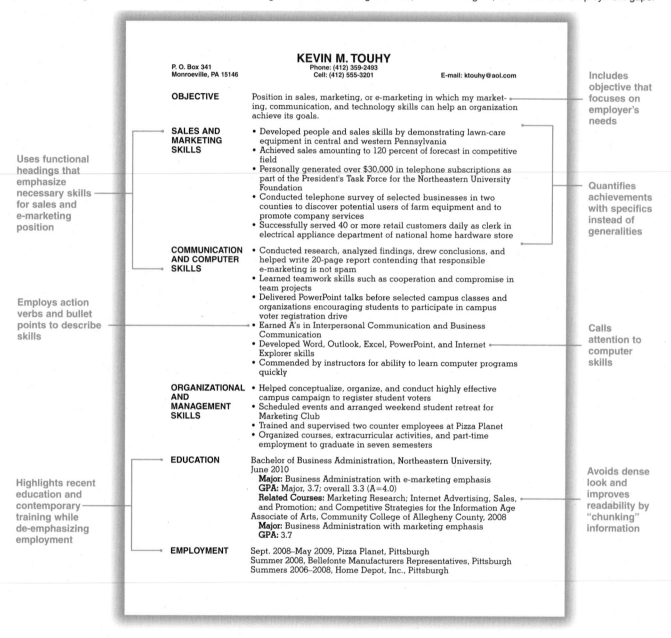

KEVIN M. TOUHY

P. O. Box 341
Monroeville, PA 15146
Phone: (412) 359-2493
Cell: (412) 555-3201
E-mail: ktouhy@aol.com

Includes objective that focuses on employer's needs

OBJECTIVE
Position in sales, marketing, or e-marketing in which my marketing, communication, and technology skills can help an organization achieve its goals.

Uses functional headings that emphasize necessary skills for sales and e-marketing position

SALES AND MARKETING SKILLS
- Developed people and sales skills by demonstrating lawn-care equipment in central and western Pennsylvania
- Achieved sales amounting to 120 percent of forecast in competitive field
- Personally generated over $30,000 in telephone subscriptions as part of the President's Task Force for the Northeastern University Foundation
- Conducted telephone survey of selected businesses in two counties to discover potential users of farm equipment and to promote company services
- Successfully served 40 or more retail customers daily as clerk in electrical appliance department of national home hardware store

Quantifies achievements with specifics instead of generalities

Employs action verbs and bullet points to describe skills

COMMUNICATION AND COMPUTER SKILLS
- Conducted research, analyzed findings, drew conclusions, and helped write 20-page report contending that responsible e-marketing is not spam
- Learned teamwork skills such as cooperation and compromise in team projects
- Delivered PowerPoint talks before selected campus classes and organizations encouraging students to participate in campus voter registration drive
- Earned A's in Interpersonal Communication and Business Communication
- Developed Word, Outlook, Excel, PowerPoint, and Internet Explorer skills
- Commended by instructors for ability to learn computer programs quickly

Calls attention to computer skills

ORGANIZATIONAL AND MANAGEMENT SKILLS
- Helped conceptualize, organize, and conduct highly effective campus campaign to register student voters
- Scheduled events and arranged weekend student retreat for Marketing Club
- Trained and supervised two counter employees at Pizza Planet
- Organized courses, extracurricular activities, and part-time employment to graduate in seven semesters

Highlights recent education and contemporary training while de-emphasizing employment

EDUCATION
Bachelor of Business Administration, Northeastern University, June 2010
Major: Business Administration with e-marketing emphasis
GPA: Major, 3.7; overall 3.3 (A=4.0)
Related Courses: Marketing Research; Internet Advertising, Sales, and Promotion; and Competitive Strategies for the Information Age
Associate of Arts, Community College of Allegheny County, 2008
Major: Business Administration with marketing emphasis
GPA: 3.7

Avoids dense look and improves readability by "chunking" information

EMPLOYMENT
Sept. 2008–May 2009, Pizza Planet, Pittsburgh
Summer 2008, Bellefonte Manufacturers Representatives, Pittsburgh
Summers 2006–2008, Home Depot, Inc., Pittsburgh

electronically, nearly every job candidate will want to have an attractive traditional résumé handy for human readers.

Preparing a Scannable Résumé

A scannable résumé is one that is meant to be printed on plain white paper and read by a computer. To screen incoming résumés, many mid- and large-sized companies use automated applicant-tracking software. These systems scan an incoming résumé with optical character recognition (OCR) looking for keywords. The most sophisticated programs enable recruiters and hiring managers to search for keywords, rank résumés based on the number of "hits," and generate reports. Information from your résumé is stored, usually from six months to a year.

Applicant-tracking software scans incoming résumés searching for keywords.

Before sending your résumé, find out whether the recipient uses scanning software. If you can't tell from the job announcement, call the company to ask whether it scans résumés electronically. If you don't get a clear answer and you have even the slightest suspicion that your résumé might be read electronically, you will be smart to prepare a plain, scannable version as shown in Figure 13.11.

FIGURE 13.11 Scannable Résumé

Letitia P. Lopez prepared this "plain Jane" résumé free of graphics and fancy formatting so that it would scan well if read by a computer. With the résumé, she included many job titles, skills, traits, and other descriptive keywords that scanners are programmed to recognize. To improve accurate scanning, she avoided bullets, italics, underlining, and columns. If she had more information to include, she could have gone to a second page because a résumé to be scanned need not be restricted to one page.

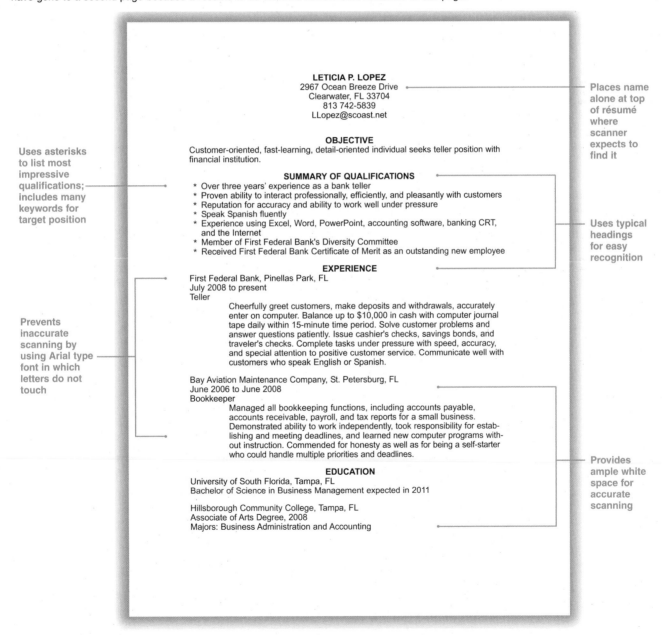

Places name alone at top of résumé where scanner expects to find it

Uses asterisks to list most impressive qualifications; includes many keywords for target position

Prevents inaccurate scanning by using Arial type font in which letters do not touch

Uses typical headings for easy recognition

Provides ample white space for accurate scanning

LETICIA P. LOPEZ
2967 Ocean Breeze Drive
Clearwater, FL 33704
813 742-5839
LLopez@scoast.net

OBJECTIVE
Customer-oriented, fast-learning, detail-oriented individual seeks teller position with financial institution.

SUMMARY OF QUALIFICATIONS
* Over three years' experience as a bank teller
* Proven ability to interact professionally, efficiently, and pleasantly with customers
* Reputation for accuracy and ability to work well under pressure
* Speak Spanish fluently
* Experience using Excel, Word, PowerPoint, accounting software, banking CRT, and the Internet
* Member of First Federal Bank's Diversity Committee
* Received First Federal Bank Certificate of Merit as an outstanding new employee

EXPERIENCE
First Federal Bank, Pinellas Park, FL
July 2008 to present
Teller
    Cheerfully greet customers, make deposits and withdrawals, accurately enter on computer. Balance up to $10,000 in cash with computer journal tape daily within 15-minute time period. Solve customer problems and answer questions patiently. Issue cashier's checks, savings bonds, and traveler's checks. Complete tasks under pressure with speed, accuracy, and special attention to positive customer service. Communicate well with customers who speak English or Spanish.

Bay Aviation Maintenance Company, St. Petersburg, FL
June 2006 to June 2008
Bookkeeper
    Managed all bookkeeping functions, including accounts payable, accounts receivable, payroll, and tax reports for a small business. Demonstrated ability to work independently, took responsibility for establishing and meeting deadlines, and learned new computer programs without instruction. Commended for honesty as well as for being a self-starter who could handle multiple priorities and deadlines.

EDUCATION
University of South Florida, Tampa, FL
Bachelor of Science in Business Management expected in 2011

Hillsborough Community College, Tampa, FL
Associate of Arts Degree, 2008
Majors: Business Administration and Accounting

Tips for Maximizing Scannability.
A scannable résumé must sacrifice many of the graphic enhancements you might have used to make your traditional print résumé attractive. To maximize scannability, follow these steps:

Scannable résumés use plain formatting, large fonts, quality printing, and white space.

- **Use 10- to 14-point type.** Because touching letters or unusual fonts are likely to be misread, using a large, well-known font such as 12-point Times New Roman or Arial is safest. This may mean that your résumé will require two pages. After printing, inspect your résumé to see whether any letters touch—especially in your name.

- **Avoid unusual typefaces, underlining, and italics.** Moreover, don't use borders, shading, or other graphics to highlight text. These features don't scan well. Most applicant-tracking programs, however, can accurately read bold print, solid bullets, and asterisks.

- **Be sure that your name is the first line on the page.** Don't use fancy layouts that may confuse a scanner. Reports generated by applicant-tracking software usually assume that the first line of a résumé contains the applicant's name.

- **List each phone number on its own line.** Your landline and cell phone numbers should appear on separate lines to improve recognition.

- **Provide white space.** To ensure separation of words and categories, leave plenty of white space. For example, instead of using parentheses to enclose a telephone area code, insert blank spaces, such as 212 799-2415. Leave blank lines around headings.

- **Avoid double columns.** When listing job duties, skills, computer programs, and so forth, don't tabulate items into two- or three-column lists. Scanners read across and may convert tables into nonsensical output.

- **Use smooth white paper, black ink, and quality printing.** Avoid colored or textured paper, and use a high-quality laser or ink-jet printer.

- **Don't fold or staple your résumé.** Send it in a large envelope so that you can avoid folds. Words that appear on folds may not be scanned correctly.

Tips for Maximizing "Hits."
In addition to paying attention to the physical appearance of your résumé, you must also be concerned with keywords that produce "hits" or recognition by the scanner. To maximize hits, do the following:

Scanners produce "hits" when they recognize targeted keywords such as nouns describing skills, traits, tasks, and job titles.

- **Focus on specific keywords.** Study carefully any advertisements and job descriptions for the position you want. Select keywords that describe skills, traits, tasks, and job titles. Because interpersonal traits are often requested by employers, consult Figure 13.12. It shows the most frequently requested interpersonal traits, as reported by Resumix, a pioneer in résumé-scanning software.

- **Incorporate words from the advertisement or job description.** Describe your experience, education, and qualifications in terms associated with the job advertisement or job description for this position.

- **Use typical headings.** Include expected categories such as *Objective, Summary of Qualifications, Education, Work Experience, Skills,* and *Accomplishments.* Scanning software looks for such headings.

- **Be careful of abbreviations.** Minimize unfamiliar abbreviations, but maximize easily recognized abbreviations—especially those within your field, such as CAD, JPG, or JIT. When in doubt, though, spell out! Computers are less confused by whole words.

- **Describe interpersonal traits and attitudes.** Hiring managers look for keywords and phrases such as *time management skills, dependability, high energy, leadership, sense of responsibility,* and *team player.*

- **Use more than one page if necessary.** Computers can easily handle more than one page so include as much as necessary to describe your qualifications and maximize hits.

FIGURE 13.12 Interpersonal Keywords Most Requested by Employers Using Résumé-Scanning Software*

Ability to delegate	Creative	Leadership	Self-accountable
Ability to implement	Customer oriented	Multitasking	Self-managing
Ability to plan	Detail minded	Open communication	Setting priorities
Ability to train	Ethical	Open minded	Supportive
Accurate	Flexible	Oral communication	Takes initiative
Adaptable	Follow instructions	Organizational skills	Team building
Aggressive work	Follow through	Persuasive	Team player
Analytical ability	Follow up	Problem solving	Tenacious
Assertive	High energy	Public speaking	Willing to travel
Communication skills	Industrious	Results oriented	
Competitive	Innovative	Safety conscious	

*Reported by Resumix, a leading producer of résumé-scanning software.
Source: Joyce Lain Kennedy and Thomas J. Morrow, *Electronic Résumé Revolution* (New York: John Wiley & Sons), 70. Reprinted by permission of John Wiley & Sons, Inc.

Preparing a Plain-Text Résumé for E-Mailing

A plain-text résumé (also called an ASCII résumé) is an electronic version suitable for e-mailing or pasting into online résumé bank submission forms. Employers prefer plain-text résumés because they avoid possible e-mail viruses and word processing incompatibilities. Usually embedded within an e-mail message, a plain-text résumé, shown in Figure 13.13, is immediately searchable. You should prepare a plain-text résumé if you want the fastest and most reliable way to contact potential employers. Follow these suggestions to create a plain-text résumé:

- **Observe all the tips for a scannable résumé.** A plain-text résumé requires the same attention to content, formatting, and keywords as that recommended for a scannable résumé.
- **Reformat with shorter lines.** Many e-mail programs wrap lines longer than 60 characters. To avoid having your résumé look as if a chain saw attacked it, use a short line length (such as 4 inches).
- **Think about using keyboard characters to enhance format.** In addition to using capital letters and asterisks, you might use spaced equals signs (= = =) and tildes (~ ~ ~) to create lines that separate résumé categories.
- **Move all text to the left.** Do not center items; start all text at the left margin. Remove tabs.
- **Save your résumé in plain text (.txt) or rich text format (.rtf).** Saving your résumé in one of these formats will ensure that it can be read when pasted in an e-mail message.
- **Test your résumé before sending it to an employer.** After preparing and saving your résumé, copy and paste a copy of it into an e-mail message and send it to yourself and check to see whether any non-ASCII characters appear. They may show up as question marks, square blocks, or other odd characters. Make any necessary changes.

When sending a plain-text résumé to an employer, be sure that your subject line clearly describes the purpose of your message. In addition, use the professional e-mail techniques you learned in Chapter 5.

> Employers prefer plain-text résumés because they are immediately searchable and they do not require employers to open attachments, which might carry viruses or create software incompatibilities.

FIGURE 13.13 Plain-Text Résumé

To be sure her plain-text résumé would transmit well when within an e-mail message, Leticia prepared a special version with all lines starting at the left margin. She used a 4-inch line length to avoid awkward line breaks. To set off her major headings, she used the tilde character on her keyboard. She saved the document as a text file (.txt or .rtf) so that it could be read by different computers. At the end she included a statement saying that an attractive, fully formatted hard copy of her résumé was available on request.

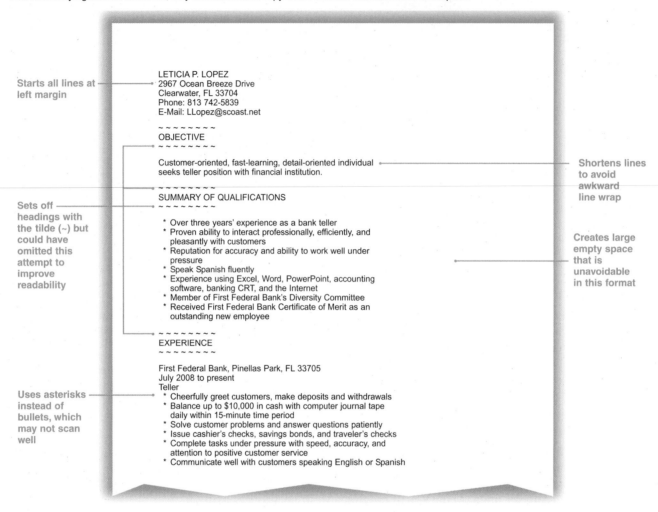

Starts all lines at left margin

Shortens lines to avoid awkward line wrap

Sets off headings with the tilde (~) but could have omitted this attempt to improve readability

Creates large empty space that is unavoidable in this format

Uses asterisks instead of bullets, which may not scan well

```
LETICIA P. LOPEZ
2967 Ocean Breeze Drive
Clearwater, FL 33704
Phone: 813 742-5839
E-Mail: LLopez@scoast.net

~ ~ ~ ~ ~ ~ ~ ~
OBJECTIVE
~ ~ ~ ~ ~ ~ ~ ~

Customer-oriented, fast-learning, detail-oriented individual
seeks teller position with financial institution.

~ ~ ~ ~ ~ ~ ~ ~
SUMMARY OF QUALIFICATIONS
~ ~ ~ ~ ~ ~ ~ ~

   * Over three years' experience as a bank teller
   * Proven ability to interact professionally, efficiently, and
     pleasantly with customers
   * Reputation for accuracy and ability to work well under
     pressure
   * Speak Spanish fluently
   * Experience using Excel, Word, PowerPoint, accounting
     software, banking CRT, and the Internet
   * Member of First Federal Bank's Diversity Committee
   * Received First Federal Bank Certificate of Merit as an
     outstanding new employee

~ ~ ~ ~ ~ ~ ~ ~
EXPERIENCE
~ ~ ~ ~ ~ ~ ~ ~

First Federal Bank, Pinellas Park, FL 33705
July 2008 to present
Teller
   * Cheerfully greet customers, make deposits and withdrawals
   * Balance up to $10,000 in cash with computer journal tape
     daily within 15-minute time period
   * Solve customer problems and answer questions patiently
   * Issue cashier's checks, savings bonds, and traveler's checks
   * Complete tasks under pressure with speed, accuracy, and
     attention to positive customer service
   * Communicate well with customers speaking English or Spanish
```

Showcasing Your Qualifications in an E-Portfolio

An e-portfolio offers links to examples of a job candidate's performance, talents, and accomplishments in digital form.

As the workplace becomes increasingly digital, you have yet another way to display your qualifications to prospective employers—the e-portfolio. Resourceful job candidates in certain fields—writers, models, artists, and graphic artists—have been creating print portfolios to illustrate their qualifications and achievements for some time. Now business and professional job candidates in the technology industry in particular are using electronic portfolios to show off their talents.

An e-portfolio is a collection of digital files that can be navigated with the help of menus much like a personal Web site. It provides viewers with a snapshot of a candidate's performance, talents, and accomplishments. A digital portfolio may include a copy of your résumé, reference letters, special achievements, awards, certificates, work samples, a complete list of your courses, thank-you letters, and anything else that

"I want my résumé to be the one you remember. It's also available as a music video, interpretive dance, and a haiku."

touts your accomplishments. An advanced portfolio might include links to electronic copies of your artwork, film projects, blueprints, and photographs of classwork that might otherwise be difficult to share with potential employers.

Digital portfolios are generally accessed on Web sites, where they are available around the clock to employers. Some colleges and universities not only make Web site space available for student e-portfolios, but also provide instruction and resources for scanning photos, digitizing images, and preparing graphics. E-portfolios may also be burned onto CDs and DVDs that you can mail to prospective employers.

E-portfolios have many advantages. On Web sites they can be viewed at employers' convenience. Let's say you are talking on the phone with an employer in another city who wants to see a copy of your résumé. You can simply refer the employer to the Web address where your résumé is posted. E-portfolios can also be seen by many individuals in an organization without circulating a paper copy. But the real reason for preparing an e-portfolio is that it shows off your talents and qualifications more thoroughly than a print résumé does.

Tech-savvy applicants even use videos to profile their skills. A professional-grade video résumé may open doors and secure an interview when other techniques have failed.[33] However, some recruiters are skeptical about digital or video portfolios because they fear that such applications will take more time to view than paper-based résumés do. Nontraditional applications may end up at the bottom of the pile or be ignored. Worse yet, lack of judgment can lead to embarrassment. Aleksey Vayner's video résumé somehow ended up on YouTube in late 2006, causing him to be widely ridiculed. The Yale senior and budding investment banker concocted a six-minute video titled "Impossible Is Nothing," showing him boisterously lifting weights, ballroom dancing, and playing tennis, all the while engaging in shameless puffery.[34]

Experts agree that the new medium will need to mature before smart use guidelines can be established. You can learn more about video résumés by searching the Web.

> **Job candidates generally offer e-portfolios at Web sites, but they may also burn them onto a CD or a DVD.**

> **OFFICE INSIDER**
>
> *I think the video résumé debate is going to be hot for the next few years. Typically, they are frowned upon because of [Equal Employment Opportunity Commission] regulation. Companies are scared to death of getting sued.*

Applying the Final Touches to Your Résumé

Because your résumé is probably the most important message you will ever write, you will revise it many times. With so much information in concentrated form and with so much riding on its outcome, your résumé demands careful polishing, proofreading, and critiquing.

As you revise, be certain to verify all the facts, particularly those involving your previous employment and education. Don't be caught in a mistake, or worse, a distortion of previous jobs and dates of employment. These items likely will be checked, and the consequences of puffing up a résumé with deception or flat-out lies are simply not worth the risk.

Being Honest and Ethical

A résumé is expected to showcase a candidate's strengths and minimize weaknesses. For this reason, recruiters expect a certain degree of self-promotion. Some résumé writers, however, step over the line that separates honest self-marketing from deceptive half-truths and blatant lies. Distorting facts on a résumé is unethical; lying is illegal. Either practice can destroy a career.

Given the competitive job market, it might be tempting to puff up your résumé. What's more, you wouldn't be alone in telling fibs or outright whoppers. One study found that 44 percent of applicants lied about their work histories, 23 percent fabricated licenses or credentials, and 41 percent falsified their educational backgrounds.[35] Another recent study revealed an even higher number of résumé cheats; over 50 percent of applicants lie.[36] Although recruiters can't check all information, most will verify previous employment and education before hiring candidates. Over half will require official transcripts.

WORKPLACE IN FOCUS

Despite the temptation to fudge the facts a little when applying for a job, it doesn't pay to pad one's résumé. Celebrity chef Robert Irvine, who rose to fame by preparing meals on the Food Network's *Dinner: Impossible* program, lost his spot when executives discovered the TV chef had cooked up far more than sumptuous soufflés and dynamite desserts. Numerous qualifications listed on Irvine's résumé—such as the claim to have cooked for U.S. presidents and Britain's royal family—proved greatly exaggerated or untrue. *What common pitfalls should job seekers avoid when preparing résumés?*

"I typed up my résumé on the computer. The spell-checker accidentally changed 'Mid-State Junior College' to 'Harvard.'"

After hiring, the checking process may continue. If hiring officials find a discrepancy in GPA or prior experience and the error is an honest mistake, they meet with the new-hire to hear an explanation. If the discrepancy wasn't a mistake, they will likely fire the person immediately. No job seeker wants to be in the unhappy position of explaining résumé errors or defending misrepresentation. Avoiding the following common problems can keep you off the hot seat:

- **Inflated education, grades, or honors.** Some job candidates claim degrees from colleges or universities when in fact they merely attended classes. Others increase their grade point averages or claim fictitious honors. Any such dishonest reporting is grounds for dismissal when discovered.
- **Enhanced job titles.** Wishing to elevate their status, some applicants misrepresent their titles. For example, one technician called himself a programmer when he had actually programmed only one project for his boss. A mail clerk who assumed added responsibilities conferred upon herself the title of supervisor. Even when the description seems accurate, it is unethical to list any title not officially granted.
- **Puffed-up accomplishments.** Some job seekers inflate their employment experience or achievements. One clerk, eager to make her photocopying duties sound more important, said that she assisted the *vice president in communicating and distributing employee directives*. An Ivy League graduate who spent the better part of six months watching rented movies on his DVD player described the activity as *Independent Film Study*. That statement may have helped win an interview, but it lost him the job. In addition to avoiding puffery, guard against taking sole credit for achievements that required the efforts of many people. When recruiters suspect dubious claims on résumés, they nail applicants with specific—and often embarrassing—questions during their interviews.
- **Altered employment dates.** Some candidates extend the dates of employment to hide unimpressive jobs or to cover up periods of unemployment and illness. Let's say that several years ago Cindy was unemployed for 14 months between working for Company A and being hired by Company B. To make her employment history look better, she adds seven months to her tenure with Company A and seven months to Company B. Now her employment history has no gaps, but her résumé is dishonest and represents a potential booby trap for her.
- **Hidden keywords.** One of the latest sneaky tricks involves inserting invisible keywords in electronic résumés. To fool scanning programs into ranking their résumés higher, some job hunters use white type on a white background or they use Web coding to pack their résumés with target keywords. However, newer recruiter search tools detect such mischief, and those résumés are tossed.[37]

If your honest qualifications aren't good enough to get you the job you want, start working now to improve them.

Polishing Your Résumé

While you continue revising, look for other ways to improve your résumé. For example, consider consolidating headings. By condensing your information into as few headings as possible, you will produce a clean, professional-looking document. Study other résumés for valuable formatting ideas. Ask yourself what graphic highlighting techniques you can use to improve readability: capitalization, underlining, indenting, and bulleting. Experiment with headings and styles to achieve a pleasing, easy-to-read message. Moreover, look for ways to eliminate wordiness. For example, instead of *Supervised two employees who worked at the counter*, try *Supervised two counter employees*. Review Chapter 4 for more tips on writing concisely.

In addition to making your résumé concise, make sure that you haven't included any of the following information, which doesn't belong on a résumé:

- Any basis for discrimination (age, marital status, gender, national origin, religion, race, marital status, number of children, disability)
- A photograph
- Reasons for leaving previous jobs
- The word *résumé*
- Social security number
- Salary history or requirements
- High school information
- References
- Full addresses of schools or employers (include city and state only)

Above all, make sure your print-based résumé look professional. Avoid anything humorous or "cute," such as a help-wanted poster with your name or picture inside. Eliminate the personal pronoun *I* to ensure an objective style. Use high-quality paper in a professional color, such as white, off-white, or light gray. Print your résumé using a first-rate laser or ink-jet printer. Be prepared with a résumé for people to read as well as one for a computer to read.

Study résumé models for ideas on improving your format.

Proofreading Your Résumé

After revising, you must proofread, proofread, and proofread again for spelling, mechanics, content, and format. Then have a knowledgeable friend or relative proofread it yet again. This is one document that must be perfect. Because the job market is so competitive, one typo, misspelled word, or grammatical error could eliminate you from consideration.

By now you may be thinking that you'd like to hire someone to write your résumé. Don't! First, you know yourself better than anyone else could know you. Second, you will end up with a generic or a one-time résumé. A generic résumé in today's highly competitive job market will lose out to a customized résumé nine times out of ten. Equally useless is a one-time résumé aimed at a single job. What if you don't get that job? Because you will need to revise your résumé many times as you seek a variety of jobs, be prepared to write (and rewrite) it yourself.

In addition to being well written, a résumé must be carefully formatted and meticulously proofread.

Submitting Your Résumé

If you are responding to a job advertisement, be sure to read the job listing carefully to make sure you know how the employer wants you to submit your résumé. Not following the prospective employer's instructions can eliminate you from consideration before your résumé is even reviewed. Employers will probably ask you to submit your résumé in one of the following ways:

- **Word document.** Recruiters may still ask candidates to send their résumés and cover letters by snail mail. They may also allow applicants to attach their résumés as MS Word documents to e-mail messages, despite the fear of viruses.
- **Plain-text, ASCII document.** As discussed earlier, some employers expect applicants to submit résumés and cover letters as plain-text documents. This format is widely used for posting to an online job board or for e-mail delivery. Plain-text résumés may be embedded within or attached to e-mail messages.
- **PDF document.** For the sake of safety, many hiring managers prefer PDF (portable document format) files. A PDF résumé will look exactly like the original

Send your résumé in the format the employer requests.

and cannot be easily altered. Newer computers come with Adobe Acrobat Reader preinstalled for easy reading. Converting your MS Word and other documents to a PDF file requires Adobe software.

- **Company database.** Some organizations prefer that you complete an online form with your résumé information. This enables them to plug your data into their formats for rapid searching. You might be able to cut and paste your information into the form.
- **Fax.** Although still a popular way of sending résumés, faxing presents problems in blurring and lost information. If you must fax your résumé, use at least a 12-point font to improve readability. Thinner fonts—such as Times, Palatino, New Century Schoolbook, Arial, and Bookman—are clearer than thicker ones. Avoid underlines, which may look broken or choppy when faxed. Follow up with your polished, printed résumé.

Whether you are mailing your résumé the traditional way, submitting it by e-mail, or transmitting it by fax, don't send it on its own. Regardless of the submission format, in most cases a résumé should be accompanied by a cover letter, which will be discussed in the next section.

Creating a Customized, Persuasive Cover Letter

Cover letters introduce résumés, relate writer strengths to reader benefits, and seek an interview.

Job candidates often labor over their résumés but treat the cover letter as an afterthought. This critical mistake could destroy a job search. Even if an advertisement doesn't request one, be sure to distinguish your application with a persuasive cover letter (also called a *letter of application*). It has three purposes: (a) introducing the résumé, (b) highlighting your strengths in terms of benefits to the reader, and (c) gaining an interview. In many ways your cover letter is a sales letter; it sells your talent and tries to beat the competition. It will, accordingly, include many of the techniques you learned for sales letters in Chapter 8, especially if your letter is unsolicited.

Recruiting professionals disagree about how long to make a cover letter. Many prefer short letters with no more than three paragraphs. Others desire longer letters that supply more information, thus giving them a better opportunity to evaluate a candidate's qualifications. These recruiters argue that hiring and training new employees is expensive and time consuming; therefore, they welcome extra data to guide them in making the best choice the first time. Follow your judgment in writing a brief or a longer cover letter. If you believe, for example, that you need space to explain in more detail what you can do for a prospective employer, do so.

Regardless of its length, a cover letter should have three primary parts: (a) an opening that introduces the message and identifies the position, (b) a body that sells the candidate and focuses on the employer's needs, and (c) a closing that requests an interview and motivates action. When putting your cover letter together, remember that the biggest mistake job seekers make when writing cover letters is making them sound too generic. You should, therefore, write a personalized, targeted cover letter for every position you apply for.

Gaining Attention in the Opening

The opening in a cover letter gains attention by addressing the receiver by name.

Your cover letter will be more appealing, and will more likely be read, if it begins by addressing the reader by name. Rather than sending your letter to the *Hiring Manager* or *Human Resources Department*, try to identify the name of the appropriate individual. Call the organization for the name of the person in charge of hiring for the position, and always verify spelling. If that fails, says workplace expert Liz Ryan, look on the company Web site under **About Us**. "Either the VP/leader of the function you are interested in (e.g., marketing or engineering)," suggests Ryan, "or the VP/leader of HR is a great person to call or write to."[38] If you still cannot find the name of a person to address, you might use the simplified letter style and replace the salutation with a subject line such as "Application for Position of . . . ."

How you open your cover letter depends largely on whether the application is solicited or unsolicited. If an employment position has been announced and applicants are being solicited, you can use a direct approach. If you do not know whether a position is open and you are prospecting for a job, use an indirect approach. Whether direct or indirect, the opening should attract the attention of the reader. Strive for openings that are more imaginative than *Please consider this letter an application for the position of . . .* or *I would like to apply for. . . .*

Openings for Solicited Jobs. Here are some of the best techniques to open a cover letter for a job that has been announced:

- **Refer to the name of an employee in the company.** Remember that employers always hope to hire known quantities rather than complete strangers:

  > Mitchell Sims, a member of your Customer Service Department, told me that IntriPlex is seeking an experienced customer service representative. The enclosed summary of my qualifications demonstrates my preparation for this position.

  > At the suggestion of Ms. Jennifer Larson of your Human Resources Department, I submit my qualifications for the position of staffing coordinator.

Openers for solicited jobs refer to the source of the information, the job title, and qualifications for the position.

- **Refer to the source of your information precisely.** If you are answering an advertisement, include the exact position advertised and the name and date of the publication. For large organizations it is also wise to mention the section of the newspaper where the ad appeared:

  > Your advertisement in Section C-3 of the June 1 *Daily News* for an accounting administrator greatly appeals to me. With my accounting training and computer experience, I believe I could serve Quad Graphics well.

  > From your company's Web site, I learned about your need for a sales representative for the Ohio, Indiana, and Illinois regions. I am very interested in this position and believe that my education and experience are appropriate for the opening.

  > Susan Butler, placement director at Sierra University, told me that DataTech has an opening for a technical writer with knowledge of Web design and graphics.

- **Refer to the job title and describe how your qualifications fit the requirements.** Human resources directors are looking for a match between an applicant's credentials and the job needs:

  > Will an honors graduate with a degree in recreation and two years of part-time experience organizing social activities for a convalescent hospital qualify for your position of activity director?

  > Because of my specialized training in computerized accounting at Boise State University, I am confident that I have the qualifications you described in your advertisement for a cost accountant trainee.

Openings for Unsolicited Jobs. If you are unsure whether a position actually exists, you may wish to use a more persuasive opening. Since your goal is to convince this person to read on, try one of the following techniques:

- **Demonstrate interest in and knowledge of the reader's business.** Show the hiring officer that you have done your research and that this organization is more than a mere name to you:

  > Because Signa HealthNet, Inc., is organizing a new information management team for its recently established group insurance division, could you use the services of a well-trained information systems graduate who seeks to become a professional systems analyst?

Openers for unsolicited jobs show interest in and knowledge of the company, as well as spotlight reader benefits.

- **Show how your special talents and background will benefit the company.**
  Human resource managers need to be convinced that you can do something for
  them:

> Could your rapidly expanding publications division use the services of an
> editorial assistant who offers exceptional language skills, an honors degree
> from the University of Maine, and two years' experience in producing a cam-
> pus literary publication?

In applying for an advertised job, Kendra Hawkins wrote the solicited cover
letter shown in Figure 13.14. Notice that her opening identifies the position and
the newspaper completely so that the reader knows exactly what advertisement
Kendra means. Using features on her word processing program, Kendra designed
her own letterhead that uses her name and looks like professionally printed letterhead paper.

FIGURE 13.14 Solicited Cover Letter

Uses personally designed letterhead

Kendra A. Hawkins

1770 Hawthorne Place, Boulder CO 80304
(303) 492-1244, khawkins@yahoo.com

May 23, 200x

Ms. Courtney L. Donahue — Addresses proper person by name and title
Director, Human Resources
Del Rio Enterprises
4839 Mountain View Avenue
Denver, CO 82511

Dear Ms. Donahue:

Identifies job and exact page where ad appeared

Your advertisement for an assistant product manager, appearing May 22 in
Section C of the *Denver Post*, immediately caught my attention because my education and training closely parallel your needs.

According to your advertisement, the job includes "assisting in the coordination of a
wide range of marketing programs as well as analyzing sales results and tracking
marketing budgets." A recent internship at Ventana Corporation introduced me to — Relates her experiences to job requirements
similar tasks. Assisting the marketing manager enabled me to analyze the promo-
tion, budget, and overall sales success of two products Ventana was evaluating. My
ten-page report examined the nature of the current market, the products' life cycles,
and their sales/profit return. In addition to this research, I helped formulate a product merchandising plan and answered consumers' questions at a local trade show.

Discusses education and experience as they relate to the position

Intensive course work in marketing and management, as well as proficiency in
computer spreadsheets and databases, has given me the kind of marketing and
computer training that Del Rio probably demands in a product manager.
Moreover, my recent retail sales experience and participation in campus organizations have helped me develop the kind of customer service and interpersonal
skills necessary for an effective product manager.

After you have examined the enclosed résumé for details of my qualifications, I — Refers reader to enclosed résumé
would be happy to answer questions. Please call me at (303) 492-1244 to arrange

Asks for interview and repeats main qualifications

an interview so that we may discuss how my marketing experience, computer
training, and interpersonal skills could contribute to Del Rio Enterprises.

Sincerely,

Kendra A. Hawkins

Kendra A. Hawkins

Enclosure

More challenging are unsolicited cover letters, such as Donald Vinton's shown in Figure 13.15. Because he hopes to discover or create a job, his opening must grab the reader's attention immediately. To do that, he capitalizes on company information appearing in an online article. Donald purposely kept his cover letter short and to the point because he anticipated that a busy executive would be unwilling to read a long, detailed letter. Donald's unsolicited letter "prospects" for a job. Some job candidates believe that such letters may be even more productive than efforts to secure advertised jobs, since "prospecting" candidates face less competition and show initiative. Notice that Donald's letter uses a personal business letter format with his return address above the date.

Selling Your Strengths in the Body

Once you have captured the attention of the reader and identified your purpose in the letter opening, you should use the body of the letter to promote your qualifications for

> The body of the cover letter promotes the candidate's qualifications for the targeted job.

FIGURE 13.15 Unsolicited Cover Letter

Uses personal business style with return address above date

Shows resourcefulness and knowledge of company

Uses bulleted list to make letter easier to read

Refers to enclosed résumé

Addresses proper person by name and title

Keeps letter brief to retain reader's attention

Takes initiative for follow-up

2250 Turtle Creek Drive
Monroeville, PA 15146
May 29, 200x

Mr. Richard M. Jannis
Vice President, Operations
Sports World, Inc.
4907 Allegheny Boulevard
Pittsburgh, PA 16103

Dear Mr. Jannis:

Today's *Pittsburgh Examiner* reports that your organization plans to expand its operations to include national distribution of sporting goods, and it occurs to me that you will be needing highly motivated, self-starting sales representatives and marketing managers. Here are three significant qualifications I have to offer:

- Four years of formal training in business administration, including specialized courses in sales management, retailing, marketing promotion, and consumer behavior

- Practical experience in demonstrating and selling consumer products, as well as successful experience in telemarketing

- Excellent communication skills and a strong interest in most areas of sports (which helped me become a sportscaster at Penn State radio station WGNF)

May we talk about how I can put these qualifications, and others summarized in the enclosed résumé, to work for Sports World as it develops its national sales force? I'll call during the week of June 5 to discuss your company's expansion plans and the opportunity for an interview.

Sincerely yours,

Donald W. Vinton

Donald W. Vinton

Enclosure

this position. If you are responding to an advertisement, you will want to explain how your preparation and experience fill the stated requirements. If you are prospecting for a job, you may not know the exact requirements. Your employment research and knowledge of your field, however, should give you a reasonably good idea of what is expected for this position.

It is also important to stress reader benefits. In other words, you should describe your strong points in relation to the needs of the employer. Hiring officers want you to tell them what you can do for their organizations. This is more important than telling what courses you took in college or what duties you performed in your previous jobs. Instead of *I have completed courses in business communication, report writing, and technical writing,* try this:

> Courses in business communication, report writing, and technical writing have helped me develop the research and writing skills required of your technical writers.

Choose your strongest qualifications and show how they fit the targeted job. Remember that students with little experience are better off spotlighting their education and its practical applications, as these candidates did:

> Because you seek an architect's apprentice with proven ability, I submit a drawing of mine that won second place in the Sinclair College drafting contest last year.

> Composing e-mail messages, business letters, memos, and reports in my business communication and office technology courses helped me develop the writing, language, proofreading, and computer skills mentioned in your ad for an administrative assistant.

In the body of your letter, you may choose to discuss relevant personal traits. Employers are looking for candidates who, among other things, are team players, take responsibility, show initiative, and learn easily. Don't just list several personal traits, though; instead, include documentation that proves you possess these traits. Notice how the following paragraph uses action verbs to paint a picture of a promising candidate:

> In addition to developing technical and academic skills at Mid-State University, I have gained interpersonal, leadership, and organizational skills. As vice president of the business students' organization, Gamma Alpha, I helped organize and supervise two successful fund-raising events. These activities involved conceptualizing the tasks, motivating others to help, scheduling work sessions, and coordinating the efforts of 35 diverse students in reaching our goal. I enjoyed my success with these activities and look forward to applying such experience in your management trainee program.

Finally, in this section or the next, you should refer the reader to your résumé. Do so directly or as part of another statement, as shown here:

> As you will notice from my enclosed résumé, I will graduate in June with a bachelor's degree in business administration.

> Please refer to the attached résumé for additional information regarding my education, experience, and references.

Motivating Action in the Closing

After presenting your case, you should conclude by asking confidently for an interview. Don't ask for the job. To do so would be presumptuous and naive. In requesting an interview, you might suggest reader benefits or review your strongest points. Sound sincere and appreciative. Remember to make it easy for the reader to agree by supplying your telephone number and the best times to call you. In addition, keep in mind that some hiring officers prefer that you take the initiative to call them. Avoid expressions like *I hope,* which will weaken your closing. Here are possible endings:

This brief description of my qualifications and the additional information on my résumé demonstrate my genuine desire to put my skills in accounting to work for you. Please call me at (405) 488-2291 before 10 a.m. or after 3 p.m. to arrange an interview.

To add to your staff an industrious, well-trained administrative assistant with proven word processing and communication skills, call me at (350) 492-1433 to arrange an interview. I can meet with you at any time convenient to your schedule.

I look forward to the opportunity to discuss my qualifications more fully in an interview. You can reach me on my cell phone at (213) 458-4030.

Next week, after you have examined the enclosed résumé, I will call you to discuss the possibility of arranging an interview.

Sending Your Cover Letter by E-Mail or by Fax

More than 90 percent of résumés at Fortune 500 companies arrive by e-mail or are submitted through the corporate Web site.[39] Many applicants using technology make the mistake of not including cover letters with their résumés submitted by e-mail or by fax. A résumé that arrives without a cover letter makes the receiver wonder what it is and why it was sent. Recruiters want you to introduce yourself, and they also are eager to see some evidence that you can write. Some candidates either skip the cover letter or think they can get by with one-line cover letters such as this: *Please see attached résumé, and thanks for your consideration.*

If you are serious about landing the job, take the time to prepare a professional cover letter. If you are sending your résumé by e-mail, you may use the same cover letter you would send by snail mail but shorten it a bit. As illustrated in Figure 13.16, an inside address is unnecessary for an e-mail recipient. Also move your

> Serious job candidates send a professional cover letter even if the résumé is submitted online, by e-mail, or by fax.

FIGURE 13.16 E-Mail Cover Letter

To: Courtney L. Donahue <courtney.donahue@delrio.com>
From: Kendra A. Hawkins <khawkins@yahoo.com>
Subject: Application for Assistant Product Manager Position Advertised 5-22-09
Cc:
Attached: HawkinsRésumé.doc (150 Kb)

Provides complete subject line identifying purpose

Dear Ms. Donahue:

Your advertisement for an assistant product manager, appearing May 22 in Section C of the DENVER POST, immediately caught my attention because my education and training closely parallel your needs. The advertisement says the job involves coordinating marketing programs, analyzing sales results, and tracking marketing budgets.

Addresses proper person by name

Transfers traditional cover letter to e-mail

I would like to discuss my qualifications with you and answer any questions you have about my résumé, which is embedded below. The best way to reach me is to call my cell at (713) 343-2910 during business hours. I look forward to putting my skills to work for Del Rio Enterprises.

Calls attention to résumé embedded in same message

Sincerely,

Kendra A. Hawkins
1770 Hawthorne Place
Boulder, CO 80304
E-Mail; khawkins@yahoo.com
Cell: (713) 343-2910

Uses signature block for all contact information

Plain-text résumé embedded below. Attractive print résumé available on request.

Reminds receiver that attractive print résumé is available

return address from the top of the letter to just below your name. Include your e-mail address and phone number. Remove tabs, bullets, underlining, and italics that might be problematic in e-mail messages. If you are submitting your résumé by fax, you can use the same cover letter you would send by the U.S. Postal Service, just indicate the delivery method by writing BY FAX above the recipient's address.

Final Tips for Successful Cover Letters

As you revise your cover letter, notice how many sentences begin with *I*. Although it is impossible to talk about yourself without using *I*, you can reduce "I" domination with this writing technique. Make activities and outcomes, and not yourself, the subjects of sentences. For example, rather than *I took classes in business communication and computer applications*, say *Classes in business communication and computer applications prepared me to . . . .* Instead of *I enjoyed helping customers*, say *Helping customers was a real pleasure.*

Because the beginning of a sentence is a prominent position, avoid starting sentences with *I* whenever possible. Use the "you" view (*You are looking for a hardworking team player . . .*), or try opening with phrases that de-emphasize you, the writer, for example, *All through college, I worked full time at . . . .* Above all, strive for a comfortable style. In your effort to avoid sounding self-centered, don't write unnaturally.

Like the résumé, your cover letter must look professional and suggest quality. This means using a traditional letter style, such as block or modified block. Also, be sure to print it on the same quality paper as your résumé. As with your résumé, proofread it several times yourself; then have a friend read it for content and mechanics. Don't rely on spell check to find all the errors. Just like your résumé, your cover letter must be perfect.

Visit www.meguffey.com

- Chapter Review Quiz
- Flash Cards
- Grammar Practice

- PowerPoint Slides
- Personal Language Trainer
- Beat the Clock Quiz

Summing Up and Looking Forward

In today's competitive job market, an employment search begins with identifying your interests, evaluating your qualifications, and choosing a career path. Finding the perfect job will mean a concentrated effort devoted to searching online job listings, checking classified advertisements, and networking. In applying for jobs, you will want to submit a customized, persuasive résumé that sells your skills and experience. Whether you choose a chronological or a functional résumé style, you should tailor your assets to fit the position sought. If you think your résumé might be scanned, emphasize keywords and keep the format simple. A persuasive cover letter should introduce your résumé and describe how your skills and experiences match those required.

Now, if your résumé and cover letter have been successful, you will proceed to the employment interview, one of life's most nerve-wracking experiences. The last chapter in this book provides helpful suggestions for successful interviewing and follow-up communication.

Critical Thinking

1. How has the Internet changed job searching for individuals and recruiters? Has the change had a positive or a negative effect?

2. How is a résumé different from a company employment application?

3. Some job candidates think that applying for unsolicited jobs can be more fruitful than applying for advertised positions. Discuss the advantages and disadvantages of letters that "prospect" for jobs.

4. Discuss the advantages and disadvantages of unconventional job applications that use "gimmicks" or a video résumé to get noticed.

5. Ethical Issue: Job candidate Karen accepts a position with Company A. One week later she receives a better offer from Company B. She wants very much to accept it. What should she do?

Chapter Review

6. How should the job-search process begin? By writing a résumé?

7. Using the Web, where should job candidates look in addition to using the big job board sites?

8. What is a chronological résumé, and what are its advantages and disadvantages?

9. Describe a functional résumé and discuss its advantages and disadvantages.

10. List five tips for writing an effective career objective on your résumé.

11. Describe a summary of qualifications, and explain why it is increasingly popular on résumés.

12. Has searching for a job online replaced traditional job-search methods?

13. What changes must be made in a typical résumé to make it effective for computer scanning?

14. When you send a cover letter within an e-mail message, what changes should you make to the format of the letter?

15. What is an e-portfolio, and what are its advantages?

Activities and Cases

13.1 Revising Janet's Résumé

One effective way to improve your writing skills is to critique and edit the résumé of someone else.

Your Task. Analyze the following poorly organized résumé. List its weaknesses. Your instructor may ask you to revise sections of this résumé before showing you an improved version.

Résumé
Janet P. Garza
530 N. Comanche St., Apt. B • San Marcos, TX 78666
Phone (512) 396-5182 • E-Mail: Hotchilibabe08@gmail.com

OBJECTIVE
I would love to find a first job in the "real world" with a big accounting company that will help me get ahead in the accounting field

SKILLS
Word processing, Internet browsers (Explorer and Google), Powerpoint, Excel, type 30 wpm, databases, spreadsheets; great composure in stressful situations; 3 years as leader and supervisor and 4 years in customer service

EDUCATION
Austin Community College Lamar Center. San Marcos, Texas. AA degree Fall 2007

Now I am pursuing a BA in Accounting at TSU-San Marcos, majoring in Accounting; my minor is Marketing. Expected degree date is June 2009; I recieved a Certificate of Completion in Entry Level Accounting in June 2007

I went to Scranton High School, Scranton, PA. I graduated in June 2004.

Highlights:

- Named Line Manager of the Month at Home Depot, 09/2004 and 08/2003
- Obtained a Certificate in Entry Level Accounting, June 2005
- Chair of Accounting Society, Spring and fall 2007
- Dean's Honor List, Fall 2008
- Financial advisor training completed through Primerica (May 2008)
- Webmaster for M.E.Ch.A., Spring 2009

Part-Time Employment

Financial Consultant, 2008 to present

I worked only part-time (January 2008-present) for Primerica Financial Services, San Marcos, TX to assist clients in obtaining a mortgage or consolidating a current mortgage loan and also to advise clients in assessing their need for life insurance.

Home Depot, Kyle, TX. As line manager, from September 2004–March 2008, I supervised 50 cashiers and front-end associates. I helped to write schedules, disciplinary action notices, and performance appraisals. I also kept track of change drawer and money exchanges; occasionally was manager on duty for entire store.

Penn Foster Career School-Scranton, PA where I taught flower design, I supervised 15 florists, made floral arrangements, sent them to customers, and restocked flowers.

List at least six weaknesses in this résumé.

13.2 Revising Janet's Cover Letter

The following cover letter accompanies Janet Garza's résumé (Activity 13.1).

Your Task. Analyze each section of the following cover letter written by Janet and list its weaknesses. Your instructor may ask you to revise this letter before showing you an improved version.

To Whom It May Concern:

I saw your internship position yesterday and would like to apply right away. It would be so exciting to work for your esteemed firm! An internship would really give me much needed real-world experience and help my career.

I have all the qualifications you require in your ad and more. I am a junior at Texas State University-San Marcos and an Accounting major (with a minor in Finance). Accounting and Finance are my passion and I want to become a CPA and a financial advisor. I have taken Intermediate I and II and now work as a financial advisor with Primerica Financial Services in San Marcos. I should also tell you that I was at Home Depot for four years. I learned a lot, but my heart is in accounting and finance.

I am a team player, a born leader, motivated, reliable, and I show excellent composure in stressful situation, for example, when customers complain. I put myself through school and always carry at least 15 units while working part time.

You will probably agree that I am a good candidate for your internship position, which should start July 1. I feel that my motivation, passion, and strong people skills will serve your company well.

Best regards,

List at least six weaknesses in the cover letter.

13.3 Identifying Your Employment Interests

Your Task. In a memo or e-mail addressed to your campus career counselor or to a professional job expert you would like to hire, answer the questions in the section "Identifying Your Interests" at the beginning of the chapter. Draw a conclusion from your answers. What kinds of career, company, position, and location seem to fit your self-analysis? Explore options on your campus in career placement and advising; find out if you have access to personality and aptitude testing to help you flesh out a likely career path.

13.4 Evaluating Your Qualifications

Your Task. Prepare four worksheets that inventory your qualifications in the areas of employment, education, capabilities and skills, and honors and activities. Use active verbs when appropriate.

a. **Employment.** Begin with your most recent job or internship. For each position list the following information: employer; job title; dates of employment (months and years); and three to five duties, activities, or accomplishments. Emphasize activities related to your job goal. Strive to quantify your achievements.

b. **Education.** List degrees, certificates, and training accomplishments. Include courses, seminars, or skills that are relevant to your job goal. Calculate your grade point average in your major.

c. **Capabilities and skills.** List all capabilities and skills that recommend you for the job you seek. Use words such as *skilled, competent, trained, experienced*, and *ability to*. Also list five or more qualities or interpersonal skills necessary for a successful individual in your chosen field. Write action statements demonstrating that you possess some of these qualities. Empty assurances aren't good enough; try to show evidence (*Developed teamwork skills by working with a committee of eight to produce a . . .*).

d. **Awards, honors, and activities.** Explain any awards so that the reader will understand them. List campus, community, and professional activities that suggest you are a well-rounded individual or possess traits relevant to your target job.

13.5 Choosing a Career Path

Many people know surprisingly little about the work done in various occupations and the training requirements.

Your Task. Use the online *Occupational Outlook Handbook* at **http://www.bls.gov/oco**, prepared by the Bureau of Labor Statistics, to learn more about an occupation of your choice. Find the description of a position for which you could apply now or after you graduate. Learn about what workers do, the nature of the job, working conditions, training and education needed, earnings, and expected job outlook. Print the pages from the *Occupational Outlook Handbook* that describe employment in the area in which you are interested. If your instructor directs, attach these copies to the cover letter you will write in Activity 13.10.

13.6 Locating Salary Information

What salary can you expect in your chosen career?

Your Task. Visit America's Career InfoNet at **http://www.acinet.org** or Salary.com at **www.salary.com** and select an occupation based on the kind of employment you are seeking now or will be seeking after you graduate. What wages can you expect in this occupation? Use your current geographic area or the location where you would like to work after graduation. Click to learn more about this occupation. Take notes on three or four interesting bits of information you uncovered about this career. Bring a printout of the wage information to class and be prepared to discuss what you learned.

13.7 Searching the Job Market

Where are the jobs? Even though you may not be in the market at the moment, become familiar with the kinds of available positions because job awareness should become an important part of your education.

Your Task. Clip or print a job advertisement or announcement from (a) the classified section of a newspaper, (b) a job board on the Web, (c) a company Web site, or (d) a professional association listing. Select an advertisement or announcement describing the kind of employment you are seeking now or plan to seek when you graduate. Save this advertisement or announcement to attach to the résumé you will write in Activity 13.9.

13.8 Posting a Résumé on the Web

Learn about the procedure for posting résumés at job boards on the Web.

Your Task. Prepare a list of at least three online employment sites where you could post your résumé. Describe the procedure involved and the advantages for each site.

13.9 Writing Your Résumé

Your Task. Using the data you developed in Activity 13.4, write your résumé. Aim it at a full-time job, part-time position, or internship. Attach a job listing for a specific position (from Activity 13.7). Also prepare a separate list of at least three professional references. Revise your résumé until it is perfect.

13.10 Preparing Your Cover Letter

Your Task. Write a cover letter introducing your résumé. Again, revise it until it is perfect.

13.11 Swapping Résumés

A terrific way to get ideas for improving your résumé is seeing how other students have developed their résumés.

Your Task. Bring your completed polished résumé to class. Attach a plain sheet with your name at the top. In small groups exchange your résumés for peer edits. Each reviewer should provide at least two supportive comments and one suggestion for improvement on the cover sheet. Reviewers should sign their names with their comments.

E-MAIL

13.12 Special Tips for Today's Résumé Writers

Your Task. Using electronic databases, research the topic of employment résumés. Read at least three recent articles. In an e-mail or memo to your instructor list eight or more good tips that are not covered in this chapter. Pay special attention to advice concerning the preparation of online résumés. The subject line of your memo should be *Special Tips for Today's Résumé Writers*.

13.13 Consumer: Being Wary of Career Advisory Firms With Big Promises and Big Prices

Not long ago employment agencies charged applicants 5 percent of their annual salaries to find jobs. Most agencies have quit this unethical practice, but unscrupulous firms still prey on vulnerable job seekers. Some career advisory firms claim to be legitimate, but they make puffed-up promises and charge inflated fees—an up-front payment of $4,000 is typical, with a typical hourly honorarium of $90 to $125.

Your Task. Using databases and the Web, find examples of current employment scams or danger areas for job seekers. In a presentation to the class or in team discussions, describe three examples of disreputable practices candidates should recognize. Make recommendations to job seekers for avoiding employment scams and disappointment with career advisory services.

WEB

13.14 E-Portfolios: Job Hunting in the Twenty-First Century

In high-tech fields digital portfolios have been steadily gaining in popularity and now seem to be going mainstream as universities are providing space for student job seekers to profile their qualifications in e-portfolios online. Although it is unlikely that digital portfolios will become widely used very soon, you would do well to learn about them by viewing many samples—good and bad.

Your Task. Conduct a Google search using the search term *student e-portfolios* or *student digital portfolios*. You will see long lists of hits, some of which will be actual digital document samples on the Web or instructions for creating an e-portfolio. Your instructor may assign individual students or teams to visit specific digital portfolio sites and ask them to summarize their findings in a memo or in a brief oral presentation. If this is your task, you could focus on the composition of the site, page layout, links provided, colors used, types of documents included, and so forth. A fine site to start from that offers many useful links is maintained by the Center for Excellence in Teaching (CET) at the University of Southern California. Visit **http://www.usc.edu** and type *student e-portfolios* to search the USC Web pages. Click the link to the CET site.

Alternatively, single groups or the whole class could study sites that provide how-to instructions and combine the advice of the best among them to create practical tips for making a digital portfolio. This option would lend itself to team writing, for example, with the help of a wiki.

Video Resource

Video Library 1: *Building Workplace Skills: The Job Search.* At Clifton-Harding Associates (CHA), owner Ella Clifton realizes that she needs another employee to help run the business. She places a "blind" advertisement, to which her current employee, Stephanie, responds. Ella interviews a promising candidate, Yolanda, but during the process Ella learns that Stephanie has lied on a résumé posted to a job site. In addition to the ethical dilemma, you will witness good and bad job-search and résumé techniques.

Number Style

Review Sections 4.01–4.13 in the Grammar/Mechanics Handbook. Then study each of the following pairs. Assume that these expressions appear in the context of letters, reports, or memos. Write *a* or *b* in the space provided to indicate the preferred number style and record the number of the G/M principle illustrated. When you finish, compare your response with those at the end of the book. If your responses differ, study carefully the principles in parentheses.

<u>a</u>   (4.01a)   **Example** (a) three cell phone (b) 3 cell phones

1. (a) twenty menu items   (b) 20 menu items
2. (a) Third Street Promenade   (b) 3rd Street Promenade
3. (a) 24 newspapers   (b) twenty-four newspapers
4. (a) September 1st   (b) September 1
5. (a) the sum of fifty dollars   (b) the sum of $50
6. (a) on the 15th of July   (b) on the fifteenth of July
7. (a) at 4:00 p.m.   (b) at 4 p.m.
8. (a) 5 250-pound athletes   (b) five 250-pound athletes
9. (a) over fifty years ago   (b) over 50 years ago
10. (a) 2,000,000 people   (b) 2 million people
11. (a) fifteen cents   (b) 15 cents
12. (a) a twenty-year-old student   (b) a 20-year-old student
13. (a) 2/3 of the e-mails   (b) two thirds of the e-mails
14. (a) two printers for 15 employees   (b) 2 printers for 15 employees
15. (a) 40 of the 1,000 laid-off employees   (b) forty of the 1,000 laid-off employees

The following résumé has errors in capitalization, number usage, punctuation, spelling, proofreading, and other problems. You may either (a) use standard proofreading marks (see Appendix B) to correct the errors here or (b) download the document from **www.meguffey.com** and revise at your computer. Study the guidelines in the Grammar/Mechanics Handbook to sharpen your skills.

JONATHAN M. DEMPSEY
2259 7th Avenue
Tucson, Ariz. 85021

Summary of qualifications

- Over two years experience in Office Administration interacting with customers
- Ability to keyboard (fifty-five wpm) and proficient with 10-key calculator
- Proficient with MS Word, Excel, Powerpoint, and the internet
- Enjoy working with colleagues' and customers'

Experience

Office Assistant (part time), Western mineral resources, Tucson, Arizona
June 2009 to present

- Gather and distribute data for minerals related reports
- Keyboard and format Letters, Memos and Reports in MS Word
- Respond to inquirys from the public, industry and goverment agencys

Assistant Manger, Southwest Housewares, Tucson, Arizona
July 2008 to May 2009

- Managed store in mangers absence.
- Ordered merchandise and supervised 2 employees; earned rapid promotion
- Assisted manger in opening and closing registers; balanced daily reciepts

Education

Mesa community college, Mesa, Arizona
Major: organizational leadership
Aa degree expected June 2010. GPA in major: 3.7 (4.0 = A)

Network Your Way to a Job in the Hidden Market

The "hidden" job market may account for as many as 70 to 80 percent of all positions available.[40] Companies don't always announce openings publicly because interviewing all the applicants, many of whom aren't qualified, is time consuming and costly. What's more, even when a job is advertised, companies dislike hiring "strangers." They are more comfortable hiring a person they know.

Smart job seekers won't count on the Internet or a newspaper's classified section to land a job. Recruitmax, an applicant-tracking company that powers corporate career sites, along with countless other human resources experts, admitted that "most new hires come by word of mouth and employee referrals."[41] The key to finding a good job, then, is converting yourself from a "stranger" into a known quantity. Probably the best way to become a known quantity is by networking. You can use either traditional methods or online resources.

Traditional Networking

- **Develop a list.** Make a list of anyone who would be willing to talk with you about finding a job. List your friends, relatives, former employers, former coworkers, members of your religious community, people in social and athletic clubs, present and former teachers, neighbors, and friends of your parents. Also consider asking your campus career center for alumni contacts who will talk with students.
- **Make contacts.** Call the people on your list or, even better, try to meet with them in person. To set up a meeting, say, *Hi, Aunt Martha! I'm looking for a job and I wonder if you could help me out. When could I come over to talk about it?* During your visit be friendly, well organized, polite, and interested in what your contact has to say. Provide a copy of your résumé, and try to keep the conversation centered on your job-search area. Your goal is to get two or more referrals. In pinpointing your request, ask two questions: *Do you know of anyone who might have an opening for a person with my skills?* If the person doesn't, ask, *Do you know of anyone else who might know of someone who would?*
- **Follow up on your referrals.** Call the people whose names are on your referral list. You might say something like, *Hello. I'm Eric Rivera, a friend of Meredith Medcalf. She suggested that I call and ask you for help. I'm looking for a position as a management trainee, and she thought you might be willing to spare a few minutes and steer me in the right direction.* Don't ask for a job. During your referral interview ask how the individual got started in this line of work, what he or she likes best (or least) about the work, what career paths exist in the field, and what problems must be overcome by a newcomer. Most important, ask how a person with your background and skills might get started in the field. Send an informal thank-you note to anyone who helps you in your job search, and stay in touch with the most promising contacts. Ask whether you may call every three weeks or so during your job search.

Online Networking

As with traditional networking, the goal of online networking is to make connections with people who are advanced in their fields. Ask for their advice about finding a job. Most people like talking about themselves, and asking them about their experiences is an excellent way to begin an online correspondence that might lead to "electronic mentoring," a letter of recommendation from an expert in the field, or information on an internship opportunity. Making online connections with industry professionals is a great way to keep tabs on the latest business trends and potential job leads. Here are possible online networking sources:

- **Join a career networking groups.** Build your own professional network by joining one or more of the following: **http://www.linkedin.com, http://twitter.com, http://ryze.com, http://zerodegrees.com,** and **http://itsnotwhatyouknow.com**. Some of these sites are fee based while others are free. Typically, joining a network requires creating a password, filling in your profile, and adding your business contacts. At some sites, you can specify search criteria to locate and then contact individuals directly. At other sites both parties' e-mail addresses are hidden. The site then acts as an intermediary connecting people only after they agree to share their contact information. Once you have connected with an individual, the content of your discussions and the follow-up will be similar to that of traditional networking. The medium, however, will center on electronic communication through e-mail and chat room discussions.

- **Participate in a discussion groups and mailing lists.** Two especially good discussion group resources for beginners are Yahoo! Groups (**http://groups.yahoo.com**) and Google Groups (**http://groups.google.com/**). You may choose from groups in a variety of fields including business and computer technology. For example, if you click the *Business/Finance* listing, you will see links leading to more specialized groups. Click *Employment and Work*, and you will find career groups including construction, customer service, office administration, court reporting, and interior design.
- **Locate relevant blogs.** Blogs are the latest trend for networking and sharing information. A quick Web search will result in hundreds of career-related blogs and blogs in your field of study. Many companies, such as Microsoft, also maintain employment-related blogs. A good list of career blogs can be found at **http://www.quintcareers .com/career-related_blogs.html**. You can also search a worldwide blog directory at **http://www.blogcatalog.com/**. Once you locate a relevant blog, you can read recent postings, search archives, and make replies.

Career Application. Everyone who enters the job market must develop a personal network. Assume you are ready to change jobs or look for a permanent position.

Your Task

To begin developing your personal network, do one of the following:

- Conduct at least one referral interview and report your experience to your class.
- Join one professional discussion group or mailing list. Ask your instructor to recommend an appropriate group for your field. Take notes on group discussions, and describe your reactions and findings to your class
- Find a blog related to your career or your major. After monitoring the blog for several days, describe your experience to your class.

CHAPTER 14

Interviewing and Following Up

OBJECTIVES

After studying this chapter, you should be able to

● Differentiate among screening, one-on-one, panel, group, sequential, and stress interviews.

● Describe what to do before the interview to make an impressive initial contact.

● Explain how to prepare for employment interviews, including researching the target company.

● Recognize how to fight interview fears and control nonverbal messages.

● Be prepared to answer common interview questions and know how to close an interview positively.

● Outline the activities that take place after an interview, including thanking the interviewer and contacting references.

● Write follow-up letters and other employment messages.

A job interview can change your life. Because employment is a major part of everyone's life, the job interview takes on enormous importance. Interviewing is equally significant whether you are completing your education and searching for your first serious position or whether you are in the workforce and striving to change jobs.

Everyone agrees that job interviews are extremely stressful. However, the more you learn about the process and the more prepared you are, the less stress you will feel. It is also important to realize that a job interview is a two-way street. It is not just about being judged by the employer. You, the applicant, will be using the job interview to evaluate the employer. Do you really want to work for this organization?

An interview has several purposes for you as a job candidate. It is an opportunity to (a) convince the employer of your potential, (b) find out more about the job and the company, and (c) expand on the information in your résumé. This is the time to gather information about whether you would fit into the company culture. You should also be thinking about whether this job suits your career goals.

From the employer's perspective, the interview is an opportunity to (a) assess your abilities in relation to the requirements for the position; (b) discuss your training, experience, knowledge, and qualifications in more detail; (c) see what drives and motivates you; and (d) decide whether you would fit into the organization.

This chapter presents various kinds of interviews and shows you how to prepare for them. You will learn how to project a professional image in your initial phone contact, gather information about an employer, and reduce interview jitters. You will receive advice on how to send positive nonverbal messages that will help you stay in control during an interview. You will pick up tips for responding to recruiters' favorite questions and learn how to cope with illegal questions. Moreover, you will receive pointers on significant questions you can ask during an interview. Finally, you will learn what you should do as a successful follow-up to an interview.

Yes, job interviews can be intimidating and stressful. However, you can expect to ace an interview if you know what's coming and prepare thoroughly. Remember, preparation often determines who gets the job. First, though, you need to know what types of interviews you might encounter in your job search.

Types of Employment Interviews

Job applicants generally face two kinds of interviews: screening interviews and hiring/placement interviews. You must succeed in the first to proceed to the second. Once you make it to the hiring/placement interview, you will find a variety of interview styles, including one-on-one, panel, group, sequential, and stress interviews. You will be better prepared if you know what to expect in these types of interviews.

Screening Interviews

Screening interviews do just that—they screen candidates to eliminate those who fail to meet minimum requirements. Companies use screening interviews to save time and money by weeding out lesser-qualified candidates before scheduling face-to-face interviews. Although some screening interviews are conducted during job fairs or on college campuses, most take place on the telephone.[1]

Some companies computerize their screening interviews. For example, Lowe's Home Improvement has applicants access a Web site where they answer a series of ethics-related questions, and Wal-Mart uses a multiple-choice questionnaire, which applicants answer by pushing buttons on a phone keypad, to screen cashiers, stockers, and customer service representatives.[2] Increasingly, employers use videoconferencing to interview candidates. This allows multiple hiring managers in distant locations to participate in the interview. Workplace experts predict that in the future job seekers will need video capability on their computers for interviewing.[3]

During a screening interview you will likely be asked to provide details about the education and experience listed on your résumé, so you must be prepared to sell your qualifications. Remember that the person conducting the screening interview is trying to determine whether you should move on to the next step in the interview process.

A screening interview may be as short as five minutes. Even though it may be short, don't treat it casually. If you don't perform well during the screening interview, it may be your last interview with that organization. You can use the tips that follow in this chapter to succeed during the screening process.

Hiring/Placement Interviews

The most promising candidates selected from screening interviews will be invited to hiring/placement interviews. Hiring managers want to learn whether candidates are motivated, qualified, and a good fit for the position. Their goal is to learn how the candidate would fit into their organization. Conducted in depth, hiring/placement interviews may take many forms.

> **Screening interviews are intended to eliminate those who fail to meet minimum requirements.**

> **In hiring/placement interviews, recruiters try to learn how the candidate would fit into their organization.**

"You seem intelligent, capable, level-headed and mature. That's a shame because I was really hoping you'd fit in here."

Hiring interview types include one-on-one, panel, group, sequential, and stress.

One-on-One Interviews. In one-on-one interviews, which are the most common type, you can expect to sit down with a company representative and talk about the job and your qualifications. If the representative is the hiring manager, questions will be specific and job related. If the representative is from human resources, the questions will probably be more general.

Panel Interviews. Panel interviews are typically conducted by people who will be your supervisors and colleagues. Usually seated around a table, interviewers may take turns asking questions. Panel interviews are advantageous because they save time and show you how the staff works together. For these interviews, you can prepare basic biographical information about each panel member. In answering questions, keep eye contact with the questioner as well as with the other team members. Try to take notes during the interview so that you can remember each person's questions and what was important to that individual.[4]

Group Interviews. Group interviews occur when a company interviews several candidates for the same position at the same time. Some employers use this technique to measure leadership skills and communication styles. During a group interview, stay focused on the interviewer, and treat the other candidates with respect.[5]

Sequential Interviews. Sequential interviews allow a candidate to meet individually with two or more interviewers over the course of several hours or days. For example, job candidates seeking tenure-track academic positions undergo sequential interviewing. You must listen carefully and respond positively to all interviewers. Sell your qualifications to each one; don't assume that any interviewer knows what was said in a previous interview. Keep your responses fresh, even when repeating yourself many times over.[6]

Stress Interviews. Stress interviews are meant to test your reactions during nerve-wracking situations. You may be forced to wait a long time before being greeted by the interviewer, you may be given a test with an impossible time limit, or you may be treated rudely by one or more of the interviewers. Another stress interview technique is to have interviewers ask questions at a rapid rate. If asked rapid-fire questions from many directions, take the time to slow things down. For example, you might say, *I would be happy to answer your question, Ms. X, but first I must finish responding to Mr. Z.* If greeted with silence, another stress technique, you might say, *Would you like me to begin the interview? Let me tell you about myself.* Or ask a question such as *Can you give me more information about the position?* The best way to handle stress questions is to remain calm and give thoughtful answers. However, you might also reconsider whether you would want to work for this kind of organization.

No matter what interview structure you encounter, you will feel more comfortable and better prepared if you know what to do before, during, and after the interview.

Before the Interview

Once you have sent out at least one résumé or filled out at least one job application, you must consider yourself an active job seeker. Being active in the job market means that you must be prepared to be contacted by potential employers. As discussed earlier, employers use screening interviews to narrow the list of candidates. If you do well in the screening interview, you will be invited to an in-person meeting. Here are tips for sounding professional and acting appropriately from the beginning and for preparing for a job interview once it has been scheduled.

Using Professional Phone Techniques

Even with the popularity of e-mail, most employers contact job applicants by phone to set up interviews. Employers can get a better sense of how applicants communicate by hearing their voices over the phone. Therefore, once you are actively looking for a job, anytime the phone rings, it could be a potential employer. Don't make the mistake of letting an unprofessional voice mail message or a lazy roommate ruin your chances. Here's how you can avoid such problems:

- Invest in a good answering machine or voice mail service. Make sure that your outgoing message is concise and professional, with no distracting background sounds. It should be in your own voice and include your full name for clarity. You will find more tips for creating professional outgoing messages in Chapter 11.
- Tell those who might answer your phone at home about your job search. Explain to them the importance of acting professionally and taking complete messages. Family members or roommates can affect the first impression an employer has of you.
- If you have children, prevent them from answering the phone during your job search. Children of all ages are not known for taking good messages!
- If you have put your cell phone number on your résumé, don't answer your cell phone unless you are in a good location to carry on a conversation with an employer. It is hard to pay close attention when you are driving down the highway or eating in a noisy restaurant!
- Use voice mail to screen calls. By screening incoming calls, you can be totally in control when you return a prospective employer's call. Organize your materials and ready yourself psychologically for the conversation.

Making the First Conversation Impressive

Whether you answer the phone directly or return an employer's call, make sure you are prepared for the conversation. Remember that this is the first time the employer has heard your voice. How you conduct yourself on the phone will create a lasting impression. Here are tips to make that first impression a positive one:

Job seekers who sound flustered, unprepared, or unprofessional when an employer calls may ruin their chances with that company.

- Keep a list near the telephone of positions for which you have applied.
- Treat any call from an employer just like an interview. Use a professional tone and businesslike language. Be polite and enthusiastic, and sell your qualifications.
- If caught off guard by the call, ask whether you can call back in a few minutes. Organize your materials and yourself.
- Have a copy of your résumé available so that you can answer any questions that come up. Also have your list of references, a calendar, and a notepad handy.
- Be prepared for a screening interview. As discussed earlier, this might occur during the first phone call.
- Take good notes during the phone conversation. Obtain accurate directions, and verify the spelling of your interviewer's name. If you will be interviewed by more than one person, get all of their names.
- Before you hang up, reconfirm the date and time of your interview. You could say something like *I look forward to meeting with you next Wednesday at 2 p.m.*

Researching the Target Company

After scheduling an in-person interview, you need to begin in-depth research. One of the most important steps in effective interviewing is gathering detailed information about a prospective employer. Never enter an interview cold. Recruiters are impressed by candidates who have done their homework. In an Office Team survey, 47 percent of executives polled said that the most common mistake job seekers make during interviews is having little or no knowledge about the potential employer.[7]

Before your interview, take time to research the target company and learn about its goals, customers, competitors, reputation, and so forth.

Visit the library, explore your campus career center, or search the Web for information and articles about the target company or its field, service, or product. Visit the company's Web site and read everything. Call the company to request annual reports, catalogs, or brochures. Ask about the organization and possibly the interviewer. Learn something about the company's mission and goals, size, number of employees, customers, competitors, culture, management structure and names of leaders, reputation in the community, financial condition, future plans, strengths, and weaknesses.

Analyze the company's advertising, including sales and marketing brochures. One candidate, a marketing major, spent a great deal of time pouring over brochures from an aerospace contractor. During his initial interview, he shocked and impressed the recruiter with his knowledge of the company's guidance systems. The candidate had, in fact, relieved the interviewer of his least-favorite task—explaining the company's complicated technology.

Talking with company employees is always a good idea, if you can manage it. They are probably the best source of inside information. Try to be introduced to someone who is currently employed—but not working in the immediate area where you wish to be hired. Be sure to seek out someone who is discreet.

Blogs can provide authentic information about a company's culture, current happenings, and future plans.

Blogs are also good sources for company research. Many employees maintain both formal and informal blogs, where they share anecdotes and information about their employers. You can use these blogs to learn about a company's culture, its current happenings, and its future plans. Many job seekers find that they can get a more realistic picture of a company's day-to-day culture by reading blogs than they would by reading news articles or company Web site information.[8]

In learning about a company, you may uncover information that convinces you that this is not the company for you. It is always better to learn about negatives early in the process. More likely, though, the information you collect will help you tailor your application and interview responses to the organization's needs. You know how flattered you feel when an employer knows about you and your background. That feeling works both ways. Employers are pleased when job candidates take an interest in them. Be ready to put in plenty of effort in investigating a target employer because this effort really pays off at interview time.

Preparing and Practicing

After you have learned about the target organization, study the job description or job listing. It not only helps you write a focused résumé but also enables you to match your education, experience, and interests with the employer's position. Learning about the duties and responsibilities of the position will help you practice your best response strategies.

The most successful job candidates never go into interviews cold. They prepare success stories and practice answers to typical questions. They also plan their responses to any problem areas on their résumés. As part of their preparation before the interview, they decide what to wear, and they gather the items they plan to take with them.

Practice success stories that emphasize your most strategic skills, areas of knowledge, strongest personality traits, and key accomplishments.

Prepare Success Stories. To feel confident and be able to sell your qualifications, prepare and practice success stories. These stories are specific examples of your educational and work-related experience that demonstrate your qualifications and achievements. Look over the job description and your résumé to determine what skills, training, personal characteristics, and experience you want to emphasize during the interview. Then prepare a success story for each one. Incorporate numbers, such as dollars saved or percentage of sales increase, whenever possible. Your success stories should be detailed but brief. Think of them as 30-second sound bites.

Practice telling your success stories until they fluently roll off your tongue and sound natural. Then in the interview be certain to find places to insert them. Tell stories about (a) dealing with a crisis, (b) handling a tough interpersonal situation,

WORKPLACE IN FOCUS

No longer an adornment restricted to sailors, bikers, and ruffians, tattoos have gained popularity with celebrities, pro athletes, fashion models and youth. The proliferation of the body-art trend has meant that markings and piercings are increasingly showing up in the white-collar world of business executives, accountants, and lawyers. Despite their "cool factor" within the broader culture, tattoos present unique challenges for job seekers who want to know how to dress properly for interviews. *How should individuals with tattoos or piercings dress for success in the workplace?*

(c) successfully juggling many priorities, (d) changing course to deal with changed circumstances, (e) learning from a mistake, (f) working on a team, and (g) going above and beyond expectations.[9]

Practice Answers to Possible Questions. Imagine the kinds of questions you may be asked and work out sample answers. Although you can't anticipate precise questions, you can expect to be asked about your education, skills, experience, and availability. Recite answers to typical interview questions in a mirror, with a friend, while driving in your car, or in spare moments. Keep practicing until you have the best responses down pat. Consider recording a practice session to see and hear how you answer questions. Do you look and sound enthusiastic?

Clean Up Any Digital Dirt. Many companies that recruit on college campuses are now using Google and Yahoo to screen applicants. The president of a small consulting company in Chicago was about to hire a summer intern when he discovered the student's Facebook page. The candidate described his interests as "smokin' blunts [cigars hollowed out and stuffed with marijuana], shooting people, and obsessive sex."[10] The executive quickly lost interest in this candidate. Even if the student was merely posturing, it showed poor judgment.

Teasing photographs and provocative comments about drinking, drug use, and sexual exploits make students look immature and unprofessional. Employers have the same access to the Internet as job seekers do, and they are taking a close look: "If what pops up is a ranting blog about the evils of corporate America or a picture of you topless in Cancun with a beer in your hand, you're in trouble," Cynthia Shapiro, an employment expert, says. "Your résumé will land in the trash, and you won't even know what happened."[11] Check out your online presence to see if anything needs to be cleaned up.

Expect to Explain Problem Areas on Your Résumé. Interviewers are certain to question you about problem areas on your résumé. If you have little or no experience, you might emphasize your recent training and up-to-date skills. If you have gaps in your résumé, be prepared to answer questions about them positively and truthfully. If you were fired from a job, accept some responsibility for what happened and explain what you gained from the experience. Don't criticize a previous employer, and don't hide the real reasons. If you received low grades for one term, explain why and point to your improved grades in subsequent terms.

> Make sure everything posted about you online is professional and positive.

Decide How to Dress. What you wear to a job interview still matters. Even if some employees in the organization dress casually, you should look qualified, competent, and successful. One young applicant complained to his girlfriend about having to wear a suit for an interview when everyone at the company dressed casually. She replied, "You don't get to wear the uniform, though, until you make the team!" Avoid loud colors; strive for a coordinated, natural appearance. Favorite "power" colors for interviews are gray and dark blue. Cover tattoos and conceal body piercings; these can be a turnoff for many interviewers. Don't overdo jewelry, and make sure that what you do wear is clean, pressed, odor-free, and lint-free. Shoes should be polished and scuff-free. Forget about flip-flops.

To summarize, ensure that what you wear projects professionalism and shows your respect for the interview situation.

Gather Items to Bring. Decide what you should bring with you to the interview, and get everything ready the night before. You should plan to bring copies of your résumé, your reference lists, a notebook and pen, money for parking and tolls, and samples of your work, if appropriate. Place everything in a businesslike briefcase to add that final professional touch to your look.

Traveling to and Arriving at Your Interview

The big day has arrived! Ideally you are fully prepared for your interview. Now you need to make sure that everything goes smoothly. That means arriving on time and handling that fear you are likely to feel.

On the morning of your interview, give yourself plenty of time to groom and dress. Then give yourself ample time to get to the employer's office. If something unexpected happens that will to cause you to be late, such as an accident or bridge closure, call the interviewer right away to explain what is happening. Most interviewers will be understanding, and your call will show that you are responsible. On the way to the interview, don't smoke, don't eat anything messy or smelly, and don't load up on perfume or cologne. Arrive at the interview five or ten minutes early. If possible, check your appearance before going in.

> **Allow ample time to arrive unflustered, and be congenial to everyone who greets you.**

When you enter the office, be courteous and congenial to everyone. Remember that you are being judged not only by the interviewer but by the receptionist and anyone else who sees you before and after the interview. They will notice how you sit, what you read, and how you look. Introduce yourself to the receptionist, and wait to be invited to sit. You may be asked to fill out a job application while you are waiting. You will find tips for doing this effectively later in this chapter.

Greet the interviewer confidently, and don't be afraid to initiate a handshake. Doing so exhibits professionalism and confidence. Extend your hand, look the interviewer directly in the eye, smile pleasantly, and say, *I'm pleased to meet you, Mr. Thomas. I am Constance Ferraro.* In this culture a firm, not crushing, handshake sends a nonverbal message of poise and assurance. Once introductions have taken place, wait for the interviewer to offer you a chair. Make small talk with upbeat comments, such as *This is a beautiful headquarters* or *I'm very impressed with the facilities you have here.* Don't immediately begin rummaging in your briefcase for your résumé. Being at ease and unrushed suggest that you are self-confident.

Fighting Fear

Expect to be nervous before and during the interview. It is natural! Other than public speaking, employment interviews are the most dreaded events in people's lives. One of the best ways to overcome fear is to know what happens in a typical interview. You can further reduce your fears by following these suggestions.

> **Fight fear by practicing, preparing thoroughly, breathing deeply, and knowing that you are in charge for part of the interview.**

- **Practice interviewing.** Try to get as much interviewing practice as you can—especially with real companies. The more times you experience the interview situation, the less nervous you will be. If offered, campus mock interviews also provide excellent practice, and the interviewers will offer tips for improvement.

- **Prepare thoroughly.** Research the company. Know how you will answer the most frequently asked questions. Be ready with success stories. Rehearse your closing statement. One of the best ways to reduce butterflies is to know that you have done all you can to be ready for the interview.
- **Breathe deeply.** Take deep breaths, particularly if you feel anxious while waiting for the interviewer. Deep breathing makes you concentrate on something other than the interview and also provides much-needed oxygen.
- **Know that you are not alone.** Everyone feels some level of anxiety during a job interview. Interviewers expect some nervousness, and a skilled interviewer will try to put you at ease.
- **Remember that it is a two-way street.** The interviewer isn't the only one who is gleaning information. You have come to learn about the job and the company. In fact, during some parts of the interview, you will be in charge. This should give you courage.

During the Interview

During the interview you will be answering questions and asking your own questions. Your demeanor, body language, and other nonverbal cues will also be on display. The interviewer will be trying to learn more about you, and you should learn more about the job and the organization. Although you may be asked some unique questions, many interviewers ask standard, time-proven questions, which means that you can prepare your answers ahead of time.

Sending Positive Nonverbal Messages and Acting Professionally

You have already sent nonverbal messages to your interviewer by arriving on time, being courteous, dressing professionally, and greeting the receptionist confidently. You will continue to send nonverbal messages throughout the interview. Remember that what comes out of your mouth and what is written on your résumé are not the only messages an interviewer receives from you. Nonverbal messages also create powerful impressions. Here are suggestions that will help you send the right nonverbal messages during interviews:

> Send positive nonverbal messages by arriving on time, being courteous, dressing professionally, greeting the interviewer confidently, controlling your body movements, making eye contact, listening attentively, and smiling.

- **Control your body movements.** Keep your hands, arms, and elbows to yourself. Don't lean on a desk. Keep your feet on the floor. Don't cross your arms in front of you. Keep your hands out of your pockets.
- **Exhibit good posture.** Sit erect, leaning forward slightly. Don't slouch in your chair; at the same time, don't look too stiff and uncomfortable. Good posture demonstrates confidence and interest.
- **Practice appropriate eye contact.** A direct eye gaze, at least in North America, suggests interest and trustworthiness. If you are being interviewed by a panel, remember to maintain eye contact with all interviewers.
- **Use gestures effectively.** Nod to show agreement and interest. Gestures should be used as needed, but don't overdo it.
- **Smile enough to convey a positive attitude.** Have a friend give you honest feedback on whether you generally smile too much or not enough.
- **Listen attentively.** Show the interviewer you are interested and attentive by listening carefully to the questions being asked. This will also help you answer questions appropriately.

"I'm in the middle of a job interview. What are you doing?"

An old adage of interviewing says, "You never get a second chance to make a first impression." Until recently, image consultants differed on how much time individuals have to put their best face forward. But a study conducted by two Princeton psychologists has concluded that it takes only one-tenth of a second to form judgments about the key character traits of others. In practical terms, this means employers will make inferences about one's likeability, competence, trustworthiness, and aggressiveness in the blink of an eye. *What should job candidates do to make a good first impression during an interview?*

- **Turn off your cell phone.** Avoid the embarrassment of a ringing cell phone during an interview. Turn it off or leave it at home.
- **Don't chew gum.** Chewing gum during an interview is distracting and unprofessional.
- **Sound enthusiastic and interested—but sincere.** The tone of your voice has an enormous effect on the words you say. Avoid sounding bored, frustrated, or sarcastic during an interview. Employers want employees who are enthusiastic and interested.
- **Avoid "empty" words.** Filling your answers with verbal pauses such as *um*, *uh*, *like*, and *basically* communicates that you are not prepared. Also avoid annoying distractions such as clearing your throat repeatedly or sighing deeply.

Above all, remember that employers want to hire people who have confidence in their own abilities. Let your body language, posture, dress, and vocal tone prove that you are self-assured.

Answering Typical Interview Questions

How you answer questions can be as important as the answers themselves.

The way you answer questions can be almost as important as what you say. Use the interviewer's name and title from time to time when you answer. *Ms. Lyon, I would be pleased to tell you about . . . .* People like to hear their own names. Be sure you are pronouncing the name correctly, and don't overuse this technique. Avoid answering questions with a simple *yes* or *no*; elaborate on your answers to better sell yourself.

During the interview it may be necessary to occasionally refocus and clarify vague questions. Some interviewers are inexperienced and ill at ease in the role. You may even have to ask your own question to understand what was asked, *By ____ , do you mean ____?* Consider closing out some of your responses with *Does that answer your question?* or *Would you like me to elaborate on any particular experience?*

Stay focused on the skills and traits that employers seek; don't reveal weaknesses.

Always aim your answers at the key characteristics interviewers seek: expertise, competence, motivation, interpersonal skills, decision-making skills, enthusiasm for the job, and a pleasing personality. Remember to stay focused on your strengths. Don't reveal weaknesses, even if you think they make you look human. You won't be hired for your weaknesses, only for your strengths.

Be sure to use good English and enunciate clearly. Avoid slurred words such as *gonna* and *din't*, as well as slangy expressions such as *yeah, like*, and *ya know*. As you practice answering expected interview questions, it is always a good idea to make a recording. Is your speech filled with verbal static?

FIGURE 14.1 Twelve Interview Actions to Avoid

1. **Don't be late or too early.** Arrive five to ten minutes before your scheduled interview.

2. **Don't be rude.** Treat everyone you come into contact with warmly and respectfully.

3. **Don't ask for the job.** Asking for the job is naive, undignified, and unprofessional. Wait to see how the interview develops.

4. **Don't criticize anyone or anything.** Don't criticize your previous employer, supervisors, colleagues, or job. The tendency is for interviewers to wonder if you would speak about their companies similarly.

5. **Don't be a threat to the interviewer.** Avoid suggesting directly or indirectly that your goal is to become head honcho, a path that might include the interviewer's job.

6. **Don't act unprofessionally.** Don't discuss controversial subjects, and don't use profanity. Don't talk too much.

7. **Don't emphasize salary or benefits.** Don't bring up salary, vacation, or benefits early in an interview. Leave this up to the interviewer.

8. **Don't focus on your imperfections.** Never dwell on your liabilities or talk negatively about yourself.

9. **Don't interrupt.** Interrupting is not only impolite but also prevents you from hearing a complete question or remark.

10. **Don't bring someone along.** Don't bring a friend or relative with you to the interview. If someone must drive you, ask that person to drop you off and come back later.

11. **Don't appear impatient.** Your entire focus should be on the interview. Don't glance at your watch, which can imply that you are late for another appointment.

12. **Don't act desperate.** A sure way to turn off an interviewer is to act too desperate. Don't focus on why you *need* the job; focus on how you will add value to the organization.

You can't expect to be perfect in an employment interview. No one is. But you can avert sure disaster by avoiding certain topics and behaviors such as those described in Figure 14.1.

Employment interviews are all about questions, and many of the questions interviewers ask are not new. You can anticipate a large percentage of questions that will be asked before you ever walk into an interview room. Although you can't anticipate every question, you can prepare for different types.

This section presents questions that are may be asked during employment interviews. Some questions are meant to help the interviewer become acquainted with you. Others are aimed at measuring your interest, experience, and accomplishments. Still others will probe your future plans and challenge your reactions. Your interviewer may use situational or behavioral questions and may even occasionally ask an illegal question. To get you thinking about how to respond, we have provided an answer or discussion for one or more of the questions in each of the following groups. As you read the remaining questions in each group, think about how you could respond most effectively. For additional questions and mock interviews, contact your campus career and placement center.

> You can anticipate a large percentage of the questions you will be asked in an interview.

"Yes, I think I have good people skills. What kind of idiot question is that?"

Questions to Get Acquainted. After opening introductions, recruiters generally try to start the interview with personal questions that put you at ease. They are also striving to gain an overview to see whether you will fit into the organization's culture. When answering these questions, keep the employer's needs in mind and try to incorporate your success stories.

Prepare for get-acquainted questions by practicing a short formula response.

1. Tell me about yourself.

   Experts agree that you must keep this answer short (one to two minutes tops) but on target. Use this chance to promote yourself. Stick to educational, professional, or business-related strengths; avoid personal or humorous references. Be ready with at least three success stories illustrating characteristics important to this job. Demonstrate responsibility you have been given; describe how you contributed as a team player. Try practicing this formula: *I have completed _____ degree with a major in ____. Recently I worked for _____ as a _____. Before that I worked for _____ as a ____. My strengths are _____ (interpersonal) and _____ (technical).* Try rehearsing your response in 30-second segments devoted to your education, work experience, qualifications, and skills.

2. What are your greatest strengths?

   Stress your strengths that are related to the position, such as *I am well organized, thorough, and attentive to detail.* Tell success stories and give examples that illustrate these qualities: *My supervisor says that my research is exceptionally thorough. For example, I recently worked on a research project in which I . . . .*

3. Do you prefer to work by yourself or with others? Why?

   This question can be tricky. Provide a middle-of-the-road answer that not only suggests your interpersonal qualities but also reflects an ability to make independent decisions and work without supervision.

4. What was your major in college, and why did you choose it?
5. What are some things you do in your spare time? Hobbies? Sports?

Recruiters want to know how interested you are in this organization and in this specific position.

Questions to Gauge Your Interest. Interviewers want to understand your motivation for applying for a position. Although they will realize that you are probably interviewing for other positions, they still want to know why you are interested in this particular position with this organization. These types of questions help them determine your level of interest.

1. Why do you want to work for (name of company)?

   Questions like this illustrate why you must research an organization thoroughly before the interview. The answer to this question must prove that you understand the company and its culture. This is the perfect place to bring up the company research you did before the interview. Show what you know about the company, and discuss why you desire to become a part of this organization. Describe your desire to work for this organization not only from your perspective but also from its point of view. What do you have to offer?

2. Why are you interested in this position?
3. What do you know about our company?
4. Why do you want to work in the _____ industry?
5. What interests you about our products (services)?

Questions About Your Experience and Accomplishments. After questions about your background and education and questions that measure your interest, the interview generally becomes more specific with questions about your experience and accomplishments. Remember to show confidence when you

OFFICE INSIDER

Occasionally you bump into a talented and competent candidate . . . who's so lacking in the EQ components of humility and realness that you can't take a chance. This young man had a lot of the right stuff, but when he started telling us that he had never made a mistake in his life and didn't expect to, we knew we'd heard enough.

answer these questions. If you are not confident in your abilities, why should an employer be?

1. Why should we hire you when we have applicants with more experience or better credentials?

   In answering this question, remember that employers often hire people who present themselves well instead of others with better credentials. Emphasize your personal strengths that could be an advantage with this employer. Are you a hard worker? How can you demonstrate it? Have you had recent training? Some people have had more years of experience but actually have less knowledge because they have done the same thing over and over. Stress your experience using the latest methods and equipment. Be sure to mention your computer training and use of the Web. Tell success stories. Emphasize that you are open to new ideas and learn quickly. Above all, show that you are confident in your abilities.

2. Describe the most rewarding experience of your career so far.
3. How have your education and professional experiences prepared you for this position?
4. What were your major accomplishments in each of your past jobs?
5. What was a typical workday like?
6. What job functions did you enjoy most? Least? Why?
7. Tell me about your computer skills.
8. Who was the toughest boss you ever worked for and why?
9. What were your major achievements in college?
10. Why did you leave your last position? OR: Why are you leaving your current position?

Questions About the Future. Questions that look into the future tend to stump some candidates, especially those who have not prepared adequately. Employers ask these questions to see whether you are goal oriented and to determine whether your goals are realistic.

1. Where do you expect to be five (or ten) years from now?

   Formulate a realistic plan with respect to your present age and situation. The important thing is to be prepared for this question. It is a sure kiss of death to respond that you would like to have the interviewer's job! Instead, show an interest in the current job and in making a contribution to the organization. Talk about the levels of responsibility you would like to achieve. One employment counselor suggests showing ambition but not committing to a specific job title. Suggest that you hope to have learned enough to have progressed to a position where you will continue to grow. Keep your answer focused on educational and professional goals, not personal goals.

2. If you got this position, what would you do to be sure you fit in?
3. This is a large (or small) organization. Do you think you would like that environment?
4. Do you plan to continue your education?
5. What do you predict for the future of the _____ industry?
6. How do you think you can contribute to this company?
7. What would you most like to accomplish if you get this position?
8. How do you keep current with what is happening in your profession?

Challenging Questions. The following questions may make you uncomfortable, but the important thing to remember is to answer truthfully without dwelling on your weaknesses. As quickly as possible, convert any negative response into a discussion of your strengths.

Employers will hire a candidate with less experience and fewer accomplishments if he or she can demonstrate the skills required.

Questions about your experience and accomplishments enable you to work in your practiced success stories.

When asked about the future, show ambition and interest in succeeding with this company.

1. What is your greatest weakness?

   It is amazing how many candidates knock themselves out of the competition by answering this question poorly. Actually, you have many choices. You can present a strength as a weakness (*Some people complain that I'm a workaholic or too attentive to details*). You can mention a corrected weakness (*I found that I really needed to learn about conducting Web research, so I took a course*). You could cite an unrelated skill (*I really need to brush up on my Spanish*). You can cite a learning objective (*One of my long-term goals is to learn more about international management. Does your company have any plans to expand overseas?*). Another possibility is to reaffirm your qualifications (*I have no weaknesses that affect my ability to do this job*).

2. What type of people do you have no patience for?

   Avoid letting yourself fall into the trap of sounding overly critical. One possible response is, *I have always gotten along well with others. But I confess that I can be irritated by complainers who don't accept responsibility.*

3. If you could live your life over, what would you change and why?
4. How would your former (or current) supervisor describe you as an employee?
5. What do you want the most from your job? Money? Security? Power?
6. What is your grade point average, and does it accurately reflect your abilities?
7. Have you ever used drugs?
8. Who in your life has influenced you the most and why?
9. What are you reading right now?
10. Describe your ideal work environment.
11. Is the customer always right?
12. How do you define success?

Situational Questions. Questions related to situations help employers test your thought processes and logical thinking. When using situational questions, interviewers will describe a hypothetical situation and ask how you would handle it. Situational questions differ based on the type of position for which you are interviewing.[12] Knowledge of the position and the company culture will help you respond favorably to these questions. Even if the situation sounds negative, keep your response positive. Here are just a few examples:

1. You receive a call from an irate customer who complains about the service she received last night at your restaurant. She is demanding her money back. How would you handle the situation?
2. If you were aware that a coworker was falsifying data, what would you do?
3. Your supervisor has just told you that she is dissatisfied with your work, but you think it is acceptable. How would you resolve the conflict?
4. Your supervisor has told you to do something a certain way, and you think that way is wrong and that you know a far better way to complete the task. What would you do?
5. Assume that you are hired for this position. You soon learn that one of the staff is extremely resentful because she applied for your position and was turned down. As a result, she is being unhelpful and obstructive. How would you handle the situation?
6. A work colleague has told you in confidence that she suspects another colleague of stealing. What would your actions be?
7. You have noticed that communication between upper management and first-level employees is eroding. How would you solve this problem?

Behavioral Questions. Instead of traditional interview questions, you may be asked to tell stories. The interviewer may say, *Describe a time when . . .* or *Tell me about a time when . . . .* To respond effectively, learn to use the storytelling or STAR technique. Ask yourself, what the **S**ituation or **T**ask was, what **A**ction you took, and what the **R**esults were.[13] Practice using this method to recall specific examples of your skills and accomplishments. To be fully prepared, develop a coherent and articulate STAR narrative for every bullet point on your résumé. When answering behavioral questions, describe only educational and work-related situations or tasks, and try to keep them as current as possible. Here are a few examples of behavioral questions:

1. Tell me about a time when you solved a difficult problem.

   Tell a concise story explaining the situation or task, what you did, and the result. For example, *When I was at Ace Products, we continually had a problem of excessive back orders. After analyzing the situation, I discovered that orders went through many unnecessary steps. I suggested that we eliminate much paperwork. As a result, we reduced back orders by 30 percent.* Go on to emphasize what you learned and how you can apply that learning to this job. Practice your success stories in advance so that you will be ready.

2. Describe a situation in which you were able to use persuasion to successfully convince someone to see things your way.

   The recruiter is interested in your leadership and teamwork skills. You might respond, *I have learned to appreciate the fact that the way you present an idea is just as important as the idea itself. When trying to influence people, I put myself in their shoes and find some way to frame my idea from their perspective. I remember when I . . . .*

3. Describe a time when you had to analyze information and make a recommendation.
4. Describe a time that you worked successfully as part of a team.
5. Tell me about a time you dealt with confidential information.
6. Give me an example of a time when you were under stress to meet a deadline.
7. Tell me about a time when you had to go above and beyond the call of duty in order to get a job done.
8. Tell me about a time you were able to successfully deal with another person even when that person may not have personally liked you (or vice versa).
9. Give me an example of when you showed initiative and took the lead.
10. Tell me about a recent situation in which you had to deal with an upset customer or coworker.

Illegal and Inappropriate Questions. Federal laws prohibit employment discrimination based on gender, age, religion, color, race, national origin, and disability. In addition, many state and city laws exist that prohibit employment discrimination based on such factors as sexual orientation.[14] Therefore, it is inappropriate for interviewers to ask any question related to these areas. These questions become illegal, though, only when a court of law determines that the employer is asking them with the intent to discriminate.[15] Most illegal interview questions are asked innocently by inexperienced interviewers. Some are only trying to be friendly when they inquire about your personal life and family. Regardless of the intent, how should you react?

If you find the question harmless and if you want the job, go ahead and answer it. If you think that answering it would damage your chance to be hired, try to deflect the question tactfully with a response such as *Could you tell me how my marital status relates to the responsibilities of this position?* or, *I prefer to keep my personal and professional lives separate.* If you are uncomfortable answering a question, try to determine the reason behind it; you might answer, *I don't let my personal life interfere with my ability to do my job,* or, *Are you concerned with my availability to work overtime?* Another option, of course, is to respond to any inappropriate or

Candidates who are asked illegal questions must decide whether to answer, deflect the question tactfully, or confront the interviewer.

illegal question by confronting the interviewer and threatening a lawsuit or refusing to answer. However, you could not expect to be hired under these circumstances. In any case, you might wish to reconsider working for an organization that sanctions such procedures.

Here are some inappropriate and illegal questions that you may or may not want to answer:[16]

1. What is your marital status? Are you married? Do you live with anyone? Do you have a boyfriend (or girlfriend)? (However, employers can ask your marital status after hiring for tax and insurance forms.)
2. Do you have any disabilities? Have you had any recent illnesses? (But it is legal to ask if the person can perform specific job duties, such as, *Can you carry a 50-pound sack up a 10-foot ladder five times daily?*)
3. I notice you have an accent. Where are you from? What is the origin of your last name? What is your native language? (However, it is legal to ask what languages you speak fluently if language ability is related to the job.)
4. Have you ever filed a worker's compensation claim or been injured on the job?
5. Have you ever had a drinking problem or been addicted to drugs? (But it is legal to ask if a person uses illegal drugs.)
6. Have you ever been arrested? (But it is legal to ask, *Have you ever been convicted of _____?* when the crime is related to the job.)
7. How old are you? What is your date of birth? When did you graduate from high school? (But it is legal to ask, *Are you 16 years (or 18 years or 21 years) old or older?* depending on the age requirements for the position.)
8. Of what country are you a citizen? Where were you born? (But it is legal to ask, *Are you a citizen of the United States?* or, *Can you legally work in the United States?*)
9. What is your maiden name? (But it is legal to ask, *What is your full name?* or, *Have you worked under another name?*)
10. Do you have any religious beliefs that would prevent you from working weekends or holidays? (An employer can, however, ask you if you are available to work weekends and holidays.)
11. Do you have children? Do you plan to have children? Do you have adequate child-care arrangements? (However, employers can ask for dependent information for tax and insurance purposes after you are hired.)
12. How much do you weigh? How tall are you? (However, employers can ask you about your height and weight if minimum standards are necessary to safely perform a job.)[17]

> Interview questions become illegal only if a court of law determines that the intent was to discriminate.

Asking Your Own Questions

> Your questions should impress the interviewer but also provide valuable information about the job.

At some point in the interview, usually near the end, you will be asked whether you have any questions. The worst thing you can do is say *No*, which suggests that you are not interested in the position. Instead, ask questions that will help you gain information and will impress the interviewer with your thoughtfulness and interest in the position. Remember that this interview is a two-way street. You must be happy with the prospect of working for this organization. You want a position for which your skills and personality are matched. Use this opportunity to find out whether this job is right for you. Be aware that you don't have to wait for the interviewer to ask you for questions. You can ask your own questions throughout the interview to learn more about the company and position. Here are some questions you might ask:

1. What will my duties be (if not already discussed)?
2. Tell me what it is like working here in terms of the people, management practices, workloads, expected performance, and rewards.
3. What training programs are available from this organization? What specific training will be given for this position?

4. Who would be my immediate supervisor?
5. What is the organizational structure, and where does this position fit in?
6. Is travel required in this position?
7. How is job performance evaluated?
8. Assuming my work is excellent, where do you see me in five years?
9. How long do employees generally stay with this organization?
10. What are the major challenges for a person in this position?
11. What do you see in the future of this organization?
12. What do you like best about working for this organization?
13. May I have a tour of the facilities?
14. When do you expect to make a decision?

Ending Positively

After you have asked your questions, the interviewer will signal the end of the interview, usually by standing up or by expressing appreciation that you came. If not addressed earlier, you should at this time find out what action will follow. Demonstrate your interest in the position by asking when it will be filled or what the next step will be. Too many candidates leave the interview without knowing their status or when they will hear from the recruiter. Don't be afraid to say that you want the job!

At the end of the interview summarize your strongest qualifications, thank the interviewer, and ask for the interviewer's card.

Before you leave, summarize your strongest qualifications, show your enthusiasm for obtaining this position, and thank the interviewer for a constructive interview and for considering you for the position. Ask the interviewer for a business card, which will provide the information you need to write a thank-you letter, which is discussed later. Shake the interviewer's hand with confidence, and acknowledge anyone else you see on the way out. Be sure to thank the receptionist. Leaving the interview gracefully and enthusiastically will leave a lasting impression on those responsible for making the final hiring decision.

After the Interview

After leaving the interview, immediately make notes of what was said in case you are called back for a second interview. Write down key points that were discussed, the names of people you spoke with, and other details of the interview. Ask yourself what went really well and what could have been improved. Note your strengths and weaknesses during the interview so that you can work to improve in future interviews. Next, write down your follow-up plans. To whom should you send thank-you letters? Will you contact the employer by phone? If so, when? Then be sure to follow up on those plans, beginning with writing a thank-you letter and contacting your references.

Thanking Your Interviewer

After a job interview you should always send a thank-you letter, also called a follow-up letter. This courtesy sets you apart from other applicants, most of whom will not bother. Your letter also reminds the interviewer of your visit as well as suggesting your good manners and genuine enthusiasm for the job.

A follow-up thank-you letter shows your good manners and your enthusiasm for the job.

Follow-up letters are most effective if sent immediately after the interview. Experts believe that a thoughtful follow-up note carries as much weight as the cover letter does. Almost nine out of ten senior executives admit that in their evaluation of a job candidate they are swayed by a written thank you.[18] In your thank-you letter refer to the date of the interview, the exact job title for which you were interviewed, and specific topics discussed. "An effective thank-you letter should hit every one of the employer's hot buttons," author and career consultant Wendy Enelow says.[19] Don't get carried away after a successful interview and send an ill-conceived thank-you e-mail that reads like a text message or sounds too chummy. Smart interviewees don't ruin their chances by communicating with recruiters in hasty, poorly thought-out textspeak from their mobile devices.

In addition to being respectful when following up after an interview, avoid worn-out phrases, such as *Thank you for taking the time to interview me*. Be careful, too, about overusing *I*, especially to begin sentences. Most important, show that you really want the job and that you are qualified for it. Notice how the letter in Figure 14.2 conveys enthusiasm and confidence.

If you have been interviewed by more than one person, send a separate letter to each interviewer. It is also a good idea to send a thank-you letter to the receptionist and to the person who set up the interview. Your thank-you letter will probably make more of an impact if prepared in proper business format and sent by regular mail. However, if you know the decision will be made quickly, send your follow-up message by e-mail. One job candidate now makes a follow-up e-mail a practice. She summarizes what was discussed during the face-to-face interview and adds information that she had not thought to mention during the interview.[20]

FIGURE 14.2 Interview Follow-Up Letter

Adam G. Heraud

158 Gause Blvd., Apt. E, Slidell, LA 70458
(985)726-5143, aheraud@gmail.com

May 28, 200x

Mr. Charles W. Hainsworth
Apex Tech Imaging
3855 Ridgelake Avenue
New Orleans, LA 70130

Dear Mr. Hainsworth:

Talking with you Thursday, May 27, about the graphic designer position was both informative and interesting.

Thanks for describing the position in such detail and for introducing me to Ms. Tanaka, the senior designer. Her current project designing an annual report in four colors sounds fascinating as well as quite challenging.

Now that I've learned in greater detail the specific tasks of your graphic designers, I'm more than ever convinced that my computer and creative skills can make a genuine contribution to your graphic productions. My training in design and layout using PhotoShop and InDesign ensures that I could be immediately productive on your staff.

You will find me an enthusiastic and hardworking member of any team effort. As you requested, I'm enclosing additional samples of my work. I'm eager to join the graphics staff at your New Orleans headquarters, and I look forward to hearing from you soon.

Sincerely,

Adam G. Heraud

Adam G. Heraud

Enclosures

Annotations:

- Mentions the interview date and specific job title
- Highlights specific skills for the job
- Shows appreciation, good manners, and perseverance —traits that recruiters value
- Personalizes the message by referring to topics discussed in the interview
- Reminds reader of interpersonal skills as well as enthusiasm and eagerness for the job

Contacting Your References

Once you have thanked your interviewer, it is time to alert your references that they may be contacted by the employer. You might also have to request a letter of recommendation to be sent to the employer by a certain date. As discussed in Chapter 13, you should have already asked permission to use these individuals as references, and you should have supplied them with a copy of your résumé, highlighted with sales points.

To provide the best possible recommendation, your references need information. What position have you applied for with what company? What should they stress to the prospective employer? Let's say you are applying for a specific job that requires a letter of recommendation. Professor Orenstein has already agreed to be a reference for you. To get the best letter of recommendation from Professor Orenstein, help her out. Write a letter telling her about the position, its requirements, and the recommendation deadline. Include a copy of your résumé. You might remind her of a positive experience with you that she could use in the recommendation. Remember that recommenders need evidence to support generalizations. Give them appropriate ammunition, as the student has done in the following request:

"Why do all your references scream and slam down the phone when I mention your name?"

Dear Professor Orenstein:

Recently I interviewed for the position of administrative assistant in the Human Resources Department of Host International. Because you kindly agreed to help me, I am now asking you to write a letter of recommendation to Host.

> In a reference request letter, tell immediately why you are writing. Identify the target position and company.

The position calls for good organizational, interpersonal, and writing skills, as well as computer experience. To help you review my skills and training, I enclose my résumé. As you may recall, I earned an A in your business communication class last fall; and you commended my long report for its clarity and organization.

> Specify the job requirements so that the recommender knows what to stress.

Please send your letter to Mr. James Jenkins at Host International before July 1 in the enclosed stamped, addressed envelope. I'm grateful for your support, and I promise to let you know the results of my job search.

> Provide a stamped, addressed envelope.

Following Up

If you don't hear from the interviewer within five days, or at the specified time, call him or her. Practice saying something like, *I'm wondering what else I can do to convince you that I'm the right person for this job*, or, *I'm calling to find out the status of your search for the _____ position.* You could also e-mail the interviewer to find out how the decision process is going. When following up, it is important to sound professional and courteous. Sounding desperate, angry, or frustrated that you haven't been contacted can ruin your chances. The following follow-up e-mail message would impress the interviewer:

Dear Ms. Jamison:

I enjoyed my interview with you last Thursday for the receptionist position. You should know that I'm very interested in this opportunity with Coastal Enterprises. Because you mentioned that you might have an answer this week, I'm eager to know how your decision process is coming along. I look forward to hearing from you.

> A follow-up letter inquires courteously and does not sound angry or desperate.

Sincerely,

Depending on the response you get to your first follow-up request, you may have to follow up additional times. Keep in mind, though, that some employers won't tell you about their hiring decision unless you are the one hired.[21] Don't harass the interviewer, and don't force a decision. If you don't hear back from an employer within several weeks after following up, it is best to assume that you didn't get the job and to continue with your job search.

Other Employment Documents

Although the résumé and cover letter are your major tasks, other important documents and messages are often required during the employment process. You may need to complete an employment application form and write follow-up letters. You might also have to write a letter of resignation when leaving a job. Because each of these tasks reveals something about you and your communication skills, you will want to put your best foot forward. These documents often subtly influence company officials to offer a job.

Application Form

Some organizations require job candidates to fill out job application forms instead of, or in addition to, submitting résumés. This practice permits them to gather and store standardized data about each applicant. Whether the application is on paper or online, follow the directions carefully and provide accurate information. The following suggestions can help you be prepared:

> **When applying for jobs, keep with you a card summarizing your important data.**

- Carry a card summarizing vital statistics not included on your résumé. If you are asked to fill out an application form in an employer's office, you will need a handy reference to the following data: graduation dates, beginning and ending dates of all employment; salary history; full names, titles, and present work addresses of former supervisors; full addresses and phone numbers of current and previous employers; and full names, occupational titles, occupational addresses, and telephone numbers of persons who have agreed to serve as references.
- Look over all the questions before starting.
- Fill out the form neatly, using blue or black ink. Many career counselors recommend printing your responses; cursive handwriting can be difficult to read.
- Answer all questions honestly. Write *Not applicable* or *N/A* if appropriate.
- Use accurate spelling, grammar, and punctuation.
- If asked for the position desired, give a specific job title or type of position. Don't say, *Anything* or *Open*. These answers will make you look unfocused; moreover, they make it difficult for employers to know what you are qualified for or interested in.
- Be prepared for a salary question. Unless you know what comparable employees are earning in the company, the best strategy is to suggest a salary range or to write *Negotiable* or *Open*. See the Communication Workshop at the end of this chapter for tips on dealing with money matters while interviewing.
- Be prepared to explain the reasons for leaving previous positions. Use positive or neutral phrases such as *Relocation, Seasonal, To accept a position with more responsibility, Temporary position, To continue education,* or *Career change*. Avoid words or phrases such as *Fired, Quit, Didn't get along with supervisor,* or *Pregnant*.
- Look over the application before submitting to make sure it is complete and that you have followed all instructions. Sign and date the application.

Application or Résumé Follow-Up Letter

If your résumé or application generates no response within a reasonable time, you may decide to send a short follow-up letter such as the following. Doing so (a) jogs the memory of the personnel officer, (b) demonstrates your serious interest, and (c) allows you to emphasize your qualifications or to add new information.

Dear Ms. Lopez:

Please know I am still interested in becoming an administrative support specialist with Quad, Inc.

Open by reminding the reader of your interest.

Since I submitted an application [*or* résumé] in May, I have completed my degree and have been employed as a summer replacement for office workers in several downtown offices. This experience has honed my word processing and communication skills. It has also introduced me to a wide range of office procedures.

Review your strengths or add new qualifications.

Please keep my application in your active file and let me know when I may put my formal training, technical skills, and practical experience to work for you.

Rejection Follow-Up Letter

If you didn't get the job and you think it was perfect for you, don't give up. Employment specialists encourage applicants to respond to a rejection. The candidate who was offered the position may decline, or other positions may open up. In a rejection follow-up letter, it is OK to admit you are disappointed. Be sure to add, however, that you are still interested and will contact the company again in a month in case a job opens up. Then follow through for a couple of months—but don't overdo it. You should be professional and persistent, but not a pest. Here's an example of an effective rejection follow-up letter:

Dear Mr. O'Neal:

Although I'm disappointed that someone else was selected for your accounting position, I appreciate your promptness and courtesy in notifying me.

Subordinate your disappointment to your appreciation at being notified promptly and courteously.

Because I firmly believe that I have the technical and interpersonal skills needed to work in your fast-paced environment, I hope you will keep my résumé in your active file. My desire to become a productive member of your Transamerica staff remains strong.

I enjoyed our interview, and I especially appreciate the time you and Ms. Goldstein spent describing your company's expansion into international markets. To enhance my qualifications, I have enrolled in a course in International Accounting at CSU.

Refer to specifics of your interview.

Should you have an opening for which I am qualified, you may reach me at (818) 719-3901. In the meantime, I will call you in a month to discuss employment possibilities.

Take the initiative; tell when you will call for an update.

Sincerely,

Job Acceptance and Rejection Letters

When all your hard work pays off, you will be offered the position you want. Although you will likely accept the position over the phone, it is a good idea to follow up with an acceptance letter to confirm the details and to formalize the acceptance. Your acceptance letter might look like this:

Dear Ms. Scarborough:

It was a pleasure talking with you earlier today. As I mentioned, I am delighted to accept the position of web designer with Innovative Creations, Inc., in your Seattle office. I look forward to becoming part of the IC team and to starting work on a variety of exciting and innovative projects.

Confirm your acceptance of the position with enthusiasm.

As we agreed, my starting salary will be $46,000, with a full benefits package including health and life insurance, retirement plan, stock options, and three weeks of vacation per year.

Review salary and benefits details.

I look forward to starting my position with Innovative Creations on September 15, 2011. Before that date I will send you the completed tax and insurance forms you need. Thanks again for everything, Ms. Scarborough.

Sincerely,

If you must turn down a job offer, show your professionalism by writing a sincere letter. This letter should thank the employer for the job offer and explain briefly that you are turning it down. Taking the time to extend this courtesy could help you in the future if this employer has a position you really want. Here's an example of a job rejection letter:

Dear Mr. Opperman:

Thank the employer for the job offer and decline the offer without giving specifics. Express gratitude and best wishes for the future.

Thank you very much for offering me the position of sales representative with Bendall Pharmaceuticals. It was a difficult decision to make, but I have accepted a position with another company.

I appreciate your taking the time to interview me, and I wish Bendall much success in the future.

Resignation Letter

After you have been in a position for a period of time, you may find it necessary to leave. Perhaps you have been offered a better position, or maybe you have decided to return to school full-time. Whatever the reason, you should leave your position gracefully and tactfully. Although you will likely discuss your resignation in person with your supervisor, it is a good idea to document your resignation by writing a formal letter. Some resignation letters are brief, while others contain great detail. Remember that many resignation letters are placed in personnel files; therefore, it should be formatted and written using the professional business letter writing techniques you learned earlier. Here is an example of a basic letter of resignation:

Dear Ms. Patrick:

Confirm exact date of resignation. Remind employer of your contributions.

This letter serves as formal notice of my resignation from Allied Corporation, effective Friday, August 15. I have enjoyed serving as your office assistant for the past two years, and I am grateful for everything I have learned during my employment with Allied.

Please let me know what I can do over the next two weeks to help you prepare for my departure. I would be happy to help with finding and training my replacement.

Offer assistance to prepare for your resignation. Offer thanks and end with a forward-looking statement.

Thanks again for providing such a positive employment experience. I will long remember my time here.

Sincerely,

Although this employee gave a standard two-week notice, you may find that a longer notice is necessary. The higher and more responsible your position, the longer the notice you should give your employer. You should, however, always give some notice as a courtesy.

Writing job acceptance, job rejection, and resignation letters requires effort. That effort, however, is worth it because you are building bridges that later may carry you to even better jobs in the future.

Visit www.meguffey.com
- **Chapter Review Quiz**
- **Flash Cards**
- **Grammar Practice**
- **PowerPoint Slides**
- **Personal Language Trainer**
- **Beat the Clock Quiz**

Summing Up and Looking Forward

Whether you face a screening interview or a hiring/placement interview, you must be well prepared. You can increase your chances of success and reduce your anxiety considerably by knowing how interviews are typically conducted and by researching the target company thoroughly. Practice answering typical questions, including situational, behavioral, and challenging ones. Consider audio or video recording a mock interview so that you can check your body language and improve your answering techniques.

At the end of the interview, thank the interviewer, review your main strengths for the position, and ask what the next step is. Follow up with a thank-you letter and a follow-up call or message, if appropriate. Prepare other employment-related documents as needed, including application forms, application and résumé follow-up letters, rejection follow-up letters, job acceptance and rejection letters, and resignation letters.

You have now completed 14 chapters of rigorous instruction aimed at developing your skills so that you can be a successful business communicator in today's rapidly changing world of information. Remember that this is but a starting point. Your skills as a business communicator will continue to grow on the job as you apply the principles you have learned and expand your expertise.

Critical Thinking

1. How can recruiters and job seekers connect on the Web, and what are the advantages and potential disadvantages of doing so?

2. What can you do to improve the first impression you make at an interview?

3. In employment interviews, do you think that behavioral questions (such as *Tell me about a business problem you have had and how you solved it*) are more effective than traditional questions (such as *Tell me what you are good at*)? Why?

4. Why is it important to ask one's own questions of the interviewer?

5. Why should a job candidate write a thank-you letter after an interview?

Chapter Review

6. Name the main purposes of interviews—for job candidates as well as for employers.

7. Briefly describe the types of hiring/placement interviews you may encounter.

8. How can you address problem areas on your résumé such as lack of experience, getting fired, or earning low grades?

9. You have scheduled an interview with a large local company. What kind of information should you seek about this company, and where could you expect to find it?

10. Name at least six interviewing behaviors you can exhibit that send positive nonverbal messages.

11. What is your greatest fear of what you might do or what might happen to you during an employment interview? How can you overcome your fears?

12. Should you be candid with an interviewer when asked about your weaknesses?

13. How should you respond to questions you feel are inappropriate or illegal?

14. List the steps you should take immediately following your job interview.

15. List various kinds of follow-up letters.

Activities and Cases

WEB

14.1 Researching an Organization

An important part of your preparation for an interview is finding out about the target company.

Your Task. Select an organization where you would like to be employed. Assume you have been selected for an interview. Using resources described in this chapter, locate information about the organization's leaders and their business philosophies. Find out about the organization's accomplishments, setbacks, finances, products, customers, competition, and advertising. Prepare a summary report documenting your findings.

WEB

14.2 Learning What Jobs Are Really About Through Blogs

Blogs are becoming an important tool in the employment search process. By accessing blogs, job seekers can learn more about a company's culture and day-to-day activities.

Your Task. Using the Web, locate a blog that is maintained by an employee of a company where you would like to work. Monitor the blog for at least a week. Prepare a short report that summarizes what you learned about the company through reading the blog postings. Include a statement of whether this information would be valuable during your job search.

WEB

14.3 Taking a Look at Corporate Web Videos

Would you like to know what it is like to work for the company that interests you? Check out Web videos posted by companies on their career pages, job boards, and even YouTube. Currently about 7,000 corporate videos await you on Jobing, a job board that lists openings in specific geographic regions.

Your Task. Search company recruiting Web sites, YouTube, or Jobing for videos featuring two or three companies in your chosen industry. Compare how the employers introduce themselves, which aspects they emphasize about their organizations, how they present their employees, what they offer potential applicants, and so forth. Write a short report addressed to your instructor comparing and contrasting the corporate Web videos you examined.

14.4 Building Interview Skills

Successful interviews require diligent preparation and repeated practice. To be well prepared, you need to know what skills are required for your targeted position. In addition to computer and communication skills, employers generally want to know whether a candidate works well with a team, accepts responsibility, solves problems, is efficient, meets deadlines, shows leadership, saves time and money, and is a hard worker.

Your Task. Consider a position for which you are eligible now or one for which you will be eligible when you complete your education. Identify the skills and traits necessary for this position. If you prepared a résumé in Chapter 13, be sure that it addresses these targeted areas. Now prepare interview worksheets listing at least ten technical and other skills or traits you think a recruiter will want to discuss in an interview for your targeted position.

14.5 Preparing Success Stories

You can best showcase your talents if you are ready with your own success stories that show how you have developed the skills or traits required for your targeted position.

Your Task. Using the worksheets you prepared in Activity 14.4, prepare success stories that highlight the required skills or traits. Select three to five stories to develop into answers to potential interview questions. For example, here's a typical question: *How does your background relate to the position we have open?* A possible response: *As you know, I have just completed an intensive training program in _____. In addition, I have over three years of part-time work experience in a variety of business settings. In one position I was selected to manage a small business in the absence of the owner. I developed responsibility and customer-service skills in filling orders efficiently, resolving shipping problems, and monitoring key accounts. I also inventoried and organized products worth over $200,000. When the owner returned from a vacation to Florida, I was commended for increasing sales and was given a bonus in recognition of my efforts.* People relate to and remember stories. Try to shape your answers into memorable stories.

WEB

14.6 Exploring Appropriate Interview Attire

As you prepare for your interview by learning about the company and the industry, don't forget a key component of interview success: creating a favorable first impression by wearing appropriate business attire. Job seekers often have nebulous ideas about proper interview wear. Some wardrobe mishaps include choosing a conservative "power" suit but accessorizing it with beat-up casual shoes or a shabby bag. Grooming glitches include dandruff on dark suit fabric, dirty fingernails, or mothball odor. Women sometimes wrongly assume that any black clothing items are acceptable, even if they are too tight, revealing, sheer, or made of low-end fabrics. Most image consultants agree that workplace attire falls into three main categories: business formal, business casual, and casual. Only business formal is considered proper interview apparel.

Your Task. To prepare for your big day, search the Web for descriptions and images of *business formal*. You may research *business casual* and *casual* styles, but for an interview, always dress on the side of caution—conservatively. Compare prices and look for suit sales to buy one or two attractive interview outfits. Share your findings (notes, images, and price range for suits, solid shoes, and accessories) with the class and your instructor.

14.7 Polishing Answers to Interview Questions

Practice makes perfect in interviewing. The more often you rehearse responses to typical interview questions, the closer you are to getting the job.

Your Task. Select three questions from each of these question categories discussed in this chapter: Questions to Get Acquainted, Questions to Gauge Your Interest, Questions About Your Experience and Accomplishments, Questions About the Future, and Challenging Questions. Write your answers to each set of questions. Try to incorporate skills and traits required for the targeted position, and include success stories where appropriate. Polish these answers and your delivery technique by practicing in front of a mirror or into an audio recorder.

WEB **TEAM**

14.8 Learning to Answer Situational Interview Questions

Situational interview questions can vary widely from position to position. You should know enough about a position to understand some of the typical situations you would encounter on a regular basis.

Your Task. Use your favorite search tool to locate typical job descriptions of a position in which you are interested. Based on these descriptions, develop a list of six to eight typical situations someone in this position would face; then write situational interview questions for each of these scenarios. In pairs of two students, role-play interviewer and interviewee alternating with your listed questions.

WEB **TEAM**

14.9 Developing Skill With Behavioral Interview Questions

Behavioral interview questions are increasingly popular, and you will need a little practice before you can answer them easily.

Your Task. Use your favorite search tool to locate lists of behavioral questions on the Web. Select five skills areas such as communication, teamwork, and decision making. For each skills area find three behavioral questions that you think would be effective in an interview. In pairs of two students, role-play interviewer and interviewee alternating with your listed questions. You goal is to answer effectively in one or two minutes. Remember to use the STAR method when answering.

WEB

14.10 Answering Puffball and Killer Questions in a Virtual Interview

Two Web sites offer excellent interview advice. At Monster Career Advice (**http://career-advice.monster.com/interview-tips/home.aspx**) you can improve your interviewing skills in virtual interviews. You will find questions, answers, and explanations for interviews in job fields ranging from administrative support to human resources to technology. At WetFeet (**http://www.wetfeet.com**) you can learn how to answer résumé-based questions and how to handle preinterview jitters, and see dozens of articles filled with helpful tips.

Your Task. Visit one or both of the targeted Web sites. If these URLs have been changed, use your favorite search tool to locate *Monster Interviews* and *WetFeet Interviews*.

14.11 Creating an Interview Cheat Sheet
Even the best-rehearsed applicants sometimes forget to ask the questions they prepared, or they fail to stress their major accomplishments in job interviews. Sometimes applicants are so rattled they even forget the interviewer's name. To help you keep your wits during an interview, make a "cheat sheet" that summarizes key facts, answers, and questions. Use it before the interview and also review it as the interview is ending to be sure you have covered everything that is critical.

Your Task. Prepare a cheat sheet with the following information:

Day and time of interview:
Meeting with: (Name of interviewer(s), title, company, city, state, zip, telephone, cell, fax, e-mail)
Major accomplishments: (four to six)
Management or work style: (four to six)
Things you need to know about me: (three or four items)
Reason I left my last job:
Answers to difficult questions: (four or five answers)
Questions to ask interviewer:
Things I can do for you:

14.12 Handling Inappropriate and Illegal Interview Questions
Although some questions are considered illegal by the government, many interviewers will ask them anyway—whether intentionally or unknowingly. Being prepared is important.

Your Task. How would you respond in the following scenario? You are being interviewed at one of the top companies on your list of potential employers. The interviewing committee consists of a human resources manager and the supervising manager of the department where you would work. At various times during the interview, the supervising manager asks questions that make you feel uncomfortable. For example, he asks whether you are married. You know this question is illegal, but you saw no harm in answering it. But then he asks how old you are. Because you started college early and graduated in three and a half years, you are worried that you may not be considered mature enough for this position. You have most of the qualifications required, and you are convinced you could succeed on the job. How should you answer this question?

14.13 Knowing What to Ask
When it is your turn to ask questions during the interview process, be ready.

Your Task. Decide on three to five questions that you would like to ask during an interview. Write these questions out and practice asking them so that you sound confident and sincere.

TEAM
14.14 Role-Playing in a Mock Interview
One of the best ways to understand interview dynamics and to develop confidence is to role-play the parts of interviewer and candidate in a mock interview.

Your Task. Choose a partner for this activity. Each partner makes a list of two interview questions for each of the eight interview question categories presented in this chapter. In team sessions you and your partner will role-play an actual interview. One acts as interviewer; the other is the candidate. Prior to the interview, the candidate tells the interviewer what job and company he or she is applying to. For the interview, the interviewer and candidate should dress appropriately and sit in chairs facing each other. The interviewer greets the candidate and makes the candidate comfortable. The candidate gives the interviewer a copy of his or her résumé. The interviewer asks three (or more, depending on your instructor's time schedule) questions from the candidate's list. The interviewer may also ask follow-up questions if appropriate. When finished, the interviewer ends the meeting graciously. After one interview, reverse roles and repeat.

14.15 Video Recording an Interview
Seeing how you look during an interview can help you improve your body language and presentation style. Your instructor may act as the interviewer, or an outside businessperson may be asked to conduct mock interviews in your classroom.

Your Task. Engage a student or campus specialist to videotape each interview. Review your performance, and critique it looking for ways to improve. Your instructor may ask class members to offer comments and suggestions on individual interviews. Alternatively, visit your campus career center and sign up for a mock interview. Ask if your session could be recorded for subsequent viewing.

14.16 Saying Thanks for the Interview

You have just completed an exciting employment interview, and you want the interviewer to remember you.

Your Task. Write a follow-up thank-you letter to Ronald T. Ranson, Human Resources Development, Electronic Data Sources, 1328 Peachtree Plaza, Atlanta, GA 30314 (or a company of your choice). Make up any details needed.

14.17 Refusing to Take *No* for an Answer

After an excellent interview with Electronic Data Sources (or a company of your choice), you are disappointed to learn that someone else was hired. However, you really want to work for EDS.

Your Task. Write a follow-up letter to Ronald T. Ranson, Human Resources Development, Electronic Data Sources, 1328 Peachtree Plaza, Atlanta, GA 30314 (or a company of your choice). Indicate that you are disappointed but still interested.

14.18 Following Up After Submitting Your Résumé

A month has passed since you sent your résumé and cover letter in response to a job advertisement. You are still interested in the position and would like to find out whether you still have a chance.

Your Task. Write a follow-up letter that doesn't offend the reader or damage your chances of employment.

14.19 Requesting a Reference

Your favorite professor has agreed to be one of your references. You have just arrived home from a job interview that went well, and you must ask your professor to write a letter of recommendation.

Your Task. Write to the professor requesting that a letter of recommendation be sent to the company where you interviewed. Explain that the interviewer asked that the letter be sent directly to him. Provide data about the job description and about yourself so that the professor can target its content.

14.20 Saying *Yes* to a Job Offer

Your dream has come true: you have just been offered an excellent position. Although you accepted the position on the phone, you want to send a formal acceptance letter.

Your Task. Write a job acceptance letter to an employer of your choice. Include the specific job title, your starting date, and details about your compensation package. Make up any necessary details.

E-MAIL **WEB**

14.21 Searching for Advice

You can find wonderful, free, and sometimes entertaining job-search strategies, career tips, and interview advice on the Web.

Your Task. Use an electronic database or search the Web to locate articles or links to job-search and résumé sites. Make a list of at least five good job search pointers—ones that were not covered in this chapter. Send an e-mail message to your instructor describing your findings, or post your findings to a class discussion board to share with your classmates.

Video Resource

Video Library 1: *Building Workplace Skills: Sharpening Your Interview Skills.* In this video you see the job interview of Betsy Chin. Based on what you learned in this chapter and your own experience, critique her performance. What did she do well, and what could she improve?

Grammar/Mechanics Checkup 14

Punctuation Review

Review Sections 1.17 and 2.01–2.29 in the Grammar/Mechanics Handbook. Study the following groups of sentences. In the space provided write the letter of the one that is correctly punctuated. When you finish, compare your responses with those at the end of the book. If your responses differ, study carefully the principles in parentheses.

1. a. Our products will not be ready for the first month of the holiday shopping season, therefore we must hire additional seasonal workers.

   b. We know that the extra staff will cut into our slim profit margin; however, not delivering the goods on time could hurt us more in the longer term.

   c. Our company could pick up the slack by instituting extra shifts in our flagship plant, or by subcontracting at least part of the lot to our Mexican partner plant.

2. a. Our accounting team makes a point of analyzing your business operations, and getting to know what's working for you and what's not.

   b. We are dedicated to understanding your business needs over the long term, and taking an active role when it comes to creating solutions.

   c. We understand that you may be downsizing or moving into new markets, and we want to help you make a seamless transition.

3. a. If you decide to use throwaway batteries, or fear the high upfront cost of incandescent lamps, you can still be somewhat "green" by disposing of hazardous waste safely.

   b. When the batteries are fully charged, unplug the battery chargers to save power.

   c. Although they are switched off many office appliances continue to draw a small amount of power.

4. a. There is a direct relationship between fuel economy and carbon dioxide emissions; therefore, a car that produces less carbon dioxide will cost less to fill up.

   b. Although tangible advantages exist; the decision to buy a hybrid vehicle is not easy or clear-cut.

   c. Efforts to clean up automotive emissions started as an attempt to cut smog, and also to slow global warming.

5. a. One of the reasons we are decreasing the number of our ATMs, is that two thirds of the bank's customers depend on tellers for transactions.

   b. We are looking for an article titled, "Online Banking."

   c. Banks are at this time competing with nontraditional rivals that can provide extensive financial services.

6. a. We care deeply about the environment; but we also care about safety and good customer service.

   b. The president worked with environmental concerns; the vice president focused on customer support.

   c. Our Web site increases our productivity, it also improves customer service.

7. a. Employees who will be receiving salary increases are: Terri, Mark, Rob, and Ellen.

   b. The following employees are eligible for bonuses: Robin, Jeff, Bill, and Jose.

   c. Our consulting firm is proud to offer Web services for: site design, market analysis, e-commerce, and hosting.

8. a. Independent Web workers' schedules tend to be very flexible.

   b. The two supervisors irresponsibility caused injury on the shop floor.

   c. Several smaller suppliers trucks and passenger vans are running on CNG to substitute for expensive gasoline.

9. a. Our committee considered convention sites in Scottsdale, Arizona, Palm Springs, California; and Dallas, Texas.

   b. Serena was from Columbus, Ohio; Josh was from Denver, Colorado, and Rachel was from Seattle, Washington.

   c. The following engineers were approved: J. W. Ellis, civil; Dr. Thomas Lee, structural; and W. R. Verey, mechanical.

10. a. The package from Albany, New York was never delivered.

    b. We have scheduled an inspection tour on Tuesday, March 5, at 4 p.m.

    c. Send the check to M. E. Williams, 320 Summit Ridge, Ogden, Utah 84404 before the last mail pickup.

The following letter has faults in grammar, punctuation, spelling, capitalization, wordiness, and other problems. Correct the errors with standard proofreading marks (see Appendix B) or revise the message online at **www.meguffey.com**.

842 New Durham Rd.
Edison, NJ 08817
June 4, 200x

Mr. Frederick M. Eadgar
Human Resources Department
Marketing and Sales Pros
1050 Avenue of the Americas
New York, NY 10036

Dear Mr. Edgar:

I would really wellcome the opportunity to work for you. I appriciated the interview yesterday for the newly-listed Position of Sales Trainee. It was really a pleasure meeting yourself and learning more about Marketing and Sales Pros, you have a fine staff and a sophisticated approach to marketing.

You are organization appears to be growing in a directional manner that parralels my interests' and career goals. The interview with yourself and your staff yesterday confirmed my initale positive impressions of Marketing and Sales Pros and I want to reiterate my strong interest in working with and for you. My prior Retail sales experience as a sales associate with The Gap; plus my recent training in Microsoft Word and Excel would enable me to make progress steadily through your programs of training and become a productive member of your sales team in no time at all.

Again, thank-you for your kind and gracius consideration. In the event that you need any additional information from me, all you have to do is give me a jingle at (732) 598-3557.

Sincerly yours,

Communication Workshop: Career Skills

Let's Talk Money: Negotiating a Salary

When to talk about salary causes many job applicants concern. The important thing to remember is that almost all salaries are negotiable. Research conducted by the Society for Human Resource Management and *CareerJournal.com* shows that approximately 90 percent of human resources professionals say salaries are negotiable, and 78 percent of employees report negotiating salary.[22] If you have proved your worth throughout the interview process, employers will want to negotiate with you. To discuss compensation effectively, though, you must be prepared for salary questions, and you should know what you are worth. You also need to know basic negotiation strategies. As negotiation expert Chester L. Karrass said, "In business, you don't get what you deserve, you get what you negotiate."[23] The following negotiating rules, recommended by various career experts, can guide you to a better beginning salary.[24]

Rule No. 1: Avoid discussing salary for as long as possible in the interview process.
The longer you delay salary discussion, the more time you will have to convince the employer that you are worth what you are asking for. Ideally, you should try to avoid discussing salary until you know for sure that the interviewing company is making a job offer. The best time for you to negotiate your salary is between the time you are offered the position and the time you accept it. Wait for the employer to bring salary up first. If salary comes up and you are not sure whether the job is being offered to you, it is time for you to be blunt. Here are some things you could say:

Are you making me a job offer?

What salary range do you pay for positions with similar requirements?

I'm very interested in the position, and my salary would be negotiable.

Tell me what you have in mind for the salary range.

Rule No. 2: Know in advance the probable salary range for similar jobs in similar organizations.
Many job-search Web sites provide salary information. But it is probably better for you to call around in your area to learn what similar jobs are paying. The important thing here is to think in terms of a wide range. Let's say you are hoping to start at between $45,000 and $50,000. To an interviewer, you might say, *I was looking for a salary in the high forties to the low fifties.* This technique is called bracketing. In addition, stating your salary range in an annual dollar amount sounds more professional than asking for an hourly wage. Be sure to consider such things as geographic location, employer size, industry standards, the strength of the economy, and other factors to make sure that the range you come up with is realistic.

Rule No. 3: When negotiating, focus on what you are worth, not on what you need.
Throughout the interview and negotiation process, focus continually on your strengths. Make sure that the employer knows everything of value that you will bring to the organization. You have to prove that you are worth what you are asking for. Employers pay salaries based on what you will accomplish on the job and contribute to the organization. When discussing your salary, focus on how the company will benefit from these contributions. Don't bring personal issues into the negotiation process. No employer will be willing to pay you more because you have bills to pay, mouths to feed, or debt to get out of.

Rule No. 4: Never say *no* to a job before it is offered.
Why would anyone refuse a job offer before it is made? It happens all the time. Let's say you were hoping for a salary of, say, $45,000. The interviewer tells you that the salary scheduled for this job is $40,000. You respond, *Oh, that is out of the question!* Before you were offered the job, you have, in effect, refused it. Instead, wait for the job offer; then start negotiating your salary.

Rule No. 5: Ask for a higher salary first, and consider benefits.

Within reason, always try to ask for a higher salary first. This will leave room for this amount to decrease during negotiations until it is closer to your original expectations. Remember to consider the entire compensation package when negotiating. You may be willing to accept a lower salary if benefits such as insurance, flexible hours, time off, and retirement are attractive.

Rule No. 6: Be ready to bargain if offered a low starting salary.

Many salaries are negotiable. Companies are often willing to pay more for someone who interviews well and fits their culture. If the company seems right to you and you are pleased with the sound of the open position but you have been offered a low salary, say, *That is somewhat lower than I had hoped but this position does sound exciting. If I were to consider this, what sorts of things could I do to quickly become more valuable to this organization?* Also discuss such things as bonuses based on performance or a shorter review period. You could say something like, *Thanks for the offer. The position is very much what I wanted in many ways, and I am delighted at your interest. If I start at this salary, may I be reviewed within six months with the goal of raising the salary to ____?*

Another possibility is to ask for more time to think about the low offer. Tell the interviewer that this is an important decision, and you need some time to consider the offer. The next day you can call and say, *I am flattered by your offer, but I cannot accept because the salary is lower than I would like. Perhaps you could reconsider your offer or keep me in mind for future openings.*

Rule No. 7: Be honest.

Be honest throughout the entire negotiation process. Don't inflate the salaries of your previous positions to try to get more money. Don't tell an employer that you have received other job offers unless it is true. These lies can be grounds for being fired later on.

Rule No. 8: Get the final offer in writing.

Once you have agreed on a salary and compensation package, get the offer in writing. You should also follow up with a position acceptance letter, as discussed earlier in the chapter.

Career Application. You have just passed the screening interview and have been asked to come in for a personal interview with the human resources representative and the hiring manager of a company for which you are very eager to work. Although you are delighted with the company, you have promised yourself that you will not accept any position that pays less than $45,000 to start.

Your Task

In teams of two, role-play the position of interviewer and interviewee. The interviewer sets the scene by discussing preliminaries and offers a salary of $42,500. The interviewee responds to preliminary questions and to the salary offer of $42,500. Then, reverse roles so that the interviewee becomes the interviewer, and repeat the scenario.

Business communicators produce numerous documents that have standardized formats. Becoming familiar with these formats is important because business documents actually carry two kinds of messages. Verbal messages are conveyed by the words chosen to express the writer's ideas. Nonverbal messages are conveyed largely by the appearance of a document and its adherence to recognized formats. To ensure that your documents carry favorable nonverbal messages about you and your organization, you'll want to give special attention to the appearance and formatting of your e-mail messages, letters, envelopes, and fax cover sheets.

E-Mail Messages

E-mail messages are sent by computers through networks. After reading e-mail messages, receivers may print, store, or delete them. E-mail is an appropriate channel for *short* messages. E-mail should not replace business letters or memos that are lengthy, require permanent records, or transmit confidential or sensitive information. Chapter 5 presented guidelines on using e-mail smartly and safely. This section provides information on formats and usage. The following suggestions, illustrated in Figure A.1 and also in Figure 5.2 on page 104, may guide you in setting up the parts of any e-mail message. Always check, however, with your organization so that you can follow its practices.

To **Line.** Include the receiver's e-mail address after *To*. If the receiver's address is recorded in your address book, you just have to click on it. Be sure to enter all addresses very carefully since one mistyped letter prevents delivery.

From **Line.** Most mail programs automatically include your name and e-mail address after *From*.

Cc **and** *Bcc***.** Insert the e-mail address of anyone who is to receive a copy of the message. *Cc* stands for carbon copy or courtesy copy. Don't be tempted, though, to send needless copies just because it is easy. *Bcc* stands for blind carbon copy. Some writers use *bcc* to send a copy of the message without the addressee's knowledge. Writers also use the *bcc* line for mailing lists. When a message is sent to a number of people and their e-mail addresses should not be revealed, the *bcc* line works well to conceal the names and addresses of all receivers.

Subject. Identify the subject of the e-mail message with a brief but descriptive summary of the topic. Be sure to include enough information to be clear and compelling. Capitalize the initial letters of main words. Main words are all words except (a) the articles *a, an,* and *the*; (b) prepositions containing two or three letters (such as *at, to, on, by, for*); (c) the word *to* in an infinitive (*to work, to write*); and (d) the word *as*—unless any of these words are the first or last word in the subject line.

Salutation. Include a brief greeting, if you like. Some writers use a salutation such as *Dear Erica* followed by a comma or a colon. Others are more informal with *Hi, Erica; Hello, Erica; Good morning;* or *Greetings.* See Chapter 5 for a more complete discussion of e-mail salutations.

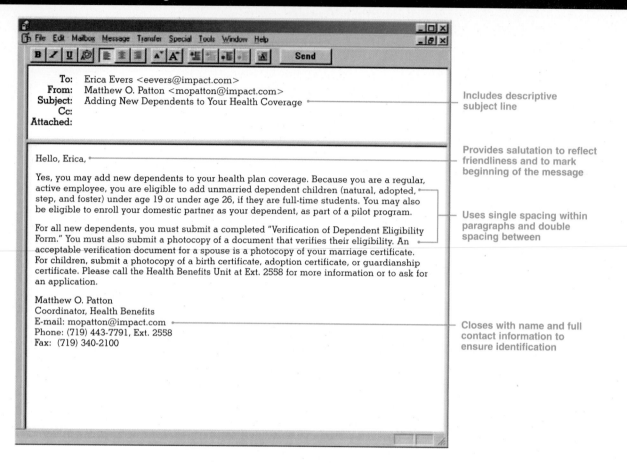

Message. Cover just one topic in your message, and try to keep your total message under two or three screens in length. Single-space and be sure to use both upper- and lowercase letters. Double-space between paragraphs.

Closing. Conclude an e-mail message, if you like, with *Cheers, Best wishes,* or *Warm regards,* followed by your name and complete contact information. Some people omit their e-mail address because they think it is provided automatically. However, some programs and routers do not transmit the address automatically. Therefore, always include it along with other identifying information in the closing.

Attachment. Use the attachment window or button to select the path and file name of any file you wish to send with your e-mail message. You can also attach a Web page to your message.

Business Letters

Business communicators write business letters primarily to correspond with people outside the organization. Letters may go to customers, vendors, other businesses, and the government, as discussed in Chapters 6, 7, and 8. The following information will help you format your letters following conventional guidelines.

Spacing and Punctuation

For some time typists left two spaces after end punctuation (periods, question marks, and so forth). This practice was necessary, it was thought, because typewriters did not have proportional spacing and sentences were easier to read if two spaces separated them. Professional typesetters, however, never followed this practice because they used proportional spacing, and readability was not a problem. Influenced by the look of typeset publications, many writers now leave only one space after end punctuation. As a practical matter, however, it is not wrong to use two spaces.

Letter Placement and Line Endings

The easiest way to place letters on the page is to use the defaults of your word processing program. In Microsoft Word 2003, default side margins are set at 1¼ inch; in Word 2007 they are set at 1 inch. Many companies today find these margins acceptable. If you want to adjust your margins to better balance shorter letters, use the following chart:

Words in Body of Letter	Margin Settings	Blank Lines After Date
Under 200	1.5 inches	4 to 10
Over 200	1 inch	2 to 3

Experts say that a ragged-right margin is easier to read than a justified (even) margin. You might want to turn off the justification feature of your word processing program if it automatically justifies the right margin.

Business Letter Parts

Professional-looking business letters are arranged in a conventional sequence with standard parts. Following is a discussion of how to use these letter parts properly. Figure A.2 illustrates the parts of a block style letter. (See Chapter 6 for additional discussion of letters and their parts.)

Letterhead. Most business organizations use 8½ × 11-inch paper printed with a letterhead displaying their official name, street address, Web address, e-mail address, and telephone and fax numbers. The letterhead may also include a logo and an advertising message.

Dateline. On letterhead paper you should place the date one blank line below the last line of the letterhead or 2 inches from the top edge of the paper (line 13). On plain paper place the date immediately below your return address. Because the date goes on line 13, start the return address an appropriate number of lines above it. The most common dateline format is as follows: *June 9, 2010.* Don't use *th* (or *rd, nd* or *st*) when the date is written this way. For European or military correspondence, use the following dateline format: *9 June 2010.* Notice that no commas are used.

Addressee and Delivery Notations. Delivery notations such as *FAX TRANSMISSION, FEDERAL EXPRESS, MESSENGER DELIVERY, CONFIDENTIAL,* or *CERTIFIED MAIL* are typed in all capital letters two blank lines above the inside address.

Inside Address. Type the inside address—that is, the address of the organization or person receiving the letter—single-spaced, starting at the left margin. The number of lines between the dateline and the inside address depends on the size of the letter body, the type size (point or pitch size), and the length of the typing lines. Generally, one to nine blank lines are appropriate.

Be careful to duplicate the exact wording and spelling of the recipient's name and address on your documents. Usually, you can copy this information from

Letterhead ——————

Island Graphics
893 Dillingham Boulevard
Honolulu, HI 96817-8817

(808)493-2310
http://www.islandgraphics.com

↓ Dateline is 2 inches from the top or 1 blank line below letterhead

Dateline ——————— September 13, 200x

↓ 1 to 9 blank lines

Inside address ——————
Mr. T. M. Wilson, President
Visual Concept Enterprises
1901 Kaumualii Highway
Lihue, HI 96766

↓ 1 blank line

Salutation ——————— Dear Mr. Wilson:

↓ 1 blank line

Subject line ——————— Subject: Block Letter Style

↓ 1 blank line

This letter illustrates block letter style, about which you asked. All typed lines begin at the left margin. The date is usually placed 2 inches from the top edge of the paper or one blank line below the last line of the letterhead, whichever position is lower.

Body ———————
This letter also shows mixed punctuation. A colon follows the salutation, and a comma follows the complimentary close. Open punctuation requires no colon after the salutation and no comma following the close; however, open punctuation is seldom seen today.

If a subject line is included, it appears one blank line below the salutation. The word *SUBJECT* is optional. Most readers will recognize a statement in this position as the subject without an identifying label. The complimentary close appears one blank line below the end of the last paragraph.

↓ 1 blank line

Complimentary close ———————
Sincerely,

↓ 3 blank lines

Mark H. Wong

Signature block ———————
Mark H. Wong
Graphic Designer

↓ 1 blank line

Reference initials ———————
MHW:pil

**Modified block style,
Mixed punctuation**

In the modified block style letter shown at the left, the date is centered or aligned with the complimentary close and signature block, which start at the center. Mixed punctuation includes a colon after the salutation and a comma after the complimentary close, as shown above and at the left.

the letterhead of the correspondence you are answering. If, for example, you are responding to *Jackson & Perkins Company*, do not address your letter to *Jackson and Perkins Corp.*

Always be sure to include a courtesy title such as *Mr., Ms., Mrs., Dr.,* or *Professor* before a person's name in the inside address—for both the letter and the envelope. Although many women in business today favor *Ms.*, you should use whatever title the addressee prefers.

In general, avoid abbreviations such as *Ave.* or *Co.* unless they appear in the printed letterhead of the document being answered.

Attention Line. An attention line allows you to send your message officially to an organization but to direct it to a specific individual, officer, or department. However, if you know an individual's complete name, it is always better to use it as the first line of the inside address and avoid an attention line. Here are two common formats for attention lines:

The MultiMedia Company
931 Calkins Avenue
Rochester, NY 14301

Attention Marketing Director

The MultiMedia Company
Attention: Marketing Director
931 Calkins Avenue
Rochester, NY 14301

Attention lines may be typed in all caps or with upper- and lowercase letters. The colon following *Attention* is optional. Notice that an attention line may be placed two lines below the address block or printed as the second line of the inside address. Use the latter format so that you may copy the address block to the envelope and the attention line will not interfere with the last-line placement of the zip code. Mail can be sorted more easily if the zip code appears in the last line of a typed address. Whenever possible, use a person's name as the first line of an address instead of putting that name in an attention line.

Salutation. For most letter styles place the letter greeting, or salutation, one blank line below the last line of the inside address or the attention line (if used). If the letter is addressed to an individual, use that person's courtesy title and last name (*Dear Mr. Lanham*). Even if you are on a first-name basis (*Dear Leslie*), be sure to add a colon (not a comma or a semicolon) after the salutation. Do not use an individual's full name in the salutation (not *Dear Mr. Leslie Lanham*) unless you are unsure of gender (*Dear Leslie Lanham*).

For letters with attention lines or those addressed to organizations, the selection of an appropriate salutation has become more difficult. Formerly, writers used *Gentlemen* generically for all organizations. With increasing numbers of women in business management today, however, *Gentlemen* is problematic. Because no universally acceptable salutation has emerged as yet, you could use *Ladies and Gentlemen* or *Gentlemen and Ladies*.

Subject and Reference Lines. Although experts suggest placing the subject line one blank line below the salutation, many businesses actually place it above the salutation. Use whatever style your organization prefers. Reference lines often show policy or file numbers; they generally appear one blank line above the salutation. Use initial capital letters for the main words or all capital letters.

Body. Most business letters and memorandums are single-spaced, with double-spacing between paragraphs. Very short messages may be double-spaced with indented paragraphs.

Complimentary Close. Typed one blank line below the last line of the letter, the complimentary close may be formal (*Very truly yours*) or informal (*Sincerely* or *Cordially*).

Signature Block. In most letter styles the writer's typed name and optional identification appear three or four blank lines below the complimentary close. The combination of name, title, and organization information should be arranged to achieve a balanced look. The name and title may appear on the same line or on separate lines, depending on the length of each. Use commas to separate categories within the same line, but not to conclude a line.

Sincerely yours,

Jeremy M. Wood

Jeremy M. Wood, Manager
Technical Sales and Services

Cordially yours,

Casandra Baker-Murillo

Casandra Baker-Murillo
Executive Vice President

Courtesy titles (*Ms., Mrs.,* or *Miss*) should be used before names that are not readily distinguishable as male or female. They should also be used before names containing only initials and international names. The title is usually placed in parentheses, but it may appear without them.

Yours truly,

Ms. K.C. Morris

(Ms.) K. C. Morris
Project Manager

Sincerely,

Mr. Leslie Hill

(Mr.) Leslie Hill
Public Policy Department

Some organizations include their names in the signature block. In such cases the organization name appears in all caps one blank line below the complimentary close, as shown here:

Cordially,
LIPTON COMPUTER SERVICES

Ms. Shelina A. Simpson

Ms. Shelina A. Simpson
Executive Assistant

Reference Initials. If used, the initials of the typist and writer are typed one blank line below the writer's name and title. Generally, the writer's initials are capitalized and the typist's are lowercased, but this format varies.

Enclosure Notation. When an enclosure or attachment accompanies a document, a notation to that effect appears one blank line below the reference initials. This notation reminds the typist to insert the enclosure in the envelope, and it reminds the recipient to look for the enclosure or attachment. The notation may be spelled out (*Enclosure, Attachment*), or it may be abbreviated (*Enc., Att.*). It may indicate the number of enclosures or attachments, and it may also identify a specific enclosure (*Enclosure: Form 1099*).

Copy Notation. If you make copies of correspondence for other individuals, you may use *cc* to indicate carbon copy or courtesy copy, *pc* to indicate photocopy, or merely *c* for any kind of copy. A colon following the initial(s) is optional.

Second-Page Heading. When a letter extends beyond one page, use plain paper of the same quality and color as the first page. Identify the second and succeeding pages with a heading consisting of the name of the addressee, the page number, and the date. Use the following format or the one shown in Figure A.3:

Ms. Sara Hendricks   2   May 3, 2010

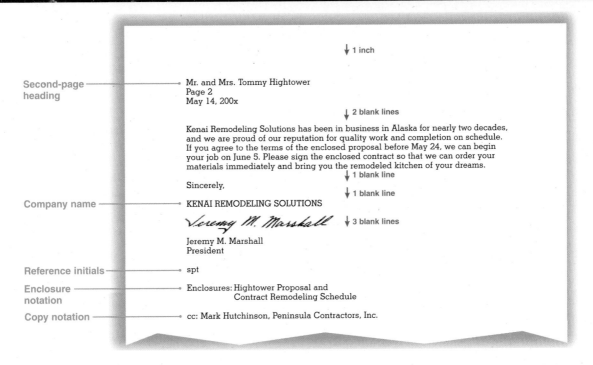

Both headings appear six blank lines (1 inch) from the top edge of the paper followed by two blank lines to separate them from the continuing text. Avoid using a second page if you have only one line or the complimentary close and signature block to fill that page.

Plain-Paper Return Address. If you prepare a personal or business letter on plain paper, place your address immediately above the date. Do not include your name; you will type (and sign) your name at the end of your letter. If your return address contains two lines, begin typing so that the date appears 2 inches from the top. Avoid abbreviations except for a two-letter state abbreviation.

580 East Leffels Street
Springfield, OH 45501
December 14, 2010

Ms. Ellen Siemens
Escrow Department
TransOhio First Federal
1220 Wooster Boulevard
Columbus, OH 43218-2900

Dear Ms. Siemens:

For letters in the block style, type the return address at the left margin. For modified block style letters, start the return address at the center to align with the complimentary close.

Letter and Punctuation Styles

Most business letters today are prepared in either block or modified block style, and they generally use mixed punctuation.

Block Style. In the block style, shown in Figure A.2, all lines begin at the left margin. This style is a favorite because it is easy to format.

Modified Block Style. The modified block style differs from block style in that the date and closing lines appear in the center, as shown at the bottom of Figure A.2. The date may be (a) centered, (b) begun at the center of the page (to align with the closing lines), or (c) backspaced from the right margin. The signature block—including the complimentary close, writer's name and title, or organization identification—begins at the center. The first line of each paragraph may begin at the left margin or may be indented five or ten spaces. All other lines begin at the left margin.

Mixed Punctuation Style. Most businesses today use mixed punctuation, shown in Figure A.2 on page A-4. It requires a colon after the salutation and a comma after the complimentary close. Even when the salutation is a first name, a colon is appropriate.

Envelopes

An envelope should be of the same quality and color of stationery as the letter it carries. Because the envelope introduces your message and makes the first impression, you need to be especially careful in addressing it. Moreover, how you fold the letter is important.

Return Address. The return address is usually printed in the upper left corner of an envelope, as shown in Figure A.4. In large companies some form of identi-

---

FIGURE A.4 Envelope Formats

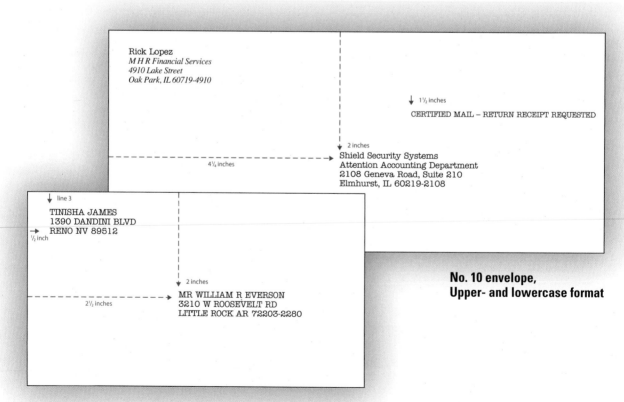

No. 6³/₄ envelope, Postal Service uppercase format

No. 10 envelope,
Upper- and lowercase format

fication (the writer's initials, name, or location) may be typed above the company name and address. This identification helps return the letter to the sender in case of nondelivery.

On an envelope without a printed return address, single-space the return address in the upper left corner. Beginning on line 3 on the fourth space (½ inch) from the left edge, type the writer's name, title, company, and mailing address. On a word processor, select the appropriate envelope size and make adjustments to approximate this return address location.

Mailing Address. On legal-sized No. 10 envelopes (4⅛ × 9½ inches), begin the address on line 13 about 4¼ inches from the left edge, as shown in Figure A.4. For small envelopes (3⅝ × 6½ inches), begin typing on line 12 about 2½ inches from the left edge. On a word processor, select the correct envelope size and check to be sure your address falls in the desired location.

The U.S. Postal Service recommends that addresses be typed in all caps without any punctuation. This Postal Service style, shown in the small envelope in Figure A.4, was originally developed to facilitate scanning by optical character readers (OCRs). Today's OCRs, however, are so sophisticated that they scan upper- and lowercase letters easily. Many companies today do not follow the Postal Service format because they prefer to use the same format for the envelope as for the inside address. If the same format is used, writers can take advantage of word processing programs to copy the inside address to the envelope, thus saving keystrokes and reducing errors. Having the same format on both the inside address and the envelope also looks more professional and consistent. For those reasons you may choose to use the familiar upper- and lowercase combination format. But you will want to check with your organization to learn its preference.

In addressing your envelopes for delivery in this country or in Canada, use the two-letter state and province abbreviations shown in Figure A.5. Notice that these abbreviations are in capital letters without periods.

Folding. The way a letter is folded and inserted into an envelope sends additional nonverbal messages about a writer's professionalism and carefulness. Most businesspeople follow the procedures shown here, which produce the least number of creases to distract readers.

For large No. 10 envelopes, begin with the letter face up. Fold slightly less than one third of the sheet toward the top, as shown in the following diagram. Then fold down the top third to within ⅓ inch of the bottom fold. Insert the letter into the envelope with the last fold toward the bottom of the envelope.

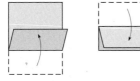

For small No. 6¾ envelopes, begin by folding the bottom up to within ⅓ inch of the top edge. Then fold the right third over to the left. Fold the left third to within ⅓ inch of the last fold. Insert the last fold into the envelope first.

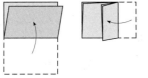

FIGURE A.5 Abbreviations of States, Territories, and Provinces

State or Territory	Two-Letter Abbreviation	State or Territory	Two-Letter Abbreviation
Alabama	AL	North Dakota	ND
Alaska	AK	Ohio	OH
Arizona	AZ	Oklahoma	OK
Arkansas	AR	Oregon	OR
California	CA	Pennsylvania	PA
Canal Zone	CZ	Puerto Rico	PR
Colorado	CO	Rhode Island	RI
Connecticut	CT	South Carolina	SC
Delaware	DE	South Dakota	SD
District of Columbia	DC	Tennessee	TN
Florida	FL	Texas	TX
Georgia	GA	Utah	UT
Guam	GU	Vermont	VT
Hawaii	HI	Virgin Islands	VI
Idaho	ID	Virginia	VA
Illinois	IL	Washington	WA
Indiana	IN	West Virginia	WV
Iowa	IA	Wisconsin	WI
Kansas	KS	Wyoming	WY
Kentucky	KY		
Louisiana	LA		
Maine	ME	**Canadian Province**	
Maryland	MD	Alberta	AB
Massachusetts	MA	British Columbia	BC
Michigan	MI	Labrador	LB
Minnesota	MN	Manitoba	MB
Mississippi	MS	New Brunswick	NB
Missouri	MO	Newfoundland	NF
Montana	MT	Northwest Territories	NT
Nebraska	NE	Nova Scotia	NS
Nevada	NV	Ontario	ON
New Hampshire	NH	Prince Edward Island	PE
New Jersey	NJ	Quebec	PQ
New Mexico	NM	Saskatchewan	SK
New York	NY	Yukon Territory	YT
North Carolina	NC		

Fax Cover Sheet

Documents transmitted by fax are usually introduced by a cover sheet, such as that shown in Figure A.6. As with memos, the format varies considerably. Important items to include are (a) the name and fax number of the receiver, (b) the name and fax number of the sender, (c) the number of pages being sent, and (d) the name and telephone number of the person to notify in case of unsatisfactory transmission.

When the document being transmitted requires little explanation, you may prefer to attach an adhesive note (such as a Post-it fax transmittal form) instead of a full cover sheet. These notes carry essentially the same information as shown in our printed fax cover sheet. They are perfectly acceptable in most business organizations and can save considerable paper and transmission costs.

FIGURE A.6 Fax Cover Sheet

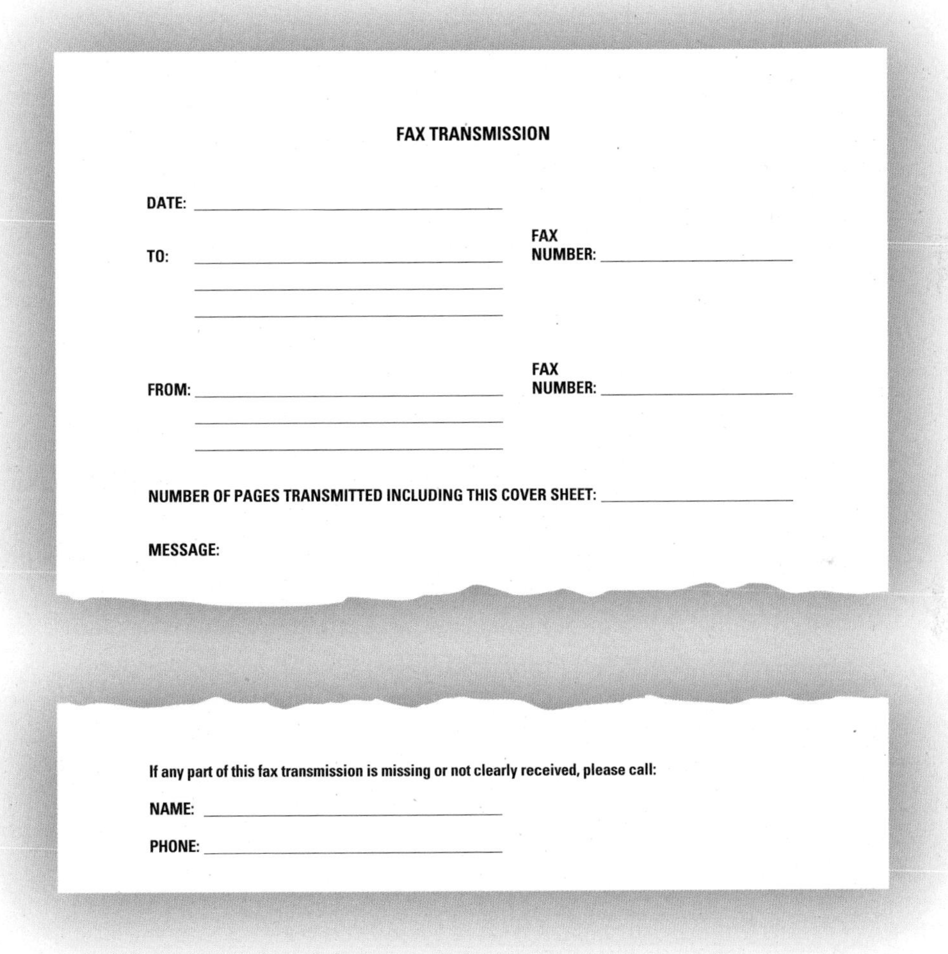

FAX TRANSMISSION

DATE: _____

TO: _____   FAX NUMBER: _____
_____
_____

FROM: _____   FAX NUMBER: _____
_____
_____

NUMBER OF PAGES TRANSMITTED INCLUDING THIS COVER SHEET: _____

MESSAGE:

If any part of this fax transmission is missing or not clearly received, please call:

NAME: _____

PHONE: _____

In marking your papers, your instructor may use the following symbols or abbreviations to indicate writing weaknesses. Studying these symbols and suggestions will help you understand your instructor's remarks. Knowing this information can also help you evaluate and improve your own memos, e-mail, letters, reports, and other writing. These symbols are keyed to your Grammar/Mechanics Handbook and to the text.

Adj	Hyphenate two or more adjectives that are joined to create a compound modifier before a noun. See G/M 1.17e.
Adv	Use adverbs, not adjectives, to describe or limit the action. See G/M 1.17d.
Apos	Use apostrophes to show possession. See G/M 2.20.
Assgn	Follow the assignment instructions.
Awk	Recast to avoid awkward expression.
Bias	Use inclusive, bias-free language. See Ch. 2, page 42.
Cap	Use capitalization appropriately. See G/M 3.01–3.16.
CmConj	Use a comma before the coordinating conjunction in a compound sentence. See G/M 2.05.
CmDate	Use commas appropriately in dates, addresses, geographical names, degrees, and long numbers. See G/M 2.04.
CmIn	Use commas to set off internal sentence interrupters. See G/M 2.06c.
CmIntr	Use commas to separate introductory clauses and certain phrases from independent clauses. See G/M 2.06.
CmSer	Use commas to separate three or more items (words, phrases, or short clauses) in a series. See G/M 2.01.
Coh	Improve coherence between ideas. Repeat key ideas, use pronouns, or use transitional expressions. See Ch. 3, page 65.
Cl	Improve the clarity of ideas or expression so that the point is better understood.
CS	Avoid comma-splice sentences. Do not use a comma to splice (join) two independent clauses. See Ch. 3, page 60.
CmUn	Avoid unnecessary commas. See G/M 2.15.
:	Use a colon after a complete thought that introduces a list of items. Use a colon in business letter salutations and to introduce long quotations. See G/M 2.17–2.19.
Direct	Use the direct strategy by emphasizing the main idea. See Ch. 3, page 56.
Dash	Use a dash to set off parenthetical elements, to emphasize sentence interruptions, or to separate an introductory list from a summarizing statement. See G/M 2.26.
DM	Avoid dangling modifiers by placing modifiers close to the words they describe or limit. See Ch. 3, page 64.
Frag	Avoid fragments by expressing ideas in complete sentences. A fragment is a broken-off part of a sentence. See Ch. 3, page 59.

Filler	Avoid fillers such as *there are* or long lead-ins such as *this is to inform you that.* See Ch. 4, page 77.
Format	Choose an appropriate format for this document.
GH	Use graphic highlighting (bullets, lists, indentions, or headings) to enhance readability. See Ch. 4, page 83.
MM	Avoid misplaced modifiers by placing modifiers close to the words they describe or limit. See Ch. 3, page 64.
Num	Use number or word form appropriately. See G/M 4.01–4.13.
Ob	Avoid stating the obvious.
Org	Improve organization by grouping similar ideas.
Par	Express ideas in parallel form. See Ch. 3, pages 62–63.
Paren	Use parentheses to set off nonessential sentence elements such as explanations, directions, questions, or references. See G/M 2.27.
Period	Use one period to end a statement, command, indirect question, or polite request. See G/M 2.23.
Pos	Express an idea positively rather than negatively. See Ch. 2, page 41.
PosPro	Use possessive-case pronouns to show ownership. See G/M 1.07 and 1.08d.
Pro	Use nominative-case pronouns as subjects of verbs and as subject complements. Use objective-case pronouns as objects of prepositions and verbs. See G/M 1.07–1.08.
ProAgr	Make pronouns agree in number and gender with the words to which they refer (their antecedents). See G/M 1.09.
ProVag	Be sure that pronouns such as *it, which, this,* and *that* refer to clear antecedents. See G/M 1.09i.
?	Use a question mark after a direct question and after statements with questions appended. See G/M 2.24.
Quo	Use quotation marks to enclose the exact words of a speaker or writer, to distinguish words used in a special sense, or to enclose titles of articles, chapters, or other short works. See G/M 2.28.
Redun	Avoid expressions that repeat meaning or include unnecessary words. See Ch. 4, pages 77–78.
RunOn	Avoid run-on (fused) sentences. A sentence with two independent clauses must be joined by a coordinating conjunctions (*and, or, nor, but*) or by a semicolon (;). See Ch. 3, page 60.
Sp	Check misspelled words.
Self	Use *self*-ending pronouns only when they refer to previously mentioned nouns or pronouns. See G/M 1.08h.
;	Use a semicolon to join closely related independent clauses. A semicolon is also an option to join separate items in a series when one or more of the items contain internal commas. See G/M 2.16.
Shift	Avoid a confusing shift in verb tense, mood, or voice. See G/M 1.15c.
Trans	Use an appropriate transition. See Ch. 3, page 65, and Ch. 12, page 344.
Tone	Use a conversational, positive, and courteous tone that promotes goodwill. See Ch. 2, page 41.
You	Focus on developing the "you" view. See Ch. 2, pages 38–39.
VbAgr	Make verbs agree with subjects. See G/M 1.10.
VbMood	Use the subjunctive mood to express hypothetical (untrue) ideas. See G/M 1.12.

VbTnse	Use present-tense, past-tense, and part-participle forms correctly. See G/M 1.13	
VbVce	Use active- and passive-voice verbs appropriately. See G/M 1.11.	
WC	Focus on precise word choice. See Ch. 4, pages 80–81.	
Wordy	Avoid wordiness including fillers, long lead-ins, redundancies, compound prepositions, wordy noun phrases, and empty words. See Ch. 4, pages 76–78.	

Proofreading Marks

Proofreading Mark	Draft Copy	Final Copy
⌐ Align horizontally	TO: Rick Munoz	TO: Rick Munoz
‖ Align vertically	166.32 132.45	166.32 132.45
≡ Capitalize	Coca-cola sending a pdf file	Coca-Cola sending a PDF file
⊂ Close up space	meeting at 3 p. m.	meeting at 3 p.m.
⊐⊏ Center	⌐Recommendations⌐	Recommendations
ℓ Delete	in my final judgement	in my judgment
⋎ Insert apostrophe	our companys product	our company's product
⋏ Insert comma	you will of course	you will, of course,
⌃ Insert hyphen	tax free income	tax-free income
⊙ Insert period	Ms Holly Hines	Ms. Holly Hines
⋎ Insert quotation mark	shareholders receive a bonus.	shareholders receive a "bonus."
# Insert space	wordprocessing program	word processing program
/ Lowercase (remove capitals)	the Vice President HUMAN RESOURCES	the vice president Human Resources
⊏ Move to left	⌐I. Labor costs	I. Labor costs
⊐ Move to right	A. Findings of study ⌐	A. Findings of study
○ Spell out	aimed at 2 depts	aimed at two departments
⌐ Start new paragraph	¶Keep the screen height of your computer at eye level.	Keep the screen height of your computer at eye level.
····· Stet (don't delete)	officials talked openly	officials talked openly
∿ Transpose	accounts recievable	accounts receivable
bf Use boldface	Conclusions bf	**Conclusions**
ital Use italics	The Perfect Résumé ital	*The Perfect Résumé*

Documentation Formats

For many reasons business writers are careful to properly document report data. Citing sources strengthens a writer's argument, as you learned in Chapter 10. Acknowledging sources also shields writers from charges of plagiarism. Moreover, good references help readers pursue further research.

Source Notes and Content Notes

Before we discuss specific documentation formats, you must understand the difference between *source* notes and *content* notes. Source notes identify quotations, paraphrased passages, and author references. They lead readers to the sources of cited information, and they must follow a consistent format. Content notes, on the other hand, enable writers to add comments, explain information not directly related to the text, or refer readers to other sections of a report. Because content notes are generally infrequent, most writers identify them in the text with a raised asterisk (*). At the bottom of the page, the asterisk is repeated with the content note following. If two content notes appear on one page, a double asterisk identifies the second reference.

Your real concern will be with source notes. These identify quotations or paraphrased ideas in the text, and they direct readers to a complete list of references (a bibliography) at the end of your report. Source notes are usually cited in two places: a brief citation appears in the text and a complete citation appears in a bibliography at the end of the report. How you arrange your source notes depends on the documentation system you choose.

Which System Is Best?

Students frequently ask, "But what documentation system is most used in business?" That is not an easy question to answer because no one method dominates. Researchers have struggled for years to develop the perfect documentation system, one that is efficient for the writer and crystal clear to the reader. As a result, various systems exist, each with its advantages.

Some businesses have developed their own hybrid systems. These companies generally supply guidelines illustrating their in-house style to employees. Before starting any research project on the job, you will want to inquire about your organization's preferred documentation style. You can also look in the files for examples of previous reports.

A number of databases now provide ready-made bibliographic citation formats. When you find articles in databases, you might copy the suggested format. However, the formats are not always accurate, so be sure you know the conventions of your style.

The two most common formats for citations and bibliographies in academic work are those of the Modern Language Association (MLA) and the American Psychological Association (APA). Each has its own style for textual references and bibliography lists. The citations in this textbook are based on the APA style, which is increasingly the standard in business communication.

Modern Language Association Format

Writers in the humanities frequently use the MLA format, as illustrated in Figure C.1. In parentheses close to the textual reference appears the author's name and page cited. If no author is known, a shortened version of the source title is used. At the end of the

FIGURE C.1 Portions of MLA Text Page and Bibliography

Peanut butter was first delivered to the world by a St. Louis physician in 1890. As discussed at the Peanut Advisory Board's Web site, peanut butter was originally promoted as a protein substitute for elderly patients ("History"). However, it was the 1905 Universal Exposition in St. Louis that truly launched peanut butter. Since then, annual peanut butter consumption has zoomed to 3.3 pounds a person in the United States (Barrons 46).

America's farmers produce 1.6 million tons of peanuts annually, about half of which is used for oil, nuts, and candy. Lisa Gibbons, executive secretary of the Peanut Advisory Board, says that "peanuts in some form are in the top four candies: Snickers, Reese's Peanut Butter Cups, Peanut M & Ms, and Butterfingers" (Meadows 32).

Works Cited

Barrons, Elizabeth Ruth. "A Comparison of Domestic and International Consumption of Legumes." *Journal of Economic Agriculture* 23 (2006): 45–49.

"History of Peanut Butter." *Peanut Advisory Board.* Retrieved 19 Jan. 2009 <http://www.peanutbutterlovers.com/History/index.html>.

Meadows, Mark Allen. "Peanut Crop Is Anything but Peanuts at Home and Overseas." *Business Monthly*, 30 Sept. 2008, 31–34.

report, the writer lists alphabetically all references in a bibliography called *Works Cited*. For more information consult Joseph Gibaldi, *MLA Handbook for Writers of Research Papers*, 6e (New York: The Modern Language Association of America, 2003).

MLA In-Text Format. In-text citations generally appear close to the point where the reference is mentioned or at the end of the sentence inside the closing period. Follow these guidelines:

- Include the last name of the author(s) and the page number. Omit a comma, as (*Smith 310*).
- If the author's name is mentioned in the text, cite only the page number in parentheses. Do not include either the word *page* or the abbreviations *p.* or *pp.*
- If no author is known, refer to the document title or a shortened version of it, as (*"Facts at Fingertips" 102*).

MLA Bibliographic Format. The works-cited bibliography lists all references cited in a report. Some writers include all works consulted. A portion of an MLA bibliography is shown in Figure C.1. An expanded list of model references appears in Figure C.2. Following are selected guidelines summarizing important points regarding MLA bibliographic format:

- Use italics or underscores for the titles of books, magazines, newspapers, and journals. Check with your organization or instructor for guidance. Capitalize all main words.
- Enclose the titles of magazine, newspaper, and journal articles in quotation marks. Include volume and issue numbers for journals only.
- For Internet citations, include a retrieval date. Although MLA format does not include the words *Retrieved* or *Accessed*, such wording helps distinguish the retrieval date from the document date.
- In citing online documents, list only the search term and main search site page for URLs that are impractically long and complicated (e.g., *"Wendy's International," Hoovers.com*).

FIGURE C.2 MLA Sample Works Cited

Works Cited

American Airlines. *2009 Annual Report.* Fort Worth, TX: AMR Annual Corporation. •————— Annual report

Atamian, Richard A., and Ellen Ferranto. *Driving Market Forces.* New York: •————— Book, two authors
    HarperCollins, 2007.

Berss, Marcia. "Protein Man," *Forbes* 24 Oct. 2009: 65–66. •————— Magazine article

Cantrell, Mark R., and Hilary Watson. "Violence in Today's Workplace." •————— Magazine article, online,
    PDF version. 10 Jan. 2007 *Office Review:* 24–29.   PDF version

"Information Processing." *Encyclopaedia Britannica.* 2007. Encyclopaedia
    Britannica Online. 19 Oct. 2007. <http:www.britannica.com/eb/ •————— Encyclopedia, online
    article-61669>.

Lancaster, Hal. "When Taking a Tip From a Job Network, Proceed With Caution." •————— Newspaper article,
    The Wall Street Journal 7 Feb. 2008: B1.   one author

Morris, Mark. "Privacy Rules Proposed." *The Washington Post* 14 July 2007. •————— Newspaper article, online
    18 July 2007 <http://www.washingtonpost.com>.

Patton, James C. "Key Trends in Systems Development." *Journal of Global* •————— Journal article with volume
    Information Management 3.2. (2007): 5–20.   and issue numbers
    ["3.2" signifies volume 3, issue 2]

Pensky, D. (2009, February 10). "Ad Agencies Unchained," *BusinessWeek,* 54. •————— Database article with
    March 1, 2009. Business Source Premier database (32587601).   accession number

Procter & Gamble home page. 28 Nov. 2008 <http://www.pg.com>. •————— Web site

Rivera, Francisco. Personal interview. 16 May 2009. •————— Interview

"Spam: Eliminate It From the Workplace." *SmartPros.* 8 Aug. 2006. 12 Sept. 2008 •————— Web document, no author
    <http://accounting.smartpros.com/>.

Tillman, Ann. "Avoiding Plagiarism." 9 July 2007. University of British Columbia •————— Web document, with author
    <http://www.ubc/ca/pbg/plagiarism.htm>.

Trillion, Andrew. "Corporations and Guilt by Association." Weblog entry. Business •————— Weblog entry
    Ethics Blog. 20 Jan. 2009. 10 Feb. 2009. <http://www.businessethicsblog.com/>.

Uhrich, Trisha. "How to Lose Money." Video weblog posted to Youtube.com. 3 May •————— Video weblog entry
    2009. 10 June 2009 <http://www.youtube.com/watch?v+Vja83KLQXZs>.

U.S. Dept. of Labor. *Child Care as a Workforce Issue.* Washington, DC. •————— Government publication
    Government Printing Office, 2008.

Yellin, Mike. "Re: Managing Managers and Cell Phones." Online posting. 9 Sept. •————— Online forum posting
    2008. 15 Sept. 2008. Message 44 posted to <http://groups.yahoo.com/groups
    /ecommerce/message44>.

Note 1: Where italics are shown, MLA style originally prescribed the use of underlines. With today's word processors, most writers use italics.

Note 2: To prevent confusion, you might add the words *Accessed* or *Retrieved* preceding the date you accessed an online source.

Note 3: Although MLA style prescribes double spacing for the works cited, we show single spacing to conserve space and to represent preferred business usage.

- If you are working from a database that provides citation formats, you may copy the suggested format for your reference, but know the style conventions to catch errors.

American Psychological Association Format

Popular in the social and physical sciences, the American Psychological Association (APA) documentation style uses parenthetic citations. That is, each author reference is shown in parentheses when cited in the text, as shown in Figure C.3. At the end of the report, all references are listed alphabetically in a bibliography called *References*. For more information about APA formats, see the *Publication Manual of the American Psychological Association*, 5e (Washington, DC: American Psychological Association, 2001), *Concise Rules of APA Style* (Washington, DC: American Psychological Association, 2005), or *APA Style Guide to Electronic References* (2007, available in PDF format from **http://www.apa.org/books/**).

APA In-Text Format. Within the text, document each specific textual source with a short description in parentheses. Following are selected guidelines summarizing important elements of APA style:

- Include the last name of the author(s), date of publication, and page number, as (*Jones, 2007, p. 36*). Use *n.d.* if no date is available.
- If no author is known, refer to the first few words of the reference list entry and the year, as (*Computer Privacy, 2008, p. 59*).
- Omit page numbers for general references, but always include page numbers for direct quotations.

APA Reference Format. List all citations alphabetically in a section called *References*. A portion of an APA reference page is shown in Figure C.3. A more complete list of model references appears in Figure C.4. APA style requires specific capitalization and sequencing guidelines, some of which are summarized here:

- Include an author's name with the last name first followed by initials, such as *Smith, M. A.* First and middle names are not used.

FIGURE C.3 Portions of APA Text Page and References

Peanut butter was first delivered to the world by a St. Louis physician in 1890. As discussed at the Peanut Advisory Board's Web site, peanut butter was originally promoted as a protein substitute for elderly patients ("History," n.d.). However, it was the 1905 Universal Exposition in St. Louis that truly launched peanut butter. Since then, annual peanut butter consumption has zoomed to 3.3 pounds a person in the United States (Barrons, 2006, p. 46).

America's farmers produce 1.6 million tons of peanuts annually, about half of which is used for oil, nuts, and candy. Lisa Gibbons, executive secretary of the Peanut Advisory Board, says that "peanuts in some form are in the top four candies: Snickers, Reese's Peanut Butter Cups, Peanut M & Ms, and Butterfingers" (Meadows, 2008, p. 32).

References

Barrons, E. (2006, November). A comparison of domestic and international consumption of legumes. *Journal of Economic Agriculture*, 23(3), 45–49.

Meadows, M. (2008, September 30). Peanut crop is anything but peanuts at home and overseas. *Business Monthly*, *14*, 31–34.

History of peanut butter. (n.d.). Peanut Advisory Board. Retrieved January 19, 2009, from http://www.peanutbutterlovers.com/History/index.html

FIGURE C.4 APA Sample References

References

American Airlines. (2009). *2009 Annual Report.* Fort Worth, TX: AMR Corporation. ●——— Annual report

Atamian, R. A., & Ferranto, E. (2007). *Driving market forces.* New York: ●——— Book, two authors
   HarperCollins.

Berss, M. (2009, October 24). Protein man. *Forbes,* 65–66. ●——— Magazine article

Cantrell, M. R., & Watson, H. (2007, January 10). Violence in today's workplace ●——— Magazine article,
   [PDF version]. *Office Review,* 24–29.   PDF version

Information processing. (2007). In *Encyclopaedia Britannica.* Retrieved
   October 19, 2007, from Encyclopaedia Britannica Online: http//www. ●——— Encyclopedia, online
   britannica.com/eb/article-61669

Lancaster, H. (2008, February 7). When taking a tip from a job network, proceed ●——— Newspaper article
   with caution. *The Wall Street Journal,* p. B1.

Morris, M. (2007, July 14). Privacy rules proposed. *The Washington Post.* Retrieved ●——— Newspaper article, online
   July 18, 2009, from http://www.washingtonpost.com

Patton, J. C. (2007, May). Key trends in systems development. *Journal of Global* ●——— Journal article with volume
   Information Management, 3(2), 5–20.   and issue numbers
   [3(2) signifies volume 3, series or issue 2]

Pensky, D. (2009, February 10). Ad agencies unchained. *BusinessWeek,* 54. ●——— Database article with
   Retrieved March 1, 2009, from Business Source Premier database.   accession number
   (32587601)

Procter & Gamble home page. (2008). Retrieved November 28, 2008, from ●——— Web site
   http://www.pg.com

Spam: Eliminate it from the workplace. (2006, August 8). *SmartPros.* Retrieved ●——— Web document, no author
   September 12, 2008, from http://accounting.smartpros.com/

Tillman, A. (2006). Avoiding plagiarism. Retrieved July 9, 2007, from University ●——— Web document, with author
   of British Columbia: http://www.ubc/ca/pbg/plagiarism.htm

Trillion, M. (2009, January 20). Corporations and guilt by association. Message ●——— Weblog post
   posted to http://www.businessethicsblog.com/

Uhrich, T. (2009, May 3). How to lose money [Video file]. Video posted to ●——— Video weblog post
   http://www.youtube.com/watch?v+Vja83KLQXZs

U.S. Department of Labor. (2008). *Child care as a workforce issue.* Washington, ●——— Government publication
   DC: Government Printing Office.

Yellin, M. (2008, September 9). Managing managers and cell phones. [Msg 44]. ●——— Online forum or
   Message posted to http://groups.yahoo.com/group/ecommerce/message44   discussion group

---

- Show the date of publication in parentheses immediately after the author's name, as *Smith, M. A. (2008).*
- Italicize the titles of books. Use "sentence-style" capitalization. This means that only the first word of a title, proper nouns, and the first word after an internal colon are capitalized.
- Do not italicize or underscore the titles of magazine and journal articles. Use sentence-style capitalization for article titles.
- Italicize the names of magazines, newspapers, and journals. Capitalize the initial letters of all main words.
- In citing online documents, list only the search term and main search site page for URLs that are impractically long and complicated.

- To reference a published article that you viewed only in its electronic form, add in brackets after the article title [*Electronic version*]. Use this form only if the electronic version is identical to the published version.
- To reference an online article that you have reason to believe has been changed (e.g., the format is different from that of the print version or page numbers are not indicated), add the date you retrieved the document and the URL. Do not include a period after a URL that appears at the end of a line.
- For excellent examples of current electronic sources in APA style, visit *The OWL at Purdue* (**http://owl.english.purdue.edu/owl/resource/560/01/**).

Grammar/Mechanics Handbook

Because many students need a quick review of basic grammar and mechanics, we provide a number of resources in condensed form. The Grammar/Mechanics Handbook, which offers you a rapid systematic review, consists of four parts:

- **Grammar/Mechanics Diagnostic Test.** This 65-point pretest helps you assess your strengths and weaknesses in eight areas of grammar and mechanics. Your instructor may later give you a posttest to assess your improvement.
- **Grammar/Mechanics Profile.** The G/M Profile enables you to pinpoint specific areas in which you need remedial instruction or review.
- **Grammar/Mechanics Review.** Provided here is a concise review of basic principles of grammar, punctuation, capitalization, and number style. The review also provides reinforcement and quiz exercises that help you interact with the principles of grammar and test your comprehension. The guidelines not only provide a study guide for review but will also serve as a reference manual throughout the writing course. The grammar review can be used for classroom-centered instruction or for self-guided learning.
- **Confusing Words and Frequently Misspelled Words.** A list of selected confusing words, along with a list of 160 frequently misspelled words, completes the Grammar/Mechanics Handbook.

Some of you want all the help you can get in improving your language skills. For additional assistance with grammar and language fundamentals, *Essentials of Business Communication,* 8e, offers you unparalleled interactive and print resources at **www.meguffey.com**.

- **Your Personal Language Trainer.** In this self-paced learning tool, Dr. Guffey acts as your personal trainer in helping you pump up your language muscles. *Your Personal Language Trainer* provides the rules plus hundreds of sentence applications so that you can try out your knowledge and build your skills with immediate feedback and explanations.
- **Sentence Competency Skill Builders** offer interactive exercises similar to the grammar/mechanics checkups in this book. These drills focus on common writing weaknesses so that you can learn to avoid them.
- **Speak Right!** reviews frequently mispronounced words. You'll hear correct pronunciations from Dr. Guffey so that you will never be embarrassed by mispronouncing these terms.
- **Spell Right!** presents frequently misspelled words along with exercises to help you improve your skills.
- **Advanced Grammar/Mechanics Checkups** take you to the next level in developing language confidence. These self-teaching exercises provide challenging sentences that test your combined grammar, punctuation, spelling, and usage skills.

More comprehensive treatment of grammar, punctuation, and usage can be found in Clark and Clark's *A Handbook for Office Workers* or Guffey's *Business English.*

The first step in your systematic review of grammar and mechanics involves completing a diagnostic pretest found on the next page.

Grammar/Mechanics Diagnostic Pretest

This diagnostic pretest is intended to reveal your strengths and weaknesses in using the following:

plural nouns	adjectives	punctuation
possessive nouns	adverbs	capitalization style
pronouns	prepositions	number style
verbs	conjunctions	

The pretest is organized into sections corresponding to the preceding categories. In Sections A through H, each sentence is either correct or has one error related to the category under which it is listed. If a sentence is correct, write C. If it has an error, underline the error and write the correct form in the space provided. When you finish, check your answers with your instructor and fill out the Grammar/Mechanics Profile at the end of the test.

A. Plural Nouns

copies

Example All CPAs must keep backup <u>copys</u> of their files.

1. Since the early 2000s, most attornies have invested in software packages that detect computer viruses.
2. Four freshmans discussed the pros and cons of using laptops and cell phones in their classes.
3. Both of Mark's sister-in-laws worked as secretaries at different companies.
4. Neither the Cortezes nor the Morris's knew about the changes in beneficiaries.
5. All job candidates are asked whether they can work on Sunday's.

B. Possessive Nouns

6. We sincerely hope that the jurys judgment reflects the stories of all the witnesses.
7. In a little over two months time, the analysts finished their reports.
8. Ms. Hartmans staff is responsible for all accounts receivable for customers purchasing electronics parts.
9. At the next stockholders meeting, we will discuss benefits for employees and dividends for shareholders.
10. For the past 90 days, employees in the sales department have complained about Mr. Logan smoking.

C. Pronouns

me

Example Whom did you ask to replace Francisco and <u>I</u>?

11. The chief and myself were quite willing to send copies to whoever requested them.
12. Much of the project assigned to Samantha and I had to be reassigned to Matt and them.
13. Although it's CPU was noisy, the computer worked for Jeremy and me.
14. Just between you and me, only you and I know that she will be transferred.
15. My friend and I applied at GM because of their excellent benefits.

D. Verb Agreement

Example The list of payments <u>have</u> to be approved by the boss.   has _____

16. This cell phone and its calling plan costs much less than I expected. _____
17. A description of the property, together with several other legal documents, were submitted by my attorney. _____
18. There are a wide range of proposals for taming spam. _____
19. Neither the manager nor the employees in the office think the solution is fair. _____
20. Because of the holiday, our committee were unable to meet. _____

E. Verb Mood, Voice, and Tense

21. If I was in charge, I would certainly change things. _____
22. To make a copy, first open the disk drive door and then you insert the disk. _____
23. If I could chose any city, I would select Hong Kong. _____
24. Those contracts have laid on his desk for more than two weeks. _____
25. The auditors have went over these accounts carefully, and they have found no discrepancies. _____

F. Adjectives and Adverbs

26. Until we have a more clearer picture of what is legal, we will proceed cautiously. _____
27. Britney thought she had done good in her job interview. _____
28. A recently appointed official was in charge of monitoring peer to peer file-sharing systems. _____
29. Robert only has two days before he must submit his end-of-the-year report. _____
30. The architects submitted there drawings in a last-minute attempt to beat the deadline. _____

G. Prepositions and Conjunctions

31. Can you tell me where the meeting is scheduled at? _____
32. It seems like we have been taking this pretest forever. _____
33. Our investigation shows that cell phones may be cheaper then landlines. _____
34. My courses this semester are totally different than last semester's. _____
35. Do you know where this shipment is going to? _____

H. Commas

For each of the following sentences, insert any necessary commas. Count the number of commas that you added. Write that number in the space provided. All punctuation must be correct to receive credit for the sentence. If a sentence requires no punctuation, write C.

Example Because of developments in theory and computer applications, management is becoming more of a science.   1 _____

36. For example management determines how orders assignments and responsibilities are delegated to employees. _____
37. Your order Ms. Lee will be sent from Memphis Tennessee on July 1. _____
38. When you need service on any of your equipment we will be happy to help you Mr. Lopez. _____
39. Michelle Wong who is the project manager at TeleCom suggested that I call you. _____
40. You have purchased from us often and your payments in the past have always been prompt. _____

I. Commas and Semicolons 1

Add commas and semicolons to the following sentences. In the space provided, write the number of punctuation marks that you added.

41. The salesperson turned in his report however he did not indicate the time period it covered.

42. Interest payments on bonds are tax deductible dividend payments are not.

43. We are opening a branch office in Scottsdale and hope to be able to serve all your needs from that office by the middle of January.

44. As suggested by the committee we must first secure adequate funding then we may consider expansion.

45. When you begin to research a report consider many sources of information namely the Internet, books, periodicals, government publications, and databases.

J. Commas and Semicolons 2

46. After our chief had the printer repaired it jammed again within the first week although we treated it carefully.

47. Our experienced courteous staff has been trained to anticipate your every need.

48. In view of the new law that went into effect on April 1 our current liability insurance must be increased therefore we need to adjust our budget.

49. As stipulated in our contract your agency will supervise our graphic arts and purchase our media time.

50. As you know Ms. Mears we aim for long-term business relationships not quick profits.

K. Other Punctuation

Each of the following sentences may require colons, question marks, quotation marks, periods, parentheses, and underscores, as well as commas and semicolons. Add the appropriate punctuation to each sentence. Then in the space provided, write the total number of marks that you added or changed.

Example Fully recharging your digital camera's battery (see page 6 of the instruction manual) takes only 90 minutes.

51. The following members of the department volunteered to help on Saturday Kim Carlos Dan and Sylvia.

52. Mr Phillips, Miss Reed, and Mrs Garcia usually arrived at the office by 830 a m.

53. We recommend that you use hearing protectors see the warning on page 8 when using this electric drill.

54. Did the president really say "All employees may take Friday off

55. We are trying to locate an edition of Newsweek that carried an article titled Who Is Reading Your E-Mail

L. Capitalization

For each of the following sentences, underline any letter that should be capitalized. In the space provided, write the number of words you marked.

Example vice president daniels devised a procedure for expediting purchase orders from area 4 warehouses.

56. although english was his native language, he also spoke spanish and could read french.

57. on a trip to the east coast, uncle henry visited the empire state building.

58. karen enrolled in classes in history, german, and sociology.

59. the business manager and the vice president each received a new dell computer.

60. james lee, the president of kendrick, inc., will speak to our conference in the spring.

M. Number Style

Decide whether the numbers in the following sentences should be written as words or as figures. Each sentence either is correct or has one error. If it is correct, write C. If it has an error, underline it and write the correct form in the space provided.

Example   The bank had <u>5</u> branches in three suburbs.   five _____

61. More than 2,000,000 people have visited the White House in the past five years.   _____

62. Of the 28 viewer comments we received regarding our TV commercial, only three were negative.   _____

63. We set aside forty dollars for petty cash, but by December 1 our fund was depleted.   _____

64. The meeting is scheduled for May 5th at 3 p.m.   _____

65. In the past five years, nearly fifteen percent of the population changed residences at least once.   _____

Grammar/Mechanics Profile

In the spaces at the right, place a check mark to indicate the number of correct answers you had in each category of the Grammar/Mechanics Diagnostic Pretest.

		Number Correct				
		5	4	3	2	1
1–5	Plural Nouns	___	___	___	___	___
6–10	Possessive Nouns	___	___	___	___	___
11–15	Pronouns	___	___	___	___	___
16–20	Verb Agreement	___	___	___	___	___
21–25	Verb Mood, Voice, and Tense	___	___	___	___	___
26–30	Adjectives and Adverbs	___	___	___	___	___
31–35	Prepositions and Conjunctions	___	___	___	___	___
36–40	Commas	___	___	___	___	___
41–45	Commas and Semicolons 1	___	___	___	___	___
46–50	Commas and Semicolons 2	___	___	___	___	___
51–55	Other Punctuation	___	___	___	___	___
56–60	Capitalization	___	___	___	___	___
61–65	Number Style	___	___	___	___	___

Note: 5 = have excellent skills; 4 = need light review; 3 = need careful review; 2 = need to study rules; 1 = need serious study and follow-up reinforcement.

Grammar/Mechanics Review

Parts of Speech (1.01)

1.01 Functions. English has eight parts of speech. Knowing the functions of the parts of speech helps writers better understand how words are used and how sentences are formed.

  a. **Nouns:** name persons, places, things, qualities, concepts, and activities (for example, *Kevin, Phoenix, computer, joy, work, banking*).

b. **Pronouns:** substitute for nouns (for example, *he, she, it, they*).

c. **Verbs:** show the action of a subject or join the subject to words that describe it (for example, *walk, heard, is, was jumping*).

d. **Adjectives:** describe or limit nouns and pronouns and often answer the questions *what kind? how many?* and *which one?* (for example, *red* car, *ten* items, *good* manager).

e. **Adverbs:** describe or limit verbs, adjectives, or other adverbs and frequently answer the questions *when? how? where?* or *to what extent?* (for example, *tomorrow, rapidly, here, very*).

f. **Prepositions:** join nouns or pronouns to other words in sentences (for example, desk *in* the office, ticket *for* me, letter *to* you).

g. **Conjunctions:** connect words or groups of words (for example, you *and* I, Mark *or* Jill).

h. **Interjections:** express strong feelings (for example, *Wow! Oh!*).

Nouns (1.02–1.06)

Nouns name persons, places, things, qualities, concepts, and activities. Nouns may be classified into a number of categories.

1.02 Concrete and Abstract. Concrete nouns name specific objects that can be seen, heard, felt, tasted, or smelled. Examples of concrete nouns are *telephone, dollar, IBM,* and *tangerine*. Abstract nouns name generalized ideas such as qualities or concepts that are not easily pictured. *Emotion, power,* and *tension* are typical examples of abstract nouns.

Business writing is most effective when concrete words predominate. It's clearer to write *We need 16-pound copy paper* than to write *We need office supplies*. Chapter 4 provides practice in developing skill in the use of concrete words.

1.03 Proper and Common. Proper nouns name specific persons, places, or things and are always capitalized (*General Electric, Baltimore, Jennifer*). All other nouns are common nouns and begin with lowercase letters (*company, city, student*). Rules for capitalization are presented in Sections 3.01–3.16.

1.04 Singular and Plural. Singular nouns name one item; plural nouns name more than one. From a practical view, writers seldom have difficulty with singular nouns. They may need help, however, with the formation and spelling of plural nouns.

1.05 Guidelines for Forming Noun Plurals

a. Add *s* to most nouns (*chair, chairs; mortgage, mortgages; Monday, Mondays*).

b. Add *es* to nouns ending in *s, x, z, ch,* or *sh* (*bench, benches; boss, bosses; box, boxes; Lopez, Lopezes*).

c. Change the spelling in irregular noun plurals (*man, men; foot, feet; mouse, mice; child, children*).

d. Add *s* to nouns that end in *y* when *y* is preceded by a vowel (*attorney, attorneys; valley, valleys; journey, journeys*).

e. Drop the *y* and add *ies* to nouns ending in *y* when *y* is preceded by a consonant (*company, companies; city, cities; secretary, secretaries*).

f. Add *s* to the principal word in most compound expressions (*editors in chief, fathers-in-law, bills of lading, runners-up*).

g. Add *s* to most numerals, letters of the alphabet, words referred to as words, degrees, and abbreviations (*5s, 2000s, Bs, ands, CPAs, qts.*).

h. Add *'s* only to clarify letters of the alphabet that might be misread, such as *A's, I's, M's,* and *U's* and *i's, p's,* and *q's*. An expression like *c.o.d.s* requires no apostrophe because it would not easily be misread.

1.06 Collective Nouns. Nouns such as *staff, faculty, committee, group,* and *herd* refer to a collection of people, animals, or objects. Collective nouns may be considered singular or plural depending on their action. See Section 1.10i for a discussion of collective nouns and their agreement with verbs.

Review Exercise A—Nouns

In the space provided for each item, write *a* or *b* to complete the following statements accurately. When you finish, compare your responses with those provided. Answers are provided for odd-numbered items. Your instructor has the remaining answers. For each item on which you need review, consult the numbered principle shown in parentheses.

1. Two of the contest (a) *runner-ups*, (b) *runners-up* protested the judges' choice.
2. Several (a) *attorneys*, (b) *attornies* worked on the case together.
3. Please write to the (a) *Davis's*, (b) *Davises* about the missing contract.
4. The industrial complex has space for nine additional (a) *companys*, (b) *companies*.
5. That accounting firm employs two (a) *secretaries*, (b) *secretarys* for five CPAs.
6. Four of the wooden (a) *benches*, (b) *benchs* must be repaired.
7. The home was constructed with numerous (a) *chimneys*, (b) *chimnies*.
8. Tours of the production facility are made only on (a) *Tuesdays*, (b) *Tuesday's*.
9. We asked the (a) *Lopez's*, (b) *Lopezes* to contribute to the fund-raising drive.
10. Both my (a) *sister-in-laws*, (b) *sisters-in-law* agreed to the settlement.
11. The stock market is experiencing abnormal (a) *ups and downs*, (b) *up's and down's*.
12. Three (a) *mouses*, (b) *mice* were seen near the trash cans.
13. This office is unusually quiet on (a) *Sundays*, (b) *Sunday's*.
14. Several news (a) *dispatchs*, (b) *dispatches* were released during the strike.
15. Two major (a) *countries*, (b) *countrys* will participate in arms negotiations.
16. Some young children have difficulty writing their (a) *bs and ds*, (b) *b's and d's*.
17. The (a) *board of directors*, (b) *boards of directors* of all the major companies participated in the surveys.
18. In their letter the (a) *Metzes*, (b) *Metzs* said they intended to purchase the property.
19. In shipping we are careful to include all (a) *bill of sales*, (b) *bills of sale*.
20. Over the holidays many (a) *turkies*, (b) *turkeys* were consumed.

---

1. b (1.05f)   3. b (1.05b)   5. a (1.05e)   7. a (1.05d)   9. b (1.05b)   11. a (1.05g)   13. a (1.05a)
15. a (1.05e)   17. b (1.05f)   19. b (1.05f) (Only odd-numbered answers are provided. Consult your instructor for the others.)

Pronouns (1.07–1.09)

Pronouns substitute for nouns. They are classified by case.

1.07 Case. Pronouns function in three cases, as shown in the following chart.

Nominative Case *(Used for subjects of verbs and subject complements)*	Objective Case *(Used for objects of prepositions and objects of verbs)*	Possessive Case *(Used to show possession)*
I	me	my, mine
we	us	our, ours
you	you	your, yours
he	him	his
she	her	her, hers
it	it	its

Nominative Case	Objective Case	Possessive Case
(Used for subjects of verbs and subject complements)	*(Used for objects of prepositions and objects of verbs)*	*(Used to show possession)*
they	them	their, theirs
who, whoever	whom, whomever	whose

1.08 Guidelines for Selecting Pronoun Case

a. Pronouns that serve as subjects of verbs must be in the nominative case:

> *He* and *I* (not *Him* and *me*) decided to apply for the jobs.

b. Pronouns that follow linking verbs (such as *am, is, are, was, were, be, being, been*) and rename the words to which they refer must be in the nominative case.

> It must have been *she* (not *her*) who placed the order. (The nominative-case pronoun *she* follows the linking verb *been* and renames *it*.)

> If it was *he* (not *him*) who called, I have his number. (The nominative-case pronoun *he* follows the linking verb *was* and renames *it*.)

c. Pronouns that serve as objects of verbs or objects of prepositions must be in the objective case:

> Mr. Andrews asked *them* to complete the proposal. (The pronoun *them* is the object of the verb *asked*.)

> All computer printouts are sent to *him*. (The pronoun *him* is the object of the preposition *to*.)

> Just between you and *me*, profits are falling. (The pronoun *me* is one of the objects of the preposition *between*.)

d. Pronouns that show ownership must be in the possessive case. Possessive pronouns (such as *hers, yours, ours, theirs,* and *its*) require no apostrophes:

> I bought a cheap cell phone, but *yours* (not *your's*) is expensive.

> All parts of the machine, including *its* (not *it's*) motor, were examined.

> The house and *its* (not *it's*) contents will be auctioned.

> Don't confuse possessive pronouns and contractions. Contractions are shortened forms of subject–verb phrases (such as *it's* for *it is, there's* for *there is,* and *they're* for *they are*).

e. When a pronoun appears in combination with a noun or another pronoun, ignore the extra noun or pronoun and its conjunction. In this way pronoun case becomes more obvious:

> The manager promoted Jeff and *me* (not *I*). (Ignore *Jeff and*.)

f. In statements of comparison, mentally finish the comparative by adding the implied missing words:

> Next year I hope to earn as much as *she*. (The verb *earns* is implied here: . . . *as much as she earns.*)

g. Pronouns must be in the same case as the words they replace or rename. When pronouns are used with appositives, ignore the appositive:

> A new contract was signed by *us* (not *we*) employees. (Temporarily ignore the appositive *employees* in selecting the pronoun.)

> *We* (not *us*) citizens have formed our own organization. (Temporarily ignore the appositive *citizens* in selecting the pronoun.)

h. Pronouns ending in *self* should be used only when they refer to previously mentioned nouns or pronouns:

> The CEO *himself* answered the telephone.

> Robert and *I* (not *myself*) are in charge of the campaign.

i. Use objective-case pronouns as objects of the prepositions *between, but, like,* and *except:*

> Everyone but John and *him* (not *he*) qualified for the bonus.

> Employees like Miss Gillis and *her* (not *she*) are hard to replace.

j. Use *who* or *whoever* for nominative-case constructions and *whom* or *whomever* for objective-case constructions. In making the correct choice, it's sometimes helpful to substitute *he* for *who* or *whoever* and *him* for *whom* or *whomever:*

> For *whom* was this book ordered? (*This book was ordered for him/whom?*)

> *Who* did you say would drop by? (*Who/he . . . would drop by?*)

> Deliver the package to *whoever* opens the door. (In this sentence the clause *whoever opens the door* functions as the object of the preposition *to*. Within the clause itself *whoever* is the subject of the verb *opens*. Again, substitution of *he* might be helpful: *He/Whoever opens the door.*)

1.09 Guidelines for Making Pronouns Agree With Their Antecedents. Pronouns must agree with the words to which they refer (their antecedents) in gender and in number.

a. Use masculine pronouns to refer to masculine antecedents, feminine pronouns to refer to feminine antecedents, and neuter pronouns to refer to antecedents without gender:

> The man opened *his* office door. (Masculine gender applies.)

> A woman sat at *her* desk. (Feminine gender applies.)

> This computer and *its* programs fit our needs. (Neuter gender applies.)

b. Use singular pronouns to refer to singular antecedents:

Common-gender pronouns (such as *him* or *his*) traditionally have been used when the gender of the antecedent is unknown. Sensitive writers today, however, prefer to recast such constructions to avoid the need for common-gender pronouns. Study these examples for alternatives to the use of common-gender pronouns:*

> Each student must submit *a* report on Monday.

> All students must submit *their* reports on Monday.

> Each student must submit *his or her* report on Monday. (This alternative is least acceptable since it is wordy and calls attention to itself.)

c. Use singular pronouns to refer to singular indefinite subjects and plural pronouns for plural indefinite subjects. Words such as *anyone, something,* and *anybody* are considered indefinite because they refer to no specific person or object. Some indefinite pronouns are always singular; others are always plural.

Always Singular			**Always Plural**
anybody	either	nobody	both
anyone	everyone	no one	few
anything	everything	somebody	many
each	neither	someone	several

---

*See Chapter 2, page 42, for additional discussion of common-gender pronouns and inclusive language.

Somebody in the group of touring women left *her* (not *their*) purse in the museum.

Either of the companies has the right to exercise *its* (not *their*) option to sell stock.

d. Use singular pronouns to refer to collective nouns and organization names:

The engineering staff is moving *its* (not *their*) facilities on Friday. (The singular pronoun *its* agrees with the collective noun *staff* because the members of *staff* function as a single unit.)

Jones, Cohen, & James, Inc., *has* (not *have*) canceled *its* (not *their*) contract with us. (The singular pronoun *its* agrees with *Jones, Cohen, & James, Inc.,* because the members of the organization are operating as a single unit.)

e. Use a plural pronoun to refer to two antecedents joined by *and*, whether the antecedents are singular or plural:

Our company president and our vice president will be submitting *their* expenses shortly.

f. Ignore intervening phrases—introduced by expressions such as *together with, as well as,* and *in addition to*—that separate a pronoun from its antecedent:

One of our managers, along with several salespeople, is planning *his* retirement. (If you wish to emphasize both subjects equally, join them with *and*: One of our managers *and* several salespeople are planning *their* retirements.)

g. When antecedents are joined by *or* or *nor*, make the pronoun agree with the antecedent closest to it.

Neither Jackie nor Kim wanted *her* (not *their*) desk moved.

Review Exercise B—Pronouns

In the space provided for each item, write *a*, *b*, or *c* to complete the statement accurately. When you finish, compare your responses with those provided. For each item on which you need review, consult the numbered principle shown in parentheses.

1. Send e-mail copies of the policy to the manager or (a) *me*, (b) *myself*.
2. James promised that he would call; was it (a) *him*, (b) *he* who left the message?
3. Much preparation for the seminar was made by Mrs. Washington and (a) *I*, (b) *me* before the brochures were sent out.
4. The Employee Benefits Committee can be justly proud of (a) *its*, (b) *their* achievements.
5. A number of inquiries were addressed to Jeff and (a) *I*, (b) *me*, (c) *myself*.
6. (a) *Who*, (b) *Whom* did you say the letter was addressed to?
7. When you visit Sears Savings Bank, inquire about (a) *its*, (b) *their* certificates.
8. All e-mail messages for Taylor and (a) *I*, (b) *me*, (c) *myself* will become part of the lawsuit.
9. Apparently one of the female applicants forgot to sign (a) *her*, (b) *their* application.
10. Both the printer and (a) *it's*, (b) *its* cover are missing.
11. I've never known any man who could work as fast as (a) *him*, (b) *he*.
12. Just between you and (a) *I*, (b) *me*, the stock price will fall by afternoon.
13. Give the supplies to (a) *whoever*, (b) *whomever* ordered them.
14. (a) *Us*, (b) *We* employees have been given an unusual voice in choosing benefits.
15. On her return from Mexico, Mrs. Sanchez, along with many other passengers, had to open (a) *her*, (b) *their* luggage for inspection.

16. Either James or Robert must submit (a) *his,* (b) *their* report next week.

17. Any woman who becomes a charter member of this organization will be able to have (a) *her,* (b) *their* name inscribed on a commemorative plaque.

18. We are certain that (a) *our's,* (b) *ours* is the smallest smart phone available.

19. Everyone has completed the reports except Debbie and (a) *he,* (b) *him.*

20. Lack of work disturbs Mr. Thomas as much as (a) *I,* (b) *me.*

---

1. a (1.08h)   3. b (1.08c)   5. b (1.08c, 1.08e)   7. a (1.09d)   9. a (1.09b)   11. b (1.08f)
13. a (1.08j)   15. a (1.09f)   17. a (1.09b)   19. b (1.08i)

Cumulative Editing Quiz 1

Use proofreading marks (see Appendix B) to correct errors in the following sentences. All errors must be corrected to receive credit for the sentence. Check with your instructor for the answers.

Example   Nicholas and ~~him~~ *he* made all ~~there~~ *their* money in the 1990~~'~~s.

1. Just between you and I, whom do you think would make the best manager?

2. Either Stacy or me is responsible for correcting all errors in news dispatchs.

3. Several attornies asked that there cases be postponed.

4. One of the secretarys warned Bill and I to get the name of whomever answered the phone.

5. The committee sent there decision to the president and I last week.

6. Who should Susan or me call to verify the three bill of sales received today?

7. Several of we employees complained that it's keyboard made the new computer difficult to use.

8. All the CEO's agreed that the low interest rates of the early 2000s could not continue.

9. Every customer has a right to expect there inquirys to be treated courteously.

10. You may send you're contribution to Eric or myself or to whomever is listed as your representative.

Verbs (1.10–1.15)

Verbs show the action of a subject or join the subject to words that describe it.

1.10 Guidelines for Agreement With Subjects. One of the most troublesome areas in English is subject–verb agreement. Consider the following guidelines for making verbs agree with subjects.

a. A singular subject requires a singular verb:

> The stock market *opens* at 10 a.m. (The singular verb *opens* agrees with the singular subject *market.*)

> He *doesn't* (not *don't*) work on Saturday.

b. A plural subject requires a plural verb:

> On the packing slip several items *seem* (not *seems*) to be missing.

c. A verb agrees with its subject regardless of prepositional phrases that may intervene:

> This list of management objectives *is* extensive. (The singular verb *is* agrees with the singular subject *list.*)

> Every one of the letters *shows* (not *show*) proper form.

d. A verb agrees with its subject regardless of intervening phrases introduced by *as well as, in addition to, such as, including, together with,* and similar expressions:

> An important memo, together with several contracts, *is* missing. (The singular verb *is* agrees with the singular subject *memo*.)

> The president as well as several other top-level executives *approves* of our proposal. (The singular verb *approves* agrees with the subject *president*.)

e. A verb agrees with its subject regardless of the location of the subject:

> Here *is* one of the contracts about which you asked. (The verb *is* agrees with its subject *one*, even though it precedes *one*. The adverb *here* cannot function as a subject.)

> There *are* many problems yet to be resolved. (The verb *are* agrees with the subject *problems*. The word *there* does not function as a subject.)

> In the next office *are* several printers. (In this inverted sentence the verb *are* must agree with the subject *printers*.)

f. Subjects joined by *and* require a plural verb:

> Analyzing the reader and organizing a strategy *are* the first steps in letter writing. (The plural verb *are* agrees with the two subjects, *analyzing* and *organizing*.)

> The tone and the wording of the letter *were* persuasive. (The plural verb *were* agrees with the two subjects, *tone* and *wording*.)

g. Subjects joined by *or* or *nor* may require singular or plural verbs. Make the verb agree with the closer subject:

> Neither the memo nor the report *is* ready. (The singular verb *is* agrees with *report*, the closer of the two subjects.)

h. The following indefinite pronouns are singular and require singular verbs: *anyone, anybody, anything, each, either, every, everyone, everybody, everything, many a, neither, nobody, nothing, someone, somebody,* and *something*:

> Either of the alternatives that you present *is* acceptable. (The verb *is* agrees with the singular subject *either*.)

i. Collective nouns may take singular or plural verbs, depending on whether the members of the group are operating as a unit or individually:

> Our management team *is* united in its goal.

> The faculty *are* sharply divided on the tuition issue. (Although acceptable, this sentence sounds better recast: The faculty *members* are sharply divided on the tuition issue.)

j. Organization names and titles of publications, although they may appear to be plural, are singular and require singular verbs.

> Clark, Anderson, and Horne, Inc., *has* (not *have*) hired a marketing consultant.

> *Thousands of Investment Tips is* (not *are*) again on the best-seller list.

1.11 Voice. Voice is that property of verbs that shows whether the subject of the verb acts or is acted upon. Active-voice verbs direct action from the subject toward the object of the verb. Passive-voice verbs direct action toward the subject.

Active voice: Our employees *send* many e-mail messages.
Passive voice: Many e-mail messages *are sent* by our employees.

Business writers generally prefer active-voice verbs because they are specific and forceful. However, passive-voice constructions can help a writer be tactful. Chapter 3 presents strategies for effective use of active- and passive-voice verbs.

1.12 Mood. Three verb moods express the attitude or thought of the speaker or writer toward a subject: (a) the indicative mood expresses a fact; (b) the imperative mood expresses a command; and (c) the subjunctive mood expresses a doubt, a conjecture, or a suggestion.

Indicative:	I *am looking* for a job.
Imperative:	*Begin* your job search with the want ads.
Subjunctive:	I wish I *were* working.

Only the subjunctive mood creates problems for most speakers and writers. The most common use of subjunctive mood occurs in clauses including *if* or *wish*. In such clauses substitute the subjunctive verb *were* for the indicative verb *was*:

If he *were* (not *was*) in my position, he would understand.

Mr. Simon acts as if he *were* (not *was*) the boss.

We wish we *were* (not *was*) able to ship your order.

The subjunctive mood can maintain goodwill while conveying negative information. The sentence *We wish we were able to ship your order* sounds more pleasing to a customer than *We cannot ship your order,* although, for all practical purposes, both sentences convey the same negative message.

1.13 Tense. Verbs show the time of an action by their tense. Speakers and writers can use six tenses to show the time of sentence action; for example:

Present tense:	I *work;* he *works.*
Past tense:	I *worked;* she *worked.*
Future tense:	I *will work;* he *will work.*
Present perfect tense:	I *have worked;* he *has worked.*
Past perfect tense:	I *had worked;* she *had worked.*
Future perfect tense:	I *will have worked;* he *will have worked.*

1.14 Guidelines for Verb Tense

a. Use present tense for statements that, although introduced by past-tense verbs, continue to be true:

What did you say his name *is*? (Use the present tense *is* if his name has not changed.)

b. Avoid unnecessary shifts in verb tenses:

The manager *saw* (not *sees*) a great deal of work yet to be completed and *remained* to do it herself.

Although unnecessary shifts in verb tense are to be avoided, not all the verbs within one sentence have to be in the same tense; for example:

She *said* (past tense) that she *likes* (present tense) to work late.

1.15 Irregular Verbs. Irregular verbs cause difficulty for some writers and speakers. Unlike regular verbs, irregular verbs do not form the past tense and past participle by adding *-ed* to the present form. Here is a partial list of selected troublesome irregular verbs. Consult a dictionary if you are in doubt about a verb form.

Troublesome Irregular Verbs

Present	Past	Past Participle *(always use helping verbs)*
begin	began	begun
break	broke	broken
choose	chose	chosen
come	came	come
drink	drank	drunk
go	went	gone
lay (to place)	laid	laid
lie (to rest)	lay	lain
ring	rang	rung
see	saw	seen
write	wrote	written

a. Use only past-tense verbs to express past tense. Notice that no helping verbs are used to indicate simple past tense:

> The auditors *went* (not *have went*) over our books carefully.

> He *came* (not *come*) to see us yesterday.

b. Use past-participle forms for actions completed before the present time. Notice that past-participle forms require helping verbs:

> Steve *had gone* (not *had went*) before we called. (The past-participle *gone* is used with the helping verb *had*.)

c. Avoid inconsistent shifts in subject, voice, and mood. Pay particular attention to this problem area because undesirable shifts are often characteristic of student writing.

> **Inconsistent:** When Mrs. Taswell read the report, the error was found. (The first clause is in the active voice; the second, passive.)
>
> **Improved:** When Mrs. Taswell read the report, she found the error. (Both clauses are in the active voice.)

> **Inconsistent:** The clerk should first conduct an inventory. Then supplies should be requisitioned. (The first sentence is in the active voice; the second, passive.)
>
> **Improved:** The clerk should first conduct an inventory. Then he or she should requisition supplies. (Both sentences are in the active voice.)

> **Inconsistent:** All workers must wear security badges, and you must also sign a daily time card. (This sentence contains an inconsistent shift in subject from *all workers* in the first clause to *you* in the second clause.)
>
> **Improved:** All workers must wear security badges, and they must also sign a daily time card.

> **Inconsistent:** Begin the transaction by opening an account; then you enter the customer's name. (This sentence contains an inconsistent shift from the imperative mood in the first clause to the indicative mood in the second clause.)
>
> **Improved:** Begin the transaction by opening an account; then enter the customer's name. (Both clauses are now in the imperative mood.)

Review Exercise C—Verbs

In the space provided for each item, write *a* or *b* to complete the statement accurately. When you finish, compare your responses with those provided. For each item on which you need review, consult the numbered principle shown in parentheses.

1. Our directory of customer names and addresses (a) *was* (b) *were* out-of-date.

2. There (a) *is*, (b) *are* a customer service engineer and two salespeople waiting to see you.

3. Improved communication technologies and increased global competition (a) *is*, (b) *are* changing the world of business.

4. Crews, Meliotes, and Bove, Inc., (a) *has*, (b) *have* opened an office in Boston.

5. Yesterday Mrs. Phillips (a) *choose*, (b) *chose* a new office on the second floor.

6. The man who called said that his name (a) *is*, (b) *was* Johnson.

7. *U.S. News & World Report* (a) *is*, (b) *are* beginning a campaign to increase readership.

8. Either of the flight times (a) *appears*, (b) *appear* to fit my proposed itinerary.

9. If you had (a) *saw*, (b) *seen* the rough draft, you would better appreciate the final copy.

10. Across from our office (a) *is*, (b) *are* the parking structure and the information office.

11. Although we have (a) *began*, (b) *begun* to replace outmoded equipment, the pace is slow.

12. Specific training as well as ample experience (a) *is*, (b) *are* important for that position.

13. Changing attitudes and increased job opportunities (a) *is*, (b) *are* resulting in increased numbers of working women.

14. Neither the organizing nor the staffing of the program (a) *has been*, (b) *have been* completed.

15. If I (a) *was*, (b) *were* you, I would ask for a raise.

16. If you had (a) *wrote*, (b) *written* last week, we could have sent a brochure.

17. The hydraulic equipment that you ordered (a) *is*, (b) *are* packed and will be shipped Friday.

18. One of the reasons that sales have declined in recent years (a) *is*, (b) *are* lack of effective advertising.

19. Either of the proposed laws (a) *is*, (b) *are* going to affect our business negatively.

20. Merger statutes (a) *requires*, (b) *require* that a failing company accept bids from several companies before merging with one.

1. a (1.10c) 3. b (1.10f) 5. b (1.15a) 7. a (1.10j) 9. b (1.15b) 11. b (1.15b) 13. b (1.10f)
15. b (1.12) 17. a (1.10a) 19. a (1.10h)

Review Exercise D—Verbs

In the following sentence pairs, choose the one that illustrates consistency in use of subject, voice, and mood. Write *a* or *b* in the space provided. When you finish, compare your responses with those provided. For each item on which you need review, consult the numbered principle shown in parentheses.

1. (a) You need more than a knowledge of technology; one also must be able to interact well with people.

   (b) You need more than a knowledge of technology; you also must be able to interact well with people.

2. (a) Tim and Jon were eager to continue, but Bob wanted to quit.

   (b) Tim and Jon were eager to continue, but Bob wants to quit.

3. (a) The salesperson should consult the price list; then you can give an accurate quote to a customer.

   (b) The salesperson should consult the price list; then he or she can give an accurate quote to a customer.

4. (a) Read all the instructions first; then you install the printer program.

   (b) Read all the instructions first, and then install the printer program.

5. (a) She was an enthusiastic manager who always had a smile for everyone.

   (b) She was an enthusiastic manager who always has a smile for everyone.

1. b (1.15c)   3. b (1.15c)   5. a (1.14b)

Cumulative Editing Quiz 2

Use proofreading marks (see Appendix B) to correct errors in the following sentences. All errors must be corrected to receive credit for the sentence. Check with your instructor for the answers.

1. Assets and liabilitys is what my partner and myself must investigate.
2. If I was you, I would ask whomever is in charge for their opinion.
3. The faculty agree that it's first concern is educating students.
4. The book and it's cover was printed in Japan.
5. Waiting to see you is a sales representative and a job applicant who you told to drop by.
6. Every employee could have picked up his ballot if he had went to the cafeteria.
7. Your choice of hospitals and physicians are reduced by this plan and it's restrictions.
8. My uncle and her come to visit my parents and myself last night.
9. According to both editor in chiefs, the tone and wording of all our letters needs revision.
10. The Davis'es, about who the article was written, said they were unconcerned with the up's and down's of the stock market.

Adjectives and Adverbs (1.16–1.17)

Adjectives describe or limit nouns and pronouns. They often answer the questions *what kind? how many?* or *which one?* Adverbs describe or limit verbs, adjectives, or other adverbs. They often answer the questions *when? how? where?* or *to what extent?*

1.16 Forms. Most adjectives and adverbs have three forms, or degrees: positive, comparative, and superlative.

	Positive	**Comparative**	**Superlative**
Adjective:	clear	clearer	clearest
Adverb:	clearly	more clearly	most clearly

Some adjectives and adverbs have irregular forms.

	Positive	**Comparative**	**Superlative**
Adjective:	good	better	best
	bad	worse	worst
Adverb:	well	better	best

Adjectives and adverbs composed of two or more syllables are usually compared by the use of *more* and *most*; for example:

The Payroll Department is *more efficient* than the Shipping Department.

Payroll is the *most efficient* department in our organization.

1.17 Guidelines for Use

a. Use the comparative degree of the adjective or adverb to compare two persons or things; use the superlative degree to compare three or more:

> Of the two plans, which is *better* (not *best*)?

> Of all the plans, we like this one *best* (not *better*).

b. Do not create a double comparative or superlative by using *-er* with *more* or *-est* with *most*:

> His explanation couldn't have been *clearer* (not *more clearer*).

c. A linking verb (*is, are, look, seem, feel, sound, appear,* and so forth) may introduce a word that describes the verb's subject. In this case be certain to use an adjective, not an adverb:

> The characters on the monitor look *bright* (not *brightly*). (Use the adjective *bright* because it follows the linking verb *look* and modifies the noun *characters*.)

> The company's letter made the customer feel *bad* (not *badly*). (The adjective *bad* follows the linking verb *feel* and describes the noun *customer*.)

d. Use adverbs, not adjectives, to describe or limit the action of verbs:

> The business is running *smoothly* (not *smooth*). (Use the adverb *smoothly* to describe the action of the verb *is running*. *Smoothly* tells how the business is running.)

> Don't take his remark *personally* (not *personal*). (The adverb *personally* describes the action of the verb *take*.)

> Serena said she did *well* (not *good*) on the test. (Use the adverb *well* to tell how she did.)

e. Two or more adjectives that are joined to create a compound modifier before a noun should be hyphenated:

> The *four-year-old* child was tired.

> Our agency is planning a *coast-to-coast* campaign.

Hyphenate a compound modifier following a noun only if your dictionary shows the hyphen(s):

> Our speaker is very *well-known*. (Include the hyphen because most dictionaries do.)

> The tired child was four years old. (Omit the hyphens because the expression follows the word it describes, *child*, and because dictionaries do not indicate hyphens.)

f. Keep adjectives and adverbs close to the words they modify:

> She asked for *a cup of hot coffee* (not *a hot cup of coffee*).

> Patty *had only two days* of vacation left (not *only had two days*).

> Students may sit in the *first five rows* (not *in five first rows*).

> He *has saved almost* enough money for the trip (not *has almost saved*).

g. Don't confuse *there* with the possessive pronoun *their* or the contraction *they're*:

> Put the documents *there*. (The adverb *there* means "at that place or at that point.")

> *There* are two reasons for the change. (The pronoun *there* is used as function word to introduce a sentence or a clause.)

We already have *their* specifications. (The possessive pronoun *their* shows ownership.)

They're coming to inspect today. (The contraction *they're* is a shortened form of *they are*.)

Review Exercise E—Adjectives and Adverbs

In the space provided for each item, write *a*, *b*, or *c* to complete the statement accurately. If two sentences are shown, select *a* or *b* to indicate the one expressed more effectively. When you finish, compare your responses with those provided. For each item on which you need review, consult the numbered principle shown in parentheses.

1. After the interview, Tim looked (a) *calm*, (b) *calmly*.
2. If you had been more (a) *careful*, (b) *carefuler*, the box might not have broken.
3. Because we appointed a new manager, the advertising campaign is running (a) *smooth*, (b) *smoothly*.
4. To avoid a (a) *face to face*, (b) *face-to-face* confrontation, she sent an e-mail.
5. Darren completed the employment test (a) *satisfactorily*, (b) *satisfactory*.
6. I felt (a) *bad*, (b) *badly* that he was not promoted.
7. Which is the (a) *more*, (b) *most* dependable of the two cars?
8. Can you determine exactly what (a) *there*, (b) *their*, (c) *they're* company wants us to do?
9. Of all the copiers we tested, this one is the (a) *easier*, (b) *easiest* to operate.
10. (a) Mr. Aldron almost was ready to accept the offer.
    (b) Mr. Aldron was almost ready to accept the offer.
11. (a) We only thought that it would take two hours for the test.
    (b) We thought that it would take only two hours for the test.
12. (a) Please bring me a glass of cold water.
    (b) Please bring me a cold glass of water.
13. (a) The committee decided to retain the last ten tickets.
    (b) The committee decided to retain the ten last tickets.
14. New owners will receive a (a) *60-day*, (b) *60 day* trial period.
15. The time passed (a) *quicker*, (b) *more quickly* than we expected.
16. We offer a (a) *money back*, (b) *money-back* guarantee.
17. Today the financial news is (a) *worse*, (b) *worst* than yesterday.
18. Please don't take his comments (a) *personal*, (b) *personally*.
19. You must check the document (a) *page by page*, (b) *page-by-page*.
20. (a) We try to file only necessary paperwork.
    (b) We only try to file necessary paperwork.

---

1. a (1.17c)   3. b (1.17d)   5. a (1.17d)   7. a (1.17a)   9. b (1.17a)   11. b (1.17f)   13. a (1.17f)
15. b (1.17d)   17. a (1.17a)   19. a (1.17e)

PREPOSITIONS (1.18)

Prepositions are connecting words that join nouns or pronouns to other words in a sentence. The words *about*, *at*, *from*, *in*, and *to* are examples of prepositions.

1.18 Guidelines for Use

a. Include necessary prepositions:

What type *of* software do you need (not *what type software*)?

I graduated *from* high school two years ago (not *I graduated high school*).

b. Omit unnecessary prepositions:

Where is the meeting? (Not *Where is the meeting at?*)

Both printers work well. (Not *Both of the printers.*)

Where are you going? (Not *Where are you going to?*)

c. Avoid the overuse of prepositional phrases.

Weak: We have received your application for credit at our branch in the Fresno area.
Improved: We have received your Fresno credit application.

d. Repeat the preposition before the second of two related elements:

Applicants use the résumé effectively by summarizing their most important experiences and *by* relating their education to the jobs sought.

e. Include the second preposition when two prepositions modify a single object:

George's appreciation *of* and aptitude *for* computers led to a promising career.

Conjunctions (1.19)

Conjunctions connect words, phrases, and clauses. They act as signals, indicating when a thought is being added, contrasted, or altered. Coordinate conjunctions (such as *and, or, but*) and other words that act as connectors (such as *however, therefore, when, as*) tell the reader or listener in what direction a thought is heading. They're like road signs signaling what's ahead.

1.19 Guidelines for Use

a. Use coordinating conjunctions to connect only sentence elements that are parallel or balanced.

Weak: His report was correct and written in a concise manner.
Improved: His report was correct and concise.

Weak: Management has the capacity to increase fraud, or reduction can be achieved through the policies it adopts.
Improved: Management has the capacity to increase or reduce fraud through the policies it adopts.

b. Do not use the word *like* as a conjunction:

It seems *as if* (not *like*) this day will never end.

c. Avoid using *when* or *where* inappropriately. A common writing fault occurs in sentences with clauses introduced by *is when* and *is where*. Written English ordinarily requires a noun (or a group of words functioning as a noun) following the linking verb *is*. Instead of acting as conjunctions in these constructions, the words *where* and *when* function as adverbs, creating faulty grammatical equations (adverbs cannot complete equations set up by linking verbs). To avoid the problem, revise the sentence, eliminating *is when* or *is where*.

Weak: A bullish market is when prices are rising in the stock market.
Improved: A bullish market is created when prices are rising in the stock market.

Weak: A flowchart is when you make a diagram showing the step-by-step progression of a procedure.
Improved: A flowchart is a diagram showing the step-by-step progression of a procedure.

Weak: Word processing is where you use a computer and software to write.
Improved: Word processing involves the use of a computer and software to write.

A similar faulty construction occurs in the expression *I hate when*. English requires nouns, noun clauses, or pronouns to act as objects of verbs, not adverbs.

Weak: I hate when we're asked to work overtime.
Improved: I hate it when we're asked to work overtime.
Improved: I hate being asked to work overtime.

d. Don't confuse the adverb *then* with the conjunction *than*. *Then* means "at that time"; *than* indicates the second element in a comparison:

We would rather remodel *than* (not *then*) move.

First, the equipment is turned on; *then* (not *than*) the program is loaded.

Review Exercise F—Prepositions and Conjunctions

In the space provided for each item, write *a* or *b* to indicate the sentence that is expressed more effectively. When you finish, compare your responses with those provided. For each item on which you need review, consult the numbered principle shown in parentheses.

1. (a) The chief forgot to tell everyone where today's meeting is.
   (b) The chief forgot to tell everyone where today's meeting is at.

2. (a) She was not aware of nor interested in the company insurance plan.
   (b) She was not aware nor interested in the company insurance plan.

3. (a) Mr. Samuels graduated college last June.
   (b) Mr. Samuels graduated from college last June.

4. (a) "Flextime" is when employees arrive and depart at varying times.
   (b) "Flextime" is a method of scheduling worktime in which employees arrive and depart at varying times.

5. (a) Both employees enjoyed setting their own hours.
   (b) Both of the employees enjoyed setting their own hours.

6. (a) I hate when my cell loses its charge.
   (b) I hate it when my cell loses its charge.

7. (a) What style of typeface should we use?
   (b) What style typeface should we use?

8. (a) Business letters should be concise, correct, and written clearly.
   (b) Business letters should be concise, correct, and clear.

9. (a) Mediation in a labor dispute occurs when a neutral person helps union and management reach an agreement.
   (b) Mediation in a labor dispute is where a neutral person helps union and management reach an agreement.

10. (a) It looks as if the plant will open in early January.
    (b) It looks like the plant will open in early January.

11. (a) We expect to finish up the work soon.
    (b) We expect to finish the work soon.

12. (a) At the beginning of the program in the fall of the year at the central office, we experienced staffing difficulties.
    (b) When the program began last fall, the central office experienced staffing difficulties.

13. (a) Your client may respond by e-mail or a telephone call may be made.
    (b) Your client may respond by e-mail or by telephone.

14. (a) A résumé is when you make a written presentation of your education and experience for a prospective employer.

    (b) A résumé is a written presentation of your education and experience for a prospective employer.

15. (a) Stacy exhibited both an awareness of and talent for developing innovations.

    (b) Stacy exhibited both an awareness and talent for developing innovations.

16. (a) This course is harder then I expected.

    (b) This course is harder than I expected.

17. (a) An ombudsman is an individual hired by management to investigate and resolve employee complaints.

    (b) An ombudsman is when management hires an individual to investigate and resolve employee complaints.

18. (a) I'm uncertain where to take this document to.

    (b) I'm uncertain where to take this document.

19. (a) By including accurate data and by writing clearly, you will produce effective messages.

    (b) By including accurate data and writing clearly, you will produce effective messages.

20. (a) We need computer operators who can load software, monitor networks, and files must be duplicated.

    (b) We need computer operators who can load software, monitor networks, and duplicate files.

1. a (1.18b)   3. b (1.18a)   5. a (1.18b)   7. a (1.18a)   9. a (1.19c)   11. b (1.18b)
13. b (1.19a)   15. a (1.18e)   17. a (1.19c)   19. a (1.18d)

Cumulative Editing Quiz 3

Use proofreading marks (see Appendix B) to correct errors in the following sentences. All errors must be corrected to receive credit for the sentence. Check with your instructor for the answers.

1. If Cindy works faster then her, shouldn't Cindy be hired?

2. We felt badly that Mark's home was not chose for the tour.

3. Neither the company nor the workers is pleased at how slow the talks seems to be progressing.

4. Just between you and I, it's better not to take his remarks personal.

5. After completing there floor by floor inventory, managers will deliver there reports to Mr. Quinn and I.

6. If my cell phone was working, Jean and myself could have completed our calls.

7. Powerful software and new hardware allows us to send the newsletter to whomever is currently listed in our database.

8. The eighteen year old girl and her mother was given hot cups of tea after there ordeal.

9. We begun the work two years ago, but personnel and equipment has been especially difficult to obtain.

10. Today's weather is worst then yesterday.

Punctuation Review

Commas 1 (2.01–2.04)

2.01 Series. Commas are used to separate three or more equal elements (words, phrases, or short clauses) in a series. To ensure separation of the last two elements, careful writers always use a comma before the conjunction in a series:

> Business letters usually contain a dateline, address, salutation, body, and closing. (This series contains words.)

> The job of an ombudsman is to examine employee complaints, resolve disagreements between management and employees, and ensure fair treatment. (This series contains phrases.)

> Trainees complete basic keyboarding tasks, technicians revise complex documents, and editors proofread completed projects. (This series contains short clauses.)

2.02 Direct Address. Commas are used to set off the names of individuals being addressed:

> Your inquiry, *Mrs. Johnson,* has been referred to me.

> We genuinely hope that we may serve you, *Mr. Lee.*

2.03 Parenthetical Expressions. Skilled writers use parenthetical words, phrases, and clauses to guide the reader from one thought to the next. When these expressions interrupt the flow of a sentence and are unnecessary for its grammatical completeness, they should be set off with commas. Examples of commonly used parenthetical expressions follow:

all things considered	however	needless to say
as a matter of fact	in addition	nevertheless
as a result	incidentally	no doubt
as a rule	in fact	of course
at the same time	in my opinion	on the contrary
consequently	in the first place	on the other hand
for example	in the meantime	therefore
furthermore	moreover	under the circumstances

> *As a matter of fact,* I wrote to you just yesterday. (Phrase used at the beginning of a sentence.)

> We will, *in the meantime,* send you a replacement order. (Phrase used in the middle of a sentence.)

> Your satisfaction is our first concern, *needless to say.* (Phrase used at the end of a sentence.)

Do not use commas if the expression is necessary for the completeness of the sentence:

> Kimberly had *no doubt* that she would finish the report. (Omit commas because the expression is necessary for the completeness of the sentence.)

2.04 Dates, Addresses, and Geographical Items. When dates, addresses, and geographical items contain more than one element, the second and succeeding elements are normally set off by commas.

a. Dates:

The conference was held February 2 at our home office. (No comma is needed for one element.)

The conference was held February 2, 2009, at our home office. (Two commas set off the second element.)

The conference was held Tuesday, February 2, 2009, at our home office. (Commas set off the second and third elements.)

In February 2009 the conference was held. (This alternate style omitting commas is acceptable if only the month and year are written.)

b. Addresses:

The letter addressed to Mr. Jim W. Ellman, 600 Via Novella, Agoura, CA 91306, should be sent today. (Commas are used between all elements except the state and zip code, which in this special instance act as a single unit.)

c. Geographical items:

She moved from Toledo, Ohio, to Champaign, Illinois. (Commas set off the state unless it appears at the end of the sentence, in which case only one comma is used.)

In separating cities from states and days from years, many writers remember the initial comma but forget the final one, as in the examples that follow:

The package from Austin, Texas{,} was lost.

We opened June 1, 2004{,} and have grown steadily since.

Review Exercise G—Commas 1

Insert necessary commas in the following sentences. In the space provided write the number of commas that you add. Write C if no commas are needed. When you finish, compare your responses with those provided. For each item on which you need review, consult the numbered principle shown in parentheses.

1. As a rule we do not provide complimentary tickets.
2. You may be certain Mr. Martinez that your policy will be issued immediately.
3. I have no doubt that your calculations are correct.
4. The safety hazard on the contrary can be greatly reduced if workers wear rubber gloves.
5. Every accredited TV newscaster radio broadcaster and blogger had access to the media room.
6. Deltech's main offices are located in Boulder Colorado and Seattle Washington.
7. The employees who are eligible for promotions are Terry Evelyn Vicki Rosanna and Steve.
8. During the warranty period of course you are protected from any parts or service charges.
9. Many of our customers include architects engineers attorneys and others who are interested in database management programs.
10. I wonder Mrs. Stevens if you would send my letter of recommendation as soon as possible.
11. The new book explains how to choose appropriate legal protection for ideas trade secrets copyrights patents and restrictive covenants.
12. The factory is scheduled to be moved to 2250 North Main Street Ann Arbor Michigan 48107 within two years.

13. You may however prefer to correspond directly with the manufacturer in Hong Kong.

14. Are there any alternatives in addition to those that we have already considered?

15. The rally has been scheduled for Monday January 12 in the football stadium.

16. A check for the full amount will be sent directly to your home Mr. Jefferson.

17. Goodstone Tire & Rubber for example recalled 400,000 steelbelted radial tires because some tires failed their rigorous tests.

18. Kevin agreed to unlock the office open the mail and check all the equipment in my absence.

19. In the meantime thank you for whatever assistance you are able to furnish.

20. Research facilities were moved from Austin Texas to Santa Cruz California.

1. rule, (2.03)   3. C (2.03)   5. newscaster, radio broadcaster, (2.01)   7. Terry, Evelyn, Vicki, Rosanna, (2.01)   9. architects, engineers, attorneys, (2.01)   11. ideas, trade secrets, copyrights, patents, (2.01)   13. may, however, (2.03)   15. Monday, January 12, (2.04a)   17. Rubber, for example, (2.03)   19. meantime, (2.03)

Commas 2 (2.05–2.09)

2.05 Independent Clauses. An independent clause is a group of words that has a subject and a verb and that could stand as a complete sentence. When two such clauses are joined by *and, or, nor,* or *but,* use a comma before the conjunction:

> We can ship your merchandise July 12, but we must have your payment first.

> Net income before taxes is calculated, and this total is then combined with income from operations.

Notice that each independent clause in the preceding two examples could stand alone as a complete sentence. Do not use a comma unless each group of words is a complete thought (that is, has its own subject and verb).

> Our CPA calculates net income before taxes *and* then combines that figure with income from operations. (No comma is needed because no subject follows *and*.)

2.06 Dependent Clauses. Dependent clauses do not make sense by themselves; for their meaning they depend on independent clauses.

a. **Introductory clauses.** When a dependent clause precedes an independent clause, it is followed by a comma. Such clauses are often introduced by *when, if,* and *as*:

> *When your request came,* we responded immediately.

> *As I mentioned earlier,* Mrs. James is the manager.

b. **Terminal clauses.** If a dependent clause falls at the end of a sentence, use a comma only if the dependent clause is an afterthought:

> We have rescheduled the meeting for October 23, *if this date meets with your approval.* (Comma used because dependent clause is an afterthought.)

> We responded immediately *when we received your request.* (No comma is needed.)

c. **Essential versus nonessential clauses.** If a dependent clause provides information that is unneeded for the grammatical completeness of a sentence, use commas to set it off. In determining whether such a clause is essential or nonessential, ask yourself whether the reader needs the information contained in the clause to identify the word it explains:

Our district sales manager, *who just returned from a trip to the Southwest District,* prepared this report. (This construction assumes that there is only one district sales manager. Since the sales manager is clearly identified, the dependent clause is not essential and requires commas.)

The salesperson *who just returned from a trip to the Southwest District* prepared this report. (The dependent clause in this sentence is necessary to identify which salesperson prepared the report. Therefore, use no commas.)

The position of assistant sales manager, *which we discussed with you last week,* is still open. (Careful writers use *which* to introduce nonessential clauses. Commas are also necessary.)

The position *that we discussed with you last week* is still open. (Careful writers use *that* to introduce essential clauses. No commas are used.)

2.07 Phrases. A phrase is a group of related words that lacks both a subject and a verb. A phrase that precedes a main clause is followed by a comma if the phrase contains a verb form or has five or more words:

Beginning November 1, Worldwide Savings will offer two new combination checking/savings plans. (A comma follows this introductory phrase because the phrase contains the verb form *beginning.*)

To promote our plan, we will conduct an extensive direct mail advertising campaign. (A comma follows this introductory phrase because the phrase contains the verb form *to promote.*)

In a period of only one year, we were able to improve our market share by 30 percent. (A comma follows the introductory phrase—actually two prepositional phrases—because its total length exceeds five words.)

In 2009 our organization installed a multiuser system that could transfer programs easily. (No comma needed after the short introductory phrase.)

2.08 Two or More Adjectives. Use a comma to separate two or more adjectives that equally describe a noun. A good way to test the need for a comma is this: Mentally insert the word *and* between the adjectives. If the resulting phrase sounds natural, a comma is used to show the omission of *and*:

We're looking for a *versatile, error-free* operating system. (Use a comma to separate *versatile* and *error-free* because they independently describe *operating system. And* has been omitted.)

Our *experienced, courteous* staff is ready to serve you. (Use a comma to separate *experienced* and *courteous* because they independently describe *staff. And* has been omitted.)

It was difficult to refuse the *sincere young* telephone caller. (No commas are needed between *sincere* and *young* because *and* has not been omitted.)

2.09 Appositives. Words that rename or explain preceding nouns or pronouns are called *appositives.* An appositive that provides information not essential to the identification of the word it describes should be set off by commas:

James Wilson, *the project director for Sperling's,* worked with our architect. (The appositive, *the project director for Sperling's,* adds nonessential information. Commas set it off.)

Review Exercise H—Commas 2

Insert only necessary commas in the following sentences. In the space provided, indicate the number of commas that you add for each sentence. If a sentence requires no commas, write C. When you finish, compare your responses with those provided. For each item on which you need review, consult the numbered principle shown in parentheses.

1. A corporation must register in the state in which it does business and it must operate within the laws of that state.

2. The manager made a point-by-point explanation of the distribution dilemma and then presented his plan to solve the problem.

3. If you will study the cost analysis you will see that our company offers the best system at the lowest price.

4. Molly Epperson who amassed the greatest number of sales points won a bonus trip to Hawaii.

5. The salesperson who amasses the greatest number of sales points will win a bonus trip to Hawaii.

6. To promote goodwill and to generate international trade we are opening offices in South Asia and in Europe.

7. On the basis of these findings I recommend that we retain Jane Rada as our counsel.

8. Scott Cook is a dedicated hardworking employee for our company.

9. The bright young student who worked for us last summer will be able to return this summer.

10. When you return the completed form we will be able to process your application.

11. We will be able to process your application when you return the completed form.

12. The employees who have been with us over ten years automatically receive additional insurance benefits.

13. Knowing that you wanted this merchandise immediately I took the liberty of sending it by FedEx.

14. The central processing unit requires no scheduled maintenance and has a self-test function for reliable performance.

15. A tax credit for energy-saving homes will expire at the end of the year but Congress might extend it if pressure groups prevail.

16. Stacy Wilson our newly promoted office manager has made a number of worthwhile suggestions.

17. For the benefit of employees recently hired we are offering a two-hour seminar regarding employee benefit programs.

18. Please bring your suggestions and those of Mr. Mason when you attend our meeting next month.

19. The meeting has been rescheduled for September 30 if this date meets with your approval.

20. Some of the problems that you outline in your recent memo could be rectified through more stringent purchasing procedures.

---

1. business, (2.05)   3. analysis, (2.06a)   5. C (2.06c)   7. findings, (2.07)   9. C (2.08)   11. C (2.06b)   13. immediately, (2.07)   15. year, (2.05)   17. hired, (2.07)   19. September 30, (2.06b)

Commas 3 (2.10–2.15)

2.10 Degrees and Abbreviations. Degrees following individuals' names are set off by commas. Abbreviations such as *Jr.* and *Sr.* are also set off by commas unless the individual referred to prefers to omit the commas:

Anne G. Turner, *MBA,* joined the firm.

Michael Migliano, *Jr.,* and Michael Migliano, *Sr.,* work as a team.

Anthony A. Gensler *Jr.* wrote the report. (The individual referred to prefers to omit commas.)

The abbreviations *Inc.* and *Ltd.* are set off by commas only if a company's legal name has a comma just before this kind of abbreviation. To determine a company's practice, consult its stationery or a directory listing:

Firestone and Blythe, *Inc.,* is based in Canada. (Notice that two commas are used.)

Computers *Inc.* is extending its franchise system. (The company's legal name does not include a comma before *Inc.*)

2.11 Omitted Words. A comma is used to show the omission of words that are understood:

On Monday we received 15 applications; on Friday, only 3. (Comma shows the omission of *we received.*)

2.12 Contrasting Statements. Commas are used to set off contrasting or opposing expressions. These expressions are often introduced by such words as *not, never, but,* and *yet:*

The president suggested cutbacks, *not* layoffs, to ease the crisis.

Our budget for the year is reduced, *yet* adequate.

The greater the effort, the greater the reward.

If increased emphasis is desired, use dashes instead of commas, as in *Only the sum of $100—not $1,000—was paid on this account.*

2.13 Clarity. Commas are used to separate words repeated for emphasis. Commas are also used to separate words that may be misread if not separated:

The building is a long, long way from completion.

Whatever is, is right.

No matter what, you know we support you.

2.14 Quotations and Appended Questions

a. A comma is used to separate a short quotation from the rest of a sentence. If the quotation is divided into two parts, two commas are used:

The manager asked, "Shouldn't the managers control the specialists?"

"Not if the specialists," replied Tim, "have unique information."

b. A comma is used to separate a question appended (added) to a statement:

You will confirm the shipment, won't you?

2.15 Comma Overuse. Do not use commas needlessly. For example, commas should not be inserted merely because you might drop your voice if you were speaking the sentence:

One of the reasons for expanding our East Coast operations is{,} that we anticipate increased sales in that area. (Do not insert a needless comma before a clause.)

I am looking for an article entitled{,} "State-of-the-Art Communications." (Do not insert a needless comma after the word *entitled*.)

Customers may purchase many food and nonfood items in convenience stores *such as*{,} 7-Eleven and Stop-N-Go. (Do not insert a needless comma after *such as*.)

We have{,} at this time{,} an adequate supply of parts. (Do not insert needless commas around prepositional phrases.)

Review Exercise I—Commas 3

Insert only necessary commas in the following sentences. Remove unnecessary commas with the delete sign (⌐). In the space provided, indicate the number of commas inserted or deleted in each sentence. If a sentence requires no changes, write C. When you finish, compare your responses with those provided. For each item on which you need review, consult the numbered principle shown in parentheses.

1. We expected Anna Cortez not Tyler Rosen to conduct the audit.
2. Brian said "We simply must have a bigger budget to start this project."
3. "We simply must have" said Brian "a bigger budget to start this project."
4. In August customers opened at least 50 new accounts; in September only about 20.
5. You returned the merchandise last month didn't you?
6. In short employees will now be expected to contribute more to their own retirement funds.
7. The better our advertising and recruiting the stronger our personnel pool will be.
8. Mrs. Delgado investigated selling her stocks not her real estate to raise the necessary cash.
9. "On the contrary" said Mr. Stevens "we will continue our present marketing strategies."
10. Our company will expand into surprising new areas such as, women's apparel and fast foods.
11. What we need is more not fewer suggestions for improvement.
12. Randall Clark Esq. and Jonathon Georges MBA joined the firm.
13. "America is now entering" said President Saunders "the Age of Information."
14. One of the reasons that we are inquiring about the publisher of the software is, that we are concerned about whether that publisher will be in the market five years from now.
15. The talk by D. A. Spindler PhD was particularly difficult to follow because of his technical and abstract vocabulary.
16. The month before a similar disruption occurred in distribution.
17. We are very fortunate to have, at our disposal, the services of excellent professionals.
18. No matter what you can count on us for support.
19. Mrs. Sandoval was named legislative counsel; Mr. Freeman executive advisor.
20. The data you are seeking can be found in an article entitled, "The Fastest Growing Games in Computers."

1. Cortez, Rosen, (2.12)   3. have," said Brian, (2.14a)   5. month, (2.14b)   7. recruiting, (2.12)
9. contrary," Stevens, (2.14a)   11. more, not fewer, (2.12)   13. entering," Saunders, (2.14a)
15. Spindler, PhD, (2.10)   17. have at our disposal (2.15)   19. Freeman, (2.11)

Cumulative Editing Quiz 4

Use proofreading marks (see Appendix B) to correct errors and omissions in the following sentences. All errors must be corrected to receive credit for the sentence. Check with your instructor for the answers.

1. Business documents must be written clear, to ensure that readers comprehend the message quick.
2. Needless to say the safety of our employees have always been most important to the president and I.
3. The Small Business Administration which provide disaster loans are setting up an office in Miami Florida.
4. Many entrepreneurs who want to expand there markets, have choosen to advertise heavy.
5. Our arbitration committee have unanimously agreed on a compromise package but management have been slow to respond.
6. Although the business was founded in the 1970's its real expansion took place in the 1990s.
7. According to the printed contract either the dealer or the distributor are responsible for repair of the product.
8. Next June, Lamont and Jones, Inc., are moving their headquarters to Denton Texas.
9. Our company is looking for intelligent, articulate, young, people who has a desire to grow with an expanding organization.
10. As you are aware each member of the jury were asked to avoid talking about the case.

Semicolons (2.16)
2.16 Independent Clauses, Series, Introductory Expressions

a. **Independent clauses with conjunctive adverbs.** Use a semicolon before a conjunctive adverb that separates two independent clauses. Some of the most common conjunctive adverbs are *therefore, consequently, however,* and *moreover*:

> Business messages should sound conversational; *therefore,* writers often use familiar words and contractions.

> The bank closes its doors at 5 p.m.; *however,* the ATM is open 24 hours a day.

> Notice that the word following a semicolon is *not* capitalized (unless, of course, that word is a proper noun).

b. **Independent clauses without conjunctive adverbs.** Use a semicolon to separate closely related independent clauses when no conjunctive adverb is used:

> Bond interest payments are tax deductible; dividend payments are not.

> Ambient lighting fills the room; task lighting illuminates each workstation.

> Use a semicolon in *compound* sentences, not in *complex* sentences:

> After one week the paper feeder jammed; we tried different kinds of paper. (Use a semicolon in a compound sentence.)

> After one week the paper feeder jammed, although we tried different kinds of paper. (Use a comma in a complex sentence. Do not use a semicolon after *jammed.*)

The semicolon is very effective for joining two closely related thoughts. Don't use it, however, unless the ideas are truly related.

c. **Independent clauses with other commas.** Normally, a comma precedes *and, or,* and *but* when those conjunctions join independent clauses. However, if either clause contains commas, change the comma preceding the conjunction to a semicolon to ensure correct reading:

> If you arrive in time, you may be able to purchase a ticket; but ticket sales close promptly at 8 p.m.

> Our primary concern is financing; and we have discovered, as you warned us, that money sources are quite scarce.

d. **Series with internal commas.** Use semicolons to separate items in a series when one or more of the items contains internal commas:

> Delegates from Miami, Florida; Freeport, Mississippi; and Chatsworth, California, attended the conference.

> The speakers were Kevin Lang, manager, Riko Enterprises; Henry Holtz, vice president, Trendex, Inc.; and Margaret Slater, personnel director, West Coast Productions.

e. **Introductory expressions.** Use a semicolon when an introductory expression such as *namely, for instance, that is,* or *for example* introduces a list following an independent clause:

> Switching to computerized billing are several local companies; namely, Ryson Electronics, Miller Vending Services, and Black Advertising.

> The author of a report should consider many sources; for example, books, periodicals, databases, and newspapers.

Colons (2.17–2.19)
2.17 Listed Items

a. **With colon.** Use a colon after a complete thought that introduces a formal list of items. A formal list is often preceded by such words and phrases as *these, thus, the following,* and *as follows.* A colon is also used when words and phrases like these are implied but not stated:

> Additional costs in selling a house involve *the following*: title examination fee, title insurance costs, and closing fee. (Use a colon when a complete thought introduces a formal list.)

> Collective bargaining focuses on several key issues: cost-of-living adjustments, fringe benefits, job security, and work hours. (The introduction of the list is implied in the preceding clause.)

b. **Without colons.** Do not use a colon when the list immediately follows a *to be* verb or a preposition:

> The employees who should receive the preliminary plan are James Sears, Monica Spears, and Rose Lopez. (No colon is used after the verb *are*.)

> We expect to consider equipment for Accounting, Legal Services, and Payroll. (No colon is used after the preposition *for*.)

2.18 Quotations. Use a colon to introduce long one-sentence quotations and quotations of two or more sentences:

> Our consultant said: "This system can support up to 32 users. It can be used for decision support, computer-aided design, and software development operations at the same time."

2.19 Salutations. Use a colon after the salutation of a business letter:

Gentlemen: Dear Mrs. Seaman: Dear Jamie:

Review Exercise J—Semicolons, Colons

In the following sentences, add semicolons, colons, and necessary commas. For each sentence indicate the number of punctuation marks that you add. If a sentence requires no punctuation, write C. When you finish, compare your responses with those provided. For each item on which you need review, consult the numbered principle shown in parentheses.

1. Technological advances make full-motion video viewable on small screens consequently mobile phone makers and carriers are rolling out new services and phones.

2. Our branch in Sherman Oaks specializes in industrial real estate our branch in Canoga Park concentrates on residential real estate.

3. The sedan version of the automobile is available in these colors Olympic red metallic silver and Aztec gold.

4. If I can assist the new manager please call me however I will be gone from June 10 through June 15.

5. The individuals who should receive copies of this announcement are Jeff Doogan Alicia Green and Kim Wong.

6. We would hope of course to send personal letters to all prospective buyers but we have not yet decided just how to do this.

7. Many of our potential customers are in Southern California therefore our promotional effort will be strongest in that area.

8. Since the first of the year we have received inquiries from one attorney two accountants and one information systems analyst.

9. Three dates have been reserved for initial interviews January 15 February 1 and February 12.

10. Several staff members are near the top of their salary ranges and we must reclassify their jobs.

11. Several staff members are near the top of their salary ranges we must reclassify their jobs.

12. Several staff members are near the top of their salary ranges therefore we must reclassify their jobs.

13. If you open an account within two weeks you will receive a free cookbook moreover your first 500 checks will be imprinted at no cost to you.

14. Monthly reports from the following departments are missing Legal Department Human Resources Department and Engineering Department.

15. Monthly reports are missing from the Legal Department Human Resources Department and Engineering Department.

16. Since you became director of that division sales have tripled therefore I am recommending you for a bonus.

17. The convention committee is considering Portland Oregon New Orleans Louisiana and Phoenix Arizona.

18. Several large companies allow employees access to their personnel files namely General Electric Eastman Kodak and Infodata.

19. Sherry first asked about salary next she inquired about benefits.

20. Sherry first asked about the salary and she next inquired about benefits.

---

1. screens; consequently, (2.16a)   3. colors: Olympic red, metallic silver, (2.01, 2.17a)
5. Doogan, Alicia Green, (2.01, 2.17b)   7. California; therefore, (2.16a)   9. interviews: January 15, February 1, (2.01, 2.17a)   11. ranges; (2.16b)   13. weeks, cookbook; moreover, (206a, 2.16a)   15. Department, Human Resources Department, (2.01, 2.17b)   17. Portland, Oregon; New Orleans, Louisiana; Phoenix, (2.16d)   19. salary; (2.16b)

Apostrophes (2.20–2.22)

2.20 Basic Rule. The apostrophe is used to show ownership, origin, authorship, or measurement.

Ownership: We are looking for *Brian's keys*.
Origin: At the *president's suggestion*, we doubled the order.
Authorship: The *accountant's annual report* was questioned.
Measurement: In *two years' time* we expect to reach our goal.

a. **Ownership words not ending in s.** To place the apostrophe correctly, you must first determine whether the ownership word ends in an *s* sound. If it does not, add an apostrophe and an *s* to the ownership word. The following examples show ownership words that do not end in an *s* sound:

the employee's file	(the file of a single employee)
a member's address	(the address of a single member)
a year's time	(the time of a single year)
a month's notice	(notice of a single month)
the company's building	(the building of a single company)

b. **Ownership words ending in s.** If the ownership word does end in an *s* sound, usually add only an apostrophe:

several employees' files	(files of several employees)
ten members' addresses	(addresses of ten members)
five years' time	(time of five years)
several months' notice	(notice of several months)
many companies' buildings	(buildings of many companies)

A few singular nouns that end in *s* are pronounced with an extra syllable when they become possessive. To these words, add *'s.*

   my boss's desk   the waitress's table   the actress's costume

Use no apostrophe if a noun is merely plural, not possessive:

All the sales representatives, as well as the assistants and managers, had their names and telephone numbers listed in the directory.

2.21 Names. The writer may choose either traditional or popular style in making singular names that end in an *s* sound possessive. The traditional style uses the apostrophe plus an *s*, whereas the popular style uses just the apostrophe. Note that only with singular names ending in an *s* sound does this option exist.

Traditional style	Popular style
Russ's computer	Russ' computer
Mr. Jones's car	Mr. Jones' car
Mrs. Morris's desk	Mrs. Morris' desk
Ms. Horowitz's job	Ms. Horowitz' job

The possessive form of plural names is consistent: the Joneses' car, the Horowitzes' home, the Lopezes' daughter.

2.22 Gerunds. Use *'s* to make a noun possessive when it precedes a gerund, a verb form used as a noun:

Mr. Smith's smoking prompted a new office policy. (*Mr. Smith* is possessive because it modifies the gerund *smoking*.)

It was Betsy's careful proofreading that revealed the discrepancy.

Review Exercise K—Apostrophes

Insert necessary apostrophes in the following sentences. In the space provided for each sentence, write the corrected word. If none were corrected, write C. When you finish, compare your responses with those provided. For each item on which you need review, consult the numbered principle shown in parentheses.

1. In five years time Lisa hopes to repay all of her student loans.

2. If you go to the third floor, you will find Mr. Londons office.

3. All the employees personnel folders must be updated.

4. In a little over a years time, that firm was able to double its sales.

5. The Harrises daughter lived in Florida for two years.

6. An inventors patent protects his or her invention for 17 years.

7. Both companies headquarters will be moved within the next six months.

8. That position requires at least two years experience.

9. Some of their assets could be liquidated; therefore, a few of the creditors received funds.

10. All secretaries workstations were equipped with Internet access.

11. The package of electronics parts arrived safely despite two weeks delay.

12. Many nurses believe that nurses notes are not admissable evidence.

13. According to Mr. Cortez latest proposal, all employees would receive an additional holiday.

14. Many of our members names and addresses must be checked.

15. His supervisor frequently had to correct Jacks financial reports.

16. We believe that this firms service is much better than that firms.

17. Mr. Jackson estimated that he spent a years profits in reorganizing his staff.

18. After paying six months rent, we were given a receipt.

19. The contract is not valid without Mrs. Harris signature.

20. It was Mr. Smiths signing of the contract that made us happy.

---

1. years' (2.20b)   3. employees' (2.20b)   5. Harrises' (2.21)   7. companies' (2.20b)   9. C (2.20b)
11. weeks' (2.20b)   13. Cortez' or Cortez's (2.21)   15. Jack's (2.21)   17. year's (2.20a)
19. Harris' or Harris's (2.21)

Cumulative Editing Quiz 5

Use proofreading marks (see Appendix B) to correct errors and omissions in the following sentences. All errors must be corrected to receive credit for the sentence. Check with your instructor for the answers.

1. The three C's of credit are the following character capacity and capital.

2. We hope that we will not have to sell the property however that may be our only option.

3. As soon as the supervisor and her can check this weeks sales they will place an order.

4. Any of the auditors are authorized to proceed with an independent action however only the CEO can alter the councils directives.

5. Although reluctant technicians sometimes must demonstrate there computer software skills.

6. On April 6 2009 we opened an innovative fully-equipped fitness center.

7. A list of maintenance procedures and recommendations are in the owners manual.

8. The Morrises son lived in Flint Michigan however there daughter lived in Albany New York.

9. Employment interviews were held in Dallas Texas Miami Florida and Chicago Illinois.

10. Mr. Lees determination courage and sincerity could not be denied however his methods was often questioned.

Other Punctuation (2.23–2.29)

2.23 Periods

a. **Ends of sentences.** Use a period at the end of a statement, command, indirect question, or polite request. Although a polite request may have the same structure as a question, it ends with a period:

> Corporate legal departments demand precise skills from their workforce. (End a statement with a period.)

> Get the latest data by reading current periodicals. (End a command with a period.)

> Mr. Rand wondered whether we had sent any follow-up literature. (End an indirect question with a period.)

> Would you please reexamine my account and determine the current balance. (A polite request suggests an action rather than a verbal response.)

b. **Abbreviations and initials.** Use periods after initials and after many abbreviations.

R. M. Johnson	c.o.d.	Ms.
p.m.	a.m.	Mr.
Inc.	i.e.	Mrs.

The latest trend is to omit periods in degrees and professional designations: BA, PhD, MD, RN, DDS.

Use just one period when an abbreviation falls at the end of a sentence:

> Guests began arriving at 5:30 p.m.

2.24 Question Marks. Direct questions are followed by question marks:

> Did you send your proposal to Datatronix, Inc.?

Statements with questions added are punctuated with question marks.

> We have completed the proposal, haven't we?

2.25 Exclamation Points. Use an exclamation point after a word, phrase, or clause expressing strong emotion. In business writing, however, exclamation points should be used sparingly:

> Incredible! Every terminal is down.

2.26 Dashes. The dash (constructed at a keyboard by striking the hyphen key twice in succession) is a legitimate and effective mark of punctuation when used according to accepted conventions. As an emphatic punctuation mark, however, the dash loses effectiveness when overused.

a. **Parenthetical elements.** Within a sentence a parenthetical element is usually set off by commas. If, however, the parenthetical element itself contains internal commas, use dashes (or parentheses) to set it off:

> Three top salespeople—Tom Judkins, Tim Templeton, and Mary Yashimoto—received bonuses.

b. **Sentence interruptions.** Use a dash to show an interruption or abrupt change of thought:

> News of the dramatic merger—no one believed it at first—shook the financial world.

> Ship the materials Monday—no, we must have them sooner.

Sentences with abrupt changes of thought or with appended afterthoughts can usually be improved through rewriting.

c. **Summarizing statements.** Use a dash (not a colon) to separate an introductory list from a summarizing statement:

> Sorting, merging, and computing—these are tasks that our data processing programs must perform.

2.27 Parentheses. One means of setting off nonessential sentence elements involves the use of parentheses. Nonessential sentence elements may be punctuated in one of three ways: (a) with commas, to make the lightest possible break in the normal flow of a sentence; (b) with dashes, to emphasize the enclosed material; and (c) with parentheses, to de-emphasize the enclosed material. Parentheses are frequently used to punctuate sentences with interpolated directions, explanations, questions, and references:

> The cost analysis (which appears on page 8 of the report) indicates that the copy machine should be leased.

> Units are lightweight (approximately 13 oz.) and come with a leather case and operating instructions.

> The latest laser printer (have you heard about it?) will be demonstrated for us next week.

A parenthetical sentence that is not embedded within another sentence should be capitalized and punctuated with end punctuation:

> The Model 20 has stronger construction. (You may order a Model 20 brochure by circling 304 on the reader service card.)

2.28 Quotation Marks

a. **Direct quotations.** Use double quotation marks to enclose the exact words of a speaker or writer:

> "Keep in mind," Mrs. Frank said, "that you'll have to justify the cost of networking our office."

> The boss said that automation was inevitable. (No quotation marks are needed because the exact words are not quoted.)

b. **Quotations within quotations.** Use single quotation marks (apostrophes on the keyboard) to enclose quoted passages within quoted passages:

> In her speech, Mrs. Deckman remarked, "I believe it was the poet Robert Frost who said, 'All the fun's in how you say a thing.'"

c. **Short expressions.** Slang, words used in a special sense, and words following *stamped* or *marked* are often enclosed within quotation marks:

> Jeffrey described the damaged shipment as "gross." (Quotation marks enclose slang.)

> Students often have trouble spelling the word "separate." (Quotation marks enclose words used in a special sense.)

Jobs were divided into two categories: most stressful and least stressful. The jobs in the "most stressful" list involved high risk or responsibility. (Quotation marks enclose words used in a special sense.)

The envelope marked "Confidential" was put aside. (Quotation marks enclose words following *marked*.)

In the four preceding sentences, the words enclosed within quotation marks can be set in italics, if italics are available.

d. **Definitions.** Double quotation marks are used to enclose definitions. The word or expression being defined should be underscored or set in italics:

The term *penetration pricing* is defined as "the practice of introducing a product to the market at a low price."

e. **Titles.** Use double quotation marks to enclose titles of literary and artistic works, such as magazine and newspaper articles, chapters of books, movies, television shows, poems, lectures, and songs. Names of major publications—such as books, magazines, pamphlets, and newspapers—are set in italics (underscored) or typed in capital letters.

Particularly helpful was the chapter in Smith's EFFECTIVE WRITING TECHNIQUES entitled "Right Brain, Write On!"

In the *Los Angeles Times* appeared John's article, "E-Mail Blunders"; however, we could not locate it in a local library.

f. **Additional considerations.** In this country periods and commas are always placed inside closing quotation marks. Semicolons and colons, on the other hand, are always placed outside quotation marks:

Mrs. James said, "I could not find the article entitled 'Cell Phone Etiquette.'"

The president asked for "absolute security": All written messages were to be destroyed.

Question marks and exclamation points may go inside or outside closing quotation marks, as determined by the form of the quotation:

Sales Manager Martin said, "Who placed the order?" (The quotation is a question.)

When did the sales manager say, "Who placed the order?" (Both the incorporating sentence and the quotation are questions.)

Did the sales manager say, "Ryan placed the order"? (The incorporating sentence asks a question; the quotation does not.)

"In the future," shouted Bob, "ask me first!" (The quotation is an exclamation.)

2.29 Brackets. Within quotations, brackets are used by the quoting writer to enclose his or her own inserted remarks. Such remarks may be corrective, illustrative, or explanatory:

Mrs. Cardillo said, "OSHA [Occupational Safety and Health Administration] has been one of the most widely criticized agencies of the federal government."

Review Exercise L—Other Punctuation

Insert necessary punctuation in the following sentences. In the space provided for each item, indicate the number of punctuation marks that you added. Count sets of parentheses, dashes, and quotation marks as two marks. Emphasis or de-emphasis will be indicated for some parenthetical elements. When you finish, compare your responses with those provided. For each item on which you need review, consult the numbered principle shown in parentheses.

1. Will you please send me your latest catalog
2. (Emphasize) Three of my friends Carmen Lopez, Stan Meyers, and Ivan Sergo were all promoted.
3. Mr Lee, Miss Evans, and Mrs Rivera have not responded.
4. We have scheduled your interview for 4 45 p m
5. (De-emphasize) The appliance comes in limited colors black, ivory, and beige, but we accept special orders.
6. The expression de facto means exercising power as if legally constituted.
7. Was it the president who said "This, too, will pass
8. Should this package be marked Fragile
9. Did you see the Newsweek article titled How Far Can Wireless Go
10. Amazing All sales reps made their targets

---

1. catalog. (2.23a)   3. Mr. Mrs. (2.23a)   5. colors (black, ivory, and beige) (2.26a)
7. said, pass"?   9. *Newsweek* "How Go?" (2.28e)

Cumulative Editing Quiz 6

Use proofreading marks (see Appendix B) to correct errors and omissions in the following sentences. All errors must be corrected to receive credit for the sentence. Check with your instructor for the answers.

1. Although the envelope was marked Confidential the vice presidents secretary thought it should be opened.
2. Would you please send my order c.o.d?
3. To be eligible for an apartment you must pay two months rent in advance.
4. We wanted to use Russ computer, but forgot to ask for permission.
5. Wasnt it Jeff Song not Eileen Lee who requested a 14 day leave.
6. Miss. Judith L. Beam is the employee who the employees council elected as their representative.
7. The Evening Post Dispatch our local newspaper featured an article entitled The Worlds Most Expensive Memo.
8. As soon as my manager or myself can verify Ricks totals we will call you, in the meantime you must continue to disburse funds.
9. Just inside the entrance, is the receptionists desk and a complete directory of all departments'.
10. Exports from small companys has increased thereby affecting this countrys trade balance positively.

Style and Usage

Capitalization (3.01–3.16)
Capitalization is used to distinguish important words. However, writers are not free to capitalize all words they consider important. Rules or guidelines governing capitalization style have been established through custom and use. Mastering these guidelines will make your writing more readable and more comprehensible.

3.01 Proper Nouns. Capitalize proper nouns, including the *specific* names of persons, places, schools, streets, parks, buildings, religions, holidays, months, agreements, programs, services, and so forth. Do not capitalize common nouns that make only *general* references.

Proper nouns	Common nouns
Michael DeNiro	a salesperson in electronics
Germany, Japan	U.S. trading partners
El Camino College	a community college
Sam Houston Park	a park in the city
Phoenix Room, Statler Inn	a meeting room in the hotel
Catholic, Presbyterian	two religions
Memorial Day, New Year's Day	two holidays
Express Mail	a special package delivery service
George Washington Bridge	a bridge
Consumer Product Safety Act	a law to protect consumers
Orlando Chamber of Commerce	a chamber of commerce
Will Rogers World Airport	a municipal airport

3.02 Proper Adjectives. Capitalize most adjectives that are derived from proper nouns:

Greek symbol	British thermal unit
Roman numeral	Norwegian ship
Xerox copy	Hispanic markets

Do not capitalize the few adjectives that, although originally derived from proper nouns, have become common adjectives through usage. Consult your dictionary when in doubt:

manila folder	diesel engine
india ink	china dishes

3.03 Geographic Locations. Capitalize the names of *specific* places such as cities, states, mountains, valleys, lakes, rivers, oceans, and geographic regions:

New York City	Great Salt Lake
Allegheny Mountains	Pacific Ocean
San Fernando Valley	Delaware Bay
the East Coast	the Pacific Northwest

3.04 Organization Names. Capitalize the principal words in the names of all business, civic, educational, governmental, labor, military, philanthropic, political, professional, religious, and social organizations:

Matrix Steel Company	Board of Directors, Midwest Bank
*The Wall Street Journal**	San Antonio Museum of Art
New York Stock Exchange	Securities and Exchange Commission
United Way	National Association of Letter Carriers
Commission to Restore the Statue of Liberty	Association of Information Systems Professionals

---

*Note: Capitalize *the* only when it is part of the official name of an organization, as printed on the organization's stationery.

3.05 Academic Courses and Degrees. Capitalize particular academic degrees and course titles. Do not capitalize general academic degrees and subject areas:

> Professor Bernadette Ordian, *PhD,* will teach *Accounting* 221 next fall.
>
> Mrs. Snyder, who holds *bachelor's* and *master's degrees,* teaches *marketing* classes.
>
> Jim enrolled in classes in *history, business English,* and *management.*

3.06 Personal and Business Titles

a. Capitalize personal and business titles when they precede names:

Vice President Ames	Uncle Edward
Board Chairman Frazier	Councilman Herbert
Governor G. W. Thurmond	Sales Manager Klein
Professor McLean	Dr. Samuel Washington

b. Capitalize titles in addresses, salutations, and closing lines:

Mr. Juan deSanto	Very truly yours,
Director of Purchasing	
Space Systems, Inc.	Clara J. Smith
Boxborough, MA 01719	Supervisor, Marketing

c. Generally, do not capitalize titles of high government rank or religious office when they stand alone or follow a person's name in running text.

> The president conferred with the joint chiefs of staff and many senators.
>
> Meeting with the chief justice of the Supreme Court were the senator from Ohio and the mayor of Cleveland.
>
> Only the cardinal from Chicago had an audience with the pope.

d. Do not capitalize most common titles following names:

> The speech was delivered by Robert Lynch, *president,* Academic Publishing.
>
> Lois Herndon, *chief executive officer,* signed the order.

e. Do not capitalize common titles appearing alone:

> Please speak to the *supervisor* or to the *office manager.*
>
> Neither the *president* nor the *vice president* could attend.

However, when the title of an official appears in that organization's minutes, bylaws, or other official document, it may be capitalized.

f. Do not capitalize titles when they are followed by appositives naming specific individuals:

> We must consult our *director of research,* Ronald E. West, before responding.

g. Do not capitalize family titles used with possessive pronouns:

my mother	your father
our aunt	his cousin

h. Capitalize titles of close relatives used without pronouns:

> Both *Mother* and *Father* must sign the contract.

3.07 Numbered and Lettered Items. Capitalize nouns followed by numbers or letters (except in page, paragraph, line, and verse references):

Flight 34, Gate 12	Plan No. 2
Volume I, Part 3	Warehouse 33-A
Invoice No. 55489	Figure 8.3
Model A5673	Serial No. C22865404-2
State Highway 10	page 6, line 5

3.08 Points of the Compass. Capitalize *north, south, east, west,* and their derivatives when they represent *specific* geographical regions. Do not capitalize the points of the compass when they are used in directions or in general references.

Specific regions	General references
from the South	heading north on the highway
living in the Midwest	west of the city
Easterners, Southerners	western Nevada, southern Indiana
going to the Middle East	the northern part of the United States
from the East Coast	the east side of the street

3.09 Departments, Divisions, and Committees. Capitalize the names of departments, divisions, or committees within your own organization. Outside your organization capitalize only *specific* department, division, or committee names:

The inquiry was addressed to the *Legal Department* in our *Consumer Products Division.*

John was appointed to the *Employee Benefits Committee.*

Send your résumé to their *human resources division.*

A *planning committee* will be named shortly.

3.10 Governmental Terms. Do not capitalize the words *federal, government, nation,* or *state* unless they are part of a specific title:

Unless *federal* support can be secured, the *state* project will be abandoned.

The *Federal Deposit Insurance Corporation* protects depositors from bank failure.

3.11 Product Names. Capitalize product names only when they refer to trademarked items. Except in advertising, common names following manufacturers' names are not capitalized:

Magic Marker	Dell computer
Kleenex tissues	Swingline stapler
Q-tips	3M diskettes
Levi 501 jeans	Sony dictation machine
DuPont Teflon	Canon camera

3.12 Literary Titles. Capitalize the principal words in the titles of books, magazines, newspapers, articles, movies, plays, songs, poems, and reports. Do *not* capitalize articles (*a, an, the*), short conjunctions (*and, but, or, nor*), and prepositions of fewer than four letters (*in, to, by, for*) unless they begin or end the title:

Jackson's *What Job Is for You?* (Capitalize book titles.)

Gant's "Software for the Executive Suite" (Capitalize principal words in article titles.)

"Performance Standards to Go By" (Capitalize article titles.)

"The Improvement of Fuel Economy With Alternative Fuels" (Capitalize report titles.)

3.13 Beginning Words. In addition to capitalizing the first word of a complete sentence, capitalize the first word in a quoted sentence, independent phrase, item in an enumerated list, and formal rule or principle following a colon:

The business manager said, "*All* purchases must have requisitions." (Capitalize first word in a quoted sentence.)

Yes, if you agree. (Capitalize an independent phrase.)

Some of the duties of the position are as follows:
1. *Editing* and formatting Word files
2. *Arranging* video and teleconferences
3. *Verifying* records, reports, and applications (Capitalize items in an enumerated list.)

One rule has been established through the company: *No* smoking is allowed in open offices. (Capitalize a rule following a colon.)

3.14 Celestial Bodies. Capitalize the names of celestial bodies such as *Mars, Saturn,* and *Neptune.* Do not capitalize the terms *earth, sun,* or *moon* unless they appear in a context with other celestial bodies:

Where on *earth* did you find that manual typewriter?

Venus and *Mars* are the closest planets to *Earth.*

3.15 Ethnic References. Capitalize terms that refer to a particular culture, language, or race:

Asian	Hebrew
Caucasian	Indian
Latino	Japanese
Persian	Judeo-Christian

3.16 Seasons. Do not capitalize seasons:

In the *fall* it appeared that *winter* and *spring* sales would increase.

Review Exercise M—Capitalization

In the following sentences correct any errors that you find in capitalization. Underscore any lowercase letter that should be changed to a capital letter. Draw a slash (/) through a capital letter that you wish to change to a lowercase letter. In the space provided, indicate the total number of changes you have made in each sentence. If you make no changes, write *0.* When you finish, compare your responses with those provided. For each item on which you need review, consult the numbered principle shown in parentheses.

Example Bill McAdams, currently Assistant Manager in our Personnel department, will be promoted to Manager of the Employee Services division.   5

1. The social security act, passed in 1935, established the present system of social security.

2. Our company will soon be moving its operations to the west coast.

3. Marilyn Hunter, mba, received her bachelor's degree from Ohio university in athens.

4. The President of Datatronics, Inc., delivered a speech entitled "Taking off into the future."

5. Please ask your Aunt and your Uncle if they will come to the Attorney's office at 5 p.m.

6. Your reservations are for flight 32 on american airlines leaving from gate 14 at 2:35 p.m.

7. Once we establish an organizing committee, arrangements can be made to rent holmby hall.

8. Bob was enrolled in history, spanish, business communications, and physical education courses.

9. Either the President or the Vice President of the company will make the decision about purchasing xerox copiers.

10. Rules for hiring and firing Employees are given on page 7, line 24, of the Contract.

11. Some individuals feel that american companies do not have the sense of loyalty to their employees that japanese companies do.

12. Where on Earth can we find better workers than Robots?

13. The secretary of state said, "we must protect our domestic economy from Foreign competition."

14. After crossing the sunshine skyway bridge, we drove to Southern Florida for our vacation.

15. All marketing representatives of our company will meet in the empire room of the red lion motor inn.

16. Richard Elkins, phd, has been named director of research for spaceage strategies, inc.

17. The special keyboard for the Dell Computer must contain greek symbols for Engineering equations.

18. After she received a master's degree in electrical engineering, Joanne Dudley was hired to work in our product development department.

19. In the Fall our organization will move its corporate headquarters to the franklin building in downtown los angeles.

20. Dean Amador has one cardinal rule: always be punctual.

---

1. Social Security Act (3.01) 3. MBA University Athens (3.01, 3.05) 5. aunt uncle attorney's (3.06e, 3.06g) 7. Holmby Hall (3.01) 9. president vice president Xerox (3.06e, 3.11) 11. American Japanese (3.02) 13. We foreign (3.10, 3.13) 15. Empire Room Red Lion Motor Inn (3.01) 17. computer Greek engineering (3.01, 3.02, 3.11) 19. fall Franklin Building Los Angeles (3.01, 3.03, 3.16)

Cumulative Editing Quiz 7

Use proofreading marks (see Appendix B) to correct errors and omissions in the following sentences. All errors must be corrected to receive credit for the sentence. Check with your instructor for the answers.

1. The Manager thinks that you attending the three day seminar is a good idea, however we must find a replacement.

2. We heard that professor watson invited edward peters, president of micropro, inc. to speak to our business law class.

3. Carla Jones a new systems programmer in our accounting department will start monday.

4. After year's of downsizing and restructuring the u.s. has now become one of the worlds most competitive producers.

5. When our company specialized in asian imports our main office was on the west coast.

6. Company's such as amway discovered that there unique door to door selling methods was very successful in japan.

7. If you had given your sony camera to she or I before you got on the roller coaster it might have stayed dry.

8. Tracy recently finished a bachelors degree in accounting, consequently she is submitting many résumé's to companys across the country.

9. The Lopezs moved from San Antonio Texas to Urbana Illinois when mr lopez enrolled at the university of illinois.

10. When we open our office in montréal we will need employees whom are fluent in english and french.

Number Style (4.01–4.13)

Usage and custom determine whether numbers are expressed in the form of figures (for example, *5, 9*) or in the form of words (for example, *five, nine*). Numbers expressed as figures are shorter and more easily understood, yet numbers expressed as words are necessary in certain instances. The following guidelines are observed in expressing numbers in written sentences. Numbers that appear on business forms—such as invoices, monthly statements, and purchase orders—are always expressed as figures.

4.01 General Rules

a. The numbers *one* through *ten* are generally written as words. Numbers above *ten* are written as figures:

The bank had a total of *nine* branch offices in *three* suburbs.

All *58* employees received benefits in the *three* categories shown.

A shipment of *45,000* light bulbs was sent from *two* warehouses.

b. Numbers that begin sentences are written as words. If a number beginning a sentence involves more than two words, however, the sentence should be written so that the number does not fall at the beginning.

Fifteen different options were available in the annuity programs.

A total of 156 companies participated in the promotion (not *One hundred fifty-six companies participated in the promotion*).

4.02 Money. Sums of money $1 or greater are expressed as figures. If a sum is a whole dollar amount, omit the decimal and zeros (whether or not the amount appears in a sentence with additional fractional dollar amounts):

We budgeted *$300* for a digital camera, but the actual cost was *$370.96*.

On the invoice were items for *$6.10, $8, $33.95,* and *$75*.

Sums less than $1 are written as figures that are followed by the word *cents*:

By shopping carefully, we can save *15 cents* per unit.

4.03 Dates. In dates, numbers that appear after the name of the month are written as cardinal figures (*1, 2, 3,* etc.). Those that stand alone or appear before the name of a month are written as ordinal figures (*1st, 2nd, 3rd,* etc.):

The Personnel Practices Committee will meet *May 7*.

On the *5th* day of February and again on the *25th,* we placed orders.

In domestic business documents, dates generally take the following form: *January 4, 2009.* An alternative form, used primarily in military and foreign correspondence, begins with the day of the month and omits the comma: *4 January 2009.*

4.04 Clock Time. Figures are used when clock time is expressed with *a.m.* or *p.m.* Omit the colon and zeros in referring to whole hours. When exact clock time is expressed with the contraction *o'clock,* either figures or words may be used:

Mail deliveries are made at *11 a.m.* and *3:30 p.m.*

At *four* (or *4*) *o'clock* employees begin to leave.

4.05 Addresses and Telephone Numbers

a. Except for the number *one,* house numbers are expressed in figures:

540 Elm Street	17802 Washington Avenue
One Colorado Boulevard	2 Highland Street

b. Street names containing numbers *ten* or lower are written entirely as words. For street names involving numbers greater than *ten,* figures are used:

330 Third Street	3440 Seventh Avenue
6945 East 32nd Avenue	4903 West 23rd Street

c. Telephone numbers are expressed with figures. When used, the area code is placed in parentheses preceding the telephone number:

Please call us at *(818) 347-0551* to place an order.

Mr. Sims asked you to call *(619) 554-8923,* Ext. 245, after 10 a.m.

4.06 Related Numbers. Numbers are related when they refer to similar items in a category within the same reference. All related numbers should be expressed as the largest number is expressed. Thus if the largest number is greater than *ten,* all the numbers should be expressed in figures:

Only *5* of the original *25* applicants completed the processing. (Related numbers require figures.)

The *two* plans affected *34* employees working in *three* sites. (Unrelated numbers use figures and words.)

Exxon Oil operated *86* rigs, of which *6* were rented. (Related numbers require figures.)

The company hired *three* accountants, *one* customer service representative, and *nine* sales representatives. (Related numbers under ten use words.)

4.07 Consecutive Numbers. When two numbers appear consecutively and both modify a following noun, generally express the first number in words and the second in figures. If, however, the first number cannot be expressed in one or two words, place it in figures also (*120 37-cent* stamps). Do not use commas to separate the figures.

Historians divided the era into *four 25-year* periods. (Use word form for the first number and figure form for the second.)

We ordered *ten 30-page* color brochures. (Use word form for the first number and figure form for the second.)

Did the manager request *150 100-watt* bulbs? (Use figure form for the first number since it would require more than two words.)

4.08 Periods of Time. Seconds, minutes, days, weeks, months, and years are treated as any other general number. Numbers above ten are written in figure form. Numbers below ten are written in word form unless they represent a business concept such as a discount rate, interest rate, or warranty period.

This business was incorporated over *50* years ago. (Use figures for a number above ten.)

It took *three* hours to write this short report. (Use words for a number under ten.)

The warranty period is limited to *2* years. (Use figures for a business term.)

4.09 Ages. Ages are generally expressed in word form unless the age appears immediately after a name or is expressed in exact years and months:

At the age of *twenty-one*, Elizabeth inherited the business.

Wanda Tharp, *37*, was named acting president.

At the age of *4 years and 7 months*, the child was adopted.

4.10 Round Numbers. Round numbers are approximations. They may be expressed in word or figure form, although figure form is shorter and easier to comprehend:

About *600* (or *six hundred*) stock options were sold.

It is estimated that *1,000* (or *one thousand*) people will attend.

For ease of reading, round numbers in the millions or billions should be expressed with a combination of figures and words:

At least *1.5 million* readers subscribe to the ten top magazines.

Deposits in money market accounts totaled more than *$115 billion*.

4.11 Weights and Measurements. Weights and measurements are expressed with figures:

The new deposit slip measures *2* by *6 inches*.

Her new suitcase weighed only *2 pounds 4 ounces*.

Toledo is *60 miles* from Detroit.

4.12 Fractions. Simple fractions are expressed as words. Complex fractions may be written either as figures or as a combination of figures and words:

Over *two thirds* of the stockholders voted.

This microcomputer will execute the command in *1 millionth* of a second. (A combination of words and numbers is easier to comprehend.)

She purchased a *one-fifth* share in the business.*

4.13 Percentages and Decimals. Percentages are expressed with figures that are followed by the word *percent*. The percent sign (%) is used only on business forms or in statistical presentations:

We had hoped for a *7 percent* interest rate, but we received a loan at *8 percent*.

Over *50 percent* of the residents supported the plan.

---

*Note: Fractions used as adjectives require hyphens.

Decimals are expressed with figures. If a decimal expression does not contain a whole number (an integer) and does not begin with a zero, a zero should be placed before the decimal point:

The actuarial charts show that *1.74* out of 1,000 people will die in any given year.

Inspector Norris found the setting to be *.005* inch off. (Decimal begins with a zero and does not require a zero before the decimal point.)

Considerable savings will accrue if the unit production cost is reduced *0.1* percent. (A zero is placed before a decimal that neither contains a whole number nor begins with a zero.)

Quick Chart—Expression of Numbers

Use Words	Use Figures
Numbers *ten* and under	Numbers *11* and over
Numbers at beginning of sentence	Money
Ages	Dates
Fractions	Addresses and telephone numbers
	Weights and measurements
	Percentages and decimals

Review Exercise N—Number Style

Circle *a* or *b* to indicate the preferred number style. Assume that these numbers appear in business correspondence. When you finish, compare your responses with those provided. For each item on which you need review, consult the numbered principle shown in parentheses.

1. (a) 2 alternatives (b) two alternatives
2. (a) Seventh Avenue (b) 7th Avenue
3. (a) sixty sales reps (b) 60 sales reps
4. (a) November ninth (b) November 9
5. (a) forty dollars (b) $40
6. (a) on the 23rd of May (b) on the twenty-third of May
7. (a) at 2:00 p.m. (b) at 2 p.m.
8. (a) 4 two-hundred-page books (b) four 200-page books
9. (a) at least 15 years ago (b) at least fifteen years ago
10. (a) 1,000,000 viewers (b) 1 million viewers
11. (a) twelve cents (b) 12 cents
12. (a) a sixty-day warranty (b) a 60-day warranty
13. (a) ten percent interest rate (b) 10 percent interest rate
14. (a) 4/5 of the voters (b) four fifths of the voters
15. (a) the rug measures four by six feet (b) the rug measures 4 by 6 feet
16. (a) about five hundred people attended (b) about 500 people attended
17. (a) at eight o'clock (b) at 8 o'clock
18. (a) located at 1 Wilshire Boulevard (b) located at One Wilshire Boulevard
19. (a) three computers for twelve people (b) three computers for 12 people
20. (a) 4 out of every 100 licenses (b) four out of every 100 licenses

1. b (4.01a)   3. b (4.01a)   5. b (4.02)   7. b (4.04)   9. a (4.08)   11. b (4.02)   13. b (4.13)
15. b (4.11)   17. a or b (4.04)   19. b (4.06)

Cumulative Editing Quiz 8

Use proofreading marks (see Appendix B) to correct errors and omissions in the following sentences. All errors must be corrected to receive credit for the sentence. Check with your instructor for the answers.

1. The president of the U.S. recommended a 30 day cooling off period in the middle east peace negotiations.
2. Please meet at my attorneys office at four p.m. on May 10th to sign our papers of incorporation.
3. A Retail Store at 405 7th avenue had sales of over one million dollars last year.
4. Every new employee must receive their permit to park in lot 5-A or there car will be cited.
5. Mr thompson left three million dollars to be divided among his 4 children rachel, timothy, rebecca and kevin.
6. Most companys can boost profits almost one hundred percent by retaining only 5% more of there current customers.
7. Although the bill for coffee and doughnuts were only three dollars and forty cents Phillip and myself had trouble paying it.
8. Only six of the 19 employees, who filled out survey forms, would have went to hawaii as their vacation choice.
9. Danielles report is more easier to read then david because her's is better organized and has good headings.
10. At mcdonald's we devoured 4 big macs 3 orders of french fries and 5 coca colas for lunch.

Confusing Words

accede:	to agree or consent	*apprise:*	to inform
exceed:	over a limit	*ascent:*	(n) rising or going up
accept:	to receive	*assent:*	(v) to agree or consent
except:	to exclude; (prep) but	*assure:*	to promise
adverse:	opposing; antagonistic	*ensure:*	to make certain
averse:	unwilling; reluctant	*insure:*	to protect from loss
advice:	suggestion, opinion	*capital:*	(n) city that is seat of government; wealth of an individual; (adj) chief
advise:	to counsel or recommend		
affect:	to influence		
effect:	(n) outcome, result; (v) to bring about, to create	*capitol:*	building that houses state or national lawmakers
all ready:	prepared	*cereal:*	breakfast food
already:	by this time	*serial:*	arranged in sequence
all right:	satisfactory	*cite:*	to quote; to summon
alright:	unacceptable variant spelling	*site:*	location
		sight:	a view; to see
altar:	structure for worship	*coarse:*	rough texture
alter:	to change	*course:*	a route; part of a meal; a unit of learning
appraise:	to estimate		

complement:	that which completes	loose:	not fastened
compliment:	(n) praise, flattery; (v) to praise or flatter	lose:	to misplace
		miner:	person working in a mine
conscience:	regard for fairness		
conscious:	aware	minor:	a lesser item; person under age
council:	governing body		
counsel:	(n) advice, attorney; (v) to give advice	patience:	calm perseverance
		patients:	people receiving medical treatment
credible:	believable		
creditable:	good enough for praise or esteem; reliable	personal:	private, individual
		personnel:	employees
desert:	arid land; to abandon	plaintiff:	(n) one who initiates a lawsuit
dessert:	sweet food		
device:	invention or mechanism	plaintive:	(adj) expressive of suffering or woe
devise:	to design or arrange	populace:	(n) the masses; population of a place
disburse:	to pay out		
disperse:	to scatter widely	populous:	(adj) densely populated
elicit:	to draw out		
illicit:	unlawful	precede:	to go before
envelop:	(v) to wrap, surround, or conceal	proceed:	to continue
		precedence:	priority
envelope:	(n) a container for a written message	precedents:	events used as an example
every day:	each single day	principal:	(n) capital sum; school official; (adj) chief
everyday:	ordinary		
farther:	a greater distance		
further:	additional	principle:	rule of action
formally:	in a formal manner	stationary:	immovable
formerly:	in the past	stationery:	writing material
grate:	(v) to reduce to small particles; to cause irritation; (n) a frame of crossed bars blocking a passage	than:	conjunction showing comparison
		then:	adverb meaning "at that time"
		their:	possessive form of *they*
great:	(adj) large in size; numerous; eminent or distinguished	there:	at that place or point
		they're:	contraction of *they are*
hole:	an opening	to:	a preposition; the sign of the infinitive
whole:	complete		
imply:	to suggest indirectly	too:	an adverb meaning "also" or "to an excessive extent"
infer:	to reach a conclusion		
lean:	(v) to rest against; (adj) not fat		
		two:	a number
lien:	(n) a legal right or claim to property	waiver:	abandonment of a claim
liable:	legally responsible		
libel:	damaging written statement	waver:	to shake or fluctuate

Grammar/Mechanics Handbook

160 Frequently Misspelled Words

absence	desirable	independent	prominent
accommodate	destroy	indispensable	qualify
achieve	development	interrupt	quantity
acknowledgment	disappoint	irrelevant	questionnaire
across	dissatisfied	itinerary	receipt
adequate	division	judgment	receive
advisable	efficient	knowledge	recognize
analyze	embarrass	legitimate	recommendation
annually	emphasis	library	referred
appointment	emphasize	license	regarding
argument	employee	maintenance	remittance
automatically	envelope	manageable	representative
bankruptcy	equipped	manufacturer	restaurant
becoming	especially	mileage	schedule
beneficial	evidently	miscellaneous	secretary
budget	exaggerate	mortgage	separate
business	excellent	necessary	similar
calendar	exempt	nevertheless	sincerely
canceled	existence	ninety	software
catalog	extraordinary	ninth	succeed
changeable	familiar	noticeable	sufficient
column	fascinate	occasionally	supervisor
committee	feasible	occurred	surprise
congratulate	February	offered	tenant
conscience	fiscal	omission	therefore
conscious	foreign	omitted	thorough
consecutive	forty	opportunity	though
consensus	fourth	opposite	through
consistent	friend	ordinarily	truly
control	genuine	paid	undoubtedly
convenient	government	pamphlet	unnecessarily
correspondence	grammar	permanent	usable
courteous	grateful	permitted	usage
criticize	guarantee	pleasant	using
decision	harass	practical	usually
deductible	height	prevalent	valuable
defendant	hoping	privilege	volume
definitely	immediate	probably	weekday
dependent	incidentally	procedure	writing
describe	incredible	profited	yield

Key to Grammar/Mechanics Checkups

Chapter 1
1. inquiries (1.05e) 2. C (1.05g) 3. companies (1.05e)
4. Saturdays (1.05a) 5. turkeys (1.05d) 6. Bushes (1.05b)
7. 2000s (1.05g) 8. editors in chief (1.05f) 9. complexes (1.05b)
10. counties (1.05e) 11. Cassidys (1.05a) 12. C (1.05d) 13. liabilities (1.05e) 14. C (1.05h) 15. women (1.05c)

Chapter 2
1. she (1.08b) 2. his (1.09b) 3. him (1.08c) 4. whom (1.08j)
5. hers (1.08d) 6. me (1.08c) 7. I (1.08a) 8. yours (1.08d)
9. whoever (1.08j) 10. me (1.08i) 11. he (1.08f) 12. us (1.08g)
13. her (1.09c) 14. its (1.09g) 15. his or her (1.09b)

Chapter 3
1. *was* for *were* (1.10c) 2. *were* for *was* (1.12) 3. *is* for *are* (1.10c) 4. *was* for *were* (1.10d) 5. *knows* for *know* (1.10g)
6. *written* for *wrote* (1.15b) 7. *are* for *is* (1.10f) 8. C (1.10g)
9. *begun* (1.15b) 10. *seen* (1.15b) 11. *gone* for *went* (1.15b)
12. b (1.15c) 13. b (1.15c) 14. a (1.15c) 15. b (1.15c)

Chapter 4
1. state-of-the-art (1.17e) 2. work-related (1.17e) 3. equally (1.17d) 4. their (1.17g) 5. had only (1.17f) 6. point-by-point (1.17e) 7. their (1.17g) 8. spur-of-the-moment (1.17e) 9. C (1.17e) 10. well-thought-out (1.17e) 11. change-of-address (1.17e) 12. case-by-case (1.17e) 13. were nearer (1.17b) 14. bad (1.17c) 15. smoothly (1.17d)

Chapter 5
1. a (1.18b) 2. b. (1.19c) 3. b (1.19d) 4. b (1.19c) 5. a (1.19a)
6. b (1.18a) 7. a (1.19d) 8. b (1.18c) 9. a (1.19c) 10. b (1.18e)
11. b (1.19a) 12. b (1.19b) 13. b (1.19c) 14. a (1.18b)
15. b (1.19c)

Chapter 6
1. (2) not, rule, (2.03) 2. (2) sure, Mr. Sanchez, (2.02) 3. (2) reliable, conscientious, (2.01) 4. (0) 5. (1) fact, (2.03) 6. (3) Memphis, Tennessee, Des Moines, (2.04c) 7. (1) meantime, (2.03) 8. (2) February 4, 2008, (2.04a) 9. (2) Mr. Loh, Mrs. Adams, (2.01) 10. (4) Ms. Leslie Holmes, 3430 Larkspur Lane, San Diego, CA 92110, (2.04b) 11. (2) feels, needless to say, (2.03) 12. (2) supplies, inventories, (2.01) 13. (1) business, (2.02) 14. (2) feels, however, (2.03) 15. (0)

Chapter 7
1. (1) culture, (2.06a) 2. (1) world, (2.05) 3. 0 (2.05) 4. (2) Tolstaya, 2007, (2.06c) 5. (1) imaginative, (2.08) 6. (0) (2.06c) 7. (2) Manning, Generation, (2.09) 8. (1) year, (2.07) 9. (1) language, (2.06a) 10. (1) successful, (2.01) 11. (2) automation, cutting, (2.01) 12. (3) hired, Monday, June 2, (2.06a, 2.04a) 13. (1) Sunnyvale, (2.06c) 14. (3) telephone, Thursday, March 4, (2.06a, 2.04a) 15. (1) clasp, (2.05)

Chapter 8
1. (2) gains," Franklin, (2.14a) 2. (3) Krahnke, PhD, Kostiz, (2.10) 3. (1) site, (2.14b) 4. (0) (2.15) 5. (1) monitor, (2.12)
6. (3) know, work, travel, (2.06a, 2.01) 7. (2) think, however, (2.03) 8. (2) position, Robinson, (2.07, 2.06c) 9. (3) considered,

Vegas, Scottsdale, (2.03, 2.01) 10. (2) closely, Friday, (2.06a, 2.11) 11. (2) years, individuals, (2.07, 2.09) 12. (2) Rubey, week, (2.06c, 2.15) 13. (0) (2.06c) 14. (4) weapons, report, companies, more robots, (2.06c, 2.01) 15. (2) fact, unprotected, (2.03, 2.08)

Chapter 9
1. (3) informational; reports, hand, (2.03, 2.16b) 2. (2) delayed; however, (2.16a) 3. (3) months: June, July, (2.01, 2.17a) 4. (1) are [delete colon] (2.17b) 5. (1) handbook, (2.06a, 2.16b) 6. (3) credit; resort, however, (2.03, 2.16b) 7. (3) credit: commercial, paper, (2.01, 2.17a) 8. (9) businesspeople: Lynne Krause, financial manager, American International Investments; Patrick Coughlin, comptroller, NationsBank; and Shannon Daly, legal counsel, (2.16d, 2.17) 9. (1) site, (2.05) 10. (5) charges; for example, average daily balance, adjusted balance, two-cycle average daily balance, (2.16e, 2.01) 11. (3) rating, loan; however, (2.06c, 2.16a) 12. (2) Union Bank, to [delete colon] (2.06a, 2.17b) 13. (2) high; therefore, (2.16a) 14. (2) 18 percent, prohibitive, (2.06a, 2.16c) 15. (1) high; (2.16b)

Chapter 10
1. Hanley's (2.20) 2. weeks' (2.20b) 3. year's (2.20b)
4. Peterson's (2.21) 5. employees' (2.20b) 6. witness's (2.20b)
7. Robin's (2.22) 8. money's (2.20a) 9. C (2.20a) 10. month's (2.20a) 11. boss's (2.20b) 12. secretary's (2.20a) 13. C (2.20a)
14. company's (2.20a) 15. businesses' (2.20b)

Chapter 11
1. (2) four key areas—education, experience, hard skills, and soft skills— (2.26a) 2. (3) please, Eddie, five o'clock. (2.02, 2.23a)
3. (2) (see Figure 5.1) (2.27) 4. (3) "Web site" two, (2.06a, 2.28c)
5. (3) Mars—these U.S. (2.23b, 2.26c) 6. (2) said, "Why like?" (2.28f) 7. (4) *The Wall Street Journal* "Oracle's Study"? (2.28e, 2.28f) 8. (2) states—California Oregon—are- (2.26a) 9. (5) Ms. Alice Theodor, Mr. Ron P. Gill, and Dr. Wei Li Chin? (2.23b, 2.24) 10. (3) "The Meeting" *The Etiquette Advantage in Business* (2.28e) 11. (2) task"; however, (2.16a, 2.28f) 12. (2) "gross." (2.28c) 13. (3) 9 a.m.? (2.23b, 2.24) 14. (3) Wow! techniques, you? (2.24, 2.25) 15. (3) *speculator* "one changes." (2.28d)

Chapter 12
1. (7) Suzuki branch Suite Yorba Linda Fire Department (3.01, 3.02, 3.07) 2. (6) Europe dollar; French accounting director Hotels (3.01, 3.02, 3.04, 3.06d) 3. (3) chauffeur limo service (3.01) 4. (5) German history, geography, and political science (3.05) 5. (4) Harry Potter Endless Cash (3.12) 6. (4) Dell Inspiron notebook computer (3.11) 7. (4) federal government state county (3.10) 8. (4) United States We foreign (3.01, 3.06c, 3.13) 9. (8) comptroller president board directors Securities Exchange Commission company (3.01, 3.04, 3.06e) 10. (5) father Death Valley moon stars (3.03, 3.06g, 3.14) 11. (7) marketing director manager ad campaign wireless phone (3.01, 3.06d, 3.06e, 3.09, 3.11) 12. (7) summer faculty advisor Japan, Korea, and China sponsors (3.01, 3.06a, 3.16) 13. (4) Park island River Bridge (3.01, 3.03) 14. (3) Accounting Department master's (3.05, 3.07, 3.09) 15. (5) Figure Chapter Census Bureau English (3.02, 3.04, 3.07)

Chapter 13

1. b (4.01a) **2.** a (4.05b) **3.** a (4.01a) **4.** b (4.03) **5.** b (4.02) **6.** a (4.03) **7.** b (4.04) **8.** b (4.07) **9.** b (4.08) **10.** b (4.10) **11.** b (4.02) **12.** b (4.08) **13.** b (4.12) **14.** a (4.06) **15.** a (4.06)

Chapter 14

1. b (2.16a) **2.** c (2.05) **3.** b (2.06) **4.** a (2.16a) **5.** c (2.15) **6.** b (2.16b) **7.** b (2.17a) **8.** a (2.20) **9.** c (2.16d) **10.** b (2.04a)

Notes

Chapter 1

1. Kinsman, M. (2004, February 1). Are poor writing skills holding back your career? *California Job Journal*. Retrieved January 22, 2008, from http://www.jobjournal.com/article_full_text.asp?artid=1039. See also Smerd, J. (2007, December 10). New workers sorely lacking literacy skills. *Workforce Management*, 6; Stevens, B. (2005, March). What communication skills do employers want? Silicon Valley recruiters respond. *Journal of Employment Counseling*, 42, 1; Gray, F., Emerson, L., & MacKay, B. (2005). Meeting the demands of the workplace: Science students and written skills. *Journal of Science Education and Industry*, 14, 425–435; Tucker, M. L., & McCarthy, A. M. (2001, Summer). Presentation self-efficacy: Increasing communication skills through service-learning. *Journal of Managerial Issues*, 227–244; Cohen, A. (1999). The right stuff. *Sales and Marketing Management*, 151; and Messmer, M. (1999, August). Skills for a new millennium. *Strategic Finance*, 10–12.

2. Moody, J., Stewart, B., & Bolt-Lee, C. (2002, March). Showcasing the skilled business graduate: Expanding the tool kit. *Business Communication Quarterly*, 65(1), 23.

3. Vance, E. (2007, February 2). College graduates lack key skills, report says. *The Chronicle of Higher Education*, p. A30.

4. Robinson, T. M. (2008, January 26). Quoted in Same office, different planets. *The New York Times*, p. B5.

5. Messmer, M. (2001, January). Enhancing your writing skills. *Strategic Finance*, 8. See also Staples, B. (2005, May 15). The fine art of getting it down on paper, fast. *The New York Times*, p. WK13(L).

6. The National Commission on Writing. [press release] (2004, September 14). Writing skills necessary for employment, says big business. Retrieved January 22, 2008, from http://www.writingcommission.org/pr/writing_for_employ.html

7. Survey shows workers should write better. (2004, September 14). Associated Press. Retrieved May 18, 2008, from MSNBC at http://www.msnbc.msn.com/id/6000685

8. The National Commission on Writing. [press release] (2004, September 14). Writing skills necessary for employment, says big business. Retrieved January 22, 2008, from http://www.writingcommission.org/pr/writing_for_employ.html

9. Laff, M. (2006, December). Wanted: CFOs with communications skills. *T + D*, 20. PDF file retrieved January 22, 2008, from Business Source Premier database.

10. Stranger, J. (2007, July). How to make yourself offshore-proof. *Certification Magazine*, 9(7), 34–40. Retrieved January 22, 2008, from Business Source Premier database.

11. Marsan, C. D. (2007, December 31). Job skills that matter: Where you can leave a mark. *Network World*, 24(50), 38–40. Retrieved January 23, 2008, from Business Source Premier database.

12. Professional demeanor and personal management. (2004, January). *Keying In*, National Business Education Association Newsletter, 1.

13. Daniels, C. (2004, June 28). 50 best companies for minorities. *Fortune*, 136.

14. Burgoon, J., Coker, D., & Coker, R. (1986). Communicative explanations. *Human Communication Research*, 12, 463–494.

15. Birdwhistell, R. (1970). *Kinesics and context*. Philadelphia: University of Pennsylvania Press.

16. Nolen W. E. (1995, April). Reading people. *Internal Auditor*, 48–51.

17. Hall, E. T. (1966). *The hidden dimension*. Garden City, NY: Doubleday, pp. 107–122.

18. Wilkie, H. (2003, Fall). Professional presence. *The Canadian Manager*, 28(3), 14–19. Retrieved January 28, 2008, from Business Source Premier database.

19. Hall, E. T., & Hall, M. R. (1990). *Understanding cultural differences*. Yarmouth, ME: Intercultural Press, pp. 183–184.

20. Chaney, L. H., & Martin, J. S. (2000). *Intercultural business communication* (2nd ed.). Upper Saddle River, NJ: Prentice Hall, p. 83.

21. Beamer, L., & Varner, I. (2008). *Intercultural communication in the global workplace*. Boston: McGraw-Hill Irwin, p. 129.

22. Sheer, V. C., & Chen, L. (2003, January). Successful Sino-Western business negotiation: Participants' accounts of national and professional cultures. *The Journal of Business Communication*, 40(1), 62; see also Luk, L., Patel, M., & White, K. (1990, December). Personal attributes of American and Chinese business associates. *The Bulletin of the Association for Business Communication*, 67.

23. Gallois, C., & Callan, V. (1997). *Communication and culture*. New York: Wiley, p. 24.

24. Jarvis, S. S. (1990, June). Preparing employees to work south of the border. *Personnel*, 763.

25. Gallois, C., & Callan, V. (1997). *Communication and culture*. New York: Wiley, p. 29.

26. Copeland, L., & Griggs, L. (1985). *Going international*. New York: Penguin, p. 94. See also Beamer, L. & Varner, I. (2008). *Intercultural communication in the global workplace*. Boston: McGraw-Hill Irwin, p. 340.

27. Copeland, L., & Griggs, L. (1985). *Going international*. New York: Penguin, p. 12.

28. Flannery, R. (2005, May 10). China is a big prize. *Forbes*, 173(10), 163.

29. Martin, J. S., & Chaney, L. H. (2006). *Global business etiquette*. Westport, CT: Praeger, p. 36.

30. Based on 2000 U.S. Census figures, as reported by Little, J. S., & Triest, R. K. (2001). Proceedings from the Federal Reserve Bank of Boston Conference Series. The impact of demographic change on U.S. labor markets. *Seismic shifts: The economic impact of demographic change*. Retrieved January 29, 2008, from http://www.bos.frb.org/economic/conf/conf46/conf46a.pdf

31. Neff, J. (1998, February 16). Diversity. *Advertising Age*, S1.

32. Terhune, C. (2005, April 19). Pepsi, vowing diversity isn't just image polish, seeks inclusive culture. *The Wall Street Journal*, p. B4.

33. Schwartz, J., & Wald, M. L. (2003, March 9). Smart people working collectively can be dumber than the sum of their

brains. Appeared originally in *The New York Times*. Retrieved January 28, 2008, from http://www.mindfully.org/Reform/2003/Smart-People-Dumber9mar03.htm

34 Simons, G., & Dunham, D. (1995, December). Making inclusion happen. *Managing Diversity*. Retrieved January 28, 2008, from http://www.jalmc.org/mk-incl.htm

35 Kerrey, B. (2004). Quoted in National Commission on Writing: Writing skills necessary for employment, says big business. Retrieved January 28, 2008, from http://www.writingcommission.org/pr/writing_for_employ.html

36 What's the universal hand sign for 'I goofed'? (1996, December 16). *Santa Barbara News-Press*, p. D2.

37 Makower, J. (1995, Winter). Managing diversity in the workplace. *Business & Society Review, 92*, 48–54. Retrieved February 2, 2008, from Business Source Premier database.

Chapter 2

1 Arnold, V. D. (1986, August). Benjamin Franklin on writing well. *Personnel Journal*, 17.

2 Bacon, M. (1988, April). Quoted in Business writing: One-on-one speaks best to the masses. *Training*, 95. See also Danziger, E. (1998, February). Communicate up. *Journal of Accountancy*, 67.

3 Pomerenke, P. J. (1999). A short introduction to the plain English movement. *Issues in Writing, 10*(1), 30. See also Letunic, N. (2007, October). Beyond plain English: Ten best practices for creating citizen-friendly planning documents. *Planning, 73*(9), 4. Retrieved February 9, 2008, from InfoTrac College Edition database.

4 Center for Plain Language home page. Retrieved February 10, 2008, from http://www.centerforplainlanguage.org

5 Pickens, J. E. (1985, August). Communication: Terms of equality: A guide to bias-free language. *Personnel Journal*, 5.

Chapter 3

1 National Commission on Writing. (2004, September 14). Writing skills necessary for employment, says big business. Retrieved February 13, 2008, from http://www.writingcommission.org/pr/writing_for_employ.html

2 Adapted from Conaway, R. N., & Fernandez, T. L. (2000, March). Ethical preferences among business leaders: Implications for business schools. *Business Communication Quarterly*, 23–38.

Chapter 4

1 Cook, C. K. (1985) *Line by line*. Boston: Houghton Mifflin, p. 17.

2 Lague, L., *People* magazine editor (personal communication with Mary Ellen Guffey, February 5, 1992).

3 Moore, R. (2007, July). Beyond spell check. *Officeproletter.com*, p. 6.

Chapter 5

1 Sandberg, J. (2006, September 26). Employees forsake dreaded email for the beloved phone. *The Wall Street Journal*, p. B1.

2 More clicks than conversations: Shift to e-mail in business makes crafting meaningful messages more important. (2007, December 12). *PR Newswire*. Retrieved March 30, 2008, from InfoTrac College Edition database.

3 Maney, K. (2003, July 24). How the big names tame e-mail. *USA Today*, p. 2A.

4 Hogan, R. C. (2006, February 16). Cure for an epidemic of bad e-mail—explicit business writing. *PR Newswire*. Retrieved March 30, 2008, from InfoTrac College Edition database.

5 Brown, P. B. (2008, January 26). Same office, different planets. *The New York Times*, p. B5.

6 Improving workplace safety. (2007, June). *Officepro Newsletter*, p. 6.

7 DeLisser, E. (1999, September 27). One-click commerce: What people do now to goof off at work. *The Wall Street Journal*. Retrieved April 11, 2008, from http://www.kenmaier.com/wsj19990927.htm

8 Ibid.

9 The 2007 electronic monitoring and surveillance survey. (2008, February 29). Retrieved April 10, 2008, from http://www.gpsdaily

Chapter 6

1 Fallows, J. (2005, June 12). Enough keyword searches. Just answer my question. *The New York Times*, p. BU3.

2 Mascolini, M. (1994, June). Another look at teaching the external negative message. *The Bulletin of the Association of Business Communication*, 46.

3 Emily Post Institute. (2008). Conveying sympathy Q & A. Retrieved May 5, 2008, from 1-800-flowers.com

4 Caddell, M. H. (2003, November/December). Is letter writing dead? *OfficePro*, p. 22.

5 Fallows, J. (2005, June 12). Enough keyword searches. Just answer my question. *The New York Times*, p. BU3.

Chapter 7

1 American Management Association. 2004 survey on workplace e-mail and IM reveals unmanaged risks. (2004). Retrieved May 9, 2008, from http://www.amanet.org/press/amanews/im_survey.htm

2 McCord, E. A. (1991, April). The business writer, the law, and routine business communication: A legal and rhetorical analysis. *Journal of Business and Technical Communication*, 183.

3 Ibid.

4 Shuit, D. P. (2003, September). Do it right or risk getting burned. *Workforce Management*, 80.

5 Brodkin, J. (2007, March 19). Corporate apologies don't mean much. *Networkworld, 24*(11), 8. PDF file retrieved May 9, 2008, from Business Source Premier database.

6 Schweitzer, M. E. (2006, December). Wise negotiators know when to say "I'm sorry." *Negotiation*, 4. PDF file retrieved June 6, 2007, from Business Source Premier database.

7 Brodkin, J. (2007, March 19). Rating apologies. *Networkworld, 24*(11), 14. PDF file retrieved June 6, 2007, from Business Source Premier database.

8 Neeleman, D. (2007). An apology from David Neeleman. Retrieved June 10, 2007, from http://www.jetblue.com/about/ourcompany/apology/index.html

9 Letters to Lands' End. (1991, February). 1991 Lands' End catalog. Dodgeville, WI: Lands' End, 100.

10 Mowatt, J. (2002, February). Breaking bad news to customers. *Agency Sales*, 30; and Dorn, E. M. (1999, March). Case method instruction in the business writing classroom. *Business Communication Quarterly, 62*(1), 51–52.

11 Forbes, M. (1999). How to write a business letter. In K. Harty (Ed.), *Strategies for business and technical writing*. Boston: Allyn and Bacon, p. 108.

12 Browning, M. (2003, November 24). Work dilemma: Delivering bad news a good way. *Government Computer News*, p. 41; and Mowatt, J. (2002, February). Breaking bad news to customers. *Agency Sales*, 30.

[13] Engels, J. (2007, July). Delivering difficult messages. *Journal of Accountancy, 204*(1), 50–52. Retrieved May 11, 2008, from Business Source Premier database. See also Lewis, B. (1999, September 13). To be an effective leader, you need to perfect the art of delivering bad news. *InfoWorld,* 124. Retrieved May 11, 2008, from http://www.infoworld.com/columnists/archive/survival_guide_bob.html

[14] O'Neal, S. (2003, November). Quoted in Need to deliver bad news? How & why to tell it like it is. *HR Focus,* 3.

[15] Granberry, M. (1992, November 14). Lingerie chain fined $100,000 for gift certificates. *Los Angeles Times,* p. D3.

[16] Based on Lee, L. (2007, June 11). A smoothie you can chew on. *BusinessWeek,* 64.

[17] Based on Sloan, G. (1996, November). Under 21? Carnival says cruise is off. *USA Today*; Sieder, J. (1996, October 16). Full steam ahead: Carnival Cruise Line makes boatloads of money by selling fun. *U.S. News & World Report,* 72; and Fun ship fleet. Retrieved July 2, 2005, from http://www.carnival.com/CMS/Ships/FunShips.aspx

[18] Based on Burbank, L. (2007, June 8). Personal items can be swept away between flights. *USA Today,* p. 3D.

[19] Sorkin, A. (1999, November 11). J. Crew web goof results in discount. *The New York Times,* p. D3.

[20] Based on Harari, O. (1999, July-August). The power of complaints. *Management Review,* 31.

[21] Based on SUV Surprise. (2004, June 15). *The Wall Street Journal,* p. W7.

Chapter 8

[1] How to ask for—and get—what you want! (1990, February 1). *Supervision,* p. 11. Retrieved March 2, 2008, from http://www.allbusiness.com/human-resources/workforce-management/117804–1.html

[2] Rieck, D. (1998, June). Great letters and why they work. *Direct Marketing,* pp. 20–24. See also Graham, J. R. (2002, January). Improving direct mail. *Agency Sales,* pp. 47–50; and Weitzer, S. (2004, April 19). The secret's out: Private sales spur big returns. *Twice: This Week in Consumer Electronics,* p. 18. Retrieved March 1, 2008, from Academic Search Premier (EBSCO).

[3] Nicastro, E. W. (2006, May 12). Five deadly sales letter mistakes. *SalesVantage.com.* Retrieved March 2, 2008, from http://www.salesvantage.com/article/view.php?w=934

[4] Chambers, D. (1998). *The agile manager's guide to writing to get action.* Bristol, VT: Velocity Press, p. 86; Kennedy, D. S. (2006). *The ultimate sales letter: Attract new customers.* Avon, MA: Adams Media.

[5] McLaughlin, K. (1990, October). Words of wisdom. *Entrepreneur,* p. 101; and Lowenstein, M. (2007, September 24). Make both an emotional and rational appeal to your customers: Inside-out and outside-in commitment and advocacy. *CustomerThink.net.* Retrieved March 2, 2008, from http://www.customerthink.net/article/make_emotional_rational_appeal_customers

[6] To learn more about this tool, visit http://www.hp.com/phinfo/blogs/

[7] *PR Week* and Burson Marsteller study cited in Rubel, S. (2005, November 7). Study: 47% of CEOs say blogs useful for PR. *Micro Persuasion Blog.* Retrieved March 1, 2008, from http://www.micropersuasion.com/2005/11/study_47_of_ceo.html

[8] Based on Asbrand, D. (2007, August 30). Designing a new way to connect. *Microsoft Business & Industry.* Retrieved March 1, 2008, from http://www.microsoft.com/business/peopleready/business/operations/insight/portals.mspx

[9] Pilgrim, M. (2002, December 18). What is RSS. O'Reilly XML.com. Retrieved March 1, 2008, from http://www.xml.com/pub/a/2002/12/18/dive-into-xml.html

[10] Based on Heffernan, V. (2005, June 17). For the age of do-it-yourself finance, she wrote the book(s) and the programs. *The New York Times,* p. E30. Retrieved March 1, 2008, from LexisNexis.

[11] Grant, K. B. (2008, February 29). Seven places to retire during an economic downturn. SmartMoney.com. Retrieved March 24, 2008, from http://finance.yahoo.com

[12] Rubel, S. (2005, November 7). *PR Week* and Burson Marsteller study cited in Study: 47% of CEOs say blogs useful for PR. *Micro Persuasion Blog.* Retrieved March 1, 2008, from http://www.micropersuasion.com/2005/11/study_47_of_ceo.html

[13] Federal Trade Commission. (2002, April 18). FTC warns Internet marketers about making misleading claims about the benefits of gas-saving and other energy-related devices. Retrieved March 24, 2008, from http://www.ftc.gov

Chapter 9

[1] Takeuchi Cullen, L. (2007, April 26). Employee diversity training doesn't work. *Time.com.* Retrieved May 29, 2008, from http://www.time.com/time/magazine/article/0,9171,1615183,00.html

Chapter 10

[1] Holtz, H. (1998). *Proven proposal strategies to win more business.* Chicago: Upstart Publishing Company/Dearborn Publishing Group, pp. 104–107.

[2] Based on Grinyer, M., Raytheon proposal consultant (personal communication with Mary Ellen Guffey, July 23, 2007).

[3] From an online RTF by OMRI company: Basor, B. (June 6, 2008). OMNI Website RFP. *The RFP Database.* Retrieved June 8, 2008, from http://www.rfpdb.com/view/document/id/4415

[4] Netcraft Ltd., *November 2006 Web Server Survey.* Retrieved June 6, 2008, from http://news.netcraft.com/archives/2006/11/01/november_2006_web_server_survey.html and Killmer, K. A., & Koppel, N. B. (2002, August). So much information, so little time: Evaluating Web resources with search engines. *THE Journal.* Retrieved June 6, 2008, from http://www.thejournal.com/articles/16051

[5] Brooks Suzukamo, L. (2002, July 3). Search engines become popular for fact-finding, game playing. *Knight-Ridder/Tribune News Service,* p. K6110

[6] Integrated Web services: Technologies and definitions. (2008). Cornell University. Retrieved June 6, 2008, from http://iws.cit.cornell.edu/iws2/technology/techinfo.cfm

[7] Bulkeley, W. M. (2005, June 23). Marketers scan blogs for brand insights. *The Wall Street Journal,* p. B1. Retrieved June 6, 2008, from http://online.wsj.com/public/us

[8] Pimentel, B. (2001, June 13). Writing the codes on blogs: Companies figure out what's OK, what's not in online realm. *San Francisco Chronicle,* p. E1. Retrieved June 6, 2008, from http://www.sfgate.com/cgi-bin/article.cgi?file=/c/a/2005/06/13/BLOG.TMP

[9] Beutler, W. (2007, April 10). Yes, but how many blogs are there really? *Blog, P. I.* Retrieved June 6, 2008, from http://www.blogpi.net/yes-but-how-many-blogs-are-there-really

[10] Baker, S., & Green, H. (2008, May 22). Beyond blogs: What business needs to know. *BusinessWeek Online.* Retrieved June 6, 2008, from http://www.businessweek.com/magazine/content/08_22/b4086044617865.htm?chan=search

[11] Ibid.

12 Ibid.

13 Baltimore Sun columnist quits amid plagiarism charges. (2006, January 4). *Associated Press/FoxNews.com*. Retrieved June 6, 2008, from http://www.foxnews.com/story/0,2933,180569,00 .html; Large, J. (2004, March 29). Jayson Blair and Jack Kelley are journalism's unbelievable problem. *The Seattle Times*. Retrieved June 6, 2008, from http://seattletimes. nwsource.com/html/living/2001889442_jdl28.html; and Snyder, G. (2004, January 19). Journalists devour their own in eager scrutiny. *Variety*, p. 3.

14 Writing Tutorial Services, Indiana University, Plagiarism: What it is and how to recognize and avoid it. Retrieved June 6, 2008, from http://www.indiana.edu/~wts/pamphlets/ plagiarism.shtml; Learning Center. (2008). *iParadigms, LLC*. Retrieved June 7, 2008, from http://www.plagiarism.org

15 Brady, D. (2006, December 4). *!#?@ the e-mail. Can we talk? *BusinessWeek*, 109.

16 Based on Sterkel, K. S. (1988). Integrating intercultural communication and report writing in the communication class. *The Bulletin of the Association for Business Communication*, pp. 14–16.

17 Activity is based on Skidmore, S. (2008, June 10). Some retailers give vinyl records a spin. *The Los Angeles Times*, p. C6.

18 Tapscott, D., & Williams, A. D. (2007, March 26). *BusinessWeek Online*. Retrieved June 10, 2008, from http://www.businessweek.com/innovate/content/mar2007/ id20070326_237620.htm

Chapter 11

1 Buhler, P. M. (2003, April). Workplace civility: Has it fallen by the wayside? *SuperVision*, p. 20. Retrieved June 24, 2008, from ProQuest database.

2 Wikipedia: Civility. (2008, June 18). Wikipedia. Retrieved June 20, 2008, from http://en.wikipedia.org/wiki/Wikipedia:CIV

3 Johnson, D. (1988–2006). Dine like a diplomat. Seminar Script. The Protocol School of Washington.

4 Albrecht, K. (2005). *Social intelligence: The new science of success*. San Francisco: Pfeiffer, p. 3.

5 Chismar, D. (2001). Vice and virtue in everyday (business) life. *Journal of Business Ethics*, 29, 169–176.

6 Hughes, T. (2008). Being a professional. *Wordconstructions.com*. Retrieved June 16, 2008, from http://www.wordconstructions .com/articles/business/professional.html; Grove, C., & Hallowell, W. (2002). The seven balancing acts of professional behavior in the United States: A cultural values perspective. *Grovewell.com*. Retrieved July 18, 2008, from http://www .grovewell.com/pub-usa-professional.html

7 Brent, P. (2006, November). Soft skills speak volumes. *CA Magazine*, 139, 112. Retrieved June 16, 2008, from ProQuest database.

8 Laff, M. (2006, December). Wanted: CFOs with communications skills. *ASTD*, 60(12), 20. Retrieved June 16, 2008, from http://store.astd.org/product.asp?prodid=4282

9 Martin, C. (2007, March 6). The importance of face-to-face communication at work. *CIO.com*. Retrieved June 16, 2008, from http://www.cio.com/article/29898/The_Importance_ of_Face_to_Face_Communication_at_Work; Duke, S. (2001, Winter). E-Mail: Essential in media relations, but no replacement for face-to-face communication. *Public Relations Quarterly*, p. 19

10 Brenner, R. (2007, October 17). Virtual conflict. *Point Lookout*, Chaco Canyon Consulting. Retrieved June 16, 2008, from http://www.chacocanyon.com/pointlookout/071017 .shtml; Drolet, A. L., & Morris, M. W. (2000, January). Rapport in conflict resolution: Accounting for how face-to-

face contact fosters mutual cooperation in mixed-motive conflicts. *Journal of Experimental Social Psychology*, p. 26.

11 Miculka, J. (1999). *Speaking for success*. Cincinnati: South-Western, p. 19.

12 Motivational and Inspirational Corner. (2005, June 27). Retrieved June 16, 2008, from http://www.motivational-inspirational-corner.com/getquote.html?startrow=11& categoryid=207

13 Burge, J. (2002, June). Telephone safety protocol for today. *The National Public Accountant*. FindArticles.com. Retrieved June 17, 2008, from http://findarticles.com/p/articles/mi_ m4325/is_2002_June/ai_n25049376

14 Lanman, S. (2005, July 9). Mobile-phone users become a majority. *San Francisco Chronicle*, p. C1.

15 Sidener, J. (2008, January 27). Cell phones taking on many roles, transforming market, generation. *SignOnSanDiego.com*. Retrieved June 17, 2008, from http://www.signonsandiego .com/news/metro/20080127–9999–1n27phone.html

16 Hockenberry, J., Adaora, U., & Colgan, J. (2008, May 20). For many Americans, cell phones are supplanding the landline. Retrieved June 17, 2008, from http://www.thetakeaway.org/ archives/2008/05/20/7

17 Ennen, S. (2003, April). Red Baron soars with teamwork: New pizza products sate lifestyle needs. *Food Processing*, 64, p. 40. Retrieved June 17, 2008, from Factiva database.

18 Edmondson, G. (2006, October 16). BMW's dream factory. *BusinessWeek*, p. 80. Retrieved June 17, 2008, from http:// www.businessweek.com/magazine/content/06_42/b4005072 .htm

19 Brown, M. K., Huettner, B., & James-Tanny, C. (2007). *Managing virtual teams: Getting the most of wikis, blogs, and other collaborative tools*. Plano, TX: Wordware Publishing; Lipnack, J., & Stamps, J. (2000). *Virtual teams: People working across boundaries with technology* (2nd ed.). New York: Wiley, p. 18.

20 Kiger, P. J. (2006, September 25). Flexibility to the fullest: Throwing out the rules of work—Part 1 of 2. *Workforce Management*, 85(18), 1. See also Holland, K. (2006, December).When work time isn't face time. *The New York Times*, p. BU3.

21 Cutler, G. (2007, January–February). Mike leads his first virtual team. *Research-Technology Management*, 50(1), 66. Retrieved June 17, 2008, from ABI/INFORM database.

22 Amason, A. C., Hochwarter, W. A., Thompson, K. R., & Harrison, A. W. (1995, Autumn). Conflict: An important dimension in successful management teams. *Organizational Dynamics*, 24(2), 1. Retrieved June 17, 2008, from EBSCO database; Romando, R. (2006, November 9). Advantages of corporate team building. *Ezine Articles*. Retrieved June 17, 2008, from http://ezinearticles.com/?Advantages-of-Corporate-Team-Building&id=352961

23 Ruffin, B. (2006, January). T.E.A.M. work: Technologists, educators, and media specialists collaborating. *Library Media Connection*, 24(4), 49. Retrieved June 20, 2008, from EBSCO database.

24 Katzenbach, J. R., & Smith, K. (1994). *The wisdom of teams*. New York: HarperBusiness, p. 45.

25 Holstein, W. J. (2008, May 30). Getting the most from management teams. *BusinessWeek*. Retrieved June 21, 2008, from http://www.businessweek.com/managing/content/may2008/ ca20080530_775110.htm?chan=search

26 Gale, S. F. (2006, July). Common ground. *PM Network*, p. 48. Retrieved June 17, 2008, from EBSCO database.

27 Bayot, J. (2000, November 8). Developers bet on theaters in glutted L.A. *The Wall Street Journal*, Eastern edition, p. C1.

28 Katzenbach, J. R., & Smith, K. (1994). *The wisdom of teams.* New York: HarperBusiness, p. 50.

29 Dull meeting? I'd rather see the dentist. (2004, October 19). *Personnel Today*, p. 1. Retrieved June 17, 2008, from LexisNexis database.

30 Maher, K. (2004, January 13). The jungle: Focus on recruitment, pay and getting ahead. *The Wall Street Journal*, p. B6.

31 Schechtman, M. quoted in Lancaster, H. (1998, May 26). Learning some ways to make meetings less awful. *The Wall Street Journal*, p. B1; How to stand out at meetings. (n. d.) *eHow.com*. Retrieved June 17, 2008, from http://www.ehow.com/how_2096879_stand-out-meetings.html

32 ThinkExist.com. Retrieved June 16, 2008, from http://en.thinkexist.com/quotation/by_failing_to_prepare_you_are_preparing_to_fail/199949.html

33 Bruening, J. C. (1996, July). There's good news about meetings. *Managing Office Technology*, pp. 24–25. Retrieved June 17, 2008, from ProQuest database.

34 Marquis, C. (2003, July 13). Doing well and doing good. *The New York Times*, p. BU 2.

35 Imperato, G. (2007, December 19). You have to start meeting like this! *FastCompany.com*. Retrieved June 17, 2008, from http://www.fastcompany.com/magazine/23/begeman.html

36 Schabacker, K. (1991, June). A short, snappy guide to meaningful meetings. *Working Women*, p. 73.

37 Hamilton, C., & Parker, C. (2001). *Communicating for success* (6th ed.). Belmont, CA: Wadsworth, pp. 311–312.

38 Marquis, C. (2003, July). Doing well and doing good. *The New York Times*, p. BU 2.

39 Gerke, S. Cited in The two sides of conflict. (2008). *Team Building.* Retrieved June 24, 2008, from http://www.teambuildingportal.com/articles/team-failure/good-bad-conflict.php

40 Dörnyei, Z., & Murphey, T. (2004). *Group dynamics in the language classroom.* Cambridge, UK: Cambridge University Press, p. 142.

41 Steinway, T. E. as quoted by Gerke, S. (2008). Useful quotes: Conflict. *Gerke Consulting & Development LLC.* Retrieved June 21, 2008, from http://www.susangerke.com/

42 LeBaron, M., & Pillay, V. (2007). *Conflict across cultures.* Boston: Intercultural Press, p. 16.

43 Based on Thomas, K., & Killman, R. as quoted by Podmoroff, D. (2006, May 23). Be positive: Resolve conflict. *Mind Tools.* Retrieved June 22, 2008, from http://www.mindtools.com/pages/Newsletters/23May06.htm#article2

44 Hamilton, E. A., Gordon, J. R., & Whelan-Berry, K. S. (2006). Understanding the work-life conflict of never-married women without children. *Women in Management Review*, 21(5), 397–398. Retrieved June 22, 2008, from ProQuest database.

Chapter 12

1 Hooey, B. (2005). Speaking for success! *Speaking success.* Retrieved June 24, 2008, from Toastmasters International Web site, http://members.shaw.ca/toasted/speaking_succes.htm

2 Barrington, L., Casner-Lotto, J., & Wright, M. (2008, May). Are they really ready to work? *The Conference Board.* Retrieved June 26, 2008, from http://www.conference-board.org/pdf_free/BED-06-Workforce.pdf

3 Pincus, A. (2007, July 3). The fear factor, and the alpha boss. *BusinessWeek.* Retrieved June 24, 2008, from http://www.businessweek.com/careers/content/jul2007/ca2007073_045947.htm?chan=search

4 Ginsberg, S. (2006). I'm such a moron—self-deprecating humor basics. *Ezinearticles.* Retrieved June 25, 2008, from http://ezinearticles.com/?Im-Such-a-Moron–Self-Deprecating-Humor-Basics&id=385150

5 Wharton Applied Research Center. (1981). A study of the effects of the use of overhead transparencies on business meetings, final report cited in Visual Being Blog Archive. (2005, July 14). The 1981 Wharton study. Retrieved June 26, 2008, from http://www.visualbeing.com

6 Pope, J. (2007, August 5). Business school requires PowerPoint. *Oakland Tribune*, p. 1. Retrieved July 1, 2008, from ProQuest database.

7 Nass, C. quoted in Simons, T. (2001, July). When was the last time PowerPoint made you sing? *Presentations*, 6. See also Tufte, E. R. (2006). *The cognitive style of PowerPoint: Pitching out corrupts within.* Cheshire, CT: Graphics Press.

8 Booher, D. (2003). *Speak with confidence: Powerful presentations that inform, inspire, and persuade.* New York: McGraw-Hill Professional, p. 126. See also http://www.indezine.com/ideas/prescolors.html

9 Bates, S. (2005). *Speak like a CEO: Secrets for commanding attention and getting results.* New York: McGraw-Hill Professional, p. 113.

10 Sommerville, J. (n. d.). The seven deadly sins of PowerPoint Presentations. *About.com: Entrepreneurs.* Retrieved June 26, 2008, from http://entrepreneurs.about.com/cs/marketing/a/7sinsofppt.htm

11 Burrows, P., Grover, R., & Green, H. (2006, February 6). Steve Jobs' magic kingdom. *BusinessWeek*, 62. Retrieved June 26, 2008, from http://www.businessweek.com; see also Gallo, C. (2006, April 6). How to wow 'em like Steve Jobs. *BusinessWeek.* Retrieved June 26, 2008, from http://www.businessweek.com

12 See http://www.tlccreative.com/images/tutorials/PreShowChecklist.pdf

13 Ellwood, J. (2004, August 4). Less PowerPoint, more powerful points. *The Times* (London), p. 6.

14 Ozer, J. (2006, January 11). Ovation for PowerPoint. *PC Magazine.* Retrieved July 18, 2007, from http://www.pcmag.com/article2/0,1759,1921436,00.asp; See more information at http://www.adobe.com/products/ovation/

15 Boeri, R. J. (2002, March). Fear of flying? Or the mail? Try the Web conferencing cure. *Emedia Magazine*, 49.

16 Booher, D. (2003) *Speak with confidence.* New York: McGraw-Hill, p. 14; and Booher, D. (1991). *Executive's portfolio of model speeches for all occasions.* Englewood Cliffs, NJ: Prentice Hall, p. 259.

17 Jackson, M. quoted in Garbage in, garbage out. (1992, December). *Consumer Reports*, 755.

Chapter 13

1 Ryan, L. (2007). Online job searching. *BusinessWeek.* Video interview retrieved July 6, 2008, from http://feedroom.businessweek.com/index.jsp?fr_story=5e1ec1bacf73ae689d381f30e80dfea30cd52108; Wolgemuth, L. (2008, February 25). Using the Web to search for a job. *U.S. News & World Report.* Retrieved July 6, 2008, from http://www.usnews.com/articles/business/careers/2008/02/25/using-the-web-to-search-for-a-job.html

2 Jansen, J. (n. d.) What's keeping you from changing careers? *CareerJournal.com.* Retrieved July 6, 2008, from http://208.144.115.170/jobhunting/change/20030225-jansen.html

3 O'Connell, B. (2003). *The career survival guide.* New York: McGraw-Hill, pp. 11–12.

4 Kimmit, R. M. (2007, January 23). Why job churn is good. *Washingtonpost.com*. Retrieved July 6, 2008, from http://www.washingtonpost.com/wp-dyn/content/article/2007/01/22/AR2007012201089.html

5 Kharif, O. (2007, January 3). Online job sites battle for share. *BusinessWeek*. Retrieved July 8, 2008, from http://www.businessweek.com/technology/content/jan2007/tc20070103_369308.htm

6 Korkki, P. (2007, July 1). So easy to apply, so hard to be noticed. *The New York Times*. Retrieved July 8, 2008, from LexisNexis database.

7 Marquardt, K. (2008, February 21). 5 tips on finding a new job. *U.S. News & World Report*. Retrieved July 6, 2008, from http://www.usnews.com/articles/business/careers/2008/02/21/5-tips-on-finding-a-new-job.html; Wolgemuth, L. (2008, February 25). Using the Web to search for a job. *U.S. News & World Report*. Retrieved July 6, 2008, from http://www.usnews.com/articles/business/careers/2008/02/25/using-the-web-to-search-for-a-job.html

8 Crispin, G., & Mehler, M. (2003, January). Impact of the Internet on source of hires—2002. *CareerXroads.com*. Retrieved July 6, 2008, from http://www.careerxroads.com/news/03sourceofhire.html

9 Ryan, L. (2007). Online job searching. *BusinessWeek*. Video interview retrieved July 6, 2008, from http://feedroom.businessweek.com/index.jsp?fr_story=5e1ec1bacf73ae689d381f30e80dfea30cd52108

10 Top job boards. (2006, November/December). *Office Pro*, 66(8), 5. Retrieved July 6, 2008, from Business Source Premier (EBSCO) database.

11 Pont, J. (2005, November 7). Leading job boards address challenges of globalization. *Workforce Management*, 49. Retrieved July 7, 2008, from http://www.workforce.com/archive/feature/24/21/06/index.php

12 Farquharson, L. (2003, September 15). Technology special report: The best way to find a job. *The Wall Street Journal*, p. R8. Retrieved July 8, 2008, from http://www.taleo.com/news/media/pdf/74En_20030916_WallStreetJournal.pdf

13 Ryan, L. (2007). Online job searching. *BusinessWeek*. Video interview retrieved July 6, 2008, from http://feedroom.businessweek.com/index.jsp?fr_story=5e1ec1bacf73ae689d381f30e80dfea30cd52108

14 Kharif, O. (2007, January 3). Online job sites battle for share. *BusinessWeek*. Retrieved July 8, 2008, from http://www.businessweek.com/technology/content/jan2007/tc20070103_369308.htm

15 McConnon, A. (2007, August 30). Social networking graduates and hits the job market. *BusinessWeek*. Retrieved July 8, 2008, from http://www.businessweek.com/innovate/content/aug2007/id20070830_886412.htm?chan=search

16 Ibid.

17 Cheeseman, J. quoted by Wolgemuth, L. (2008, February 25). Using the Web to search for a job. *U.S. News & World Report*. Retrieved July 6, 2008, from http://www.usnews.com/articles/business/careers/2008/02/25/using-the-web-to-search-for-a-job.html

18 Feldman, D. quoted by Marquardt, K. (2008, February 21). 5 tips on finding a new job. *U.S. News & World Report*. Retrieved July 6, 2008, from http://www.usnews.com/articles/business/careers/2008/02/21/5-tips-on-finding-a-new-job.html

19 Brown, D. J., Cober, R. T., Kane, K., Levy, P. E., & Shalhoop, J. (2006). Proactive personality and the successful job search: A field investigation with college graduates. *Journal of Applied Psychology, 91*(3), 717–726. Retrieved July 8, 2008, from Business Source Premier (EBSCO) database.

20 Koeppel, D. (2006, December 31). Those low grades in college may haunt your job search. *The New York Times*, p. 1. Retrieved July 8, 2008, from Academic Search Premier (EBSCO) database.

21 Black, D. quoted by Brandon, E. (2007, January 31). Tips for getting that first job. *U.S. News & World Report*. Retrieved July 8, 2008, from http://www.usnews.com/usnews/biztech/articles/070131/31firstjob.htm

22 Korkki, P. (2007, July 1). So easy to apply, so hard to be noticed. *The New York Times*. Retrieved July 8, 2008, from LexisNexis database.

23 The Creative Group. (2008, February 21). Substance over style: Survey shows off-the-wall job-hunting tactics can be risky. Press Release. Retrieved July 9, 2008, from http://www.creativegroup.com/portal/site/tcg-us/template.PAGE/menuitem.926b08198c67974b735e0c5c02f3dfa0/

24 Jones, C. (2007). What do recruiters want anyway? *Yahoo HotJobs Exclusive*. Retrieved July 8, 2008, from http://hotjobs.yahoo.com/jobseeker/tools/article_print.html?id=What_Do_Recruiters_Want_Anyway__20021114-1412.xml

25 Blackburn-Brockman, E., & Belanger, K. (2001, January). One page or two?: A national study of CPA recruiters' preferences for résumé length. *The Journal of Business Communication*, 29–57. Retrieved July 8, 2008, from Sage Journals Online.

26 Isaacs, K. (2005, July 27). How to decide on résumé length. *Monster Career Advice*. Retrieved July 8, 2008, from http://career-advice.monster.com/resume-writing-basics/How-to-Decide-on-Resume-Length/home.aspx

27 Fisher, A. (2007, March 29). Does a resume have to be one page long? *CNNMoney.com*. Retrieved July 8, 2008, from http://money.cnn.com/2007/03/28/news/economy/resume.fortune/index.htm

28 Hansen, K. (n. d.). Should you use a career objective on your résumé? *Quintessential Careers*. Retrieved July 8, 2008, from http://www.quintcareers.co/resume_objectives.html; Domkowski, D., & Saunders, D. (2007). Career objective guide. (2007). *Career Center*, Florida State University. Retrieved July 8, 2008, from http://www.career.fsu.edu/advising/guides.html

29 Korkki, P. (2007, July 1). So easy to apply, so hard to be noticed. *The New York Times*. Retrieved July 8, 2008, from LexisNexis database.

30 Koeppel, D. (2006, December 31). Those low grades in college may haunt your job search. *The New York Times*, p. 1. Retrieved July 8, 2008, from Academic Search Premier (EBSCO) database.

31 Locke, A. (2008, June 18). Is your resume telling the wrong story? *The Ladders.com*. Retrieved July 9, 2008, from http://www.theladders.com/career-advice/Is-Your-Resume-Telling-the-Wrong-Story-

32 Washington, T. (n. d.) Effective resumes bring results to life. *HM Price*. Retrieved July 9, 2008, from http://www.hmprice.com/resume.html#3

33 The video resume technique. (2007). Retrieved July 9, 2008, from http://www.collegegrad.com/jobsearch/guerrilla-insider-techniques/the-video-resume-technique/

34 Peter, T. A. (2007, March 26). Résumés get a technology makeover. *Christian Science Monitor*, p. 13. Retrieved July 8, 2008, from LexisNexis database.

35 Kidwell Jr., R. E. (2004, May). "Small" lies, big trouble: The unfortunate consequences of résumé padding from Janet Cooke to George O'Leary. *Journal of Business Ethics*, 175.

36 Korver, C. D. (2008, May 19). The ethics of resume writing. *BusinessWeek/Harvard Business Online*. Retrieved July 9,

2008, from http://www.businessweek.com/print/managing/content/may2008/ca20080527_367723.htm

37 Needleman, S. E. (2007, March 6). Why sneaky tactics may not help résumé. *The Wall Street Journal*, p. B8.

38 Ryan, L. (2007). For job-hunters: How to find a contact name inside a target company. *Ezine Articles*. Retrieved July 9, 2008, from http://ezinearticles.com/?For-Job-Hunters:-How-to-Find-a-Contact-Name-Inside-a-Target-Company&id=101910

39 Korkki, P. (2007, July 1). So easy to apply, so hard to be noticed. *The New York Times*. Retrieved July 8, 2008, from LexisNexis database.

40 Safani, B. (2007, October 24). Seven rules for networking success. *The Ladders.com*. Retrieved July 9, 2008, from http://www.theladders.com/career-advice/Networking

41 Dussert, B. quoted in Shuit, D. P. (2003, November). Monster's competitors are nipping at its heels. *Workforce Management*. Retrieved July 9, 2008, from http://www.workforce.com/archive/feature/23/55/14/index.php?ht=

Chapter 14

1 Wilmott, N. (n. d.). Interviewing styles: Tips for interview approaches. *About.com: Human Resources*. Retrieved July 10, 2008, from http://humanresources.about.com/cs/selectionstaffing/a/interviews.htm

2 Ibid.

3 Needleman, S. E. (2008, February 12). Need a new situation? Check the Internet: Recruiters and job seekers find each other through Facebook, "fan" pages, videos. *The Wall Street Journal*, p. B6. Retrieved July 20, 2008, from ProQuest database.

4 Panel interview. (2007). *Job-Employment-Guide.com*. Retrieved July 11, 2008, from http://www.job-employment-guide.com/panel-interview.html

5 Niznik, J. S. (2002). What's a group interview? *About.com: Tech Careers*. Retrieved July 11, 2008, from http://jobsearchtech.about.com/od/interview/l/aa121602.htm

6 Dorio, M. (2000). *The complete idiot's guide to the perfect interview*. Indianapolis: Alpha Books, pp. 217–218.

7 Domeyer, D. (2007, January/February). *OfficePro*, 5.

8 Maher, K. (2004, September 28). Blogs catch on as online tool for job seekers and recruiters. *The Wall Street Journal* (Eastern Edition), p. B10. Retrieved July 19, 2008, from ProQuest database.

9 Ryan, L. (2006, February 9). Job seekers: Prepare your stories. *EzineArticles.com*. Retrieved July 19, 2008, from http://ezinearticles.com/?Job-Seekers:-Prepare-Your-Stories&id=142327

10 Finder, A. (2006, June 11). For some, online persona undermines a résumé. *The New York Times*. Retrieved July 19, 2008, from http://www.nytimes.com/2006/06/11/us/11recruit.html?_r=1&scp=1&sq=For%20some,%20online%20persona%20undermines&st=cse&oref=slogin

11 Needleman, S. E. (2008, February 12). Need a new situation? Check the Internet: Recruiters and job seekers find each other through Facebook, "fan" pages, videos. *The Wall Street Journal*, p. B6. Retrieved July 20, 2008, from ProQuest database.

12 Situational interview. (2004–2008). *Money-Zine.com*. Retrieved July 19, 2008, from http://www.money-zine.com/Definitions/Career-Dictionary/Situational-Interview

13 Wright, D. (2004, August/September). Tell stories, get hired. *OfficePro*, 64(6), 32–33. Retrieved July 19, 2008, from Business Source Premier (EBSCO).

14 Illegal interview questions. (n. d.). *FindLaw.com*. Retrieved July 19, 2008, from http://www.employment.findlaw.com/employment/employment-employee-hiring/employment-employee-hiring-interview-questions.html; Employment discrimination. (n. d.). *YourLawyer.com*. Retrieved July 19, 2008, from http://www.yourlawyer.com/topics/overview/employment_discrimination

15 Doyle, A. (n. d.). Illegal interview questions. *About.com*. Retrieved July 19, 2008, from http://jobsearchtech.about.com/od/interview/l/aa022403.htm

16 Illegal interview questions. (2001, January 29). *USA Today.com*. Retrieved July 19, 2008, from http://www.usatoday.com/careers/resources/interviewillegal.htm; Illegal interview questions. (2007). *FindLaw.com*. Retrieved July 19, 2008, from http://employment.findlaw.com/employment/employment-employee-hiring/employment-employee-hiring-interview-questions.html

17 Illegal interview questions. (2001, January 29). *USA Today.com*. Retrieved July 19, 2008, from http://www.usatoday.com/careers/resources/interviewillegal.htm; Sack, S. M. (1998). Illegal interview questions: Special considerations for women. *The Working Woman's Legal Survival Guide*. Retrieved July 19, 2008, from http://employment.findlaw.com/articles/2446.html; Asking the right question. (n. d.). *Lawyers.com*. Retrieved July 19, 2008, from http://labor-employment-law.lawyers.com/human-resources-law/Asking-the-Right-Questions.html

18 Lublin, J. S. (2008, February 5). Notes to interviewers should go beyond a simple thank you. *The Wall Street Journal*, p. B1. Retrieved July 19, 2008, from ProQuest database.

19 Ibid.

20 Needleman, S. E. (2006, February 7). Be prepared when opportunity calls. *The Wall Street Journal*, p. B4.

21 Bazen, K. L. (n. d.). The art of the follow-up after job interviews. *QuintCareers.com*. Retrieved July 19, 2008, from http://www.quintcareers.com/job_interview_follow-up.html

22 Patterson, V. (2004, March 30). Earning the salary you want in today's tough economy. *The Wall Street Journal*. Retrieved July 20, 2008, from ProQuest database.

23 About Karrass: The Karrass Story. (n. d.). Retrieved July 20, 2008, from http://www.karrass.com/kar_eng/about.htm

24 Boardman, J. (n. d.). Know what you're worth BEFORE your salary negotiation. *CBsalary.com*. Retrieved July 20, 2008, from http://www.cbsalary.com; Dawson, R. (2006). *Secrets of power salary negotiating*. Franklin Lakes, NJ: Career Press, pp. 117–125. Hansen, R. S. (n. d.). Job offer too low? Use these key salary negotiation techniques to write a counter proposal letter. *Quintessential Careers*. Retrieved July 20, 2008, from http://www.quintcareers.com/salary_counter_proposal.html; Hansen, R. S. (n. d.). Salary negotiation do's and don'ts. *Quintessential Careers*. Retrieved July 20, 2008, from http://www.quintcareers.com/salary-dos-donts.html; Ireland, S. (n. d.). Salary negotiation guide. Retrieved July 20, 2008, from http://susanireland.com/salarywork.html; Powell, J. (n. d.). Salary negotiation: The art of the deal. *Resume-Resource*. Retrieved July 20, 2008, from http://www.resume-resource.com/article16.html

Acknowledgments

Chapter 1

p. 4 Office Insider based on Hendricks, M. (2007, July 2). *Entrepreneur, 35*(7), 85–86. Retrieved January 22, 2008, from Business Source Premier database.

p. 6 Source to Figure 1.3, Chao, E. L. (2007, September 3). Knowledge fuels U.S. work force. *Santa Barbara News-Press*, p. A9.

p. 12 Office Insider based on Bucero, A. (2006, July). Listen and learn. PM Network. Retrieved February 1, 2008, from Business Source Premier database.

Chapter 2

p. 32 Office Insider based on Stevens, B. (2005, March). What communication skills do employees want? Silicon Valley recruiters respond. *Journal of Employment Counseling, 42*, 3. Retrieved January 24, 2008, from Business Source Premier database.

p. 34 Office Insider based on step up to the soft skills. (2004, January). Marilyn Mackes, National Association of Colleges and Employers, quoted in *Keying In*, Newsletter of the National Business Education Association, p. 1.

p. 41 Office Insider based on Blake, G. (2002, November 4). Insurers need to upgrade their employees' writing skills. *National Underwriter Life & Health-Financial Services Edition, 106* (44), 35. Retrieved February 8, 2008, from InfoTrac College Edition database.

p. 42 Office Insider based on La Corte, R. (2006, December 11). Wash. state sees results from 'plain talk' initiative. *USA Today*, p. 18A.

p. 43 Figure 2.5 based on U.S. Securities and Exchange Commission. (1998, August). A plain English handbook. Retrieved February 4, 2008, from http://www.sec.gov/pdf/handbook.pdf

Chapter 3

p. 53 Office Insider based on National Commission on Writing. (2004, September). Writing: A ticket to work . . . or a ticket out. Retrieved February 11, 2008, from http://www.writingcommission.org/prod_downloads/writingcom/writing-ticket-to-work.pdf

p. 56 Office Insider based on National Commission on Writing. (2003). The neglected "R": The need for a writing revolution. Retrieved February 10, 2008, from http://www.writingcommission.org/prod_downloads/writingcom/neglectedr.pdf

Chapter 4

p. 76 Office Insider based on Powell, E. (2003, November/December). Ten tips for better business writing. *Office Solutions, 20*(6), 36. Retrieved March 2, 2008, from ProQuest database.

p. 78 Office Insider based on Ilja van Roon, quoted in Sorry, no more excuses for bad business writing. (2006, May 23). *PR Newswire*. Retrieved March 30, 2008, from InfoTrac College Edition.

Chapter 5

p. 99 Workplace in Focus based on Hunter, G. (2008, January 30). GM's Lutz on hybrids, global warming and cars as art. *D Magazine*. Retrieved May 20, 2008, from http://frontburner.dmagazine.com/2008/01/30/gms-lutz-on-hybrids-global-warming-and-cars-as-art; Lutz, B. (2008, February 21). Talk about a crock. GM Fastlane blog. Retrieved May 20, 2008, from http://fastlane.gmblogs.com/archives/2008/02/talk_about_a_cr.html

p. 100 Office Insider based on Domeyer, D. (2007, December 12). Quoted in More clicks than conversations: Shift to e-mail in business makes crafting meaningful messages more important. Retrieved April 10, 2008, from InfoTrac College Edition database.

p. 107 Office Insider based on Sandberg, J. (2006, September 26). Employees forsake dreaded e-mail for the beloved phone. *The Wall Street Journal*, p. B1.

p. 109 Workplace in Focus based on Lashinsky, A. (2006, June 1). Razr's edge: How a team of engineers and designers defied Motorola's own rules to create the cellphone that revived their company. *Fortune*. Retrieved May 13, 2008, from http://money.cnn.com/2006/05/31/magazines/fortune/razr_greatteams_fortune/index.htm

p. 110 Office Insider based on Anderson, T. M. (2008, January 26). Quoted in Same office, different planets. *The New York Times*, p. B5.

p. 114 Office Insider based on Bloch, M. (n.d.). Instant messaging and live chat etiquette tips. Retrieved June 20, 2008, from http://www.tamingthebeast.net/articles6/messaging-chat-etiquette.htm

Chapter 6

p. 134 Office Insider based on Caddell, M. H. (2003, November/December). Is letter writing dead? OfficePro, 22–23.

p. 134 Workplace in Focus based on Department of the Treasury, Internal Revenue Service. (2008, March). Economic stimulus payment notice. Retrieved May 29, 2008, from http://www.irs.gov/pub/irs-utl/economic_stimulus_payment_notice.pdf

p. 141 Office Insider based on Kerrey, B. (2004, September 14). Writing skills necessary for employment, says big business. The National Commission on Writing. Retrieved April 27, 2008, from http://www.writingcommission.org/pr/writing_for_employ.html

p. 142 Workplace in Focus based on Goldman, D., & and Musante, K. (2008, April 12). American: Back to normal on Sunday. *CNNMoney*. Retrieved May 29, 2008, from http://money.cnn.com/2008/04/11/news/companies/airline_woes/index.htm; Stoller, G. (2008, May 19). How satisfied are travelers with their services? *USA Today*. Retrieved May 29, 2008, from http://www.usatoday.com/money/industries/travel/2008-05-19-customer-satisfaction_N.htm

p. 144 Office Insider based on Ashton, R. (2008, April 11). To whom it may concern. Utility Week. Retrieved April 27, 2008, from InfoTrac College Edition database.

Chapter 7

p. 161 Office Insider based on Engels, J. (2007, July). Delivering difficult messages. *Journal of Accountancy, 204*(1), 50. Retrieved May 11, 2008, from Business Source Premier database.

p. 162 Workplace in Focus based on Bouton, D. (2008, January 24). Letter from Societe General CEO Daniel Bouton. Retrieved June 10, 2008, from http://www.marketwatch.com; Report spreads blame at Societe Generale. (2008, May 23). *The Boston Globe.* Retrieved June 10, 2008, from http://www.boston.com/business/articles/2008/05/23/report_spreads_blame_at_societe_generale/

p. 168 Photo essay based on Demos, T. (2008, May 12). Bag Revolution. *Fortune,* p.18.

p. 175 Office Insider based on Mishory, J. (2004, June). Don't shoot the messenger: How to deliver bad news and still keep customers satisfied. *Sales & Marketing Management, 156*(6), 18. Retrieved May 8, 2008, from Business Source Premier database.

Chapter 8

p. 194 Office Insider based on [Ms. pg. 395] Mortensen, K. W. (2006, June 9). The ultra-prosperous study persuasion. *EzineArticles.* Retrieved March 2, 2008, from http://ezinearticles.com/?The-Ultra-Prosperous—Study—Persuasion&id=216435

p. 196 Office Insider based on Sandler, P. M. (2003, March 31). Cited in Power of persuasion. *SourceWatch.* Retrieved March 2, 2008, from http://www.sourcewatch.org/index.php?title=Power_of_persuasion

p. 198 Office Insider based on how to create and structure a winning complaint: Being positive and fair gets you more. (2008, January 4). *The Travel Insider.* Retrieved March 2, 2008, from http://www.thetravelinsider.info/info/howtocomplain2.htm

p. 201 Photo Essay based on Kim, V. (2008, January 27). Saving the world from paper tyranny. *The Los Angeles Times,* p. C2.

p. 205 Office Insider based on Stevenson, V. S. (2007, August 7). New VSS forecast released: Shift to alternative media strategies will drive U.S. communications spending growth in 2007–2011 period. Retrieved March 2, 2008, from http://www.vss.com/news/index.asp?d_News_ID=166ad sales forecast; Green, H. (2007, August 7). Blog, podcast, RSS online sales to be nearly half size of mobile sales. *Blogspotting. BusinessWeek Online.* Retrieved March 2, 2008, from www.businessweek.com

Chapter 9

p. 226 Office Insider based on The College Board: The National Commission on Writing. (2004, September). Writing: A ticket to work . . . or a ticket out. Retrieved April 6, 2008, from http://www.writingcommission.org/report.html

p. 233 Office Insider based on The College Board: The National Commission on Writing. (2004, September). Writing: A ticket to work . . . or a ticket out. Retrieved April 6, 2008, from http://www.writingcommission.org/report.html

Chapter 10

p. 255 Office Insider based on Piecewicz, M., proposal manager, Hewlett-Packard (personal communication with Mary Ellen Guffey, January 12, 1999).

p. 267 Office Insider based on Believe it or not . . . (2008). Learning Center. iParadigms. Retrieved June 7, 2008, from http://www.plagiarism.org

Chapter 11

p. 305 Office Insider based on Bosrock, R. M. (2005, October 5). Business forum: Good manners bring good results. *Star Tribune.com.* Retrieved June 16, 2008, from http://www.startribune.com/146/v-print/story/70672.html

p. 306 Office Insider based on Chismar, D. (2001). Vice and virtue in everyday (business) life. *Journal of Business Ethics,* 29, 169–176.

p. 310 Office Insider based on Johnson, D. (1988–2006). Dine like a diplomat. Seminar Script. The Protocol School of Washington.

p. 311 Office Insider based on Andrew Carnegie quoted in Johnson, D. (1988–2006). Dine like a diplomat. Seminar Script. The Protocol School of Washington.

p. 320 Office Insider based on Andrew Carnegie quoted in HeartQuotes: Quotes of the Heart. Retrieved June 17, 2008, from http://www.heartquotes.net/teamwork-quotes.html

p. 322 Office Insider based on Meeting Quotes. (2004). *Management by Meetings.* Retrieved June 17, 2008, from http://www.managementbymeetings.com/links/quotes/quotes.htm

Chapter 12

p. 337 Office Insider based on Dlugan, A. (2008, April 10). 10 ways your presentation skills generate career promotions. *Six Minutes.* Retrieved June 26, 2008, from http://sixminutes.dlugan.com/2008/04/10/career-promotions-presentation-skills

p. 339 Office Insider based on Booher, D. (2003). On speaking. Quotes by Dianna Booher. *Booher Consultants.* Retrieved June 26, 2008, from http://www.booher.com/quotes.html#speaking

p. 348 Office Insider based on Paradi, D. (2004). PowerPoint sucks! No it doesn't!! multimedia presentations. *Think Outside The Slide.* Retrieved July 1, 2008, from http://www.thinkoutsidetheslide.com/articles/powerpointnotsucks.htm

p. 359 Office Insider based on Booher, D. (2003). On speaking. Quotes by Dianna Booher. *Booher Consultants.* Retrieved June 26, 2008, from http://www.booher.com/quotes.html#speaking

Chapter 13

p. 378 Office Insider based on Granovetter, M. quoted in Wells, S. J. (1998, March 12). Many jobs on Web. *The New York Times,* p. A12.

p. 395 Office Insider based on Cheesman, J. quoted in Wolgemuth, L. (2008, February 25). Using the Web to search for a job. U. S. News & World Report. Retrieved July 6, 2008, from http://www.usnews.com/articles/business/careers/2008/02/25/using-the-web-to-search-for-a-job.html

p. 397 Office Insider based on Enelow, W. S. quoted in Korkki, P. (2007, July 1). So easy to apply, so hard to be noticed. *The New York Times.* Retrieved July 8, 2008, from LexisNexis database.

p. 404 Office Insider based on Patrick Beausoleil, Bouma Construction Company. (2008, March 3). E-mail message to Mary Ellen Guffey.

Chapter 14

p. 424 Office Insider based on Welch, J., & Welch, S. (2008, July 7). Hiring is hard work. *BusinessWeek,* 80.

p. 427 Office Insider based on Welch, J., & Welch, S. (2008, April 7). Getting to know your next CEO. *BusinessWeek,* 124.

p. 430 Office Insider based on Carol Roth quoted in Bachel, B. (2007, February/March). Fantastic follow-ups: Touching base after a good interview can give you an edge. *Career World,* p. 20. Retrieved July 19, 2008, from Academic Search Premier (EBSCO).

Index

Low-text business communicators, comparing high-and, *17*

M

Mail, report delivery by, 228
Mailing address, A-9
Main idea, opening with, 101
Malware, 113
Management
  flattened hierarchies of, 7
  more participatory, 7
Manual searches, 55
Manuscript format, 226
Maps, photographs, and illustrations, *271, 275–276*
Margins
  memo forms and, 105–106
  understanding, 81
Marketing messages
  writing sales and, 200–204
  writing online sales and, 204–207
Measurements, number style of, GM-45
Media richness, 35
Meeting location and materials, preparing, 323
Meetings
  agenda, *323*
  avoid issues that sidetrack, 325
  conducting professional, 321–327
  ending and following up on, 326–327
  etiquette checklist for leaders and participants of, *324*
  minutes of, 234, 238–239, *240*
  purpose and number of participants in, *323*
Memo format, 102–107, 226
Memo forms and margins, 105–106
Memo requests
  making direct, 117–118
  replying to, 118
Memorandums. *See* Memos
Memos, *36*
  as e-mail attachments, 107
  components of, 101–102
  e-mail cover note with attached persuasive, *197*
  hard-copy, 105
  interoffice, 99, 105–107, *106*
  knowing when to send, 100–101
  organizing, 100–102
  writing information and procedure, 114–116
  writing request and reply, 116–118
Messages
  audience focus, 38
  bad news follow-up, *174*
  collecting information to compose, 53–55
  communicating with electronic, 99–100
  communicating with paper-based, 99
  e-mail, 103–105, *117*, 148, A-1, *A-2*
  evaluating, 34

goodwill, 145–148
organizations exchange, 98–100
paper-based and electronic 98
sender focus, 38
sending positive written, outside your organization, 133–135
silent, 13–14, 15
writing online sales and marketing, 204–207
writing sales and marketing, 200–204
Metaphors, 343
Microsoft PowerPoint, 347
Minutes of meetings, 234, 238–240
  distribution of, 327
  report format, *239*
Miscommunication and intercultural audiences
  oral, 20
  written, 20–21
Misplaced modifiers, avoiding dangling and, 64
Misspelled words, GM-49
Mixed punctuation style, A-8
Modern Language Association (MLA), 267, A-15–A-17
  bibliographic format, A-16–A-17
  in-text format, A-16
  referencing format, 288
  text page and bibliography, *A-16*
  works cited, *A-17*
Modified block style, A-8
Money, number style of, GM-43
Monster, 377
Multifunctional printers, *8*
Multimedia presentation
  adapting text and color selections, 349
  designing an impressive, 347–356
  eight steps to making powerful, 355–356
  slides, *346*, 349, *353*
Multiple line chart, *273*

N

Names
  apostrophes with, GM-32
  proofreading for, 85–86
National Commission on Writing, 3
National origin, capitalizing on workforce diversity, 21–22
Neeleman, 167
Negative remarks, 310
Negative team behavior, 318, *319*
Netiquette, e-mail, 110
Niche Web sites, 377
Noise, 10
Nominative case, GM-7–GM-8
Non profit organization, volunteer with, 375
Nonverbal communication skill, enhancing of, 12–15
Nonverbal meanings out of context, avoid assigning, 15
Nonverbal messages, 344–345
  different cultures interpret verbal and, 15

different meanings in different cultures, 13
Nonverbal skills, keys to building strong, 15
Nouns, GM-6–GM-7
  abstract, GM-6
  as search words, 261
  collective, GM-7
  common, GM-6
  concrete, GM-6
  function of, GM-5
  plural, GM-6
  proper, GM-6
  singular, GM-6
Number of participants, meeting purpose and, *323*
Number style, GM-43–GM-46
  general rules, GM-43
Numbered items, capitalization of, GM-40
Numbered lists, 83
  for quick comprehension, 83
Numbers
  cite carefully, 21
  proofreading for, 85–86

O

Objective case, GM-7–GM-8
Observation, 264
  facts for reports from, 229
Observe yourself on video, 15
Official style, 42
Offshoring, 374
Omitted words, commas with, GM-27
One-on-one interviews, 416
Online
  report delivery by, 228
  résumé information, company database for, 398
  sales and marketing messages, 204–207
Open offices, *8*
Opening
  buffering of, 165–166
  claim letter with clear statement, 137
  cover letter, 398–401
  for solicited jobs, 399
  for unsolicited jobs, 399–401
  reveal good news in, 142
  with information reader wants, 140
Opinion, separate fact from, 230
Optical character recognition (OCR), 390
Oral miscommunication and intercultural audiences, 20
Oral presentation, 337
  building audience rapport, 343–345
  identifying purpose, 337
  outline, *341*
  understanding audience, 337
  writing process for, 33–34
Organization chart, *271*, 276, 275
Organizational patterns for reports, 223–226, *268*

Organizational stationery, 165
Organizational strategies, 267–269
Organizations, 163
  capitalization of names of, GM-38
  delivering bad news within, 177–179
  exchange messages and information, 98–100
  persuasion within, 196–198
  to show relationships, 55–58
Organize information, 108
Outlines, *56, 269*
Outsourcing, 374

P

Panel interviews, 416
Paper-based messages, 98, 99
Paragraph
  building coherence, 65
  controlling length, 65
  drafting powerful, 64–65
Parallel construction, 232
Parallelism, 83
  achieving, 62–63
Paraphrase, 264
Paraphrasing, 266
Parentheses, GM-35
Parenthetical expressions, commas with, GM-22–GM-23
Participants of meeting, number of, 322–323
Parts of speech, GM-5–GM-6
Passive voice, 62, *63*, GM-12
  in bad news messages, 169
PDF document, résumé as, 397–398
Percentages, number style of, GM-45
Periodicals provide limited current coverage, 259, 260
Periods, GM-34
Periods of time, number style of, GM-45
Person, report delivery in, 228
Personal anecdotes, 343
Personal appearance, 15
Personal data on résumé, 384
Personal digital assistants (PDAs), 315
Personal titles, capitalization of, GM-39
Personal use of company computers, 111
Personal zone, *14*
Personalized statistics, 344
Persuasion within organizations, 196–198
Persuasive favor request, *195*
Persuasive memo, e-mail cover note with attached, *197*
Persuasive requests, 193–199
Phishing schemes, 113
Phone call, *36*
Photographs, maps, and illustrations, *271, 275–276*
Phrases, commas with, GM-25
Physical ability, capitalizing on workforce diversity, 21–22
Pie charts, *271, 274*